THE TODAS

THE TODAS

W. H. R. RIVERS

GYAN

Published by

Gyan Publishing House
5, Ansari Road
Daryaganj, New Delhi-110002
Phone: 011-47034999, 9811692060
E-mail: books@gyanbooks.com

Distribution Network
gyanbooks.com
India, USA, Canada, UK, Australia

ISBN: 978-93-7447-106-7 (PB)

First Published, 1906

2nd Impression 2026

Printed at: Gyan Press, Delhi.

THE TODAS

Author: W. H. R. RIVERS

THE TODAS

rers's Todas.

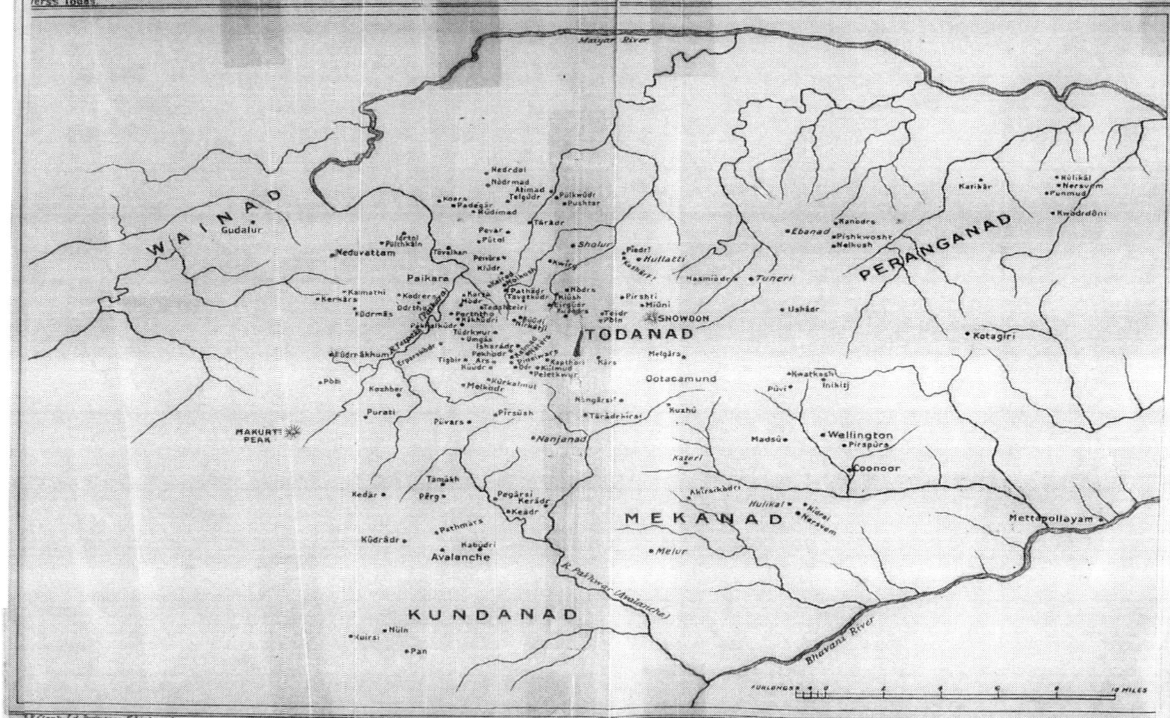

WAINAD
Gudalur
Neduvattam
Paikara
TODANAD
SNOWDON
Ootacamund
PERANGANAD
Kotagiri
Wellington
Coonoor
Mettupollayam
MEKANAD
KUNDANAD
Avalanche
MAKURTI PEAK
Moyar River
Bhavani River
R. Pakhwar (Avalanche)
Sholur
Hullatti
Tuneri
Ebanad
Nanjanad
Melur
Hulikal
10 MILES

THE TODAS

BY

W. H. R. RIVERS

FELLOW OF ST. JOHN'S COLLEGE, CAMBRIDGE

WITH ILLUSTRATIONS

London

MACMILLAN AND CO., LIMITED

NEW YORK: THE MACMILLAN COMPANY

1906

PREFACE

It has been my object in writing this book to make it, not merely a record of the customs and beliefs of a people, but also a demonstration of anthropological method. The great need of anthropology at the present time is for more exact method, not only in collecting material, but also in recording it, so that readers may be able to assign its proper value to each fact, and may be provided with definite evidence which will enable them to estimate the probable veraciousness and thoroughness of the record.

With this idea in my mind I have tried to describe as fully as possible the way in which my account has been built up, and have been careful to point out the different degrees of trustworthiness of different portions of my story. Perhaps I have been so anxious to make it clear when my record is of doubtful value that sometimes I may have laid undue stress on its uncertainties and deficiencies.

I have tried to make a clear distinction between my description of Toda custom and belief, and any theoretical conclusions drawn by myself, and have kept the latter for sections at the ends of chapters or for special chapters, of which those numbered xi, xix, xxix and xxx are the most important.

It may be thought by some that the book is unduly loaded with minute detail, and I am myself aware that I have often complicated, perhaps even obscured, the story I am telling by the mass of detail with which it is accompanied. I have had, however, no scruples on this score, partly because I wished my readers thoroughly to grasp the nature of the material on which my account is based, but still more, because details which may seem insignificant or trivial are often of great importance in the comparative study of custom and belief.

I have not attempted such a comparative study of Toda institutions. It was often very tempting to suggest resemblances with the practices of other peoples of the present or the past, but the result would have been to swell the book to unwieldy dimensions, and perhaps to have obscured the description of the life of the people. In giving parallels for Toda custom I have therefore limited myself to examples from other parts of India, and even here I have only dealt with a few resemblances which illustrate certain suggestions made in the final chapter on the origin and affinities of the Toda people.

In conclusion, I am very glad to express my gratitude for help received from many sources. The researches on which the book is based were undertaken in consequence of the award to myself of the income of the Gunning Fund of the Royal Society for the years 1901–2, and my work was also assisted by a grant from the British Association. In India I received every assistance from those whose official positions gave them the means of helping me, and my thanks are especially due to Mr. Edgar Thurston, whose kind interest and assistance I cannot sufficiently acknowledge. I owe much to the care and attention with which my two interpreters, P. Samuel and Albert Urrilla, performed their duties, and I am greatly indebted to the managers of the Church of England Zenana Missionary Society at Ootacamund for the services of the former, and to Mr. C. M. Mullaly and Mr. Hadfield for giving the latter leave from his forest duties in order that he might help me.

Of friends in England I am especially indebted to Dr. C. S. Myers, who kindly read nearly the whole of the book in proof; to Syed Ali Bilgrami for information on various points connected with Indian custom; to Don M. da Zilva

Wickramasinghe for reading Chapter xxv, dealing with the language; and to Mr. H. N. Webber for help, especially in the revision of the genealogical tables.

Most of the illustrations in the book are from photographs taken under my direction by Messrs. Wiele and Klein of Madras, and I am indebted to H M. India Office for permission to make use of illustrations from "An Account of the Primitive Tribes and Monuments of the Nilagiris," by the late J. Williamson Breeks (1873), and to Messrs. Longmans Green and Co., for permission to make use of illustrations from "A Phrenologist amongst the Todas," by the late Colonel William E. Marshall (1873).

W. H. R. R.

CONTENTS

CHAPTER X

CHAPTER XI

CHAPTER XII

CHAPTER XIII

CHAPTER XIV

CHAPTER XV

CHAPTER XVI

CHAPTER XVII

CHAPTER XVIII

CHAPTER XIX

CHAPTER XX

CHAPTER XXI

CHAPTER XXII

CHAPTER XXIII

CHAPTER XXIV

CHAPTER XXV

CHAPTER XXVI

CHAPTER XXVII

CHAPTER XXVIII

CHAPTER XXIX

CHAPTER XXX

LIST OF ILLUSTRATIONS

PHONETIC SYSTEM

THE following is the phonetic system which has been used in this book. The use of many of the signs is more fully described in Chapter XXV.

Vowels.

ā, the a of father.
a, the u of hut.
ä, the a of hat.
ē, the ei of their.
e, the e of met.
ī, the ee of meet.
i, the i of hit.
ō, the o of post.
o, the o of pot.
ö, the o of word.

ò, the aw of law.
ū, the oo of moon.
u, the u of full.
ü, the German vowel.
ai, the i of bite.
au, the ou of house.
ei, the a of date.
eu, the French diphthong.
oi, the oy of boy.

Consonants.

b, as in English.
ch, the ch of church.
d, used in the text for the English sound and also for the lingual consonant *ḍ*.[1]
f, as in English.
g, the g of sing.
gg, the g of finger.
gh, the ch of ich.

h, used for a sound of doubtful nature (see p. 611).
j, as in English.
k, as in English.
kh, the ch of auch.
l, used in the text for the English sound and for the lingual consonant *ḷ*.

[1] One of the most frequent consonantal sounds in the Toda language is ***dr*** which in the text always stands for *ḍr*; when *d* comes before *sh*, it also represents the lingual sound. In both cases the *ḍ* was hardly appreciated by my ear, and the European will perhaps most nearly imitate the Toda sound if he pronounces ***dr*** and ***dsh*** as *r* and *sh*.

m,	as in English.	*t*,	as in English and also for the lingual *ṭ*.
n,	as in English.	*th*	the th both of though and throw.
ñ,	a nasal n, as in French.	*v*, *w*,	as in English.
p, *r*,	as in English.	*z*,	the z of zeal.
s,	a sound resembling the English s.	*zh*,	the si of occasion.
sh,	as in English.		

Sounds represented by *ch*, *s*, *sh*, and *th*, very frequently inserted euphonically in Toda words, have usually been omitted. I have also omitted the signs showing the long vowels whenever a word occurs frequently throughout the book, and the glossary should be consulted to ascertain the correct method of pronouncing such words. Similarly, Appendices III and IV should be consulted to ascertain the proper pronunciation of the names of places and plants.

I do not use the plurals of Toda words, either in the English form or in that proper to the Toda language; thus, I write "the two *palol*" and not "the two *palols*" or "the two *palolam*."

MAP.

The names printed in the same type as **Kâra** are those of Toda villages; the names in italics, as *Nanjanad* are those of Badaga villages; the names in small black type, as **Ootacamund** are those of towns with a general population, or of *dâk* bungalows.

THE TODAS

CHAPTER I

INTRODUCTION

THE people whose manners and customs I am about to describe live on the undulating plateau of the Nilgiri Hills in Southern India. The hills were visited by a Portuguese missionary in 1602, and have been invaded by Indian tribes on various occasions, but, at the beginning of the last century, the plateau and its inhabitants were absolutely unknown to Europeans. The earliest definite information about the hills at this time is given in a letter from William Keys, an assistant revenue surveyor, written in 1812, but it was not till several years later that further information about the people began to be published.

Of the various tribes inhabiting the hills, the Todas excited the greatest interest, and this interest has continued, partly because the people are so different from any other of the races by which they are surrounded, but still more because both they and their customs are so picturesque and, in many ways, so unique.

A very large literature[1] has accumulated about the Todas and their customs. This literature is so extensive that when I determined to go to the Nilgiri Hills, I was reproached by more than one anthropologist for going to people about whom we already knew so much; and one even said that, so far as his department of knowledge was concerned, he was sure that we had all the information we could expect to get.

[1] The bibliography of this literature is given in Appendix II.

A review of the literature, however, showed me that there were certain subjects about which our information was of the scantiest. This was especially the case in matters connected with the social organisation. Little was known of the system of kinship, and it was not known whether there was any definite system of exogamy. The Todas furnish one of the best existing examples of the custom of polyandry, but scarcely anything was known about the various social regulations which must be associated with such a practice.

I had not worked long among the Todas before I discovered the existence of many customs and ceremonies previously undescribed, and I was able to obtain much more detailed accounts of others which had already been repeatedly recorded. I found that there was so much to be done that I gave up an intention of working with several different tribes, and devoted the whole of my time to the Todas.

This book is not intended to be a complete account of all that is known about the Toda people. Their physical anthropology has been so ably dealt with by Mr. Edgar Thurston that I leave this subject almost untouched, and I omit all but a brief mention of my own psychological observations which I have published in detail elsewhere.[1] The book deals almost exclusively with the religion and sociology of the people. Even here, however, the account will be far from complete. After several months' work among a people about whom "we knew all there was to be known," I came away knowing that there were subjects of which I had barely touched the fringe, and many others on which my information could have been made far more complete with greater opportunity. About certain subjects the Todas are extremely reticent, and my information is in consequence very defective. There are many points on which I know my information to be far from complete, and doubtless there are far more numerous examples of deficiency of which I am not aware.

Some deficiencies of the record are due to certain untoward events which occurred during my visit. After I had been working among the Todas for about four months, various misfortunes befell some of those who had

[1] See *British Journal of Psychology*, 1905, vol. i., p. 321.

been my chief guides to Toda lore. One man who had pointed out to me certain sacred places fell ill and made up his mind that he was going to die. Another man lost his wife a few days after he had shown me the method of performing one of the most sacred of Toda ceremonies. A third man who had revealed to me the details of the ceremonial of the most sacred Toda dairy, suffered the loss of his own village dairy by fire.

The Todas consulted their diviners, who ascribed these events to the anger of the gods because their secrets had been revealed to the stranger. In consequence my sources of information ran dry to a large extent, and the difficulties in the way of the investigation of the more sacred topics were greatly increased. By the time it was settled that I was to blame I was nearly at the end of my visit, but it was in the last two or three weeks that I had hoped to overcome the scruples of the people and to obtain information on many doubtful points about which I had to come away unsatisfied.

One of the subjects on which my material is defective is the folk-lore. I have a number of tales, but they are only a small part of the store of Toda legend. I regret especially the incompleteness of my work in this respect because I believe that the Todas are rapidly forgetting their folk-tales and the legends of their gods, while their ceremonial remains to a large extent intact, and seems likely to continue so for some time.

I was especially struck by this because, in previous anthropological experience in the islands of Torres Straits with Dr. Haddon, we had found the exact opposite to be the case. In these islands, the ceremonial had disappeared, and the only record of it to be obtained was that derived from the memories of the oldest inhabitants. Nevertheless in Torres Straits the store of legend was still ample, and the agreement of the stories obtained from different individuals was so great that it was evident that the people had preserved their folklore with fidelity.

The difference between the two communities is easily explained. In Torres Straits missionary influence is strong, and missionary effort is always directed to break down the practices associated with belief. The ceremonial in Torres Straits had been swept away, while the stories of the legendary heroes were almost all that remained to the people of the old life and were in consequence still cherished.

Among the Todas missionary influence, whether of Christian or Hindu, has had little effect, and the ritual of the Todas in some parts of the hills is almost, if not quite, untouched by outside influences.[1] The effect of intercourse with other peoples seems to be showing itself largely in the form of loss of interest in the stories of the past.

One of the most striking aspects of the customs and ceremonies of the Todas is that these have in many cases no exact parallels in other places. Perhaps the most definite result which modern research in anthropology has brought out is the extraordinary similarity of custom throughout the world. Customs apparently identical are found in races so widely separated geographically and so diverse ethnologically that it seems certain the customs must have developed in total independence of one another. There seems to be an identity of idea actuating custom in peoples very different from one another in their surroundings and conditions of life.

The nearest parallels to Toda custom and ceremonial are undoubtedly to be found in the Indian peninsula, but even here, though there is often a general resemblance, this breaks down on going into detail. Even when the resemblance is so close as to suggest a common origin, the differences in detail are often very great.[2]

One clue to this exceptional nature of Toda custom and belief is to be found in the geographical position of the people, which has to a large extent isolated them from the world in general.

The plateau on which they live, broken by numerous hills and valleys, is the top of a scarp formed by the meeting of the Eastern and Western Ghats. Some of the hills project

[1] As we shall see later, this is only true of some parts of the hills and some institutions.

[2] With more exact knowledge of Indian customs and ceremonies which have lingered on side by side with, though often obscured by Brahmanism, it is possible that these differences would be found to be much slighter than the evidence at present available suggests.

more than the rest above the general level of the plateau, which ranges from 6,000 to 7,500 feet above the sea, and the loftiest of these hills reaches the height of 8,760 feet. The plateau is so high that, though it is situated only about eleven degrees from the equator, the thermometer rarely rises above 70° F., and in the nights of the cold season may touch the freezing point.

In every direction the sides of the hills leading up to the plateau are steep and often precipitous. To the south-east, east, and north-east there is a rapid fall of about 5,000 feet to the plains of the Coimbatore district, though to the south this plain only forms a gap about twenty miles in breadth between the Nilgiri and the Anaimalai Hills. On the north-west the slope is more gradual and is broken by the Wainad district about 3,000 feet above the sea. To the north there is a steep fall, but only for about 4,000 feet, to the plateau of Mysore, which is about 3,000 feet above the sea.

The south-western part of the hills is known as the Kundahs and may be regarded as a range separate from the greater part of the plateau, from which it is divided by a wide valley, the Avalanche Valley. From the Kundahs there is an extremely precipitous fall to the Malabar district.

The steep sides leading up to the plateau on which the Todas live are clothed with thick, almost impenetrable jungle, which is extremely malarious, so that a night spent on the way to the summit is very likely to produce fever.

The hills appear to have been for long an object of reverence to Hindus on account of their height and inaccessibility. Dubois states that "as it is very difficult to reach the top of this mountain, a view of the summit alone (and it is visible a long way off) is considered sufficient to remove the burden of sin from the conscience of any person who looks at it."[1]

When the hills were first visited by Europeans, their use as a sanatorium was long delayed owing to the difficulty of making roads, and it was not till after many years that the hills became a regular resort of the European population. We shall see later that the isolation of the Todas has certainly

[1] *Hindu Manners, Customs, and Ceremonies*, part ii., chap. v.

not been complete, and that the hills have been invaded by strangers, especially from the side of the Wainad; but the isolation has probably been considerable, and, for long periods, it may have been complete.

In their isolation from the world in general, however, the Todas have not been alone. Two other tribes, the Kotas and the Badagas, occupy the plateau with them, and the peculiar relations between the three tribes are among the most interesting features of the social life of the Nilgiris. The Todas are a purely pastoral people, limiting their activities almost entirely to the care of their buffaloes and to the complicated ritual which has grown up in association with these animals. The Badagas are chiefly agriculturists; the Kotas are artisans and mechanics; and both supply the Todas with part of their produce. There is here a well-marked instance of division of labour, in which the labour of the Todas is reduced to a minimum. Their privileged position is usually held to be due to the tradition that they are the "lords of the soil," and the produce which the Todas receive from the other tribes is supposed to be of the nature of tribute.

The jungle on the slopes of the hills is inhabited by two wild, dwarfish tribes, the Kurumbas and Irulas, who have a general resemblance to the many other jungle tribes of Southern India. These people are much feared by the tribes of the plateau for their supposed magical powers, but they have little to do with the complex social life of the others.

The district in which the three tribes live is not extensive. The extreme length of the plateau, from east to west, is about forty-two miles, and its average breadth, from north to south, about ten miles, the maximum breadth being fifteen miles in the centre of the district. The total area of the plateau is less than 500 square miles. In this district there live about 800 Todas, 1,200 Kotas, and 34,000 Badagas. In addition, there are now extensive European settlements, the largest of which is Ootacamund, the seat of the Madras Government for six months of the year. The other large European settlements are Coonoor and Kotagiri, while Wellington, near Coonoor, is a military station.

The plateau of the Nilgiris is divided into four districts,

ordinarily known by the names, Todanad, Mekanad, Peranganad, and Kundanad, and these districts are recognised by the Todas. The Todanad is the largest district, and is the part where the majority of the Todas live. Their own name for it is Marsâdr.

The Mekanad is called by the Todas Karâdr, and is now very sparsely inhabited, though there are many old villages in the district.

The Peranganad is the eastern part of the hills, and is called by the Todas Purgòdr, and is the chief seat of a few of their clans.

The fourth district, or Kundanad, is that already mentioned as the Kundahs in the south-west part of the hills. It is the chief seat of one Toda clan, but it also contains villages belonging to others. It is especially visited in the dry season, since its large rainfall often provides ample pasturage when this is burnt up on other parts of the hills. The Toda name of the district is Mêdr.

A few Todas live near Gudalur in the Wainad, some 3,000 feet lower than the main plateau.

METHODS

The description of Toda life to be given in this book is the outcome of an attempt to apply rigorous methods in the investigation of sociology and religion. In the brief time which was at my disposal, it was essential to employ methods of investigation which would enable me to tell with some certainty whether I was obtaining accurate and trustworthy information. Two great sources of error in anthropological investigation are the dependence on the evidence of only a few individuals and the necessity of paying for information.

The first source of error was easily avoided, and I was able to obtain my information from a large body of witnesses, usually independently of one another. As regards the second source, the Todas are inveterate beggars, and are now thoroughly accustomed to receive payment for every service rendered to the European, even of the most trivial kind. Payment for information was inevitable, but I minimised the danger by arranging that every man who came to me for work should receive a definite stipulated sum as a recompense for his time and trouble. I paid, not for the information, but for the trouble taken in giving a day or half a day to my service. As a general rule, anything like payment by results was carefully avoided. The sum paid was for coming to me, and if anyone was reluctant to talk about one subject, we passed on to another. Only at the end of my visit did I depart from this rule on a few occasions, and offered rewards to one or two individuals for certain items of information; but by this time I was in a position to judge the value of the information I received, and I only employed this procedure in cases where I knew the degree of trustworthiness of my informant.

Definite methods for the verification of the evidence obtained were the more necessary in my work among the Todas, in that I was obliged throughout to depend on interpreters. I was, however, very fortunate in my assistants. I first worked with a forest ranger, Albert Urrilla, who knew the Todas very well, though he had no special knowledge of their customs. He translated faithfully, and, owing to his wide knowledge of the hills, he was extremely useful in helping me to become familiar with the names and positions of the many Toda villages. After about six weeks' work, Albert had to return to his forest duties, and, except for a week towards the end of my visit, the interpreter for the rest of my work was P. Samuel, a catechist who had been endeavouring for ten years to convert the Todas to Christianity, under the auspices of the Church of England Zenana Missionary Society. When he began to work with me, Samuel had a very limited acquaintance with Toda ceremonies, but he was very familiar with the general life of the people, and was especially acquainted with the actual working of many of their social customs. Some of the Todas at first objected strongly to his helping me, probably on account of his missionary efforts, but he soon overcame this initial difficulty and gained the general confidence of the people. He was well acquainted with the Toda language, and soon became a very careful inquirer into customs and beliefs, and I owe much to his help. He often obtained independent information about customs, and I was put by him on the track of much that might otherwise have escaped me. I had hoped that he would have continued to make inquiries for me after I had left the hills, and soon after my departure, he forwarded to me a very valuable account of a ceremony which I had not been able to witness and other important material. While with me he had discovered, however, how little progress he had made with the people during his ten years' work among them, and how little he had known of their beliefs, and, soon after my departure, he asked to be given a new sphere of work and was removed to the Wainad, so that I have not had the opportunity for which I hoped, of making further inquiries into the many doubtful points which always arise in working up the notes of anthropological investigation.

One of the chief dangers arising from the use of interpreters is that they will often transmit, not what they are told, but their own versions of what they are told. They interpret the meaning as well as the words of the informants. I think I can be certain that this danger was avoided with both my interpreters, and that they gave me as accurate an account as possible of what the Todas told them. We always used the Toda names for all specific objects, individuals, and places, so that the information transmitted to me by the interpreters was often in such a form that nearly every noun was Toda in a setting of English verbs, adverbs, and pronouns. Thus, referring to one of my notebooks at random, I find the following: "After cleansing the *poh* in this manner, each *palol* puts salt in the *ponmukeri*, and takes it and the *karpun* to the *upunkudi*, taking also five pieces of *tudrpül*, five sprigs of *puthimul*, and a bundle of *taf*." In fact, we habitually used so many Toda words that the Todas sometimes obviously knew the general drift of my questions before they were interpreted to them, and, similarly, I could often understand the general drift of the answer.

The first principle of my investigation was to obtain independent accounts from different people; I then compared these independent accounts and cross-examined into any discrepancies. The general result of this method was highly satisfactory from the point of view of Toda veracity. The general agreement of the accounts obtained from different individuals was very striking, and, whenever discrepancies occurred, it was nearly always found that they were due either to misunderstanding or to differences in the practices of different sections of the Toda people. These differences are so great that in many cases it made a rigorous application of the method of direct corroboration impossible. There are distinct differences in the ceremonial and social customs of the two chief divisions of the Todas and some differences in the practices of different clans. In the investigation of the dairy ritual, there were found to be great differences in the practices of different dairies, and, for the practice of any one dairy, I had sometimes to be content with the information of one native only; but I did not content myself with such independent accounts till I had satisfied myself of the trustworthiness of the witness, and had learnt enough of the customs in question to be in a position to weigh the evidence. As regards the differences in the customs of different sections of the community, many of my informants were able to describe the practices not only of their own section but also of others.

After a time I managed to put myself on such terms with my chief informants that they were always ready to confess any deficiencies in their knowledge and would refer me to others whose special experience would make them more satisfactory informants. Occasionally, however, they carried this a little too far and pleaded ignorance of a subject when they were really only reluctant to reveal the more esoteric knowledge.

Still more important than this method of direct corroboration of independent accounts is what I may call the method of indirect corroboration. By this I mean the method of obtaining the same information in different ways. Often this indirect corroboration occurred accidentally. The whole of Toda ceremonial and social life forms such an intricate web of closely related practices that I rarely set out to investigate some one aspect of the life of the people without obtaining information bearing on many other wholly different aspects, and the information so gained often afforded valuable corroboration of what I had been told on other occasions and by other individuals. Thus, in obtaining a prayer, various matters would arise which would confirm the accuracy of a legend obtained weeks earlier, or the investigation of a funeral custom would lead to the indirect corroboration of evidence concerning the regulation of marriage.

The most important way in which this method of indirect corroboration may be intentionally applied is by obtaining the same information first in an abstract form and then by means of a number of concrete instances. As an example of what I mean I may cite the method by which I inquired into the laws of inheritance of property. I first obtained an account of what was done in the abstract—of the laws governing the inheritance of houses, the division of the buffaloes and other property among the children, &c. Next I gave a number of hypothetical concrete instances; I took cases of men with so many children and so many buffaloes, and repeating the cases I found that my informant gave answers which were consistent not only with one another but also with the abstract regulations previously given. Finally I took real persons and inquired into what had actually happened when A or B died, and again obtained a body of information consistent in itself and agreeing with that already obtained.

By far my most valuable instrument of inquiry was that provided by the genealogical method.[1] The Todas preserve in their memories the names of all their ancestors and relatives extending back for several generations. In the tables given at the end of this book, I have recorded the pedigrees of seventy-two families, including the whole of the Toda community. Whenever the name of a man was mentioned in connexion with ceremony or social custom, his name was found in the genealogical record and the relation was ascertained in which he stood towards others participating in the ceremony or custom. By this means a concrete element was brought into the work which greatly facilitated inquiry.

[1] See chapter XX and *Journ. Anthrop. Inst.*, 1900, vol. xxx., p. 74.

Customs and rites were investigated by means of concrete examples in which the people taking part were real people to me as well as to my informants. In a later chapter I shall consider more fully the *rôle* of the genealogies in anthropological investigation. I mention them here to give a preliminary indication of the extensive part they played in my investigations. In order to give my readers the opportunity of following my method in some measure for themselves, I have given after the name of any individual mentioned in the book the number of the genealogical table in which his name occurs; thus "Kòdrner (7)" means that Kòdrner is a member of the family of which the pedigree is recorded in Table 7.

I have already referred to the trustworthiness of the evidence given by the Todas. I must now speak of the great differences in this respect shown by different individuals. Some would give full and elaborate accounts of ceremonial which close investigation showed to be, so far as one could tell, thoroughly accurate. Others gave careless and slovenly accounts, full of omissions and inaccuracies of detail, though they rarely said anything which was distinctly untrue.

After some experience had been gained, one day's work was usually sufficient to enable me to make up my mind whether a man was a careful witness, and if he did not seem to be so, he was not again called upon for help. Different men were known to have especial acquaintance with certain branches of knowledge, and I always endeavoured to obtain such people. In the case of the religious ritual, it was not practicable to make use, to any great extent, of men actually holding any of the sacred offices, but I always had recourse to people who had held these offices and were personally familiar with the ceremonial.

Among the many aspects of social life and religion, I soon found that there were some about which there was no reticence, and these could be discussed in public with men, women, or children standing by and perhaps taking part. There were others which were of a more sacred nature, and, if they were approached in public, it was immediately obvious that the people were ill at ease and their answers became hesitating and unsatisfactory. After a short time I adopted the practice of devoting the mornings to my psychological work and to the discussion of affairs of a non-sacred character. In the afternoons I had private interviews with one individual at a time, or occasionally two. If I approached any dangerous topic during the morning, my guide made me a sign and I changed the subject, to return to it at an afternoon sitting.

In the investigation of all the more sacred ceremonies, it was found to be best that the narrator should be alone. He knew that he was telling what should not be told and was embarrassed if any other Todas were there to hear him.

One of the difficulties of anthropological inquiry is that the good and trustworthy narrators are often the most reticent. They are trustworthy because they are honest and pious members of their community, and are therefore naturally reluctant to offend against the sanctity of their religious customs by talking of them to a stranger. Some of my best informants were such men, who were gradually led on to tell me far more than they had ever intended, and then, having told me so much about a given subject, they would sometimes throw reticence to the winds and tell me all. It was very instructive in such a case to start a fresh topic which I knew to be forbidden ground and observe the complete change of attitude. One old man who had entirely lost his scruples in our absorption in the details of dairy ritual absolutely refused to speak a word when I turned to the subject of animal sacrifice, and for this and some other topics I had to be content with less scrupulous but at the same time less trustworthy witnesses.

I only found one Toda who was deliberately untruthful, and yet he was so much less reticent and less scrupulous than others that I often had to have recourse to his services. After I had been able to convict him more than once of having given unsatisfactory evidence, he was more accurate, but I was especially careful to check and obtain independent accounts of everything he told me, and I have only made use of so much of his evidence as I believe to be trustworthy. His knowledge was not deep or accurate, but he often told me enough to enable me to extract the full account from others, who, seeing I knew something, thought they might as well tell me all. On one or two subjects, the whole of my information is derived from this man, but whenever this is the case I mention the fact, so that my readers may know the doubtful nature of the evidence. I only give such information, however, when I believe it to be correct. The informant in question was one of the cleverest of the Todas, and his usual fault was not that he deliberately deceived, but that he supplied the lacunæ in his knowledge by having recourse to his imagination. In the matter of folk-tales, where the difficulties of checking an account are especially great, I was obliged wholly to reject his assistance.

An altogether different type of witness was my constant attendant, Kòdrner. His special business was to bring me people as the subjects for my psychological work and to act as my guide in visiting various parts of the hills. He did not profess to any wide knowledge of custom or ceremonial, and was always diffident about the information he gave; but he was a good observer, and could give an excellent account of any ceremony which he had witnessed or of any procedure in which he had been involved.

Except in a few cases the Todas were quite unable to give any explanations of their customs, the answer to nearly every inquiry being that the custom in question was ordained by the goddess Teikirzi. In the few cases in which an explanation was forthcoming, it seemed to me that it was usually a recent invention. The explanations of customs given in this book are therefore almost invariably those arrived at by myself from the study of the available evidence.

While I was working I had by me the books or papers of Harkness, Marshall, Breeks, and Thurston, the chief previous writers on the Todas, and I inquired into most of the details mentioned by them; but I have not attempted any criticism or comment on the work of others except on special occasions when my own information is lacking or when I am uncertain as to the truth of their statements. Except in those cases in which I definitely refer to the work of others, every statement made in this book is the outcome of my own inquiry or observation. Whenever my account differs from those of others, it may be accepted that I have inquired into the discrepancy and that my account represents the result of a careful investigation.

As some of the accounts of the Todas were written many years ago, there is always the possibility that two dissimilar accounts may both be true and that the differences may represent changes in custom with lapse of time. There is one fact, however, which makes it probable that this explanation of discrepancies is not the true one. The accounts of the Todas which show the closest correspondence with my own are some of the earliest, especially the book of Captain Harkness, published in 1832, and the papers of Bernhard Schmid and C. F. Muzzy, published in 1837 and 1844 respectively. In many cases my work agrees more closely with these than with the accounts of later observers.

This is, perhaps, a suitable place to mention what I believe to be the chief source of error in previous accounts of the Todas. In their extensive intercourse with the Badagas, the Todas use the language of this people, with which they appear to be perfectly familiar. The Toda language is very difficult to understand, and the literature shows that from the first, most of those who have investigated Toda customs have used the Badaga language or Tamil as their means of communication. Every Toda village, every Toda institution or office, and nearly every object used by the Todas has its Badaga name as well as its proper Toda name, and, owing to intercourse through the intermediation of the Badagas, these names have come to be used not only by nearly all who have written on the Todas, but also in official documents connected with the people.

The names by which the Toda villages are known to Europeans are always the Badaga names and not those of the Todas, and similarly with the names of institutions such as clans, dairies, or ceremonies. The practice of giving Badaga names in their intercourse with Europeans has become so engrained that a Toda invariably uses these names when speaking to a European. During the first few weeks of my work, I received exclusively Badaga names, and to the end of my visit, whenever I visited a new district, the Badaga names would crop up till the people found that I wanted Toda and not Badaga. Kiunievan, who was the chief informant of Mr. Breeks in 1872, is still alive, and when I asked him why he gave Mr. Breeks the Badaga names in every case, he answered "He did not seem to want anything else," and this answer seems to me to give the clue to much of the error which has found its way into many of the accounts which have been given of the Todas.

One of the most serious errors which has arisen in this way is one connected with the Toda clans. Every account which has been given of the clan-system of the Todas is that of a system which is current among the Badagas as the Toda system, but has only a limited correspondence with the actual system as it is in use among the Todas themselves. Every Toda, if asked by a European to what clan or division he belongs, will promptly give his division according to the Badaga classification, and this has led to the incorporation of this classification in all the accounts of the Todas which deal with their social organisation.

Some words are necessary about the general plan of the book. I should have preferred to begin with the social organisation, and to approach the religious aspect of the life of the Todas through the ceremonies accompanying the chief incidents of life, including birth, marriage, and death. The ideas borrowed from the ritual of the dairy, however, so pervade the whole of Toda ceremonial, that I have been obliged to consider the ritual of the dairy at an early stage. After a preliminary chapter sketching the general character and life of the people, I have therefore given a full description of the elaborate ceremonial which centres round the dairy; and on this follow the accounts of other ceremonies and sacred institutions and a general discussion of the religion of the people. I then turn to the social aspect of life, and consider kinship, marriage, and the various factors upon which the social organisation depends. Then, after some chapters on diverse topics, I describe the relations of the Todas with the other tribes of the Nilgiris, and in the final chapters discuss certain special problems, including the origin and affinities of the Toda people.

CHAPTER II

THE TODA PEOPLE

I DO not propose to describe at any length the physical characters of the Todas.[1] It must be sufficient to say here that the people differ remarkably in general appearance, and perhaps still more remarkably in general bearing, from the other inhabitants of Southern India. The average height of the men is about 5 ft. 7 in., and that of the women 5 ft. 1 in.; both are well-proportioned, and the men robustly built. Their heads are distinctly dolichocephalic, the cephalic index of the men being 73·3. The shaved heads of the children show very well the great length, and probably owing to the special method of shaving (see Figs. 63 and 64), this feature is in them exaggerated so as to seem almost abnormal.

The nose is usually well-formed and not especially broad, the nasal index being 74·9. It is often distinctly rounded in profile. The skin is of a rich brown colour, distinctly lighter than that of most of the Dravidian inhabitants of Southern India. The skins of the women are lighter than those of the men. There is much hair on the bodies of the men, who usually grow thick beards, and the hair of the head is luxuriant in both men and women. The men are strong and very agile; the agility being most in evidence when they have to catch their infuriated buffaloes at the funeral ceremonies. They stand fatigue well, and often travel great distances. One day I met an old man about seventy years of age going to the market at Gudalur for a supply

[1] Those who wish for information on this point should consult the articles by Mr. Edgar Thurston in the *Bulletins* of the Madras Museum, vol. i., pp. 148 and 207, and vol. iv., p. 2.

of grain, and in the evening I met him on his return carrying a large and heavy bag. He had travelled over thirty miles, had gone down and again come up some 3,000 feet, and most of his journey had been in a climate much warmer than that of his native hills.

FIG. 1.—TODA MAN. FULL FACE.

My guide at the end of the day would sometimes go a distance of eight or ten miles and back to arrange for my supply of men for the next day's work, and I have seen him on these occasions running at a steady pace which he would keep up for miles. In going from one part of the hills to another, a Toda always travels as nearly as possible in a straight line, ignoring altogether the influence of gravity, and mounting the steepest hills with no apparent effort.

In all my work with the men, it seemed to me that they were extremely intelligent. They grasped readily the points of any inquiry upon which I entered, and often showed a

FIG. 2.—TODA MAN. SIDE FACE.

marked appreciation of complicated questions. They were interested in the customs of other parts of the world, and appeared to grasp readily the essential differences between their own ways and those of other peoples. It is very difficult to estimate general intelligence, and to compare definitely the intelligence of different individuals, still more of people of different races. I can only record my impression, after several months' close intercourse with the Todas, that they were just as intelligent as one would have found any average body of educated Europeans. There were marked individual differences, just as there are among the more civilised, and it is probable that I saw chiefly the more intelligent members of the community.

FIG. 3.—TODA WOMAN. FULL FACE.

My time was largely devoted to experimental work, especially on the nature of the sensory and perceptual processes. The people entered readily into this work, quickly grasped the nature of the methods employed, and showed the same power of close attention and careful observation which, as I have found in other races, enable even more definite and consistent results to be obtained from uncultured races than from most classes of a civilised community.

I had slighter opportunities of estimating the intelligence of the women than that of the men, but, as a general rule, it seemed to me that there was a very marked difference between the

FIG. 4.—TODA WOMAN. SIDE FACE.

two sexes. Some of the younger women, when examined by various tests, showed as ready a grasp of the methods as any of the men, but most of the elder women gave me the impression of being extremely stupid. It was often obvious that they were not attending and were thinking far more of their personal appearance and of the effect it was having on the men of the party than of the task they were being set, but even when a liberal discount was made for this, it seemed to me that they were distinctly less intelligent than the men.

The characteristic note in the demeanour of the people is given by their absolute belief in their own superiority over the surrounding races. They are grave and dignified, and yet thoroughly cheerful and well-disposed towards all. In their intercourse with Europeans, they now recognise the superior race so far as wealth and the command of physical and mental resources are concerned, but yet they are not in the slightest degree servile, and about many matters still believe that their ways are superior to ours, and, in spite of their natural politeness, could sometimes not refrain from showing their contempt for conduct which we are accustomed to look upon as an indication of a high level of morality. It is in the matter of ethical standards that the difference between the Todas and ourselves comes out most strongly.

THE VILLAGE AND THE HOUSE

The Todas live in little villages scattered about the hills. The greater part of the plateau consists of grass-covered hills separated by valleys, sometimes narrow, more often of wide extent. In every valley there are streams and in many places swamps. In the hollows of the hills are small woods, generally known as sholas, and it is usually near these sholas that the Toda villages are to be found. Some parts of the hills are much more thickly beset with villages than others, and this is especially the case in the neighbourhood of the part known as Governor Shola, about six to eight miles west and north-west of Ootacamund.

In other parts one may go considerable distances without finding a Toda village, but relics of the former history of the Todas may be found widely scattered over the hills, and I think there can be little doubt that at one time the Toda habitations were much more generally distributed than they are at present. The bazaar at Ootacamund has now become an important place in the economic life of the Todas; they sell there the ghi or clarified butter in which form their dairy produce chiefly goes to the market, and they procure in return at the bazaar the rice and grain and other things which have now taken their places among the necessaries of life. In consequence there exists a tendency for the larger part of the Todas, especially those of the Todanad, to live within an easy distance of Ootacamund, and many of the villages in the more distant parts of the hills are now only occupied for a few weeks in the year.

The Toda name for a village is *mad*,[1] but this is now often replaced by the Badaga form of the word, *mand*, and the latter word is used exclusively by the Europeans and others living on the Nilgiri hills. A *mad* usually consists of several huts. In some villages there may be only one hut, and the maximum number I have seen is six. At some places where there was formerly a village with dwelling-huts there is now only a dairy, but the term *mad* is still applied to the place at which the dairy is situated. The term *mad* is also given to the funeral-places of the Todas. Sometimes the funeral-place is also a village at which people live; sometimes it has only a dairy; while in other places there may be no trace of human habitations; but the term *mad* is equally applied in all three cases. The term is also used for the dairies and accessory buildings connected with the most sacred herds of buffaloes (the *ti*). Each group of buildings is called a *mad* or *ti mad*. The term has therefore a wider significance than "village" and denotes rather a "place"—a place connected in any way with the active life of the Todas. The chief village of a clan and certain other sacred or important villages are called *etudmad* and other villages are often known as *kinmad*.

A typical Toda village consists of a small group of huts (*ars*), often on a piece of ground slightly raised above the surrounding level and enclosed by a wall (*katu*). In this wall there are two or three narrow openings, large enough to admit a man but not a buffalo. In most villages there is a dairy or there may be several dairies. Each of these buildings is also enclosed by a wall, usually higher than that surrounding the dwelling-huts. The dairies may be near the huts, but more commonly are at some little distance from

[1] The word *marth* is also occasionally used.

FIG. 5.—THE VILLAGE OF TARADR, SHOWING TWO DAIRIES IN THE FOREGROUND AND THREE HOUSES IN THE BACKGROUND.

the latter. Somewhere near the dairy will be found a circular enclosure, the buffalo-pen, or *tu*,[1] in which the buffaloes are enclosed at night, and there may be more than one *tu* for use on different occasions or for different kinds of buffalo. There will be a small pen for the calves which is called *kadr*, and there may also be a house for the calves (*kwotars*). A small structure called *kush* (? *kudsh*), used as an enclosure for calves less than fifteen days old, may often be seen, situated between the spreading roots of a tree.

Close to the village there will be at least one stream (*nipa*), and very often there are two streams. If possible, there should be two streams, in order that one may be used for the sacred purposes of the dairy, the *pali nipa*, while the other is used for household purposes, the *ars nipa*. Where there is only one stream, different parts are used for the two purposes, and the two parts of the stream then receive the names *pali nipa* and *ars nipa*. In this case the *pali nipa* is always above the *ars nipa*, so as to avoid the danger that the water used for the dairy shall have been contaminated by contact with household vessels. At some villages there may even be a third stream, or part of a stream, used in the ordination ceremonies of the dairymen.

It has often been a subject of remark by visitors to the Nilgiri Hills that the Todas have chosen the most beautiful spots for their dwellings, and interest has been taken in the love of beauty in nature which this choice shows. I think there can be little doubt that the choice of suitable dwelling-places has been chiefly determined by the necessity of a good water-supply, and if possible of a double water-supply, and the Todas have chosen the beautiful spots, not because they are beautiful, but because they are well watered. Their choice has been dictated, not by a love of beautiful scenery, but by the practical necessities of their daily life.

In the immediate neighbourhood of a village there are usually well-worn paths by which the village is approached, and some of these paths or *kalvol* receive special names.

[1] Harkness and others have called this pen *tuel*, but repeated inquiry on my part failed to elicit this form of the word. *Tuelu* would mean "where is the *tu*?" and it is possible that Harkness heard the word in this form.

Some may not be traversed by women. When I first visited the village of Taradr, nearly the whole population of the village met me at the spot where the path to the village leaves the road. We all went along together till I suddenly found that I was walking with the men and boys only, while the women and girls were following another path. We were going by the way over which the sacred buffaloes travel

FIG. 6.—THE VILLAGE OF TARADR, SHOWING THE HOUSES SURROUNDED BY A WALL, IN WHICH THERE IS ONE OPENING IN THE MIDDLE.

when leaving or approaching the village, and the women might not tread this path, but had another appointed way by which they were to reach their home.

Within the village there are also certain recognised paths, of which two are especially important. One, the *punetkalvol*, is the path by which the dairyman goes from his dairy to milk or tend the buffaloes ; the other is the *majvatitthkalvol*, the path which the women must use when they go to the dairy to receive buttermilk (*maj*) from the dairyman. Women are not allowed to go to the dairy or to other places connected with it, except at appointed times when they receive buttermilk given out by the dairyman, and when going for this purpose they must keep to the *majvatitthkalvol.* This path is sometimes indicated by a stone, the *majvatitthkars*, and the spot where the women stand to receive the buttermilk is called the *majvatvaiidrn.*

At many villages there are other stones which have definite

FIG. 7.—THE CHIEF HOUSE OF THE VILLAGE OF KIUDR.

names and mark the sites where certain ceremonial functions are performed.

The house is called *ars*, and is of the kind shown in Fig. 7. It is shaped like half a barrel, with the barrel-like roof and sides projecting for a considerable distance beyond the front partition containing the door. The size of the hut is by no means constant; in some cases it is sufficiently roomy to enable people to move about with ease and comfort, while in others it is so small that it is unbearably stuffy, and the smoke from the fire, which is always burning, makes it difficult to believe that anyone can long live in it. The entrance to the hut is always very small, and is closed by a door which slides over the opening on its inner side.

Some houses are much longer than others, with a door at each end and a central partition, so as to form a double hut which is called *epotirikhthars*, *i.e.*, "both-ways-turned house." This kind of hut did not seem to be common, and I only saw three or four examples, of which one is shown in Fig. 8.

A much more common kind of double hut is called *merkalars*, *i.e.*, "other-side house," in which the back part of the hut is partitioned off, with a door at one side.

FIG. 8.—THE VILLAGE OF PEIVÒRS, SHOWING A DOUBLE HUT (IN THE BACKGROUND). THE TWO BUILDINGS ON THE LEFT ARE DAIRIES, AND THE STRUCTURE IN THE CENTRE IS A CALF-HOUSE.

In some Toda villages there may now be found huts of the same kind as those of the Badagas. In the cases in which I found such huts, I was told that they had been built by Badagas who had lived in the villages while the Toda occupants were away. Todas may also occasionally be found living away from their own villages, usually near tea plantations. They do this because there is a demand for buffalo manure at the plantations, and when living in this way they not uncommonly use huts of the Badaga pattern.

In front of the hut on either side of the door there are usually raised seats called *kwottün*, and there are similar raised portions, called *tün*, within the huts on which the people sleep. The floor of the hut is divided into two parts, which are marked off from one another by the hole in which grain is pounded by the women. The part in front of this is often used for churning, and with this part women have nothing to do, their operations being limited to the hinder part.

FIG. 9.—A TODA MAN, SIRIAR (20), WITH HIS WIFE AND CHILD, SHOWING THE ORDINARY METHOD OF WEARING THE 'PUTKULI.'

There is little difference between the dress of men and women. Each wears a mantle called the *putkuli*, which is worn thrown round the shoulders without any fastening. Under it is worn a loin-cloth called *tadrp*, and the men also wear a perineal band called *kuvn*, corresponding to the Hindu *languti*. The *kuvn* is kept in position by a string round the waist called *pennar*, a string which, we shall see later, is of considerable ceremonial importance.

There are various ways of wearing the cloak which will be

more fully described in Chapter XXIV. It will be sufficient to say here that when showing reverence, a Toda bares his right arm, this method of wearing the cloak so that the arm is exposed being called *kevenarut*. It is shown in Figs. 1 and 10.

THE DAILY LIFE OF THE TODAS

The daily life of the Toda men is largely devoted to the care of their buffaloes and to the performance of the dairy operations. As we shall see later, much of the dairy work is the duty of certain men set aside to look after the sacred buffaloes and the sacred dairies connected with them. A large proportion, however, of the Toda buffaloes are not sacred, and their care falls on the ordinary Todas. The milking and churning is chiefly the duty of the younger men and boys, but the older men also take their part, while the head of the family exercises a general superintendence.

FIG. 10.—KÒDRNER PERFORMING THE SALUTATION CALLED 'KAIMUKHTI.' HIS RIGHT ARM IS BARED ('KEVENARUT'), AND HE HAS REMOVED HIS TURBAN.

On rising in the morning, the men salute the sun with the gesture called *kaimukhti*, shown in Fig. 10, and then they turn to their work of milking the buffaloes and churning the milk.

When the dairy operations of the morning are over, the buffaloes are driven to the grazing ground, the people take their food and go about any business of the day. Some may collect firewood and procure the leaves used as plates and drinking vessels; others may carry out any necessary tendance which the buffaloes require, or may go to fetch grain or rice from Badaga villages or from the bazaar. The chief men of the village may perhaps have to attend a meeting of the *naim*, or council, which holds very frequent sittings to adjudicate upon the many disputed points which arise in connexion with the intricate social organisation of the people.

While the men are doing their work, the women will have been seeing to their special tasks, of which three, represented in Fig. 11, have come to be regarded as pre-eminently woman's work.

They pound the grain with the *wask* in a hole situated in the middle of the floor of the hut,[1] and when the pounding is finished the grain is sifted with the *murn*, or sieve, and the hut is swept with the *kip*. It seemed that pounding grain is normally performed wearing the *tadrp* only.

Though these are the three operations which are regarded as pre-eminently woman's work, the women have other things to do. They rub the seats or beds both inside and outside the hut with dried buffalo-dung, and use the same material to cleanse the various household utensils. They mend the garments of the family, and some women devote much time to the special embroidery with which they adorn their cloaks.

The ordinary routine of the day is often broken by the visits of people from other villages, who may have come to talk over a proposed marriage or transference of wives; to announce some approaching ceremony; to discuss some business connected with the buffaloes, or perhaps, but probably rarely, to pay a friendly call. Such a visit will probably give the opportunity of observing the characteristic Toda salutation shown in Fig. 12.[2] This is essentially a salutation between a woman and her male relatives older than herself. If a man

[1] For the purpose of photography, a hole was made outside the hut exactly like that within the hut. The picture must not be taken to indicate that pounding is ever normally performed out of doors.

[2] The old man on the right in this picture shows a very characteristic Toda attitude, in which a person crouches down completely enveloped in the cloak.

visits a village in which he has any female relatives younger than himself, these will go out to meet him as he approaches the house, and each bows down before the man, who raises his

FIG. 11.—WOMEN POUNDING AND SIFTING. THE BROOM IS ON THE GROUND TO THE RIGHT.

foot, while the woman places her hand below the foot and helps to raise it to her forehead, and the same salutation is repeated with the other foot. This mode of greeting is called *kalmelpudithti*,[1] or "leg up he puts." It is usually a salutation in which women bow down before men, but it may also take place between two men or between two women, while on certain occasions a male may bow down and have his forehead touched by the feet of a woman.

In the evening the buffaloes again find their way to the milking-place, and the operations of the morning are repeated. When these are finished the buffaloes are shut up in the enclosure, or *tu*, for the night; the lamp is now lighted and saluted by the men who use the same gesture as that with which the sun had been saluted in the morning. The people then take their food and retire to rest.

Sketch of Social Organisation

I shall consider the social organisation in detail at a much later stage, but it is necessary to give here a brief sketch in order to make its main features clear before going on to describe the Toda ceremonial, which often shows differences according to the division or clan with which the ceremony is connected. The fundamental feature of the social organisation is the division of the community into two perfectly distinct groups, the Tartharol and the Teivaliol. As we shall see more fully later, there is a certain amount of resemblance between these two divisions and the castes of the Hindus. There is a certain amount of specialisation of function, certain grades of the priesthood being filled only by members of the Teivaliol. Further, marriage is not allowed between members of the two divisions, though certain irregular unions are permitted; a Tarthar man must marry a Tarthar woman, and a Teivali man a Teivali woman. The Tartharol and Teivaliol are two endogamous divisions of the Toda people.

Each of these primary divisions is subdivided into a number of secondary divisions. These are exogamous, and I shall speak of them throughout this book as 'clans,' using this word as the best general term for an exogamous division of a tribe or community.

[1] This salutation has been previously known by its Badaga name, *adabuddiken*.

FIG. 12.—THE 'KALMELPUDITHTI' SALUTATION TAKING PLACE AT THE VILLAGE OF NÒDRS. ON THE LEFT IS THE HOUSE; ON THE RIGHT IS THE LESS IMPORTANT DAIRY OF THE VILLAGE (THE 'TARVALI'), AND IN FRONT OF IT IS THE STONE CALLED 'MENKARS.'

Each clan possesses a group of villages and takes its name from the chief of these villages, the *etudmad*, and the people of a clan are known as *madol*, or village people.

The Tartharol are divided into twelve clans, which take their names from the villages of Nòdrs, Kars, Pan, Taradr, Keradr, Kanòdrs, Kwòdrdoni, Päm, Nidrsi, Melgars, Kidmad, and Karsh.[1] The people of each clan are known as Nòdrsol, Karsol, Panol, &c. The Kidmadol and Karshol are much less important than the other ten clans, having split off from the Melgarsol in comparatively recent times. The original number of Tarthar clans appears to have been ten, and I have no record that any clan of this division has become extinct.

The Teivaliol are divided into six clans, or *madol*, taking their names from the villages of Kuudr, Piedr, Kusharf, Keadr, Pedrkars, and Kulhem. The people of Kuudr are called both Kuudrol and Kuurtol, and similarly the people of Piedr and Keadr are often called the Piertol and Keartol.

Here again two clans, the Pedrkarsol and the Kulhemol, are less important than the others. They are offshoots of the Kuudrol, but the separation is of very long standing.

There was some doubt as to the existence of another clan, the Kwaradrol, but it seemed certain that these people, who have now died out, formed a subdivision of the Keadrol.

One Teivali clan has become extinct, its last member having died, it was said, about a hundred years ago. This clan took its name from the village of Kemen, which was near Kiudr, but no trace of this village exists at present and I think it probable that the Kemenol have been extinct longer than the Todas suppose.

The villages of each clan are usually situated in the same part of the hills, though there are very often outlying villages far from the main group. At any one period of the year, only some of the villages of the clan are occupied. The people may move about from one village to another accord-

[1] In these names and throughout the text the signs to indicate long vowels are generally omitted. In order to ascertain the exact method of pronunciation, the map or the list of villages in Appendix III. should be consulted.

ing to the need for pasturage, and the villages in the Kundahs and other outlying parts of the hills appear only to be visited during the dry season before the south-west monsoon sets in.

Each clan is further subdivided, these subdivisions being of two kinds. One, called the *kudr*, is only of ceremonial importance, and we shall meet with it first in the chapter dealing with offerings. The other, called the *pòlm*, is of more practical importance, and is the basis of the machinery for regulating any expenses which fall on the clan as a whole.

CHAPTER III

DAIRIES AND BUFFALOES

THE milking and churning operations of the dairy form the basis of the greater part of the religious ritual of the Todas. The lives of the people are largely devoted to their buffaloes, and the care of certain of these animals, regarded as more sacred than the rest, is associated with much ceremonial. The sacred animals are attended by men especially set apart who form the Toda priesthood, and the milk of the sacred animals is churned in dairies which may be regarded as the Toda temples and are so regarded by the people themselves. The ordinary operations of the dairy have become a religious ritual and ceremonies of a religious character accompany nearly every important incident in the lives of the buffaloes.

Among the buffaloes held by the Toda to be sacred there are varying degrees of sanctity, and each kind of buffalo is tended at its own kind or grade of dairy by its own special grade of the priesthood; buffaloes and dairies forming an organisation the complexities of which were far from easy to unravel.

Each kind of dairy connected with its special kind of buffalo has its own peculiarities of ritual. The dairies form an ascending series in which we find increasing definiteness and complexity of ritual; increasing sanctity of the person of the dairyman-priest, increasing stringency of the rules for the conduct of his daily life, and increasing elaboration of the ceremonies which attend his entrance upon office. There are also certain dairies in which the ritual has developed in special directions, and there are special features of the organisation of buffaloes and dairies not only in each of the two chief divisions of the Toda people, but also in many of the clans of which each division is composed.

I propose in this chapter to sketch some of the chief features of the buffalo and dairy organisation, and in succeeding chapters there will follow detailed accounts of the different dairies and of the ceremonial which accompanies the daily work of the dairy and the important events of buffalo life.

THE DAIRY ORGANISATION

The first distinction to be made concerns the buffaloes. These animals are divided into those of a sacred character and those which may be called 'ordinary buffaloes.' The latter are known as *putiir*; they may be kept at any village, are tended by the men and boys of the village—in Toda language, they are tended by *perol*, or ordinary persons—and their milk is churned in the front part of the dwelling-hut. There is no special ritual of any kind connected with these buffaloes or with their milk, and there are no restrictions on the use of the milk or its products.

The classification of the sacred buffaloes is very different in the two divisions of the Toda people. The Teivaliol possess only one class of sacred buffalo and these buffaloes are called collectively *pasthir*. The Tartharol, on the other hand, have several classes of sacred buffalo, and, so far as I could ascertain, they have properly no collective term for all of them, though they are often spoken of by the Teivali term, *pasthir*.

Possessing only one kind of sacred buffalo, the dairy organisation of the Teivaliol is comparatively simple. The milk of the *pasthir* is churned in dairies at the more important villages of each clan. The dairy is, in general, called *pali*,[1] and the dairyman is called *palikartmokh*, 'dairy watch-boy,' or *palikartpol*, 'dairy watch-man,'[2] according to his age; but,

[1] This word should probably be *paḷḷi* and was usually pronounced *paḷthḷi*, but I have adopted the spelling of the text for the sake of simplicity.

[2] According to some Todas, *kart* was a shortened form of *karitht*, milking or milked.

probably owing to the general custom of employing youths or young men to fill the office of dairyman, the term *palikartmokh* is in far more general use, and is often employed even when the dairyman is an elderly man.

At many of the chief Teivali villages, there are two dairies; a large dairy, called *etudpali*, and a smaller, called *kidpali*. Each of these dairies should have its own *palikartmokh*, and this is still the case when both dairies are used, but at most villages at the present time one of the two dairies has been disused and there is in consequence only one dairyman.

Both ordinary and sacred buffaloes are the property, not of the whole clan, but of families or individuals, and the buffaloes tended at the dairy of a village are, in general, the property of the family living at that village. A large clan with many villages, such as that of Kuudr, has many dairies in working order and a corresponding number of dairymen.

Among the Tartharol the organisation is far more complicated. Most Tarthar clans have more than one kind of sacred buffalo in addition to the ordinary buffaloes or *putiir*. In every clan there is one kind of sacred herd which may be said to correspond to the *pasthir* of the Teivaliol. The milk of these buffaloes is churned in a dairy called *pali* by a dairyman called *palikartmokh* or *palikartpol*. There are, however, two grades of dairy corresponding to these buffaloes. The lower grade is called the *tarpali*, or more commonly *tarvali*, and is served by a *tarvalikartmokh*. The higher grade is called *kudrpali*, tended by a *kudrpalikartmokh*. There is no distinction of buffaloes corresponding to this distinction of dairies, the same buffaloes being tended sometimes at a *kudrpali* and sometimes at a *tarvali*. The distinguishing feature of a *kudrpali* is the possession of a *mani*, or sacred bell, and the greater elaboration and stringency of its ritual is due to the presence of this sacred object.

In addition to the buffaloes tended at the *tarvali* or *kudrpali*, most Tarthar clans possess other sacred buffaloes called *wursulir*. These buffaloes are tended by a dairyman called *wursol* and their milk is churned in a dairy called *wursuli* or *wursulipali*. One point which marks off this branch of the dairy organisation from the preceding is that the dairyman, or *wursol*, must belong either to the Teivaliol or to the Melgars clan of the Tartharol. Both *tarpalikartmokh* and *kudrpalikartmokh* are chosen from the Tartharol, either of the same or of a different clan from that of the dairy, but the *wursol* must be taken either from the members of the other chief division of the Todas or from one special clan of the Tartharol, a clan which has many other peculiar privileges and occupies a position in some ways intermediate between Tartharol and Teivaliol.

The ritual of the *wursuli* is distinctly more elaborate than than that of either *tarvali* or *kudrpali*, and the *wursol* is a more sacred personage, so far as one can judge from his rules of conduct and the elaboration of his ordination ceremonies.

Two Tarthar clans have dairies of especial importance and sanctity, in both of which there are distinctive features of ritual.

The people of Taradr possess a herd of buffaloes called *kugvalir* which take their name from the dairy, the *kugvali* or *kugpali*, meaning the chief or great dairy. The *kugvalir* are tended by a *kugvalikartmokh*, who must belong to the Taradrol. The six chief families of this clan take charge of the buffaloes for periods of three years in rotation, and the head of the family in charge selects the *kugvalikartmokh*.

The other Tarthar dairy which occupies an exceptional position is that of *Kanòdrs*, which is called a *poh*, and is tended by a dairyman called *pohkartpol*. The ritual both of this dairy and of the *kugvali* of Taradr resembles in some respects that of the most sacred Toda dairies, the dairies of the institution called the *ti*.

The number and nature of the dairies are different in the different Tarthar clans and in different villages of the same clan. The Melgars clan has only one kind of dairy, the *tarvali*. The Nòdrs clan now has a *tarvali* and a *wursuli*, and at most Kars villages there are both *kudrpali* and *wursuli*, but formerly both at Nòdrs and Kars there were three kinds of dairy, *tarvali*, *kudrpali*, and *wursuli*. Some Pan villages have *tarvali* and *wursuli*, others *kudrpali* and *wursuli*. At Taradr there are both *tarvali* and *wursuli* in addition to the special institution of that clan, the *kugvali*.

All these various kinds of dairy are situated at the villages where the people live. In addition, five Tarthar clans possess dairies where are kept herds of great sanctity, the herds of the *ti* or the *tiir*. These buffaloes are kept at special dairies far from any village where people live. A place where such a dairy is situated is called a *ti mad*, or *ti* village, and each sacred herd moves about from one *ti mad* to another at different seasons of the year, and the group of places, together with the herds connected with it, is known collectively as a *ti*.[1] The *ti* is thus the name of a special institution comprising buffaloes, dairies, grazing grounds, and the various buildings and objects connected with the dairies.

The *ti* is presided over by a dairyman-priest called *palol*, who is assisted by a boy or youth called *kaltmokh* or, more rarely, *kavelol*. Formerly it was the custom in most cases that a *ti* should have two *palol*, each of whom had his own herd of buffaloes and his own dairy, so that each *ti mad* had two dairies. This custom now persists in full at one *ti* only, though in other cases there are still two dairies, of which one is not used, or is only used on special occasions.

Though the *ti* is, in every case, regarded as the property of a Tarthar clan, the *palol* must be chosen from the Teivaliol, and in some cases the choice is restricted to certain Teivali clans. The *kaltmokh* must belong either to the Teivaliol or to the Melgars clan of the Tartharol. The dairy of a *ti* is always called a *poh*.

The ritual of the *ti* reaches a far higher degree of complexity than is attained in any village dairy. The *palol* is a far more sacred personage than the *wursol* or the *palikartmokh*; his life is far more strictly regulated, and the ceremonies attendant on his entrance into office are far more elaborate. The ceremonies connected with dairy or buffaloes are more numerous, and when they correspond to ceremonies performed at the lower grades of dairy, they are much more elaborate and prolonged.

[1] In previous accounts of the Todas, the place where these sacred herds are kept has always been called a *tirieri*. This is not properly a Toda term, but is that used by the Badagas.

THE DAIRY

There are two forms of Toda dairy. One resembles very closely the ordinary hut, and, but for its situation and the higher wall which surrounds it, it might often be supposed to be one of the huts. The vast majority of dairies are now of this form. The other kind of dairy is circular with a conical roof. There are now only three or four of these buildings in existence, though others have only fallen into ruins in recent times. Breeks, who wrote in 1873, says[1] that at that time there were four, and a fifth in ruins.

The best known of these dairies is that at Nòdrs (the Manboa of Breeks), shown in Fig. 13. It has received the name of "the Toda Cathedral," and is one of the show places of the Nilgiris. Another (shown in Fig. 25) is at Kanòdrs (the Mutterzhva of Breeks). Both are village dairies of especial sanctity; the Nòdrs building is in full working order, while that of Kanòdrs is only occupied occasionally. A third dairy of the conical form is at the *ti* place of Anto near Sholur (the Kiurzh of Breeks) and should be regularly visited once a year, though the year in which I was on the Nilgiris was an exception. The fourth dairy of the kind (called by Breeks Tarzhva) is at Tarsòdr on the Kundàhs. It is also a *ti* dairy, but is now falling into ruins, having been disused for about twenty years. The ruined dairy mentioned by Breeks (Katedva) is said to be still in the same condition. It was used as a *ti* dairy, and is near Makurti Peak.

There is no doubt that conical dairies were at one time more numerous. There was one at the *ti* place of Enòdr, not far from Ootacamund. There was another at the village of Kars, and the circular wall which once surrounded the dairy still remains, and has been converted into a buffalo pen.

The various names given to the Toda dairies are at first sight very confusing. We have already seen that each kind of dairy is named according to the kind of buffalo connected with it—according to its position in the dairy-series connecting *tarvali* with *ti*. Each dairy has also its own special or indi-

[1] *An Account of the Primitive Tribes and Monuments of the Nilagiris*, 1873, p. 14.

FIG. 13.—THE CONICAL DAIRY OF NÒDRS. THE STONE AT THE RIGHT-HAND END OF THE WALL IS THE 'TEIDRTOLKARS' (see p. 439).

vidual name; thus the *kudrpali* of Kars is called Tarziolv, and the *wursuli* of the same village, Karziolv.

In addition to these two sets of names, there is another distinction of a more general kind. There are two general names, *poh* and *pali*, and every dairy is one or other of these. The former name is given to every *ti* dairy, to every dairy of the conical form,[1] and to certain other dairies at the older and more important villages. Some of the latter are ordinarily called *pali*, but the name *poh* lingers in the name employed for the dairies in prayer (see Chapter X), or in the individual names of the dairies; thus the dairy at the ancient village of Nasmiòdr is ordinarily called a *pali*, but its individual name is *Tilipoh*. I think it probable that originally *poh* and *pali* were the names of the two forms of dairy, the conical kind being called *poh* and the ordinary kind *pali*. At the present time every existing conical dairy is a *poh*, and every dairy which is said to have been in the past of the conical form is called *poh*. It seems probable that in many cases a dairy, originally of the conical form, has been rebuilt in the same form as the dwelling-hut, owing to the difficulty and extra labour of reconstruction in the older shape; and that in some of these cases the dairy of the new form has retained the name of the old and is still called *poh*, at any rate on certain occasions. All the dairies to which the name *poh* is ever given are either *ti* dairies or are situated in villages of especial antiquity and sanctity.

There is now no definite rule as to the grade of dairymen who shall serve at a dairy called *poh*. The *poh* of a *ti* is, of course, occupied by a *palol* and *kaltmokh*. The conical *poh* of Nòdrs, the old conical *poh* of Kars, and several old dairies which are still called *poh* in the prayers are, or were, tended by dairymen of the rank of *wursol*, while several *poh* of the ordinary shape belonging to the Teivaliol are occupied by dairymen called *palikartmokh*. The only place at which the dairyman takes his name from the *poh* is Kanòdrs, where the conical dairy is occupied by a *pohkartpol*.

[1] This word, in the forms *boa*, *boath*, &c., has by previous writers been limited to dairies of the conical shape. There is no doubt that it has at present a far wider application.

There is a considerable degree of uniformity in the orientation of dairies of all grades. The doors usually face in an easterly direction, and in the majority of those I observed

FIG. 14.—THE LOWER PART OF THE CONICAL DAIRY OF NÒDRS, WHICH IS HIDDEN BY THE WALL IN FIG. 13. THE 'WURSOL' IS SHOWN EATING 'AL' FROM A LEAF-PLATE.

the door faced north of east, the most frequent direction being some point between east and north-east. In one case, that of the *ti poh* at Mòdr, the door of the dairy faces south-east; but in front of the door there is a screen, and on leaving his dairy the *palol* always turns to the left, so that he faces north-east as he goes towards his buffaloes. In a few dairies the door faces directly west, and, according to Breeks, this is the case at the conical dairy of Anto.

THE TODA BUFFALO

The Toda buffalo is a variety of the Indian water-buffalo, but the life on the hills seems to have produced a much finer animal than that of the plains. Although thoroughly under the control of the Todas, the buffaloes are semi-wild and often attack people of a different race from their owners, and Europeans have frequently been severely injured by the onslaught of these animals.

The Toda name for the male buffalo is *er*, and for the female *ir*, but either term may be used when the people speak of buffaloes collectively. Calves have different designations at different ages. A young calf is *kar*, one from one to two years of age is *pòl*, and a three-year-old calf is *nakh*.

Defective buffaloes, and especially those with only one horn, are called *kwadrir*, and those whose horns bend downwards are *kughir*. Barren buffaloes are called *maiir*.

There are considerable differences of colour among the buffaloes. Those much lighter than the rest are called *nerir* or *pushtir*, and there is a legend about the origin of these buffaloes, which, however, I failed to obtain. The only obvious way in which the animals differ from one another in marking is that some have a black stripe running down either side of the neck very much in the position which would be occupied by the chain suspending a bell.

There do not seem to be any physical differences between the buffaloes of different classes, and, as we shall see shortly, the nature of the breeding of the Toda buffaloes is such as would have entirely destroyed any distinctions of the kind if they had ever existed.

Every adult female buffalo has an individual name, which is usually given when her first calf is born. The number of buffalo names is limited, so that many buffaloes bear the same name.

The following are among the buffalo names of which I have records:—Kûdzi or Kûrsi, Kâsimi, Pän or Pern, Kiûd or Kiûdz, Enmon, Koisi, Keien, Ilsh or Idrsh, Kârsthum, Perûv or Perov, Kebân, Enmars, Persud, Nerûv, Kôzi, Perith, Pülkoth, Persuth, Tòthi, Kerâni, Keirev, Püthiov, Peires, Nersâdr, Tâlg, Ûf, Köji, Persv, Arvatz, Kòjiû, Pundrs, Purkîsi, and Òrsum.

Both Tartharol and Teivaliol have the same names for their buffaloes, and it seemed that a buffalo of any village herd might have the same name as one belonging to the *ti*. It is possible, however, that certain names may be restricted to the *ti* herds. I collected some names which occurred only in these herds, but I cannot say positively that they might not also be used for less sacred buffaloes.

Male buffaloes are unnamed and appear to have little or no sanctity even when born of cows of the most sacred herds. The greater number of male calves are either killed at *erkumpthtiti* ceremonies (Chap. XIII) or given away to the Kotas. A few are kept for breeding purposes, usually in the proportion of two to every hundred females.

There is a singular absence of care about the breeding of the buffaloes. The Todas have many herds of which every female has some degree of sacredness, and it might have been expected that the bulls of a sacred herd would have been carefully chosen from the male calves of that herd. So far as I could ascertain after repeated inquiries, there was no restriction of any kind in the mating of the sacred animals; a bull of the ordinary buffaloes (*putiir*) of a village might even mate with the highly sacred animals of a *ti* dairy. No importance seemed to be attached to the question of paternity among the buffaloes, and so far as I could ascertain the people were quite indifferent whether the male was related or unrelated to the female, whether of the same or of another herd.

I did not hear of the existence of any ceremonies connected with the chosen male buffaloes. Marshall states[1] that a bull new from one of the sacred *ti* herds undergoes a process of sanctification before he is permanently installed,

[1] *A Phrenologist among the Todas*, 1873, p. 132.

by being isolated for a day and night in a small pen in the sacred woods of the *ti*, during which time he is deprived of food, though allowed access to water. Marshall also states that it is permissible to introduce a bull from an ordinary drove "after due sanctification." Though I failed to obtain definite confirmation of Marshall's statement, it is possible that something of the kind may at one time have taken place or may even still take place.

At the present time the buffaloes are tended entirely by males, and males only are allowed to take any part either in the work of the dairy or in those dairy operations which are performed in the house. There is a tradition that at one time women attended to the buffaloes at the time of calving, and one incident is recorded in which women performed Cæsarian section on a dying buffalo (p. 78), but this custom has now long ceased to be followed.

The first buffaloes were created by one of the chief Toda gods, Ön, and his wife. The buffaloes created by the male deity were the progenitors of the sacred buffaloes, while the ordinary buffaloes or *putiir* are descended from those created by the wife. Certain other buffaloes are descended from ancestors created by other gods, but the account of their various creations may be deferred till the chapter containing the legends of the gods. I was told by some that the sacred buffaloes were descended from a sambhar deer, but it was later found that this was only believed to be true of one special group of buffaloes belonging to one clan.

Dairy Procedure

The general plan of the dairy procedure is the same in all dairies, the difference between different dairies lying chiefly in certain formalities accompanying certain stages of the procedure.

The day's operations begin with the churning of the milk drawn on the previous evening. The milk is poured from the milking-vessels into earthenware pots, and during the night it will have coagulated. The coagulated mass is first broken up by the churn; water and butter already made are added, and then the churning is continued till the milk separates into a solid part, which I shall speak of as 'butter,' and a liquid, which I shall call 'buttermilk.' It must be remembered, however, that these do not correspond to the butter and buttermilk of a European dairy. The milk coagulates before the cream has risen in any quantity, and there is no skimming. The 'butter' consists of both the fat and casein of the milk, while the 'buttermilk' ought perhaps rather to be called 'whey.'

In order to avoid this ambiguity in the use of the words 'butter' and 'buttermilk,' it might have seemed desirable to use the Toda terms for these products; but I have not done so, partly in order to avoid the too frequent use of Toda words, partly because the names are not constant among the Todas themselves, different terms being used in different dairies.

When the churning is finished, the butter and buttermilk are put into their appropriate vessels, and the dairyman goes out to milk the buffaloes, using for this purpose a bamboo milking-vessel, into which he has put some buttermilk from the previous churning. The newly drawn milk is poured into the earthenware vessels, in which it stands till the afternoon. By this time the milk will have become solid, and is churned as in the morning.

The 'butter' is used chiefly in the form of ghi, or clarified butter, for which the Toda name is *nei.* The butter is clarified by keeping it over the fire after the addition of grain or rice. The latter sinks to the bottom of the vessel, while the *nei* consists of the liquefied fat of the milk. The *nei* or ghi is partly used by the Todas, but is largely sold at the bazaar. The deposit of grain or rice is called *al*, and is one of the chief Toda foods. It is, no doubt, mixed with part of the proteid constituents of the milk precipitated during the process of clarification.

The milking-vessel is of bamboo, and several of the small vessels used in the dairy procedure are also made from bamboo of various sizes. The vessels into which the milk is poured and in which it is churned are of earthenware, and the vessels in which the butter and buttermilk are kept are also

FIG. 15.—ÒD (26) CHURNING.

of this kind. The earthenware vessels used in the ordinary dairy-work are made by the Kotas.

The names of the different dairy vessels vary according to the dairy in which they are used, and these, together with a complete list of the dairy vessels and implements, will be reserved till later.

The method of churning is shown in Fig. 15. The churning is always done within the hut or dairy, but in order to obtain a photograph of the process a staff was put in the ground outside a hut, so that the figure shows exactly the method used within the hut or dairy. The upright staff is called *palmän*, or 'milk-tree'; the two rings by means of which the churning-stick is fastened to the *palmän* are called *palkati*, or 'milk-ties.' The cord by which the churning-stick, or *madth* is revolved is called *kudinan* or *palv*.

The general plan of the dairy operations appears to be much the same as that practised elsewhere in India. There are, however, two special features of the Toda procedure which, so far as I know, are not in general use elsewhere. One of these is the addition of buttermilk from a previous churning. This addition probably hastens the process of coagulation, and has a material use, but in the hands of the Todas it has become of great ceremonial importance, and forms the basis of some of the most interesting features of the dairy ritual.

The other special feature which does not seem to be generally found in India is the addition of grain or rice when clarifying the butter. Unlike the addition of buttermilk, this has no ceremonial value, and is chiefly important in providing the Todas with one of their favourite foods.

THE CARE OF THE ORDINARY BUFFALOES

The ordinary buffaloes, or *putiir*, of a village are looked after and milked by the males of the village; by those who in Toda terminology are *perol*, or ordinary men, as compared with those who have been ordained to one of the sacred dairy offices.

When the people rise in the morning, the buffaloes are

released from the pen, or *tu*, in which they have been enclosed for the night, and the animals make their way at once to the place where they are accustomed to be milked, the *irkarmus*. At the same time, or a little later, the calves are released from their enclosure, the *kadr*, and each calf runs to its mother. The milk of the previous night is churned in the interior of the dwelling-hut, usually by one of the youths of the family.

FIG. 16.—THE MORNING MILKING AT THE VILLAGE OF MOLKUSH. IN THE BACKGROUND IS A MODERN 'TU' MADE OF WOODEN PALINGS.

In the dairy one man has to carry out all the dairy operations, and here the churning is always finished before the milking begins; but in the case of the ordinary buffaloes, where many take part in the work, the two operations may go on simultaneously, and while one man or boy is churning, others will be milking the buffaloes and carrying the milk into the hut. Usually it seemed that each of the males of the family was taking his part in the proceedings.

Whenever I watched the milking operations, I saw one

man, the head of the family, walking about and superintending the operations, while several other men and youths were milking the buffaloes or churning the milk within the hut. It seemed as if in general each buffalo gave very little milk, and a man soon left one buffalo to go to another, and as the bamboo milking-vessels are small and have soon to be emptied, there was a constant moving about from one buffalo to another

FIG. 17.

and from the milking-place to the hut. A typical milking scene is shown in Fig. 16. Each man carries a stick, with which he keeps off troublesome calves who may come to suck while the milking is going on (see Fig. 17). If a buffalo and its calf are troublesome, milk is sometimes smeared on the back of the calf, and the buffalo occupies herself with licking the calf, a process which keeps both quiet. At other times, a man may pour milk into his hollowed hand which he gives to one of the buffaloes to drink.

When the milking is over, the buffaloes are driven to their grazing-ground, where they remain till the afternoon, when they return, often spontaneously, to the milking-place, and the operations of the morning are repeated.

While at the pasturage, one or two small boys are often in attendance to keep the buffaloes from straying beyond the proper grazing-ground.

CHAPTER IV

THE VILLAGE DAIRY

THIS chapter will be devoted to a description of the various kinds of dairy which are found at the Toda villages. An account will be given of the daily course of the dairy operations and of the ritual accompanying it. The description of special ceremonies which occur in connexion with the dairy will be reserved till future chapters, in which ceremonies of the same nature occurring in all grades of dairy can be considered together.

A village dairy is often situated at some little distance from the huts in which the people live, though sometimes it is in their immediate neighbourhood. When of the same form as the hut, it may not at once be distinguished from the latter, but it is usually enclosed by a higher wall which surrounds the building more closely, so that there is very little room between the two. The door seemed to me to be usually smaller than that of most of the huts, and it is always capable of being closed by a shutter on the inner side.

The dairy is usually divided into compartments completely separated from one another by a partition extending to the roof, one room being entered from another by a small door of the same kind as that by which the dairy itself is entered. The majority of dairies have two rooms, an inner room called ***ulkkursh*** and an outer room called ***pòrmunkursh***. Many dairies, especially among the kind called ***wursuli***, have only one room. At five Tarthar villages, viz., Nòdrs, Taradrkirsi, Keradr, Akirsikòdri, and Tim, there are dairies which have three rooms, the inner and outer rooms being separated by a third, called the *nedrkursh*. Each of the five villages at which these dairies are found is the funeral-place for males of the clan to which the village belongs, and the body of a dead man is placed in the outer room of the dairy at each place during the funeral ceremonies.

At Nòdrs and Tedshteiri (villages of the Nòdrs clan) it is said that there were at one time dairies each of which had seven rooms. The ruins of these, which were of the grade called *kudrpali*, are still to be seen.

Sometimes the same building serves for two dairies, especially at the less important villages of a clan. In these cases the building resembles that kind of hut which is called *merkalars*, one compartment of the hut opening at the side. At the villages at which I found dairies of this kind, the front part of the hut was a *kudrpali* and the part with the door at the side was a *wursuli*. In these cases each dairy has only one room.

In every dairy which has more than one room, the dairy vessels are kept in the inner room and the actual dairy operations are performed by the dairyman in this room. He only is allowed to go into the inner room, while other men may go into the outer room and, in those cases in which there are three rooms, into the middle room.

When a village dairy has two or more rooms, the outer room first entered from the outside is often used as a sleeping-place and in this case usually has two of the couches called *tün*, one on each side with a fireplace between them. That on the right-hand side as one enters is called the *meitün* (*meiltün*), or high (superior) bed, and that on the left-hand side is the *kitün*, or low (inferior) bed.

In the outer room is kept the *kepun* or *kaipun* (hand vessel), used to hold the water with which the dairyman washes his hands. The *masth*, or axe used for cutting firewood, and the *tek* or *tekh*, a basket used to bring rice or grain into the dairy, are also kept in this room.

The fireplace between the two sleeping-places is usually made of four stones and is called *kudrvars*. At the *wursuli* it is made of three stones and is called *waskal*.

The room of the dairy which contains the dairy vessels is divided into three parts: the *patatmar*, the *ertatmar*, and the *kalkani*.

The *patatmar* takes its name from the *patat*, an earthenware vessel into which the milk is poured from the milking vessel and in which it is churned. The vessels kept in this part of the inner room, which are known collectively as *patatpur*, are those which are actually used in the milking and churning.

The *ertatmar* takes its name from the *ertat*, a bamboo vessel used to carry buttermilk or butter out of the dairy. The *ertat* and the vessels kept with it, known collectively as the *ertatpur*, are those which receive the products of the churning or are used to convey these products out of the dairy. The lamp and the fire-sticks used for making fire by friction are also kept in this part of the dairy.

In the third part of the room, called the *kalkani*, are kept leaves, firewood, knives, and various sticks or wands. According to some accounts, the vessel called *penpariv* is also kept here.

When the dairy vessels are taken into a new dairy (see Chap. VI.), they are placed on ferns. I do not know whether they always rest on a bed of ferns or whether the ferns are only used when the vessels are first placed in the dairy.

The following is a list of the *patatpur*, the vessels and other objects which are kept in the part of the dairy called *patatmar*:

Patat or *tat*. Earthenware vessels into which the freshly drawn milk is poured and in which it is churned (Fig. 18, F). There are several of these vessels, one of which may be used to hold water.

Irkartpun or *patatpun*. The bamboo milking-vessel (Fig. 18, I).

Parskadrvenmu or *parskadrpenmu*, *i.e.*, milk churn butter *mu* (Fig. 18, H). This is also sometimes called *kazhmu*, and is a small earthenware vessel in which is kept the butter (*pen*) which is added while churning. Except when the churning is in progress, it is used as a cover for the *patat*.

Adimu. An earthenware vessel (Fig. 18, K) into which

FIG. 18.—THE CHIEF DAIRY VESSELS.

A. The *palmän*.
B. The *palkati*.
C. The *madth*.
D. A *tedshk*.
E. The *ertatpun*.
F. The *patat*.
G. The *pòlmachok*.
H. The *parskadrvenmu*.
I. The *irkartpun*.
K. The *adimu*.

some of the coagulated milk may be poured while churning. It may also be used to fetch water from the dairy stream.

Madth or *parskartmadth*. Churning-stick (Fig. 18, C).

Palkati. Bamboo rings for holding the churning-stick while churning.

Parskurs or *ularwurthkurs*. Stick or wand used chiefly for driving off calves while milking.

Tatkich. The cut-up ends of a churning-stick, used for cleaning the *patat*.

Tedshk. Rings made of rattan (Fig. 18, D), used in carrying the dairy vessels.

The garment of the dairyman, called *tuni*, is also kept here. and when there is a *mani* (bell), it is kept on the *patatmar*. The churning-stick is kept on a stand called *agar*.

The following are the objects kept on the *ertatmar*:

Majpariv. Vessel in which buttermilk is kept.

Penpariv. Vessel in which butter is kept. (According to some, this vessel is kept in the part called *kalkani*.)

Ertatpun. Vessel used to take buttermilk or butter out of the dairy (Fig. 18, E).

Majertkudriki. A small earthenware pot used like a ladle to take buttermilk out of the *majpariv*. It is also called *ashkiok*.

Pòlmachok. A bamboo vessel (Fig. 18, G) used to hold the buttermilk which is distributed to the people of the village.

Nirsi. The fire-sticks for making fire by friction.

Pelk. The lamp.

Tòratthadi. Cooking vessel which may be used for anything except barley.

Put, a stirring-stick.

When there is only one room, the *masth*, axe for cutting firewood, may be kept on the *ertatmar*; otherwise it is kept in the outer room.

The vessels and other objects of the *patatmar* are those which come directly into contact with the milk of the buffaloes or which may at any time come into contact with the buffaloes themselves.

The vessels and objects of the *ertatmar*, on the other hand, are those which contain the dairy products which are going out to ordinary people (*perol*), or which come into contact with food or other materials obtained from ordinary people.

The things of the *patatmar* are always kept apart from those of the *ertatmar*. When the buffaloes migrate from one grazing-place to another, the things of the *patatmar* are carried by one man and those of the *ertatmar* by another.

In connexion with many dairies there is a house in which calves are kept, the *kwotars*, and a place for very young calves, called *kush* or *kudsh*, which is sometimes partly formed by the spreading roots of a tree.

I am in some doubt as to whether the buffaloes belonging to a village dairy ever have a special *tu* in which they are enclosed for the night. In general, however, there is no doubt that the sacred buffaloes of the dairy occupy the same pen as the ordinary buffaloes. Similarly I am not clear whether the dairy always has its own *irkarmus*, or milking-place, or whether ordinary and sacred buffaloes are not often milked at the same spot, the dairyman recognising the buffaloes committed to his charge and milking them only.

Every dairy has its own place from which water is drawn the *pali nipa*. This may be a different stream from that used for household purposes, but is, perhaps, most commonly part of the same stream, the higher part being used for dairy purposes. When a village has more than one dairy, each dairy has its own place for drawing water, usually different parts of the same stream.

The foregoing account holds good of all kinds of village dairy. The different grades of village dairy present differences in the daily procedure, in the qualifications and rules of conduct of the dairyman, and in other respects. I will begin with the *tarvali* of the Tartharol.

The Tarvali

This is the name applied to the lowest grade of Tarthar dairy and may mean "the ordinary dairy," the first syllable being probably the same as in the word "Tarthar."

The *tarvali* is always of the ordinary form and is never called *poh*. The dairyman, or *tarvalikartmokh*, is often a youth or man of the village to which the dairy belongs, but he may be taken from any other village of the clan or from other Tarthar villages, the choice in some cases being restricted to certain clans. The only Tarthar clan which is strictly limited to its own members in the choice of *tarvalikartmokh* is that of Melgars. In all cases this grade of dairyman must be one of the Tartharol; he is never taken from the other division of the Toda people.

When the dairyman is taken from another clan, he may receive certain wages, viz., two cloaks (*putkuli*) in the year and six rupees, together with the loan of a milking buffalo for the use of his family. I have no definite information whether anything is given to dairymen who are members of the clan or family to which the dairy belongs.

The dairyman is regarded by the Todas as a servant, especially when taken from another clan. I was often told that a man was working for another and was his servant, and always found that the so-called servant was *palikartmokh* at the dairy of the village at which the master lived. Correspondingly, there seemed to be no doubt that the dairyman was treated with very scant respect, except on ceremonial occasions and when actually performing the ritual of his office.

The *tarvalikartmokh* wears nothing but the *kuvn*, or perineal band, when he is in the dairy, and wears a loincloth called *irkarthtadrp* when milking. When away from his work or when looking after his buffaloes on the grazing-ground, he wears the ordinary cloak, or *putkuli*. He usually sleeps in the outer room of the dairy, but is allowed to sleep at any time in the dwelling-hut. When he goes there he may only touch the sleeping-place (*idrtül*) and the floor (*kuter*). If he touches any other part of the hut, he at once loses his office and becomes an ordinary person. There are no restrictions on the intercourse of the *tarvalikartmokh* with women.

When the *tarvalikartmokh* rises in the morning, he leaves the dairy, raising one or both hands to his face as in Fig. 10 and saying *Sami* or *Swami*. He often also says this word when getting up from the sleeping-place. He first lets the buffaloes out of the pen (*tu*) in which they had been put for the night and then goes into the dairy to churn. He does not light the

FIG. 19.—THE 'WURSOL' OF NŌDRS CARRYING THE 'ADIMU' AND 'PATATPUN' TO FETCH WATER.

lamp in the morning unless it is dark, nor does he pray. The milk poured into the *patat* overnight will have coagulated, so that it forms a solid mass called *adrpars*. The dairyman puts the churning-stick into the *patat* and churns for a little time till he has broken up the *adrpars*.[1] Then he pours off most of the semi-fluid milk into another vessel (also a *patat*), leaving about one *kudi*[2] in the churning-vessel. He adds to this some butter from a previous churning, which he takes from the *parskadrvenmu*, adds also some water, and churns the mixture till butter is formed. He pours out the buttermilk into the *majpariv*, keeping the butter in the *patat*, adds more coagulated milk and water, and churns again, transferring the buttermilk to its vessel when butter is formed. He continues in this way till all the milk has been churned, and he then transfers the butter which has been formed to the vessel called *penpariv*, also putting a small portion in the *parskadrvenmu*.

The *palikartmokh* then goes out to milk, with the *irkarthpun* and the wand called *parskurs* or *ularwurthkurs*. He puts into the milking-vessel some buttermilk, the buttermilk used for this purpose being called *pep*, and he also smears some butter on the edge of the vessel to put on the teats of the buffaloes. When he goes out, he salutes by raising the *irkarthpun* and *parskurs* to his forehead in the same manner as is shown in Fig. 27. When he has filled the milking-vessel, he goes into the dairy and empties the milk into the *patat* and returns to the buffaloes. This is repeated till all the buffaloes have been milked, after which the dairyman takes food and buttermilk, but with no prescribed ritual as in the case of more sacred dairies. He also gives out buttermilk to the people of the village. After the work of the morning is over, the *palikartmokh* may go out to look after the buffaloes, or may collect firewood, leaves, or other things necessary for his work. During the later hours of the morning the *palikartmokh* may often be seen lying down taking a rest before he begins the work of the afternoon, which is more ceremonial than that of the morning.

[1] This is literally 'cooked milk.' It probably receives this name because the coagulation is often hastened by heating.

[2] About four pints.

About three o'clock in the afternoon he goes to the dairy, bows down and touches the threshold with his forehead (*pavnersatiti*, Fig. 20), enters and touches a vessel on the *patat* side, and then a vessel on the *ertat* side. He then lights the fire and inspects the milk drawn in the morning. If it has not become solid, he puts it on the fire for a few minutes to hasten the coagulation. He lights the lamp and prays,

FIG. 20.—THE 'PALIKARTMOKH' SALUTING THE THRESHOLD OF THE DAIRY AT KIUDR 'PAVNERSATITI.'

using the prayer of the dairy (see Chap. X), and then churns as in the morning. When he has finished churning, he clears the churning-stick of the butter clinging to it, and after holding it to his forehead and uttering the sacred word "*Oñ*," he puts it in the stand called *agar*. He then goes out to milk as in the morning, taking buttermilk in the milking-vessel. When the milking is over, he shuts up the buffaloes in the pen for the night, and as he does so, he repeats the prayer of the dairy, the prayer being exactly the same as that used when lighting the lamp. He then takes food and goes to sleep, often saying *Swami* as he lies down for the night.

The *tarvali* of the Melgars people is in some ways regarded as superior to the other *tarvali* of the Tartharol. The Melgars *tarvalikartmokh* may not go to the *tarvali* of another Tarthar clan, though the *tarvalikartmokh* of another clan may go to a Melgars *tarvali*. This was said to be due to the higher degree of sanctity of the Melgars dairy and office, but there do not appear to be any differences of ritual corresponding to this different degree of sanctity.

THE KUDRPALI

The special feature of the *kudrpali* is that it contains one or more of the bells called *mani*. This involves several additions to the ceremonial of the dairy, and these are accompanied by more stringent rules of conduct for the dairyman.

Whenever engaged in his work, the *kudrpalikartmokh* must be naked except for the *kuvn*. In the cold Nilgiri mornings it must often be a very unpleasant task to have to milk the buffaloes with no covering, and I was told that at some places, and especially at Nòdrs, the people gave up the maintenance of a *kudrpali* on account of the difficulty experienced in obtaining men to undertake the office of dairyman.

When the *kudrpalikartmokh* is taking his meals, he must hold his food in his hands till he has finished. He is not allowed to put it down on the ground, as may be done by the dairyman of the *tarvali*.

Soon after beginning to churn, the *kudrpalikartmokh* takes up some of the broken-up curd (*adrpars*) and puts it on the bell (*mani*) three times, saying "*Oñ*" each time, and milk from the vessel first brought into the dairy is also put on the bell in the same manner.

At the *kudrpali* of Kars, the dairyman puts the curd and milk on a board called *pato*. The bells of this dairy have been lost, and the dairyman puts the milk on the board on which the bells used to hang. The process of putting milk on the bells is properly called *terzantirikiti*, but the Todas often speak of the process as "feeding the bell." At the *kudrpali* of Kuzhu, belonging to the Kars clan, milk is put in the same way on a gold bracelet.

When making butter, it will be remembered that the dairyman of the *tarvali* makes a certain amount, and then pours away the buttermilk, and repeats this till all the *adrpars* has been converted into butter and buttermilk. Whenever the *kudrpalikartmokh* pours away buttermilk, he takes a piece of

FIG. 21.—THE 'KUDRPALI' OF KARS, WITH THE 'KUDRPALIKARTMOKH' STANDING ON THE WALL. IN THE FOREGROUND IS THE MOUND CALLED 'IMUDRIKARS' IN THE BACKGROUND ON THE RIGHT IS THE CALF-HOUSE.

the bark of the sacred *tudr* tree (*Meliosma pungens* and *Wightii*) and beats three times on the *patat*, saying "*Oñ*" each time. This ceremony is called *pepeirthti*, and is the exclusive privilege of the *kudrpalikartmokh*. If this ceremony should be omitted, the buttermilk may not be drunk by any one.

The *kudrpalikartmokh* is allowed to sleep in the ordinary hut, but only on special days—viz., Sunday, Wednesday, and Saturday—and on these days he must, like the *tarvalikartmokh*, avoid touching anything in the hut except the sleeping-place and the floor on pain of losing his office. He is allowed intercourse with any Tarthar woman, but must have nothing to do with the women of his own division, the Teivaliol.

While in office, the *kudrpalikartmokh* is not allowed to visit the bazaar,[1] and if he does so he becomes an ordinary person at once. One afternoon when I was working with Parkurs (8), one of the elders of the Kars clan, Sakari (7), who had been *kudrpalikartmokh* at Kuzhu, came to announce that he had visited the bazaar at Ootacamund. He was therefore no longer *palikartmokh*, and he came to tell Parkurs that a successor must be appointed. It seemed to me in this case that Sakari had visited the bazaar because he was tired of office and wished to become free. I had a suspicion also that he wished to become acquainted with my proceedings, for he came straight to me from the bazaar and was one of my most regular attendants for some time after his deprivation. The *kudrpalikartmokh* is prohibited from entering a *tarvali*, though the *tarvalikartmokh* may enter a *kudrpali*.

The milk of buffaloes connected with a *kudrpali* is more sacred than that of buffaloes milked at a *tarvali*. Any one may drink milk from a *tarvali*, but the milk of the *kudrpali* may only be drunk by the *palikartmokh*. If any one else drink the milk of the *kudrpali* it is believed that he will die. I could learn of no case in which a man had taken this milk, but Kòdrner (7) had seen a cat die on the day it had drunk milk of the *martir*, the buffaloes of the *kudrpali* of Kars. Kòdrner was somewhat of a sceptic in connexion with many of the beliefs of his people, but he was very much in earnest on this occasion, and when my interpreter said he should like to drink some of the milk, Kòdrner offered to give him one hundred rupees if he drank the milk of *martir* for four days and remained alive.

The buffaloes tended at the *tarvali* and *kudrpali* are of several named kinds. According to tradition, each clan at the original distribution of buffaloes by Teikirzi (see p. 186) was given a certain kind. To Kars were given the buffaloes

[1] I am not sure whether this restriction does not also apply to the *tarvalikartmokh*.

called *martir*; to Nòdrs were given *nashperthir*; to Pan, *pineipir*; to Melgars, *persasir*; these buffaloes originally given being called in general *nòdrodvaiir*; lit. "buffaloes who rule."

In various ways the buffaloes originally given to one clan have passed into the possession of other clans. This has happened when buffaloes have been purchased, but is chiefly due to the existence of several customs which involve gifts of buffaloes. The tradition also runs that soon after the buffaloes were originally given, the Nòdrs people built the *kudrpali* with seven rooms to which I have already referred and begged the Kars people for *martir* to milk at this dairy. Similarly the people of Kanòdrs borrowed *martir* from Kars to milk at their conical dairy, and similar transferences of buffaloes may have occurred between other clans. In these and possibly in other ways buffaloes have passed from one clan to another, and as the buffaloes have in many cases kept their original names, most clans now possess buffaloes of several kinds.

I was for a long time very doubtful about the relation of the *kudrpali* and *tarvali* to one another, and had very great difficulty in finding out which buffaloes belonged to each kind of dairy. Finally, it became quite clear that the same buffaloes might be milked either at a *kudrpali* or a *tarvali*, and that the possession of a *mani* was the chief point which determined whether a given dairy was a *kudrpali* or a *tarvali*.

The same kind of buffalo may be milked at one kind of dairy in one clan and at the other kind in another clan. The *nashperthir* of Nòdrs are milked at the *tarvali* of that place, but those of Kars are milked at the *kudrpali* together with the *martir*. Further, in at least one case, the same buffaloes might be milked in one village of a clan at a *kudrpali* and in another village at a *tarvali*. The Pan people now live chiefly at Naters and the chief villages of the clan in the Kundahs, Pan and Kuirsi, are deserted during the greater part of the year. When these villages are occupied the *pineipir* are milked at their *kudrpali* dairies, but when the people are at Naters the same buffaloes are milked at the *tarvali*. The *mani* is left at Pan, and I was told that if the bell were to be brought to Naters a *kudrpali* would have to be built for its reception and the *pineipir* would then be milked at this dairy.

At the present time the only clan which has a *kudrpali* in constant use is that of Kars. The Pan clan only uses its *kudrpali* during the few months that the villages in the Kundahs are occupied. The Nòdrs clan is said to have had a *kudrpali* at one time, but the fact that they had to borrow buffaloes for it from Kars points to the especial connexion of the *kudrpali* with the latter clan.

Although the Karsol and Panol are the only clans which have a *kudrpali*, the special feature of which is the possession of a *mani*, these are not the only clans which own these sacred bells. In other cases the *mani* belongs to the next higher grade of dairy, the *wursuli*, and the Kars clan itself also possesses *mani* kept at this grade of dairy. Indeed, although the Kars *kudrpali* is said to have bells as its special feature, these bells do not really exist, having been stolen some years ago. The fiction of their presence is, however, kept up, and, as we have seen, the place where they should hang is still 'fed' with curd and milk.

In one case, that of the Kars *kudrpali*, I worked out in detail the ownership and care of the buffaloes called *martir*. There were altogether forty-eight of these buffaloes kept at six places and tended by seven dairymen, who were chosen from the Karsol or from the people of Nòdrs, Pan, Taradr or Keradr.

The distribution at the time of my visit was as follows :—

Kutadri (7)	possessed	8	buffaloes	kept at	Kars	tended by	Idjen of Taradr (22)
Kutthurs (12)	,,	8	,,	,,	,,	,,	Tilipa of Kars (12)
Parkurs (8)	,,	8	,,	,,	Isharadr	,,	Kosners of Nòdrs (6)
Pidrvan (9)	,,	6	,,	,,	Pakhalkudr	,,	Tidjkudr of Nòdrs (6)
Kuinervan (14)	,,	6	,,	,,	Peletkwur	,,	Pons of Keradr (26)
Potheners (10)	,,	6	,,	,,	Keshker	,,	Palpa of Pan (16)
Nudriki (8)	,,	3	,,	,,	Kuzhu	,,	Mutkudr of Kars (15)
Mongeithi (15)	,,	3	,,	,,	,,	,,	,, ,,

It will be noticed that in only two of the dairies did the *palikartmokh* belong to the Karsol, and in each case he looked after the buffaloes of his own father, Mutkudr also tending the buffaloes of Nudriki. Idjen was the son-in-law of

Kutadri, and Palpa had married a Kars woman, who was not, however, closely related to Potheners, to whom he was acting as dairyman. Kosners and Tidjkudr were given to me as examples of a practice in which a man of one clan works for one of another,[1] and they received the same wages as in the case of the *tarvalikartmokh* (see p. 62).

These facts show clearly that the *kudrpalir* are not regarded as the property of the whole clan, but belong to different families, and the same is true of the buffaloes milked at the *tarvali*. Each family possesses its own sacred buffaloes as well as its ordinary buffaloes or *putiir*, and in some cases the buffaloes of each family have their own dairyman, even when the milk of two herds is churned in the same dairy.

THE WURSULI

Most of the Tarthar clans possess herds of buffaloes called collectively *wursulir*, each herd being tended by a diaryman called *wursol* at a dairy called *wursuli* or *wursuli pali*. The buffaloes of different clans have special names. At Nòdrs, they are called *mersgursir*; at Kars and Taradr, *püdrshtipir*; at Pan, *kudeipir*; at Keradr, *miniapir*; and at Nidrsi and Kwòdrdoni, *keitankursir*. The people of Päm, Kanòdrs, and Melgars have no *wursulir*; Päm and Kanòdrs both had buffaloes of this kind at one time, but they have been allowed to die out. Melgars, on the other hand, never had *wursulir*, the tradition being that none of these buffaloes were assigned to the clan at the original partition by Teikirzi.

The *wursulir* are said to have been given to most clans at the original partition of buffaloes, but no reason could be given for the creation of this special kind of buffalo. The Keradr clan are believed to have received their *wursulir* from Korateu (see Chap. IX), the buffaloes being descended from a sambhar calf given by this god.

A special feature of the *wursuli* is that the dairyman or *wursol* of this Tarthar dairy has to be taken either from the Teivaliol or from the Melgars clan of the Tartharol. The

[1] See Chapter XXIII.

Melgars people could hold the office of *wursol*, but had no *wursulir* themselves. At the present time the majority of men who hold this office are drawn from the Teivaliol, only two belonging to Melgars, and it seemed that it was only when the supply ran short among the Teivaliol that the Tarthar people had recourse to members of their own division. The Melgarsol do not share fully the privileges of the Teivaliol in respect of this office, for though they may perform the ordinary work of the dairy, there are certain duties of the *wursol*, such as those at the funeral ceremonies, which may only be performed by a Teivali occupant of the office.

The *wursol* has to go through more complicated ordination ceremonies than the *palikartmokh*, and has a distinctly higher degree of sanctity so far as one can judge from the rules for his conduct. He may not be touched by any ordinary person, and in general the rules regulating his conduct are more stringent than those for the ordinary dairyman.

The *wursol* has two dresses; one, the grey garment called *tuni*, which is worn at his dairy work and kept in the dairy; the other, the ordinary *putkuli*, which he wears when not engaged at his special work.

The *wursol* does not sleep in his own dairy, but in one of a different kind, a village which has a *wursuli* always having at least one other dairy. At Kars he sleeps in the *kudrpali*, and at Nòdrs in the *tarvali*. He is allowed to sleep in the hut of a Tarthar village on two nights in the week—viz., Sunday and Wednesday—and on these occasions he may have intercourse with any Tarthar woman. Except on these occasions he loses his office even if touched by a woman. He is not allowed to have intercourse with any Teivali woman, even with his wife if he is married, on pain of becoming an ordinary person.

He may go to any Tarthar village, but to no Teivali village—*i.e.*, if one of the Teivaliol, he is allowed to visit none of his own people.

When he goes to the dwelling-hut, care is taken to remove from the hut the objects shown in Fig. 11—viz., the *murn* or sieve, the *wask* or pounder, and the *kip* or broom. It seems as if these three objects are removed because they are used by women. The emblems of womanhood are not allowed to contaminate the house while the *wursol* is present, although, at the same time, he is not restricted from intercourse with the women themselves. On the mornings after he has slept in the hut he bathes from head to foot before going to the dairy, and prostrates himself at the threshold before he enters.

If the cloak of the *wursol* requires cleaning or mending, it may only be taken to the hut for these purposes on the same days as those on which the *wursol* may sleep there—viz., Sunday or Wednesday.

The food of the *wursol* is prepared for him by the *palikartmokh* of the dairy in which he sleeps. The *wursol* never prepares food either for himself or others, except on the occasion of the festival called *irpalvusthi* (see Chap. VIII).

Most *wursuli* have only one room, the exception being the *poh* at Nòdrs, and the *wursuli* of Nasmiòdr and Òdr. It is noteworthy that these, however, are three of the most ancient and important dairies of the Todas. The reason why the other *wursuli* have one room is probably the fact that the *wursol* is not allowed to sleep in the dairy, and consequently there is no necessity for an outer room. When these dairies have been rebuilt, or new dairies have been made, the Todas have probably not thought it worth while to keep two rooms except at the especially important and sacred places. I was also told, however, that each of the three places which have two rooms had been at one time a *ti* dairy, and, as we shall see later, dairies of this, the highest, grade always have two rooms.

Another indication of the special sanctity of these three dairies is that at them, and also at the *wursuli* at Kozhtudi, the *wursol* must never turn his back on the contents of the dairy—*i.e*, he must do all his work and go in and out of the dairy facing the place where the *mani* is kept. The Todas call this proceeding in which the back is never turned on the contents of the dairy "*kabkaditi*."

The vessels of the *wursuli* are divided, like those of the ordinary dairy, into those of the *patatmar* and those of the *ertatmar*. The following sketch of the arrangement was made by Kòdrner, but I do not feel confident of its accuracy.

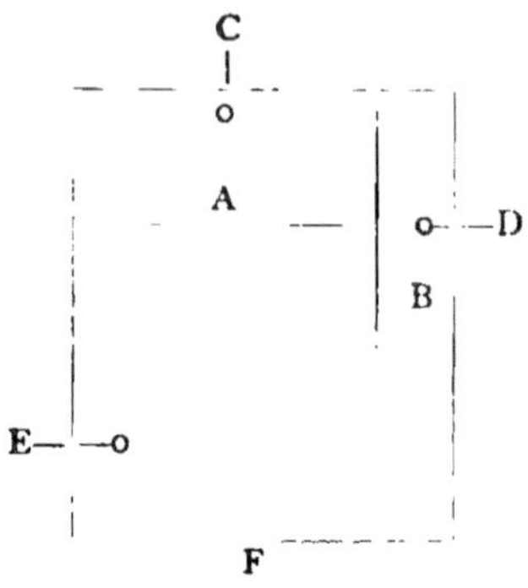

A. *Patatmar*.
B. *Ertatmar*.
C. The *mani* or bell.
D. The *pelk* or lamp.
E. *Waskal* or fireplace.
F. The door.

FIG. 22.

The lamp is of iron, bought in the bazaar: it is called *tudrkpelk* or *tagarspelk*, according as it is hung by a hook or on a chain. This distinction probably holds for other village dairies.

THE DAILY LIFE OF THE WURSOL

The dairy work of the *wursol* is carried out on the same general lines as that of the *palikartmokh*, but the order and method of the various operations are more strictly regulated. Before the *wursol* goes into the dairy in the morning he washes his hands with water from the vessel called *kepun*,[1] bows down at the threshold and enters the dairy; salutes the *mani* (*kaimukhti*), goes to the *ertatmar* and touches the *majpariv*; then to the *patatmar* and touches the *patat*. Then, after lighting the fire, he takes the *mu* off the *patat*, and, if the milk has coagulated, he begins to churn. After churning for a little while he puts some of the coagulated milk on the *mani*. After the churning is over, he milks, putting some of the first milk on the bell.

After the milking is finished, buttermilk is distributed to the women, and a mixture of milk and buttermilk is given to the men, who come to drink it standing outside the dairy. The *wursol* then drinks buttermilk and eats. When taking

[1] Probably a corruption of *kaipun*, hand vessel.

buttermilk he pours it from the vessel called *ertatpun* into the leaf[1] from which he drinks. When he goes to attend to the buffaloes, he leaves the *tuni* in the dairy and puts on his *putkuli* in a special way which is only adopted by the *wursol* and only by him when engaged in looking after the buffaloes. Placing one end of the cloak over the left shoulder, he brings the other end under the right arm, and, taking this end in his right hand, throws it round the back of his neck so that it

FIG. 23.—THE 'WURSOL' OF KARS, KERNPISI (56), STANDING BY THE SIDE OF HIS DAIRY.

rests on the left shoulder. The result of this adjustment is that the front part of his body is uncovered as shown in Fig. 23. I could not ascertain why the *wursol* should wear his cloak in this special way, nor why this method of wearing the garment should be peculiar to his office.[2]

[1] This is done by folding a leaf in such a way that it forms a cup.

[2] The method of wearing the cloak adopted by the *wursol* is not unlike that shown in a picture at the Guimet Museum in Paris, which represents a Brahman engaged in prayer.

In the afternoon the *wursol* again washes his hands, bows down to the threshold and enters the dairy, salutes the *mani*, touches the *majpariv* and *patat* as in the morning, and lights the fire. He then lights the lamp, and prays, using the prayer of the village. Then he churns and "feeds the bell," but his procedure differs from that of the morning in that he distributes the buttermilk at this stage of the proceedings. When he milks he puts some of the first milk on the bell, and when he shuts up the buffaloes in their enclosure (*tu*) for the night, he recites the same prayer as when lighting the lamp. He then takes his food, eating it outside the dairy, puts his *tuni* on the *patatmar*, and goes to rest.

The procedure thus differs from that of the *tarvali* and *kudrpali* in that the dairy vessels are touched ceremonially at the beginning of both morning and evening operations. The *wursuli* resembles the other dairies, however, in that prayer is offered in the evening only. The differences are less pronounced in ritual than in the rules of conduct.

THE KUGVALI OF TARADR

The people of Taradr have a special institution which is in many ways intermediate between the dairies of the village and the institution to be described in the next chapter—the *ti*.

The buffaloes connected with this institution are known as the *kugvalir*. They are said to belong to the whole of the Tartharol, but this only seems to mean that they are so important that every Toda looks up to them and feels that they are in some measure his. It does not mean that every Toda has a voice in their management or share in their produce.

The people of Taradr are divided into six families (*pòlm*), and each family has charge of the *kugvalir* in turn for periods of three years, the head of the family having the chief direction. At the present time they are in charge of Siriar (20), having only recently passed to his family.

The head of the family in charge appoints the dairyman, who is called *kugvalikartmokh*. This dairyman must be a member of the Taradr clan, but need not necessarily be a member of the family in charge.

Each of the chief Taradr villages has a special dairy for the *kugvalir*. It is called the *kugvali* (*kugpali*) or chief dairy (*kug* = *etud* = chief), and it was said to be the chief of all the dairies. All these dairies have one room only, except that at Taradr itself, where there are two rooms. These dairies do not at present differ in form or general appearance from

FIG. 24.—THE 'KUGVALI' OF TARADR. ON ITS LEFT IS THE 'KWOTARS,' AND ON THE EXTREME RIGHT, UNDER THE TREE, IS THE 'KUSH.' THE FLAT STONE TO THE RIGHT OF THE 'KUGVALI' IS THE 'PÜDRSHTIKARS' (see p. 654).

dairies of other kinds. The *kugvali* at Taradr is shown in Fig. 24, and it is the dairy on the right-hand side of Fig. 5.

The *kugvalir* have one feature peculiar to themselves. They are never recruited from any other herd. Even the buffaloes of the *ti* often have additions to their number, especially through the ceremony of *irnörtiti* (Chap. XIII), but in no circumstances are any additions from outside made to the *kugvalir*.

There is a legend that the original buffaloes of this herd

were sent from Amnòdr[1] by the god Ön to the people of Taradr. A long time after they came to Taradr the herd was on the point of dying out, only one cow buffalo remaining, which was so old that it had lost its teeth. This sole survivor was pregnant, and when about to calve the delivery was much delayed, and it seemed that the buffalo would die before the calf was born. Only women were present and they cut open the belly of the buffalo and took out the calf, which was tended very carefully and lived, and the existing *kugvalir* are descended from this calf.

This story preserves a tradition of the practice of women attending to the buffaloes at the time of calving, which is said to have been at one time the regular practice.

The *kugvalikartmokh* sleeps in the *kwotars* or calf-house, except at Taradr, at which place he sleeps in the outer room of his dairy. He is allowed to sleep in the ordinary hut on certain nights in the week, and may only have intercourse with Tarthar women.

He wears the grey garment, or *tuni*, which he ties round his waist when churning and wears over his shoulders when milking.

The work of the dairy is carried out on the same general lines as that already described, but with certain distinguishing features.

All the work is done *kabkaditi*; the dairyman never turns his back to the contents of the dairy. In those villages in which he sleeps in the calf-house he goes naked (except for the *kuvn*) to the *kugvali*, washes his hands, prostrates himself at the threshold, enters, and puts on his *tuni* which is kept on the *patatmar*. He salutes the *mani*, which he feeds with curd and milk as in other dairies. He also knocks on the *patat* three times, saying "*Oñ*" each time.

As in the other village dairies, he only prays and lights the lamp in the evening. When he gives out buttermilk, he must use the vessel called *pòlmachok*. He drinks buttermilk (*peputi*) in a distinctly more ceremonial manner than in the ordinary dairy, sitting on the seat (*kwottün*) outside the dairy, and pouring from the *ertatpun* into a leaf-cup made of two

[1] The world of the dead.

leaves of the kind called *kakuders*. He drinks three times only, raising the leaves to his forehead and saying "*Oñ*" each time.

In this more definite ceremonial when drinking buttermilk, we have a transition to the ritual of the *ti*, and this resemblance to the procedure of the *ti* is still more marked in the following features. In addition to the *kugvalir*, the *kugvalikartmokh* has certain ordinary buffaloes, *putiir*, to provide milk for his personal use, and these buffaloes are milked in a special vessel called *kuvun* (*kupun*). This vessel is also used to transfer butter and buttermilk from the *patatmar* to the *ertatmar*, *i.e.*, buttermilk is not poured directly from the *patatpun* into the *majpariv*, but poured from the former into the *kuvun* and from this into the *majpariv*, and similarly the butter is transferred from *patatpun* to *penpariv* by means of the same vessel.

The Dairy of Kanòdrs

Another dairy-temple which occupies an exceptional position is the *poh* at Kanòdrs. This is a dairy of the conical form, shown in Fig. 25, which differs from that of Nòdrs in being surrounded by two walls (*katu*), both of which are shown in the photograph.

According to one account the people of Kanòdrs borrowed *martir* from Kars to be milked at this dairy, but at the present time, when the dairy is occupied, the cattle milked are those called *nashperthir*.

The dairyman at this *poh* is called *polhkartpol* and must be a Kanòdrs man. During my visit, the dairy was not occupied and the office of *polhkartpol* was vacant. At the present time a dairyman is appointed about once a year and holds office for thirty or forty days only. So far as I could ascertain, the failure to occupy the dairy constantly is due to the very considerable hardships and restrictions which have to be endured by the holder of the office of dairyman, and the time is probably not far distant when this dairy, one of the most sacred among the Todas, will cease altogether to be used.

When a *pohkartpol* is in office he is allowed to have one companion, who is a *perol*, or ordinary person, *i.e.*, he undergoes no special ordination ceremony. With the exception of the two men, no one is allowed to go near the building for any purpose. When I visited the place, my guide stayed a considerable distance away from and out of sight of the dairy while I went with my interpreter to inspect the building and its surroundings. The *pohkartpol* and his companion

FIG. 25.—THE 'POH' OF KANÒDRS. THE TWO WALLS ARE SHOWN.

sleep in the *kwotars*, or calf-house, in which there is a bed (*tün*) for each. This building has no door and is a very flimsy structure, so that sleeping in it can differ very little from sleeping in the open air. There is a fireplace between the two beds, but its warmth can hardly be sufficient for any degree of comfort. Further, the *pohkartpol* may only wear the *tuni*, a very scanty garment as compared with the *putkuli*. The *pohkartpol* must be celibate while in office, and his companion, must also be celibate while at the dairy. The *pohkartpol* must take his food sitting on the outer wall which surrounds the dairy. He must not put his hand to his mouth, but must throw his food in ; nor must he put the leaf used as a cup to his lips, but must pour into his mouth from above.

Several of these rules and restrictions are even more severe than those for the *palol*, to be considered in the next chapter. The reason given for the strictness of ritual is that the god Kwoto or Meilitars "had done so many wonderful things on that side" (see Chapter IX).

One feature peculiar to the Kanòdrs dairy is that milk receives the special name *persin*. This is the name of the churning-vessel of the *ti*, but is not used for milk in any other dairy. Otherwise the names used at Kanòdrs are the same as at other village dairies.

THE TEIVALI DAIRY

Among the Teivaliol, the various grades of dairy and dairymen so far considered have no existence. Many Teivali villages have two dairies, but each is served by a *palikartmokh* of the same rank.

The general procedure of the Teivali dairy does not appear to differ in any very marked respect from that of the Tarthar *tarvali*. The most marked difference which I could discover is in the clothing of the dairyman. When engaged in the dairy operations, the Teivali *palikartmokh* wears, at any rate in some cases, the *tuni*, or garment of dark grey cloth of the same kind as that worn by the *wursol*.

The sacred buffaloes of the Teivaliol are known as *pasthir*, and there are no differences corresponding to the different grades of the Tartharol. Similarly with one exception, the Teivali *pasthir* of each clan have no special names like the *martir*, *nashperthir*, &c., of the Tartharol. The exception is that the buffaloes of the Piedr clan are called *kudeipir* or *kudipir*, apparently the same name as that of the *wursulir* of Pan.

The village of Kiudr, belonging to the Kuudrol, possesses a dairy of special sanctity (see Fig. 31). It is served by a *palikartmokh*, and it does not appear to have any special complexities of ritual except in connexion with certain bells which this dairy contains. There are six of these bells, two kept on the *patatmar*, called *patatmani*, and four kept on the *ertatmar*, called *ertatmani*. During the dairy ceremonial these bells are 'fed' by the *palikartmokh*, the *patatmani* receiving milk and the *ertatmani* buttermilk. I only became aware of the existence of these bells incidentally, and had not the opportunity of ascertaining their history or meaning. It is clear, however, that they differ from the *mani* of the Tartharol and from those of the Piedr clan among the Teivaliol in that they are never used at a funeral (see p. 352).

CHAPTER V

THE TI DAIRY

THE *ti* is the name of an institution which comprises a herd of buffaloes with a number of dairies and grazing districts tended by a dairyman-priest or priests called *palol* with an assistant called *kaltmokh*. Each dairy with its accompanying buildings and pasturage is called a *ti mad*, or *ti* village.

In most cases there are two kinds of buffaloes at each *ti*, and each kind should properly be tended by its own *palol* and *kaltmokh*. There is, however, only one *ti* which possesses two *palol* at the present time, and they share a *kaltmokh* between them, though a second is appointed on certain ceremonial occasions. In other cases one *palol* tends both kinds of buffalo, and in others, again, the dairies are unoccupied for the greater part of the year and the office of *palol* is only filled for certain limited periods.

Each *ti* is regarded as the property of a Tarthar clan, but the *palol* has to be taken from the Teivaliol, the choice being in some cases restricted to one or two Teivali clans; thus, the *palol* of the Nòdrs *ti* must belong either to Piedr or Kusharf. The *palol* is chosen by the Tarthar owners, but the latter do not seem to gain any material advantage from their possession. In fact, it involves them in some expense owing to the necessity of giving certain feasts, and this expense was put forward as one reason why a *ti* is often unoccupied. Never-

G 2

theless the Tartharol are very proud of the fact that the institution of the *ti* belongs to their division, and whenever I asked a Tarthar man why he considered his people superior to the Teivaliol, the answer always ran that they had the *ti* and that the Teivaliol who tended the *ti* were their servants.

The buffaloes belonging to a *ti* are of two kinds, distinguished as *persinir* and *punir*. The former are the sacred buffaloes, and the elaborate ceremonial of the *ti* dairy is concerned with their milk. The *punir* correspond in some respects to the *putiir* of the ordinary village dairy, and their milk and its products are largely for the personal use and profit of the *palol* and are not treated with any special ceremony. The *persinir* are usually of various kinds, but the nature of their classification is different at each *ti* and its consideration may be postponed till later.

I obtained most of my information from people connected with the Nòdrs *ti*. During the whole of my visit the herds of this *ti* were at Mòdr, which is only about a mile from the Paikara bungalow. Owing to the restrictions on intercourse with so sacred a personage as a *palol*, it was not practicable to obtain all my information from those actually in office, and I found it best to work with men who had formerly held the post and had retired. I worked chiefly with Kaners (63), an old man who had been *palol* at the Nòdrs *ti*, and with Koboners (58), who had been at the Kars *ti*. For some time I worked with one or other of these two men every day, paying occasional visits to Mòdr to observe as much of the ceremonial as I was allowed to see. On these occasions I was also able to consult Karkievan, the chief *palol*, on points about which the ex-officials were doubtful.

Both Kaners and Koboners were trustworthy witnesses, but Kaners was old and had given up his office some time before, and in consequence often committed faults of omission. Koboners was an admirable informant, and the fulness of the account of the *ti* ceremonial is largely due to him. It must be remembered that I was only able to see for myself a few superficial features of the ceremonial, and that my account is based on the descriptions given by these and other men, but nevertheless I have a considerable degree of confidence in its essential accuracy.

The dairy of a *ti* is always called *poh*, whatever its shape may be, and at those places where there is, or should be, more than one *palol*, each has his own dairy. In these cases the work of one dairy goes on quite independently of the other, each *palol* being only allowed to enter and work in his own building. In addition to the dairy, or dairies, there is at each *ti mad* a hut in which the *palol* and *kaltmokh* sleep and in which the latter takes his food. When there are two *palol*, both sleep in the same hut. There is a house for the calves called *karenpoh*, corresponding to the *kwotars* of the village dairy.

The milking-place of a *ti mad* is called *pepkarmus* instead of *irkarmus*, as at the ordinary dairy, and is usually enclosed so that the buffaloes are screened from the eyes of ordinary people.

There is always one buffalo-pen, or *tu*,[1] for ordinary use, and at some places two others, called *pon tu*, or festival pens, used on the ceremonial occasions of migration from one place to another and of salt-giving.

The surroundings of the dairy are called *pül*, and there is a special part of the *pül* to which alone the ordinary Toda is allowed to go, and he may only go there by a special path. Each *ti* dairy which I visited was by the side of a wood and the place for ordinary Todas was in the wood.

At a little distance from the dairy there is the source from which the water for sacred purpose is drawn. This source is called *kwoinir*, and at Mòdr, where there was a *kwoinir* for each *palol*, it was a spring built in with stones, and not a stream as at most villages. In addition to the *kwoinir* there is also a stream from which water is taken by the *kaltmokh*, who is not allowed to go to the sacred spring.

There are various stones and other objects of ceremonial importance at most *ti* places, but the description of these may be given with that of the ceremonies in which they play a part.

[1] The proper name for the pen at the *ti* was *mukadr*, and for the calf-pen, *tülk-kadr*, but my informants always used the ordinary words *tu* and *kadr*.

At Mòdr, the diary place I know best, all the buildings and objects of the *ti mad* are shut off from the outer world either by walls or by the natural configuration of the ground or forest. Within this screen, partly natural and partly artificial, there is the large milking-ground which may be entered by the buffaloes from two directions, and on one side of this are the three pens, the two dairies, and other buildings.

The more important of the two dairies has situated close to it the sleeping-hut and two huts for the calves, and this small group of buildings, shown in Fig. 27, is surrounded by a wall like that round the ordinary village dairy, leaving little space between the wall and buildings. These buildings, being within the outer boundaries of the *ti mad*, are already well screened from the world, and in consequence the surrounding wall is low. The other dairy is situated on the boundary, so that it can be seen by anyone outside the *ti mad*, and the wall around it is therefore high, so that a person standing outside can see nothing of the proceedings of the dairyman. At Mòdr the water springs are at some distance from the dairies and there is a special path by which the *palol* goes from the dairy to fetch water.

At another dairy, that of Anto, there is one path by which the *palol* goes to fetch water and another by which he returns, but I do not know if this is so at all dairies.

Although I visited Mòdr on many occasions, I never had an opportunity to investigate the buildings closely. I was never allowed to go within the walls enclosing the dairies, much less to go inside these buildings. If the annual programme of the *ti* had been carried out, the buffaloes would have left this place before the end of my visit, and I intended to make a thorough inspection after they had gone; but owing to various causes I mention elsewhere (see Chap. VI) the herds stayed at Mòdr till after my departure, and I had no opportunity of ascertaining the exact plan of the dairies and their surroundings.

The dairy of a *ti* always has two rooms, an inner room, the *ulkkursh*, and an outer room, the *pòrmunkursh*. These are divided from one another by a screen, or *patun*, which stretches about two-thirds of the way across the breadth of the building and is about three feet high. The *palol* stands in the outer room and performs the dairy operations proper to the inner room leaning over the top of the screen. The object of the screen is to keep the sacred objects of the dairy from the gaze of anyone who may look in, and especially from that of the *kaltmokh*; but in the only dairy of the kind into which I had the chance of looking, the screen was made of vertical sticks with wide intervals between them, so that I could easily see through. This dairy was, however, unoccupied, and if dairy vessels had been there, it is possible that they would

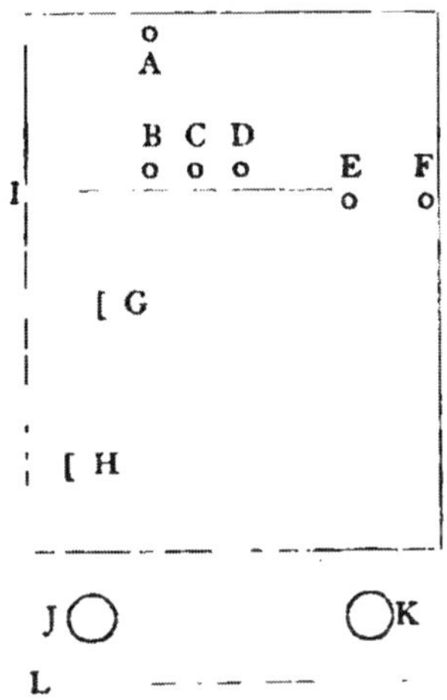

A. *Mani.*

B, C, D. The three *persin.*

E. The *idrkwoi.*

F. The lamp.

G. The *pelkkatitthwaskal.*

H. The *tòratthwaskal.*

I. The *patun.*

J, K. The *pohvelkars.*

L. The screen in front of the dairy.

FIG. 26.—SHOWING THE GENERAL PLAN OF THE TI DAIRY.

have been screened from view in some way. In this dairy the screen extended from the right-hand wall as one looked in, but at Mòdr I was told that the screen was attached to the left-hand wall, and there were certain facts which make it almost certain that this statement is correct, though I had not the opportunity of confirming it by actual observation.

I did not discover whether there were any differences between the internal arrangements of the conical dairies and those of the dairies of the ordinary form. Breeks has given a description of the conical dairy at Anto, and from this it would seem that the dairy is divided into two rooms by a partition extending to the roof, the two rooms communicating by a door. There are two possibilities as to procedure. It is possible that only one room of this dairy is used for the ceremonial and that it is again divided by an incomplete screen into inner and outer rooms, or it may be that the dairyman churns in the inner room. I have no information on this point, but the general nature of the churning procedure at the *ti* dairy makes it highly probable that the former supposition is correct and that the inner room is divided into two parts.

In the plan on p. 87, I have adopted the arrangement in which the *patun*, or screen, is attached to the left-hand side of the building, but this is certainly not the case in all diaries. In some dairies also the fireplaces are on the other side.

THE CONTENTS OF THE POH

(*a*) In the inner room.	One *mani*. Three *persin*. Two *tòrzum*. Two *kòghlag*. One *persinkudriki*. One *pohvet* or *pohpet*. One *kwoi*. One *kwoinörtpet*. Several *tedshk*.
(*b*) Between inner and outer rooms.	*Pelk*, or lamp. *Idrkwoi*.
(*c*) In the outer room.	Two fireplaces { *Pelkkatitthwaskal*. / *Tòratthwaskal*. } Several *alug*. *Uppun*. *Mòrkudriki*. *Karpun*. *Turavali*. *Guduboi*. Unused *kòghlag*.

Another vessel, the *mòrpun*, is kept in the sleeping-hut, where two or more horns are also kept which are blown by the *kaltmokh* every night before going to rest.

The things of the inner room correspond in general to those of the *patatmar* in the ordinary dairy, and the things of the outer room correspond to those of the *ertatmar*. The things of the outer room are sometimes called the *alugpur*, just as those in the village dairy are called *ertatpur*, but I did not hear of any corresponding term for the things of the inner room. I have no record of the place where the fire-sticks (*nirsi*) are kept, but they will almost certainly belong to the outer room, since, in the village, they belong to the *ertatmar*.

The nature of each of the vessels and other objects of the dairy is as follows:

Persin. This is an earthenware vessel containing about five *kudi*, *i.e.*, 2½ gallons. The freshly churned milk is poured into and churned in three of these vessels. The *persin* corresponds to the *patat* of the village dairy.

Tòrzum. This is an earthenware vessel containing two or three *kudi*. Two of these vessels are kept in the inner room, one, called the *karitòrzum*, to hold water, and the other to hold the butter added while churning. The latter is called the *peptòrzum* because it is also used to give butter-milk to the buffaloes on certain occasions. When not in use the two *tòrzum* are placed on and act as covers for two of the *persin*. The *tòrzum* corresponds to the *mu* of the ordinary dairy.

Kòghlag. This is the churning-stick which corresponds to the *madth*. Both *kòghlag* and *madth* are alike in having the peculiar shape shown in Fig. 18 (see also p. 111). The thong by means of which the stick is turned, ordinarily called *palv*, is here called *poinurs*, and consists of a strip of the skin of a male calf. The *kòghlag* is made by the *palol* from bamboo growing on the Nilgiris. In addition to two used and kept in the inner room, five or six new churning-sticks are kept in the outer room.

Persinkudriki. This is a small piece of bamboo with a handle called *tutth*, used to knock against the *persin* when praying.

Pohvet (*pohpet*). A wand used when praying.

Kwoi. A bamboo vessel containing about three *kudi*. It is the vessel taken out by the *palol* to milk the buffaloes. It corresponds to the *irkartpun* of the village dairy and is made by the *palol* from bamboo obtained by the *kaltmokh*.

Kwoinörtpet. A wand carried by the *palol* with the *kwoi* and used to keep away the calves when milking.

Tedshk. Rattan rings used when carrying the dairy vessels.

Idrkwoi. A bamboo vessel containing about one *kudi.* It is used to transfer butter and buttermilk from the vessels of the inner room to the vessels of the outer room, and is kept midway between the two rooms. There is nothing corresponding to it in the village dairy, except at the *kugvali,* where the *kuvun* is used in the same way.

Alug. Earthenware vessels used as receptacles for buttermilk and butter in the outer room. There are at least two of these vessels, usually more. This vessel corresponds to the *pariv* of the village dairy.

Uppun. A bamboo vessel which is used to hold the buttermilk which the *palol* drinks.

Mòrkudriki. A vessel used like a ladle to transfer buttermilk from the *alug* to the *uppun* or the *mòrpun.* It corresponds to the *majertkudriki* or *ashkiok* of the ordinary dairy.

Karpun. A bamboo vessel used to milk the *punir,* or ordinary buffaloes of the *ti* herds.

Turavali. The cooking-pot of which the ordinary name is *tòratthadi.*

Guduboi. An earthenware pot to hold *nei* or ghi. Its ordinary name is *pathrs.*

The *mòrpun,* kept in the sleeping-hut, is a bamboo vessel used by the *kaltmokh* to hold buttermilk both for himself and for certain privileged visitors called *mòrol.*

The earthenware vessels of the inner room are not obtained from the Kotas, like the ordinary vessels, but are made by Hindus, and are procured through the Badagas.

The *palol* has two garments, one of which, the *kubuntuni,* he wears when not engaged in dairy-work, while the other, the *pòdrshtuni,* is worn during the dairy-work or other ceremonial. The latter is kept in the outer room when not in use.

There are usually two kinds of bell at the *ti,* one kind connected with the more sacred buffaloes and another belonging to the *punir.* The bells of the first kind, called *mani,* are kept in the inner room, and are tied on the necks of certain buffaloes for a short time on special occasions. The other bells, called *kudrs mani*, are kept outside the door of the dairy and are put on the necks of the *punir* on the same occasions.

There were several points of interest about the lamps used to light the dairies. At one time it seems that every *palol* was provided with an iron lamp with a number of cavities, each cavity being fitted with a wick. These lamps are reputed to have been as old as the foundation of the *ti* dairies. One of the lamps which is still in existence at the Nòdrs *ti* (that of the *warspoh*) is said to have been brought from Amnòdr. There is some doubt about the exact number of cavities and wicks in these lamps, but in the existing lamp of the Nòdrs *ti* there seems to be little doubt that there are seven cavities and wicks, and the lamp is called *önavpelk*, "the lamp of the seven holes." All the seven wicks are only lighted on special occasions (*ponnol*), and on most days only one is used. At some dairies these iron lamps have been long lost, and in these cases the *palol* used to make lamps of the bark of the *tudr* tree. According to Marshall (p. 141), these lamps have five wicks, and this appears to be still the case at the Kars *ti*, where there were formerly two iron lamps, one with five cavities and one with four, and in the lamp now used at this *ti* they still keep up the use of five wicks on special occasions, using only two on ordinary days. It is possible that Marshall derived his information from a man who had been *palol* at this *ti*. At one of the dairies of the Pan *ti* there is an old iron lamp with seven cavities, and at the other, where a bark lamp is used, it has three wicks. At the present time the dairymen rarely trouble to make bark lamps, but are content with earthenware lamps procured from the bazaar. If these are broken and cannot be replaced at once, bark lamps are used during the interval. The wicks of the lamps, for whichever lamp they may be used, are always made of *tuni* taken from the garments worn by the *palol*, and the substance used in the lamps is butter.

Of the two fireplaces in the outer room, the *tòratthwaskal* is used for ordinary purposes, for cooking food, &c. The other, called *pelkkatitthwaskal*, or sometimes *persinkaftthwaskal*, is used for lighting the lamp or for any other purpose directly connected with the vessels of the inner room.

THE DAILY LIFE AT THE TI

The inhabitants of the *ti* rise before it is light, probably about five a.m., and on getting up from the bed some say "*ekirzam meidjam.*"[1] The *kaltmokh* goes at once to open the *tu* in which the buffaloes have been penned for the night. The *palol* salutes with hand to forehead when he leaves the sleeping-hut and goes to the front of the dairy, where there is water standing in a bamboo vessel called *papun*, corresponding to the *kepun* of the village dairy. He washes his hands and face, and then washes out his mouth by taking up water with his right hand, pouring into his left, and taking the water into his mouth from the latter. It is noticeable that the *palol* uses his left hand for this purpose of personal cleanliness, and not the right hand, which is chiefly used in his sacred work. He then ties up his straggling hair at the back of his head, bows down at the threshold of his dairy and enters, in some cases saying "*ekirzam meidjam*" as he does so.

When the *palol* enters the outer room of the dairy, he transfers fire from the *tòratthwaskal*, where it has been burning all night, to the other fireplace, the *pelkkatitthwaskal*, and then takes off the *kubuntuni*, which has been his covering during the night and puts the *pòdrshtuni* round his loins. He lights the lamp by means of three pieces of wood of the kind called *kid*, taken from the *pelkkatitthwaskal*, and while so doing begins to pray, using the prayer of the *ti*. After lighting the lamp, and while still continuing to pray, he takes up the *persinkudriki* and knocks with it on the middle of the three vessels called *persin*, going from one *persin* to another, when he pauses to take breath. I had the greatest difficulty in finding out exactly what happened in connexion with this

[1] These are the *kwarzam*, or prayer names (see Chapter X) of Teikirzi and Tirshti. They were used by Naburs (64) who had been *palol* at the Pan *ti*, but it is doubtful whether their use or the use of any other *kwarzam* on these occasions is an established custom.

prayer, but after I had settled on the foregoing description as correct I was allowed one day by the *kaltmokh* to go near the dairy while the *palol* was praying, and was able to hear the beating on the earthenware vessel with each word of the prayer.

The next step is to take up the *pohvet* and place it against the wall, and then the *palol* begins to churn the coagulated milk in the middle *persin*, milk in this state being here called *kudabpol* instead of *adrpars*, as in the ordinary dairy.

In those cases in which the *mani* is 'fed,' the *palol* puts *kudabpol* on the bell shortly after beginning to churn. This is done three times, the syllable *On* being uttered each time. When the *palol* does anything three times in this way, he says that he does it *mushtiu*. This expression for 'thrice' is not used in the ordinary dairy.

The next steps are to pour into the *kwoi* and *karitòrzum* most of the coagulated milk which has been broken up by the churning, to add to the milk remaining in the *persin* some *persinpen*, or butter especially kept for the purpose in the *peptòrzum*, to add water, and to churn the mixture of coagulated milk, water, and butter in the middle *persin*. When the new butter is formed, the *palol* pours out the buttermilk into the vessel called *idrkwoi*, keeping back the butter with his hand. The buttermilk is transferred from the *idrkwoi* to one of the *alug* in the outer room. Some of the milk which had been put into the *kwoi* or *karitòrzum* is then poured back into the middle *persin*, more water is added, and the mixture is churned, after which the buttermilk is again transferred by means of the *idrkwoi* to the *alug*, while the butter is kept in the *persin*. This procedure is repeated till all the milk of the middle *persin* has been churned.

The *persin* on the right-hand side of the *palol* is then taken, and its position exchanged with that of the vessel hitherto used, and the churning is continued in exactly the same manner. The buttermilk is transferred to the *alug*, but the butter when formed is transferred to the *persin*, which had been originally in the middle. When the contents of the second *persin* have been churned, the third *persin* is placed in the middle and the same procedure is followed, so that when the churning is over all the butter which has been formed will be in the *persin* which was originally in the middle. Some of this butter is put into the *peptòrzum* to act as *persinpen* on another occasion, and the remainder is transferred to the butter *alug* by means of the *idrkwoi*. The two *tòrzum* are then put on the tops of two of the *persin* as covers, the *peptòrzum* being placed on the middle *persin* and the *palol* takes the milking-vessel (*kwoi*) and wand (*kwoinörtpet*) in his right hand and goes out to milk, having first put some buttermilk, called *pep*, into the *kwoi*.

When the *palol* leaves the dairy, he raises the milking-vessel and wand to his forehead and salutes in the way shown in Fig. 27. The Todas say that he is saluting the sun and the buffaloes. It is probable that, in general, the *palol* faces approximately east as he salutes, but there is no doubt that, at the present time, his salutation is chiefly to the buffaloes. He salutes in the same direction both morning and evening, and certainly pays no attention to the direction in which the sun lies.

This salutation is now often done in a very perfunctory manner. The vessel and wand may be raised hastily to the forehead for a few seconds only as the *palol* goes towards his buffaloes, and I am doubtful whether the salutation is ever performed exactly as shown in the figure, for the vessel contains some of the buttermilk called *pep*, which might be spilt if the vessel were held quite horizontally.

When the *palol* salutes, he says "*Oñ*" three times, and repeats two or three clauses of the dairy prayer, usually the *kwarzam* of the more important gods of the dairy.

When going to milk and when going from one buffalo to another, the *kwoi* and *kwoinörtpet* are always held together in the right hand. When the *kwoi* is filled, it is taken into the dairy. If it is the custom of the dairy to put milk on the *mani*, this is now done three times, saying "*Oñ*" each time, and then the milk is poured into the middle *persin*, the *kwoi* being held in the left hand, and the *palol* goes out again to refill the *kwoi*. When all the *persinir* have been milked, the milk of the three *persin* is mixed together by pouring from one to the other. The reason for this is that the buttermilk, called *pep*, is only taken out in the *kwoi* on first going to milk, and in consequence the *pep* would affect the milk of the middle *persin* only if its contents were not mixed with those of the vessels filled later.

The *palol* next goes out to milk the *punir*, taking for this

FIG. 27.—THE 'PALOL,' KARKIEVAN, SALUTING AT MÒDR. HE IS STANDING IN THE 'PEPKARMUS.' THE BUILDING NEXT TO THE 'PALOL' IS THE 'TI POH'; THAT ON THE RIGHT IS THE 'KARENPOH,' AND BETWEEN IT AND THE 'TI POH' CAN BE SEEN THE HUT WHERE THE INHABITANTS OF THE 'TI MAD' SLEEP.

purpose the vessel called *karpun* and an ordinary wand, the *kwoi* and *kwoinörtpet* being only used for the more sacred buffaloes. There was some difference of opinion as to what should be done with the milk of the *punir*. According to some it may be used to fill the *persin* if these are not filled by the milk of the *persinir*; according to others it is wrong to do this, and the milk of *punir* should on no account be put in the more sacred vessels of the inner room. I think there is no doubt that at the Nòdrs *ti* at any rate the first procedure is followed. At this *ti* the *punir* outnumber the *persinir* by far, and it is probable that the milk of the former is used to supplement that of the more sacred buffaloes, although it is contrary to tradition that this should be done.

FIG. 28.—TO SHOW THE ATTITUDE ADOPTED BY THE 'PALOL' WHEN PRAYING.

The three *persin* being filled, the *tòrzum* are again put on as covers, and the *palol* takes up the wand called *pohvet*, and prays, standing in front of the screen (*patun*) with his hands lying over one another crosswise on the top of the stick as shown in Fig. 28. He recites the full prayer of the *ti*, then replaces the *pohvet* between the *persin* and the *patun* and this act of replacing the wand marks the end of the more sacred part of the dairy operations. If a Toda wishes to ascertain if the work of the dairy is over, he asks, "Has he taken the *pohvet*?"

The *palol* now unties his hair, sees to anything necessary in connexion with his food, fills the *uppun* with buttermilk, and then leaves his dairy and goes to sit on the seat called *pohvelkars* on one side of the door of the dairy, viz., on the opposite side to that on which the *mani* is placed. At Mòdr he sits on the stone on the right side of the door when going in (K in Fig. 26), and the fact that he does so is one of the reasons which make it probable that the arrangement of the *poh* of that place is as I have given it in the plan.

When the *palol* has seated himself on the *pohvelkars*, he calls out to the *kaltmokh* "*Kaizhvatitva*," "Come here and pour buttermilk!" When the *kaltmokh* comes, the *palol* gives the *uppun* to the boy, who says three times "*Kaizhvatkina*," "Shall I pour buttermilk?" and the *palol* replies each time, "*Vat!*" The *kaltmokh* pours from the *uppun* into a cup made of the leaf called *kakuders* held by the *palol*, who drinks after raising to his forehead. This is repeated till the *palol* is satisfied, when the leaf-cup from which he has been drinking is thrown away,[1] and he goes again into the outer room to get food. He gives food to the *kaltmokh*, who eats it in the sleeping-hut, while the *palol* himself eats sitting on the *pohvelkars*. If any *mòrol* (see p. 107) are present, they are fed at this stage with buttermilk and food by the *kaltmokh*, who gives them the buttermilk out of the *mòrpun*, pouring it into leaf-cups as when giving to the *palol*.

The rest of the morning is passed in looking after the buffaloes, cutting firewood, plucking leaves used as cups and plates, or doing any other work connected with the *ti*.

In the afternoon the *palol* returns to his dairy and goes through the same operations as in the morning, except that he fetches water from the *kwoinir* early in the proceedings, usually bringing enough for the work of that afternoon and of the next morning. He churns the milk drawn in the morning, and when the time for milking has arrived, the buffaloes will have returned to the milking-place, and as soon as they arrive their calves are let out from the house (*karenpoh*) in which they have been kept.

When the churning and milking are over, the buffaloes are shut up in the *tu* for the night. The *palol* then takes buttermilk as in the morning, and both he and the *kaltmokh* take their food. The latter eats his food in the sleeping-hut as in

[1] In the story of Kwoto and the Keradr *ti* (Chap. IX) the *kaltmokh* has to pour away buttermilk at an appointed spot. It is probable that this buttermilk is that unfinished by the *palol*, and possibly this custom is still followed but was not mentioned by my informants.

the morning, and the *palol* does not enter till the boy has finished. As the *palol* enters, the *kaltmokh* says "*Oñ*" thrice, takes the horn or horns, and standing at the door blows three times (if there are two horns, three times on each horn), and then re-enters the hut and all go to rest.

In the afternoon the *palol* prays three times; when lighting the lamp, and after milking and filling the three *persin* as in the morning, and again after shutting up the buffaloes in the *tu* for the night, when he stands in front of the entrance to the pen. In each case he uses the whole of the ordinary prayer of the dairy. He also utters a few clauses of the prayer when going out to milk. These prayers will be given in Chap. X.

The Palol

The *palol*, who must belong to the Teivaliol, is chosen by the members of the Tarthar clan to which the *ti* belongs. He may hold office for as long as he pleases up to eighteen years, and, according to some accounts, he might continue in office even after this period, though there is no case known in which this has happened.

The usual duration of office seems now to be only two or three years, though a man may often be reappointed either to the same or another *ti*. At the time of my visit, one *palol* had been continuously in office for sixteen years, another for six years, and the rest for shorter periods. At the present time the office of *palol* is vacant at several dairies owing to the difficulty of obtaining qualified occupants.

During the whole time he holds office, the *palol* may not visit his home or any other ordinary village, though he may visit another *ti* village. Any business with the outside world is done either through the *kaltmokh* or with people who come to visit him at the *ti*. All business with the Badagas is transacted through a special man of this caste called the *tikelfmav*. If the *palol* has to cross a river, he may not pass by a bridge, but must use a ford; and it appears that he may only use certain fords; thus it is easy to cross the Paikara river just above the bridge, but the *palol* of the Nòdrs *ti* was not allowed to do so and had to use a ford nearer to the dairy at Mòdr.

The *palol* must be celibate, and if married, he must leave his wife, who is in most cases also the wife of his brother or brothers. According to the account given by Finicio in 1603, the *palol* could send for his wife and meet her in a wood every week or so and might also send for the wives of any other Todas. It is possible that this may still happen, but I failed to obtain an account of it and understood that the *palol* was really celibate. According to Finicio the restriction to which the *palol* is subject is that he may not touch a woman in the house. We have seen that in the lowest rank of the dairyman-priesthood intercourse with women in the house is allowed at any time and in the higher ranks only on certain days of the week. It is quite consistent with this that in the highest rank intercourse in the house should be altogether forbidden, but might still be allowed in the forest, and it is quite possible that Finicio is correct. I was unacquainted with his account at the time of my visit, and all other writers had been so unanimous as to the complete celibacy of the *palol* that I did not press my inquiries on this point very closely.

If a death occurs in the clan of a *palol*, he cannot attend any of the funeral ceremonies unless he gives up his office. If he resigns he is not again eligible for the office till the second funeral ceremonies have been completed. When a man of one clan gives up his office in this way, his place must be taken by a man of some other clan. Karkievan of Piedr was *palol* of the Nòdrs *ti* eighteen years ago and resigned when his wife died, his place being taken by Tulchievan of Kusharf. Two years later Karkievan resumed office and has been *palol* continuously since that time. Though there have been many deaths among the Piedrol, he has not attended a funeral, and has not, therefore, had to resign his post again.

In old times, it seems probable that it was usual to give up the office of *palol* when there was a death in the clan. According to tradition, the division of the Keadrol into the Keadrol and Kwaradrol by Kwoten (see Chap. IX) was ordained in order that there might still be men to undertake the office of *palol* when there was a death in the clan, the men of the

Keadrol taking office when there was a death among the Kwaradrol and *vice versa*.

It has been stated by several writers on the Todas that the *palol* does not profit in any way by his sacred office. I made most careful inquiries on this point, and there seemed to be no doubt that the *palol* may often make a considerable income from the sale of the ghi made from the milk of the herd under his charge; one *palol* was stated to make six rupees a week in this way, and while he has been in office is said to have increased his own herd (*i.e.*, that of his own family) by no less than twenty-five buffaloes. In one recent case, a man has resigned the post of *palol* to the Pan *ti* because he found the income was too small.

According to my informant, Kaners, a man used always to accept the office of *palol* unwillingly. When the offer came to him, he would say, "I cannot leave my buffaloes; I cannot leave my wife and my children." Then the people would say, "You are born for the *ti*; it is your birthright; you must not refuse"; and the man would reluctantly consent. Now the Todas are in more need of money than they used to be, and there is no difficulty in obtaining candidates for those dairies at which the pecuniary advantages are sufficiently great, so that people will now beg to be appointed as *palol* to certain dairies, and it is even whispered that bribes have been offered in order to obtain office. There is no doubt whatever that the pecuniary reward is the chief inducement to people to undertake the charge.

The Nòdrs *ti* has the largest herd of buffaloes, and I was told that this *ti* is very much coveted, while others which have few buffaloes are unable to obtain a *palol* at all. My Teivali friends invariably talked about the *ti* in exactly the same kind of way that an Englishman talks about a benefice.

At the present time there are several instances in which the office of *palol* is vacant, and there seems to be a growing difficulty in filling many of these places. There is little doubt that the chief reason for this is that the herds have become very small, so that the resulting profit does not offer sufficient inducement; but there is also no doubt that the exclusion from the home and the limitation of intercourse with the world in general act as deterrents to those who are thinking of becoming candidates for the vacant places.

Another point about which several writers have erred is in supposing that the *palol* is important in the general government of the Todas and in stating that the Todas go to him for counsel and advice. I inquired into this very carefully, and there seemed to be no doubt whatever that the *palol* has absolutely no functions outside the management of his dairy and of ceremonies connected with it. He has no place on the *naim*, or council, and only appears before it as defendant or witness in matters connected with the *ti*. I could not ascertain that any one ever consults the *palol* on any business except that of the *ti*, and outside his office he has nothing whatever to do, and is little thought of by the Todas. The sanctity attaching to the *palol* and the reverence paid to him are attached and paid wholly to the holder of the office and not at all to the man.

The ordinary Toda may only approach the *palol* on two days of the week, Monday and Thursday. On other days, if he wishes to communicate, he must stand a considerable distance from the *ti*—it was said as much as a quarter of a mile—and carry on his conversation from this distance. I had, however, the opportunity of observing that the distance was diminished on some occasions.

On no account may a *palol* ever be touched by an ordinary person. A *palol* becomes himself an ordinary person, or *perol*, if either he or his dairy should be touched by any unconsecrated person. Recently 'Nòdrners (67) lost the office of *palol* to the *warsir* at the Nòdrs *ti*, because a Tamil man went to his dairy while he was out looking after his buffaloes; he was soon reappointed, but to another *ti*.

The Toda who approaches the *palol* must go *kevenarut*, *i.e.*, with his right arm out of the cloak, and there is a definite form of salutation which is different for Tartharol and Teivaliol. When one of the former approaches, the *palol* says "*Bañ*," and the Tarthar man replies "*Ir kañdâ*," literally "Buffalo, calf, have you?" To one of the Kuudrol, the chief Teivali clan, the *palol* says the *kwarzam*, or sacred name of Kuudr, followed by the word *idith*, *i.e.*, he utters the words *Ivikanmokh kûtmeil teu idith.* When any other Teivali man approaches, the *palol* says "*Pekein*," but all the Teivaliol reply with the same formula as the Tartharol. If a Tarthar man and a Teivali man approach the *palol* together, the former will be greeted first. The *palol* greets the man to whose division the buffaloes belong before the man of his own clan or division.

If a Toda is in the condition called *ichchil*, *i.e.*, has been defiled in connexion with funeral or other ceremonies, it was said that he might not approach the *palol.* I had an interesting example, however, of the way in which a regulation of this kind is observed. While Teitnir (52) had *ichchil*, owing to the fact that the funeral ceremonies of a relative had not been completed, he went with me to the Mòdr *ti* one day and approached within a few yards of the *palol.* He had taken off the semi-European clothing he often wore, and had his right arm bare, but no greeting of any kind took place between him and the *palol*; the latter did not recognise his presence in any way and behaved as if Teitnir were not there. On this occasion Teitnir was *ichchil* on account of the death of a more or less distant relative. Later his wife died, and then there seemed to be no doubt that he would not under any circumstances have approached the *ti* or the *palol.*

There are several regulations concerning the food of the *palol.* Any grain he eats must be that provided by the Badagas. At the present time more rice is eaten than was formerly the case. This is not grown by the Badagas, but nevertheless the rice for the *palol* must be obtained through them. The *palol* may drink milk, but only that from the buffaloes called *punir.* He must take his food sitting on the seat, or *pohvelkars*, outside the dairy, and, as we have seen, he uses for this purpose the seat which is not on the same side as the *mani.* He usually prepares the food himself and cooks it on the fireplace called *tòratthwaskal* in the outer room of dairy; but there is also a fireplace outside the dairy which is used sometimes, especially when food has to be prepared for many people, and then the *palol* may be assisted by the *kaltmokh.* If food is prepared by the *kaltmokh*, the fireplace outside the dairy must be used.

The only food which the *palol* is altogether forbidden is chillies.

The *palol* wears garments of the kind called *tuni*, of a dark grey material made at Nulturs in the Coimbatore district. They are brought to the *palol* by the Badaga called *tikelfmav.*[1] Each *palol* has two of these garments. One is worn as a loincloth and is called *pòdrshtuni.* It is only worn when definitely engaged in dairy-work and on certain ceremonial occasions, and at other times is kept in the outer room of the dairy. The other garment is called *kubuntuni*, and is worn like the ordinary cloak, but always with the right arm out (*kevenarut*). It is worn when not engaged on sacred business, and on a few occasions is worn together with the *pòdrshtuni*. The small perineal cloth ordinarily called *kuvn* is made of the same material as the *tuni* and is called *kagurs* at the *ti*, while the string which passes round the waist and holds the *kagurs* in place is called *kwainur* or *kwoinur*.

I was told that the *palol* should never cut his hair or his nails while he is in office.

If a *palol* has held office for eighteen years without a break, he performs a special ceremony. The essential feature of this ceremony is that the *palol* has intercourse in the daytime with a girl or young woman who must belong to the Tartharol. The woman is chosen by the *palol* and the matter is arranged by the clan to which the *ti* belongs. On the appointed day the woman is brought to a village near the dairy at which the *palol* is living; if he is at Mòdr, for instance, the woman will come to the adjacent village of Perththo. She must bathe carefully and be adorned with all possible ornaments and fine clothing. After the work of the morning is over, the *palol* gives rice and milk to the *kaltmokh* and tells him to have food ready for him when he returns at night. He then goes covered with his *kubuntuni* to a wood near the village, where the woman will be awaiting him. Later the woman returns to the village and the *palol* remains in the

[1] According to Breeks (p. 14) these garments are made by the Badagas of Jakaneri. This may be correct, but it is much more probable that they are procured through the Badagas living in this village.

wood completely naked till sunset, when he dresses and returns to the neighbourhood of his dairy, but remains in an adjoining wood till midnight. He then bathes in a stream and going to the dairy calls "*Kaltmokhia*!" twice. The *kaltmokh* comes out of the sleeping hut and brings a stone resembling the *pohvelkars*, on which the *palol* sits, and the *kaltmokh* pours buttermilk (*kaizhvatiti*) for the *palol* according to the customary ritual. Then the *kaltmokh* brings the *papun*, and the *palol* washes his hands and goes to rest. There was some difference of opinion among the Todas as to whether the *palol* would continue to hold office after this ceremony. He undoubtedly returns to his work; but it seemed probable that he would retire after a short time and his place be taken by another. In this ceremony the celibate priest after eighteen years of office has intercourse with a woman belonging to the division not his own. This takes place in the day-time, the *palol* thus committing an act which is ordinarily regarded by the Todas as immoral.[1]

The last occasion on which this ceremony was performed was when it was done by Kodrizbon, who lived before the time of the grandfather of Kaners, who is himself an old man. Karkievan has now been *palol* of the Nòdrs *ti* for sixteen years, and there was already at the time of my visit much talk among the Todas about the ceremony which he might be expected to perform two years later.

A man who has given up the office of *palol* is known as *patol*. It was quite clear that, on resigning office, he entirely lost his sanctity, and it did not seem that he derived any great social importance from having held the sacred office. I could find no instance of a man who had been *palol* having any special influence or power either in his clan or among the Todas generally. Only in one way are the *patol* important, and that is as repositories of the knowledge of the dairy ritual, and any man about to enter on the office of *palol* will learn the details of the ritual from those who have held office before him.

I could learn of one privilege only pertaining to a *patol*.

[1] It is possible that Finicio was told of this custom, and that his statement about the relations of the *palol* to women only refer to this ceremony.

He is allowed to go to the *ti mad* on the day called *upkarvnol*, after the *ponup* ceremony (see Chap. VIII), and on that occasion he receives food from the *palol*.

THE KALTMOKH

The *kaltmokh* is usually a boy, but he may occasionally continue to hold office till he is about twenty years of age. He must belong either to the Teivaliol or to the Melgarsol. He is a general assistant to the *palol*, and has also certain definitely assigned duties, such as giving buttermilk to the *palol* and blowing the horns at night. He also takes part in several important ceremonies.

When away from the dairy and its immediate surroundings he wears an ordinary cloak, but always with his right arm outside. When engaged in his work at the dairy or in the *pül* of the *ti*, he must be naked except for the *kuvn*. When he has been away from the *ti* he may not return by the path used by the *palol*, but must use a special path, carrying the cloak folded and hung over his shoulder. At the Mòdr dairy, however, I noticed that the *kaltmokh* sometimes kept his cloak in a tree just outside the *ti mad*, and then went in and out by the same path as the *palol*.

The *kaltmokh* sleeps in the same hut as the *palol*, from whom he receives his food. When there are two *palol* and only one *kaltmokh*, the two dairymen divide the duty of feeding the boy between them.

The *kaltmokh* never goes into the dairy, but he may put his hand into the outer room to take out those vessels which he is allowed to touch. He may never touch the vessels of the inner room.

There are two grades in the office of *kaltmokh*, a lower called *perkursol* and a higher called *tunitusthkaltmokh* or full *kaltmokh*. The latter wears a piece of *tuni* called *petuni* on the left side of the string (*kerk*) supporting the perineal cloth.

The *perkursol* is allowed to go to certain places and do certain things which are not allowed to the full *kaltmokh*. Whenever it is necessary that the *kaltmokh* should do any of the forbidden things, or even if he is likely to be in such a position that he may have to do these things, he becomes *perkursol.* This he does by throwing off the *petuni* and dipping one leg either into the pool of water called *tarupunkudi* (see p. 177) or into the dairy stream (*pali nipa*) of an ordinary dairy (if he dipped his leg into the *ars nipa*, or part of a stream used for ordinary household purposes, he would at once lose his office entirely and become an ordinary person). As soon as he has dipped his foot, he becomes *perkursol* and may do the following things summed up in the general expression *tarskwarârkûdthodi.* He may pass a village where there is a woman in the seclusion-hut (*puzhars*), or where the relics of the dead are being kept between the two funeral ceremonies; he may go to a place where the people have been in communication with a village in which either of these conditions exist; he may pass a river by a bridge, and he may go to the *wursuli* of a Tarthar village. If the full *kaltmokh* does any of these things, even unwittingly, he would at once become an ordinary person (*perol*). The *kaltmokh* degrades himself to the rank of *perkursol* even when there is merely the danger that he may infringe any of the restrictions; thus, one day when there was a woman at Karia who was in seclusion after childbirth, the *kaltmokh* at Mòdr, Katsog (55), was going to the hut of the forest guard near Paikara. He would not have to pass Karia, but there was a chance that the forest guard might have been in communication with the people of Karia, and therefore Katsog became *perkursol.* A *perkursol* is regarded as of the same rank as a *wursol*, and the people spoke of *perkursol* as a *ti* word for *wursol*—*i.e*, a *wursol* at the *ti* was called *perkursol*, just as a *madth* (churn) at the *ti* was called *kòghlag.* In order to regain his rank as full *kaltmokh*, the *perkursol* has to perform the same ceremony as that which takes place at the end of the ordination to this office (see Chap. VII).

While the *kaltmokh* is degraded to the rank of *perkursol* he may not touch any dairy vessels; he may not pour buttermilk for the *palol*, nor may he blow the horns—*i.e.*, he may do none of the more important and sacred duties of his office.

THE MÒROL

I have said that no ordinary Toda is allowed to approach the *palol* except on certain days, and then may only go to a certain place in the surroundings of the *ti*. There is, however, one very remarkable exception to this rule, the members of certain clans having the privilege of going to the *ti* at any time and taking buttermilk (*mòr*). Owing to the latter privilege they are always known as *mòrol*.

The most important *mòrol* are the members of the Melgars clan, and at the Nòdrs *ti* they are the only people possessing these peculiar rights. A Melgars man may go to the *ti* on every day of the week, when he enters the small enclosure in which the dairy is situated, going, however, by a special opening at the back so that he does not actually pass the dairy and sits down in front of or may enter the sleeping hut. He is given buttermilk by the *kaltmokh* after it has been given to the *palol*, and he also receives food. At the Nòdrs *ti* the two *palol* divide the responsibility of providing food between them ; if four *mòrol* come, each *palol* gives food for two men.

The rights of the Melgarsol appear to be exercised very constantly. I rarely visited the Mòdr *ti* without finding several *mòrol* present, and so far as I could observe they made the most of their privileges and enjoyed themselves well. It was very remarkable to see several Todas making themselves quite at home at the *ti*, while other Todas were standing outside wholly prohibited from entering into the life of the place. On one occasion when I visited Mòdr, the brother of one *palol* was standing without at the appointed spot waiting till the business of the morning was over, while several *mòrol* were within enjoying their privileges to the full.

The Melgarsol have certain other rights and duties in connexion with the *ti*, and especially on the occasion of the procession which takes place when the buffaloes migrate from one place to another (see Chap. VI), after which ceremony the *mòrol* sleep at the *ti mad*. At some dairies members of other clans may act as *mòrol*, but in no case do they occupy quite so privileged a position as the people of Melgars. Thus, at the Kars and the Pan *ti* the people of Kars are *mòrol*, but they may only visit the *ti* and take buttermilk and are not allowed to sleep there, nor have they any of the special ceremonial duties of the Melgarsol.

When the dairy of a *ti mad* needs to be repaired or rebuilt, this is done by Melgars men, who must previously undergo an ordination ceremony of the same character as that for the office of *wursol*, and the men rank as *wursol* while engaged in the work. The hut of the *ti mad* is also repaired or rebuilt by the Melgarsol, but in this case the work is done without any special ceremony. In either case the Melgars men are not allowed to leave the *ti mad*, and they sleep in the living hut while the work is being done.

Another duty of the Melgarsol is to assist in carrying the corpse of a *palol* who has died in office.

On the occasion of the *teutütusthchi* ceremony in 1902, when the *palol* and *kaltmokh* left the dairy at Mòdr for several hours, I found a Melgars man in the neighbourhood of the dairy, and it seemed to me that he was watching the dairy while the regular guardians were away. I was told however, that this was not one of the recognised duties of a *mòrol*, and I suspected that he was stationed at Mòdr at the time of my visit, because it was feared that I might take advantage of the absence of the *palol* to make a closer inspection of the dairy than was allowed.

New Dairy Vessels

The earthenware vessels of the inner room (*persin* and *tòrzum*) are procured from Hindus through the Badagas. They were formerly obtained from a place called Kulpet (Kundapeta), near Nanjankudi in Mysore, and I was told that the Todas used to go down to fetch them.

The earthenware vessels of the outer room (*alug*) are obtained from the Kotas like those of the ordinary dairy. The churn or *kòghlag* is made by the Todas themselves from the slender bamboo growing on the hills.

The material out of which the bamboo vessels (*kwoi*, *idrkwoi*, *karpun*, *uppun*) are made, is procured from a place called Ebenput (?) near Musinigudi. When new vessels are required, and there is only one *kaltmokh*, a second is appointed, who goes to Ebenput, where he cuts bamboo called *kôli*, which is large enough for the dairy vessels. The bamboo is taken by the *kaltmokh* to the *ti*, and the new vessels are manufactured by the *palol*.

It is possible for the *kaltmokh* to go to Ebenput and back in one day, but if unable to do this he may stay the night at Taradr, the nearest *etudmad* to Musinigudi. The bamboo for the new vessels, however, must not be taken to Taradr, but must be left in a wood near the village, and taken on to the *ti mad* on the following day.

Any new vessels or implements must be purified before being used. The earthenware vessels of the inner room are taken from the Badagas who bring them, and are rubbed over, inside and out, with the bark of the *tudr* tree, after which the bark is put inside the vessel, water is poured in three times, saying "*Oñ*," and the contents rinsed round and poured out. Water is then put in the vessel, which is placed for a time on the fireplace to make it look old, the fireplace used being the *pelkkatitthwaskal*. The *kòghlag* or churning stick is purified by rubbing *tudr* bark over it and pouring water all over it three times. The churning stick and the earthenware vessels of the inner room are both purified in the outer room of the dairy, and the purification must be performed on a Sunday.

The *kwoi* is purified on the same day of the week in front of the buffalo enclosure or *tu*. After churning, the *palol* takes the new *kwoi*, and a *tòrzum* full of water, and purifies the former with *tudr* bark and water three times in the way already described. He then milks into the new *kwoi* for the first time, and on this occasion he must be careful not to fill the vessel completely.

The *idrkwoi* is purified in the same manner as the other vessels and also on a Sunday, but the purification is performed at the junction of the inner and outer rooms of the dairy.

New vessels and other objects belonging to the outer room are purified with the same procedure in their own room, but on a Tuesday or Wednesday.

The *kwoi* or milking vessel is the only vessel which is not purified inside the dairy. With the exception of this vessel all the other objects used in the dairy are purified in the outer room or at the junction of the inner and outer rooms.

All old, broken or worn-out vessels or implements are thrown away except the *kwoi*, which must be buried in a wood near a dairy. Thus this vessel is treated unlike other contents of the dairy, both when being purified and when rejected as of no further use. I could obtain no explanation of this, and can only suggest that the exceptional treatment is due to the fact that it comes into actual contact with the sacred buffaloes.

The Five Ti

At present there are only five *ti* in existence, belonging to the clans of Nòdrs, Kars, Pan, Kwòdroni, and Nidrsi. The Keradrol are said to have had a *ti* at one time which was spirited away by the god Kwoto (see Chap. IX) and the name of one of its places, Tikîrs, is still preserved.

The most important *ti* belongs to Nòdrs and this is one of the original institutions, the *ti* of Kars and that of Kwòdrdoni being the others. The Pan *ti* is derived from that of Nòdrs (see story of Kwoten), and the Nidrsi *ti* is an offshoot of the Kwòdrdoni institution.

Of these five *ti*, that of Nòdrs is the only one which still has two *palol*. The Kars *ti* has only one *palol*, and similarly that of Pan. The *ti* of Kwòdrdoni and Nidrsi are at present unoccupied. At the Kwòdrdoni *ti* the office is filled once a year for a limited period in order to satisfy certain requirements of the Kotas.

No *ti* is allowed to be vacant when the final funeral ceremonies are performed for any member of the clan to which the *ti* belongs, and it is only on the occasion of these ceremonies that a *palol* is now appointed to the Nidrsi *ti*.

Each *ti* has certain features of organisation and procedure peculiar to itself. There are certain differences of ritual and differences in the names and kinds of the buffaloes and sacred objects. The history and special features of each *ti* will now be considered.

THE NÒDRS TI

The goddess Teikirzi lived at Nòdrs and was its ruler, and Nòdrs was in consequence especially favoured when the various buffaloes were distributed by this deity. When Püv died and Ön went away to Amnòdr (see p. 185), the Nòdrs *ti* and its buffaloes went with him. Teikirzi, who remained behind, found after a time that it was not good to rule a country without a *ti*, so she complained to Ön and asked him to send the buffaloes back. He consented and people were sent from Nòdrs to Amnòdr to fetch the buffaloes. Ön gave them the buffaloes and all the things of the *ti*, and he also gave a milking vessel and a churning stick made of gold. When the men started to bring back the buffaloes, they went some way and then found that they had forgotten the gold vessel and churn given to them by Ön. So they went back and asked Ön for the two things. Ön refused to give them up as they had not been taken at first, and it is believed that they are still in the dairy at Amnòdr.

Ön told the men who returned to ask for the things they had forgotten that the Todas were to make the vessel and churn of bamboo. They were to go to the hill called Teikhars or Kulinkars, where they would find a flower called *kavulpuv*, and he told them to make a new *kòghlag* of the same shape as that flower. They did so, and ever since that time the churning-stick both at the *ti* and at the ordinary village has been made so that it is like the flower *kavulpuv*.

Another incident which occurred during the journey of the *ti* buffaloes back from Amnòdr was the birth of a *mani*. One of the two *palol* was carrying the dairy vessels of the inner room, and the other was carrying the *mani* called Keu. When they were about half-way back to this world, the *palol* who was carrying the dairy vessels found that they had become very heavy, so he put them down, and, taking off the *tòrzum* which was covering one of the *persin*, he found a bell in the milk of the *persin*. So they called the bell Persin because it was the son of a *persin*, and to this day the bell is fed with milk because it was born in milk. It is the *mani* which is kept in the *ti poh* of the Nòdrs *ti*, while the other *mani*, Keu, carried by the other *palol*, is kept in the *wars poh* and this bell, Keu, is not fed with milk.

When the buffaloes of the Nòdrs *ti* returned from Amnòdr, they talked like men. One day when the *palol* told the *kaltmokh* to bring the calves, the buffaloes used bad language such as may not be uttered before women; they would not obey the *palol*, and refused to allow him to milk them. Then Teikirzi found that it was bad that buffaloes should have the tongues of men, and she dragged the tongues out of the mouths of the buffaloes and made them new tongues of *tudr* bark. The buffaloes could then talk no longer, and they allowed themselves to be milked.

Originally the Nòdrs *ti* had three places, or *ti mad*, given to it by Teikirzi: Anto, Òdrtho, and Kulâdrtho. Later the people made other *ti mad*, and at one time, in addition to the three, they had the following places:—Mòdr, Kudreiil, Majòdr, Mûkòdr, Tîdj, Pûth, and Pòos. Several of these are now disused or have disappeared altogether, but are still mentioned in the prayer of the *ti*. Of the three original places, Kulâdrtho has disappeared and its place is occupied by the Prospect tea estate. The sites of Tîdj and Pûth are also occupied by tea estates. The way to Pòos has been blocked by a Kota village, so that the buffaloes would be unable to reach it without being defiled by going through the village, and, in consequence, this dairy is not used. Mukòdr is very close to another *ti mad*, probably Majòdr, and the *palol* "were lazy" and allowed it to fall into ruins. There is a conical dairy, now in ruins, near Makurti Peak, which belonged to the Nòdrs *ti*, and it is possible that this is the dairy of Mukòdr.

The herds now spend the greater part of the year at Mòdr, but still go in most years to Anto, Òdrtho, Kudreiil, and Majòdr at certain seasons.

The Nòdrs *ti* has two kinds of *persinir*, the *tiir* and the *warsir*, each of which has its own *palol*. There are also the *punir* for the special use of the *palol*. The *tiir* have three subdivisions, the *unir*, the *atir*, and the *teirtir*, so called because descended from certain buffalo ancestors, or *nòdrkutchi*, who were connected with Anto, Tîdj, and Teir. The *warsir*, are divided into two groups, the *kulatir* and the *perithir*, so called because their *nòdrkutchi* were connected with Kulâdrtho and Perithi respectively. Teir is close to Mòdr, but does not seem at any time to have been itself a *ti mad*, and I could not ascertain why it should have given its name to one group of the buffaloes. Perithi is near Gudalur, and in the prayer of Anto (see p. 225), there is a reference to a *ti* dairy at this place from which the buffaloes evidently took their name.

At most of the dairies the buffaloes stand together and the two *palol* occupy the same *ti mad*, though each has his own dairy; but when one herd, that of the *tiir*, goes to Òdrtho, the other herd, that of the *warsir*, goes to another place called Kudreiil. These two places are quite close to one another, but are regarded as separate *ti mad*. The reason given for this separation was that at one time the *warsir* did not behave properly at Òdrtho, and Teikirzi ordered that they should not stand there again, but should go to another place. I could not ascertain what the buffaloes did to merit this punishment.

I obtained a full account of the buffaloes of the Nòdrs *ti* at the time of my visit. There were seven *unir*; four adult buffaloes, called Kôzi, Perith, Kâsimi, and Uf, and three young buffaloes not yet named; five *atir*, Persuth, Enmars, Tòthi, and two unnamed; three *teirtir*, Pülkoth, Köji, and one unnamed. Of *kulatir* there were four, Köji, Keirev, and two young buffaloes; of *perithir* five, Kâsimi, Kiûd, Persv, and two unnamed. Thus the *ti palol* had fifteen *persinir*, and in addition about thirty *punir*, while the *wars palol* had nine *persinir* and about fifteen *punir*.

The dairy of the *tiir* is often called the *ti poh*, and that of the *warsir*, the *wars poh*, and every dairy has also its special name; thus, at Anto the dairy of the *tiir* is called Medrpoh, and the dairy of the *warsir* is called Kadpoh or Kadvoh. One of these dairies is of the conical form, but my record does not tell me which. According to Breeks the name of the conical dairy is Kiurzh. This is possibly the same word as Kad(poh), the name of the dairy of the *warsir*. The two dairies at Mòdr are Pänpoh and Känpoh. The name of the ruined conical dairy near Makurti Peak which belonged to the Nòdrs *ti* was Kateidipoh (Breeks, Katedva).

The *palol* of the Nòdrs *ti* must be chosen either from the people of Piedr or from those of Kusharf. Originally it was ordained that the *palol* should be chosen from the Piedrol, but later the Kuudr people obtained the right of becoming *palol*. This lasted till about seven or eight generations ago, when there is a story that the people of Kwurg (Coorg) came to fight the Todas and drove off the buffaloes of the Nòdrs *ti*, which were standing at Mòdr. The *palol* was touched by the Kwurg people and in consequence ceased to be *palol*, but instead of pursuing the invaders, he sat down by the *ti* waiting till he could be reinstated in his office. The *kaltmokh*, who belonged to Piedr, followed the Kwurg people, who had carried off a large *mani* called Kän, and some people of Nòdrs and Kusharf also followed with the boy. The Kwurg people saw the *kaltmokh* and told him that he might have the buffaloes back if he would give them as many rupees as Kän would hold. The *kaltmokh* had inside his loincloth a little gold coin called *pirpanm*, which he took out and put into Kän and immediately the bell became full of rupees and the gold coin fell out. The Kwurg people took the rupees, and the *kaltmokh* took the bell and drove the buffaloes back to Mòdr.

As the Kwurg people were making their way home, they suddenly found that all the rupees had disappeared, so they turned and pursued the *kaltmokh* and the buffaloes. Then the *kaltmokh* prayed :

Per wadrth vêdrmâ, kârs wadrth vêdrmâ, män mas vêdrmâ.

"May the high hills be broken, may the rocks be broken, may the trees fall down."

Directly there was a loud noise, the hills were divided, stones rattled, and trees fell down. Then the Kwurg people were afraid and returned to their own homes.[1] The Todas held a council, and it was decided that, as the *palol* had not

[1] This legendary account probably preserves a tradition of a real invasion of the Nilgiri Hills by the people of Coorg. The Todas put the date of the occurrence at about seven or eight generations ago. In 1774 Linga Raja, with 3,000 Coorgs, invaded the Wainad and remained there for five years. During this time it is highly probable that the Coorgs would have explored the Nilgiri Hills. (See *Mysore and Coorg*, by Lewis Rice, Bangalore, 1878, vol. iii., p. 110.)

followed the buffaloes, the Kuudr people should no longer have the privilege of becoming *palol* of the Nòdrs *ti*, and that in future the *palol* of this *ti* should be taken either from Piedr or Kusharf.

At the present time[1] the *palol* of the *tiir* is Karkievan of Piedr, who has now been continuously in office for sixteen years, having also had a previous period of office as *palol*. The *palol* of the *warsir* is Nerponers of Kusharf (66), who had been in office for about a year at the time of my visit. The *kaltmokh* is Katsog of Kuudr (55).

Although now one *palol* belongs to Piedr and the other to Kusharf, it is not necessary that this should be so and it has happened frequently that both *palol* have belonged to the Piedrol.

The *mani* of the *tiir*, which is said to be made of iron, is that called Persin, of whose miraculous birth an account has been given. The *mani* of the *warsir* is called Keu, and is said to be made partly of gold, partly of silver, and partly of iron. Milk is put on the former bell by the *palol* at every churning and milking, but Keu is not 'fed.'

In addition there are four *mani* of the kind called *kudrs*, which are tied to the *punir* and kept outside the door of the dairy. Three of these belong to the *punir* of the *ti palol*, and are called Arvatz, Kiûdz, and Kerâni, and should be tied to buffaloes named Püthiov, Peires, and Nersâdr respectively. The fourth bell belongs to the *punir* of the *wars palol*, and is called Kerâni. It should be tied to a buffalo named Tâlg.

The lamp of the *wars poh* is one of those made of iron, and is said to have come from Amnòdr. It is called Ònâvpelk, the lamp of the seven holes. The *ti poh* had a similar lamp at one time, but it has been lost.

Three horns are kept in the sleeping-hut of the Nòdrs *ti*. Two belong to the *tiir*, and are called Kiûdrkûdr and Pudothkûdr. The third belongs to the *warsir*, and is called Teigun. (For the origin of these horns see the story of Korateu or Kuzkarv in Chap. IX.)

One feature of the *ti poh* at Mòdr, which is certainly not

[1] In 1902.

general, is the presence of a screen in front of the door. The effect of this screen is to protect the *palol* from the gaze of the ordinary Todas when they are standing in their appointed place. When I visited Mòdr I was allowed to go into the enclosure where the buffaloes are milked, but this privilege was not accorded to my Toda guides, and in consequence I was often able to observe the doings of the *palol* when they were hidden from my guides by the screen.

The *wars poh*, on the other hand, has no such screen, but the wall surrounding this dairy is much higher than at the *ti poh* and effectually screens the *palol* from the public gaze. The door of the *wars poh* faces between north and north-east, and that of the *ti poh* south-east, but owing to the presence of the screen the *palol* has on coming out to turn to the left, and therefore faces north-east when saluting.

THE KARS TI

The following story gives the traditional origin of the *ti mad* at Makârs, one of the chief places of the Kars *ti*, but I could not ascertain definitely whether it was supposed to give the origin of the *ti* as a whole or only of the *ti mad* at Makârs. The story runs that Anto created buffaloes, one of which came to Makârs, where a *tudr* tree was standing. The buffalo rubbed against the tree and part of the bark came off, and that is why the place became a *ti*. When the buffalo found that there was no *palol* at Makârs and no *kaltmokh*, it was very angry and raged about furiously. While it was doing this, it jumped some stones and fell into the river called Kitheri, and it also jumped a stream called Warwar. In spite of its falling into the river, however, it did not die, but got out and pushed stones together with its horns so as to make a *tu*. Later a dairy was built near the *tudr* tree. Whether this was the origin of the *ti* or only of the *ti mad* of Makârs, it seemed quite clear that the Kars *ti* is believed to be one of the very early institutions of the Todas. Its two ancient places were Enòdr and Makârs. At each there were two dairies, and one at least of those at Enòdr was of the conical variety and had the special name of Medrpoh. Enòdr has now fallen into disuse. It was a few miles to the north-east of Ootacamund, and it was no longer visited because the buffaloes would have had to pass through Ootacamund in going from Makârs to Enòdr and would have been defiled. Makârs, which is near the Nanjanad valley, is now the chief place of the *ti*, and the buffaloes were there at the time of my visit.

Another important and ancient place of the Kars *ti* is Kòn (Lingmand) in the Kundahs. In the story of Kwoto (see p. 204) the buffaloes were going to Enòdr from Kòn when the boy showed his miraculous knowledge of the buffalo *kwarzam*. Two other places are Nerâdr and Pars. Both Kòn and Nerâdr are still used, but Pars, which is not far from Ootacamund, is no longer used, having been given up because Badagas went to live near it.

As at the Nòdrs *ti*, there are two kinds of *persinir* in addition to the *punir*. The two kinds are called *pürsir* and *parsir*, the former being also sometimes called *enòdrir*. Although there are two kinds of sacred buffalo with their corresponding dairies, there has never been more than one *palol*. When a *palol* is appointed to this *ti*, he is ordained to the office of *palol* to the *parsir*, and, for the first month, he attends to these buffaloes only and enters their dairy, the *parspoh*, only. At the end of the month, he becomes *palol* to the *pürsir*, with certain ceremonies, to be described later, and from that time to the end of his period of office he works in the *pürspoh* only and never enters the *parspoh*, although he continues to attend to the *parsir* as well as to the *pürsir*. The milk of the *parsir* is mixed with that of the *pürsir* in the vessels of the dairy belonging to the latter kind of buffalo. This dairy, which is usually called *pürspoh* after the buffaloes, has also the special name of Kakanmudri.

There is one bell belonging to the *pürsir* which has three names, Perner, Uner, and Persagan, but it is also often called Ner. Koboners told me that this bell is usually quite black, but that he had once rubbed off the thick layer of soot and dust with which it is covered and had found that it was made of gold. It seems to have been of a light colour and may have been made of bronze. There is also a bell belonging to the *parsir* called Talg.

Formerly the *palol* of the Kars *ti* was chosen from the Melgarsol, but this clan lost the privilege owing to the misbehaviour of one of their number when holding the sacred office. The buffaloes were standing at Enòdr, and the Melgars *palol* was milking a buffalo, when he saw a honey-bee. He got up, left the buffalo, and went after the bee, leaving his milking-vessel behind. He followed the bee, found the nest, took the comb, ate some of the honey, gave the remainder to the *kaltmokh* to put in the hut, and then went back and continued to milk the buffalo, whose name was Kän. When he had finished milking, he was taking the milk into the dairy when a plank fell on his head and he was killed. Then it was decided that Melgars people should no longer be *palol*, and that the office in future should be filled from the Teivaliol. Whenever the Todas wish to refer to the fact that the Melgars people have lost the right of being *palol*, they say, "*Kän kârvûk kiûztheniz ûpi vûchi*," or, "Kän milking, bee he followed after."

The *palol* is now taken from Piedr, Kusharf or Kuudr, and the present holder of the office is Nòdrners (67) of Kusharf. The dairies of this *ti* are always near those of the Pan *ti*, and the two *palol* share one *kaltmokh* between them, the present holder of this office being Teitun (64) of Piedr.

THE PAN TI

The legend of the origin of this *ti* will be given in full in the story of Kwoten (Chap. IX). When this hero was reproved by his wife because the Pan people had no *ti*, he obtained buffaloes from the Nòdrs *ti*, so that the Pan *ti* appears to have been later in origin than those of Nòdrs and Kars, and to have been derived from the former.

Certain of the buffaloes are reputed to be descended from an ancestor made by Teikhars or Kulinkars (see the story of this god in Chap. IX).

The most important dairy of this *ti* appears to have been situated at Tarsòdr or Tazòdr in the Kundahs, which is the place to which the buffalo created by Teikhars found its way. Tarsòdr is about two miles from Kòn, and there is still a dairy of the conical kind at this place which is probably one of those mentioned by Breeks under the name of Tarzhva. Its special name was Pôhûjpoh or Pûverizpoh, and it belonged to the group of buffaloes of the *ti* called *tarsir*. It is now falling into ruins, having been disused for about twenty years. The last *palol* who went there was Pethovan (70) of the Kwaradr division of the Keadrol. He died at Tarsòdr soon after going there in perfect health from Kudòdr. His son, Kiudners, later became *palol* to the *tarsir*, but was afraid to go to Tarsòdr because his father had died there. Like his father, Kiudners died in office at Kudòdr, and the death of both father and son while holding the office of *palol* so alarmed the Todas that no one has been to the dairy of Tarsòdr since. I was told that the dairy had been given up because the gods of Tarsòdr were so severe, *i.e.*, it was assumed that both father and son had been killed by the gods for some infringement of dairy regulations. New dairies have since been built near Kòn, the seat of the Kars *ti* in the Kundahs.

The place at which the buffaloes were standing at the time of my visit was Kudòdr, near Makârs, and this is the *ti mad* which is occupied during the greater part of the year. Another dairy is at Nerâdr, again near the *ti mad* of the same name belonging to the Kars *ti*.

A fourth place, Uterâdr, is now rarely visited, since the buffaloes may only go there when there are two *palol*.

There seems to be a very close association between the *ti* institutions of Kars and Pan. The buffaloes of the two always move about together, and the dairies are so close to one another that, at present, they are able to share the same *kaltmokh*.

The Pan *ti* has two kinds of buffalo in addition to the *punir*, viz., the *tarsir* and the *warsir*. At one time the *warsir* belonged to one division of the Pan clan, called the Panol, and the *tarsir* belonged to the other division, the Kuirsiol. At Kòn there are two dairies, one for each kind of buffalo, and each kind should also have its own *palol*. At the present time there is only one *palol*, who looks after the *tarsir*.

The dairy of the *warsir*, or the *warspoh*, is closed and may not be entered by the *palol*, and he is not allowed to milk the *warsir*, though he may milk the *punir* belonging to the *warspoh*.

Formerly the *palol* of the *tarsir* was chosen from the Kwaradr division of the Keadrol and the *palol* of the *warsir* from the other division of this clan, this arrangement being said to have been ordained by Kwoten.

The Kwaradr division is now extinct and the remainder of the Keadrol are not very numerous, and the present *palol* of the *tarsir* is Peilet (64) of Piedr. A few years ago both dairies were occupied, the *palol* of the *tarsir* being Naburs (64) of Piedr, and the *palol* of the *warsir*, Pichievan (69) of Keadr. The latter is said to have thrown up his office because the income was not large enough.

If there should be a death among the Panol, the second funeral ceremonies (the *marvainolkedr*, or so-called 'dry funeral') could not take place unless both dairies were occupied. Since Pichievan resigned, no Pan man has died, but when this happens a second *palol* would have to be appointed before the *marvainolkedr* could be held.

The *tarsir* have two bells, called Kòsi and Pongg. The former is tied on a buffalo called Kòsi, and Pongg on one called Enmars. Milk is only put on the bell called Kòsi. At the dairy of these buffaloes there is an iron lamp of the ancient kind with seven cavities and seven wicks, and the horn is called Kwatadr. The *warsir* have one bell, called Keituzan, which is put round the neck of a buffalo called Kòjiu. The old iron lamp belonging to these buffaloes has been lost and an earthenware or bark lamp is used in its stead. The horn is called Persagan, but as these buffaloes have no *palol*, this horn is not now blown.

The people of Pan are *mòrol* at this *ti*.

THE KWÒDRDONI TI

There was some difference of opinion as to the origin of this *ti*, which is often called the Arsaiir *ti* by the Todas. According to one account, given to me by Kwòdrdoni people, the buffaloes called *arsaiir* came from the sea and were the mothers of all the *tiir*. Another account, which seemed to be more generally accepted, was that the Kwòdrdoni *ti* was instituted by Ön, like those of Nòdrs and Kars, but that one day, when the *palol* was milking, the *mani*, called Pushodipongg, came from the sea and sat on the side of the milking-vessel.

The chief place of this *ti* is Pursâs, situated between Kwòdrdoni and Kotagiri. The other dairies in the past were at Kakwai, Karküln, Pobkars, and Kadrin, but only the first of these, which is close to Kwòdrdoni, is now used.

At the time of my visit there was no *palol*, and the buffaloes, only about eight in number, were standing at Kakwai, but were not being milked.

A *palol* is appointed every year shortly before the ceremony in honour of the god Kamataraya, which is celebrated by the Kotas in January. When the Kotas announce that they are about to hold this ceremony, a *palol* and *kaltmokh* are appointed who go to Pursâs. The buffaloes are milked and the ghi which is obtained from the milk is given to the Kotas. The *palol* remains in office for about twenty days, and his appointment is made altogether on behalf of the Kotas, who would be very angry if it were not done. It seemed that the success of the Kota ceremony would be seriously impaired if there were no *palol* at the Kwòdrdoni *ti*.

A *palol* would also be appointed if it were wished to hold the second funeral ceremonies, or *marvainolkedr*, of a Kwòdrdoni person.

The Kwòdrdoni *ti* has never had more than one kind of buffalo, and never more than one *palol* or *kaltmokh*. The buffaloes, or *arsaiir*, are those which disobeyed the commands of Ön (see Chap. IX), and are said to be responsible for the dangers suffered by buffaloes from tigers.

The people of Nòdrs and Kars have the privilege of taking buttermilk and food at the *ti*, and are known as *mòrol*, but they may not sleep at the *ti mad*, nor do they take any part in the buffalo migration. According to one account, the people of Pan are also *mòrol*, and may even sleep at the *ti*.

THE NIDRSI TI

This is an offshoot of the Kwòdrdoni *ti*. One evening, after the buffaloes and calves of the Kwòdrdoni *ti* had been shut up for the night, the women of an adjoining village were pounding the grain called *ragi*. When the calves heard the noise of the pounding, they ran out of their pen and made their way to Pursâs. One of the wooden *tasth* which bar the entrance of the pen became entangled in the neck of one of the calves, and when the calf reached a place near Edrpali village, the *tasth* dropped and became a wood, and the place is now called Tasthnòdrpem. From here the calf went on to Pursâs. The Kwòdrdoni people went to Pursâs to fetch back the calf, but when they got to the place they changed their minds and said that the calf should stop at Pursâs, and that the Nidrsi people should make a *ti* there and appoint a *palol*; and this was the origin of the Nidrsi *ti*, which is called *kar ti* because it was derived from a calf, while the *ti* of Kwòdrdoni is called *ir ti*. The two institutions have different dairies, but both are at Pursâs.

I could obtain little satisfactory information about the customs of the Nidrsi *ti*. There is only one *ti mad*, viz., that at Pursâs near the dairy of the Kwòdrdoni *ti*. Any of the Teivaliol may hold the office of *palol*, but at the time of my visit there was no *palol*, and the six buffaloes, which are all that remain of the herd, are being looked after, though not milked, by a Tarthar man, Todrigars (41), at one of the ordinary villages. A *palol* would have to be appointed before the second funeral ceremonies of one of the Nidrsiol could be performed, but apparently he would only hold office for a short time.

CHAPTER VI

BUFFALO MIGRATIONS

AT certain seasons of the year it is customary that the buffaloes both of the village and the *ti* should migrate from one place to another. Sometimes the village buffaloes are accompanied by all the inhabitants of the village; sometimes the buffaloes are only accompanied by their dairyman and one or more male assistants.

There are two chief reasons[1] for these movements of the buffaloes, of which the most urgent is the necessity for new grazing-places. During the dry season, lasting from about December to March, the pasturage around the villages where the Todas usually live becomes very scanty, and the buffaloes are taken to places where it is more abundant. Many of these places are in or near the Kundahs, where the rainfall is greater than over the rest of the hills, and others are scattered here and there about the hills in spots where, owing to favourable conditions, the ground is less parched than elsewhere. At other seasons of the year it may happen that the grazing in the neighbourhood of a village becomes exhausted, and it becomes necessary to take the buffaloes to another place.

The other chief reason for the migrations is that certain villages and dairies, formerly important and still sacred, are visited for ceremonial purposes, or out of respect to ancient custom. Some of these places, such as the villages of Piedr

[1] The buffaloes may also move from one village to another if sickness should break out among them, but I do not know whether this would become the same ceremonial occasion as in the other kinds of migration.

and Kusharf, are in outlying parts of the hills, and are entirely unoccupied except on the occasion of these ceremonial visits. Another example is the ancient and sacred village of Nasmiòdr, of which there now only remains a dairy, situated in a grove in the middle of a valley cultivated by Badagas. It is visited once a year by the *wursulir* of Kars for about a month, and, as there is only scanty pasturage available, there is little doubt that the visit to this dairy has no utilitarian motive.

At the *ti* the same reasons hold good. Several of the *ti* herds have dairies in or near the Kundahs, to which they go during the dry months of the year, while other dairies of special sanctity are visited only for a short time in each year. The dairy of Anto is a good example of the latter case; it is in an outlying part of the hills, and should be visited for one month every year, because it is the most sacred dairy of the *ti*.

The migrations of the *ti* buffaloes are more strictly regulated than are those of the village herds, and there are definitely prescribed rules for the order in which the dairies of the *ti* shall be visited, and for the duration of the stay at each, though, as we shall see later, these rules are not always followed.

As a general rule, the more ancient and sacred the dairy to which the buffaloes are going, the more elaborate are the ceremonies on reaching the new destination.

The day of migration is called *irskidithbutnol* or *irnödrthnol*.

MIGRATIONS OF THE VILLAGE BUFFALOES

My account of the ceremonial accompanying the migration from one village to another is unfortunately very incomplete. The following accounts were given by Teivali men, and I cannot guarantee that they hold good for both divisions and for all clans.

When it is decided to move to a fresh village certain men are chosen to help in the removal, and are told to come on the appointed day, which must not be one of the sacred days of the village (see Chap. XVII). On the morning of this day

FIG. 29.—TO SHOW THE METHOD OF CARRYING THE CONTENTS OF THE DAIRY. THE BOY KALMAD (64) IS CARRYING THE 'PATATPUR'; KARSÜLN (15) THE 'ERTATPUR.' IN FRONT OF KALMAD IS THE ENTRANCE OF THE PEN AT KARS CALLED 'ALTHFTU' (see p. 649).

the *palikartmokh* abstains from food. He does the ordinary work of his dairy, and gives out buttermilk and butter to the women as usual. He then calls to the chosen men who have come to the village, and they stand outside the door of the dairy. The *palikartmokh* comes out, holding in his right hand the milking-vessel (*irkartpun*) and churning-stick (*madth*). He stands facing the sun, and salutes holding the vessel and churn to his forehead, and says "*ekirzam meidjam*," the *kwarzam* of Teikirzi and Tirshti. Then all present pray, using the prayer of the dairy. The *palikartmokh* puts the milking-vessel and the churning-stick at the back of the dairy (the *palimerkal*), and then brings the other dairy things, carrying out those of the *patatmar* first and then those of the *ertatmar*. Two stout sticks are prepared, each called *püusht*, and the various objects of the *patatmar* are fastened on one stick and those of the *ertatmar* on the other, in the way shown in Figs. 29 and 30.[1] When the things have been fastened on the sticks, all go to the front of the huts of the village and take food, after which the procession starts. It is headed by the buffaloes, followed by the dairyman and the men carrying the dairy vessels. Each of the latter carries the staff on his left shoulder and has the right arm out of the mantle. The man carrying the things of the *patatmar* walks in front of the man carrying those of the *ertatmar*, as shown in the figures. After the buffaloes, the dairyman, and the dairy vessels, there follow any men who are accompanying the procession, and if all the inhabitants of the village are migrating, the women and children follow the men.

On leaving the village the women and girls may have to go for a certain distance by a different path from that taken by the buffaloes, but during the greater part of the journey there does not seem to be any regulation to prevent the women following in the wake of the sacred animals.

On reaching the new village, the *palikartmokh* purifies

[1] The vessels used for the purposes of these photographs were not the real vessels of the dairy, but those of the house. The method of fastening the earthenware vessels does not correspond to that described for the *ti* dairy, and I am doubtful whether the method of fastening for real dairy vessels would not have corresponded to the procedure of the *ti* rather than to that shown in the figures.

FIG. 30.—1. A. The *mædth.* B. A *patat.* C. Another *patat.* D. The *parskadrvenmu.* E. The *irkartpun.*
2. A. The axe. B. The fire-sticks. C. The *majpariv.* D. The *pdlmachok.* E. The *ertatpun.* F. A *tek.* G. The lamp.

the dairy by throwing into it water mixed with *tudr* bark.[1] The dairy things are taken off the sticks at an appointed spot. The *palikartmokh* salutes the sun with *irkarthpun* and *madth* as in the morning, and then all pray. After the prayer, the *palikartmokh* takes some ferns (*taf*) and puts them on the place within the dairy where the things of the *patatmar* are to stand, and these are put in their places on the ferns. The things of the *ertatmar* are then arranged in the same way. The *palikartmokh* makes fire by friction, lights the lamp, and then goes to milk the buffaloes. If he has brought milk with him, he will churn it. Meanwhile a ceremony called *nòtiteiti* will have been performed by a little girl about six or seven years of age in those cases in which all the inhabitants of the village are migrating. Before leaving the village from which the people are coming this girl will have been given food in the dairy. On reaching the new place, the girl plucks three blades of the slender grass called *kakar* and goes to the front of the dairy and sweeps the threshold with the grass. She does this with her right arm outside her cloak, and when she has swept she bows down with her forehead to the threshold three times. If there is more than one dairy, she sweeps the threshold of each. The *palikartmokh* then gives her a small handful of butter and the girl goes to the huts. Up to this time the women will have been waiting near the village, but when they see that the girl has performed her ceremony, they go to the huts and prepare the food called *ashkkartpimi*.[2]

When the *palikartmokh* has finished milking, he also prepares food, and when it is ready he throws some into the fire, *tòrtütrsersthi*, "food into the fire he throws," and then gives out the food to the people, and they eat both this and that prepared by the women.

At some places the ceremonial is more complicated than at others, the degree of elaboration depending on the sacredness of the dairy to which the buffaloes are going. When they migrate to the especially sacred village of Kiudr the extra

[1] This is probably only true of Teivali dairies.

[2] This is a special food used on important ceremonial occasions, the mode of preparation of which is given in Chapter XXIV.

complexity seems to depend on the presence of the bells of the dairy of that village. When the *palikartmokh* reaches Kiudr, he puts the dairy things he has brought with him at the back of the dairy. Another *palikartmokh* goes into the inner room and brings out the bells called *patatmani* and lays them by stones called *neurzülnkars* at one side of the dairy (see Fig. 31). He enters again and brings out four *ertatmani*, which he lays by the side of another group of stones called *neurzülnkars* (see Fig. 32). The second *palikartmokh* then

FIG. 31.—THE DAIRY OF KIUDR WITH THE 'PALIKARTMOKH' ETAMUDRI (58); ON THE RIGHT OF THE DAIRY ABOVE AND TO THE LEFT OF THE HEAD OF ETAMUDRI IS THE STONE CALLED 'NEURZÜLNKARS,' BY WHICH THE 'PATATMANI' IS LAID.

purifies the dairy with *tudr* bark and puts the vessels which have been brought to Kiudr in their places on a bed of ferns in the way which has been described. After all the vessels are in their places, he takes the *patatmani* to the dairy stream, while the first *palikartmokh* brings *tudr* bark. The *tudr* bark is pounded and the juice squeezed over the bells. The two *patatmani*, having thus been purified, are then put on a forked stick and carried to their usual place in the dairy. The same procedure is repeated with the *ertatmani*, which are strung on a piece of bamboo and hung on another piece of bamboo which projects from the wall on the *ertat* side of the dairy. Then milk is put on the *patatmani* and buttermilk on the *ertatmani* as usual.

FIG. 32.—THE 'NEURZÜLNKARS' OF KIUDR, BY THE SIDE OF WHICH THE 'ERTATMANI' ARE LAID.

MIGRATION OF THE TI BUFFALOES

I obtained a very full account of the migration of the buffaloes of the Nòdrs *ti* and will first give an account of the proceedings for this herd.

The Toda year begins during October with the ceremony of *teutütusthchi* (see Chap. XIII) and at this time the buffaloes should be standing at Mòdr, near Paikara. Soon after this ceremony, the herd goes to Anto, the most important and sacred of the *ti* places. They stay here for a month and then go to Majòdr, not far from Makurti Peak, where they stay during the dry season, stopping about three months or longer, according to the nature of the weather. It is often not until May is reached that the buffaloes return to Mòdr and stay there till August, when they cross the Paikara river to the two dairies, Òdrtho and Kudreiil, on the opposite bank. The *tiir* stay at Òdrtho and the *warsir* at Kudreiil for a month and then both return to Mòdr.

In 1902 this plan was very much disturbed. In order to go from Mòdr to Òdrtho and Kudreiil the herds and their attendants have to cross the river, and under no circumstances is the *palol* allowed to cross by the bridge. He usually watches his opportunity till the river is low enough at a certain ford to allow him to cross, but the summer of 1902 was unusually wet and the river was never sufficiently low to allow the passage, and in consequence Òdrtho and Kudreiil were not visited in that year.

Later it was arranged that the migration to Anto should take place on November 2nd. I was told that I might accompany the procession for part of the way, and was looking forward greatly to the occasion, as it was evident that it was my only chance of seeing and photographing the contents of the dairy. As the day approached, the migration was postponed because Teitnir, who was celebrating the funeral ceremonies of his wife and was therefore *ichchil*, had crossed the way by which the procession would have to pass. The ceremony was next arranged for November 23rd, but was then further postponed till the 30th. This was the last Sunday before the day on which I intended to leave the hills, and again I made arrangements to see the proceedings. No sooner had I done so than I was told that the procession was postponed for a week and was to take place on the day after I had left Ootacamund. I at once altered my plans and arranged to see the procession on December 7th. A new obstacle at once intervened, and I was told that the journey to Anto was deferred indefinitely, and, as I learnt afterwards from Samuel, the buffaloes did not go to Anto at all that year, but went direct from Mòdr to Majòdr on Wednesday, January 7th. All this occurred after the misfortunes had happened to which I have already referred—misfortunes which were believed to be the direct consequence of my investigations—and it seemed quite clear that the various postponements and final abandonment of the journey to Anto were due to the fear that some misfortune might befall the sacred herd if I saw the procession.

It will be noticed that the herd of the Nòdrs *ti* may pass the greater part of the year at Mòdr, which is not one of the three most ancient dairies of the *ti*. It has become the most frequented because it is the most convenient, occupying a more central situation than most of the other dairies. Majòdr is also not one of the most ancient dairies, but is visited purely on account of grazing necessities. Anto and Òdrtho, the two out of the three places given originally by Teikirzi according to the legend, are visited not from necessity, but on account of their sanctity, and, as we have seen, it may happen under exceptional circumstances that neither place may be visited and the whole year passed at Mòdr and Majòdr.

It is only when going to Anto and Òdrtho that some of the most remarkable features of the buffalo migration ceremonies are carried out, and if these dairies should fall into disuse, as would seem not improbable, these features of the migration ceremonies would certainly vanish.

As we have seen, the migration to the relatively unimportant dairy of Majòdr may take place on a Wednesday, but when going to the more important places a Sunday must be chosen. The orthodox day is the first Sunday after the new moon, but so far as I could gather from the various days appointed for the migration during my visit there is no very strict adherence to the rule. A week before the migration a second *kaltmokh* is appointed who goes through the customary ordination ceremony. It is also arranged that a Melgars man (*mòrol*) shall come to carry some of the contents of the dairy. When the buffaloes are going either to Anto or Òdrtho it is absolutely necessary that a *mòrol* shall be present, who goes in front of both *palol* and *kaltmokh* and has certain well defined duties. The procession may also be accompanied by any Toda who has no *ichchil* and these people may help in driving the buffaloes and in carrying the less important things from the dairy. Badagas may also accompany the procession.

The day of the migration is called *irnödrthnol*, and on the morning of this day the churning is done as usual, and sufficient milk is drawn to provide as much as can be safely carried in one of the *persin* without spilling it. All who take part in the procession must go without food on the morning of this day, and the *palol* does not take buttermilk as usual. The various objects which are to be taken with the buffaloes are brought out of the dairy and laid by a stone called the *pepkusthkars*, which in some places, and possibly everywhere, is in or near the wall of the *tu*.

The dairy vessels are carried according to well-defined rules. The things of the inner room and the intermediate objects, the lamp and the *idrkwoi*, are carried by the *palol*. The *mòrol* carries some of the things of the outer room and one of the horns. The two *kaltmokh* carry the other things of the outer room, the other horns and their own possessions.

The dairy vessels, &c., are carried by each man on a staff cut from the *mòrs* tree, the staff being called *pepkati* (the *pütusht* of the village migration). Each of the *persin* and *alug* is fixed on the staff by placing it on a roll of *kakhudri*, called a *tedshk*, round which six pieces of the string called *twadrinar* are tied. The six strings are passed round the vessel and fastened to the staff. The *palol* fastens on the three *persin* in such a way that when the staff is on his shoulder two of the vessels will be in front of him and the other behind his back, one of the vessels in front containing milk. The *tòrzum* are placed on the top of the *persin* as when they are in the dairy, and the *persinkudriki* is carried in the *peptòrzum*. The *kwoi* is fastened on in front, and the *kòghlag* and wands are placed along the staff. The lamp is put inside the *idrkwoi* and the latter tied to the end of the stick, so that it is behind the back of the *palol* when being carried. Care is taken that an interval is left between the *idrkwoi* and the other things; even when being carried from one dairy to another the objects intermediate between those of the inner and those of the outer room are kept separate from and not allowed to touch the more sacred vessels of the inner room. The staff with its burdens is carried by the *palol* on his left shoulder in the same way as is shown in Fig. 29, illustrating the method of carrying the things of the village dairy.

The *mani* is carried by the *palol* on his right side. A staff of *kiaz* wood is cut, about five cubits (*mogoi*) in length, which must be perfectly straight with a fork at one end. The bell is covered completely with *kiaz* leaves tied with rattan fastenings, and put on the fork of the staff by its ring. The staff is carried upright in the right hand of the *palol*; if he becomes tired he may rest it on his shoulder, but this must be done in such a way that the forked end of the stick carrying the bell comes in front of his body, otherwise the *palol* would be presenting his back to the sacred object.

At the Nòdrs *ti* there is an exception to the ordinary rule in the case of the *mani* of the *tiir*. It will be remembered that this bell is reputed to have been born in a *persin* during the migration from Amnòdr, and the bell is therefore carried in one of the *persin* during the migration from one dairy to another. In its place the *palol* of the *tiir* carries in his right hand the churning stick with its churning end upwards.

The *mani* is the only object of the inner room which is covered with leaves, so that it may not be exposed to the vulgar gaze. The lamp is also hidden from view within the *idrkwoi*, but I do not know whether this is for the same reason or merely because it is a convenient way of carrying it.

The *mòrol* carries the large earthenware vessels of the outer room (*alug*), which are at least four in number. They are tied on a staff by means of *tedshk* in the same manner as are the *persin*. This is done by the *kaltmokh*, who puts the staff and its burden on the left shoulder of the *mòrol*, taking particular care that the vessels do not touch the man. The *mòrol* carries one of the horns in his right hand.

Before the procession starts each *mani* is hung on the neck of a calf, left on for a minute or so, taken off and put on its staff. The *mani* of the *tiir* called Persin is put on the neck of a two-year-old calf of the *unir*, and that of the *warsir*, Keu, is put on the neck of one of the *perithir*.

If any dairy vessels or implements are not taken with the buffaloes, they are not left in the dairy, but hidden in a wood.

The procession then starts with the *mòrol* at its head. In some cases a halt is made when passing certain places, and prayer is offered by the *palol*. In going from Mòdr to Anto the procession stops first at Pòrstib near Tedshteiri village (belonging to the Nòdrsol), where the *wars palol* puts the staff carrying the *mani* on a stone and prays while touching the staff with his hands. The next halt is made at Ponvtüt, where the buffaloes separate from the *palol* and follow a slightly different route, and here the *wars palol* again prays. The procession halts for a third time at a place called Teirpül, near Anto, but this time it is the *ti palol* who prays after having placed the churning stick and bell on a stone.

On its way to Anto the procession passes near the village of Kiudr. When the buffaloes are seen to be coming, the women leave the house and go to the outskirts of the village, taking with them the pounder, sieve and broom, and wait there while the procession is going by. All the people of Kiudr fast on this day till after the buffaloes have passed.

It was said that on this day the *palikartmokh* of Kiudr used to rub clarified butter on the stones called *neurzülnkars*, but there was some doubt about this, and if the custom ever existed it seems to have fallen into disuse.

According to some accounts, certain clauses especially referring to the migration of the *ti* buffaloes are used in the prayer of the Kiudr dairy (see Chap. X).

On reaching the outskirts of the new place, the Todas who have accompanied the procession go away. The staff carried by the *mòrol* is taken off by the *kaltmokh*, who is again very careful that the vessels do not touch their bearer. Although the *mòrol* is allowed to carry some of the less sacred vessels, care is taken throughout that the vessels shall not be contaminated by touching his body or his clothing.

All the dairy vessels are taken off and laid by a stone called the *perskars*, and then follows the ceremony of *peputi*. Each *palol* has carried with him some milk in one of the *persin*. Some of this is poured into the *peptòrzum*[1] and given to certain buffaloes, one of each kind belonging to the *ti*; thus, at the Nòdrs *ti*, the milk is given to five buffaloes, to three by one *palol*

[1] The vessel derives its name from this ceremony.

and to two by the other. The milk may be given to buffaloes directly from the *tòrzum*, or it may be poured into the hands of the *palol* from which the appointed buffaloes drink.

The next business is the purification of the dairy, called *nòdrkorsi arspishpimi—i.e.*, we wash with *nòdrkorsi*. The *palol* goes to the dairy spring or *kwoinir* with the *karitòrzum*, carrying the *kwoinörtpet* under his left arm. He throws *tudr* bark into the spring, fills the *karitòrzum* and returns. He puts *tudr* bark into the *karitòrzum* and also into the *idrkwoi* and then pours the water from the *karitòrzum* into the *idrkwoi*, which he takes to the dairy and throws the water with his hands first over the dairy vessels and then well into the dairy itself so that it penetrates to the inner room. He throws the water first on the floor, then to the roof and to the sides, three times to each. Next he takes three sprigs of the plant ordinarily called *kabudri* (*Euphorbia Rothiana*), but at the *ti* called *nòdrkorsi* and ties it over the door of the dairy.

The dairy vessels, which have been untied and placed on the ground near the *perskars*, are then purified and put in their places. The *palol* first takes up the *peptòrzum* with the *persinkudriki* within it, the *kòghlag*, the *kwoi* and *kwoinörtpet*, all in the right hand, and carries them to the front of the dairy, where he repeats certain *kwarzam* of the prayer, then turns to the east and says the whole prayer of the dairy, salutes the dairy holding the four things to his forehead, enters, puts the things except the *kwoinörtpet* in their places, comes out with the *kwoinörtpet* under his left arm and without turning his back to the interior of the dairy, and shuts the door of the building. He then takes in the other vessels of the inner room, carrying the *kwoinörtpet* under his left arm and without repeating the prayer. One *persin* is taken in first, then the others, the *karitòrzum* and the *tedshk*. Then the *mani* is taken, being carried in the right hand and laid temporarily on the floor near the *persin*; when taking in the bell certain *kwarzam* are said.

The wand called *pohvet* is next taken in and laid in its place, and then the things intermediate between the inner and outer room—viz., the lamp, which is hung in its place, and the *idrkwoi*, which is put exactly at the line of junction of the two rooms.

After this the things of the outer room are put in their places. Fire is made by friction, and the *tòratthwaskal* lighted, light transferred from this to the *pelkkatitthwaskal*, and with the fire so made the *palol* lights the lamp.

In most cases the buffaloes are then milked, but at Anto and Òdrtho, before milking, the *palol* begins an extraordinary ceremony, in which the *kaltmokh* is concerned, which is continued till the following day.

For this ceremony food is especially prepared by the *palol*. He mixes husked grain (*patcherski*), brought by the Badagas who accompany the procession, with buttermilk and jaggery,[1] spreads butter on the mixture, and, putting it on a *kakud* leaf, takes it out to one of the two *kaltmokh* who is sitting in a given place about ten yards from the dairy. The *kaltmokh* must now stay on this spot till the evening.

After the *palol* has milked, he takes food himself and gives it to the *mòrol*. Before going to rest for the night a ceremony is performed called *irtupadrchiti*, "he prays for the buffaloes at the *tu*." The two *palol* go to the front of the *tu* [2] in which the buffaloes have been put for the night and they pray, using the *kwarzam* of the *ti* and of the gods only. They then go to the sleeping hut, where the second *kaltmokh* has swept the floor and prepared a fire. When the *palol* come to the hut they bawl out in a high key three times and the *kaltmokh* does the same and they go to bed, the two *palol* occupying one bed (*tün*) and the *mòrol* and the second *kaltmokh* the other. After they have been in the hut some time, the first *kaltmokh*, who has been sitting till now outside at the place where he was given food, creeps into the hut and lies down to sleep between the two beds without any covering. No notice of him must be taken by the other occupants of the hut.

The following day is called *punirsnol*. In the early morning, before the others are awake, the first *kaltmokh* must get

[1] Palm juice sugar.

[2] At Anto, and probably at some other dairies, there is a special *tu* for use on this occasion.

up, light the fire, warm himself, and then go out and sit on the same spot as on the previous evening. He remains there till the two *palol* come to him to continue the ceremony in which he is concerned.

When the *palol* rise they do their usual work, and when they have milked they perform a ceremony called *karkutkîrsiti*,[1] in which the calves are prayed for in the same way that the buffaloes were prayed for on the previous evening. The second *kaltmokh* collects the calves in the *pepkarmus*, or milking-place of the buffaloes, and the two *palol*, each with empty *kwoi* and with *kwoinörtpet*, pray as on the previous evening using the *kwarzam* of the *ti* and some of the *kwarzam* of the gods, and then bawl out in a high key three times in order to scatter the calves.

The ceremony with the *kaltmokh* is then continued. Each of the *palol* takes the vessel used for ladling buttermilk (*mòrkudriki*); one *palol* fills his vessel with the milk of *punir* and the other fills with *nei* (clarified butter). Each leaves his dairy, and they both call to the *kaltmokh*, who comes to the threshold of the *ti poh*, and stands there while the two *palo*, mix the milk and *nei*. The *kaltmokh* is then told to hold out his hands, and each *palol* pours out the mixture into the hands of the boy, who rubs it over his head first, and then all over his body. After the *kaltmokh* has thus been bathed in milk and *nei*, the three people walk in procession to the spot where the *kaltmokh* had been sitting, the *kaltmokh* going first, followed by the *wars palol* and the *ti palol* in order. As they walk, the two *palol* say the following words:—

Köda *mâ*; *pîrzi* *puti* *vurmâ*; *pob* *ers* *vurmâ*;
die may (he); tiger catch (him) may; snake bite (him) may;

per *pûdith* *vurmâ* *pûkh* *pûdith* *vurmâ* *pudi*
steep hill fall down (on him) may; river fall (on him) may[2]; wild boar

eri *mâ*; *kûdr* *pat* *mâ*; *keirman* *par* *mâ*.
bite may; wild beast hold (catch him) may; bear carry (him) away may.

---

[1] This word was translated "he prays for the calves." One verb is used in naming the ceremony of praying for the calves and another in the case of praying for the adult buffaloes.

[2] Probably this should be translated "may the river (when in flood) swallow him.

When they come to the spot where the *kaltmokh* had been given the food, the boy remains standing there while the two *palol* turn round and walk back in the dairy, saying:—

Köda mâ, idvaik, ultâmâ; pirzi par mâ,
die may (he), as was said, may he be well; tiger carry away may,

idvaik para vômâ; per pur mâ, idvaik,
as was said, carry away may not; steep hill fall may, as was said,

puva vômâ; pòb eri mâ, idvaik, eria vômâ; pâkh pur mâ,
fall may not; snake bite may, as was said, bite may not; river fall may,

idvaik, puva vômâ; kâdr pat mâ, idvaik, pata
as was said, fall may not; wild beast catch may, as was said, catch

vômâ; kedrman par mâ, idvaik, para vômâ;
may not; bear carry away may, as was said, carry away may not;

pudi eri mâ, idvaik, eria vômâ.
wild boar bite may, as was said, bite may not.

The *ti palol* then enters his dairy and brings out an especially large ball of the food called *ashkkartpimi*, more than can possibly be eaten at one sitting. It is given to the *kaltmokh*, who sits on the same spot as before, and eats as much of it as he can.

All this ceremony has been done after milking, and before drinking buttermilk (*kaizhvatiti*), which is now poured out by the second *kaltmokh* for the *palol*, who then go about their usual business. When the first *kaltmokh* has eaten as much as he can of his ball of food he leaves it on the spot where he has been sitting, and goes with the *palol*. The Todas say that the food left behind will never be touched by the crows, who will eat any other food.

In the afternoon the *palol* transact their ordinary dairy business and the *kaltmokh* returns to his place and resumes the consumption of his ball of food, staying on the spot till the end of the day. When the two *palol* have gone into the sleeping hut for the night, the *kaltmokh* goes into the hut after them and may then talk to the other occupants, and after this follows the usual routine.

During the whole of this ceremony the *kaltmokh*, who takes so prominent a part in it, is called the *neurzutpol*.

At the other dairies of the Nòdrs *ti* a ceremony which is obviously closely connected with that which has been described is performed at certain stones called *neurzülnkars*. At Mòdr there are four of these stones (shown in Fig. 33), and three of them are rounded and worn quite smooth, probably by much repetition of the ceremony about to be described.

On the day following the migration each *palol* takes a *mòrkudriki*, which one fills with milk and the other with butter (*pen*, not *nei*, as when rubbed on the *kaltmokh*). The two *palol* put milk on the stones and then rub them with butter. There is no cursing and the *kaltmokh* plays no part in the ceremony. There can be little doubt that the stones are regarded as taking the place of the *kaltmokh*, for while the latter is performing his ceremony he is called *neurzutpol*, and the stones anointed in the same way are called *neurzülnkars*.

The ceremony with the *kaltmokh* which follows the migration to the dairies of Anto and Òdrtho is one of the most extraordinary of Toda ceremonies. The leading feature of the ceremony appears to be the cursing of the *kaltmokh*, followed immediately by the removal of the curse. I was wholly unable to obtain any explanation of the ceremony from the Todas, but it seems probable that the *kaltmokh* is being made responsible for any offence which may have been committed against the very sacred dairies of Anto and Òdrtho. The *kaltmokh* having been cursed, and so made responsible, the curse is then removed in order to avoid the evil consequences which would befall the boy if this were not done.

It is possible that the *kaltmokh* is chosen as the person to be made responsible merely because he is the most convenient person to act as the recipient of any evil consequences. It is, however, probable that on this day the *kaltmokh* does something which he does not do on ordinary days, and thus commits an offence which has to be expiated. On the day of migration the *kaltmokh* does, as a matter of fact, see the sacred vessels of the inner room which are ordinarily hidden from his gaze behind the screen of the dairy. He sees the *mani* in its leafy covering, and he may even see the bell itself before it is covered. He also touches some of the vessels of the outer room which he does not

FIG. 33.—THE FOUR 'NEURZÜLNKARS' AT MÒDR. BEHIND THE STONES ON THE RIGHT IS KARKIEVAN, THE 'PALOL' OF THE 'TIIR'; ON THE LEFT IS NERPONERS, THE 'PALOL' OF THE 'WARSIR'; IN THE CENTRE IS THE 'KALTMOKH,' KATSOG, CARRYING A SICKLE-SHAPED KNIFE.

ordinarily touch, and it may be that the cursing and other features of the ceremony are intended to obviate the possible evil consequences of these acts. At the ancient and sacred dairies of Anto and Òdrtho the ceremony is still carried out in its entirety, but at other dairies many of the chief features of the ceremony have disappeared and all that remains is the anointing of the *neurzülnkars*, which take the place of the head of the *kaltmokh*.

When the *kaltmokh* comes into the sleeping hut on the first night of the ceremony, my informants laid great stress on the fact that the other occupants of the hut must take no notice of the boy, who creeps in after the others have taken their places on the beds, and he must go out in the morning before they show signs of waking. It is probable that the boy had originally to sit all the night in the open air at the appointed spot, and though he is now allowed to come into the hut, no notice is taken of him because theoretically he is not there. It is quite in accordance with Toda ideas that this should be done and other instances of similar procedure will be given.

Another noteworthy feature of the ceremony is the act of giving the *kaltmokh* a larger portion of food than can possibly be consumed at one meal. This feature occurs in other Toda ceremonies, and especially in connexion with the ordination of the *palol*, to be described in the next chapter. I know nothing of the significance of this procedure.

At some time during the day following the arrival at the new *ti mad*, the dairy is well cleansed with dried buffalo-dung. Soon after the migration—on the following Wednesday at the Nòdrs *ti* and on Sunday at the Kars and the Pan *ti*—a special ceremony called *ponup* is performed, in which salt is given to certain sacred buffaloes, but this will be described, together with the other salt-giving ceremonies, in Chapter VIII.

The Melgars man who accompanies the procession of the Nòdrs *ti* stays at Anto till the following Wednesday; at other places he only stays till the day after the procession. The Toda way of putting this is that at Anto he stays *erdpunrs*—*i.e.*, "two *punrs*." One *punrs* is a day and its next day, so that *erdpunrs* is equal to four days. At other places the Melgars man stays only one *punrs*—*i.e.*, he leaves the *ti mad* on the day following the migration.

The foregoing account applies to the Nòdrs *ti*. The general procedure is the same at the migration of other herds, but the ceremonial is, in general, less elaborate. At no other *ti* is there anything corresponding to the ceremonies in which the *kaltmokh* plays so important a part, and at no other *ti* is it absolutely necessary that a *mòrol* should take part in the procession, though, as a matter of fact, he usually also leads the way at the migrations of the Pan *ti*.

At the Kars *ti* the buffaloes pass the greater part of the year at Makars. They usually go to Neradr, where they stay about a month, and then go to Kòn for the dry season, returning to Makars in April. Sometimes they again stop at Neradr on their way from Kòn to Makars. It is probable that when the sacred dairy of Enòdr was still in use the ceremonial was more elaborate than it is at present. In the legend of Kwoto (see Chap. IX) an account is given of a ceremonial which occurred in former times during the migration from Kòn to Enòdr, and it is possible that this persisted until Enòdr was given up as a *ti mad*.

The herds of the Pan *ti* usually migrate with those of the Kars *ti*. They stand during the greater part of the year at Kudòdr, near Makars, and go to Neradr and Kòn as the dry season approaches.

In the case of the Pan *ti*, it seems that the bells travel on the necks of buffaloes; the *mani* called Kòsi on the neck of a buffalo called Kòsi, Pongg on a buffalo called Enmars, and Keituzan on one called Kòjiu. In this procession a *mòrol* goes first, followed by the *tars palol*, the *wars palol*, and the two *kaltmokh* in order.

At the present time there are no migrations of the buffaloes of the Kwòdrdoni *ti* or of the Nidrsi *ti*, and I have no information about the past. At Pursas, the present dairy of the Kwòdrdoni *ti*, there is a stone called *neurzülnkars*. I was told that nothing was done to it in connexion with the migrations of the buffaloes, but that it was rubbed with clarified butter and milk whenever the *irnörtiti* ceremony (see Chap. XIII) was performed at the *ti*.

CHAPTER VII

ORDINATION CEREMONIES

BEFORE a dairyman enters upon office he has to undergo certain initial rites, which may fitly be spoken of as "ordination ceremonies." These ceremonies vary greatly in their elaborateness, according to the dairy in which the candidate is to serve.

In the case of the ordinary dairyman, or *palikartmokh*, the proceedings are simple and may be accomplished in a few minutes, while for the highest grade of the priesthood they are extremely elaborate and prolonged over more than a week.

The essential feature of all the ordination ceremonies is a process of purification by drinking and washing with the water of a stream or spring used for sacred purposes only (*palinipa* or *kwoinir*). In every case the water is drunk out of certain leaves, and the body is rubbed with water mixed with the juice of young shoots or bark.

A general name for ordination is *pelkkodichiti* or *pelkkatthtiti*, "lamp he lights." This name is derived from the fact that the first act in connexion with the dairy work which a new dairyman has to perform is to light the lamp of the dairy. The former of the two names given above was used especially in the case of the ordinary dairy and the latter in the case of the *ti*, but I am doubtful whether there is any strict limitation of the terms in these senses.

Another general name used for the ceremony of ordination is *niròditi*, which in a more limited sense is applied to the drinking and purification at the dairy stream or spring which is the essential feature of the ceremony. This term was very often used for the ceremony of ordination to the office of *palol.*

THE PALIKARTMOKH

The ceremony of ordination of the *palikartmokh* is called *pelkkodichiti* and very often *muliniròditi*, the latter being derived from the *muli* leaves used in the ceremony. The ordination may take place on Sunday, Wednesday, or Saturday. On the day before the ceremony the candidate goes to the dairy, takes his food there, and sleeps at night in the outer room. His food is prepared and given to him either by the outgoing *palikartmokh* or by some other man holding this office.

On the morning of the ceremony the candidate washes his hands in the *pali nipa* and goes to the front of the dairy, having a piece of the ordinary mantle round his waist. The assisting *palikartmokh* will have placed a small piece of the dark cloth called *tuni* on the threshold of the dairy, this small piece being called *petuni*. The candidate bows down (*nersatiti*), as in Fig. 20, at the threshold to the *petuni*, which he then raises to his forehead and puts in the string of his *kuvn* on the left side.

The candidate then plucks seven leaves of the kind called *muliers—i.e.*, leaves of a plant called *muli* (*Rubus ellipticus*). This plant is also often called *pelkkodsthmul*, after the ceremony in which it is used. He also plucks a handful of young shoots or *nan* of the same plant, and takes the leaves and shoots to the dairy stream. At the stream he pounds the shoots with water on a stone, takes up some water from the stream with the pounded shoots, drops this water into one of the leaves three times, raises the leaf to his forehead, drinks (see Fig. 34), throws the leaf over his head and puts the shoots down on one side. When he squeezes the water from the shoots into the leaf-cup he holds the former in his right hand and the latter in his left, but when about to raise the leaf-cup to his forehead and drink he transfers it to his right hand. The candidate then takes a fresh piece of the pounded shoots and repeats with a second leaf, and so on till the seven leaves are finished, throwing the leaf over his head in each case after drinking.

He then takes all the pounded shoots which he has placed on one side, dips them in water, rubs them over his face and body three times, and puts them in his back hair, whence they are allowed to drop anywhere. In the only case in which I saw this ceremony I noticed that they remained in the hair till the end of the day.

The candidate then goes to the dairy, bows down at the

FIG. 34.—PUNATVAN (53) DRINKING DURING HIS ORDINATION AS 'PALIKARTMOKH' OF KARIA.

threshold as in Fig. 20, and enters. If there are two rooms, he bows down in the same way at the threshold of the inner room. If there is a *mani*, he salutes it (*kaimukhti*) with hand to forehead. He next bows down to the *patatmar* and to the *ertatmar*, and finally touches a vessel of the *ertatmar*, usually the *majpariv*, and a vessel of the *patatmar*, the *patat*, and by doing this becomes a full *palikartmokh*. He proceeds to light the fire and the lamp and goes to milk the buffaloes.

There are a few small points in which the ordination of a Teivali dairyman differs from that of the Tartharol. The Teivaliol use three pieces of the grass called *kakar*, with which the candidate sweeps the threshold of the dairy before bowing down and entering, the grass being left on the threshold. Among the Teivaliol also the place of the *petuni* may be taken by the special kind of cloth called *twadrinar*, which is manufactured by the Todas, and in the case in which I saw the ceremony, the candidate wore this instead of *petuni*. The Tartharol must use *petuni*.

In the only case in which I saw this ceremony the ordination was to a Teivali dairy and the candidate was completely naked except for the *kuvn*. The Tarthar *tarpalikartmokh* wears part of an ordinary mantle as a loincloth during his ordination. The ceremony is the same for the *kudrpalikartmokh* as for the *tarvalikartmokh*, except that the former is quite unclothed except for the *kuvn* and that he alone has a *mani* to salute.

THE WURSOL

The ceremony begins either on Tuesday or Friday and lasts two days. On the first day the candidate goes early in the morning to the ordinary dairy of the village at which he is to be *wursol*; at Kars he goes to the *kudrpali*. He receives food from the *palikartmokh* and eats it sitting on the seat (*kwottün*) outside the dairy. He stays near the dairy till the afternoon. When the *palikartmokh* has finished his afternoon work and has distributed butter and buttermilk, one of the men of the village comes to the candidate and says, "*Niròd*!" The candidate throws off his cloak and is given either a full *tuni* or a piece of this garment called *petuni*. The *palikartmokh* then stands in front of the door of his dairy, and the candidate stands opposite to him and asks three times "*Tunivatkina?*"—"Shall I put on the *tuni?*" The *palikartmokh* replies each time "*Vat!*"—"Put on!" Then the candidate raises the garment to his forehead and if he has been given a complete *tuni* he puts it on; if only a *petuni* he puts it in the string of his *kuvn*. This string is ordinarily called *pennar*, but is now called *kerk*, and this part of the ceremony is called *kerkatiti*. The fact that this name is given seems to indicate that properly the complete garment should not be given till a later stage of the proceedings.

The candidate then finds seven leaves called *muliers* and seven shoots or *nau* of the same plant and goes through exactly the same ceremony at the stream as in the ordination of *palikartmokh*, putting the shoots in his back hair at the end. This part of the ceremony is called *muliniròditi*, and its object is to make the candidate a *palikartmokh* as a step towards becoming *wursol*. He is taken through the lower degree on his way to the higher.

After *muliniròditi* the candidate goes to the wall of the dairy and stands outside it. The *palikartmokh* brings a firebrand from the dairy and lights with it a fire of *muli* wood, at which the candidate warms himself. The firebrand must be one of the three following kinds—*kid*, *pasòr* or *kiaz*. After warming himself, the candidate goes to fetch bark of the *tudr* tree, which must not be cut, but knocked off with a stone. He also brings seven perfect *tudr* leaves, and goes again to the dairy stream. He pounds the bark on a stone and dips it in water, squeezes the water into one of the *tudr* leaves, drinks, throws over his head and puts the bark on one side exactly in the same way as before, but using *tudr* bark and leaves instead of the shoots and leaves of *muli*. After doing this seven times he dips the pounded bark in water, sprinkles his head and face three times, puts the bark in his hair, and, going a little way off, shakes his head.

The candidate then goes again to find bark and leaves of *tudr*, and repeats the whole ceremony and continues to repeat it till he has done it seven times—*i.e.*, he drinks out of the *tudr* leaves seven times seven. After this he goes to the wood near the stream (at Kars, called Tarskars) and the *palikartmokh* comes to him there with the *ertatpun* filled with buttermilk, and with four leaves of the kind called *kakuders*. Two leaves are given to the candidate and two kept by the dairyman, and each folds the leaves in the usual way to make a cup (*ersteiti*). The dairyman then puts the *ertatpun* between his thighs and, holding it there, depresses it so that he can pour buttermilk into his leaf-cup; from this he pours into the leaf-cup of the candidate who then drinks, and this is repeated till the latter is satisfied. The *palikartmokh* brings food and fire from the dairy and both stay in the wood for the night, being allowed to have companions. The place where they sleep is called *tavarpali*.

In the morning the candidate again goes for *tudr* bark and leaves, and carries out the whole ceremony seven times as on the previous evening. He then goes to the *tavarpali* and waits there till the *palikartmokh* has finished his morning work, when the candidate again receives buttermilk and food. Then both go out together to look after the buffaloes.

When they return in the afternoon the candidate goes to the dairy stream and bathes from head to foot. This bathing is called *tudraspipini* (*tudr* I have washed), its object being to wash off the *tudr* bark previously used. After this he takes a piece of the cloth called *twadrinar* and, using it as a girdle in addition to that he already wears, he goes to the wall of the dairy while the *palikartmokh* digs up a vessel called *mu* which is buried in the buffalo pen. (At Kars the *mu* which is used is that of the *tarvali*.) The *palikartmokh* then puts the *mu* on the ground and stands by it. The candidate asks three times, "*Muvatkina?*" "Shall I touch the *mu?*" and the *palikartmokh* replies each time "*Muvat!*" The candidate then touches the *mu*, and by doing so becomes a full *wursol*. The *mu* is reburied by the *palikartmokh*.

All the ceremonies so far have taken place at or near the ordinary dairy, either *tarvali* or *kudrpali*, or at the stream belonging to one or other of these dairies. The candidate now for the first time goes to the dairy in which he is to be *wursol* (the *wursuli*) and prostrates himself at the threshold. He next enters and prostrates himself to the *patatmar* and then to the *ertatmar*. He takes up and puts in its place one of the vessels of the *ertatmar* and then one of the vessels of the *patatmar*. He salutes the *mani* (*kaimukhti*), lights the fire and the lamp and prays, using the prayer of the village. He then cleans the vessels and goes to milk, doing *mani terzantirikiti* with the first milk as usual.

I was especially told that if the candidate for the office of *wursol* wishes to scratch his head during his ordination ceremonies he must do so with a stick, but this is probably a feature of all ordination rites.

In the case of the *wursol*, it seemed that there is a difference in the ceremonial according to whether the dairy is occupied or not when the new dairyman enters upon office. The foregoing account applies to the case in which the dairy is already occupied and the new dairyman replaces another, so that there is no break in the continuity of the dairy proceedings. If the dairy should be unoccupied, I was told that the candidate would have to sleep for two nights in the wood, and there would almost certainly be additional purifications, but I did not learn the exact nature of the proceedings in this case.

Though I was only told of this difference of procedure in the case of the *wursol*, it is not unlikely that there is a corresponding difference of procedure in the case of other dairies when the dairy has been unoccupied. There will certainly be a ceremony of purification of the dairy, such as takes place when the buffaloes migrate to a new village, and probably the dairy vessels will also have to be purified.

The Kugvalikartmokh of Taradr and the Pohkartpol of Kanòdrs

The ordination ceremonies of these two dairymen appear to be almost identical. So far as I could ascertain, the feature which the *kugvalikartmokh* of Taradr and the *pohkartpol* of Kanòdrs have in common is that they serve institutions to which a high degree of sanctity is attached. The ritual of both dairies bears some resemblance to that of the *ti* and, as we have already seen, the regulations for the conduct of the *pohkartpol* are, in some respects, even more stringent than those of the *palol*.

The *kugvalikartmokh* is ordained either on Wednesday or Sunday, the *pohkartpol* on Tuesday. On the night preceding the ordination the candidate sleeps in the wood. Seven leaves are used of the following kinds: *pelkkodsthmul*,[1] *puthimul*, *änmul*, *takmul*, *kadakmul*, *tòrimul*, and *pathanmul*. One leaf of each kind is taken and the leaves pounded together and used in the same way as the shoots of *muli* or the bark of the *tudr* tree, water being dropped from them into leaves of *puthimul*. The pounded leaves are then placed in the back hair as usual. This is followed by the ceremony of drinking water three times out of a leaf containing water and some buffalo-dung. The bark of the *tudr* tree is then rubbed all over the body, though no *tudr* leaves are used for drinking. The candidate attains his full office by touching a *mu*, prostrates himself at his dairy, enters and begins his work as in the dairies of a lower grade.

The Kaltmokh

The ordination of the *kaltmokh* begins either on Sunday, Wednesday or Thursday. In the case of a *kaltmokh* of the Nòdrs *ti*, the first part of the ceremony takes place at the village of Nòdrs, while in some cases it seems that the candidate may go to the same village of Òdr which is visited by the *palol* during his ordination. I have no information about the place of ordination in the case of the other *ti* dairies.

A boy who is to become *kaltmokh* of the Nòdrs *ti* goes to Nòdrs either on Sunday, Wednesday, or Thursday, and, going to the ordinary dairy of that place (*tarvali*), he is given water by the *palikartmokh* in the vessel called *pòlmachok*. The boy washes his hands with this water and puts on a *tuni* which the *palikartmokh* gives him, after saying the same formula as in the ordination of *wursol*. He then does *muliniròditi* and so reaches the grade of *palikartmokh*. This and the following ceremony are done at a special stream at Nòdrs called *niròdigudr*. The purification ceremony is then performed with *tudr* bark and leaves till the candidate has drunk seven times seven. Food and buttermilk are given by the *palikartmokh*, and then the boy together with the

[1] This is the ordinary *muli* used in the ordination of the *palikartmokh*.

palikartmokh and the *wursol* of Nòdrs pass the night in the wood near that place.

The next morning the candidate goes to the ordination stream and washes himself from head to foot. This is called *tudraspipini*, its object being the same as in the ordination of the *wursol*. The boy next goes to the front of the *tarvali*, where the *palikartmokh* gives him a special string made of *twadrinar*, which he puts round his waist as *kerk*, and then warms himself at a fire of *muli* wood. The *palikartmokh* brings a *mu*, which the candidate touches with the same formalities as in the ordination of *wursol*, and by so doing reaches the grade called *perkursol*, which is of the same rank as that of *wursol*. The *perkursol* then takes the *mu* into the *tarvali*, prostrating himself at the threshold before entering. He prostrates himself to the *patatmar* and to the *ertatmar*, puts the *mu* on the *patatmar* and comes out. He then goes to the *poh*, or conical dairy of Nòdrs, prostrates himself at the threshold, enters, and prostrates himself before *patatmar*, *ertatmar* and, finally, before the *mani*. Up to the point of saluting the bell in this way he keeps on the *tuni* but at this stage he throws it down and comes out of the dairy naked (except for the *kuvn*), puts on the ordinary cloak and goes to the dairy at which the *ti* buffaloes are standing.

When he reaches the *ti mad*, the candidate goes to the *palol*, whom he salutes with the words "*îr kar ûdâ*," this salutation being called *pîrwadrikpini*. He goes to the sleeping hut, prostrates himself before the horns which are kept in this building, and then goes to the front of the dairy. He is now *perkursol*, and in order that he shall become full *kaltmokh* or *tunitusthkaltmokh*, the *palol* gives him a piece of *tuni* (*petuni*). The boy asks three times, "*Tunitusthvaskina?*"—"Shall I go to wash the *tuni?*"—to which the *palol* answers each time "*Tusthva!*"—"Wash, go!" The boy takes the *petuni* to the stream for ordinary use (not the *kwoinir*) and bathes from head to foot. He puts to himself three times the question, "*tunitoikina?*" and laying the piece of *tuni* on a stone, he pours water on it three times and returns with the *petuni* in his hand to the *palol*, who will be sitting on his *pohvelkars* in front of the dairy. The *palol* asks three times, "*Tunitusthpacha?*"—"Have you returned from washing the *tuni?*"—and each time the boy replies, "*tunitusthpuspini*"—"I have come from washing the *tuni.*" Then both *palol* and boy go to the front of the *kadr* in which the calves are kept and the *palol* puts into the gate three bars (*tasth*), which shut the opening of the enclosure. The boy asks three times, "*Tasthvatkina?*"—"Shall I touch the *tasth?*"—and each time the *palol* replies "*Tasthvat!*" The boy, who hitherto has been *perkursol*, now touches the *tasth*, and by so doing attains the full rank of *kaltmokh*, and at once goes and pours buttermilk (*kaizhvatiti*) for the *palol*.

The latter parts of the ordination ceremonies of the *kaltmokh*, from the point at which he receives *petuni* from the *palol* to the touching of the *tasth*, are always performed whenever the *kaltmokh* returns to the *ti* after a journey in which it has been necessary to degrade himself to the rank of *perkursol* (see p. 106). The initial stages of becoming a *kaltmokh* are known in general as *niròdibudnudr*.

The Ordination of the Palol

In accordance with the fact that the *palol* belongs to the highest and most sacred grade of the dairy-priesthood, we find that the ceremonies preceding his entrance upon office are far more elaborate and prolonged than for the minor grades.

In order that a Teivali man may become a candidate for the office of *palol* he must first have gone through a preliminary qualifying ceremony called *tesherst*. When the office of *palol* becomes vacant, the people of the clan to which the *ti* belongs are restricted in their choice to those men who have been through this ceremony. When one of these qualified men has been selected, he then goes through the proper ordination ceremonies, known as *niròditi*.

In the case of a *palol* of the Nòdrs *ti*, the *niròditi* ceremonies are performed partly at Nòdrs, partly at Òdr, one of the most sacred villages of the Nòdrs clan, and finally at the *ti mad* where he is to hold office.

The Tesherst Ceremony

This qualifying ceremony for the office of *palol* is always performed by a number of men at the same time. The number taking part must be three, five, seven or nine. There seemed to be no doubt that it was not permissible for four, six or eight men to perform the ceremony together. One or two Todas told me that an even number of men might do the ceremony, but all the more trustworthy witnesses were agreed that there must be an uneven number, and on all the occasions of which I could obtain records of actual ceremonies, an uneven number of men had done *tesherst* together. The ceremony may not be performed while the funeral ceremonies of any Teivali person are uncompleted.

At the time of my visit there were only nine or ten men who had been through the *tesherst* ceremony, including those who were holding or had held the office of *palol*. It was proposed that a number of the younger men should perform the ceremony about this time, but it had to be delayed till the second funeral ceremonies of two Teivali women had been held.

The *tesherst* ceremony always begins on a Monday after the new moon. It takes place at certain villages where people are living, and in all the cases of which I obtained records it had been done at Kudrnakhum, belonging to the Nòdrsol, or at Pushtar, belonging to the Taradrol. People must be living at the village at the time the ceremony is performed.

The candidates go to the village on Monday evening, accompanied by two or three Nòdrs men. All go to a stream by a wood and the ceremony begins after sunset, when all the candidates throw off their cloaks and stand in a row. A man of the Nòdrs clan has a *tuni* in his hand and each candidate asks three times, "*Tunivatkina?*"—"Shall I touch the *tuni*?"—and each time the Nòdrs man replies, "*Tunivat!*" The first man in the row touches the *tuni* and then the others in order. The Nòdrs man then gives the *tuni* to the first man who touched it, and he tears it into as many pieces as there are candidates, giving a piece to each man, who puts it in the string of his *kuvn*. All then go in search of the leaves of *muli* and each plucks seven leaves and seven shoots. They go to the stream, one by one, and each drinks and rubs himself with the shoots seven times, as in the ordination ceremony, and puts the shoots in his back hair.

While they are doing this, the Nòdrs man will have made fire by friction, using the wood of *muli*, and the men warm themselves at the fire. Each man then goes in search of seven *tudr* leaves and *tudr* bark and carries out the usual purification ceremony once only, drinking out of each of the seven leaves, after which the men take food prepared by another of the Nòdrs men, and all pass the night in the wood. Next morning the men fetch *tudr* bark and leaves and repeat the drinking and rubbing ceremony of the previous evening, but on this occasion each man says "*Tesh-niròdinem*," as he throws the leaf over his head after drinking. All then bathe completely in the stream.

While they are doing this, the Nòdrs men have been cooking a large amount of food, more than the candidates can readily eat, and an old woman of the Tartharol who is to take part in the ceremony has bathed and dressed in her best clothes and put on all the ornaments she can procure: gold earrings, necklace, bracelets, and rings. When the men have bathed, they wait till the message comes that the food is ready, and then each man takes off his piece of *tuni* and his *pennar* and his *kuvn*, so that he is completely naked. The Nòdrs man portions out the food and puts it on *tudr* leaves, the portion for each man being more than he can possibly eat at one sitting, and the portions of food are given to the old woman, who sits down with her back to the men. Each man goes up behind the back of the old woman, and she gives him his portion of food by putting her hand behind her back so that she does not look at him, and in doing so she says three times "*Teshtòrtudenk?*"—"*Tesh* food have I not given?" The men take the food, go into the thickest part of the wood and eat it. None of the food prepared on this occasion may be eaten by the Nòdrs men or by the old woman, but though the amount is excessive, the whole of it must be eaten by the candidates during the day. After each man has eaten to the full he may put on his cloak. The Nòdrs men and the old woman go back to their villages and they must hold no communication of any kind with the candidates after the food has been given. The men remain in the wood all day, and when it is getting dark they go to the nearest village at which any of them live, taking care that no one sees them on the way.

One of the most remarkable features of this ceremony is the part taken by the old woman. She must be one of the Tartharol; she must be past the age of child-bearing, and she must never have had intercourse with one of her own clan. In the last particular the word of the woman is trusted, for it was said that she would never deceive in such a matter. Every woman believed that if she did not speak the truth she would die, and all those concerned in the ceremony would either die or have serious illness. I was told that it was by no means easy to find a woman who fulfilled this requirement, and in each of the cases of which I have records the same woman officiated—viz. Naspilthi of Taradr (21).

Other remarkable features of this ceremony are that the men should be given more food than they are readily able to eat, as in the ceremony connected with the *kaltmokh* after the migration (p. 139), and that they receive this food in a condition of complete nudity, a condition which only occurs in one other dairy ceremonial.

The *tesherst* ceremony is one in which candidates for the office of *palol* go through certain of the rites which ordinarily form part of the process of ordination, with the addition of special ceremonies, in which a superabundant portion of food is given by a woman who fulfils certain peculiar conditions.

When the office of *palol* becomes vacant, the clan to which the *ti* belongs chooses from among those who have been through the *tesherst* ceremony, and the chosen man has then to undergo the ordination ceremonies proper, or *niròditi*.

The Niroditi Ceremony

The ceremony begins on a Saturday evening, after the new moon, when the chosen candidate goes to a village of the clan to which his future *ti* belongs and sleeps there in the ordinary hut.

On the following morning he goes before daybreak to the front of the dairy of the village, naked except for his *kuvn*, and a man of the village stands at the door of the dairy holding a *tuni* in his hand, and says three times, "*Tunivatkia!*"—"Touch the *tuni!*" The candidate answers, "*Tunivatkin*," and takes the *tuni*. If the garment is a complete one, he puts it on; if only a piece, he puts it in his *pennar*, and taking seven *tudr* leaves and *tudr* bark he goes to the stream of the dairy and performs the usual drinking and rubbing ceremony, and after putting the *tudr* bark in his hair, goes a little way off and shakes his head so that the bark falls out. He repeats the ceremony twice, so that it is performed three times altogether—*i.e.*, he drinks from the *tudr* leaves three times seven. This ceremony is called *teshnir*, and is done in view of the inhabitants of the village. The candidate stays for the rest of the day at the village. If there is a *wursol* there, the food of the candidate is prepared by this dairyman[1]; if no *wursol* is present, it is prepared by the *palikartmokh*. The food is grain boiled in milk, and is only eaten in the evening. The candidate sleeps that night in a wood near the village, but not the same wood as that by the stream where *teshnir* had been done. Either the *wursol* or the *palikartmokh* must pass the night in the wood with the candidate, and other men of the village may also be their companions. Until the candidate lies down to sleep he must remain naked (except for the *kuvn*), but when sleeping he may cover himself with his ordinary cloak.

Next morning (Monday) the candidate gets up at sunrise,

[1] This is inconsistent with the statement made on p. 73 that the *wursol* never prepares food except at the *irpalvusthi* ceremony. It is possible that the food is only given to the candidate by the *wursol* and is not prepared by him.

lays aside his cloak, and goes to bathe completely in the stream, saying three times, "*Tudraspinem*,"[1]—"*Tudr* I have washed," thus washing off the *tudr* of the previous day. He then returns to the place where he had slept, puts on his ordinary cloak with the right arm out, and goes to the front of the dairy. He is given food by the *wursol*, or, in his absence, by the *palikartmokh*, and eats it outside the dairy, after which he washes. He then goes to the ordinary stream of the village (*ars nipa*) and takes up water with his hand, and by so doing he becomes *perol*—*i.e.*, he loses any sanctity he has acquired by the ceremony of the previous day.

The candidate then goes direct to the village of Òdr and stays near that village till the evening, when he makes his way to the front of the dairy of that place. He stands about ten yards from the dairy and throws off his cloak. A man of the clan to which his future *ti* belongs now gives him a complete *tuni* of the kind worn in the village dairy (a *mad tuni*, not a *ti tuni*), saying three times, "*Tunivatkia*," to which is replied "*Tunivatkin*." The man who gives the *tuni* now remains as assistant and companion till the candidate reaches his future dairy. The candidate puts the *tuni* round his loins, goes to the stream of the dairy, and performs the drinking and rubbing ceremony with *muli* leaves and shoots as in the ordination of *palikartmokh*. The assistant makes fire by friction and lights a fire of *muli* wood, at which the candidate warms himself.

The drinking ceremony with *tudr* is then carried out in the same way as at *teshnir*, and then the *wursol* of Òdr brings buttermilk in an *ertatpun* and gives it in cups of *kakud* leaves to both the candidate and his assistant. They also receive food from the *wursol*, while any other men present go to the ordinary hut for their meal. That night is passed at a special spot under a tree not far from the dairy at Òdr, the *wursol* and assistant being the companions of the candidate. On that night the candidate may not

[1] This has not the same form as the word uttered by the *wursol* and *kaltmokh* in the corresponding ceremony. In some cases different verbal forms are used at the *ti*, and this may be an instance.

touch his ordinary cloak and has to be content with the scanty covering of the *tuni*.[1]

On the next day (Tuesday), the ceremony with *tudr* leaves and bark is repeated three times as on the previous days, and after the *wursol* has finished his dairy work he gives buttermilk and food to both the candidate and his assistant. On the afternoon of this day the *tudr* ceremony is performed again, but on this occasion seven times, so that the candidate drinks from the *tudr* leaves seven times seven. In the evening buttermilk and food are again given by the *wursol* and the three men pass the night in the wood.

On the next day (Wednesday) the candidate fetches bark of the tree from which the material called *twadrinar* is made and makes for his temporary use a rough *kuvn*. When it is ready, he bathes in the dairy stream, takes off the old *pennar* and *kuvn* and puts on the newly made garment, together with the *tuni*, and goes with the *wursol* to the dairy where the buffaloes of his *ti* are standing. When they approach the *ti mad* the *wursol* goes away and leaves the candidate to go to the dairy alone, where he sits on the outskirts (*pül*) of the *ti mad*. When the *kaltmokh* sees the candidate approaching, he collects the buffaloes at the milking place (*pepkarmus*) and catches hold of the tails of certain buffaloes which are to be taken in charge by the new *palol*, saying to himself three times for each buffalo, "*Tover vatkina?*"—"Tail shall I hold?"—and replying to himself each time, "*Vat!*" At the Nòdrs *ti* if the candidate is to be *palol* of the *tiir*, the *kaltmokh* holds the tails of three buffaloes, one of each kind; if he is to be *palol* of the *warsir*, two buffaloes only take part (see p. 112). After this the *kaltmokh* prepares food in the *pül* of the dairy and gives it to the *palol* designate. While the *kaltmokh* is attending to the new *palol* he must become a *perkursol*—*i.e.*, he degrades himself to this rank before undertaking these duties. During the night the candidate together with the *kaltmokh* and the other *palol* already in office

[1] It has been stated by Harkness, Marshall and others that when the *palol* is entering on his office he has to sleep in the wood completely naked. This is not strictly correct, though the covering afforded by the *tuni* is so meagre that the statement is almost justified.

(if there are two, as at the Nòdrs *ti*) sleep in the hut of the *ti mad*.

The next day (Thursday) the new *palol* goes to the stream and performs the *tudr* ceremony three times in the morning and nine times in the afternoon; *i.e.*, he drinks from the *tudr* leaves three and nine times seven. On this day the *kaltmokh* milks the *punir*, takes the milk to the *pül*, churns there and gives buttermilk, butter and other food to the new *palol*. On that night all sleep in the *karenpoh* or calf-house.

The proceedings of Friday, Saturday, and Sunday are the same as those of Thursday, except that the new *palol* may now drink the milk of the *punir* like the full *palol*.

On Monday morning the new *palol* enters on his office. In the morning he bathes and then takes off the temporary *pennar* and *kuvn* he has been wearing and replaces them by others made in the same way. A Badaga (the *tikelfmav*) then brings one of the two cloaks of the *palol*, that called *pòdrshtuni*, and lays it down at the outskirts of the dairy. It is taken up by the *kaltmokh* and given to the new *palol*, who spreads it out on the place where the buffaloes are milked. He then takes pounded *tudr* bark, says the *kwarzam* of the gods, of the *ti* and of the buffaloes (see Chap. X) and throws the pounded bark on the garment. He turns the garment over so as to expose the other surface and purifies this in the same way. He then asks himself, "*Pòdrshtuni tutkina?*"—"Shall I tie the *pòdrshtuni*?"—and throwing off the *mad tuni* he has been wearing hitherto, he puts on the *pòdrshtuni*. The *kaltmokh* returns the *mad tuni* to the Nòdrs people, who come on this day and stand on the outskirts of the place.

The new *palol* then purifies his dairy by sprinkling it with water and *tudr* bark in the same way as is done when going to a new dairy (see p. 136). He next takes the *uppun*, puts into it water and *tudr* bark, and turning towards the Nòdrs people with the vessel to his forehead, says three times to them, "*Poh pûkhkina?*"—"Shall I enter the dairy?" All the Nòdrs people cry "*Pûkh!*" and the new *palol* enters his dairy with the full rights of his position.

At some period before entering into office as full *palol*

the candidate touches a *tasth* or bar of the entrance into the *tu.* This ceremony is similar to that performed by the *kaltmokh*, and as in this case it seemed to be the special indication of entrance on full office, but unfortunately my notes do not make it clear exactly when this touching of the *tasth* is done nor with what ceremonial it is accomplished.

For a month from this day there will be what is called *pon*, nothing being either sold or given from the dairy. At the end of the month, on a Monday, a *tuni* of the kind called *kubuntuni* is brought by the *tikelfmav*, and is put on in the usual way. (During the previous month the *pòdrshtuni* will have been used both as a cloak and as a loincloth, and will have been taken into the sleeping hut.) The *palol* is visited by the dairymen of his rank from the other *ti* dairies, and there will be many visitors from all the Todas, who come and sit in the *pül* of the dairy and feast. The new *palol* also receives greetings on this day from the Todas for the first time since his entry upon office. He greets the Tartharol first, saying "*Bañ*" in the usual way, and then the Teivaliol, saying "*Pekein*," and each reply in the customary manner.

The ordination ceremonies of the *palol* are thus very prolonged. There is a preliminary qualifying ceremony in which the would-be candidates receive pieces of *tuni*, perform both the *muli* and the *tudr* purificatory ceremonies, each once only, and on the following day go through the very peculiar ceremonial in which they are given superabundant food by an old woman while in a condition of complete nudity.

The proper ordination ceremonies begin on a Sunday, when the candidate receives *tuni*, performs the purificatory ceremony with *tudr* three times seven, and sleeps in a wood. On Monday he washes off the *tudr*, becomes a *perol*, and goes to the village of Òdr, where he again receives *tuni*, goes through the *muliniròditi* ceremony which makes him a *palikartmokh*, and then performs the *tudr* ceremony three times seven and sleeps in the open, covered only with the *tuni*. On Tuesday he performs the *tudr* purification three times seven in the morning and seven times seven in the evening and again sleeps in the open. On Wednesday he bathes and assumes a special *kuvn* and goes to his future dairy, where the *kaltmokh* performs the tail-holding ceremony and the candidate sleeps in the hut. On the four next days the *tudr* ceremony is performed three times seven in the mornings and nine times seven in the afternoons, and the calf-house is used as a sleeping-place. On the following Monday the *palol* enters upon office, assuming the *pòdrshtuni*, touching a *tasth*, and entering his dairy.

The foregoing description of the ordination of the *palol* applies primarily to the Nòdrs *ti*, but in its main details it holds good for other places.

I am doubtful as to the part taken by the village of Òdr, and am not clear whether part of the ordination ceremony is performed at this place by every *palol* or only by those of the Nòdrs *ti*. It is possible that it is only the latter who visit the village, but I do not know of any corresponding village visited by the candidates for the post of *palol* at other *ti* dairies. My impression is that every candidate for the office of *palol* visits this village.

The only definite modification of the ceremonies attendant on entrance into office of which I know occurs at the Kars *ti*. Here the *palol* is first ordained to the *parsir*—*i.e.*, he becomes the *palol* of this herd of buffaloes and tends them only. At the end of a month he becomes *palol* of the *pürsir*, and the ceremony of entrance upon this office was spoken of as *pelkkatthtiti* to the *pürspoh*. In this case the ceremony of ordination to the *parspoh* is called *niròditi*, and that of removal to another dairy *pelkkatthtiti*.

On the afternoon of the appointed day the *palol* churns the milk of the morning in the *parspoh* and then shuts the door of this dairy, which he never re-enters as long as he is in office. He could only do so if he should cease to be *palol* and be re-ordained to the same *ti*.

A new *pòdrshtuni* is brought by a Badaga and is assumed by the *palol* after purification in the usual manner. At the same time he puts on a new *kagurs*,[1] which has been purified by the *kaltmokh*, who has also cut a new *kwoinörtpet* on the hill of Kulinkars which the *palol* then purifies with *tudr* bark in the usual manner, saying the names of the four deities, Anto, Nòtirzi, Kulinkars, and Kuzkarv.

[1] The *ti* name of the *kuvn*.

The *palol* then digs up earth from the footprints of one of the *pürsir*, saying the whole prayer of the *ti* as he does so. He drives the buffalo slightly to one side by touching it with the wand, and takes earth from the exact place where the foot of the buffalo had been resting and puts the earth into a cup which he has made of *tudr* leaves. He adds pounded *tudr* bark and goes to the spring (*kwoinir*) of the dairy, where he mixes water with the earth and bark. He then goes to the stone called *pepkusthkars*, where he has previously laid a complete set of new dairy vessels and implements of the inner room, together with the lamp and the bell (Ner) of the *pürspoh*. The bell is laid on the stone, the other things by its side.

Wearing the *pòdrshtuni* and holding the *kwoinörtpet* under his left arm, the *palol* sprinkles the contents of the leaf-cup over the dairy vessels and other objects, beginning with the bell, and as he does so he prays, using the whole prayer of the dairy. He then ties all the vessels and other contents of the dairy on a staff called *pepkati* in exactly the same manner as when taking them from one *ti mad* to another. The bell is tied up in a leafy covering of *kiaz* and everything is done as in the migration from one place to another, and the staff with its burden is then borne by the *palol* from the *pepkusthkars* to the stone called *perskars*, by the side of which the dairy vessels are laid, while the *mani* is uncovered and laid on the stone. The staff is then placed at the back of the dairy.

Having untied the dairy vessels and arranged them by the stone, the *palol* pounds fresh *tudr* bark, and with the *kwoinörtpet* under his left arm goes with the *karitòrzum* to the sacred spring, into which he throws the bark, takes water, and returns. Taking more pounded bark, he puts it in the *idrkwoi* and pours water into this vessel from the *karitòrzum*. He takes the *idrkwoi* with its contents to the front of the dairy, and with his right hand sprinkles the water over the outside of the dairy and then into its interior till the vessel is emptied. The dairy vessels are not again purified, but are taken into the dairy with the same procedure as that described in the last chapter. The vessels of the outer room, which have been purified by the *kaltmokh*, are then taken to their places. Fire is made by friction; one fireplace is lighted and fire transferred to the other, and from this the lamp is lighted, and the *palol*, who is now *palol* of the *pürsir*, goes out to look after and milk his new charges. On this evening no food is taken, nor does the *palol* drink buttermilk as usual, and the *kaltmokh* does not blow the horn in the evening. On the following day, which is the occasion of a feast for all Todas, the usual routine is followed.

The most interesting feature of this ceremony at the Kars *ti* is that the vessels of the inner room are taken by the *palol* from the *pepkusthkars* to the *perskars*, a distance said to be about fifty yards, in exactly the same manner as that in which they are carried from one dairy to another during the migrations when the distance may be many miles.

The essential feature of the various ordination ceremonies is purification by drinking water from certain leaves and rubbing the body with the juice of certain plants or the bark of a tree mixed with water from a dairy stream or spring. The ordinary dairyman uses the leaves and shoots of *muli;* the dairymen of the Taradr *kugvali* and the Kanòdrs *poh* use seven kinds of leaves and rub themselves with *tudr* bark, while the three grades of dairyman open only to Teivali or Melgars people not only rub with the juice of *tudr* bark, but use *tudr* leaves for the purificatory drinking.

The *palikartmokh* drinks and rubs himself seven times only, the *wursol* and *kaltmokh* seven times seven, while at various stages in his ordination the *palol* uses *tudr* bark three times seven, seven times seven, and nine times seven.

The final stage of ordination or induction is marked by touching some sacred object of the dairy. The ordinary dairyman touches one or more of the sacred vessels of the dairy; the *wursol*, *kugvalikartmokh*, and the *pohkartpol* of Kanòdrs touch the *mu*, a dairy vessel buried in the buffalo pen, which is dug up for the ordination ceremony. The *kaltmokh* and the *palol* touch a *tasth*, the former touching a bar of the calf enclosure and the latter one in the opening of the pen used for adult buffaloes.

According to one account, the Teivali *palikartmokh* also touches a *mu* on entrance into office, but it is very doubtful if this is correct. Nothing was said about it at the ordination at which I was present, and I saw nothing to indicate that this vessel was being used, but it is possible that the *mu* had been dug up earlier in the day and put inside the dairy.

Another interesting feature of the ordination ceremonies is that a dairyman of a higher grade may be taken through the lower stages on his way to the higher office. Thus both *wursol* and *palol* perform the purificatory ceremony with *muli*, which is the chief feature of the ordination of the *palikartmokh*. There did not seem to be any stage in the ordination of the *palol* when he could be said to be a *wursol*, though the ceremonies of Monday evening and Tuesday are very much like those of the *wursol*, the chief difference being in the exact number of times that the *tudr* purification is performed.

CHAPTER VIII

SPECIAL DAIRY CEREMONIES

I HAVE so far dealt with the organisation and ritual of the dairy, with the ceremonies accompanying the movements of the buffaloes from one place to another, and with the ceremonies attendant on the entrance of the dairymen into office. There remain ceremonies which accompany certain events in the course of the dairy ritual or in the lives of the buffaloes. One of these, the *pepkaricha* ceremony, is performed whenever any evil befalls a certain dairy vessel which is buried in the buffalo pen. Another ceremony celebrates the birth of a calf, and a group of ceremonies are connected with the act of giving salt to the buffaloes.

THE PEPKARICHA CEREMONY

In the account of the daily work of the dairy, it will be remembered that whenever the dairyman goes out to milk for the first time he puts some buttermilk into his milking vessel. This is done in every dairy, and the buttermilk so added is called *pep*. The milk of every day has mixed with it some of the buttermilk from the milking of the day before, and in this way continuity is kept up in the dairy operations. Under certain conditions this continuity is broken and new *pep* has to be made, and the process of doing so is the ceremony called *pepkaricha*, *pepkarichti*, or *pepkarichanudr* —*i.e.*, "*pep* he purifies," or, "if *pep* is purified."

In some cases new *pep* has to be made for the whole clan

(*madol*); in other cases it has only to be made for one of the dairies of the clan.

The ceremony is performed for the whole clan whenever anything goes wrong with a certain dairy vessel called *mu*, which is buried in the buffalo pen at the chief village of the clan. We have seen that this vessel is used in the ordination to certain dairy offices, and it is also inspected as a matter of routine about once a year. If it is broken or has been stolen or tampered with in any way, it becomes necessary to make new *pep* for the whole clan.

Among the Tartharol, new *pep* has also to be made after the funeral of a male on account of the defilement of the *mani* involved in its exposure to the ordinary people at the funeral ceremonies.

The conditions which necessitate the making of new *pep* for a single dairy are, (1) if a Tamil or other "foreigner" has entered the dairy, (2) if an ordinary Toda (*perol*) has gone into the dairy at night, (3) if the dairyman has used tobacco. In these cases the people of the village at which the offence has been committed procure a new *mu*, and, after purifying it, go to some other dairy of the clan, where they procure some buttermilk to act as *pep* and take it to their own dairy. It is only when new *pep* has to be made for the whole clan that the prolonged ceremony of *pepkarichti* has to be carried out. This ceremony differs in its details for each clan, and is more complicated in some cases than in others. As an example, I will give the proceedings for the Kuudr clan.

When it becomes necessary to make new *pep* for the whole group of dairies belonging to the clan it is necessary to take the buffaloes to one special dairy. The Kuudr people go to the dairy of Kwirg near Sholur. On the day of going to Kwirg, a feast is held at which the food called *ashkkartpimi* is eaten.

Whenever new *pep* is made it is necessary to have a new *palikartmokh*, and the man who is to undertake the duties goes to Kwirg with the milking buffaloes of the *pasthir* and is accompanied by a number of Kuudr men. The men take with them a new and complete set of dairy vessels, and reach Kwirg in the early morning of a Sunday after the new moon.

The buffaloes are at once penned in the *tu*. The first business is the ordination of the new *palikartmokh*, which is carried out as usual. When at the stream for the purification ceremony, the *palikartmokh* has with him a new *mu*, which he fills with water at the stream. He takes this vessel to the *tu* in which the buffaloes are penned, and knocks one of the buffaloes on the back with his wand (*pet*), so that it moves to one side. Then with the wand he digs some earth from the spot where the hoof of the buffalo had been resting, and mixes this earth with *tudr* bark. He places part of the mixed earth and bark in the *mu*, and puts the rest on one side; this part of the ceremony is called *mukatchkudrspini*, or purification of the *mu*, literally "*mu* purification I have purified."

The *palikartmokh* then brings all the other dairy vessels and implements, beginning with the *patat*, and purifies them by throwing on them mixed earth and *tudr* bark, sprinkling them with water from the *mu* three times, saying "*Oñ*" each time. The things of the *patatmar* are purified first and then the things of the *ertatmar*, and the purified objects are placed in the dairy. Fire is made by friction and the *palikartmokh* goes out to milk. Buttermilk is not put into the milking-vessel as usual, and the lamp is not lighted. The milk is poured into the *patat*, and the *palikartmokh* then prepares food, which he gives to the people who have come with him, but he himself fasts. All the men then go away except one or two, who are to remain as companions of the dairyman. In the evening the *palikartmokh* takes off some of the cream,[1] which has risen to the top of the milk, and puts it into the lamp which he lights, and then prays, using the *kwarzam* of Kwirg[2] and the *kwarzam* of the *pep* only.

If the milk has coagulated it is now churned, and then the buffaloes are milked as usual, but if the milk has not coagulated, it is left till next morning. In the evening the dairyman takes food as usual.

On the following day, it seems that the milk has always

[1] This is the only occasion on which this cream is used by the Todas. It is used because there are now neither butter nor ghi at the dairy. Its use here is an indication that the process of coagulation is less rapid than usual.

[2] See p. 222.

become solid and is churned. Immediately after churning and without taking food, the dairyman puts together the dairy things according to the usual method followed when going from one village to another, and goes with his buffaloes to the village of Kiudr. The dairy vessels are carried in the usual manner, the new buttermilk called *puthpep* being in the *patat* and the butter in the *mu*.

The people living at Kiudr leave the village, and the man who has been filling the office of *palikartmokh* there throws away all the old dairy things and takes the *mani* to the stones by the side of that dairy called *neurzülnkars* (see p. 129). After leaving the bells there for a little time, the dairyman takes them to the *pali nipa*, and then his office ceases and he becomes *perol*.

The new *palikartmokh*, who has come from Kwirg, purifies the dairy and his new dairy vessels and the *mani* in exactly the same way as when reaching a new dairy, and then places the bells, vessels, and other objects in the dairy. During the next month, till the following new moon, the dairyman and his companions stay alone at Kiudr doing the ordinary business of the dairy. During this time they may be visited by men of the Kuudr clan, but neither by women nor by men of other clans. At the end of the month, on the Sunday after the new moon, the *palikartmokh* drives the buffaloes (now called *ponir*, festival buffaloes) to Kuudr, taking with him the *puthpep* and the dairy vessels. When the people at Kuudr see the dairyman coming with the *ponir*, they leave the village and all go to Kiudr, which the buffaloes have just left. There they hold a feast to which many people of other clans, both men and women, are invited.

When the *palikartmokh* reaches Kuudr, he purifies the dairy as he had done at Kiudr and puts the vessels in their places.

Certain men of the clan then come, each with a new *mu*, and these vessels are laid by the side of the stones called *keinkars* and *tashtikars* in the wall of the pen. At Kuudr fifteen new *mu* should be brought by the fifteen heads of families of the Kuudr clan. The *palikartmokh* then purifies each *mu* with *tudr* bark in the usual way and places the vessels on the *patatmar* of the dairy, after which he gives food to those who have provided the vessels.

The *palikartmokh* with his companion or companions then stay at Kuudr for a month, when, again on a Sunday after the new moon, all the Kuudrol assemble at Kuudr and hold a feast. On that day a new *palikartmokh* is appointed for each dairy of the Kuudr clan. Each man goes through the usual ordination ceremony and then receives one of the new *mu* containing some of the new *pep*, which he takes to his dairy. Each new dairyman also provides new dairy vessels, and, when he reaches his dairy, purifies the *mu* and the new dairy things in the way already described. He puts the vessels into the dairy and then goes to milk, taking some of the new *pep* in his milking-vessel, and thereafter matters go on as usual. Each new dairyman fasts while going to his dairy with the new *pep*, although the rest of the people are feasting.

Those who remain at Kuudr bury the *mu* in which the *pep* was brought from Kwirg. It is buried by the side of the pen, under a tree called *teikhkwadiki*.

The ceremony of making new *pep* is carried out on the same lines in all dairies, but usually it is less complicated and fewer villages have to be visited than in the case of the Kuudrol. It seems that there is a tendency in some clans to perform the ceremony less rigidly than of old. Thus, the Kars people used to go to Keshker for new *pep*, but now they perform the ceremony at Kars itself, so that the migration to a new place with its attendant ceremonial is avoided.

There are certain differences in the procedure in the case of Teivali and Tarthar clans. One, the necessity for new *pep* after the funeral of a male, has been already mentioned.

Another difference is that there is a buried *mu* for each kind of dairy, so that a clan which has two or three kinds of dairy will have two or three *mu* buried in the pen. If it is the *mu* belonging to the *wursuli* which is broken or tampered with, the ceremony is performed by the *wursol*, who takes earth from the footprints of one of the *wursulir*. If the *mu* of the *kudrpali* is injured, the *kudrpalikartmokh* performs the ceremony, taking earth from the footprints of one of the other kinds of sacred buffaloes. Thus at Kars he takes it from the prints of the *martir*.

At Kanòdrs new *pep* has to be made at a place called Kautarmad, which I could not identify. It is a long way from Kanòdrs, but the people have to go there because the god Kwoto used to make *pep* there. There is one feature peculiar to the ceremony for this clan. Earth has to be taken from a certain spot from which it was taken by Kwoto, and this earth is mixed with that taken from the footprints of the buffalo.

Another special feature of the Kanòdrs dairy is connected with the buried *mu* and is probably the result of the fact that this dairy is now only occupied occasionally. When the *pohkartpol* leaves the dairy on vacating office, he takes up the buried *mu*, pours into it a small quantity of *pep*, and reburies the vessel, covering it on the top with a stone. When he resumes office, he takes up the *mu* and purifies it with the two kinds of earth used in the full ceremony, and puts the *pep* which has been buried into his milking-vessel when he goes out to milk for the first time. As in other Tarthar clans, the full ceremony of *pepkaricha* is only carried out when the *mu* is broken or stolen, and after the funeral of a male.

A characteristic feature of Toda dairy procedure is the coagulation of the milk before it is churned. This coagulation occurs in a few hours without the addition of rennet or other special coagulating agent, the milk drawn in the morning being nearly always solid at the time of the afternoon churning. This rapid coagulation of the milk is almost certainly assisted by the added buttermilk or *pep*, the curdling being probably an acid coagulation set up or hastened by the addition of the sour buttermilk. If this were the case, it might be expected that habitual failure of the milk to coagulate might be regarded as a reason for making new *pep*, and I therefore inquired carefully into this point. It was quite clear, however, that delay in the coagulation was not looked upon as a reason for the ceremony. If there was habitual delay, it was customary to consult the diviners, and they always gave one of two reasons for the delay: either that it was due to the action of a sorcerer, or that the dairyman had committed one of the offences against the dairy of which a list is given on p. 295.

If delay were said to be due to the first cause, the sorcerer would be invited to the village, entertained with food, and induced to remove his spell; if to the second cause, the dairyman would have to perform the *irnörtiti* or similar ceremony; but there was never any question of making new *pep*, the necessity for this ceremony being entirely dependent on the condition of the buried dairy vessel.

THE IRPALVUSTHI CEREMONY

The ceremony of *irpalvusthi* (buffalo milk he milks) is performed about the fifteenth day after the birth of a calf. It only takes place when one of the sacred buffaloes has calved, and is not performed in ordinary villages for *putiir*, nor at the *ti* for *punir*. It is performed after the birth of both male and female calves. The ceremony is carried out in the same fashion at the *wursuli*, the *kudrpali* and the *tarvali*, but has different features at the *kugvali* of Taradr and at the *ti*.

There are special days for the ceremony. At the *tarvali*, it must be performed on Sunday, Wednesday, or Saturday; at the *kudrpali* and *wursuli*, on Sunday or Wednesday; at the *kugvali*, on Saturday. The ceremony is performed at the *ti*, but I omitted to obtain any account of the proceedings at this grade of dairy.

When this ceremony is held at the village of Kuudr, a man from Ȯdr belonging to the Nodrsol must attend, and similarly a man from Kuudr must be present when the ceremony is performed at Kuudr, this regulation being the result of certain events in the histories of the buffaloes of these places (see p. 647).

At each of the three kinds of dairy which follow the same procedure, the chief part is taken by the dairyman. At the *wursuli*, the *wursol* officiates, and at the *kudrpali* and *tarvali*, the *palikartmokh*.

The first appropriate occasion after the fifteenth day from the birth of the calf is appointed and the dairy is purified with dried buffalo-dung. Contrary to the general rule, the lamp is lighted on the morning of this day. All the buffaloes are milked as usual; one or two *pun* of milk being poured into the *patat* and all the rest into the *ertat*.

The dairyman then puts some milk into the milking-vessel, and, carrying his wand, he leads the fifteen-day-old calf to its mother to be suckled. While the calf is being suckled, the dairyman strikes the mother on the right side of the back three times with the wand, saying "*Oñ*" each time. He then puts the wand on the top of the milking-vessel and, holding both in his left hand, milks the buffalo once or twice with the other hand, so that the milk splashes on the wand as it falls into the vessel. The vessel and wand are then laid at the back of the dairy, which the dairyman enters to prepare food, boiling grain or rice with milk in a special vessel (*ertat*) kept for the purpose. While the food is being cooked the dairyman takes some of the grass called *kakar* and the plant called *kabudri*, and sweeps the interior of the dairy with them, beginning at the *patatmar*. While doing this and during his other operations on this day, he must not turn his back to the contents of the dairy. After having swept the dairy, he lays the *kakar* and *kabudri* by the wall of the building, again takes the milking-vessel and wand from the back of the dairy, and, having called the people of the village, he salutes by raising the vessel and wand to his forehead and prays, all present praying with him. I am not certain whether it is the prayer of the village or a special prayer which is used on this occasion. After praying, the dairyman lays the wand on the top of the *patat* and pours the milk which he obtained from the buffalo into the *patat* over the wand. He puts the latter in its appointed place and then goes to the *ertatmar*, where he prepares a large number of leaves on which he portions out the food (*tòrkisthiti*) which he has prepared, and all the people present take this food outside the dairy. On the following day, the buffalo which has calved is milked with the rest.

When this ceremony is performed at the *wursuli* dairy, it is the only occasion on which the *wursol* prepares food; at all other times, the food of this dairyman is prepared by the *palikartmokh*. On this occasion the *wursol* not only cooks food for himself but for all those present. Another distinctive feature of this ceremony is that it is the only occasion on which the milk of the *wursulir* is ever drunk.

The day of *irpalvusthi* is the only day on which the dairymen of the three kinds of dairy, with the exception of the *wursol* of certain dairies, do their work *kabkaditi*, *i.e.*, do not turn their backs to the contents of the dairy.

At the *kugvali* of Taradr, the ceremony is more elaborate. It begins in the afternoon, when the dairy is purified with dried buffalo-dung. Three large pieces of the wood called *kid* are brought, and the dairyman ties the small piece of cloth called *petuni* to the milking-vessel and to a special wand called *irpalvusthpet*.[1] He also ties *petuni* in the form of rings round the ring and little fingers of his right hand and round the ring finger of his left hand. He then goes out with the milking-vessel and wand, and after saluting by raising them to his forehead, he goes to the place where the buffaloes are milked and prays there.

The *kugvalikartmokh* then takes the calf to its mother and milks as at the other dairies, but in this case he milks the buffalo completely, and if, by doing so, he has not filled his milking-vessel, he fills it with the milk of *putiir*. He pours this milk into the *majpariv*, which has been carefully cleaned, and puts the three pieces of *kid* wood in the fireplace. He puts into the milk three measures (*ak*) of rice, but adds neither salt nor jaggery. When the food is ready, he portions it out on leaves and gives to those present, who must on this occasion be limited to the people of the village. This ceremony occurs on Saturday evening.

On the following day, the ceremony is repeated, being called on this occasion *irpataduthti*, *i.e.*, "buffalo milk he uses publicly." When preparing food on this day the *kugvalikartmokh* puts into the milk eleven *ak* of rice[2] and adds both salt and jaggery. The number of pieces of wood used is not limited to three, but any quantity may be burnt. When the food is ready, he goes out of the dairy and finds

[1] I am doubtful whether a special wand is also used in other dairies.

[2] Eleven *ak* = one *kwa* (see p. 588).

assembled a large number of people, including guests from other villages and clans. Among them a Melgars man must be included or there could be no ceremony. When the dairyman sees the people, he says "*Ol pudra?*" "People, have you come?" They answer "*Pudspimi,*" "We have come." The dairyman then brings the stirring-stick (*put*), and, taking up some of the food on the stick, says "*Tütr erkina?*" "At the fire shall I throw?" and the people answer "*Tütr eri!*" "At the fire, throw!" The dairyman then throws the food on the stick into the fire, and portions out the rest of the food among the people, who eat it outside the dairy.

From the birth of the calf until this ceremony, the buffalo is not milked and the calf is kept, when not with its mother, in the small enclosure called *kush*. After the ceremony, the buffalo is milked like the rest of the herd, and the calf joins the others in the ordinary calf-house, or *kwotars*.

Giving Salt to Buffaloes

Salt is given to the buffaloes five times a year, both at the *ti mad* and the ordinary village. At the *ti* the salt is given with buttermilk, and the ceremony is known as *mòrup*. At the ordinary village buttermilk is not given, and there is no general name for the ceremony, though there are special names for three of the five occasions on which salt is given. These special names are also used at the *ti*. The first occasion is *kòrup*, or 'new grass salt,' which takes place in the month Nalani (February-March). The second is *marup*, or 'again salt,' a month later in Ani. The next two occasions have no special names, but in the ordinary village are known as *arsup*, 'house salt,' given in the months Ovani and Kirdivi (June-July and September-October). The last occasion is in the month Emioti (November-December), and is known as *paniup*, meaning 'frost salt.' In the case of *kòrup* and *paniup*, it seemed that salt was given shortly before the time at which the young grass and frost respectively were expected.

At the *ti* the ceremony is performed on the Sunday or Tuesday following the new moon. At the Nòdrs *ti* it should be done for the *tüir* on Sunday and for the *warsir* on Tuesday, but this now only happens when the buffaloes are at Òdrtho and Kudreiil, where the dairies of the two kinds of buffaloes are at some distance apart. At Mòdr and Anto and other dairies, the ceremony is performed for both kinds of buffalo on a Sunday. At the Pan *ti* the day for the ceremony is Tuesday, and at the Kars *ti*, Sunday.

On the day before the ceremony each *palol*[1] digs a round hole called the *upunkudi* at a prescribed spot, or more commonly enlarges the hole remaining from a previous ceremony. On the following day each *palol* carries out the usual morning churning and milking, but before drinking buttermilk the dairy is cleansed with buffalo-dung. The *palol* then pours into the vessel called *alug* two *kudi* of buttermilk and takes the vessel and some salt to the *upunkudi*. He throws bark of the *tudr* tree three times into the hole, three times into the buttermilk and on the salt, and going to the spring he throws the bark three times into the water, saying "*Oñ*" each time. The *palol* then fills the *alug* with water from the spring, mixing it with the buttermilk already in the vessel. He adds salt, saying "*Oñ*" three times, and the whole is poured into the *upunkudi*. A special buffalo is then brought to the *upunkudi*; at the Nòdrs *ti* the *ti palol* first leads up the buffalo belonging to the *unir* which is called Enmars and the *wars palol* takes the buffalo of the *perithir* called Òrsum, this act of sending a special buffalo first being called *irpârsatiti*. After this all the buffaloes are taken to drink in groups of five or six. When the hole has been emptied, it is refilled with salt and water, but this time no buttermilk is added. When all the buffaloes have drunk, each *palol* pulls some of the grass called *kargh* and throws it into the hole three times and returns to his dairy to take buttermilk from the *kaltmokh* as usual.

At the ordinary village the salt-giving ceremony is performed about a week after it has been done at the *ti*. Any day may be chosen except the *madnol*, *palinol*, or *arpatznol*.[1] Thus at Kuudr the ceremony may be performed on any day

[1] When there is only one *palol* for both kinds of buffaloes, as at the Pan *ti*, he only digs one hole.

[2] See Chapter XVII.

except Tuesday and Friday; at Kars, on any day except Tuesday, Thursday, and Friday.

On the three occasions with special names, *kòrup*, *marup*, and *paniup*, guests come from other villages, but at the *arsup* this does not happen. As in the case of the *irpalvusthi* ceremony, a man from Kuudr must be present at the salt-giving ceremony of Òdr and a man from Òdr must be present at Kuudr.

The ceremony is performed by the *palikartmokh* after the people of the village have made the hole or *upunkudi*.[1] The *palikartmokh* takes from the dairy the vessel corresponding to the *alug* of the *ti*, viz., the *tat*, but does not take buttermilk. *Tudr* bark is used in the same way as at the *ti*.

At a Teivali village, the *pasthir* drink first. At a Tarthar village at which there is a *wursol*, the *wursulir* drink first, the act of sending certain buffaloes first being called *irparsatiti* as at the *ti*. After the buffaloes have drunk, *kargh* grass is thrown into the hole, first by the dairyman and then by all the others present, but it is only thrown once by each person, who says "*Oñ*" as he throws.

The object of this ceremony is said to be that the buffaloes shall give a plentiful supply of milk.

THE PONUP CEREMONY

At the *ti* dairy salt is given to the buffaloes on certain other occasions and with a far more elaborate ritual. The ceremony is then called *ponup*, or 'festival salt,' and takes place soon after the migration from one dairy to another. At the Nòdrs *ti* the salt is given on the Wednesday following the Sunday on which the migration has occurred, and at the Kars *ti* and the Pan *ti*, on Sunday, a week later than the procession.

On the night before the ceremony the *palol* shuts up the buffaloes in the special pen called the *pon tu*.

On the morning of the appointed day, when the churning is finished, but before the buffaloes have been milked, each *palol* brings six sprigs of the shrub called *puthimul*, each sprig having on it five or six leaves. Three of these sprigs

[1] This hole at an ordinary village is sometimes known as a *tarupúnkudi*.

N

are put on one side, and the other three are used as follows:— Rice has been previously prepared and placed either on the leaf called *kakuders* or on that called *katers*. The *palol* makes a hole in this food in which he puts butter, and, taking the first sprig of *puthimul*, he plucks from it one leaf and, using it as a spoon, takes up some of the food and puts it on the fire in the fireplace called *tòratthwaskal*, saying the name of the chief *teu* or god of the *ti*. He then takes some of the butter, and holds it over the fire till it drops, when he utters the name of the same god. He repeats this with a second leaf of the *puthimul*, saying the name of the second most important god of the *ti*, and so on with the other leaves. I obtained the fullest account of *ponup* from Koboners, who had been *palol* of the Kars *ti*, and here food and butter were put on the fire six times, saying the names of Anto, Nòtirzi, Kuzkarv, Kulinkars, Onkomn, and Karmanteu.

The *kaltmokh* then brings water taken from the ordinary stream in the vessel called *mòrkudriki*, and gives it to the *palol*, who sits in the outer room facing towards the inner room, and throws some of the rice in front of him once, some behind him once, and the rest outside the dairy. He puts some salt on the fire, and taking the water brought by the *kaltmokh*, he sprinkles it before and behind him as he had done with the food.

Then follows *kaizhvatiti*, *i.e.*, the *kaltmokh* pours out buttermilk for the *palol*. This is the only occasion on which this act takes place before the buffaloes have been milked, the ceremony of drinking buttermilk on every other occasion taking place when the morning's work is over. The *palol* gives food to the *kaltmokh*, and here, again, there is a feature peculiar to this day, for the *kaltmokh* eats his food sitting in the place in the hut where the *palol* usually sits.

The buffaloes are then milked, after which the *palol* fetches three sticks of the kind ordinarily called *kwadrikurs*, but at the *ti*, *kakul*. Each is used for a special purpose and has a corresponding name, one being called *irpasthkakul*, the second *kwarkul*, and the third *parkul*.

The *palol* takes buffalo-dung in both hands and the *irpasthkakul* in the right hand, and separates certain buffaloes from the rest by knocking their backs three times with the dung and stick. At the Kars *ti* two buffaloes are separated in this way; at the Nòdrs *ti* five buffaloes are set apart, one of each kind, three by the *ti palol*, and two by the *wars palol*. These buffaloes are known as *ponir*. The dairy is then purified with the dung and water. The *irpasthkakul* is laid on one side, and the *palol* puts salt in the basket called *ponmukeri*, and takes it with the water-vessel called *karpun* to the place where salt is to be given, taking also the remaining sprigs of *puthimul* and a bundle of fern.

At the place for the ceremony there is a stone called *ponkars* (when there are two *palol* there will be two stones), and at the stone the *palol* makes a vessel of clay and water so as to resemble a milking-vessel. This clay vessel is called *teukwoi* (*teu*, god, and *kwoi*, milking-vessel).

The *palol* then takes two perfect *tudr* leaves, and fastens them together with the petioles of other leaves, so that they form a cup which is called *püvup*. Salt is placed in this leaf vessel, which is laid down by the side of the *teukwoi*. One such vessel is made for each buffalo, two at the Kars *ti* and five at the Nòdrs *ti*.

The *palol* then takes the stick called *kwarkul*, and with it makes a hole in the middle of each *teukwoi*, saying (at the Kars *ti*) "*antok teukwoi ûrtj, paln!*" ("To Anto in *teukwoi* make hole, O *palol!*"). He then makes other holes round the sides of the clay vessel, saying the names of the other gods in the same manner. (At the Kars *ti* those which have already been given. At the Nòdrs *ti* the names of five gods are mentioned—Anto, Kulinkars, Nòtirzi, Kuladrvan, and Kuzkarv.) Two pieces of *tudr* bark and a sprig of *puthimul* are then placed in each hole, saying for the first, "*Antok teukwoi et, paln!*" ("To Anto in *teukwoi* put, O *palol!*"), and this is repeated with the name of a different god for each hole.

Next the *palol* takes the stick called *parkul*, which has a sharpened end, and makes small holes called *upunkudi* as in the *mòrup* ceremony. At the Kars *ti* only two *upunkudi* are made; at the Nòdrs *ti* one *palol* makes three and the other two holes. *Tudr* bark is thrown three times into the holes and into the water of the spring. Water is taken from the spring in the *karpun*, salt is put into the water three times and the salt and water are poured into the holes, and the buffaloes previously set apart are led to the holes and drink three times, one buffalo from each hole. The leaf vessels previously made (*püvup*) are then given to the buffaloes, and are eaten by them. Care is taken to give the leaf vessels in such a way that the end of the leaf corresponding to the petiole enters the mouth of the buffalo first.

The *palol* takes Anto's leaf from the *teukwoi* and puts it in the *karpun* with water, then faces towards the place where Anto lives (Anto's hill) and pours in that direction, saying "*Antok*," "to Anto." This is repeated with the other leaves, the *palol* in each case turning and pouring towards the place where the god lives.

Then follows the ceremony called *tafkeirpudrti*, *i.e.*, "fern pool he strokes." The *palol* takes the bundle of fern which he has brought with him and goes to the stream, which is blocked up, so that the water accumulates and forms a pool. He waits till the pool is so deep that the water would come half-way up his thighs, when he steps in with the bundle of fern in his right hand and strokes the bundle over the water, saying the *kwarzam*, or prayer names of certain gods and buffaloes (at the Nòdrs *ti* the *palol* says, "*Anto idith, Kûlinkârs idith, Nòtîrzi idith, Kûlâdrvan idith, Kuzkârv idith, Mûv idith, Mòrs idith, Pan idith, Kûdreij tîdj idith*": see Chapter X). The *palol* then buries the fern at the bottom of the pool, so that there is no chance that it may come up again, and throws the grass called *kargh* into each *upunkudi* once only.

The *palol* then goes to the buffaloes and knocks one of the ordinary kind called *punir* to one side with a bush called *pîrskwadriktûr* and pours a little water on its back. This is called *punîr ûvk nîr atiti*, *i.e.*, "he pours water on the back of the *punir*."

Finally the *palol* goes to a stream near the *upunkudi* and washes there from the hands to the elbows. This final washing is called *peiaspiti*. *Pei* is the Tamil word for 'demon,' and the word suggested that there was an idea of warding off the influence of some kind of evil spirit, but it seemed that *peiaspiti* was merely the *ti* form of *kaiaspiti*, "he washes the hands."

The following day is called *ăpkărvnol*. On this day small Badaga children go to the *ti mad* and the *palol* gives them clarified butter on a leaf. On this day also any one who has been a *palol* (*patol*) may go to the *ti mad* and receive food unless the funeral ceremonies for one of his clan should still be uncompleted.

The ceremonies of *ponup* were said to be designed to invite the gods to be present by means of the clay vessels. The *tudr* bark and leaves were said to be used in order to purify these vessels after their defilement by human hands in the process of making.

CHAPTER IX

THE TODA GODS

THE ceremonies which have been described in the last five chapters make up a large part of the ritual of the Toda religion, but there is one important feature of this ritual which has so far been left on one side, or only cursorily mentioned, because its full consideration only becomes possible after an account has been given of the Toda gods.

In describing the ritual of the dairy and the various ceremonies connected with the buffaloes, it has been mentioned that at certain times the prayer of the dairy or the prayer of the village is used. In these prayers there are references to various incidents in the lives of the gods, and many of the clauses would be unintelligible without a knowledge of these lives. It therefore becomes necessary to consider this branch of Toda mythology before dealing with the prayers in detail.

The typical Toda god is a being who is distinctly anthropomorphic and is called a *teu*. In the legends he lives much the same kind of life as the mortal Toda, having his dairies and his buffaloes. The sacred dairies and the sacred buffaloes of the Todas are still regarded as being in some measure the property of the gods, and the dairymen are looked upon as their priests. The gods hold councils and consult with one another just as do the Todas, and they are believed to be swayed by the same motives and to think in the same way as the Todas themselves.

At the present time most of the gods are believed to

inhabit the summits of the hills, but they are not seen by mortals. Before the Todas were created, the gods lived on the Nilgiri Hills alone, and then it is believed that there followed a period during which gods and men inhabited the hills together. The gods ruled the men, ordained how they should live and originated the various customs of the people. The Todas can now give no definite account of their beliefs about the transition from this state of things to that which now exists.

Each clan of the Todas has a deity especially connected with it. This deity is called the *nòdrodchi* of the clan, and is believed to have been the ruler of the clan when gods and men lived together. I am doubtful whether there is at the present time any belief that the *nòdrodchi* exerts an influence over the clan with which he is connected.

There was no department of Toda lore which gave me greater difficulty than the study of the beliefs about the gods. There was no doubt that two gods stood out pre-eminent among the rest. One was a male deity whose name was Ön, and the other a female deity, Teikirzi. A simple question which I had the greatest difficulty in settling was the relation of these deities to one another. According to one account they were brother and sister; according to another, father and daughter. It seemed quite certain they were not husband and wife, and most probable that they were brother and sister. Others of the gods were believed to be related to one another, but on such points as this I found it almost impossible to obtain trustworthy information. It may have been reticence which made the difficulty, but I do not think so, and am inclined to think that the Todas have now only vague ideas about the histories of their more ancient gods, and have nothing like the definite traditions which they possess about deities of obviously more recent origin.

Sometimes there were discrepancies between different accounts which I could not clear up, and in such cases I give the account which seems to me to be the most trustworthy.

PITHI

This god is the earliest of whom any tradition is preserved. His name is Pithi or Püthi, and he is often called Pithioteu. He was born near the sacred dairy of Anto in a cave which had the same shape as the ordinary Toda hut. According to one account, Pithi created Todas and buffaloes, but there seemed to be little doubt that this is not the correct tradition, which assigns the act of creation to his son Ön. There is a suggestive resemblance between the name of this god and the Sanscrit word for earth, Prithivi, which is in common use in Southern India.

ÖN

Ön was the son of Pithi. He created the buffaloes and the Todas and became the ruler of Amnòdr, the world of the dead, where he now lives.

One day Ön went with his wife Pinârkûrs to Mêdrpem (the top of the Kundahs). There he put up an iron bar which stretched from one end of the *pem* to the other. Ön stood at one end of the bar and brought forth buffaloes from the earth, 1,600 in number. Then Pinarkurs tried to produce buffaloes and she stood at the other end of the bar and produced 1,800 buffaloes.

Behind Ön's buffaloes there came out of the earth a man, holding the tail of the last buffalo, and this was the first Toda. Ön took one of the man's ribs (*parikatelv* or *magalelv*) from the right side of his body and made a woman, who was the first Toda woman. The Todas then increased in number very rapidly so that at the end of the first week there were about a hundred.[1]

The descendants of the buffaloes created by Ön became sacred buffaloes, while the descendants of those created by his wife are the ordinary buffaloes.

[1] This account of the creation of men and buffaloes was obtained from Arsolv (27) of Kanòdrs, one of the oldest living Todas. It agrees very closely with the story as related to Mr. Breeks.

Ön had a son called Püv. One day when Püv was acting as *palikartmokh* at Kuudr, he was churning in the dairy with a ring on the little finger of his right hand. When the dairyman goes to fetch water he should always take the churning stick out of the *patat* or vessel in which the milk is churned. On this occasion Püv left it in the *patat* and went out to fetch water. As he was going a black bird called *karpüls* tried to check him, saying "*tts, tts, tts*," meaning "Don't go to the water," but Püv paid no attention and went on. When he was taking the water the ring dropped from his little finger into the spring. Püv saw the ring in the water, but could not reach it, and so he got into the spring. The water was not deep, and yet as soon as he stepped into the spring it completely covered him and he was drowned. When Ön found that his son was lost he cried very bitterly and covered himself with his cloak (*tuni*). (Ön is said to have been a *palol* at this time.) When Ön covered himself he looked downwards and saw, as through a veil, his son in Amnòdr playing with the ring, putting it on and off his finger.[1]

When Ön saw that his son was in Amnòdr he did not like to leave him there alone and decided to go away to the same place. So he called together all the people and the buffaloes and the trees to come and bid him farewell. All the people came except a man of Kwòdrdoni named Arsankutan. He and his family did not come. All the buffaloes came except the *arsaiir*, the buffaloes of the Kwòdrdoni *ti*. Some trees also failed to come. Ön blessed all the people, buffaloes and trees present, but said that because Arsankutan had not come he and his people should die by sorcery at the hands of the Kurumbas, and that because the *arsaiir* had not come they should be killed by tigers, and that the trees which had not come should bear bitter fruit. Since that time the Todas have feared the Kurumbas, and buffaloes have been killed by tigers. All the Todas and all the buffaloes appear to have suffered for the evil deeds of Arsankutan and the *arsaiir*.

Then Ön went away to Amnòdr, taking the buffaloes

[1] According to another account, Püv died from trying to catch the image of a white calf in the water. At that time, it was the custom to kill and bury any calf of a white colour, and one had been buried close to the spring.

and the *palol* of the Nòdrs *ti* with him, and since that time Ön has ruled over Amnòdr, which is sometimes called Önnòdr after him.

TEIKIRZI

This goddess is perhaps the most important of the Toda deities. She is said to have been the sister, and probably the elder sister, of Ön. I could learn very little about the story of her life, but nearly all the customs of the Todas were referred to her, and it seemed clear that when Ön left this world Teikirzi became the ruler or *nòdrodchi* of the Todas. Whenever I tried to obtain from the Todas an explanation of any ceremony or custom I nearly always received the reply, which was regarded as final, that it had been so ordained by Teikirzi.

It seems doubtful whether Teikirzi dwells in any special hill like other Toda deities, though there is a hill near Nòdrs especially connected with her. I was told that she lives everywhere in this world, and in answer to a question it was said even that her influence extends to London, where she dwells as she dwells everywhere else.

She is regarded as the ruler or *nòdrodchi* of all the Todas, and this world is often spoken of as Eikirzinòdr. At the same time Teikirzi is especially connected with Nòdrs, and she is the special *nòdrodchi* of this clan.

Five customs, or sets of customs, are ascribed especially to Teikirzi. These are :—

(i) *Madol pàkht kwadrt vai*, "Who divided and gave *madol* (clans)." Teikirzi is also said to have divided the Todas into their two chief divisions.

(ii) *Ir pàkht kwadrt vai*, "Who divided and gave buffaloes." Below Nòdrs, near a swamp called Keikudr, there is a small stream which at the present time Todas will not cross at a certain spot, and Teikirzi stood in this stream. According to one account she beat the water with a wand, saying "*Ir padri ma*" ("May buffaloes spring"), and buffaloes sprang out of the stream; but it seemed to be more generally accepted that she only divided the buffaloes on this spot by touching each animal on the back with a wand and saying the name of the clan to which it was to belong. The first portion went to Nòdrs, the second to Kuudr, the third to Kars, and the fourth to Taradr. Up to this point she used a wand of *kid* wood (*kidkurs*). For the next clan, that of Keadr, the *kidkurs* was put away and she used a wand of *tavat* wood, and several other kinds of wând were used. Teikirzi was also said to have ordained at the same time that *wursulir* should be milked by Teivaliol and to have settled the general regulations concerning the different kinds of buffalo.

(iii) *Püliol påkht kwadrt vai*, "Who divided and gave *püliol*."

Teikirzi is said to have ordained that certain people should be the *püliol* of a man, and that *püliol* should not marry one another (see Chap. XXI).

(iv) *Ir patz id vai*, "Buffalo catch who said." Teikirzi ordained that buffaloes should be caught at the funeral ceremonies (see Chap. XV).

(v) *Kwarzam pep ostht ad vai*, "Who told the *kwarzam* and gave *pep*."

Teikirzi gave to each village its *kwarzam*, or sacred name, and settled the method of making new *pep*.

The name of Teikirzi occurs frequently in other legends. One story not mentioned elsewhere is the following:—

When Teikirzi was living at Nòdrs the people of Mysore came to fight her, but as they approached, the woods made a great noise. When the Mysore people heard the noise they stopped, and then Teikirzi cursed them and said, "Let them become stones," and they were turned into stones, which are still to be seen below Nòdrs.

Teipakh, or Tirshti

I know very little about the life-history of this deity, but he is very widely mentioned in the prayers and incantations of the Todas, and is one of their most important gods. He was the brother of Teikirzi, and differs from most other Toda deities in being a river god, Teipakh being the Toda name of the Paikara river.

Teipakh is the *nòdrodchi* of the Piedr and Kusharf clans.

Although there was considerable agreement that Teipakh

and Tirshti were one and the same god, there was some doubt about it, and, according to one account, Tirshti was only another name for Teikirzi.

ANTO.

I am very doubtful about the name and identity of this god. There seemed to be little doubt that he had the same name as the chief dairy of the Nòdrs *ti* and was the chief deity connected with this dairy. According to one account he was the son of Ön, but it is possible that the two deities were identical, Anto being Önteu. His name was sometimes pronounced Anteu or perhaps more correctly Änto or Änteu.

I have only a few incidents from the life of Anto. He once rolled a huge stone with the hair of his head from Nelkòdr in the Wainad to the top of a hill called Katthvai near the dairy of Anto. The god now lives near this dairy, resting his head on a spot called Ködrs, and stretching his legs on a spot called Tudrs. These places are about two furlongs apart so that Anto is evidently a god of a large size.

Anto is said to have made buffaloes, and the buffalo which founded the *ti mad* of Makars (see p. 116) was one of his creation. The fact that Anto created buffaloes increases the probability of his identity with Ön, but this is far from conclusive for there were undoubtedly several independent creations of these animals.

KULINKARS

This deity is the *nòdrodchi* of the Kars clan. His original name appears to have been Kulin, and this was changed to Kulinkars. He is also called Teikhars. He inhabits a hill near Makurti Peak, which is so steep and rocky that "no man has ever climbed it."

The following story is told of Kulinkars or Teikhars:—He once knocked on the ground and so made two buffaloes. He then told the monsoon (*kwadr*) to drive the buffaloes to the place to which they were to go, saying, "you must push them on." As the buffaloes were being driven on by the monsoon, a tiger went after them. When they reached a certain hill, the hill divided into two and the buffaloes went between the two parts, but still the tiger followed them. Then the buffaloes came to Kwaradr and went into the pen, and the tiger also went into the pen. When the buffaloes saw that the tiger had come into the pen, they kicked it and it died. Then one of the buffaloes said to the other, "You stay here in the pen; I am going to Tarsòdr." Then the monsoon drove on this buffalo to Tarsòdr, which is one of the dairies of the Pan *ti*. The descendants of the buffalo which stayed in the pen are the *pasthir* of Kwaradr and the descendants of the other are among the buffaloes of the Pan *ti*.

Kulinkars was connected with the *erkumptthpimi* ceremony (see Chap. XIII) and was the *mokhthodvaiol* or paramour of Nòtirzi. His relation to Nòtirzi is said to have been the origin of the *mokhthoditi* custom (see Chap. XXII), but I was not able to obtain any detailed account of this part of the history of the god.

Kulinkars has a son called Teikhidap, who lives on Makurti Peak, and the proper Toda name for this hill is Teikhidap.

NÒTIRZI

I have no details of the history of this female deity. She is the *nòdrodchi* of the two important clans of Melgars and Kuudr, and lives on the hill now known as Snowdon, the Toda name of the hill being the same as that of the goddess. This hill is especially sacred, and any Toda who visits it has to salute with hand to forehead (*kaimukhti*) in all directions. Like her *mokhthodvaiol*, Kulinkars, Nòtirzi is connected with the *erkumptthpimi* ceremony. She is said to have had a son called Tikuteithi or Teukuteithi. It is possible that this is the same as Teikuteidi, who appears in the story of Kwoten (see p. 193), but they are more probably two different deities.

A stone which is said to have been thrown by this goddess from her hill is shown close to the village of Pòln, under the tree known to English visitors to the Nilgiris as the 'umbrella tree.'

KORATEU OR KUZKARV

Korateu was the son of Teikirzi. One day when Teikirzi was going from one village to another she went into a cave called Teivelkursh, by the side of a stream called Kathipa, near Kakhudri, and there gave birth to a son, who was called Azo-mazo. The afterbirth dropped into the stream and was carried down to Teipakh (the Paikara river). It travelled down the river as far as a place called Marsnavai, where there were growing two plants called *tib* and *purs* in which it became entangled. The afterbirth then slowly arose and became a boy, and the boy was Korateu. When Azo-mazo became a man he went to live at Pernòdr in the Kundahs, but Korateu lived in the river till he was eight years old. The river Teipakh was the brother of Teikirzi. As he sat in the lap of his uncle Korateu used often to play at making the buffalo horns called *tebkuter* (Fig. 35).[1] When he was eight years old he founded a *ti* and created a male and a female buffalo, making both out of earth. He also built a dairy and a buffalo pen and made the garment called *tuni*. As soon as the buffaloes had a calf, he went to fetch a churning-stick from Kaiers, beyond Makurti Peak, and took it to Nerva, near Mòdr, where his buffaloes were standing. He then went to Kurkòdr, a bamboo grove near Meipadi in the Wainad, and made a *kwoi* or milking vessel. He next made the *persin* and the

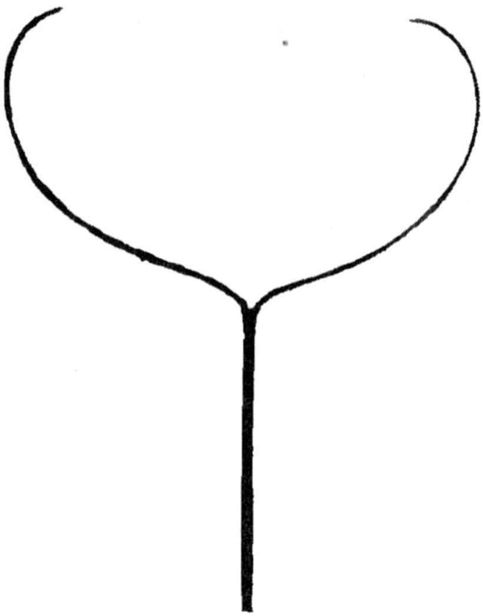

FIG. 35.—IMITATION BUFFALO HORNS.

[1] Usually called *petkuter*.

mani and all the other things of a *ti* and became *palol* of the buffaloes at Òdrtho. There was a buffalo here of the kind called *kughir*, with the horns growing downwards. Korateu cut off these horns and gave them to the *kaltmokh* at Òdrtho and they are now the horns of the Nòdrs *ti*. Korateu then made a law that the people of Piedr should fill the office of *palol* and that the *kaltmokh* should be taken from the Melgarsol. He appointed a *palol* and a *kaltmokh* from these clans, handed over the charge of the *ti* to them, and went away to the hill Korateu, where he lived in an iron cave which he called a *poh*. He used to bathe in a pool near the hill.

At this time Korateu was not recognised as a *teu*, and when the gods held council he was not summoned as a member. This made him very angry.

Near Korateu there was a wood in which there stood a tree of the kind called *mòrs* (*Michelia nilagirica*) which was about 80 feet high. Korateu ordered that honey bees (*peshtein*) should come to the tree, and after a time there were about 300 nests, which made the tree bend down with their weight. One day about twenty men came to collect honey, Todas, Irulas, and Kurumbas. The Todas made a fire under the tree, while the Irulas and Kurumbas climbed and collected honey from the nests. When they had collected the honey from all except three or four nests, the tree became so light that it sprang back and killed the Irulas and Kurumbas, and the Todas went home.

At this time Korateu was unmarried and he carried a stick of iron. One day a Kurumba woman came to the *mòrs* tree in search of honey. Korateu knocked her on the head with the iron stick and at once she became pregnant. That evening she gave birth to a daughter, who was very beautiful, and Korateu decided to marry the child and sent away the mother that night. (According to another version, the child was so beautiful that the mother was frightened and went away to her own village, and Korateu fed the child with milk and fruit and honey, and when she grew up he married her.)

Soon after the death of the Irulas and Kurumbas a sambhar calf came to Korateu, who caught it, tamed it, and kept it for a month. Then certain Todas went to Korateu and asked him for a place. Korateu gave them a place and said that it should be called Keradr. The people of Keradr then asked for buffaloes. So Korateu gave them the sambhar calf and said that it should become buffaloes for them, and he ordered that the buffaloes should be called *miniapir*, and that the calves should be called *mâvelkar*—*i.e.*, calf from a sambhar. This was the origin of Keradr and of its *wursulir*, which are still called *miniapir*, and they are the only buffaloes of the Todas which were made from sambhar.

After these things had happened the gods recognised that Korateu was a *teu*, and calling him asked him who he was. He answered that he was the son of Teikirzi, and the *manmokh* or sister's son of Teipakh. He was then admitted as one of the gods and now lives on the hill Korateu, but still sometimes sits in the lap of Teipakh. He is the *nòdrodchi* of the Keradr and Keadr clans, and the chief villages of these clans are near his hill. He is called Kuzkarv when mentioned in prayer.

Another god, called Etepi, is said to be the same god as Korateu. It appeared, however, that Korateu lived on one hill and Etepi on another, and I could not ascertain the true relation of the deities to one another.

Azo-mazo is mentioned in the prayer of the Kars *ti* as two deities, Azo and Mazo.

Puzi and Kurindo

I am very doubtful as to the identity of Puzi. According to some accounts Puzi or Purzi was merely another name for Teikirzi; according to other accounts Puzi was a male deity and the husband of Teikirzi. In the following story Puzi is a female deity, inhabiting a hill near Nòdrs. She gave birth to a son called Kurindo. As soon as Kurindo was born he became fire. Puzi did not approve of this, as it seemed to show that the boy was too powerful, so she took a leaf of the kind called *kwagal*, pounded it and mixed it with water and sprinkled it on the fire. The fire then turned back again into a boy who was bent to one side.

Puzi said, "I will put you on a hill opposite to me." So she put him on the hill called Mopuvthut, near the village of Naters, and in order to make the hill higher she put three baskets of earth on the top, so that her son might be seen by everybody.

When Kurindo was on his hill he thought to himself, "My mother has treated me badly; she sprinkled me with water and quenched my power, and she has made me bent to one side; I do not like to be opposite to her." So he went away to a hill near Kanòdrs. This was before the time of Kwoten and before the Kamasòdrolam had run away (see p. 195). While Kurindo was living on this hill a strange tribe came to the hills, so Kurindo again moved and went away to the hill of Arsnur on the Mysore side, where he still lives.

There is a hill called Puthi on which a fire is lighted at certain times (see p. 291) and the god inhabiting this hill was, according to one account, the husband of Teikirzi. It is possible that Puthi and Puzi are the same, but I think it more probable that they are two separate gods, each having his own hill, Puthi being the husband of Teikirzi, and Puzi being the deity of this legend.

The following legends differ from the preceding in that they appear almost certainly to record the lives of deified men. The first legend deals with three men of different clans, but the sons of three sisters. The second deals with the life of Kwoto, and professes to be the history of a being of miraculous birth who came to be accepted by the gods, not only as one of their number, but as superior to themselves. These two legends were known far more thoroughly and universally than any of the preceding. It seems most probable that they are records of men who really lived, and that the life of each has become a nucleus round which have grown various miraculous and portentous incidents.

Kwoten, Teikuteidi, and Elnâkhum

There were once three men, the children of three sisters. The eldest was Kwoten, who belonged to Pan, the second was Teikuteidi, who belonged to Taradr, and the youngest was Elṇâkhum of Nòdrs. (According to one account the father of Kwoten was Purten, and his mother was Tiköni of Keradr. They lived at Pan and Kiursi, and Kwoten was born at Pan. Purten died when Kwoten was thirty years old and Tiköni died six years later.)

Kwoten had a wife called Kwoterpani. She did not like her husband, but preferred a man of Kanòdrs called Parden. One day Kwoten took his wife to a place called Timukhtar (near the spot where Sandy Nullah toll-bar now stands). He gave her only the loin-cloth called *tadrp* to wear, hoping that she would be cold and uncomfortable and would sleep with him, but she refused. Kwoten then took her to Kûdrîdjpül near Mulòrs, where there was a large wood. In this wood there was a tree of the kind called *külmän*, into which Kwoten climbed and made a bed. Below him, about three feet above the ground, he made a small bed for his wife, and under the tree, close to his wife's bed, he tied a big male buffalo. He did this because he thought a tiger might come to take the buffalo during the night when his wife would be frightened and would climb up the tree to his bed. During the night a tiger came and took away the buffalo, but even this did not induce the woman to go to her husband. Next morning Kwoten took his wife to Pòlâdri, which belonged to the Panol. This village was near Miuni, and there Kwoten became a *palikartmokh*. One day Kwoten was in the dairy and his wife in the hut when Parden came from Kanòdrs. Kwoten's wife knew that her husband was in the dairy, and endeavoured to prevent Parden from going into the hut by giving him buttermilk. Kwoten found that Parden had come, and sharpened a big knife to kill him, and when he came out of the dairy, Parden ran away towards Kanòdrs and Kwoten followed with the knife.

Kwoten's sister had married a Kars man and was living with him at Nasmiòdr, and at this time Kwoten's mother was staying at this place. As Parden ran away, pursued by Kwoten, they had to pass Nasmiòdr, and Kwoten's mother saw them, and said, "How is it that my son does not catch Parden?" Then she cursed Parden, saying "*On sati udairnûdr, Kârkaḍith mul uḍith pâtmâ*"—viz., "If I have reverence to the village, may he be checked by the tree with thorns in the Kark wood." When Parden reached a stone now called Pardenkars, Kwoten caught him up and tried to kill him, but the knife struck the stone instead and split it into two pieces. Then Parden ran on to the wood called Kark, where he was caught by a tree with thorns (brambles) so that Kwoten was able to kill him.

When the news of the death of Parden reached Kanòdrs all the people were very much afraid, and all ran away except one old man and his wife. As the people were going, they sent a message to the Kotas at Tizgudr. Two Kotas took a grain pounder (*wask*) and went to Pòladri. When Kwoten was told that the Kotas were coming he went and hid himself. The Kotas came and stood near the village and were told that Kwoten had gone away. Then they told Kwoten's wife, who at this time was pregnant by Parden, to come out of the hut. She came out and went to the Kotas, who asked her where Kwoten was. She said she did not know, whereupon the Kotas were vexed, and pierced her belly with the pounder, so that she died. Her funeral took place at Tadendari, and that of Parden at Arâdr.

The people of Kanòdrs ran away to a place called Penasmalpet, near Malmathapenpet, and are known as the Kamasòdrolam. They have never been seen since, but the Todas have heard from various wandering tribes that they still exist and that they live on a hill from which they can see Kanòdrs, and that when the Kamasòdrolam see a fire at Kanòdrs they shave their heads and make a special kind of food called *ashkkarthpimi*.

When the Kanòdrs people ran away there remained behind one old man called Muturojen and his wife Muturach,[1] who were living in a village near Kanòdrs called Mìtâhârzi. When the people left, the old man went to the Kanòdrs dairy to churn the milk left there by those who had run away, and he stayed there, sleeping in the *kwotars* or calves' hut, as the dairyman should do at Kanòdrs. His wife used to come every day as far as a place called

[1] These are quite unlike Toda names, nor is the name of the village, Mîtâhârzti, like a Toda name.

Pîtipem, where she rubbed a place with buffalo-dung and sat down.

While sitting there one day an eagle (*kashk*) sat on her head, and she became pregnant, and went back to the village and gave birth to a son. When Kwoten heard of this he wished to kill the child and set out to do so. The old woman's daughter, who had married a Kars man, sent her husband to warn her parents that Kwoten was coming to kill them. The Kars man met Kwoten and ran away from him towards Kanòdrs, followed by Kwoten's dog. When he came to a hill above the village he called out that Kwoten was coming. When the old man heard him, he cursed Kwoten and those with him; the latter became stones and Kwoten himself (according to the story as told by the Kanòdrs people) was stung by honey bees and died. The people of Kanòdrs are descended from the son born to the old woman. If this old woman was not a Toda, as her name and that of her village suggest, this would seem to point to a tradition that the people of Kanòdrs are descended from an ancestor of a different race from the other Todas (see p. 640).

Owing to the behaviour of Kwoten to the Kanòdrs people there has ever since been *karaivichi* (trouble) between the people of Pan and Kanòdrs. They do not intermarry and no Kanòdrs man may go to one of the chief villages (*etudmad*) of the Pan people nor may a Pan man go to an *etudmad* of Kanòdrs.

According to the above account Kwoten died after being cursed by the old man, but this is only a feature of the story as told by the Kanòdrs people, and in the account given by others Kwoten had many other adventures and finished his life in this world in a very different manner. He married a second wife, who, like the first, objected to her husband and preferred a man of Keradr, whose name was Keradrkutan. Kwoten lived with this wife at Kazhuradr, near Isharadr. At that time women wore the garment called *än*, which is dark grey like the *tuni* of the *palol*, and is now only used as a funeral garment.

Keradrkutan used frequently to come to Kazhuradr, and this vexed Kwoten, who told his wife to have nothing to do with the man. She encouraged Keradrkutan, however, and this vexed Kwoten so much that he took off her *än* and brought a thorny bush called *peshteinmul* and beat her all over with the bush, so that she became covered with blood. Kwoten at this time wore the garment called *tuni*, which he then took off, dipped it in water, and rubbed it all over his wife so that she became the colour of *tuni*, and then he gave her back her *än* and went to his dairy. While he was in the dairy Keradrkutan came stealthily to the village. When the woman saw Keradrkutan she cried very bitterly and said, "Kwoten has beaten me very severely so that I shall die; come and see me." When Keradrkutan went into the hut, the woman died.

Before this time, when Kwoten was one day beating his wife, she abused him, saying, "*Talrs ti oditha vai, Kòlrs kûv oditha vai; en puspad*"—"You have no *ti*, you have no Kotas: why do you beat me?" This was to reproach Kwoten because the Pan people had no *ti* buffaloes and had no Kotas to make things for them. So Kwoten went and complained to his brother Teikuteidi. Teikuteidi was very sorry, and in order to remove the reproach he persuaded Elnâkhum of Nòdrs to give certain buffaloes of the kind called *unir* from the Nòdrs *ti*. Elnâkhum gave a two-year-old calf (*pòl*) and a one-year-old calf (*kar*), and also two bells (*mani*) to put on their necks. The two bells were called Tarskingg and Takhingg. The calves were then standing at Kuladrtho and were taken by Kwoten to the *tars poh* of Pan. He tied the two bells to one of the calves called Kazhi. These bells ought properly to have been tied to the buffalo called Enmars which remained behind at Kuladrtho. Then Enmars went to Anto and complained as follows:—

"*kî mûdr*,	*kî kevi*,	*ninkûlth*	*pòrâni*"[1]
"inferior neck,	inferior ear,	to your council	I will not come"

i.e., "I will not come to your presence with naked neck and

[1] ? *Pòdrâni* or *pudrâni*.

ear." Anto told him not to grieve because he had lost the *mani*, and that instead

Melgarsol	*teirpülk*	*muddâ mâ*	*nî pud*
Melgars man	pül of Anto to	in front go may	you come

Antosh	*pep ân*
at Anto	*pep* drink

i.e., "When you go to Anto, a Melgars man shall go in front of you to the *pül* of Anto; when you come to Anto you shall drink *pep*." To this day, when the buffaloes of the Nòdrs *ti* go in procession to Anto a Melgars man goes in front and the buffalo called Enmars drinks *pep* at Anto. At the same time Anto prophesied to Enmars that a misfortune would befall Teikuteidi, saying

"*wûrâdr*	*nols*	*Teikuteidi tan*	*ennâth*	*piriedkin*,	*et vokh!*"
"whole year	day	himself	without numbering	I will divide,	go away!"

When Teikuteidi heard of this prophecy he was much grieved, and was very careful to do all the following ceremonies:—*erkumptthiti*, *upatiti*, *punkudrtiti*, *tatmadthkudrtiti*, *petkudrtiti* *mukudrtiti*, *adikudrtiti*, *parivkudrtiti*, *tatòtiti*, *muòtiti*, *ponkastiti* and *irpalvusthi*—viz., sacrifice of calf, salt-giving, purification of *pun*, *tat* and *madth*, *pet*, *mu*, *adi* and *pariv*, etc.,[1] He performed all these ceremonies to escape the prophesied evil, for if he had succeeded in doing them all for the whole twelve months the prophecy would not have been fulfilled. On the very last day he forgot the prophecy and did not perform the ceremonies, but went to a place called Kirspem, where he sat under the shade of a *pülmän*. There is a flower which blossoms on this tree in the rainy season only, and then the bees come. When Teikuteidi was sitting under the tree it was not the rainy reason and he was very much surprised to hear the humming of honey bees in the tree. The noise was being made by a *kazun*[2] which had taken the form of a

[1] I do not know exactly to which ceremonies *tatòtiti* and *muòtiti* refer. The words mean "he takes the *tat*" and "he takes the *mu*," and evidently refer to some dairy ceremonial. *Ponkastiti* probably means that he kept *pon* throughout the year- *i.e.*, gave or sold nothing from his dairy during the year.

[2] A spirit which brings death (see p. 403).

bee. He looked up to see if there were any flowers to attract the bees and could not see them, neither could he see any bees. Then he thought for a little while and remembered Anto's prophecy, so he did not remain under the tree, but went away to Kirsgòrs to attend the funeral of a *wursol* of Nòdrs (see p. 439). When the funeral was over Teikuteidi set out with companions to go to Kerkars (a place near Paikara). On the way they passed Kwongudrpem (near Kuudi). There he stopped and began to count his companions ; he counted them, but forgot to include himself, saying that there were twenty when they started and now only nineteen, and he thought for a long time who the lost person could be. When he was looking in the direction of the funeral-place for the lost companion, he saw a lame man named Keikarskutan, who had a *purs* and *ab* (bow and arrow). Keikarskutan lay down and shot the arrow [1] and it came towards Teikuteidi with a sound like a bird's voice. Teikuteidi was looking to see what sort of bird it was when the arrow pierced both his eyes [2] and he died. When his companions found that he was dead, they held the funeral at Kerâs, and at the place where he died they made a mark with four stones like a cross, one for his head, one for his legs and one for each hand.

Kwoten was responsible for various features of the organisation of the Pan people. He divided them into two parts, the Panol and Kuirsiol, and also divided the *ti* into two parts, the *wars ti*, which was to belong to the Panol, and the *tars ti* to the Kuirsiol. He settled that the *palol* of the *ti* should be chosen from the people of Keadr. When there is a funeral in any clan a *palol* belonging to that clan must give up his office; hence, in order that his *ti* should never be without a *palol*, Kwoten separated the people of Keadr into two divisions, the Keadrol and the Kwaradrol, so that a member of one division might be *palol* if a member of the other division died.

[1] When Keikarskutan shot the bow and arrow he lay down. According to my informants, Keikarskutan lay down to shoot the bow and arrow because he was lame, but shot it in the ordinary way and did not use his legs in doing so. Breeks, who gives a brief version of this legend, was told that the arrow was shot by means of the legs and refers to this method as the ancient Indian custom.

[2] I give this as it was told.

This was the origin of the division of the Keadr people into the Keadrol and the Kwaradrol.

One day Kwoten went to the *wars ti* of Pan and took buttermilk and slept there, and he did the same at the *arsaiir ti* of Kwòdrdoni, and since that day the people of Pan have had the privilege of taking buttermilk and sleeping at the places of each *ti*.

Kwoten also made two *teiks* (stones or wooden posts at which buffaloes are killed at the funerals), the *parsteiks* for the Panol and the *kirshteiks* for the Kuirsiol.

It is owing to the example of Kwoten that the Todas now take meals in Kurumba villages. Before his time they had never done so, but Kwoten one day went to a Kurumba village and took food, and since that time all Todas have done so.

Kwoten was also the first Toda to go to a Kota village. He wanted one day to go to Mitur in the Wainad, and as it was getting dark and he was still on his way, he went to the Kota village of Kulgadi (Gudalur). He sat on their *tün*, or bed, got new pots and food from them, and, taking both to the stream called Marspa or Marsva, he cooked and ate the food there, and then, returning to the village, slept on a Kota *tün*. Since that time Todas have gone to that village, and have done as Kwoten did, but they will not go to any other Kota village.

One day Kwoten went with Erten of Keadr, who was spoken of as his servant, to Pòni, in the direction of Polkat (Calicut). At Pòni there is a stream called Palpa, the commencement of which may be seen on the Kundahs. Kwoten and Erten went to drink water out of the stream at a place where a goddess (*teu*) named Terkosh had been bathing. When Kwoten was about to drink from his hands, he found in the water a long golden hair; he measured the length of the hair and found it was greater than his height; he had a long stick in his hand called *pirs*, and found that the hair was longer than this stick. Then he asked Erten about it. Erten knew it was the hair of a *teu*, but thought it best not to tell Kwoten, and tried to persuade him that it was of no importance, and proposed that they should return home.

Kwoten, however, insisted on finding out from whom the hair came, so they went along the stream. Kwoten went first and Erten had to follow him. As they went they met the bird called *karpüls* going from the right side to the left,[1] uttering its cry. Kwoten asked Erten why they met the bird, why it went from right to left, and why it made a cry. Erten replied as follows:—

" *Nòdr udoi*	*kwudrpedrshai; Naraian sami kaipedrshai.*"
"Country (God) if there is	you will die; Naraian will kill you."

In spite of this warning, Kwoten persisted in going on, and finally they came to Terkosh, who said to Kwoten, "Do not come near me, I am a *teu.*" Kwoten paid no heed to this, but said, "You are a beautiful woman," and went and lay with her. Then Terkosh went away to her hill at Pòni, where she is now, and to this day the Kurumbas go there once a year and offer plantains to her and light lamps in her honour.

Kwoten and Erten returned home. Kwoten went to Kepurs, a village now in ruins, close to Nanjanad, and Erten went to a village called Kapthòri belonging to the Keadrol. Kwoten had about five hundred buffaloes grazing at Pazhmokh, near Kepurs. That night Kwoten slept on the *idrtul* over which he had spread a sambhar skin. He had on his finger a thick silver ring, which may still be seen at Naters and is used in the funeral ceremonies of men of the Pan clan. When the people awoke next morning they found that Kwoten had disappeared and that there only remained, lying on the sambhar skin, the silver ring and some *pug.*[2] Kwoten had been carried away by Terkosh and it was found that his five hundred buffaloes had also disappeared.

When Erten got up next morning he went to Kepurs and called out to the *wursol* of that place, "*Wursolia, tar tûrz-hoḍthrska*"[3]—"O *wursol*, is the man up yet?" The *wursol*

[1] To meet this bird going from right to left is a bad omen; if going from left to right, it is a good omen.

[2] I could not find out the exact meaning of this word, but it appeared to be a name for the blood-stained froth which may come from the mouth of a dying man. In a sentence which occurs later the word appears as *pògh* (blood), but my informants were certain that *pug* itself is not blood.

[3] See p. 616.

replied, "*Pülmâv tars pògh udisvichi*"—"On the sambhar skin blood is lying." Erten replied, "*Aroth pun pârs Pâlmän kwark putvai, nadrtivadr*"—"Take sixty vessels of milk to the wood of Palmän and pour out." So the *wursol* took sixty *pun* of milk and poured it out in the wood as Erten had ordered him.

Then since Kwoten had gone away, Erten did not want to live any more; he took a large creeper called *melkudri*, and tied it round his neck and tried to strangle himself, but when he pulled the creeper it broke into several pieces. He was much disappointed, but took another kind of creeper called *kakkudri*, but this broke in the same way. He then tried *teinkudri*, which also broke. Finally he took *kakhudri*,[1] and with this he succeeded in strangling himself. Then the *wursol* and all those who had helped in pouring out the milk also strangled themselves with *kakhudri*. Since this time it has been a custom among the Todas to commit suicide by strangling.

Kwoten and Terkosh are now living on twò hills near Pòni, which face one another, and Erten has also become a *teu* and lives on a smaller hill near those of Kwoten and Terkosh. Whenever a Toda sees Kwoten's hill for the first time, he lies down on his right side and sings twice the following words: "*Seizâr zon, Kwoten âr zon, Seizâr zon, Terkosh âr zon.*" I could not discover the meaning of these words, and fancy that the Todas themselves do not know exactly what they mean. It is possible that *âr* is the word meaning six.

The history and fate of Teikuteidi, the second brother of Kwoten, has been given in the story of Kwoten. He belonged to Taradr, and according to one account the *kugvalir* of that place were sent to him. Very little is related about the third brother, Elnâkhum. He had 1,800 buffaloes, but though he had so many, he was always going to other Todas and saying "I have nothing to milk; lend me a buffalo to milk," and all his life he used to beg. It is owing to his example that the Todas have begged ever since, and are not ashamed to do so even when they are rich.

[1] This is a creeper used in the funeral ceremonies.

Elnâkhum is said to have built the long wall which still exists at the village of Nòdrs.

The story of Kwoten reads very much like that of a man who really lived and was deified after his death. The minute detail with which several of the natural incidents of his life are known might be held to point in this direction, but perhaps more important is the fact that his ring can still be seen, and that his spear was, according to Breeks, in existence not long ago. It looks as if Kwoten was a man who raised Pan from a comparatively insignificant position among the Todas to be one of their chief clans, and was the means of introducing several innovations in Toda custom. It is probable that he was deified after his death, and that some of the incidents of his life have acquired miraculous characters.

Kwoto or Meilitars

There was once a man belonging to Melgars who married a woman of Kanòdrs and took her to Melgars. When she became pregnant, the woman was taken by her husband to Kanòdrs. On the way back to Melgars they passed Ushadr, the place where the funeral ceremonies of Melgars men took place. They were standing in front of the funeral hut at that place when the man found a good *twadri* tree,[1] and, cutting three or four sticks from it, brought them to his wife, who stripped the bark from the sticks. While she was doing this, the pains of labour came on, and soon after she gave birth to a gourd (*kem*). Both husband and wife were very much ashamed, and they decided to say that a child had been born and had died, and the man went round to all the villages to say that this had happened and that the funeral would be held at Ushadr. Accordingly they had the *etvainolkedr* (first funeral ceremony) at Ushadr, the gourd being covered with a *putkuli* (cloak), so that it was taken to be the body of a child.

First the buffaloes were caught and killed, and then the supposed corpse was taken to the burning-place, where a fire

[1] Probably the tree or bush from which the material called *twadrinar* is manufactured by the Todas.

was made and the gourd in its mantle was put on the fire. The fire first burnt the cloak, and when it reached the gourd, this broke into two pieces. One piece became a little baby, a boy, which took a piece of the burnt cloak and went away in the air to Neikhârs, where there is a big tree, under which it alighted. The other piece of the gourd was split into many fragments by the heat of the fire, and some of the fragments were driven with such force that they killed a kite which had come to the funeral. (To this day the kite does not eat the buffaloes at funerals at Ushadr, though it does so at other places.) The father and mother followed the child to Neikhârs, where they found it sitting on the tree.[1] The father and mother said to the child "*Ena, itvâ*"—"My son, come here," and the boy came down and went to them, and was taken away by his parents to Melgars.

As the parents and child were on their way to Melgars they met the buffaloes of the Kars *ti* going from Kòn to Enòdr. At that time the buffaloes of Melgars and Kars used to go with the *ti* buffaloes as far as a place called Irgûdrval, on the way between Kars and Enòdr. A Kars man went with the buffaloes, and he wore on his right wrist a gold bracelet (which is still kept at Kuzhu). At Irgûdrval there is a stone called Pidûtkars, and it was the duty of the man with the bracelet to sit on this stone and to make the Melgars buffaloes pass on the right side, the Kars buffaloes on the left side, and the *ti* buffaloes in the middle. When he had done this, the *palol* prayed at the stone, and then the buffaloes of Melgars and Kars turned back and the *ti* buffaloes went on to Enòdr. When the man and his wife saw the buffaloes coming, they waited near Pidûtkars, and while they were waiting the baby laughed. The father asked the boy, "Why do you laugh?" The boy answered, "I know the *kwarzam*[2]

[1] My informants could not say whether the boy went away in the air as a child or as a kite. The boy often assumed the form of a kite later, and it is tempting to suppose that the assumption of this form by the child was connected with the death of the kite, *i.e.*, that it was a case of transmigration. The fact that the child went away in the air and was found sitting on a tree makes it highly probable that it flew in the form of a kite, but my informants could not say that this was definitely part of the legend.

[2] The *kwarzam* is the name used in prayer (see Chap. X).

of the *ti* buffaloes, ***perner persagun***; I know the ***kwarzam*** of the Melgars buffaloes, ***narsüln natüln nâkh***; also I know the *kwarzam* of the Kars buffaloes, ***inâtviḍshti inâtvan***; that is why I laughed." After the buffaloes had gone on to Enòdr, the parents and child went on their way to Melgars. After they had been at Melgars fifteen days, they noticed that the child grew so rapidly that they could see him getting bigger from day to day, and he was soon grown up. He was called Kwoto.

One day Kwoto went into the buffalo pen and played there with the buffalo-dung, so that he was covered with the dust of the dung. His father rebuked him and was blowing on him to get rid of the dust when the boy changed into a kite and flew away. The next day he resumed human form, but from that time he only stayed in the village at times, and at other times stayed in the woods. This went on for about eight days, and then he refused to take food from the village and became a companion of the gods.

At this time the gods used to hold councils on the slopes below a hill called Tikalmudri. The place where they sat was called Pòlkab. When the gods were holding council at Pòlkab, Kwoto went and sat on the top of the hill Tikalmudri. Then the gods said to one another, "How is it that he sits on the top of the hill while we sit below? It is not at all good." They consulted together and decided to kill him. So three or four of the gods went to Kwoto and said in a cunning way, "We will show you your country" (*i.e.*, the place which should belong to him; each of the gods had his appointed place). So they took him to a steep precipice called Teipâper, and having deceived him that they would show him his country, they threw him down. Kwoto, however, was not killed, but took the form of a kite and flew back to Tikalmudri. Then all the gods were surprised that he was not dead, but decided to try and kill him again, and they took him to the hill Kòdrtho, near Nidrsi, and threw him down. (The hill Kòdrtho was inhabited by the god Kòdrtho.) Kwoto was not killed, but pulled up a bamboo tree with its roots, and flew back and struck Kòdrtho on the head, and Kòdrtho's head split into three pieces. One of these pieces is now the well-known hill, the Drug, seen from Coonoor, while the other two pieces are eminences on the ridge running out to the Drug.

Kwoto then returned to Tikalmudri. The gods said, "We cannot kill him; he has some power; let us try his power." So they gave him the following task:

"*Peivoi*	*tirikvâ*,	*pîdâr*	*pîrichvâ*?"
Low	turn	high	fill?

i.e., "Can he turn the low stream and fill the high stream?" (According to another account the words in which the task was given were, "*Alvoi tiriki, Kalvoi pîrsvôka*," *i.e.*, "Can he turn the stream Alvoi and fill the stream Kalvoi?")

Kwoto then took a huge stone, which may still be seen near Kanòdrs, and put it in the stream so that it flowed upwards. Then the stream begged Kwoto, "We are going upwards according to your order, but it is very difficult for us; we wish to be allowed to go our ordinary way." So Kwoto took away the stone and the stream resumed its natural course.

The gods saw what Kwoto had done and decided to try his power in another way, so they said:

"*Kânêr*	*ât*,	*kutci*	*kurs*	*ütia*?"
Sun	tie,	stone	chain	can he do?

i.e., "Can he tie the sun with a stone chain?" Kwoto then took a stone chain and tied it to the sun and brought the sun down to Nern, near Kanòdrs, and tied it to a tree. When the sun wanted to drink, Kwoto took it to the stream Kalvoi, from which the sun drank, and there is now to be seen a hole in this stream at the place where the sun drank.[1] Then Kwoto took the sun to a pool surrounded by trees called Nerpoiker, also near Kanòdrs. While the sun was tied in this way, it was dark both in this world and in Amnòdr. Then the people of Amnòdr came to the gods and asked why they allowed Kwoto to do these things, and said that they were now living in thick darkness, and they begged that Kwoto should be allowed to put the sun back in its right place. Then the gods went to Kwoto and asked him to put the sun

[1] This place is close to the spot at which the path from Pishkwosht (Bikkapattimand) to Kodanad crosses a stream soon after leaving the former village.

back, and they acknowledged that he was a god and the most powerful of the gods. They said that he should no longer be called Kwoto, but that his name should be Meilitars, because he was superior to all the gods; also that he should go "*parnur nòdr, putnur nòdr,*" "to 1,600 places, 1,800 places," *i.e.*, he should not belong to one place only, like the other gods, but should go everywhere.

Then Meilitars put back the sun in its proper place.

(According to another version, the task of tying the sun was given in the words:

"*Kûnèr*	*ât,*	*pirsagun*	*patrôkâ?*"
Male buffalo	tie,	sun	can he catch?

The sun was said to have been at this time sitting on the back of a male buffalo, and Kwoto was told to tie the buffalo and catch the sun. According to this account Kwoto first used an iron chain, *kabantagars*, which was melted by the heat of the sun. Next he tried a bronze (?) chain called *kuchtagars*, which also melted. Then he used a stone chain, or *karstagars*, which did not melt, and he succeeded in tying the sun with this. This version of the story corresponds with that given by Breeks.)

Kwoto or Meilitars was closely connected with two clans, those of Melgars and Kanòdrs. It is said to be owing to the fact that Kwoto was a Melgars man that Melgars people have the special privileges and duties which are peculiar to that clan. At any rate, this is the view held by the people of Melgars. At Kanòdrs, the name of Kwoto occupies a prominent place in the prayer of the dairy, and several of the special features of the ritual of the Kanòdrs dairy are said to exist in consequence of the many wonderful things which Kwoto had done in its neighbourhood. When new buttermilk has to be made for Kanòdrs, it is made at a place called Kautarmad, far away, because Kwoto made new buttermilk there, and in the ceremony at this place earth is taken from certain places from which Kwoto took it.

Kwoto or Meilitars is the hero of several stories, in none of which does he play a very creditable *rôle*.

At one time the Todas used to go to and fro between this

world and Amnòdr. Those who were dead stayed permanently in Amnòdr, but living people could go to visit them and return. One day Punatvan of Kars went with Meilitars to Amnòdr. They stayed there two days and two nights, and then Meilitars came away without Punatvan's knowledge. At that time the people of Kars were living at Nasmiòdr, so Meilitars went to Nasmiòdr and said that Punatvan intended to stop in Amnòdr, and wished the Kars people to perform the funeral ceremonies for him, killing thirty buffaloes. So the Kars people caught thirty buffaloes, the chief one being called Enmon. Round the neck of Enmon were hung the two bells (*wursuli mani*) called Karsod and Kòni. They cut a piece of stick and put it in a *putkuli* to represent the dead body and then killed the thirty buffaloes. As the buffaloes were on their way to Amnòdr, they met Punatvan on his way back. Punatvan asked the chief buffalo, Enmon, "Why do you come here?" Then Enmon told him what Meilitars had done. The man and buffalo put their heads together and cried, and their tears became a pool of water.[1] Then Punatvan took the two bells from the neck of Enmon and sent them back to Nasmiòdr, where they are kept to this day, but he returned to Amnòdr with the buffaloes. Then Ön, the ruler of Amnòdr, ordered that in future no one should return to the world of the living from Amnòdr, and since that day the Todas have not been able to go to and fro between the two worlds as they used to do.

At the present time the people of Keradr have no *ti*. Once they had a *ti* which they lost through the action of Kwoto, who went one day to their dairy at Tîkîrs, near Mòdr, and, hiding the *kaltmokh* in the wood, took his place. When the *palol* milks, it is the duty of the *kaltmokh* to let out the calves and send them to the *palol*. Kwoto did not do this properly, but sent more calves than were required, so the *palol* became angry and took his stick (*kwoinörtpet*) to beat the supposed *kaltmokh*, but the stroke missed and fell on the *palol* himself.

Another day the *palol* told Kwoto to pour out the re-

[1] This pool has been converted into the Marlimand reservoir, the source of the water-supply of Ootacamund.

mainder of the buttermilk at the appointed place. Instead of doing this Kwoto poured it into the stream, and the buttermilk so poured became a god called Mòraman, who sends smallpox.[1] Then the *palol* became very angry and said he would no longer be *palol*, if he had to keep such a *kaltmokh*. Then Kwoto revealed to the *palol* and to the real *kaltmokh* that he was a god, and gave them a medicine called *mûvòmad*, which has the property that anyone who takes it will never grow old.

After giving *mûvòmad* to the *palol* and *kaltmokh*, Kwoto sent them into the air, together with the dairy and the buffaloes and everything belonging to the *ti*, and they all went in the air to Kupars, near Pan; they stayed there for some time and then disappeared, and now nothing can be seen of them, but if people go near Kupars, they hear the voices of the *palol* and *kaltmokh* when they are talking to one another.

Since that time the people of Keradr have been without a *ti*.

Another story in which Kwoto played a prominent part is connected with the custom of eating flesh. I received several versions of this story and was unable to satisfy myself which was correct.

According to one account Kwoto once went to Mitur in the Wainad, where Kurumbas live. Kwoto played with these people, and one day caught and killed a wild buffalo. He said to the Kurumbas, "I have killed this buffalo; let us eat its flesh"; and he gave to each a portion. The Kurumbas ate their portions, but Kwoto only pretended to eat; he held out his *putkuli* in front of him and instead of eating dropped his portions inside the cloak. When the Kurumbas had finished, Kwoto got up and all saw on the place where he had been sitting the flesh which he had pretended to eat. Then the Kurumbas were angry and went to beat Kwoto with sticks, asking why he had not eaten the flesh, and they insisted that Kwoto should eat some of it. Kwoto ran away, and when the Kurumbas pursued him he

[1] The Hindu god who sends smallpox is Mari or Mariaman. The Toda name for buttermilk is *mòr*.

pretended that he was lame and consented to eat some of the flesh of the buffalo. He also told them that he was a god and said that he would dance before them, and did so like a lame man. He told the Kurumbas that whenever he came in the future, he would dance to the Kurumbas first and then to the Todas; and now the Kwoto *teuol*, or diviner (see Chap. XII), when he dances, does so first to the Kurumbas, and when he dances before them he does so as if he were lame.

After this Kwoto disappeared and since that time has not been seen. He is said to live in a temple at Mitur, but "wherever there is a god, there also is Kwoto, or Meilitars."

According to another account, this story was told of the people called Panins (Panyas), but in this version Kurumbas were also said to be present, though it was the Panins who were made to eat the flesh.

According to a third account, obtained, however, from an untrustworthy informant, Kwoto practised this deception on the gods themselves, and made them eat the flesh of a calf while only pretending to eat himself. This was said to have been the starting-point of the *erkumptthpimi* ceremony, and Kwoto was said to have killed the calf with the same formalities as are now used in this ceremony. All other Todas strenuously denied that Kwoto made the gods eat flesh. There was, however, so much reticence about the *erkumptthpimi* ceremony and its history, that I am not confident that Kwoto was not in some way connected with its origin, and that the version of my untrustworthy informant may in this case have been correct.

Other Gods

There are very many other deities. Of the following I can give little more than the names.

Atiato is the *nòdrodchi* of the Kwòdrdoni clan and also of Pedrkars. He lives near the chief villages of these clans, and has a temple of which the priest is said to be an Irula, and Todas sometimes give to this god offerings of clarified butter.

Konto or Konteu is the *nòdrodchi* of the Panol, and lives on the hill Konto, to which fire is set by the *palol* of the Kars or Pan *ti* (see Chap. XIII).

Kòdrtho is the *nòdrodchi* of Nidrsi. He played a part in the history of Kwoto, and according to some accounts he was the *mun*, or maternal uncle, of this god.

Near the source of the Paikara river, there is a cave in which there is a pool called Alvoi. Sometimes this pool gives forth a loud bubbling noise, and this is believed to be due to a *teu* dipping himself in the water. The name of the god is Alvoi Kalvoi, Kalvoi, situated at some distance from the pool, being a hill on which the god usually lives.

There are other gods about whose histories I have no information. Tiligush is the *nòdrodchi* of Päm and Karadr of Taradr. Pòrzo inhabits a hill near Nòdrs, and Karzo, a hill near Kars, and the names of other gods, such as Kaladrvan, Teikhun, Peigwa, Karmunteu, Kondilteu and Mundilteu, are mentioned in the prayers of the *ti* dairies.

In addition to these, who are certainly true Toda gods, the Todas also pay respect to the gods of the other tribes on the Nilgiris, while occasionally the names of Hindu gods are mentioned in their ceremonies. If a Toda be asked if he worships one of these gods, he will almost certainly assent, but at the same time he distinguishes them from his own gods. The only deity who seemed to be confused with their own gods by some of the Todas was Petkon, whose Badaga name was said to be Betakarasami. Breeks calls him Betikhan, and states that he is a hunting god; and according to some Todas Petkon was a son of Teikirzi.

Previous accounts of the Toda gods have been very erratic. Some writers have given the names of Hindu gods. Breeks gives the names of dairies as those of gods, though he also records abbreviated versions of several of the stories given in this chapter. The most curious account, however, of the Toda gods is that of Marshall, who gives[1] the following as the names of five gods which are muttered when milk is put on the sacred bells:—Ânmungâno, Godingâtho, Beligoshu, Dekulâria, and Kazudâva. We puzzled over these words for

[1] P. 142.

a long time, and could not discover the names of gods even remotely resembling them. Finally it became clear that the last was "*kars ud âva*" ("Give me one rupee"). Similarly there was little doubt that "Beligoshu, Dekulâria" stood for "*beli karsu tudkersia*" ("Will you not give me a silver coin?"), the Badaga equivalent of the last word being very much like Dekulâria. The first two names we could not identify with certainty, but the first is possibly "*en mûn gânei*" ("Do not see my face"), and the second is possibly the name of a Badaga buffalo-pen.

CHAPTER X

PRAYER

IN the chapters in which the ritual of the dairies has been described, one of the most important features of the ceremonial has been passed over which must now be fully described. This feature is the prayer which is always offered at certain stages of the dairy operations. In the village dairies, of whatever kind they may be, no prayer is offered at the morning ceremonial. In the evening the prayer of the dairy is recited twice—once when lighting the lamp, and once when shutting the buffaloes in their enclosure for the night, the prayer on this occasion being said in front of the entrance to the pen.

At the *ti* dairy the *palol* prays both morning and evening. In the morning he prays when lighting the lamp and after he has finished milking; in the evening prayer is offered on both these occasions, and also when shutting up the buffaloes for the night. The *palol* also repeats a few clauses when going out to milk. Prayers are said on certain other ceremonial occasions, and clauses from the prayers are frequently uttered during the many ceremonies of the dairy.

At the evening ceremonial of the village dairy the prayer is said when the lamp is lighted, while during the morning ceremonial, at which the lamp is usually not lighted, there is no prayer. This suggests that the prayer is especially related to the lamp-lighting, and that some idea of worship of the light is involved, but occasionally for some special reason, such as unusual darkness, the lamp may be lighted in the morning, and on these occasions the prayer is not used. Nevertheless, the relation between lamp-lighting and prayer both at the village and *ti* dairies has probably some significance, and, taken in conjunction with the undoubted salutation of the sun, it points to some degree of worship of light and its sources which may at one time have formed a more marked feature of the Toda religion than seems at present to be the case.

The prayer when shutting up the buffaloes for the night is common to both *ti* and village dairies. The night is the dangerous time for Toda buffaloes, which are not infrequently killed by tigers, and the prayer on the occasion of closing the pen is probably designed to promote their safety.

At the prayer uttered at the close of the milking at the *ti* dairy the *palol* adopts a special attitude which is shown in Fig. 28. He prays leaning on his wand, the *pohvet*, with his hands crossed over one another. This attitude is not employed in the village dairy, and only on this occasion at the *ti* dairy.

In all cases the prayer is uttered "in the throat," so that the words cannot be distinguished by any one who may hear them. Whenever I listened to the recital of a prayer as it was being offered by a dairyman within the dairy, I heard only a gurgling noise in which no words could be distinguished. On one occasion I was allowed to approach the *ti* dairy at Mòdr while the first prayer was being offered by the *palol*. I heard the beating on the *persin* (see p. 92) which accompanies this prayer, and at intervals in the monotonous sound produced by the voice of the *palol* there were pauses. As we shall see, the prayer of the *ti* has certain sections which are distinguished from one another, and it seemed possible that these pauses marked off the different portions of the prayer, but it was clear that this was not the case, the *palol* only stopping when the necessity for taking a new breath became imperative.

Each village has its own prayer, and so far as I could ascertain this prayer is used in all the dairies of the village; thus I believe that at Taradr the same prayer would be used in both *kugvali* and *tarvali*. This is not, however, a point on which I can speak positively, for there was much reluctance to talk about this subject and many of the Todas absolutely refused to discuss it. One point seemed quite clear, at any rate among the Teivaliol, viz., that the different villages of a clan had different prayers, though often with many clauses in common.

In general, the prayer of the *ti* is longer and more elaborate than that of the village dairy. Different prayers are used at different dairies of the same *ti*, though here again they may have many clauses in common.

In all cases the prayer consists of two distinct parts: a preliminary portion consisting chiefly of names known as *kwarzam*, followed by a portion which may be regarded as the prayer proper.

The prayer proper should be the same in every dairy, but it seemed to me that there was a good deal of laxity as regards this portion, and there is no doubt that it is often slurred over hastily and is less strictly regulated than the preliminary portion of the prayer.

The following is the most generally accepted form:

Tânenmâ; may it be well or may be blessed; *târmâmâ;* may it be well or may be merciful; *îr kark tânenmâ;* with the buffaloes and calves may it be well;

nâv ârk mâ; may there be no disease; *kazun ârk mâ;* may there be no destroyer; *nudri ârk mâ;* may there be no poisonous animals (snakes and insects);

kâvel ârk mâ: may there be no wild beasts (tigers, &c.); *per kârt pâ mâ:* may be kept from (falling down) steep hills; *pustht kârt pâ mâ;* may be kept from floods;

tüt ârk mâ; may there be no fire; *mâ un mâ;* may rain fall; *maj eu mâ;* may clouds rise; *pul pûv mâ;* may grass flourish;

nîr ûr mâ. may water spring.

The prayer then concludes with the names of two of the most important gods or objects of reverence, followed by the words:

âtham	*idith*	*emk*	*tânenmâ.*
them	for the sake of	for (or to) us	may it be well.

There does not seem to be any strict regulation as to the clauses of the prayer, and in different versions some of the given above were omitted, while others were added, especially requests for protection against special animals, as *pob ârk mâ*, "may there be no snakes," and *pîrzi ârk mâ*, "may there be no tigers." One man concluded with the words *erdâdrsink erdâdri ini*, "I know half to pray, I know not half to pray,"[1] but I do not know whether this was an individual peculiarity or a special feature of the prayer of his dairy.

It seemed clear that the whole prayer referred to the buffaloes. It may be summarised as follows:

"May it be well with the buffaloes, may they not suffer from disease or die, may they be kept from poisonous animals and from wild beasts and from injury by flood or fire, may there be water and grass in plenty."

The first part of the prayer contains a number of clauses each of which usually consists of the name of an object of reverence followed by the word *idith* (often contracted into *ith*). This word is said to mean "for the sake of," so that the prayer as a whole seems to consist of clauses mentioning a number of objects of reverence for the sake of which the prayer is said, followed by the prayer consisting of clauses directed to avert evils or bring blessings on the buffaloes of the dairy. The word *idith* is used in the sense of "for the sake of" in ordinary language. Thus, "for my sake, leave him," would be "*en idith, an pidr*" (me for the sake of, him leave).

The objects of more or less sanctity thus mentioned in the prayer are not called by their usual names, but are referred to by means of special names to which the general term of *kwarzam* is given. In some cases the *kwarzam* differs little from the ordinary name, while in other cases it bears no resemblance to it.

The *kwarzam* mentioned in the prayer fall into several groups: there are the *kwarzam* of the gods, of the buffaloes, of the villages, of the dairy and of its various parts, vessels and implements. In some cases, especially in the case of the *ti*, we shall find that different dairies differ in the prominence given to each kind of *kwarzam*; that the prayer of one place

[1] *Erd* means two, and this translation is a free rendering of the Toda words, though it probably conveys the proper meaning.

consists chiefly of *kwarzam* of the dairy, while in the prayer of another the *kwarzam* of the gods or of the buffaloes predominate.

In some prayers there occur *kwarzam* of a special kind containing references to incidents in legend—incidents which occurred in the life of some deity especially connected with the dairy at which the prayer is used, or other *kwarzam* may refer to incidents in the history of the dairy or of the village in which the dairy is situated.

I had great difficulty in obtaining examples of the prayers, or rather of those portions consisting of the *kwarzam* of the sacred objects. There was little objection to giving the prayer proper; it was only when the *kwarzam* were approached that the difficulty arose. It was evident that it was this portion of the prayer which was regarded as especially sacred and mysterious, and this was doubtless due to the mention of sacred beings and objects by their sacred names.

With much difficulty I succeeded in obtaining the prayers of four village dairies, three belonging to the Kuudrol, while the fourth was the prayer, or part of the prayer, of the Kanòdrs *poh*. I was also successful in obtaining two *ti* prayers and fragments of others.

THE VILLAGE PRAYER

The following are the *kwarzam* of the prayer used in the dairy of the village of Kuudr, the *etudmad* of the Kuudr clan. On the left-hand side of the page are given the *kwarzam*, each of which is followed by the word *idith* when the prayer is uttered. On the right-hand side of the page are given the objects, beings or incidents to which the *kwarzam* refer.

PRAYER OF KUUDR

Atthkâr	Kuudr village and probably also the Kuudr clan or Kuudro.
ðners	Kuudr village.
palitûdrpali	large dairy at Kuudr (*tûdrpali*).
palikidpali	small dairy at Kuudr (*kidpali*).
tûdrpalshpelk	lamp (*pelk*) of large dairy.
kidpalshpep	all the sacred objects of small dairy.

tûtòdrtho	large buffalo-pen (*tû*) at Kuudr.
tûkidtû	small buffalo-pen (*tû*) at Kuudr.
kadrtorikkadr	calf enclosure (*kadr*) at Kuudr.
keishkvet	sacred buffaloes (*pasthîr*) of Kuudr.
tarskivan	ordinary buffaloes (*putiîr*).
känpep	portion of buttermilk (*pep*) originally given by Teikirzi for *pasthîr*.
âtthpep	portion of *pep* for *putiîr*.
mutchudkars	stone in buffalo-pen at Kuudr where the vessels of the large dairy are purified.
tarskikars	stone in pen where the vessels of the small dairy are purified.
nîrkiznîr	sacred dairy spring of Kuudr.
Eikisiov	a buffalo whose milk was the origin of the spring.
Pülmâlpül	a hill near Kuudr.
Emalpûv	a buffalo which once lived at Kuudr.
Kakathûmûk	a hill near Kuudr.
Karstum	a buffalo which once died on this hill.
teikhkwadiki	a tree by which the dairy vessel called *mu* is buried (see p. 170).
manikiars	the *kiars* tree by which the sacred bell (*mani*) is laid when the dairy things are being purified.
Keikars	a hill near Kuudr.
keitnòdi	hill near which the *erkumptthiti* ceremony is performed (see Chap. XIII).
petüt pati pethût ir	chief buffaloes given when Teikirzi divided the buffaloes with wand in hand (see p. 186). Literally, "wand with divide chief buffaloes."
pûthion nâkh tarzâr maj	calf which was the ancestor of the Kuudr *putiîr*.

Thus, the prayer would run, "*Atthkâr idith; òners idith; palitûdrpali idith;* . . . . . and the translation would run, "For the sake of the village and clan of Kuudr; for the sake of the village of Kuudr; for the sake of the large dairy of Kuudr; . . . ." as far as the end of the *kwarzam* given above, and then would follow the prayer proper, "*tanenma, tarmama*, ..."

This prayer begins with two *kwarzam* of the village or clan, followed by others referring to the dairies and dairy vessels, buffalo pens and buffaloes. Then follow certain *kwarzam* of the *pep* or buttermilk which is of so much importance in the dairy ritual, and those of stones which play a part in the ceremonies attending purification of the dairy vessels. After the *kwarzam* of the dairy spring, there follow a number of *kwarzam* referring to certain incidents in the history of the dairy. *Eikisiov* is the *kwarzam* of a buffalo which was one day being milked at Kuudr when some of the milk was spilt on the ground. From that day the ground became swampy, and on digging, a spring of water was found which has ever since been used as the dairy spring and is called *kiznír*. The two following *kwarzam* refer to incidents of which I have no record. *Karstum* is the *kwarzam* of a buffalo which was one day grazing on the hill Kakathûmûk when it began to bellow and could not be induced to stop; the people tried to take it back to the pen, but it would not go and died on the hill, and has ever since been remembered in the prayer. These *kwarzam* are followed by two referring to trees of ceremonial importance—one the tree by which is buried the *mu* on the integrity of which the continuity of the dairy procedure depends, while the other is connected with the sacred bell.

Then follow the *kwarzam* of a hill on which there are cairns and that of the sacrificial place of the village. The prayer concludes with two *kwarzam* of a different kind. The first refers to the act of the goddess Teikirzi, who portioned the buffaloes and assigned to each clan its share. In so doing we have seen that she touched each buffalo on the back with her wand, saying in each case to whom the buffalo should belong, and this act is commemorated in the prayer in the form, "for the sake of the dividing of the chief buffaloes with the wand." The last *kwarzam* is that of the calf, from which the ordinary buffaloes or *putiír* of Kuudr are descended, but I was unable to ascertain the meaning of the words, except *nakh*, which is the name of a three-year-old buffalo.

In the Kuudr prayer several of the *kwarzam* refer to incidents of a more or less miraculous nature which are believed to have happened at the village where the prayer is used, while the last *kwarzam* but one refers to one of the chief events of Toda mythology.

It will be noticed that many of the *kwarzam* used in this prayer correspond very closely to the names in ordinary use. Some, such as *keitnòdi* and *teikhkwadiki*, are the same words as those in general use, while others differ from the ordinary words in the reduplication of part of the name, *tûdrpali* becoming *palitûdrpali* and *kiznîr* becoming *nîrkiznîr*.

PRAYER OF KIUDR

The following are the *kwarzam* of the prayer used at Kiudr, which is one of the most sacred of Toda villages.

	Kwarzam of
Kîlvôh	the dairy at Kiudr.
kerâni	one of the *palatmani* of Kiudr.
mêdrâni	the other *palatmani*.
pongg	one of the *ertatmani*.
nongg	another *ertatmani*.
pelteirzi	the lamp of the dairy.
îrtîrzi	also the lamp.
kinmûv	the way by which the dairyman goes from the dairy to milk; the *punetkalvol*.
nîrtâkh	the dairy stream.
nîrtîrshki	also the dairy stream.
keitu	the buffalo-pen.
tülivaners	the posts at the entrance of the buffalo-pen
tashtpâlüv	the bars of the entrance of the pen.
kadrtûlikkadr	the calf enclosure.
arkatchar	the household stream.
inerti	also the household stream.
ârsvitchkârs	the house (*ars*) at Kiudr.
eivitchâv	also the house.
nersûdrvel	the milking place.
keikû ir	the stream which runs between the house and the dairy (see 307).
kwoteiners	all of Kiudr village.
kwelthipushol	
etamûdri	
eraikin	
kârmus	
pârvakûdr	
arspem	slope of hill (*pem*) near Kiudr.

The special features of the Kiudr prayer are the large number of *kwarzam* of the village and the inclusion of the *kwarzam* of the house and household stream. The prayer of Kiudr is the only Toda prayer in which either the house or household stream is mentioned, and this fact is in accordance with the high degree of sanctity which has become attached to this village. It will be noticed also that the buffaloes are not mentioned, and that nearly all the clauses of the prayer apply to the buildings and their contents or to other parts of the village or to the village itself. Only the last *kwarzam* of the prayer applies to a place not actually in the village itself, and I could not ascertain why this place was so favoured. With this exception, the Kiudr prayer is one in which the *kwarzam* are entirely limited to those of the village and the dairy.

It will be remembered that when the buffaloes of the Nódrs *ti* migrate from Mòdr to Anto they pass by the village of Kiudr, and that the occasion is observed in various ways by the people of the village (see p. 135). I was told that certain *kwarzam* referring to this occasion are used in the Kiudr prayer. According to one man, these *kwarzam* are always recited in the prayer before those which have been already given, but others denied that they were so used. It is possible that these *kwarzam* are only said on special occasions, such as the day of migration, or it may be that they were formerly used, but are now being forgotten.

These *kwarzam* are as follow:

uner pâgit nòdr	*ti* buffaloes, come near country.
unkeu pâgit nòdr	bell of *wars* dairy, come near country.
eupalol pâgit nòdr	god *palol*, come near country.
eutuni pâgit nòdr	god *tuni*, come near country.
eitùt pâgit nòdr	hair done up, come near country (this has reference to the practice of tying the hair which is followed by the *palol* when engaged at his sacred work (p. 92).
Teigun ürpit nòdr	horn (of *warsir*) blow country.
Kiudkudr ürpit nòdr	horn (of *tiir*) blow country.

Then follow the *kwarzam* already given.

These *kwarzam* are of a different form from those used in the general form of prayer, and the various persons or objects mentioned are referred to either by their usual names or by slight modifications of them, as in *eupalol* or *euvalol* and *eutuni*. There seemed to be no doubt that these words were abbreviations of *teupalol* and *teutuni*, the omission of an initial *t* being not uncommon in the Toda language. Thus in this prayer the dairyman is called "god *palol*," and his garment "god *tuni*."

Prayer of Kwirg

Kwirg is one of the villages of the Kuudrol and is the place to which their buffaloes go when it is necessary to make new *pep* for the whole clan.

Kwatakwirg	Kwirg village.
kûlpudshol	Kwirg village.
palikeithiolv	the dairy.
tûmadshû	the pen.
kadrkeiri	the *kadr* (calf enclosure).
nîrtiûdsh	the dairy stream.
pinpunûv	a hill.
pilkûrs	a hill.
ûtthpep	see Kuudr prayer.
känpep	
mutchudpep	
keishkvet	
tarskivan	
petüt pati pethût îr	
pûthion nûkh tarzûr maj	

It will be seen that many of the clauses are common to this prayer and that of Kuudr.

The three *kwarzam* of *pep* were said to be used in every dairy of the Kuudrol, but it did not appear that they were used at Kiudr. The third, *mutchudpep*, is not included in the Kuudr prayer, but *mutchudkars* appears in its place. Two hills are mentioned in the Kwirg prayer, but there are none of the references to special events connected with the village such as exist in the prayer of Kuudr.

The Prayer of the Kanòdrs Dairy

When I was staying at Pishkwosht and visited the conical dairy at Kanòdrs with Neratkutan, he told me that the prayer of this dairy had forty *kwarzam* referring to the gods, as well as many of other kinds, but on going into detail I could only obtain the following :—

Pûr nûr teu	the 1600 gods.
pût nûr teu	the 1800 gods.
Kwoto	Kwoto or Meilitars (see p. 203).

Atioto	Atioto (see p. 210).
Kurindei teu	Kurindo (see p. 192).
Konteu	Konteu or Konto (see p. 211).
Anteu	Anto (see p. 188).
Pòrzo	Pòrzo } see p. 211.
Kòdrtho	Kòdrtho }
Kårzo	Karzo }
Teikhunteu	Teikhun }
mänpôh	Kanòdrs village.
mutlrshpôh	ditto.
tûnertû	the pen.
kânêr	the sun ? (see p. 206).
kuteikurs	the stone chain used by Kwoto (see p. 207).
aners	Kuzhu village.
tûtashki	Pishkwosht village.

This prayer is quite unlike those of the other village dairies and was much more like that of a *ti* dairy. As we have seen, the *poh* of Kanòdrs resembles a *ti* dairy both in the elaborateness of its ritual and in the high degree of sanctity of its dairyman, and this resemblance is now seen to extend to the prayer used in the dairy ritual.

Other dairies of the Tartharol which have an especial degree of sanctity are the *kugvali* of Taradr and the conical dairy of Nòdrs. I made great endeavours to obtain the prayers used in these places, but without success.

The ti Prayer

The prayers offered at the *ti* dairies are as a general rule longer and more complex than those of the ordinary village dairy. The latter portion of the prayer, or the prayer proper, does not seem to differ from that of the ordinary dairy, the differences being in the *kwarzam* recited at the beginning. The different dairies of the same *ti* may have different prayers; thus, at the Nòdrs *ti* there is a special prayer for the dairy at Anto which is longer and more complicated than that used at Mòdr, but it is probable that this is exceptional and is owing to the great antiquity and sanctity of Anto. The other dairies of this *ti* probably use much the same prayer as at Mòdr, though there may be certain slight modifications at each.

THE ANTO PRAYER

This prayer is characterised by a very large number of *kwarzam* referring to the dairy, its contents and surroundings. On ordinary days a shortened form of the prayer is used which consists wholly of *kwarzam* of this kind. On special days, such as the occasions of *ponup* and *irnödrthiti*, other *kwarzam* are said, including those of gods and buffaloes.

The following *kwarzam* are those in daily use, each being followed by the word *idith* as in the village prayer:—

	Kwarzam of
Anto	the *ti*.
eithipôh	ditto.
mëdrpôh	the *ti poh*.
pôhtîrzh	the *wars poh*.
ûv	the milking place (*pepkarmus*).
pero	the special pen used on the night before the *ponup* ceremony.
keirv	the pen used on the night before the migration of the buffaloes.
kûtû	the ordinary pen.
Teirz	a hill near the dairy on which Anto lives.
tilkav	the back of the dairy (*pohpalikef*).
îrbâr	the way by which the *kaltmokh* goes to and from the dairy.
Pîthipôh	the cave where Pithi was born (see p. 184).
nersâvul	sacred path to the dairy by which the *mani*, *pep*, &c., are taken.
karkadr	path by which ordinary people approach the dairy.
tadipül	ditto.
einpül	path by which the *palol* goes to draw water.
panpül	path by which the *palol* returns from drawing water.
Kïûln	a hill near the dairy.
Keini	another hill.
titkîn	stream at which the *palol* bathes and washes his garments.
ïltòr	stone by this stream marking the spot by which the *palol* bathes, &c.
teirpül	spot at which the *palol* halts and prays for the third time during the procession to Anto (see p. 135).
teirpôh	ditto.
nîrkûli	place at which *palol* and *kaltmokh* defecate.
Katthvai	hill near Anto (see p. 188).
Kubul	ditto.
Ködrs	place near Anto (see p. 188).
Tudrs	ditto.
teibithikars	stone rolled by Anto.
teibithival	lower part of the hill *Katthvai* (see above).

On ordinary days these *kwarzam* are followed by the prayer *tanenma tarmama*, &c. On special occasions the following *kwarzam* are inserted between those already given and the prayer proper :—

	Kwarzam of
Ekîrzam meidjam	Teikirzi, Tirshti.
Kûdreij	Kudreiil dairy.
tîdj	ditto.
Kûlâdrtho	Kuladrtho dairy.
Perithi ti vaners	*ti* dairy at Perithi in the Wainad.
Kòti	One of the hills at which fire is lighted by the *palol* at the *teutütusthchi* ceremony (see p. 291).
pagvòh	ditto.
Pûthi	another hill at which fire is lighted.
ânul	ditto.
Kûlinkârs	Kulinkars (see p. 188).
Nòtîrzivan	Nòtirzi (see p. 189).
Kuzkârv	Korateu (see p. 190).
unir	one group of *tiir* (see p. 112).
unkeu	*mani* of *wars* dairy.
Persin	*mani* of *ti* dairy.
kûdrs mani	bells of *punir*.
tadsth	axe which came from Amnòdr with the buffaloes.
tûpâr	an iron bar.
âler	the second group of *tiir* (see p. 112).
teiter	the third group of *tiir*.
Kwirz	the buffalo which has the *mani* called Keu put on its neck.
pîlti	buffaloes (*unir*).
persv	ditto.
Keirv	buffalo which drinks *pep* on day of migration (see p. 135).
Kîthi	buffalo which wears the *kudrs mani*.
kudûvòrs	the path at Mòdr by which ordinary people approach the dairy.
tadrpòrs	place near Mòdr at which the *palol* and *kaltmokh* defæcate.
tarikipül	place near Mòdr where the *erkumpîthpimi* ceremony is performed.
kidkadr	calves' hut (*karenpoh*) at Mòdr.
ponpôh	*ti* dairy at Mòdr.
kidpôh	*wars* dairy at Mòdr.
Òdrtho	*ti* dairy at Òdrtho.
Kûdreiil	*wars* dairy at Kudreiil.
munârten	a *ti* dairy.

The following is all I was able to obtain of the prayer used at Mòdr :—" *Ekîrzam meidjam idith, Anto eithipôh idith, Kûlinkârs idith, Nòtîrzivan idith, Kûlâdrvan idith, Teukuteithi idith, Kûdreij tîdj idith, Kuzkârv idith, Alvoi Kalvoi idith, tanenma tarmama,*" &c. Two of these *kwarzam*, "*Teukuteithi idith*" and "*Alvoi Kalvoi idith,*" are not mentioned in the Anto prayer. I have no doubt that the list of *kwarzam* is very incomplete.

The Prayer of Makars

The following is the prayer used at Makars, the chief dairy of the Kars *ti*. The *kwarzam* of the dairy are here comparatively few in number, but the prayer is especially rich in the *kwarzam* of gods and buffaloes, and it furnishes a very good example of the relation of the prayer formulæ to the Toda legends.

The *kwarzam* of the prayer run as follow:—

Anto	The god Anto.
Nòtïrzivan	Nòtirzi.
Kûlinkârs	Kulinkars or Teikhars.
Kuzkârv	Korateu.
Onkonm	Onkonm who lives on a hill in the Kundahs.
Ekïrzam meidjam	Teikirzi and Tirshti.
Azo } *Mazo* }	Azo and Mazo.
Katadrvanpoh	place near Kûlinkars.
Peigwa	god living on hill near Makurti Peak.
Karmunteu	Karmunteu.
Kotzgârth	the Paikara river (Teipakh).
Kondilteu	Kondilteu, a god opposite the hill of Kòti.
Mûndilteu	a god on a hill near the last.
Onâlvpoh	place near Majodr.
Kûlâdrazenteu	god on a hill near Kuladrtho.
kaban adi arten teu	"iron door shut god."
kaban kûl eiten teu	"iron stick held god."
mòrs ver arten teu	"*mòrs* tree under event god."
kûghïr kûdr kwaten teu	"crooked horned buffalo horn cut god."
tebkûter at, tan mun madrik teu	"imitation buffalo horns took, his mother's brother's lap god."
mâvel kârịtan teu	"sambhar from calved god." (The last six *kwarzam* refer to the story of Kuzkarv (see p. 190).
pülnerkûrz	buffaloes of *ti* called *pürsïr*.
tetnïrkan	ditto.
pirsk muneki potitth ir	"sun to facing that came buffalo."

nerk muneki potitth ir	"bell to facing that came buffalo."
putûdr mun kekitth ir	"*tûdr* tree back (face ?) rubbed buffalo."
Kitheri kûtk ethkitth ir	"Kitheri stream to jumped buffalo."
pûtûsh kattith ir	"desolate pen from made buffalo."
Warwark ethkitth ir	"Warwar (stream) to jumped buffalo."
ö khuberam kitj erditth êram	"seven heaps buffalo-dung fire set buffaloes."
pêrnêr	bell (*mani*) or *pürs* dairy.
unêr	ditto.
persagun	*mani* of *pars* dairy.
talg	ditto.
nârvtüls	lamp.
poikar	*pürs* dairy.
pârsvôh	*pars* dairy.
tînnudri	pen.
kakûnnudri	ditto.
nîrkar	dairy spring.
tülinîr	ditto.
pünpôh	dairy at Enòdr.
kûtû	pen at Enòdr.
pünnîr	spring at Enòdr.
Enòdr	Enòdr *ti mad.*
mêdrpôh	dairy at Pars.
peiltû	pen at Pars.
tülinîr	spring at Pars.
Pars	Pars *ti mad.*
âtârnudri	dairy at Neradr.
nêrieners	pen at Neradr.
Neradr	Neradr *ti mad*
pülvôh	dairy at Kòn.
auers	ditto.
tedrvûs	pen at Kòn.
pûvârsnîr	spring at Kòn.
Kòn	Kòn *ti mad.*

Then follow "*tanenma tarmama,*" &c.

The *kwarzam* of the prayer given above are arranged in a definite order. First come the *kwarzam* of sixteen gods or of hills or places closely connected with gods, then follow six *kwarzam* referring to various incidents in the life of the god Korateu. These are followed by two *kwarzam* of buffaloes, and then follow six referring to various features of the founding of Makars, of which an account has been given on

p. 116. Then follows a *kwarzam* relating to an incident which is probably recent. The *palol* of this *ti* used to make seven heaps of the dung of the buffaloes. There is a law that the dung should not be sold, which the *palol* disobeyed, and soon after a fire broke out suddenly from the seven heaps, and this event is commemorated in the prayer by means of the *kwarzam* meaning "seven heaps of buffalo-dung, fire set buffaloes," and is included among the *kwarzam* relating to buffaloes, probably because there was a belief that the anger of the buffaloes was the cause of the fire.

The buffalo *kwarzam* are followed by eleven referring to the bells of the *ti* and to the dairy, pen and spring of Makars, and these are followed by *kwarzam* referring to the other places of the *ti*—viz., Enòdr, Pars, Neradr, and Kòn. In each case there are said the *kwarzam* of the dairy, pen, spring, and place except in the case of Neradr, where for some reason the *kwarzam* of the spring is omitted.

The feature of the Makars prayer which is especially interesting is the reference to legend in the *kwarzam*. This reference occurs in the Kuudr prayer and in those of Kanòdrs and Anto, but the references are far more elaborate in the Makars prayer. These references were very useful in providing incidental confirmation of the details of legends previously obtained, while in other cases they put me on the track of stories which I might otherwise have failed to obtain. One point of interest connected with them is that, in the absence of the legends, they might easily be supposed to be meaningless sentences. We have seen that there is reason to believe that the Todas are forgetting much of their mythology, and if the legends referred to in the Makars prayer should be forgotten, these *kwarzam* would become meaningless formulæ. This appears to have happened already in some cases; there were certain *kwarzam* of which I could obtain no translation; thus, all the *kwarzam* of the clans and villages were of this nature and could not be explained, though they almost certainly had a definite origin. A good instance of a *kwarzam* which is on its way towards a similar fate is that at the end of the Kuudr prayer. The meaning of only one word was clear —viz., *nákh*—while *maj* was probably the word for cloud, and the *kwarzam* appears to refer to some incident of legend in which a three-year-old calf and a cloud were concerned, but I could obtain no record of the incident, nor of the legend of which the incident was a feature.

I have treated these formulæ of the dairy as prayers, and I think there can be very little doubt that they are of the nature of supplications, and are believed to invoke the aid of the gods in protecting the sacred buffaloes. It must be confessed, however, that there is no actual evidence in the formulæ of direct invocation of the gods. The name of no god is mentioned in the vocative form. In some prayers there is barely mention of a god at all, if the term 'god' be limited to the anthropomorphic beings of the hill-tops.

The exact relation between the formula and the gods largely depends on the exact meaning of the word *idith*, which is not quite clear. But, whatever the meaning of this word, it is evident that it is used in exactly the same way in the case of a god as in the case of a buffalo, a place, a dairy vessel, or other even meaner object.

Perhaps the nearest approach to an appeal to gods in the prayer is in the words at the end, in which the names of certain gods are mentioned, followed by the words *âtham idith emk tânenmâ*, "for their sake may it be well for us."

There is little doubt that the Todas offer prayers to their gods in their ordinary daily life, altogether apart from the dairy ritual. I was told by one man that when anyone leaves an *etudmad* he should pray that he may return safely, and in this case my informant said that he prayed to Teikirzi. Unfortunately I did not ask the exact form of the prayer, and do not know whether the goddess was invoked by name or whether *kwarzam* were uttered of the same form as in the prayer of the dairy. We may, however, be confident that the idea of supplication to the gods is not foreign to the Toda mind.

We shall see later that in the formulæ used in Toda sorcery, the names of gods are mentioned, followed by the same word *idith* which is used in the dairy formulæ. In the magical formulæ the evidence of appeal to deities is somewhat stronger than in the case of the dairy formulæ, which are certainly of a religious character. It seems most likely that the word *idith* was at one time used especially in connexion with the names of gods, and carried with it some idea of supplication. Gradually other sacred objects were included in the prayer, the same form being used for them as for the gods, this inclusion being prompted by the belief that the mention of any sacred object might help to promote the efficacy of the prayer. Later, when any mysterious and seemingly miraculous incident occurred at a village, it seems to have become the custom to commemorate it in the prayer.

It is quite clear that at the present time the earlier portion of the prayer, consisting of the *kwarzam*, is regarded as more important than the latter portion, which reads like the actual prayer. I suspect even that in practice the prayer proper is often omitted, or that only the first two words, *tanenma, tarmama*, are said. There certainly seemed to be no very rigorous laws as to the exact number or order of the clauses of this part of the prayer. The earlier portion, on the other hand, is very strictly regulated, and the order in which the *kwarzam* are to be uttered is definitely prescribed. Certainly there is far more reticence in connexion with the *kwarzam*, and this may safely be taken to indicate that a higher degree of sanctity attaches to them than to the words of the prayer proper.

It is probable that the alteration in the relative importance attached to the two parts of the prayer would have to go little further in order to produce a state of things in which the Toda dairyman would use the first parts of the formulæ only, and an anthropologist visiting the Todas at this stage would find them using formulæ which would not be recognisable as prayer.

If, at the same time, the process of forgetting their mythology should also have advanced, the Todas would then provide an excellent example of a people using in their religious ritual meaningless forms of words, and the Toda *kwarzam* seem to furnish one way in which people may come to use such meaningless forms.

CHAPTER XI

THE DAIRY RITUAL

IN the preceding chapters I have given an account of an elaborate ritual wholly connected with the buffalo and with the dairy. This ritual is certainly of a religious character, and, though there is much in the nature of the dairy formulæ which is uncertain, there can be little doubt that they are intercessory and that they bring the dairy operations into definite relations with the Toda deities.

It seems most probable that the general idea underlying the dairy ritual is that the dairyman is dealing with a sacred substance, the milk of the buffaloes. This sacred substance is to be converted into other substances, butter and butter-milk, which are to be used by the profane. At the present time much of the butter goes to those who are not even Todas and are regarded by the Todas as inferior beings.

It seems most probable that the elaborate ritual has grown up as a means of counteracting the dangers likely to be incurred by this profanation of the sacred substance, or, in other words, as a means of removing a taboo which prohibits the general use of the substance.

Similarly the migration ceremonies have the general underlying idea of counteracting any possible evil influence which may accompany the passage of the buffaloes through the profane world from one sacred place to another. During the migration, objects may be seen by the multitude which under ordinary circumstances are strictly screened from the general gaze, and objects may be touched, or be in danger of being touched, by people who ordinarily may not even see them.

Again, the ceremonies connected with entrance upon any dairy office are intended to purify the candidate and make him fit to see and touch and use the sacred objects.

The purpose of some of the other ceremonies is less obvious. The *irpalvusthi* ceremony seems to be of the nature of a thanksgiving, one of its most important features being a feast, but in this feast people may partake of the milk of sacred buffaloes, which is not ordinarily used by them, and there is a suggestive resemblance to those religious ceremonies in which communion is held with the divine by eating or drinking the divine.

The salt-giving ceremonies seem to point to a time when salt was difficult to procure. According to the Todas the object of these ceremonies is to ensure a plentiful supply of milk. There is a belief that salt is beneficial to the buffaloes, and the occasions on which the salt is given have become religious ceremonies which at the *ponup* of the *ti* have reached a high degree of elaboration with very special relations to the chief gods of the dairy. The ceremonies of making new *pep* are especially mysterious, and I will reserve some speculations as to the general idea underlying them till later (see p. 242).

COMPARISON OF THE PROCEDURE OF DIFFERENT DAIRIES

One of the most striking features of the ritual in all its branches is its increasing elaboration and complexity from the lowest to the highest grade of dairy.

One of the details of the ritual which runs through the whole series of dairies is the separation between the vessels and objects which come into contact with the buffaloes or their milk, and those which come into contact with the outside world, or with the products of the churning which may go to the outside world.

In the proceedings with the milk of the ordinary buffaloes in the huts where the people live, there is, so far as I know, no distinction of this kind.

In the lowest grade of dairy we already meet with the

separation. All the vessels are kept in the same room, but in different parts of the room, the *patatmar* and the *ertatmar*, and this distinction between the two sets of objects is kept up in the migration ceremonies where they are carried by different men.

There are no striking differences in this respect between the lower grades of dairy, whether *tarvali*, *kudrpali*, or *wursuli*; in all, the two sets of vessels are separated, but no strict measures are taken to prevent a vessel of the *patatmar* from coming into contact with a vessel of the *ertatmar* during the dairy operations. It is only on reaching the *kugvali* of Taradr that we find an intermediate vessel, the *kuvun*, used to transfer substances from a vessel of the more sacred to one of the less sacred kind, and to prevent possible contamination of the former by the latter.

It is in the *ti* dairy that these precautions reach their highest degree of development. Here the two sets of vessels are kept in different rooms, separated by a screen, and the dairy products are never transferred directly from a vessel of one kind to a vessel of the other, but always by means of an intermediate vessel. The butter and buttermilk produced by the churning operations in the inner room are transferred to the vessels of the outer room by means of the *idrkwoi*, which is kept on the dividing line between the two compartments. Similarly the vessels into which the butter and buttermilk are received are never allowed to come into direct contact with objects from the outside world, but their contents are transferred to vessels used outside the dairy by means of intermediate vessels, the *uppun* or the *mòrpun*.

In the migrations of the *ti* buffaloes this strict separation between the two kinds of vessel is still kept up. The things of the inner room are carried by the *palol* himself, while the things of the outer room are carried by others. The *idrkwoi*, though carried by the *palol* on the same staff as the things of the inner room, is kept apart from the rest, and is not allowed to touch them.

The fires of the *ti* dairy furnish another interesting example of the principle by which sacred objects are prevented from coming directly into relation with objects which may have been contaminated by contact with the outside world. The lamp is not lighted directly from the *tòratthwaskal*, which is probably sometimes touched by the *kaltmokh*, but fire is transferred from this fireplace to the *pelkkatitthwaskal*, from which the lamp is lighted. Here, again, the use of an intermediary object is limited to the *ti* dairy.

The principle of management by which the *palol* prevents the contamination of the sacred by the profane in the dairy is adopted by him in other ways. Whenever I paid any money to the *palol* at Mòdr, I placed it on a stone from which it was taken by the *kaltmokh* and handed to the *palol*. A similar procedure is generally adopted whenever anything is brought to, or taken from, a *ti* dairy. The *kaltmokh* in the above instance acts as the intermediate link between the *palol* and the unclean.

In the ordinary procedure of the village dairy, except at the *kugvali* of Taradr, no example occurs of this use of intermediate links, but there is such an example during the ordination of the *wursol*. When the *palikartmokh* gives the candidate milk from the *ertatpun* (p. 149), he does not pour it directly into the leaf-cup from which the candidate drinks, but first pours it into another leaf-cup and then from that into the cup used by the candidate.

Other features of the ritual in which there are differences in different grades of dairy are in the ceremonial touching of dairy vessels, in the avoidance of turning the back towards the contents of the dairy, in lamp-lighting, in the ritual connected with the bell, and in the frequency with which the prayer of the dairy is recited.

At the *tarvali* and *kudrpali*, the dairyman touches ceremonially the *majpariv* and the *patat* at the beginning of the afternoon churning, while at the *wursuli* this is done both morning and afternoon. At the *ti*, however, this ceremonial touching does not occur, or, at any rate, I failed to obtain any account of its performance.

The method of carrying out the dairy procedure *kabkaditi*, in which the back is never turned on the sacred vessels of the dairy, is not followed in the *tarvali*, except at the *irpalvusthi* ceremony. I have no record of it in the *kudrpali*, except on the same occasion, and it is only followed regularly in certain dairies of the *wursuli* grade, viz., Nòdrs, Nasmiòdr, Òdr, and Kozhtudi. The first has a conical dairy, and Nasmiòdr and Òdr are especially ancient and sacred places. At the *kugvali* and the *ti* dairy, on the other hand, the dairy ceremonial is always performed *kabkaditi*. At one ceremony, that of *irpalvusthi*, the work of the dairy is performed *kabkaditi* in every dairy of whatever grade.

The lamp-lighting is another feature which becomes more frequent and more ceremonial in the higher grades of dairy. In all the village dairies, including the *kugvali* of Taradr,[1] the lamp is only lighted ceremonially at the afternoon churning, the lighting being made the occasion of prayer. If the morning is dark, the lamp may be lighted, but it is clear that this is not done ceremonially, and the lighting is not accompanied by prayer. At the *ti* we have already seen that the lamp is lighted in a more ceremonial manner and in the morning as well as in the afternoon.

Some of the details of the ritual are definitely associated with the *mani*, and since the presence of a *mani* implies a higher grade of dairy, this leads to an increase in the elaboration of the ritual. The *mani* is treated in much the same way in all the grades of dairy which possess this sacred object.

Another feature in which the increasing sanctity of the dairy is shown is the frequency with which prayer is offered. At all the village dairies the dairyman only prays at the afternoon ceremonial when lighting the lamp, and when shutting up the buffaloes in their pen for the night. As already mentioned, there is a definite association between prayer and the ceremonial lamp-lighting.

In the *ti* dairy, prayer is offered both morning and evening; at the morning ceremonial twice and in the afternoon three times. On both occasions the first prayer begins when the lamp is being lighted and is continued while the *palol* knocks on one of the *persin* with the *persinkudriki*. The second prayer in each case is offered at the conclusion of the milking, and the third prayer of the afternoon corresponds to

[1] I am doubtful about this point at the *poh* of Kanòdrs.

the second prayer of the village dairy, being offered when shutting up the buffaloes for the night.

The increasing sanctity of the different grades of dairy is shown very clearly by the increasing stringency in the rules of conduct of the dairyman. The *tarvalikartmokh* may sleep in the living hut on any night in the week, and there are no restrictions on his intercourse with women. The *kudrpalikartmokh* may only sleep in the hut on Sundays, Wednesdays and Saturdays, and is prohibited from intercourse with Teivali women. The *wursol* is limited to two nights, Sunday and Wednesday, and, though himself a Teivali man, is prohibited from intercourse with Teivali women. The *kugvalikartmokh* has similar restrictions, but the *pohkartpol* of Kanòdrs must avoid women altogether, and this is almost certainly the case with the *palol* also.

The *tarvalikartmokh* takes his buttermilk and food without any ceremony. The *kudrpalikartmokh* must hold his food in his hands throughout his meal and must not put it on the ground.

In the case of the *wursol* we meet first with the ceremonial drinking of buttermilk, which must in this case be poured into the leaf-cup from the vessel called *ertatpun*. The *kugvalikartmokh* drinks buttermilk sitting on the seat outside his dairy and pours from the *ertatpun*, drinking three times only and saying "*Oñ*" each time.

The *pohkartpol* of Kanòdrs has to take his food with very special precautions. He sits on the wall of his dairy and his hand must not touch his mouth nor the leaf-cup his lips. At the *ti* the drinking of buttermilk has become a definite ceremony in which the *kaltmokh* pours out drink for the *palol* with prescribed formulæ, but, strangely enough, the *palol* does not suffer from the same restrictions against touching his mouth as the *pohkartpol* of Kanòdrs, though the latter holds an office which in most ways is distinctly less sacred than that of the *palol*.

The clothing of each grade is also regulated. Perhaps the most important feature here is the use of the garments called *tuni*. These are made of dark grey cloth of a quite different kind from that of the ordinary clothes worn by the Todas.

The garments are procured from the Badagas, and cloth of the same kind, called *än*, is used to enwrap the corpse in the funeral ceremonies. It is mentioned as the ordinary clothing of a woman in the legend of Kwoten, and is almost certainly the ancient clothing of the Todas still persisting in ceremonial in connexion with the dead and in the dairy ritual.

The *tuni* is only worn by the higher grades of the dairyman-priesthood and by the *palikartmokh* of the Teivaliol. The *palol* wears *tuni* only, both his loin-cloth and his mantle being of this material. The *kaltmokh* has no need for a *tuni*, for when he is engaged in his work at the *ti* he has to be naked, and when away from the *ti* and in the sleeping hut he wears a small piece of *tuni*, the *petuni*, in his girdle, the piece of cloth marking the difference between the full *kaltmokh* and the *perkursol*.

The *wursol*, the *kugvalikartmokh*, and the Teivali *palikartmokh* only wear the *tuni* when actually engaged in the dairy work and leave it inside the dairy at other times. I am doubtful whether the *pohkartpol* of Kanòdrs resembles the *palol* or the lower grades in this respect.

Although the *palikartmokh* of the *tarvali* and the *kudrpali* never wear the *tuni*, a small piece of this cloth is put in the girdle during the ordination ceremonies, and this may be a relic of a time when every dairyman wore the *tuni*.[1] In the secret language (see Chap. XXV) the word *petuni* is used in one place as the equivalent of 'uniform,' and this seems to indicate that the *petuni* is regarded as the badge of a dairyman.

The use of the leaves and bark of the sacred *tudr* tree is another feature which distinguishes different dairies. In the *tarvali* it is, so far as I know, not used at all. In the *kudrpali* it is only used in the *pepeirthti* ceremony. The *wursol* uses *tudr* in his ordination ceremonies, but not in the ordinary ritual of his dairy, nor is it used in the daily ritual of the *ti* dairy, though largely used in the purification of the dairy and of the dairy vessels, and in the ordination ceremonies of the *palol*.

[1] It is in favour of this supposition that in the legend Kwoten wore the *tuni* when acting as *palikartmokh* although he was one of the Tartharol.

The use of *tudr* in the ordination ceremonies is only allowed to the members of the Teivali division and of the Melgars clan of the Tartharol.

Special kinds of dairy or special dairies may have features peculiar to themselves; thus the *pepeirthti* ceremony, in which the dairyman beats on the *patat* with a piece of *tudr* bark, is only performed at the *kudrpali*; the prescription of nakedness when milking is confined to the *kudrpalikartmokh*; the special method of wearing the *putkuli* open in front when going to the buffaloes is only practised by the *wursol*, and the method of taking food sitting on the wall of the dairy and throwing the food into the mouth is peculiar to the *pohkartpol* of Kanòdrs.

One feature of interest in the dairy organisation is the existence of different names at different dairies for the dairy products, and for the various objects used at the dairy or in connexion with the dairy ceremonies. The chief differences are found on comparing the village dairy with the *ti*, nearly every object having a different name in the two places, though occasionally a peculiarity of nomenclature may be confined to one dairy, as at Kanòdrs, where milk is called *persin*, the name of the churning vessel of the *ti*. As a general rule it seems that the name used in the village dairy is the same as that in ordinary use; thus, the dairy vessels used in the house for the milk of the ordinary buffaloes are known by the same names as those of the village dairy.

The use of special names in the more sacred dairies is probably connected with their high degree of sanctity. The names of the dairy vessels of the village are in common use, and it would doubtless seem sacrilegious that the names of the vessels of the *ti* should be thus in everyone's mouth. Consequently nearly every object used in the ceremonial of the *ti* dairy has a special name, and in the ordinary life of the Todas these words are probably never uttered.

One striking feature of the dairy ritual is the use of the syllable *Oñ*. With one exception (p. 177) this word is always uttered thrice, and it seems to be especially connected with the act of putting curds or milk on the bells. It has a suggestive resemblance to the mystical syllable *Om* of the Hindus. It is also possible that it may be a form of the name of the god Ön, or, again, it may be a corruption of the word *mani*, of which the initial letter has been dropped, a process of which other examples have been given.

It is doubtful how much significance is attached to the right and left sides in the dairy ritual. There is no doubt that in the most sacred acts of the ritual, such as saluting the buffaloes and the sun, or feeding the bell, it is the right hand which is used. This preference of the right hand is emphasised by the action of the *palol* in washing out his mouth, when he takes the water into his mouth from the left hand, because it is his right hand which has most to do with the sacred objects. In the migration ceremonies the dairy vessels are carried on the left shoulder, but at the *ti* the choice of this shoulder by the *palol* is obviously due to the fact that either the *mani* or churning-stick is carried in the right hand, and in other cases it is probable that the choice of the left shoulder is due to the necessity of leaving the right hand free. When the candidate drinks in the ordination ceremonies he holds the cup in the right hand, and this hand certainly has the preference throughout the dairy ritual. On the other hand, the *petuni* is worn on the left side of the waist-string, both by the *kaltmokh*, as a sign of his full rank, and by the *palikartmokh* during his ordination ceremonies.

In the ordinary dairy the side which is on the right hand in entering seems to be the more sacred, and the platform on this side is the *meitün* or superior bed. In the *ti* dairy, on the other hand, there was some doubt as to the more sacred side. At Mòdr it seemed that the *mani* is on the left hand side of the *palol* as he is performing his duties, but it is doubtful whether this is so at other places, and it may be that my account of the Mòdr dairy is wrong in this respect.

The Sanctity of Milk

The different degrees of sanctity attaching to the different dairies are associated with differences in the rules regulating the use of milk, and these rules seem to show clearly that the milk of buffaloes belonging to the more sacred dairies has a higher degree of sanctity than that churned in the lower grades.

The milk of ordinary buffaloes may be drunk by anyone, man, woman, or child. The Todas do not ordinarily sell milk, but if they do so, they may only use the milk of ordinary buffaloes for this purpose. I have a note that anyone may also drink the milk of buffaloes belonging to the *tarvali*, but I suspect that this only applies to men who must drink it at the dairy.

The milk of the *kudrpali* may only be drunk by the *kudrpalikartmokh* himself. It is believed that any other person or animal who should drink milk from this dairy would die.

At the *wursuli* milk may be given to men at the dairy, but it must be mixed with buttermilk. At the *kugvali* of Taradr the milk of the *kugvalir* themselves is not drunk by anyone, the dairyman having certain ordinary buffaloes for his own use, and this is also the case at the *ti*. I believe that not even the *palol* would drink the milk of the *persinir*, the sacred buffaloes of the *ti*.

There is one exception to the rule that ordinary people may not use the milk of the sacred buffaloes of the village dairies (except in the form of butter and buttermilk). At the *irpalvusthi* ceremony at all the village dairies, including the *kugvali*, food is prepared with the milk of one of the sacred animals and this food is given to the people of the clan to which the dairy belongs and also to members of other clans.

In the case of the *wursuli*, I was especially told that this is the only occasion on which the milk of *wursulir* is used by people in general. At the *kugvali*, people of other clans are only given this food on the second day of the proceedings, and the distribution of the food is preceded by a ceremony in which some of the food is thrown into the fire. The milk used on this occasion is the milk of the buffalo which has recently calved, the ceremony being in celebration of this event.

At the *wursuli* it is noteworthy that the food is cooked by the *wursol* himself, the ceremony of *irpalvusthi* being the only occasion on which a dairyman of this grade prepares food. Thus, when the milk of the *wursulir* is used ceremonially as a food by ordinary people, the food is prepared by the dairyman-priest. One feature of the *irpalvusthi* ceremony is that the work is performed *kabkaditi* in every dairy, and it is possible that this sign of increased respect is intended to counteract the desecration which is about to take place in the use of the milk by the profane. As I have already pointed out, the *irpalvusthi* ceremony has a strong resemblance to a sacrificial feast, in which people partake of the sacred animal, but in this case it is the milk of the animal and not the animal itself which is taken.

A further indication of the sanctity of milk is given in the prohibition against the drinking of milk by a widower or widow during a period which, as we shall see later, may extend to many months.

The restrictions on the use of the milk of the sacred animals have the general characters associated with taboos, and the whole daily ritual of the dairy would seem to be designed to remove the taboo. It is possible that at one time the milk of the sacred buffaloes was not used at all, and that these animals only suckled their calves. If then the Todas had begun to milk the sacred buffaloes, it is natural that the milking and churning should have been accompanied by ritual designed to counteract the evils to be expected from the profanation of the sacred substance and the breaking of the taboo. In certain circumstances even now the Todas do not milk their sacred buffaloes, but allow them to suckle their calves only. If a *ti* dairy, or even one of a lower grade, has no dairyman, the buffaloes are not milked, though they are still tended by some unsanctified person and are kept ready to take their part in the dairy ritual if a dairyman should again be appointed.

Special Dairy Customs

The general method of treating the milk in the dairy procedure seems to be the same as that generally followed in India and other hot countries. The milk is allowed to coagulate and the curd is churned. The butter so obtained differs from that of European countries in containing the proteid as well as the fat constituents of milk. This butter is then clarified, but in this respect there is an important difference between the ordinary Hindu procedure and that of the Todas. The usual Hindu method is to heat slowly over a fire without the addition of any other substance. The Todas add grain or rice to the butter before clarification, and this sinks to the bottom of the vessel and forms a substance called by the Todas *al*, which is one of their chief foods. This deposit of grain or rice will carry down with it some, possibly all, of the proteid constituents, and the *al* will, therefore, be a nourishing food.

The only other detail in which the Toda procedure is peculiar[1] is in the addition of buttermilk from a previous churning to the newly-drawn milk, the buttermilk or *pep* being put into the vessel before milking. This addition probably hastens the process of coagulation, but its chief interest is derived from the fact that it has become the nucleus of some of the most interesting features of the dairy ceremonial.

This addition of buttermilk seems to be regarded as forming a thread of continuity in the dairy ritual, and the ceremony of *pepkaricha*, or making new *pep*, is held whenever this continuity is broken. The *pep* is connected with a dairy vessel of the kind called *mu*, which is buried in the buffalo pen, and if any evil befalls the *mu*, it is held to be a cause for making new *pep*—*i.e.*, the usual course of the dairy procedure will be interrupted, in some cases for months.

The buried dairy vessel seems to be linked in some mysterious way with the fortunes of the dairy, and especially with the buttermilk which forms the element of continuity in the dairy procedure. The buried dairy vessel, or *mu*, is not one which is now generally used to hold buttermilk. There are two kinds of *mu* in the dairy, one which contains the butter added during the churning, while the other is used,

[1] It is an Indian practice to add sour buttermilk to the milk to promote coagulation, but this is usually done after heating the milk. It is possible that in some parts of India it may be added to the milk before or immediately after it is drawn.

partly as a receptacle for the milk which is about to be churned, and partly to fetch water from the stream. It is highly probable that there was at one time a third *mu* in the dairy, which was a receptacle for the buttermilk added before milking.

At the especially sacred dairy of Kanòdrs, where ancient procedure is likely to have lingered, the buried *mu* is still used as a receptacle for buttermilk. When this dairy is unoccupied, a certain amount of buttermilk is kept in the buried *mu*, and when the dairy is again occupied, this buttermilk is used to add to the milk. In this case the continuity of the dairy procedure is directly kept up by means of the buried vessel, and this procedure of the Kanòdrs dairy is strongly in favour of the view that the buried vessel was formerly a receptacle for the *pep*.

There are other indications that the *mu* is the most sacred of the dairy vessels. It is this vessel which is touched by the *wursol* the *kugvalikartmokh* of Taradr and the *pohkartpol* of Kanòdrs, as the final act which gives them their full status at the ordination ceremonies, and we shall see later that in the funeral ceremonies at Taradr a temporary building is made to represent a dairy by placing in its inner room a *mu*. In this last case, it would seem that the *mu* is regarded as the emblem of the dairy, and that placing a *mu* in the inner room of the temporary building makes it a dairy.

The representative of the *mu* at the *ti* dairy is the *peptòrzum*, but it does not seem that this vessel is specially distinguished from the rest, and it does not appear to have the sanctity and importance which attaches to this kind of vessel at the village dairy.

There seem to be two chief possibilities in explaining the existence of the buried *mu*. It may be that it was at one time the custom to bury the *pep* while the village was unoccupied, and that this custom now only persists at Kanòdrs, the *mu* at other places being no longer used for this purpose, though it has continued to be of ceremonial importance. The other possibility is that, as the *pep* acquired increased importance in the dairy ritual, the sanctity of the buttermilk was transferred to the vessel which contained it, and the sanctity of the vessel became so great that it was not thought right to leave it exposed to the dangers it might incur in the dairy, especially in the various migrations, and it was therefore buried in the buffalo pen of the chief village of the clan. It is probable that the custom arose in the way suggested by the procedure of the Kanòdrs dairy, but that the full development of the custom has been largely due to the belief in its special sanctity.

The obscure observance of having a ball of food larger than can be eaten at one sitting occurs twice in the various dairy ceremonials. It is a feature of the ceremonies which the *kaltmokh* has to undergo on the day after the migration of the Nòdrs *ti* to Anto, and the superabundant portion of food has also to be eaten by the candidate for the office of *palol* in the preliminary ceremony called *tesherst*. In each case the food is of the ceremonial kind called *ashkkartpimi*. I can offer no suggestions as to the meaning of the observance, nor do I know of any parallel for it.

Purity and Impurity

The idea of ceremonial purity is one running through the whole of the dairy rites. Many of the details of the ritual, the purification of new vessels and of dairies revisited after a period of disuse, the ordination ceremonies of the dairyman, the elaborate ceremonies accompanying the making of new *pep*, all show a very deeply engrained idea that men and things have in themselves some degree of impurity, and that in order to be made fit for the service of the gods, they must be purified and sanctified by appropriate ceremonies.

As regards man two grades of impurity are recognised : (i.) the impurity of the ordinary man, which is perhaps an absence of ceremonial purity rather than actual impurity ; and (ii.) the special impurity which is the result of certain events and especially of those accompanying birth and death.

The impurity of the ordinary man does not prevent him from visiting the dairies of the lower grade, but it prohibits him from taking any part whatever in the actual dairy operations. With certain exceptions, he is rigorously excluded from actual contact either with dairies or dairymen of the higher grades. He is perhaps regarded as unsanctified rather than impure. The definite impurity which is the condition of those who have attended funeral ceremonies or have been in relation with a woman in the period of seclusion after childbirth is something very different. Such a man is not merely unsanctified, he is unfit to hold any sacred office; even the prolonged ceremonies of ordination would not fit him to hold office in the dairy or to perform any part in the tendance of the sacred buffaloes, and he is not allowed even to approach the members of the higher grades of the dairyman-priesthood.

WOMEN AND THE DAIRY

Women take no part in the dairy ritual, nor in the milking and churning operations which are carried on in the hut. It is said that at one time the women took charge of the buffaloes at the time of calving, but this is not the case at the present time.

Women go to the dairy to fetch buttermilk, using an appointed path and standing at an appointed spot to receive it.

Females enter dairies under two conditions only. They may enter the outermost rooms of those dairies which are used as funeral huts while the bodies of men are lying in them. Here they may sit only on one side of the room, and only when the dairy operations are not in progress. Women also enter the temporary funeral huts of men which are called *pali*, or dairies.

The other condition under which a female enters a dairy is at the migration ceremony of the village, in which a girl, seven or eight years of age, is given food in the dairy of the village which the buffaloes are leaving, and sweeps the front of the dairy of the village to which they are going. This ceremony is one in which a girl seems to take a definite part in dairy ceremonial, but the girl chosen for this office must be below the age of puberty.

The relations of women with the different grades of dairymen have already been considered; a point which may again be mentioned is that the emblems of womanhood, the pounder, sieve, and broom, may be removed from the hut while the dairyman is present, though the women themselves remain.

During certain dairy ceremonials, women must leave the village altogether, and during the passage of the buffaloes of the Nòdrs *ti* near the village of Kiudr, the women leave the village, taking with them the pounder, sieve, and broom.

Although women are thus excluded from all participation in the dairy ceremonial, we shall see later (Chapter XIV) that an artificial dairy plays a part in some of the ceremonies connected with pregnancy and childbirth.

History of the Dairy

The Todas can give very little information which throws any light on the development of this complex organisation of the dairy with its elaborate ritual. According to tradition, the most sacred dairies, and especially that of the Nòdrs *ti*, date back to the time when the gods were active on earth and were themselves dairymen.

Beyond the belief that buffaloes of different kinds were assigned to the different clans by Teikirzi, I could obtain no account of beliefs about the origin or growth of the other grades of dairy. One fact as to the past which seemed clear was that *ti* dairies were at one time more numerous than at present, and several places now possessing village dairies of the ordinary kind are said to have been at one time the seats of *ti* dairies. Thus it is believed that Kiudr was formerly a *ti* place, and the old weatherworn stones shown in Figs. 31 and 32, which are still called *neurzülnkars*, seem to provide evidence that tradition is here correct. The village of Teidr is said to have been at one time a *ti*, and here again two stones called *neurzülnkars* are to be seen about a quarter of a mile from the village.

There is another feature of the Kiudr dairy which suggests that it may at one time have been a *ti* dairy. It contains six bells called *mani*, which clearly differ in nature from the *mani* of the other village dairies, especially in the fact that they are not used at funerals. They are also distinguished as *palatmani* and *ertatmani*, a distinction not met with in any other village dairy. It seems probable that they are the representatives of the two kinds of bells of a *ti*, the *mani* proper and the *kudrsmani*. The *ertatmani* of Kiudr are 'fed' with buttermilk, a procedure not followed, so far as I know, in any other dairy, but it may be that this is a feature of the procedure of the *ti* dairy which escaped me. Certainly the most likely explanation of the existence of these bells at Kiudr is that they are survivals of its former position as a *ti* dairy.

The villages of Kiudr and Teidr both belong to the Teivaliol, and this raises the question whether this division of the Todas may not have possessed *ti* herds and *ti* dairies of their own at one time, and may not always have had to be content with providing dairymen for institutions belonging to the Tartharol. No information could be given on this point, but it seems unlikely that dairies and places belonging to a Tarthar clan should have been handed over to the Teivaliol when they were no longer used as *ti* dairies and *ti* places.

Certain Tarthar villages are also said to have had at one time *ti* dairies, especially the sacred places of Nòdrs and Òdr. This probably means that there is a tradition that the buffaloes of the Nòdrs *ti* were at one time kept at these places which, as we have seen, are still visited by the *palol* during his ordination ceremonies.

The process of extinction of *ti* institutions can be seen in progress at the present time. The Nidrsi *ti* is not now in working order; there has been no *palol* for some years and its dairies are unoccupied. It is said that a *palol* would have to be appointed temporarily if it was desired to perform the second funeral ceremonies of a Nidrsi man, but in the present condition of the Nidrsiol, it seems to me not at all unlikely, either that the rule will be disregarded, or that the second funeral ceremonies will not be performed, and that the Nidrsi *ti* will become absolutely extinct, possibly dragging down another institution into extinction with it.

The Kwòdrdoni *ti* is now only active for a short time once every year in order to satisfy a ceremonial requirement of the

Kotas, and this institution may possibly soon become little more than a name. If it were not for the Kotas, it would undoubtedly be as near extinction as the *ti* of Nidrsi. One *palol* of the Pan *ti* has recently ceased to be appointed, and the same difficulty which has led to his disappearance will probably sooner or later vacate the other office, and Pan will follow in the footsteps of the other clans. Many of the dairies belonging even to the more prosperous *ti* institutions are now disused, and some have completely vanished. The legend of Kwoto preserves a tradition of ceremonial accompanying the migration of the buffaloes of the Kars *ti* which has now entirely disappeared, and nothing is known of the special features of ritual which were practised at many *ti* dairies which have become extinct.

Of dairies of other grades, the *poh* of Kanòdrs is now only occupied for a short time once a year, and its ceremonial may soon also become extinct. The conical *poh* of Kars and the seven-roomed *kudrpali* of Nòdrs are dairies which have ceased to exist, and with the extinction of the latter have gone completely all traces of the ritual which was practised in this kind of dairy, and nothing is known as to the meaning of the seven rooms.

Some of these changes are recent, and due to the altered conditions produced by the general invasion of the Nilgiris, but others date back to a time before Europeans came to the hills, and were due to intrinsic conditions, chiefly the hardships connected with the ritual practised in certain of the dairies. The altered surroundings of the Todas are undoubtedly hastening the process of decay, and institutions which would probably have lasted for centuries will now almost certainly disappear in a few decades.

CHAPTER XII

DIVINATION AND MAGIC

THIS chapter will furnish a very good example of specialisation of religious and magical functions among the Todas. We shall find that certain Todas have the power of divination, others are sorcerers, and others again have the power of curing disease by means of spells and rites, while all three functions are quite separate from those of the priest or dairyman. The Todas have advanced some way towards specialisation of function in this respect, and have as separate members of the community their prophets, their magicians and their medicine-men in addition to their priests.

DIVINATION

Certain men among the Todas are reputed to have special powers as diviners, and are known as *teuòdipol*, "god-gesticulating men," or more commonly as *teuol*. Samuel, my interpreter, always spoke of their performances as devil-dancing and evidently regarded the *teuol* as like those whom he called the devil-dancers of his own people.

In several cases these men are said to have inherited their powers from some near relative, often a grandfather, but it seems that anyone who showed evidence of the necessary powers might become a *teuol*. All but one of the present diviners are Teivaliol, but the divining power is not limited to this division. There is no relation between the various offices of the dairy and the power of divination, and, in fact, a diviner necessarily gives up his divining if he becomes a *palol*.[1]

Each of the *teuol* is believed to be possessed by a special god when he falls into the divining frenzy, and when in this state it is said that the diviner does not, as a rule, speak in his own language, but in some other, most commonly in Malayalam or one of its dialects. The following are those who are at present credited with the power of divination :—

Midjkudr (63) of Piedr, who is inspired by the gods Kulinkars and Petkon. He speaks in Malayalam, and he does not appear to have succeeded anyone else as *teuol*. He is the most successful of those who are at present practising the art, and played the chief part in all the divining which took place during my visit.

Tadrners (60) of Kuudr, inspired by Ethrol and Arivili, succeeded his mother's father, Kasorivan (66) of Kusharf. He is said to speak the language of people whom the Todas call Mondardsetipol living in the Wainad, a language which appears to be a dialect of Malayalam.

Pangudr (66) of Kusharf, also succeeded Kasorivan, his grandfather, and is inspired by Petkon and Meilitars. There was some doubt as to the language used by him.

Ethgudr (52) of Kuudr is inspired by Arivili, and, like Tadrners, speaks the language of the Mondardsetipol.

Terkudr (63) of Piedr, inspired by Teipakh, the river god, succeeded his grandfather Keitolv. When inspired, his speech is like the babbling of a running river, "like the river's voice," and cannot be understood.

Kangudr (62) of Piedr, who lives at Kavidi in the Wainad, is inspired by Meilitars and speaks Malayalam. He succeeded Tarsvan (62), his father, and Tarsvan had succeeded his father Keithiolv.

Kobuv (61) of Kuudr, is inspired by Meilitars and Kuderol and speaks Malayalam.

Pöteners (54) of Kuudr, is inspired by Petkon and speaks the language of the Mondardsetipol.

[1] From the account of Finicio (Appendix I), it would seem that at one time the *palol* and *wursol* possessed the power of divination.

Karkievan (63), the *palol* of the Nòdrs *ti*, was formerly a *teuol*, but gave up divining when he became *palol*.

All the above belong to the Teivaliol, and the only Tarthar diviner at the present time is Mongudrvan (13) of Kars. He is said to be inspired by the god of Miuni village, and to speak the Toda language. The village of Miuni belongs to the Teivaliol, so that the only Tarthar diviner is inspired by a god connected with the division to which the majority of the diviners belong.

Two other Tarthar men, Kerveidi (5) and Tevò (3), both of Nòdrs, are said to have been *teuol* at one time, but they have ceased to divine. They succeeded another man of their clan. Kangudr, who is inspired by Meilitars, has to 'dance' or divine before the Kurumbas, and when he does so he dances as a lame man. This custom is reputed to have come down from the time of Meilitars (see p. 210), who danced as a lame man before the Kurumbas, and promised that whenever he came in the future he would dance to the Kurumbas first and then to the Todas.

It will be noticed that many of the deities by whom the diviners are inspired are not true Toda gods. Petkon, who inspires Midjkudr, Pangudr, and Pöteners, is said to be a hunting god. According to some he was a son of Teikirzi, but is almost certainly not a true Toda deity.

Arivili inspires Tadrners and Ethgudr, who are both reputed to speak the language of the Mondardsetipol, and he is probably a god of these people, a tribe of the Wainad. Ethrol, who also inspires Tadrners, is probably another deity of the same people. I do not know anything about Kuderol, by whom Kobuv is believed to be inspired.

It is noteworthy that the only existing Tarthar *teuol* speaks the Toda language when divining, and is believed to be inspired by a local Toda god; while the diviners belonging to the Teivaliol seem to speak dialects of Malayalam, and many are believed to be inspired by gods who are almost certainly not true Toda deities.

The *teuol* are consulted whenever any misfortune befalls a Toda. The following are various instances in which I have records of resort to divination: sickness or death of a Toda or of any of his family; sickness or death of a buffalo; failure of milk in a buffalo and persistent kicking of its calf; failure to make a buffalo go to the spot at which it is to be killed during a funeral ceremony; failure of milk to coagulate; burning down of a dairy; disappearance of the bells of a dairy; loss of a *tukitthkars* or lifting stone. In this last instance the stone at the village of Nidrsi was carried away some years ago by a party of English people who came to picnic near the village while the people were away. They carried the stone for some miles and then threw it down. The Nidrsi people could not find it, and consulted Midjkudr and Mongudrvan, who were able to reveal where the stone was to be found, and it was restored to the village, where it can now be seen.

The diviners usually work in pairs, though occasionally it would seem that one only may be consulted. If they are asked for an explanation of some misfortune which has befallen a man, the *teuol* usually find either that the sufferer has committed an offence against the dairy or that he is the subject of spells cast on him by a sorcerer. In the former case, they prescribe the ceremony which must be performed in order to expiate the offence. In the latter case, they name the sorcerer so that the sufferer may know with whom to make his peace.

I have already said that towards the close of my visit a number of misfortunes befell the Todas; one man fell ill, the wife of another died, and the dairy of a third was burnt down, and these events kept the diviners busy, but probably because I was implicated I was not allowed the chance of observing the diviners at work.

The only occasion on which I saw the process of divining was at a funeral. The buffalo which was to be killed had been caught at some distance from the place appointed for its slaughter. The animal was unusually refractory and at length lay down and all the natural efforts of the Todas failed to make it move. Midjkudr and Mongudrvan were then called upon to discover the cause of the obstinacy of the buffalo. Mongudrvan first began to dance slowly to and fro, away from and towards the buffalo. He had taken off his cloak and was only wearing the *tadrp*. As I already knew the man, I was able to observe that his general appearance was unaltered and that he did not appear to be in any abnormal mental condition. He was soon joined by Midjkudr, who danced up and down much more wildly (Fig. 36). His general appearance was very different to that usually presented by a Toda man. His hair seemed to stand out from his head, although it shook with each of

FIG. 36.—MIDJKUDR AND MONGUDRVAN DIVINING AT A FUNERAL.

his violent movements; his eyes were abnormally bright and his face gave every appearance of great mental excitement. I had not previously known the man, but when he came to see me a few days later I could hardly believe that the quiet, self-possessed man whom I saw before me was the same individual whom I had seen dancing at the funeral. It was obvious that he had been in a distinctly abnormal condition of frenzy during the divining process. After dancing for a time Midjkudr began to utter broken sentences in a loud and almost chanting voice, while Mongudrvan remained silent throughout. After Midjkudr had in these sentences given the reason for the obstinacy of the buffalo, and had prescribed what was to be done, he took a red cloth and dancing more violently than ever waved the cloth before the buffalo and pushed against the body of the animal. Then after the people had dragged the buffalo a little way, it rose and went quietly to the place where it was to be killed.

I had much difficulty in finding out exactly what Midjkudr had said. When he came to see me a few days later he stated that he did not know at the time what he was saying, and that his only knowledge was derived from those who had heard him, and I am inclined to believe that he was speaking the truth. His appearance during the divining was remarkably different from that of ordinary days, and strongly suggested a semi-hypnotic state, during which he might well have had no knowledge, or only a very vague knowledge, of anything he said.[1] In his ordinary condition he professed to be ignorant of Malayalam, the language which he was said to use in his frenzied condition.

My ignorance of Malayalam, and the obvious difficulties of the investigation, make me hesitate before expressing any decided opinion as to the real nature of Midjkudr's condition when divining, but I have a very strong leaning towards the idea that the man was in a genuinely abnormal condition, allied to the hypnotic state, and I am disposed to accept the statement of the Todas that he was speaking in a language of which he had only a very vague knowledge when in a normal condition. It is, of course, quite possible that the abnormal appearance of Midjkudr was merely due to the exercise of dancing and to mental excitement, and that he knew perfectly well what he was doing and saying. I can but record my impression that there was something more, and I only commit myself to this extent in regard to the special occasion on which I saw Midjkudr divining; even if I saw a genuine hypnotic or semi-hypnotic phenomenon, it does not follow that all Midjkudr's performances are wholly, or even partly,

[1] For an account of what Midjkudr seems to have said and the consequent proceedings, see p. 392.

of this nature, and still less does it follow that the performances of all the *teuol* are of this kind. Nothing struck me more than the contrast between the frenzied condition of Midjkudr and the calm, ordinary demeanour of Mongudrvan, his fellow diviner.

In the case I have described the necessity for the intervention of the diviner arose out of the funeral proceedings, but it appears to be not uncommon for divination to be practised during funerals. Both Mr. Walhouse and Mr. Thurston have seen the process of divining going on at funerals. In Mr. Thurston's case he notes that the diviners talked in Malayalam, and offered an explanation of a gigantic figure which had suddenly appeared and as suddenly disappeared some time previously.

SORCERY

I met with greater difficulties in discovering the methods of sorcery than in any other branch of my work. It was quite certain that there were men called *piliutpol* (sorcery praying people), or *pilikòren*, who had the reputation of possessing magical powers, comprised together under the title *piliutvichi* or *piliutiti*. I was able to obtain the names of these people from several sources, but when I approached any one of them on the subject he professed total ignorance and usually suggested that I should apply to some other man, who, he said, was a real *piliutpol*. Occasionally someone would give me a fragment of information, but would impress on me carefully that he had heard it from somebody else and did not know whether it was true or false.

One or two men, who were certainly not sorcerers, told me that they hoped that I should succeed in finding out the methods and would tell them, for they said that the Todas who had no magical powers were always trying to find out the methods of the sorcerers and were never successful.

I was told by two men that they believed that a sorcerer, by merely thinking of the effect he wished to produce, could produce the effect, and that it was not necessary for him to use any magical formula or practise any special rites.

It was not until my last week on the Nilgiris that I was told of some of the magical rites by Teitnir, who had previously denied all knowledge, though he was said by others to be a sorcerer, and he knew that I was aware of his reputation. He was not a trustworthy informant, but his account was consistent in itself and was in agreement with fragments which I had picked up elsewhere, and I believe it is correct, though I cannot guarantee its accuracy with the same degree of confidence which I feel in regard to most of my information.

The following men were said by various people to be *pilikòren* :—

Kaners, Kudrievan, and Teikudr (63), Ishkievan (60), Keinkursi (54), Puthion (64), and Teitnir (52), among the Teivaliol ; Keitan (6), Mudrigeidi (1), Kiunervan and Usheidi (14), and Karseidi (8), among the Tartharol. Pushteidi, the elder brother of Keitan, was a noted sorcerer who paid for the belief in his magical powers with his life. It will be noted that magical powers appear to be fairly evenly distributed between the two divisions and do not greatly predominate in one as in the case of divination.

The power of sorcery was said to belong to certain families, and I was told that it was inherited. It seemed probable that a sorcerer only communicated his methods to his sons, and usually only to one of his sons, or if he communicated his knowledge to all, it was often one of them only who obtained the credit for magical powers.

We have already seen that when a man sustains a misfortune of any kind, he consults the diviners, and they find whether the misfortune is due to a fault committed by the sufferer or whether it is the result of sorcery. In the latter case, they say by whose magic the misfortune has been produced, and the sorcerer is then propitiated and removes the spell, the nature and details of the process varying according to the method of sorcery used and the offence which had led the sorcerer to exert his powers. Thus when Pirsners (9) fell ill, he consulted Midjkudr, who said that Kudrievan had bewitched him. Pirsners went to Kudrievan and gave him food, and asked him to remove the spell, and Pirsners became well soon after.

There are two chief reasons which induce a sorcerer to work his magic on another. One is when a request by the sorcerer for assistance has been met by deception. If the sorcerer asks a rich man for a buffalo, or for money, and the rich man refuses point-blank, it does not appear that the sorcerer proceeds farther; but if the rich man promises a gift and does not give it, or if he delays giving a positive answer and puts off a decision from day to day, it is a clear case for the application of occult measures. The other chief motive for sorcery is a quarrel with a sorcerer. The methods are different in the two cases. In the first case the sorcerer procures some human hair—it may be the hair of any one, even his own hair. It is not the hair of the man he wishes to injure because it would be impossible to get it. Five small stones are taken and tied together by means of the hair, and both hair and stones are tied up in a piece of cloth. Then, holding the stones and hair in his hand, the sorcerer utters the following incantation:—

Pithioteu Ön idith, Teikirzim Tirshtim idith; â teu sati udâsnûdr;
those gods power if there be;

an nödr nödr udâsnûdr; an kar warkhi peu mâ; an îr têrgi pûti
his country country if there be; his calf sleep go may; his buffaloes wings grow

pâr mâ; ath on nîr ud puk âthm nîr un mâ; on nîkh as puk
fly may; he I water drink as he also water drink may; I thirsty am as

âthm nîkhai mâ; on eirt puk âthm eirth mâ; en mokhm
he also thirsty be may; I hungry as he also hunger may; my children

ödrth puk an mokhm ödr mâ; en tazmokh kûtm pût puk an
cry as his children cry may; my wife ragged cloth wear as his

tazmokhm kûtm pûv mâ.
wife ragged cloth wear may.

This incantation was freely rendered by Teitnir as follows: For the sake of Pithioteu, Ön, Teikirzi, and Tirshti; by the power of the gods if there be power; by the gods' country if there be a country;[1] may his calves perish; as birds fly away may his buffaloes go when the calves come to suck; as I drink water, may he have nothing but water to drink; as I am thirsty, may he also be

[1] I am very doubtful whether the meaning of this and the preceding clause is correctly given in these words.

thirsty; as I am hungry, may he also be hungry; as my children cry, so may his children cry; as my wife wears only a ragged cloth, so may his wife wear only a ragged cloth.

When he has uttered the incantation, the sorcerer takes the hair and stones in their cloth to the village of the man upon whom he wishes these misfortunes to fall, and hides them secretly in the thatch of the roof of the man's hut.

It seemed that this method of sorcery is only justified when the sorcerer is a poor man, and the references in the incantation to the poverty of the sorcerer confirm this.

When a man who has prevaricated with the request of a sorcerer suffers any evil fortune, he consults the diviners, and they may tell him not only who has produced the misfortune, but why the sorcerer has brought the misfortune upon him and they may advise the sufferer to become reconciled with his enemy and to give him what he has asked. The man goes to the sorcerer, who is usually only too ready to take the credit of the affair, and it is arranged that he shall come to the village of the sufferer. Whenever he comes a third person must be present, who is called the *nedrvol*, or intermediate man.[1] The *nedrvol* brings about the reconciliation, and arranges the terms, and then the sufferer bows down before the sorcerer and performs the *kalmelpudithti* salutation. The sorcerer then utters the following formula while his foot is resting on the head of the man:—

â	*teu*	*udâsnâdr,*	*an*	*nòdr*	*udâsnâdr;*	*taned*	*peu*	*mâ;*	*term*
Those	gods	if there be,	his	country	if there be;	cold	go	may;	mercy

ai	*peu*	*mâ;*	*in*	*ír*	*kark*	*elm*	*ultâmâ;*	*en*	*mans*	*elm*
become,	go	may;	this	buffalo	calf to	all	be well;	my	mind	all

tülsvîshpini,	*tan*	*mansm*	*tüli*	*mâ.*
cleared from guilt have I,	his	mind also	clear	may.

Teitnir rendered this freely as follows:—

By those gods if there be gods, and by their country if there be a country; as water is cold, so goes my anger; as mercy comes, may my anger go; may his buffaloes and

[1] The middle room of a three-roomed dairy is the *nedrkursh*.

calves be well; I have now nothing evil in my mind, you must also have no evil in your mind.

Food is then given to the sorcerer, who also obtains the object for which he had originally asked. Later the sorcerer goes secretly to the hut of the man and takes out the stones and hair which he had hidden in the thatch.

In removing the spell the sorcerer does not mention the names of the four gods, but speaks of them as "those gods." The object of this is that the names of the four gods whom the sorcerer invokes shall not become generally known.

If any one quarrels with a sorcerer, the method adopted by the latter is different. He obtains a bone of a man, buffalo, or some other animal, or if unable to obtain a bone, he may use a lime. He sits, holding the bone or lime in his right hand, and utters the following incantation :—

Pithioteu Ön idith, Teikirzim Tirshtim idith; a teu sati udâsnûdr, an nɔdr udâsnûdr; ank pudra pîrsk pat mâ; ank ud ultâkhâth
to him will destroy disease come may; to him one incurable

pun pâ mâ; an kal muri umâ; an kai mûri ûmâ;
sore come may; his leg broken may be; his hand broken may be;

an kan pudri ûmâ; an ârs ulrsh an kûdûpel ûvɔdink
his eye destroyed may be; his house into his family to all

sakötam pâ mâ; âth enk sakötam kasvai agi ankm
trouble come may; he to me troubles did who accordingly to him also

sakötam ö mâ; an nɔdr udi ed ariken ɔ
troubles occur may; his country there is that we shall know those

teu udi ed kanken; i elv nels alaiu
gods there is that we shall see; this bone into the ground what happens,

ai ɔlkm alâ mâ.
that man to also happen may.

The only clause of this incantation of which the meaning is not clear is the penultimate, and the free rendering of this was said to be "as there are undoubtedly gods, we shall see all this happen"; it seems that *ariken*, which means literally "we shall know," is often used in the sense "without doubt." If he is using a lime, the sorcerer substitutes *trsimitch* for *elv* in the last clause.

The bone or lime is then buried in a wood near the village of the man who is to suffer the misfortune.

When the misfortune comes, and the diviners have discovered its cause, the matter is arranged by a *nedrvol* as in the other kind of sorcery, and it is usually settled that the sufferer shall give a one- or a two-year-old calf to the sorcerer. When the matter is arranged, the sorcerer visits the village of the bewitched man, who does *kalmelpudithti* to the sorcerer, and the spell is removed with the following words:—

teu udâsnûdr, an nòdr udâsnûdr; taned peu mâ; term ai peu mâ[1]; *mokh*
son

madrik an kûdûpel elmk; in mel en mans elm tülsvînem
children to his family all to; this after my mind all cleared from guilt

in uli agi âmâ; nâv put, nudri put peu mâ.
(as I) this well be may; disease leave, troubles leave go may.

The sorcerer is then given food and goes away with his calf, and later he goes secretly and takes the bone or lime out of the ground.

I have already mentioned that these methods of casting and removing spells were obtained with great difficulty and only from one man. This man, Teitnir, was one of the most intelligent of the Todas, but was not a very trustworthy guide. In this case, however, the account he gave was so consistent in itself and with the general character of Toda customs and beliefs that I have no doubt that his methods are those actually in use. It is more than probable, however, that other sorcerers may use other methods, and even that Teitnir's account is not a wholly accurate description of the methods of any one sorcerer. The other Todas had told me that Teitnir was himself a sorcerer, but even after he had given me the above account, he denied that he had himself magical powers, but said that he had learnt the methods from Ishkievan. I had been told of one instance in which Teitnir had practised sorcery on Teikudr (63), but Teitnir gave a different account of this event. Teitnir and Teikudr had quarrelled and in consequence Teitnir had been angry with Teikudr, a condition which the Todas call *murthvichi*. Teitnir belonged to the chief family of the Kuudrol, which is known as the *mani kudupel*; "it is a bad thing for one of so im-

[1] For the meaning of this see above.

portant a family to have *murthvichi*" and any one who has been the cause of such a state of things is liable to suffer misfortunes. When therefore some of Teikudr's buffaloes died and Teikudr consulted the *teuol*, these diviners gave as the reasons for the misfortunes the *murthvichi*, not the *piliutvichi*, of Teitnir. According to Teitnir, Teikudr was himself a sorcerer and there were reports that the recent death of Teitnir's wife was due to the *piliutvichi* of Teikudr, and just before I left the hills, I was told that the *teuol* had arrived at the conclusion that Teikudr had had a hand in her death.

The Toda sorcerers are not only feared by their fellow Todas but also by the Badagas, and it is probably largely owing to fear of Toda sorcery that the Badagas continue to pay their tribute of grain.

The Badagas may also consult the Toda diviners. In one recent case a Badaga consulted Mongudrvan, who found that the misfortune from which the man was seeking relief was due to the sorcery of Kaners. Kaners was, no doubt, propitiated by the Badagas, and it is probable that the belief of the Badagas in the magical powers of the Todas is turned to good account by the latter.

In some cases Todas have been killed by the Badagas owing to this belief. About ten years ago Pushteidi of Nòdrs (6), the elder brother of Keitan, was a very notable sorcerer, much dreaded by both Todas and Badagas. He visited the Badaga village of Nanjanad on the occasion of a feast, and soon after a Badaga child died and its death was at once ascribed to the sorcery of Pushteidi. Not long after, Pushteidi's dead body was found near his village, and there seemed to be no reason to doubt that the Badagas had killed him, but owing to the fact that the Todas held the funeral and burnt the body before they made a report to the police, the crime could not be thoroughly investigated nor the murderers brought to account.

One of the events which the Todas ascribe to sorcery is failure of the milk to coagulate. If there is much trouble in getting the milk to form *adrpars*, the *teuol* are consulted, and they sometimes find that it is due to sorcery and sometimes that some offence against the dairy has been committed. I have no information, however, as to the method which the sorcerer uses to prevent the coagulation of the milk of any one who has offended him.

The only other indication of Toda methods of sorcery came to me from a Badaga source. A Badaga *maistri* said that he had been given an account by a Toda. According to this account, the sorcerer takes three leaves of each of the plants which the Badagas call *jakalmul*, *pemmul*, and *tupumul* (evidently varieties of the *muli* of the Todas), puts the nine leaves in a new earthenware pot and buries the pot in a wood after saying certain formulæ in which he wishes evil to a given man whom he mentions by name. When the man falls ill and the diviners say by whom his illness has been produced, a reconciliation is effected and the sorcerer digs up the pot of leaves when the sufferer again becomes well. This information came from a Badaga source and I could not obtain confirmation of it from the Todas but it is possibly an approximation to the method employed in one form of Toda sorcery.

The Todas dread the sorcery of the Kurumbas more than that of their own *pilikòren*. The latter can be remedied, but the sorcery of the Kurumbas, called *kurubudrchiti* (*Kurub* = Kurumba), is much more dangerous and cannot be remedied. If it is found that a Kurumba has made a man ill, the only thing to be done is to kill the Kurumba (see p. 641).

When Kutadri became ill while he was with me in the Kundahs, the first suggestion was that the Kurumbas were responsible. Soon after this I went to Kotagiri, and Kòdrner, Kutadri's brother, who was to accompany me, said that as the Kurumbas were very numerous in that part he did not like to go alone with me and made a stipulation that while I was on that side of the hills I was to provide him with a companion. Mr. Thurston[1] describes a similar experience in which his guide was afraid to walk from Ootacamund to Kotagiri lest he should come to grief at the hands of the Kurumbas. In this case it seemed that the man was using his fears as an excuse, and in my case the fear may have been

[1] *Bulletin*, i. p. 182.

used as a lever to provide occupation for a friend, but that there was a very real fear of Kurumba sorcery I have no doubt.

It is easy to see how this belief in the magical powers of the Kurumbas may have arisen, or, more probably, how its existence may have been maintained. The slopes of the hills on which the Kurumbas live are extremely malarious, and it must often have happened that a visit to a Kurumba village was followed by an attack of fever of a severe kind. We probably have here a good example of a vicious circle. Whenever two tribes of different degrees of culture live near one another, the members of the lower usually acquire the reputation of being sorcerers. For this and other reasons they are driven to a less healthy district, and the unhealthiness of the district helps to maintain and reinforce their reputation for magical powers.

The Evil Eye

Various misfortunes may befall a man if any one says that he is looking very well or is very well dressed. It is also unlucky that any one should look at a man when he is eating. Similarly it is unlucky for anyone to say that a buffalo is giving much milk; she will probably kick her calf or will suffer in some other way soon after.

This kind of misfortune is usually called *kanarvaznudr*, which was translated, "if looking anxiously." It is also often known now by the Tamil name *konduti* or *kontushti* or evil eye. One of the commonest effects of *kanarvaznudr* is indigestion. When anyone is suffering from evil effects of this kind, he calls in one of certain people called *utkòren*, or "praying people," or, probably more correctly, "saying incantations people." Piutolvan (10), Keitazvan (15), and a woman, Sinpurs (7), are *utkòren* of repute. Any one of the male *utkòren* may be spoken of as an *utpol*, but I was doubtful whether this name would also be used for a woman.

The *utpol* rubs the belly of the sick person, holds one corner of his cloak in his left hand, and, putting some salt on the cloak, strokes the salt with a thorn of the plant called *pathanmul.*[1] The thorn and some of the salt are then put into the fire, and the *utpol* utters the following incantation :—

Pithioteu Ön idith, Teikirzim Tirshtim idith,	*tan*	*âv*	*kan*	*pudrs*	*kan*
	his	mother	eye	perish	eye

pudri	*âmâ;*	*tan in kan pudrs kan pudri ûmâ;*
be destroyed	may;	father

and this formula is repeated, substituting for *av* or *in* the names of the following relatives :—*an*, *akkan*, *nòdrved*, *mun*, *mimi*, *pian*, *piav.*[2] Then follows the same formula repeated, in which the names of various tribes are substituted for those of the relatives, as "*mav kan pudrs kan pudri uma*"—Badaga eye perish, may his eye be destroyed." The people mentioned are *mav* (Badaga), *pedr* (Tamil), *suti* (? chetties), *kurub* (Kurumbas), *erl* (Irulas), *panin* (Panyas).[3] The last clause is *möditi kan pudrs kan pudri uma*, extending the imprecation to the women of all the people already mentioned. When the incantation is finished, the remainder of the salt is eaten by the sick man.

The Toda *utkòren* may practise 'absent treatment.' If a man wishes to treat a sufferer from the evil eye, and is unable to visit his patient, he puts the salt on the ground and strokes it with the thorn of *pathanmul*, repeating the above incantation as he strokes. He then sends the salt to the sick man, by whom it is eaten.

The treatment in any case is repeated till it has been done three times.

If it is a buffalo which is suffering from the evil effects of *kanarvaznudr*, the *utkòren* use the same method, and the salt is eaten by the buffalo.

In the special case in which the evil is produced by saying that a man is looking well or is well dressed, the *utkòren* have a different method. They take a piece of the root called *kabudri*,[4] and a plant called *kwagal*, and squeeze the juice of

[1] The leaves of this plant, *Solanum indicum*, are used in the ordination of the *kugvalikartmokh*.

[2] For the meaning of these kinship-terms, see Chap. XXI.

[3] It is noteworthy that the Kotas are not included.

[4] This is the plant, *Euphorbia Rothiana*, used at the purification of the *ti* dairy (p. 136).

both into a vessel. An incantation is said, the same as, or similar to, that already given, while the *utkòren* strokes the sick man with the corner of his cloak. After the incantation the sufferer drinks the juice.

Various Magical Remedies

The *utkòren* also practise various other methods of treatment.

Headache. This is called *madersnûdr*, "if head aches." For this the *utpol* places his hand on the head of the sufferer, and says the following incantation in a low voice, so that the patient may not distinguish what is being said.[1] After the names of the four gods, as in previous formulæ, it runs :—

nâkherov	*mad*	*tathi kan*	*tath mâ ;*	*ker*	*mad tathi*
cobra	head	broken into pieces	not break may ;	a snake	&c.

kan tath mâ ;

and the same formula is repeated, substituting first the names of other kinds of snake and then of other animals. The following are the animals mentioned: *kûrûpatz*, a black poisonous snake; *putpob*, a variegated snake, which is called the foolish snake, because it will not get out of the way; *taverûni*, a green snake; *pâlipob*, another green snake; *uitch*, a kind of lizard reputed to suck blood; *antîli*, a squirrel; *kapan*, a frog; *tugûli*, a crayfish (?); *kadrmad*, a water animal of some kind; *mîn*, a fish; *îgal*, an earthworm; *nelnpüf*, an insect found under stones, *âpipüf*, an insect found in buffalo dung. After all these animals have been mentioned with the same formula, the names of Pithiotcu and Ön are again uttered, followed by the words *tathkhma*. The *utpol* flicks the corner of his cloak first against the ground, and then against the forehead of the sufferer, and then, if the man is sitting, he says, "*ateuk ir*," "sit there off!" and the man moves a little way from the place where he had been sitting. If the man is unable to sit, and is lying down, the words will be "*ateuk padr*," "lie there off!" or "lie a little way off!"

[1] I think it is probable that all the incantations are said in this manner, but I only had it specifically mentioned in this case.

I could not obtain a satisfactory account of the exact meaning of the incantation; it was said to mean "may the snake's head be broken in pieces, and so may your head be broken"—*i.e.*, so may the pain go; another rendering was "may the pain go to the snake's head," the latter being by far the more probable meaning. Three divisions of the incantation are recognised: in the first, snakes only are mentioned; in the second, things which live in the water; and in the third, things which live in the earth. The treatment is repeated on one or two days, if necessary, but it is never done more than three times, "because the ailment is always cured in that time."

Another condition treated by the *utkòren* is stomach-ache, which is called *püfkwatnûdr*, "if worms bite." The *utpol* places his hand on the belly of the sufferer, and after reciting the names of the four gods, he continues:—

kërs	*pûv*	*kâdkanm*	*kâl*	*mâ*;
kërs tree	flower	fallen as fall	down	may;

and this formula is repeated, substituting the names of various trees and other plants for the name of the *kërs* tree. The trees and plants mentioned are *pirzkh* and *kûrërs*, trees having edible fruit; *pül*, *kîl*, *kwadriki*, *kid*, trees from which bees get honey; *kab*, sugarcane; *teg*, coco-nut; *patm*, samai; *ners*, rice; *eri*, ragi; *kîtj*, potato; *perigi*, chillies; *melkh*, pepper; *kwatimeli*, Coriandum sativum; *kadrkh*, mustard; and *kîri* or *kîrsi*, red amaranth.

Thus the last clause would run: *kîri pûv kâdkanm kâl mâ*, and this would be followed by the names of Pithioteu and Ön. Then the *utpol* flicks his cloak three times, first against the ground and then against the belly of the sufferer, and says, "*ateuk ir*," or "*ateuk padr*," according as the man is sitting or lying down, and the sufferer moves a little from his place.

The names of flowers are used because the Todas believe that worms come from eating honey, and the honey has come from flowers. The flowers mentioned belong to four groups;[1] (i) those of trees which bear edible fruits; (ii) those from which bees get honey; (iii) those of trees or plants part of

[1] This distinction was pointed out to me by my informant.

which are eaten; (iv) those of trees which give pungent substances like chillies and pepper.

There were various other complaints for which the *utkòren* are consulted, such as:—*elptûksnûdr*, depression in the chest of a child when it breathes (*elp* or *elv* = bone); *tekhpkâdathvüdnûdr*, pain in the side; *kankpudithnûdr*, if anything gets into the eye; *erutûthtinûdr*, if cut or wounded in any way; *pohersnûdr*, if snake bites.

Each of these has its appropriate treatment, but the only method of which I obtained an account was the last. Certain men have a special reputation for the treatment of snake-bite. A cord is made of woman's hair and this is bound tightly round the bitten limb in three places. The doctor takes a piece of *pathanmul* and strikes the bitten limb while he utters the appropriate incantation.[1] The ligature is kept on the limb for two or three days and the incantation is repeated three times a day during that period. Anyone whom a snake has bitten must not cross a stream. If it is absolutely necessary that he should cross, he must be carried over it.

If wild animals attack the buffaloes, a procedure which closely resembles those already described is carried out by the *utkòren*. The procedure is called *kâdrkatinamûdr*—*i.e.*, "wild beast tie mouth if." It is also carried out if a buffalo is lost, and in this case the charm will keep the animal from injury by wild beasts. The *utpol* takes three stones secretly and goes at night to the front either of the dairy or hut and utters the following incantation:—

Pithioteu Ön idith, Teikirzim Tirshtim idith; pef pirzi kût terz nil
big tiger teeth fastened stand

mâ; kâkh kerman mûn terz nil mâ; padr kenai amûn terz
may; black bear face crowd red dog other side

nil mâ; pob teuv terz nil mâ; pef per terz nil mâ; pef po
snake erect head big hill big river

pâ terz nil mâ; pef podi mul[2] terz nil mâ.
stream big porcupine quills

[1] I did not obtain this formula.

[2] *Mul*, which means bramble and thorn, is here used for the porcupine's quills.

Then come the names of Pithioteu and Ön, followed by

âth *âvòdin* *kati* *vaiumâ.*
these all before tie keep may.

The *utpol* then takes a piece of ragged cloth in which he ties the three stones and hides them in the thatch of the hut. If a buffalo has been lost it will come back the next day, and even if it remains in the wood no tiger would touch it while the stones are in the thatch. When the buffalo returns the stones are taken out and thrown away.

All the remedies so far described resemble one another in that they are applied by one of the people called *utkòren*. The following remedy is applied by the sufferer himself. If a man is frightened in any way, as by a sudden noise when he is passing along a road, he will go home and put the hoe (*kudali*) and a stone called *neilikal* into the fire till the hoe is red hot. He puts the hoe and stones into a brass vessel called *terg* and pours on water. He then covers himself entirely with his cloak and remains covered till the water in the vessel ceases to bubble, when he opens his cloak, drinks water from the vessel three times, and throws the rest away.

There was some difference of opinion as to the use of the stone called *neilikal* at ordinary times. It was said first to have been used for making fire before matches were introduced, and there seems to be no doubt that fire was sometimes made in this way. Others said that the *neilikal* was used for sharpening iron tools. The only *neilikal* I saw was at Nidrsi and this was a large piece of quartz, and there seemed to be no doubt that this had at one time been used for making fire.

In one of the methods of sorcery which have been described it will be remembered that human hair is used. The Todas take the same kind of precautions about hair and nail-parings which are so widely spread throughout the world, but the reasons for the precautions differed from those usually given. I was told that the Todas do not ordinarily cut their hair, but the heads of children are shaved and adults also shave their heads on special occasions. The hair removed at these times is hidden in bushes or hollows in the rocks, and the reason given is that it may not be taken by crows.

Nail-parings are buried in the ground, and this is done in order that they may not be eaten by the buffaloes, for "nails are poisonous to buffaloes," who will die or become ill if they find them when grazing.

There was some difference of opinion as to what was done with the hair cut off at the ceremony called *tersamptpimi* (see p. 333). It was clear, however, that care was taken that it should not be eaten by crows, for if crows obtained any of the hair first cut from a child's head the child would suffer from shaking of some kind.

Both at the first head-shaving and at the *tersamptpimi* ceremony special bangles are put round the wrist of the child, and these are certainly of the nature of charms, for it is believed that the child would fall ill if they were not used.

The Todas believe in certain injurious influences which they class together under the name of *pudrtvuti*,[1] but I was able to obtain very little information about them, and I suspect that belief in these influences is largely of recent growth and due to contact with Hinduism.

One variety of *pudrtvuti* is the evil influence of *Keirt* (*Keirtpudrtvuti*) at the ceremonies after childbirth (see p. 326). Another variety is *kòdipudrtvuti* (*kòdi*, demon?). The Todas now adopt as a preventative of this evil influence a round mark made with ashes above the nose. If a Toda should suffer from the effects of *kòdipudrtvuti*, two remedies are adopted. One is called *kavkal wart atpimi*—*i.e.*, "*kavkal* (a stone) grind, pour we." I did not obtain an account of the remedy, but it is possibly the same as that already described which is used by a man when frightened. The other remedy is *kwagal atpimi*. *Kwagal* (*Polygonum rude* or *P. Chinense*) is the same plant which is used in one of the remedies for the evil eye (see p. 264) and it is possible again that this remedy is the same as that already described. *Kwagal* is also the plant used by the goddess Puzi to quench the fire of her son, Kurindo.

It will have been noticed that the formulæ recorded in this

[1] *Pùdrt* is probably the Toda form of the word *bhût*.

chapter have the same general form as the prayers of the dairy ritual. They consist of sentences ending in *má*, which seem to be of the nature of supplications that certain things may come to pass, preceded by the names of certain deities followed by the word *idith*, occasionally with other sentences allied in meaning to these. The two parts of the prayer are represented, but the first part, consisting of the *kwarzam*, does not appear to have acquired the same degree of importance as in the prayer. Thus the magical formulæ of the Todas have precisely the same general form as those used in their religious ritual. In the case of the prayer, I have pointed out that the actual words leave one in doubt as to whether there is anything of the nature of a direct appeal to the gods. In the magical formulæ, on the other hand, the case for an appeal to the gods is stronger. In all the formulæ, whether used by sorcerers to bring evils on their enemies or by medicine-men to remove sufferings of various kinds, the names of the same four deities are mentioned, and these four deities, Pithioteu, Ön, Teikirzi, and Tirshti, are undoubtedly four of the most ancient and sacred of the Toda gods. It is noteworthy that the sorcerer does not say the names of these gods when he is removing his spells, but simply refers to them as "those gods," and it is clear that he does this because he does not wish his victim to learn the names of the gods by whose power his misfortunes have been brought about and are now to be removed. This procedure leaves little room for doubt that it is through the active intervention of the gods that the sorcerer is believed to work.

There still remains the question whether the words of the magical formula imply anything of the nature of supplication, or whether the sorcerer is not rather using forms of words which will compel the gods to exert their powers in the way the sorcerer wishes. I have no definite information as to the belief of the Toda sorcerer on the point, but the almost contemptuous tone of the two clauses which follow the names of the four gods might perhaps be held to point to the latter conclusion, and to indicate that the sorcerer can use the gods as his instruments of wrath much as seems to have been the case with the magicians of our mediæval times.

On the other hand, it is not unlikely that the words, "*â teu sati udâsnûdr, an nòdr nòdr udâsnûdr*," may have originally had a meaning very different from that which the bare translation seems to give to them. A similar formula occurs in the story of Kwoten (p. 194) in the curse uttered by Kwoten's mother, which has the proviso, "*on sati udairnûdr*," which was translated, "if I have reverence to the village." This makes it possible that the translation of the words of the magical incantation should rather be, "if I have proper reverence to the gods and to the gods' country." The interpretation on page 257 is that which was given to me by Teitnir, but it is not at all improbable that it is wrong, and that a translation on the lines of that given for the curse of Kwoten's mother would be more correct.

The nature of the words used makes it clear that the remedies employed by the Toda *utkòren*, or medicine-men, are of a magical kind. The words are essentially the same as those used by the *pilikòren*, or sorcerers, to remove the evils they have brought about by their previous magical incantations. The same formulæ are used to remove ills supposed to be due to natural causes as are used to remove those due to the workings of magic. It seems clear that the Todas have advanced beyond the stage of human culture in which all misfortunes are produced by magic. They recognise that some ills are not due to human intervention, but yet they employ the same kind of means to remove these ills as are employed to remove those brought about by human agency. The advance of the Todas is shown most clearly by the differentiation of function between *pilikòren* and *utkòren*, between sorcerers and medicine-men, and we seem to have here a clear indication of the differentiation between magic and medicine. The two callings are followed by different men, who are entirely distinct from one another, but both use the same kind of formula to bring about the effect they desire to produce. It seems that the powers of the *utkòren* are less definitely passed on from father to son than in the case of the *pilikòren*. There is no doubt that these powers depend largely on a knowledge of the words to be used, and especially on a knowledge of the names of the four gods, but it is probable that this knowledge is transmitted from one old person to any other who may be likely to inspire confidence. It will be noted that a woman can practise the magical remedies of the *utkòren*, but I do not know whether this is a recent innovation. It seems clear that a woman could never become one of the *pilikòren* or sorcerers.

When discussing the formulæ of the dairy ritual, it was mentioned that one difficulty in the way of regarding these formulæ as prayers is that the names of deities are not uttered in the vocative form, and that this might be held to negative the idea that they involve supplication to higher powers. In the magical formulæ there seems to be a clearer case for the presence of a distinct address to deities, though it is doubtful whether this address is of a supplicative or compelling character. If there is a distinct address in the case of the magical formulæ, which every Toda would acknowledge to be used for an evil end, it is very probable that the words of the dairy formulæ also involve the idea of an address to deities. These formulæ are always directed to avert evils from and to call down blessings on the buffaloes, and it seems almost certain that for this good end the words imply not only an address to the powers of the gods, but also one of a supplicative rather than of a compelling character.

One distinction between the formulæ of the dairy and those of the sorcerer may be pointed out. In the latter the names of the gods are those used in ordinary conversation, *i.e.*, Teikirzi, Tirshti, and are not the *kwarzam*, *i.e.*, *Ekirzam meidjam*.

One of the most interesting features of this chapter has been the clear evidence given in the formulæ of the close relation existing between magic and religion among the Todas. The formulæ of magic and of the dairy ritual are of the same nature, though the differentiation between the sorcerer and the priest who use them is even clearer than that between the sorcerer and the medicine-man. It is probable that the names of the gods with the characteristic formulæ of the prayer are later additions to the magical incantation ; that at some time the sorcerer has added the names of the most important of his deities to the spells and charms which at one time were thought to be sufficient for his purpose. It is also possible, however, that the similarity of prayer and spell points to a time when the functions of priest and sorcerer were combined in one person; that as the restrictions which hedge round the life of the dairyman-priest increased, it became impracticable for him to exert his magical functions, and that there has therefore come about a differentiation of function, though the means used continue to show a close resemblance.

It may perhaps be said that the clear evidence of the supposed influence of the gods takes the facts which have been described in this chapter out of the realm of magic and puts them in that of religion. The Toda's methods of procuring ill to his neighbours are clearly in their essential nature of a magical kind, but their close blend with religious ideas is the reason why I have considered them in their present place.

OMENS

The Todas do not pay much attention to omens, but meeting certain animals is regarded as lucky or unlucky. The most definite instance of an omen-animal is a black bird called *karpüls*, which is said to be the Indian cuckoo. If a Toda is going on an errand and sees this bird on the left side, he takes it as a bad omen and turns back; if on the right side, it is a good omen. This bird appears twice in Toda legend. It warned Püv, the son of Ön, and in the last scene of the life of Kwoten, it appeared going from left to right. It is noteworthy that when Erten is interpreting the omen in this legend, he brings in Naraian (Narayan), who is certainly not a Toda deity, and this suggests that the whole incident of the omen-bird may be an accretion to the legends, and that the belief in omens has been borrowed from the Badagas or other Hindus.

CHAPTER XIII

SACRIFICE AND OFFERINGS

IN this chapter various ceremonies will be described which may all be regarded as examples of propitiation of the higher powers by sacrifices or offerings. We shall see later that in the funeral ceremonies buffaloes are killed, but it is clear that there is no idea of propitiation or atonement connected with this slaughter, the animals being killed so that they may go to the next world for the service of the dead.

THE ERKUMPTTHPIMI CEREMONY

In this ceremony a young male calf is killed and eaten. The ordinary name is *erkumptthpimi* (" male buffalo we kill ") or *erkumptthiti*, but at the *ti* the ceremony is called *ernudrtipimi*. I met with great obstacles in obtaining a satisfactory account, the men who had told me all the details of the dairy ceremonial denying at first all knowledge of any ceremony among the Todas in which a calf was killed or eaten. As soon as they found that I knew positively of the existence of the ceremony, they acknowledged that they killed a calf, but said they could not tell me anything about it. I succeeded at last in obtaining a record of the ceremony from Teitnir, and when I was endeavouring to identify the various parts into which the sacrificial animal is divided, we met with such difficulties [1] that Teitnir agreed to allow me to see the ceremony on the condition that I would provide the cost of the calf.

[1] Our final difficulty, the laughter over which seemed to overcome Teitnir's scruples, was in the identification of the spleen, which was described as "a little tongue."

Owing to the general reluctance to talk about this ceremony, I was not able to obtain such independent accounts from other people as I should have liked, but the details of the sacrifice as given me by Teitnir agreed with those of the ceremony I witnessed, and I have no doubt as to its essential accuracy. I had hoped to have obtained independent evidence on some doubtful features at the end of my visit, but these hopes were entirely frustrated by the death of Teitnir's wife a few days after the ceremony which had been performed for my benefit, her death being generally ascribed to the anger of the gods because the secrets of *erkumptthpimi* had been revealed. After I had left the hills, however, Samuel succeeded in obtaining information on several doubtful points, and was given an independent account which entirely confirmed the accuracy of the proceedings which he had witnessed at the same time as myself.

The ceremony is performed both at the ordinary village and at the *ti* dairy. At the *ti* there is no doubt that it is performed three times a year, but there was much discrepancy in the accounts of its frequency at the village. According to some, the sacrifice only takes place once a year at each village in October, soon after the ceremony of *teutütusthchi*, to be described later in this chapter. According to others, the ceremony is performed whenever the people have a suitable male calf to sacrifice. During the ten years that my interpreter, Samuel, had been living among the Todas, he had come to the conclusion that the ceremony is performed fairly often, his opinion being based on chance remarks made by the children. I think there is very little doubt that a calf is now killed in each village more often than once a year, and the ceremony at which I was present was almost certainly one of the occasional performances, though the time of year at which it took place makes it possible that it was the chief annual occasion of that village.

There was also some doubt whether there is an annual ceremony in every village for the people living in that village, or whether the annual ceremony is only performed in the *etudmad*, or chief village of each clan, for all the people of the clan. The true state of affairs at the present time is probably that the ceremony is performed at the Nòdrs *ti* in October. Fifteen days later it is performed at the other *ti mad* and at the chief village of each clan. In addition to these annual celebrations the sacrifice is performed on two other occasions at the *ti*, while at a village it may be performed whenever the people of the village have a suitable animal.

The place at which the sacrifice is performed is called the *ernkar*, and at Karia, where I witnessed the ceremony, the *ernkar* is in a wood nearly half a mile from the village at a spot where it is very unlikely that the proceedings would be disturbed by chance visitors. It seems that there is not only a special *ernkar* for each *ti* and for each clan, but that each village has also its appointed place.

The ceremony is performed on appointed days, different for each *ti* and clan. In the case of the Kuudrol, these are Sunday, Wednesday, and Thursday, and the ceremony which I witnessed at Karia, a village of this clan, took place on a Sunday. The chief officiator at the sacrifice at an ordinary village is the *palikartmokh* of the village, who must, however, for this occasion be of the same clan as those who are celebrating the sacrifice.

On the day arranged for the ceremony at Karia the *palikartmokh* was ill, and as none of the other inhabitants of Karia was able to undertake the office, an elderly man, Punatvan (53), had to be fetched from another village. On his arrival he had first to go through the ordination ceremonies for the office of *palikartmokh*, a lucky chance which gave me the only opportunity I had during my visit of observing these proceedings.

At the *ernkar* wood for the fire is collected, and over small firewood the people place several logs about three feet in length, so that the fire is of an oblong form. The firewood must be of one or both of the kinds called *main* and *kiül*. While some of those present are making the fire, others will be fashioning sharply pointed stakes of wood on which the parts of the calf are to be impaled. These sticks are called *ko*, and must be made of one of the following four kinds of wood: *avelashki*, *karkekoi*, *kwadiki*, or *pohvet*. It was said that exactly fifty of these *ko* must be provided.

The first stage of the ceremonial is to make fire by friction, which should be done by the *palikartmokh*. The only occasion on which I saw fire made by friction during an actual ceremony was when I witnessed the sacrifice at Karia, and on this occasion both Punatvan and his chief assistant, Pichievan (69) of Keadr, twirled the firesticks alternately, but though they soon produced some smoke, they failed to light the rag

FIG. 37.—PUNATVAN AND PICHIEVAN ATTEMPTING TO MAKE FIRE AT THE 'ERKUMPTTHPIMI' CEREMONY.[1]

used as tinder. My constant attendant, Kòdrner, was called in, and with his more powerful manipulations was almost immediately successful, and the lighted rag was carried by Punatvan to the heap of firewood, which was soon in a good blaze.

As soon as the fire is alight the calf is brought to the

[1] This and the succeeding photographs were taken in a badly lighted wood, and represent the actual ceremony.

ernkar, and the *palikartmokh* goes to cut a log of *tudr* wood and three small branches of *tudr* leaves. The calf should be fifteen days old and must be without blemish. Its ears must not be split, its tail must not be cut, and its eyes must be clear.

The log of *tudr* wood is for the killing of the calf and is about four feet in length and about three inches in thickness. Such a log is usually called *tudrkud*, but on this occasion is named *erkumptthkud*. The three branches of *tudr* must consist of perfect leaves. Such branches are usually called *tudrkwunak*, but on the occasion of this ceremony they receive the name *toashtitudr*.

The *palikartmokh* then stands in front of the calf, holding the log and leaves in his right hand. He raises the log and leaves to his forehead as a salutation, and then recites the appointed prayer. This prayer is different for each clan and consists of clauses in each of which the *kwarzam* of one of the villages of the clan is followed by "——*k per mâ*." Thus the first clause of the Kuudr prayer is *atthkârk per mâ*; *atthkâr* is the *kwarzam* of Kuudr, *k* is the suffix, meaning "to," and *per mâ* is "may increase" or "may there be increase." All the clauses of the prayer are of this form except the last two, which are *karsêram parsêram*; *Nòtîrzk êr usht mâ*; the first of which is a *kwarzam* of Kulinkars, *êram* probably meaning buffaloes, while the second means, "may the buffalo appear to Nòtirzi." The calf is supposed to appear to Nòtirzi and then to go from the hill of this goddess to the hill of Kulinkars. The complete prayers of Kuudr and Kars are given on pp. 288, 289.

The *palikartmokh* touches the head of the calf with the *erkumptthkud* (Fig. 38) as he utters each *kwarzam* till he comes to the penultimate clause of the prayer, at which point he begins the following series of actions. He draws the three branches of *tudr* leaves along the back of the calf from head to tail and then drops one of the three *toashtitudr* on the ground behind the calf. The two remaining branches are drawn along the back of the calf from tail to head in the reverse direction to the first, and on reaching the head one of the two branches is dropped on the ground at the head of the animal.

The remaining branch is drawn from head to tail and dropped on the ground by the side of the first (see Fig. 39).

The animal is then killed by striking it on the head with the *erkumptthkud*. The *palikartmokh* then takes up the three *toashtitudr*, and, taking them in his right hand with the log, passes them round the calf three times. In doing this, the

FIG. 38.—PUNATVAN UTTERING THE 'ERKUMPTTHPIMI' PRAYER. HE IS HOLDING THE 'ERKUMPTTHKUD,' AND ONE OF THE 'TUDR' LEAVES IN HIS HAND CAN BE DISTINCTLY SEEN.

body of the calf rests on its side, while the log and leaves are passed between the two fore-legs, then between the two hind-legs, round the hind-quarters, and forward over the back and head, so that they make a complete circuit of the animal, and this circuit is twice repeated, so that the log and leaves are passed completely round the calf three times.

The *palikartmokh* then proceeds to cut up the calf (Fig. 40), beginning with a complete incision round the neck. The knife used is of the ordinary kind called *turi*, but on this occasion it is called *ab*, or "arrow." On the occasion on which I saw the ceremony, the calf seemed to have only been stunned by the blow on the head and began to kick as soon as this incision was made. The animal was, in con-

FIG. 39.—STROKING THE BACK OF THE CALF WITH THE 'TOASHTITUDR.' PUNATVAN IS BEGINNING THE THIRD MOVEMENT, AND ONE OF THE BRANCHES OF LEAVES CAN BE SEEN ON THE GROUND BEHIND THE CALF.

sequence, vigorously belaboured over the testicles with the log of *tudr* wood, and this was repeated till the movements of the animal ceased.

The next incision is down the mid-ventral line; incisions are made through the skin above each hoof, and the *palikartmokh* then removes the skin of the whole animal except the head and feet, beginning at the right fore-limb.

When the skin (*tars*) is removed, it is laid on the ground with its outer surface downwards a few yards from the spot at which the animal is being cut up, and the *palikartmokh* proceeds to cut the animal into the following parts:—

Kwelthkh, hoof and attached skin and bones.

Mogâl, lower segment of fore-limb (metacarpus).

FIG. 40.—PUNATVAN AND PICHIEVAN CUTTING UP THE CALF. IN THE BACKGROUND KÒDRNER IS SHARPENING UP THE 'KO.'

Kemal, or *kemalth*, upper segment of fore-limb corresponding to fore-arm.

Kanòdri, shoulder.

Mêdrkwelv, trachea and larynx.

Tòdrthars, lower segment of hind-limb (metatarsus).

Pevutth, upper segment of hind-limb (leg).

Ûrûf, liver.

Putth, gall-bladder.

Pushk, kidneys.

Kwur, small intestine.

Tütkwur, large intestine.

Mulikudri, urinary bladder.

Agelv, pelvis, including thigh bones.

Mudri, sternum and part of ribs attached.

Nüdz, heart.

Püth, lungs.

Kwotinerûf (*kwotinûrûf?*), spleen.

Pâlvîr, stomach full of milk, called *pâlvetâr* when emptied of milk.

Mutelf, lower part of backbone with parts of lower ribs attached.

Nòdi, upper half of backbone with parts of upper ribs attached.

Mad, head.

The parts of the calf are removed approximately in the order in which they are given above. The *palikartmokh* first cuts off the four feet of the animal, beginning with that of the right fore-limb and the four *kwelthkh* are placed under the skin, one at each corner.

The next part to be removed is the right *mogâl*, and then the three other corresponding parts. Up to this point, everything must be done by the *palikartmokh* himself, but after the *mogâl* have been removed any one may help, and on the occasion when I witnessed the ceremony, several operations were going on simultaneously after this point of the proceedings, and it became difficult to ascertain exactly what was being done and the exact order in which the parts were being removed. The cutting up of the calf was performed chiefly by Pichievan, while the *palikartmokh*, Punatvan, occupied himself with other operations.

After the removal of the *mogâl*, the remaining parts of the two fore-limbs are removed and placed on the skin. The larynx and windpipe are taken out together, and in doing this the large vessels of the neck are divided. The body of the animal is then taken up and held over the skin, so that the blood runs out over the parts placed on the skin, and these parts are then moved about, so that they become smeared with blood, and are then placed on the stakes (*ko*), and each *ko* with its part of the animal is stuck in the ground on one side of the skin. Some of the other parts when removed are rubbed in the blood on the skin.

When the different parts have been impaled in this manner, the *palikartmokh* cuts from each part a small piece of flesh called *mîis* and puts the pieces on a stake. From the ribs and sternum, he cuts a part called the *tütmîis*, much larger

FIG. 41.—ROASTING THE PIECES OF THE CALF.

than the other fragments, and puts this on a stake. I could not ascertain exactly of what the *tütmîis* consisted, but it seemed to be the lower end of the sternum with some of the diaphragm attached to it.[1]

After cutting off the *mîis*, the *palikartmokh* begins to put the parts round the fire (Fig. 41), beginning with the *mogâl*,

[1] The importance of the omentum in Indian animal sacrifices suggests that the *tütmîis* might have been the omentum, or have included part of the omentum. At this stage of the proceedings, so many operations were going on simultaneously that exact observation became very difficult.

which are placed, one on each side, about the middle of the fire, but rather nearer that end at which the head is to be placed later. The *mogâl* must be put in this position by the *palikartmokh* himself, but the other parts may be arranged in any order. While the *palikartmokh* is manipulating the parts first cut off and placing them round the fire, his assistants will be continuing the division of the animal. When the liver is taken out, the gall-bladder is cut from it and thrown on one side. The intestines are removed and put on stakes by transfixing every few inches of their length.

The small intestine is placed on more than one *ko*, while, so far as I could see, the large intestine is put on one stake. The urinary bladder is thrown on one side. The ribs are cut through nearer the back than the front, and the sternum and anterior parts of the ribs form one part, the *mudri*. It was from this part that the *tütmtis* was taken. The spleen is put on one side in order that it may be given to a cat, and its name is derived from this fact. The stomach when taken out of the body is filled with milk and in this state is called *pâlvtr*. Its contents are poured out and it then receives the name *pâlvetâr*.

As soon as the cutting up is completed and all the other parts have been placed round the fire, the head is put on a *ko*, and this is stuck in the ground at one end of the fire and about half a yard from it, and the four *kwelthkh* are placed on the ground round the head. Some of the parts placed round the fire may by this time have charred, and they are turned round so as to expose the opposite side to the flames.

The next step is to take up the head on its *ko* and place it in the middle of the fire for about a minute, after which it is replaced. The object of this is to singe the ears, which the *palikartmokh* then pulls off. He also takes certain fragments (*mtis*) from some of the other parts and throws them, together with the ears, into the fire, standing at one end, the opposite end to that at which the head is placed. He then takes three charred pieces of wood from the fire, and throws them over the fire and over the head, so that they fall beyond the latter, saying as he throws each time, "*Nòtirzk per mâ, mañ!*" the last exclamation being the sound which is ordinarily uttered when calling a calf.

When the flesh is sufficiently roasted the *palikartmokh* eats the *tütmtis*, while the others present may eat any portion. When enough has been eaten, the remainder of the cooked flesh is carried to the village. The *mogâl*, *agelv*, *mad*, and *kwelthkh* are carried to the dairy by the *palikartmokh* and kept there. The flesh of these parts is eaten by the dairyman or by other men, but may on no account be eaten by a woman. The other parts are taken to the hut and given into the keeping of the women, and the flesh of these parts can be eaten by any one—man, woman, or child. Butter is often put on the flesh before it is eaten.

The Sacrifice at the Ti

The sacrifice at the *ti* is called *ernudrtipimi*, and is performed at every *ti* three times in the year. The first occasion is about fifteen days after the ceremony of *teutütusthchi* in October. The second occasion is about January, when the buffaloes of the *ti* migrate to the Kundahs or elsewhere for the dry season. The third occasion is after the ceremony of giving salt, which is known as *kòrup* (see p. 175). The ceremony may take place at any *ti mad* except Anto.

The appointed days are Sunday and Wednesday. On the day before the ceremony wood is taken by the *palol* and *kaltmokh* to the sacrificial spot, called *ernkar* as at the village. At Mòdr the wood in which the sacrifice takes place is called Turikipül.

The sacrifice may be performed either in the morning or evening, and takes place, in either case, before *kaizhvatiti*, the ceremonial pouring of buttermilk. This means that the sacrifice takes place during and not after the dairy ceremonial, and thus forms part of the dairy ritual. Each *palol* wears the *pòdrshtuni*, while the *kaltmokh* is naked throughout except for the *kuvn*. The *kaltmokh* arranges the firewood and the chief *palol* (at the Nòdrs *ti*, the *ti palol*) lights the wood with fire brought from his dairy. The calf is then killed and cut up with exactly the same ritual as in the village ceremony.

After the flesh has been placed round the fire both the *palol* return to their dairies, leaving the *kaltmokh* at the *ernkar* to look after the roasting flesh. Each *palol* prays as usual and takes buttermilk without the aid of the *kaltmokh*, and then returns to the *ernkar*, the chief *palol* taking butter with him. At the place of the sacrifice the *palol* eats the *tütmîis* only, first putting it, together with butter, on leaves of *kakud*, from which he eats. The *kaltmokh* eats part of the liver at the *ernkar*, and is not allowed to touch any other part of the animal unless given to him by the *palol*. The *mogâl*, *agelv*, *mad*, and *kwelthkh* are then carried by the *palol* to the dairy where they are kept. They are eaten only by the *palol* and *kaltmokh*. Some parts are carried by the *kaltmokh* to the sleeping-hut, and are eaten by the *kaltmokh* and *mòrol*; other parts are taken to the outskirts of the *ti mad* and given to any Todas who may visit the dairy.

In connexion with the *erkumptthpimi* ceremony, I was told of a device employed to induce the mother of the sacrificed calf to continue suckling after her offspring has been killed. Several days before the sacrifice the calf to be sacrificed and a female calf of about the same age are shut up together in the *kush*, or small structure in which young calves are kept. On the floor of the *kush* are spread some of the grass called *nark*[1] and some leaves of the *kiars*[2] tree. When these have been broken up and mixed with earth by the trampling of the calves, a handful of the mixture, together with milk, is rubbed on the backs of both calves, and this is repeated for three or four days. The object is that the mother shall not know which is her own calf, and shall suckle both, and continue to suckle the female calf when her own has been taken away. During the days on which the calves are shut up together the dairyman should keep *pon*, *i.e.*, he should not sell or give away any of the produce of the dairy.

If this device is not employed or is unsuccessful the skin of the sacrificed calf is placed on the back of a female calf, and in this way the mother may be induced to suckle the latter.

[1] *Andropogon Schœnanthus*, a strongly-scented grass.

[2] ? *Kiaz*.

When Teitnir performed the *erkumptthpimi* ceremony for my benefit, he did not succeed in getting the mother to suckle another calf and demanded 60 rupees [1] as compensation for the loss of milk which he would suffer till the buffalo had another calf. When he found that I had no intention of paying this sum, he adopted the second device just described, and this expedient was successful.

The *erkumptthpimi* ceremony was first mentioned by Harkness (p. 139), who witnessed the sacrifice. The details of the ceremony which he gives agree in general with those observed by myself. He calls the sacrifice "*yerr-gompts.*" A still more complete account which agrees closely with my own was given by Muzzy in 1844. Breeks mentions the ceremony, as is usual with him, under its Badaga name of *kona shastra*, and his account contains several features which disagree with those of Harkness, Muzzy, and myself.

I could obtain no satisfactory account of the origin of the sacrifice. Teitnir gave me a circumstantial story of the way in which Kwoto or Meilitars induced the gods to eat the flesh of a male calf. Teitnir stated that when Kwoto was visiting the gods in the form of a kite, and before he had tied down the sun (see p. 206), he killed a male calf with exactly the same ceremonial as that practised since, and taking some of the flesh threw it into the midst of the gods, saying, "I have brought the flesh; it is sacred flesh; I have partaken of it, and if your counsel is to be right, you must partake of it." At this the gods were very angry and blamed Kwoto, whereupon he said, "I am not blameworthy; if you blame a man who should not be blamed, why do you not eat flesh which should not be eaten?" Kwoto was then given the task of tying down the sun, and when he succeeded in doing this and had been acknowledged by the gods as their superior, the gods agreed to eat the flesh, and since that time the Todas have sacrificed a male calf, just as Kwoto did, and have eaten the flesh of the calf.

The truth of this account, given by Teitnir, was denied by every other Toda whom I questioned, and I have not therefore included it in the story of Kwoto given in Chap. IX, but

[1] This estimate included the value of the calf four years hence!

I think it is possible that Teitnir was right, and that the denial of the other Todas was due to their reluctance that I should know the real belief about this ceremony. Even if not correct, Teitnir's account is valuable as a record of an ingenious example of Toda reȁsoning.

At the ceremony I witnessed there was one feature of some interest. When it was found that the calf had not been killed by the blow with the log of *tudr* wood, the animal was belaboured over the testicles. This procedure had not been included in the account given to me before the ceremony, and I could not discover how far it is an established custom to kill the animal in this way if it is not killed by the blow. The interest arises from the fact that in the ancient Vedic sacrifices, the animal was killed by stopping its mouth and beating it severely ten or twelve times on the testicles till it was suffocated.[1] I have not been able to discover whether this method of killing an animal is still practised in India. If so, it has probably been borrowed by the Todas; but if not, this ancient Indian method may have been preserved by the Todas. I did not observe that the mouth of the calf was stopped at the sacrifice which I witnessed, but this was probably done.

The Erkumptthpimi Prayer of Kuudr

This consists of clauses of the form *Atthkark per ma* in which the following *kwarzam* of villages are mentioned: *Atthkâr* and *Ȯners* (Kuudr), *Kidnârs* and *Toarsȯdri* (Ars), *Moskar* and *Manêthi* (Ȯdr), *Keikȯdr* and *Karsülh* (Melkȯdr), *Kwoteiners* and *Kwelpushol* (Kiudr), *Tashtakhkush* (Pirsush), *Kwotirkwirg* (Kwirg), *Toarskâria* (Karia), *Pârners* and *Tîindeuk* (Miuni). These are followed by the final two clauses, *karsêram parsêram*, *Nȯtîrzk êr usht mâ*.

The chief features of this prayer are that the chief villages of the Kuudrol have each two *kwarzam* and that two *kwarzam* of Ȯdr, a Nȯdrs village, are included (see p. 647).

[1] Haug's *Aitareya Brahmanam*, Bombay, 1863, vol. ii., p. 85, note 11.

THE KARS PRAYER

This consists of the *kwarzam* of the villages of the Karsol followed by *-k per mâ*, as in *Mutashkitik per mâ*, but in this case only one *kwarzam* is mentioned for each village. The following are the *kwarzam* with the corresponding villages in brackets: *Mutashkiti* (Kars), *Karadrners* (Kuzhu), *Kiugners* (Keshker), *Külnkars* (Taradrkirsi), *Nersmi* (Nasmiòdr), *Eḍstârs* (Tashtars), *Keiikârs* (Kerkars), *Kuzhârmûdri* (Isharadr), *Pòḍshners* (Pòdzkwar), *Peleiners* (Peletkwur), *Tarskidt, Tüli, Sing, Keitaz*. In the last four cases the *kwarzam* and ordinary name of each village are the same. These *kwarzam* are followed by *ekîrzam meidjam, Nòtîrzk êr usht mâ*. The place of *karsêram parsêram* in the Kuudr prayer is taken by *ekîrzam meidjam*, the *kwarzam* of Teikirzi, but I do not know how far this is a special feature of the Kars prayer. It may be that the Tartharol have the latter formula. It is remarkable that the Karsol should omit *karsêram parsêram*, for it is the *kwarzam* of their *nòdrodchi*, Kulinkars.

Several of the *kwarzam* of this prayer are those of villages which no longer exist. The prayer thus preserves a record of Toda institutions which have entirely disappeared.

These prayers are also interesting as records of a number of village *kwarzam*. It will be noticed that in many cases there is a considerable degree of resemblance between the ordinary name and the *kwarzam*; in other cases the words are wholly different.

In villages on the west side of the Paikara River the *palikartmokh* says, "*Teikhârsk êr usht mâ*," may the buffalo appear to Teikhars, instead of *Nòtîrzk êr usht mâ* as the last clause. Teikhars is merely another name for Kulinkars. The reason for the modification is probably connected with the fact that the calf would have to cross the sacred Paikara River in order to go to Nòtirzi (Snowdon) on its way to Kulinkars.

I was unable, as usual, to obtain any information from the Todas on the significance of the *erkumptthpimi* ceremony, but the prayer offered before the calf is killed seems to make it clear that the idea underlying the ceremony is that of promoting the general welfare of the buffaloes. The actual words of the prayer are directed to bring about an increase to the various villages of the clan, but there is, I think, no doubt that in this prayer, all have the buffaloes especially in mind and that the meaning of the prayer is, "may the buffaloes of . . . increase!" The sacrifice of the calf would seem to be of that kind in which one is killed that the rest may prosper.

There is one feature of the sacrifice which might be held to be out of harmony with this suggestion—viz., that the sacrificed calf is a young male, and hence a comparatively worthless animal. The name of the ceremony means strictly "we kill a male buffalo,"[1] and it is possible that at one time an adult male was sacrificed, but even then the sacrifice would be of an animal comparatively little valued by the Todas. As we shall see, the animals killed at funerals are always female, but there is an obvious reason for this, as the buffaloes are to be of use to the dead person in the other world. Formerly large numbers of buffaloes were killed at funerals, and it is possible that it was found impracticable to use female buffaloes also for the *erkumpthpimi* sacrifice.

There is another possible reason for the use of male buffaloes. The flesh of the sacrificed animal is eaten, and it is possible that the Todas may have preferred to use for this purpose the less sacred male buffaloes, and not to risk any possible evil effects which might follow the consumption of the flesh of the females. It is probable that utilitarian motives have played the chief part in the choice of a male, but other more religious motives may have had some influence.

THE TEUTÜTUSTHCHI CEREMONY

This is an annual ceremony in which a fire is lighted at the foot of a hill by the *palol* and *kaltmokh*. The name *teutütusthchi* or *teutütusthtiti* means "god fire he lights." It

[1] I have some reason to think, however, that *er* may be used as a term for 'buffalo' in general, whether male or female.

is performed in the month which the Todas call Tai, beginning with the new moon in October.

The two *palol* and the *kaltmokh* of the Nòdrs *ti* perform the ceremony on the first or second Sunday after the new moon, and make the fire in alternate years at the hills called Kòti and Puthi. The two *palol* of the Kars and Pan *ti* set fire together at the hill Kònto on the following Tuesday. This ceremony is not performed by the *palol* of either the Kwòdrdoni or the Nidrsi *ti*. In 1902 the Nòdrs *palol* went to the hill Kòti on the second Sunday after the new moon (October 12th).

The hills of Kòti, Puthi, and Kònto are said to be chosen because they are very high, and have the highest *teu*, who are spoken of as elder brothers.

The *palol* and *kaltmokh* set out when they have taken buttermilk after the morning work, abstaining from other food till the ceremony is over. They take with them the *nirsi* or fire-sticks, some leaves of *kakud*, a piece of *tuni*, and some dried grass from the thatch of the dairy. Each *palol* wears both the *pòdrshtuni* and the *kubuntuni*.

When they reach the foot of the hill they make a heap of firewood. They then spread the *kakud* leaves on a stone and powder the thatch of the dairy on the leaves, and each *palol* makes fire with the fire-sticks and lights the powdered thatch. Then the *kaltmokh* says, "*Teutütusthtkina ?*"—"Shall I light the god (or sacred) fire?"—and both *palol* answer "*Teutütustht !*" Then the *kaltmokh* takes the lighted thatch and applies it to the heap of firewood. As soon as the fire burns well, each *palol* takes off his *kubuntuni* and, standing some little distance from the fire, the two dairymen pray, using the usual prayer of the *ti* with the following additions:

Kòr	*pǖv*	*mā ;*	*tein*	*pǖv*	*mā ;*	*pom*
Young grass	flower	may ;	honey	flourish	may ;	fruit

purzh	*mā.*
ripen	may.

After the prayer the dairymen and their attendant return to their dairies so as to be in time for the afternoon work.

The object of the ceremony is to make the grass and honey

plentiful, as the additions to the prayer indicate. The Todas told me that in ancient times they lived largely on wild fruits, nuts, and honey, and that then the ceremony was of great importance. At the present time the Todas in general seem to take but little interest in the occasion, but its former importance is still shown by the fact that the Sunday and Tuesday on which the ceremony is performed are among the chief Toda feast days, when the people of every village eat the special kind of food which they call *ashkkartpimi*.

OFFERINGS

The ceremonies which have been described are sacrifices or offerings which occur at regulated intervals. *Teutütusthchi* is certainly an annual ceremony, and it is probable that *erkumptthpimi* was also originally an annual ceremony, though now it may be performed several times in the year. Even now, however, there seems to be little doubt that on one occasion in the year this ceremony is regarded as of special importance.

The ceremonies which remain to be described are of a different nature. They are mostly occasions on which offerings are made to avert or remove misfortune. Some are distinctly of the nature of sin offerings, but are only made when an offence which has been committed has brought some misfortune on the offender. In these cases the object of the offering seems to be propitiatory and to bring about the removal of the misfortune.

In other cases the offering may be made with the object of removing a misfortune which is not due to any fault on the part of the sufferer.

The simplest kind of offering is usually spoken of as *kwadr kwadrthpimi*—*i.e.*, we give *kwadr*. The word *kwadr* probably means gift, but seems now to be often used in the sense of 'fine.' The *kwadr* takes the form of a buffalo. When a man gives a buffalo in this way it means that he undertakes not to give or sell the buffalo to anyone and not to kill it at a funeral. The buffalo is to be allowed to die a natural death, but so long as it is alive the owner has the full use of the milk given by the animal. The idea of this offering is that the buffalo is given to the gods, according to some, or to the Amatol or people of Amnòdr, according to others. I also heard it spoken of as if the buffalo were given to the man's father or grandfather (*pia*)—*i.e.*, as if it was not given to the Amatol in general, but only to the spirit of the giver's father or grandfather. It is possible that I have confused together two or more separate things, but so far as I could learn these cases resembled one another in that the owner was not allowed to kill or part with the buffalo.

When the man devotes a buffalo in this way he mentions the buffalo by name, saying that he gives it to the gods or to his fathers, and as a sign that he has done so he bows down before an elder and performs the salutation of *kalmelpudithti*.

This offering was made at the funeral of a child at which I was present, when the diviners found that a buffalo about to be killed was of the wrong kind, and said that Kuriolv, the father of the child, should give a buffalo. In this case the diviners said that a special buffalo called Perov was to be given. Kuriolv made a vow to give this buffalo and performed the *kalmelpudithti* salutation to Perner, the grandfather of the dead child. Another example of this offering will be mentioned at the end of this chapter.

IRNÖRTITI TO THE TI

Another kind of offering is to give a buffalo to one of the *ti* dairies. This is called *irnörtiti*, but must be distinguished from another kind of *irnörtiti* to be presently described. A man gives a buffalo to a *ti* when he has committed any offence against the *ti*. In one case in which I have a record of this kind of offering, the cause was the refusal of a man to become *palol* after he had promised to undertake the office. One of the results of my visit to the Todas was a wholesale sentence from the *teuol* that the people were to do *ti irnörtiti* (see p. 310).

The Tartharol may sometimes give buffaloes to the herds of a *ti* when they have not committed any offence against the dairy. This is done when the buffaloes of the *ti* have become very few in number, and this offering is also known as *irnörtiti*, and is given with the same ceremonial as when an offence has been committed.

The gift of a buffalo to the *ti* dairy must take place on a Thursday or Sunday. On the morning of the day the man making the offering, who is called the *irnörtpol*, abstains from food and goes to the *ti mad* with a female calf between one and two years of age. He may be accompanied by other men, usually those closely related to him. The men go to the outskirts of the dairy and wait there till the morning business of the dairy is concluded, each man carrying a green stick, either a *kwadrikurs* or *avelashkikurs*. When the *palol* has finished his work he goes towards the men on the outskirts of the dairy, also carrying a stick of the same kind, and as he approaches, the other men drive the calf towards him, and when it reaches the *palol*, he drives it so that it joins the buffaloes of his herd. The *palol* then gives food to the *irnörtpol* and his companions, who eat it on the spot, where they remain till after sunset, when they return home. If the calf given belongs to the *putiir*, it becomes one of the *punir* of the *ti*, but if it is of one of the sacred kinds, *pasthir*, *wursulir*, &c., it joins one of the sacred herds of the *ti*.

IRNÖRTITI, TUNINÖRTITI AND PILINÖRTITI

We now come to three kinds of offering, with their attendant ceremonial, which are of a much more complex nature. These are *irnörtiti*, *tuninörtiti* and *pilinörtiti*, in which the offerings are a buffalo calf, a piece of the cloth called *tuni*, and a silver ring respectively. The first two offerings are made only when one of a certain number of recognised offences has been committed, and in order to bring about the removal of some misfortune which has befallen the offender. *Pilinörtiti*, on the other hand, is usually performed to bring about the cessation of some ill-fortune which is not due to any fault on the part of the sufferer, but it may also be done in expiation of an offence.

One essential feature common to all three offerings is that

the primary divisions of the clan called *kudr* (see p. 542) here become of importance.

Nearly every Toda clan is divided into two *kudr*, and the offerings in the three ceremonies always pass from one *kudr* to the other. The offering which is given by a man of one *kudr* becomes the property of the members of the other *kudr*. At the present time the *kudr* is of no importance except in connexion with these ceremonies, and, so far as I could learn, it never had any other significance. There are a few clans of recent origin which have no *kudr*, and members of these clans cannot make the offerings. In other clans, one *kudr* has become extinct, and so long as no occasion for these ceremonies should arise, nothing is done to supply the deficiency. As a general rule, it is only when some trouble arises which may require one or other of these ceremonies that a redistribution of the members of the clan is made, and it is decided that one or more of the *pòlm* or smaller sub-divisions of the clan shall be constituted a new *kudr*.

The following are the chief offences for which the *irnörtiti* or *tuninörtiti* ceremonies have to be performed :—

(i) Stealing milk, butter, buttermilk, or ghi from the dairy.

(ii) Going to the dairy after having had intercourse with a woman in the day-time.

(iii) Quarrelling between people of the same clan on a feast day.

(iv) Quarrelling in the dairy.

(v) Going to the dairy after visiting the seclusion-hut for women (see Chap. XIV).

(vi) Going to the dairy after taking food with a man who has been to the seclusion-hut,

(vii) Going to the dairy after throwing earth at a funeral (see Chap. XV).

(viii) Going to the dairy after chewing tobacco.

(ix) Buying or selling buffaloes on the *madnol* or sacred day of the village or on the *palinol*, the sacred day of the dairy (see Chap. XVII).

(x) Driving buffaloes from one place to another on these days.

Going to the buffaloes or touching the buffaloes is an offence of the same rank as going to the dairy.

The general name for all these offences is *paliwörtvichi*; they are all regarded as offences against the dairy.

For the first three of the offences it is customary that the *irnörtiti* ceremony shall be performed. For the last seven *tuninörtiti* is more usual. For the fourth offence the punishment varies according to the status of the offender. If he is a *palikartmokh*, he usually has to give the *tuni* only, but if an ordinary man he may be ordered to give a buffalo. It is a far smaller punishment to give a piece of cloth worth about one rupee four annas than to give a buffalo calf, and it would seem therefore that the first three offences are regarded as more serious than the last seven. It would seem also that if a dairyman quarrels in his dairy it is regarded as a less serious offence than in the case of an ordinary man.

The decision as to which ceremony shall be performed rests with the *teuol* or diviner, but although a diviner usually follows the rules I have given, it seems that he may order otherwise, and if he does so I was told that his decision would be followed. I have a very strong impression, however, that if a diviner ordered a man to do *irnörtiti* for one of the more trivial offences, the offender would take further advice and consult another *teuol* before obeying.

There were several other offences for which it was said by some that a man might have to perform *irnörtiti* or *tuninörtiti*; thus, if a dairyman gave up his office on any but one of the appropriate days of the week he might be ordered to do *irnörtiti*, and the same penalty might be incurred if a man assumed office on a wrong day. Similarly a dairyman might have to perform one of these ceremonies if he spoke to a woman in the day-time, and probably if he broke any other of the laws regulating his conduct or made any serious mistakes in carrying out the ritual of his office. One occasion for *irnörtiti* was said to arise if anyone crossed the Paikara or Avalanche rivers on a Tuesday, Friday, or Saturday, but this is certainly a dead letter at the present time (see p. 418).

There was some difference of opinion about the penalty for buying, selling, or driving buffaloes on the *arpatznol*, or day on which the father of a man had died. According to one account, the proper penalty for this is that the offender should give a buffalo to his ancestors—*i.e.*, that he should name a buffalo which he would neither kill at a funeral nor sell to others.

In one definite case, however, it appeared that driving buffaloes from one village to another on the *arpatznol* had been one of the offences for which a man had been ordered to do *irnörtiti*. In this case, however, other faults had been committed, and it is possible that if driving buffaloes on the *arpatznol* had been the only offence a slighter penalty would have been inflicted.

The ceremony of *irnörtiti* was performed thirty years ago after the disappearance of the sacred bells of the Kars *kudr-pali*. In this case the diviners were consulted, and they found that the bells had gone away and would not return. It was thought, however, that the *palikartmokh*, Kakarsiolv, might have committed some offence against the dairy, or have made some mistake in the performance of his duties, and it was thought best that he should perform the *irnörtiti* ceremony, though, so far as I could learn, it was not directly prescribed by the diviners.

As we shall see, the *irnörtiti* and *pilinörtiti* ceremonies may have to be performed as expiation for revealing the secret lore of Toda institutions, but this is an innovation in custom for which I am afraid I was indirectly responsible.

It does not seem that the penalties with their attendant ceremonies are inflicted merely because it is known that a man has committed any of the recognised offences. It is only when some misfortune befalls a man which obliges him to have recourse to the diviners that the ceremonies are performed.

The usual course of events is that a man, his wife, children, or his buffaloes fall ill, or the buffaloes will not give milk or kick their calves, or the milk in the dairy will not coagulate properly. Whenever any of these ills happen the man concludes that for some reason the gods are angry with him and he goes to the diviners to ascertain the cause of their displeasure.

The diviners may find that the man's misfortunes are due to the action of a sorcerer, or that he has committed some offence against the dairy, possibly some offence which it is well known he is in the habit of committing. The diviners not only announce the cause or causes of the misfortune, but also give information as to the course to be pursued to remove it. If the diviners decide that an offence has been committed and that one of the ceremonies should be performed, the offender goes on the following Sunday to the dairy or dairies of his village and makes a vow that he will perform the ceremony which has been ordered. The following is probably a typical instance. Ten years ago Kòdrner fell ill and one of his buffaloes died. He and his brother consulted the *teuol*, who said that they had bought things (*i.e.*, given money from the village) on Mondays and Thursdays, the *madnol* or sacred days of Kars and Kuzhu. They had also driven their buffaloes from Kars to Isharadr on their *arpatznol*; there had been sickness among the buffaloes and they had driven them to Isharadr without thinking that it was the *arpatznol*. The *teuol* said they must do *irnörtiti*, and on the following Sunday Kòdrner went first to the *kudrpali* of Kars (Tarziolv) and then to the *wursuli* (Karziolv) and made the following vow at each :—

Ir kar	*ultâmâ*,	*pîrsk*	*ultâkh en*,	*irnörtkin*
Buffalo calf	may it be well,	illness from	be well I,	buffalo will I give,

or "May the buffaloes and calves become well, may I recover from my illness, I will give a buffalo."[1]

From this account it seems clear that the ceremony of *irnörtiti* is not a mere punishment for offences committed. If a man commits any of the recognised offences habitually and with the knowledge of the whole community, it does not appear that anything is done. Only when some severe misfortune befalls the offender does he appeal to the diviners to learn how he has offended and how he can atone for his fault. He gives the buffalo with the definite idea of recovering from the illness or removing any other ills which his

[1] From the nature of this formula it might be expected that the ceremony would only be performed if the man's wishes are fulfilled, but, in practice, I think it is clear that the performance is not conditional on the recovery of himself or his buffaloes.

FIG. 42.—THE 'IRNÖRTKARS' AT KARS. IN THE BACKGROUND IS THE 'WURSULI.'

offences have brought upon him. Giving the buffalo is clearly of the nature of a 'sin offering,' but the offering is only made when the sin has already had evil consequences and it is made in order to remove these consequences. Its object is atonement for an offence committed. It seemed that a man only had resort to the advice of the diviners in the case of exceptionally severe misfortunes. The act of giving the buffalo is attended by ceremonial which involves considerable expense to himself and great inconvenience to all the members of his clan. The expenses and inconvenience are so great that the ceremonies of *irnörtiti* and *tuninörtiti* are rarely performed, and in some clans it is many years since they have occurred.

There is one case in which the *irnörtiti* ceremony may be performed for a reason quite different from any of those given above. Owing to a quarrel which took place many generations ago, the people of Pedrkars (and probably also those of Kulhem) may not hold the office of *palol*. They may become eligible, however, if they perform the *irnörtiti* ceremony at Kuudr or Kiudr. It would seem as if they can only hold the office by expiating the offence committed in the remote past by their ancestors.

The Irnörtiti Ceremony

This ceremony takes place at certain prescribed villages, usually at the chief village of the clan, though when a clan has several important dairies the ceremony may be performed at any of them. Thus, members of the Kuudrol may give the buffalo at Kuudr, Kiudr or Miuni.

At nearly every village there is an appointed spot, usually marked by a stone or a group of stones, called *irnörtkars*, at which the ceremony is to be performed. At Kars there is a row of stones, shown in Fig. 42. At Nòdrs the appointed spot is a pool of water (Fig. 43) by the side of a gap in the long wall of that village.

On the day before the new moon following the vow to give the buffalo, all the women leave the village at which the

FIG. 43.—GAP IN THE WALL AT NÒDRS THROUGH WHICH THE CALF IS DRIVEN AT THE 'IRNÖRTITI' CEREMONY.

ceremony is to take place, and all the men of the same *kudr* as the man who is giving the buffalo must also leave the village if they should be living there. Their place is taken by men of the *kudr* which is to receive the buffalo. If men of both *kudr* are living at the village, those of the giving *kudr* go and those of the receiving *kudr* remain ; thus, when Kòdrner, who lives at Kars, made his offering, he and his brother left and went to live at another village of the clan, while Parkurs and his brothers, who belong to the other *kudr*, remained behind. If there is a *wursuli* at the village, the *wursol* remains at his post. If the *palikartmokh* is of the same *kudr* as the offender, he leaves and a new dairyman from the other *kudr* is appointed. All the men who remain at the village sleep in the outer room of the dairy—at Kars, in the outer room of the *kudrpali*. The *palikartmokh* does his dairy work in the inner room as usual and sleeps in the outer room with the rest.

The people live thus at the village for a month, no women, no men of the offending *kudr* and no people of other clans being allowed to visit them.

The actual ceremony takes place at the end of this month, on the Sunday following the new moon. On the Saturday the man, called the *irnörtpol*, who is to make the offering brings a female calf between one and two years of age to a wood near the village and makes a rough temporary calf enclosure (*kadr*), tying the calf to a tree. If the calf is troublesome, the man and his companions may sleep in the wood by the side of the calf, but generally they leave it in the wood and go to sleep in the village where they have been living. The calf must have no blemish, its eyes must be clear, and no part of its ears or tail may be cut.[1]

On the following morning a boy between ten and fifteen years of age is chosen, who is called *ponkartvaimokh*, the boy who observes the festival. It is his duty to drive the calf.

All those who are to be present take in their hands green sticks of the kind called *kwadrikurs*. All have their right

[1] The special mention of uncut ears and tail in this and the *erkumptthpimi* ceremony suggests that the widely spread practice of cutting the ears of animals may occur among the Todas, but I have no other notes on the subject.

arms outside their cloaks (*kevenarut*), and must have bathed in the morning and abstained from food.

When the time for the ceremony comes, the *ponkartvaimokh*, who is followed by the *irnörtpol* and other men of his division, drives the calf towards the village. The people in the village then call out "*Irnört! it vos!*"—"Give the buffalo! Come here!" and they go to the appointed place and stand on the dairy side of the *irnörtkars*, or other spot appointed for the ceremony, while the calf is driven up towards the stones or other mark from the side away from the dairy. The *palikartmokh*, naked except for the *kuvn*, and the *wursol*, with the *tuni* round his loins, stand with the people of the receiving *kudr*. When the *ponkartvaimokh* has driven the calf up to the place, he asks three times, "*Irnörtkina?*"—"Shall I give the buffalo?"—and the *palikartmokh* replies each time, "*Irnört!*" The boy then drives the calf across the stones or other mark to the place where the buffaloes of the receiving *kudr* are standing. According to one account, the calf is driven direct into the *tu*, but it seems almost certain that this is wrong, though it may be that it is the practice of some clans. The calf then becomes the property of the *kudr* whose representatives have been living at the village. At Nòdrs the calf is driven through the gap in the wall and across the pool of water in the direction of the conical dairy.

All those present, both the man who has given the calf and his companions and those who have received the calf, bow down to the ground, resting their foreheads on the ends of their cloaks (as in Fig. 44), and utter a formula different for each clan. At Kars it runs:—

Swâmi, Teikirzi, Târziolv, Kârziolv, Kârzû ultâmâ; ir kark ultâmâ; irnörtvuspimi,[1] *ultâmâ.*

Then all present go to the dairy or dairies and bow down at the threshold. At Kars they go to Tarziolv (the *kudrpali*), to Karziolv (the *wursuli*), and to Karzu (the buffalo pen) and

[1] Or *irnörtpuspimi*, "buffalo giving have we come." The whole formula runs, "Swami, Teikirzi, the *kudrpali*, the *wursuli*, the buffalo pen, may it be well; may it be well with the buffaloes and calves; buffalo giving have we come, may it be well."

bow down at the threshold of each, and then all partake of a feast. The food has been prepared by the dairyman, and includes the special kind called *ashkkartpimi*, which is eaten outside the dairy. Only the men of the clan who have taken part in the ceremony may be present at this feast.

After the feast all the men belonging to the *kudr* of the *irnörtpol* must again leave the village, but the only one of

FIG. 44.—THE 'NERSATITI' SALUTATION.

their number who is subject to any special restrictions is the boy who has acted as *ponkartvaimokh*, who must avoid women and must sleep in the dairy of some village until the end of the whole business. He is spoken of as being in the condition called *pon* and derives his name from this.

The *wursol* and the *palikartmokh* of the village at which the ceremony has taken place must stay there for another month, but the men of the *kudr* which has received the calf may stay there or not as they please. No women and no people other than men of the same *kudr* may visit the village during this time.

At the end of the month the people who have been occupying the village rub the dairy or dairies thoroughly with buffalo-dung (*palikâratiti*, dairy he purifies). All the people of the village then return and another feast takes place, in which the food is rice boiled in milk. Then the usual inhabitants of the village return to their houses, and if any men of the receiving *kudr* have come from another village, they return and life resumes its normal course.

The ceremony of *irnörtiti* may thus involve the removal of the usual inhabitants from a village for about two months, and the giving of two feasts, while the man who has offended also loses a calf. The Todas probably think little of the inconvenience of removal, though probably they are more troubled by it now than in former times, especially when they have to leave a village like Kars, which is, under normal circumstances, always inhabited at the present time. It seems that the inconvenience, together with the expense of the feasts, is sufficient to render the ceremony a very unusual incident in the lives of the Todas.

TUNINÖRTITI

The smaller importance of this ceremony as compared with *irnörtiti* is shown in several ways. The ceremony may be performed at any village at which there is a dairy, and it is not necessary for the people of the receiving *kudr* to stay at the village for a month before the ceremony is performed.

The prescribed day is Sunday, and on the previous day all the people of the same *kudr* as the giver of the *tuni* leave the village, and the men of the other division come and sleep in the dairy as before the *irnörtiti* ceremony. The man who gives the *tuni* is called the *tuninörtpol*, and he procures the garment from a Badaga, paying for it about 1 rupee 4 annas.

On the Sunday morning the *tuninörtpol* comes with some companions, all having abstained from food. The *palikartmokh*, who must be of the same *kudr* as the other men at the village, goes to the front of the dairy and one of the men calls out,

"*Tuninörtpol bon!*"—"Cloth giving man, come!" The *tuninörtpol*, who is standing at an appointed spot not far off, goes to the dairy, lays the *tuni* at its threshold, and bows down, touching the cloth with his forehead. While he is doing this the *palikartmokh* prays in the inner room of the dairy and the men staying at the village pray in the outer room. Then the *tuninörtpol* enters the dairy and is given buttermilk and food by the *palikartmokh*, after which he stays in a wood near the dairy all day and returns to the village where he is living after night-fall. The people of the receiving *kudr* stay at the village for a month, at the end of which they have a feast and then all return to their own villages.

PILINÖRTITI

In this ceremony a man gives a silver ring. The offering is differentiated from those already described in that it may be given to bring about the removal of misfortunes which are not due to any offence committed by the man. In some cases, however, the ceremony may be undertaken as an atonement for an offence. Kòdrner, my guide, had to give a ring to the dairy at Kiudr in the general distribution of penalties which followed my visit.

The custom of *pilinörtiti* is limited to certain villages or clans. According to some accounts it is only followed at the villages of Kiudr and Kanòdrs, noted for the special sanctity of their dairies. According to others the ceremony is performed by the Karsol at the dairy of Kuzhu, and at Nidrsi I was shown a small stone, almost completely buried in the ground, which was called the *pilinörtkars*, and this indicates that the ceremony was also at one time performed at this village. The ceremony is certainly of especial importance at Kiudr, and the following description is of the procedure at this place.

If a man has no children, or if he becomes ill, or if his buffaloes give no milk, he may make a vow to do *pilinörtiti*. If he is a member of the Kuudrol, the people of the *kudr* to which he does not belong go to the dairy. The offerer of the ring sleeps the night before in the dairy of his village and goes in the morning with one companion to Kiudr, taking care that no one sees him by the way. Both must go without food.

On reaching Kiudr the two men go to the stream called Keikudr[1] which flows between the dairy and the dwelling-huts, and after washing hands and face in the stream they wait there. The people of the other *kudr* who are in the dairy light a lamp and place it between the two rooms, and then one goes to the door of the dairy and calls out three times "*Pilinörtpol bon!*" The men at the stream are not within sight, but they hear the summons and come to the front of the dairy. The men in the dairy lay the *tuni* of the dairyman at the threshold and the *pilinörtpol* places the ring on the cloth and bows down, touching the cloth with his forehead, and prays as follows:—

Tânenmâ,	*târmâmâ;*	*atch*	*kar*	*tâ*	*mâ,*	*atch*
May it be well,	may it be well;	little	calf	give	may,	little

mokh	*tâ*	*mâ;*	*kar*	*kulâth,*	*kar*	*kuleiti*	*tâ*
son	give	may;	calf	not refuse milk,	calf	take milk	give

mâ,	*kar*	*nesâth,*	*neseiti*	*tâ*	*mâ;*	*opath*	*âtm*
may,	calf	not kick away,	stand	give	may;	once	meal

âthi	*punerd*	*kwar*	*arki*	*madi;*	*nâ*	*ârk mâ;*
it is	twelve	years	vow	will;	may there be	no disease;

nudri	*ârk mâ;*	*kazun*	*ârk mâ;*	*per*	*ârk mâ.*
may there be	no trouble;	may there be	no *kazun*;	may there be	no Tamil.

The free rendering of this prayer was said to be as follows:—

"May it be well; may my buffaloes have calves; may I have children; may my calves have milk, and may they not be kicked away by their mothers; as surely as I am shortly to take food, do I make my vow for ever and ever; may I and my buffaloes be free from disease; may no evil befall me; may there be no *kazun* (see p. 403) to kill me; may no Tamil or other outsiders come to disturb me."

The last clause was said by Samuel to be interpreted:

[1] This is mentioned in the prayer of the Kiudr dairy (see p. 220).

"Let me not get into trouble with the government," but it is probably much older than this interpretation would indicate, and refers to the former dislike of the Todas to any intercourse with people other than the Badagas and Kotas. "Twelve years" is a common expression for an indefinitely long time, and may be translated "for ever." The practice of combining positive and negative sentences as in this prayer is one which seems to be not uncommon in the Toda language. It will be noticed that several of the clauses are identical with those of the prayer ordinarily used in the dairy.

When the *pilinörtpol* has finished his prayer he rises, and the *palikartmokh* takes up the *tuni* and the ring and puts them in the dairy. Then the *pilinörtpol* and his companions go into the outer room of the dairy and take food prepared by the dairyman, after which they go to a wood near Kiudr and stay there till after nightfall, when they make their way home, taking care not to be seen by anyone.

If the ring is given by one of the Kuudrol it becomes the property of the men of the other *kudr*, but as its value is very small, only from four annas to two rupees, it is not divided, but is usually taken by the man of the *kudr* who takes the chief part in the ceremony.

The ceremony as described above resembles those of *irnörtiti* and *tuninörtiti*, in that the offering is given by a man of one division of the clan to the members of the other division.

Pilinörtiti may also be undertaken by a man as an atonement for wrong-doing, and in the only case of the kind of which I know, the wrong-doer, although he belonged to the Kars clan of the Tartharol, had to make the offering to Kiudr. In this case there was no question of the ring passing from one *kudr* to another, and it probably became the property of the man connected with Kiudr who took the chief part in conducting the ceremony.

Various unfortunate events which occurred during my visit to the Todas illustrate very well the working of the regulations which have been described in this chapter. One of these misfortunes befell Kutadri, who went with me to visit the Kundahs, the headquarters of the Pan clan. Mr.

Mackenzie, with whom I was staying, had shot a sambhar, and Kutadri joined others in making a hearty meal on the flesh of the animal. The next day he felt far from well, and searching in his mind for the cause of his sufferings, his suspicions did not fall on the sambhar, but wavered between sorcery of the Kurumbas and the anger of the gods of the locality, because he had shown me certain sacred features of the land. He was unable to continue to act as my guide, rendering my visit to the Kundahs largely fruitless, and on his return home he frightened himself into serious illness.

Teitnir, who had told me many things, but, above all, had dared to show me the *erkumptthpimi* sacrifice, lost his wife a few days after this ceremony. She had given birth to a dead child, and in spite of obviously serious fever, she had gone through a trying ceremony connected with removal to the seclusion-hut, and had walked a long way to this hut. Two days later she died.

Kaners, who had been my chief informant on the procedure of the *ti* dairy, awoke one morning to find the dairy of his village burnt. No human agency seemed possible, and no doubt was entertained that it was another manifestation of the displeasure of the gods.

Numerous councils were held, and the diviners were consulted, on this occasion Midjkudr and Tadrners. They found that Kutadri's misfortunes were due to his having revealed to me secrets about Pan, although, as a matter of fact, his illness had prevented his telling me anything of importance. It was decided that he was to give a buffalo to the Pan *ti*.

The death of Teitnir's wife was found to have two causes.[1] The first was that Teitnir had shown me the *erkumptthpimi* ceremony; the second was that he had gone with his wife to Lake View, the house of the Zenana mission, and had stayed there for several months, Teitnir having done this in order to avoid losing his wife according to the *terersthi* custom (see Chap. XXII). For the first offence Teitnir was to do *irnörtiti* to his clan, the Kuudrol, and for the second offence he was to give a buffalo to the Amatol,

[1] According to a later finding of the *teuol*, the death of Tersveli was due to sorcery (see p. 261).

his *pia*, or grandfather, being especially singled out among them. The latter penalty was paid before I left the hills. Teitnir devoted a sacred buffalo (*pasthir*) to his grandfather, and as a sign that he had done so, he did *kalmelpudithti* to Ivievan (52), one of the chief men of his family. The giving of the buffalo was followed by a feast.

The *teuol* were also consulted on account of the burning of the dairy belonging to the village of Kaners. They decided that the loss of the dairy was due to spontaneous combustion, "had burnt of itself," because Kaners had revealed to me the secrets of the *ti*, and, as he had told me chiefly the procedure of the Nòdrs *ti*, he was sentenced to do *irnörtiti* to this institution.

Kòdrner, who had been my general assistant, was directed to perform *pilinörtiti* to Kiudr; and the *teuol* also said that all the Todas were to do *irnörtiti* to the *ti* dairies because the elders had not intervened and put an end to the revelations which the people had been making to me.

Unfortunately these decisions of the *teuol* were only given out very shortly before I left the hills. Indeed, the divination appeared to be still going on when I left, probably in order to obtain further light on the troubles. I had therefore no opportunity of witnessing the various ceremonies which were to result from my visit. I hoped that Samuel might have been able to see some of them, but the only proceedings of which he was able to give me any account took place on January 5th, nearly a month after my departure, when all the Todas assembled at the *ti mad* of Mòdr, where the buffaloes of the Nòdrs *ti* were standing, and prayed to the *ti* to pardon them for the sins they had committed in revealing its secrets. After praying, they took food in the *pül* of the dairy, and did not return home till the evening. I was not told of the existence of any such ceremony of atonement by prayer only, and I strongly suspect it was an innovation adopted in order to avoid the expense of the general *irnörtiti* to the *ti* which the diviners had prescribed.

Several of the offerings which were thus ordered by the *teuol* seem clearly to have been of the nature of punishment. Kòdrner was to do *pilinörtiti* because he had helped me, and the Todas in general were to give buffaloes to the *ti* dairies. When I was first told about these offerings, I was inclined to regard them in general as punishments and to treat them as if they were social regulations. With further knowledge it seemed clear that they were distinctly of a religious nature, and were really sin offerings designed to propitiate the gods and bring about the removal of misfortunes which had come upon the offenders. I have therefore described these offerings in the same chapter as the ceremony which is clearly a sacrifice.

The variety of the *irnörtiti* ceremony in which a buffalo is given to the *ti* dairy is that which approaches most nearly to a sacrifice; the offered animal is not killed, but in going to the sacred herd of the *ti*, it may clearly be regarded as devoted to the service of the gods. The ceremony of *pilinörtiti* to the sacred dairy of Kiudr is again an example of an offering to a higher power in those cases in which the ring is given by a man of another clan so that the mechanism of the *kudr* does not come into play.

These clear examples of offerings to gods or sacred places are, however, very closely related to the other cases in which offerings simply pass from one division of the clan to another. It seems that we have in these offerings a good example of something which is midway between a social regulation of the nature of punishment and a definitely religious rite of propitiation of higher powers.

There are two chief possibilities. The idea of offering to a higher power may be primary, and the ceremonies of *irnörtiti*, &c., in which the property merely passes from one division of the clan to the other may be secondary modifications to keep property within the clan. On the other hand, the mechanism of the *kudr* may be primary, and *irnörtiti* to the *ti* dairy and *pilinörtiti* to Kiudr may be religious developments of what was originally a social regulation.

I have no information which enables me to say that one of the two possibilities is more probable than the other. The solution probably depends on the much larger question, whether the Todas are people whose religious system has developed out of the state of many primitive people where social regulations exist without anything which can clearly be called a religious sanction, or whether they are a people whose religious system has degenerated from one higher than that they now possess.

If the former supposition is correct, it is probable that the religious sanction has been added to the system of social punishment, which seems to be all which clearly exists in the offerings when these are kept within the clan. If the latter supposition is correct, it seems more likely that the whole mechanism of the *kudr* is a device by which offerings which should be made to a higher power may remain the property of the clan.

The fact that the giving of the buffalo or other offering is accompanied by prayer and the various restrictions of a more or less religious nature which accompany the ceremonial show that at the present time the ceremony has in all cases a very definitely religious character, but it is quite possible to regard these features in two ways, either as accretions to a system of social punishment or as vestiges of what was once a purely religious sacrifice in which the offerings were given to the gods.

CHAPTER XIV

BIRTH AND CHILDHOOD CEREMONIES

THE ceremonies connected with childbirth begin before the birth of the child. These ceremonies are only performed for the first child or when the woman obtains a new husband, so that they may, from one point of view, be regarded as marriage ceremonies. Nevertheless, I prefer to consider them here, and to leave the ceremonies more strictly connected with marriage till a later chapter. These latter ceremonies are far less elaborate than those to be described in this chapter, and may be more fitly considered in connexion with the social regulation of marriage.

At or about the fifth month of pregnancy, a ceremony is performed which is called *ūr patitth kaitūtitthpimi*, "village left, hand we burnt," or more shortly, *ūrvatpimi*, "village we leave," or *kaitūtitthpimi*. The ceremony is named from its two essential features; the woman leaves the village and lives secluded in a hut and her wrists are burnt.

When it is known that the ceremony is to take place, a special hut, called *puzhars* (Fig. 45), is built in a prescribed place at some little distance from the village, or if this building already exists, it is put into good order. The word *puzhars* means "mud-house" or "earth-house," which would seem to point to a time when a temporary hut of mud was used, but at the present time it is built of wood, though it is of much simpler and rougher construction than the ordinary house.

The distance of the *puzhars* from the huts in which the people live depends on the degree of sacredness of the village. According to Breeks, the distance is greatest in those villages which have a dairy of the conical kind, but it seems that there is no real difference between these villages and any other *etudmad*. In some cases when the dairy has a high degree of sanctity, the *puzhars* may be at an adjacent village; thus, a pregnant woman of Kiudr goes into seclusion at Molkush,

FIG. 45.—THE 'PUZHARS' AT MOLKUSH.

about a quarter of a mile away, and at this village the seclusion-hut (Fig. 45) is about a hundred yards from the house in which the people live.

I may mention here that the objection to the presence of a pregnant woman in one of the more sacred villages may extend to a time when she is not in the seclusion-hut. When I visited Kiudr for the purpose of testing the people of the village for colour-blindness, Sintagars, who was pregnant and was living at Molkush, was not allowed to come to the hut to be tested like the rest, but sat on the mound shown in the foreground of Fig. 7, about thirty yards away.

The features of the hand-burning ceremony as performed by the Tartharol differ considerably from those for a Teivali woman, and I will begin with a description of the former.

On the day of the new moon, the woman goes to the *puzhars*. The husband (or in his absence his brother or other near male relative) cuts six sticks of the kind called *kwadrikurs* and sets them up so as to represent a dairy with two rooms, which is called *pülpali*. He then cuts four bamboo-reeds called *wadr*, about eighteen inches long, which represent dairy vessels; two of them are called *patatpun*, and the other two *ertatpun*. He fills these with water taken neither from the *pali nipa* nor from the *ars nipa*, for if he touched the water of either of the streams, they would be defiled and their water could not be used. He therefore fetches the water from a stream at some distance from the village.

The husband brings the reeds half filled with water and places those called *patatpun* in the inner room of the *pülpali*. He takes the other two—the *ertatpun*—to a two-year-old female calf (*pòl*), and pours out the water from one reed on the left side of the middle of the back (*ñv*) of the calf, and catches the water in the other. He then gives two leaves (*kakuders*) to the woman, who makes a leaf vessel, into which he pours three times from the *ertatpun* the water which has flowed from the back of the calf. The woman raises the leaf vessel to her forehead and then drinks, and the man puts the two *ertatpun* into the outer room of the *pülpali*.[1] The woman then bows down with her forehead to the threshold of the *pülpali*, and the man takes up the sticks forming the imitation dairy and the four reeds and throws all away.

[1] It will be noticed that the *patatpun* are placed in the inner room and the *ertatpun* in the outer room. In the ordinary dairy both would be placed in the inner room, though in different places. The procedure of this ceremony seems, therefore, to resemble that of the *ti* rather than of the ordinary dairy. It suggests that we have here a relic of a time when every dairy had at least two rooms, one for the things of the *patatmar* and another for the things of the *ertatmar*.

The woman has brought with her a new earthenware pot called *mâtkûdrik*, into which she puts food (rice or grain) and water, and places it on a small oven made on the spot with stones. When the food is cooked, the woman takes two leaves called *pelkkodsthmuliers*, *i.e.*, leaves used in the ordination of the *palikartmokh*, and portions out the food on the leaves. She then brings two pieces of wood called *parskuti* (Eleagnus latifolia), puts them in the ground and covers them with a blanket. The two leaf-plates with the food are now placed on the two pieces of wood, one on each, and the woman asks *Pîrn podia, Piri podia?* (*podia* = have you come?) My informants could tell me nothing about Pirn or Piri, except that the former was supposed to be male and the latter female.

The woman throws the *parskuti* into the bushes, this procedure being called *tapi kûrs vutpimi*, "bushes stick throw we," and then makes a little roll of threads which is called *pashti*, puts it in the fire and burns herself with the roll in four places, two on each hand, once on the prominence formed by the carpo-metacarpal joint of the thumb, and once on the prominence formed by the styloid process of the radius. The burning is sometimes done for her by the woman who is to stay in the *puzhars* with her[1] during her period of seclusion. When the ceremony is over, the woman goes into the hut with her companion and stays there for nearly a month, till three or four days before the next new moon. While in the seclusion-hut, the woman is visited by relatives and friends, who do not, however, come near the hut, but stand some way off and say *kaitütudpatia?* ("Have you had hand-burning?") They leave a present of rice for the woman and go to the people of the village, by whom they are entertained.

When the woman comes out of the *puzhars* at the end of the month, there is a ceremony called *marthk maj atpimi*, "To the village buttermilk we pour." Early in the morning of the appointed day a man of the Melgars clan comes to the village and milks one of the ordinary buffaloes (*putiir*) into the vessel called *kabanachok*. The buffalo must not have

[1] I was told at first that it might be done by her husband, but this appeared to be a mistake.

been milked by any one else since the time it last calved. The Melgars man places the milk in front of the hut where the woman usually lives, and then goes away, and the milk is taken by the people of the village. In the evening, after the day's work is over and the buffaloes are shut up for the night, a woman is chosen who has had no contact with the secluded woman, and she takes the milk drawn by the Melgars man to the *puzhars*, together with the leaves of the kind called *parsers*. She pours out the milk three times into these leaves and gives to the pregnant woman to drink. The latter has previously bathed and put on a new mantle, and after drinking she returns to the ordinary hut and may resume her household work.

The milking is done by a Melgars man for all the Tarthar clans except that of Kwòdrdoni, where the buffalo is milked by a man of that clan. I do not know why this clan forms an exception to the general rule, but Kwòdrdoni is one of the most remote Toda villages, and it is possible[1] that the difficulty of getting a Melgars man to come to them has led the people to do this part of the ceremony themselves.

For fifteen days after leaving the seclusion-hut, the woman must drink buttermilk procured from a Melgars dairy, and must take food called *peritòr*,[2] viz., grain or rice which has been cooked in Melgars buttermilk. At the end of the fifteen days she gives up taking the *peritòr*, but continues to drink Melgars buttermilk for another fifteen days.

For a woman of the Tcivaliol, the ceremony of *urvatpimi* is much more simple. No *pülpali* is made, and the husband fetches two pieces of reed only, which are called *ertatpun*. They are half filled with water, which is poured from one over the back of a calf into the other as in the Tarthar ceremony, and the woman drinks in the same way, but this is immediately followed by the hand-burning, and the rite with the two sticks and the invocation of Pirn and Piri is entirely omitted.

[1] The fact that the people of Melgars and Kwòdrdoni are not allowed to intermarry suggests, however, that there is some relation between these clans which is the cause of the exception.

[2] This may possibly be a corruption of *perithtòr*.

The Teivali ceremony on coming out of the *puzhars* takes place in the early morning. A man (not the husband) fetches water from the *ars nipa* in a brass vessel called *achok*. He takes the vessel to a pregnant buffalo and tries to milk the buffalo over the vessel of water. Although no milk comes, the attempt is supposed to convert the water in the vessel into milk. The woman then leaves the seclusion-hut and is given two leaves (*parsers*), of which she makes a leaf cup, and the man pours the water which is supposed to be milk into the cup three times, and the woman drinks each time after raising the cup to her forehead. The woman and her companion then go to another special hut, called *aliars*, and stay there for a week, or if there is in the village a house of the kind called *merkalars* (see p. 29), the woman may go to the hinder part of this house instead of to the *aliars*, but in this case all the household things have to be removed from the *merkalars*.

At the end of the week in the *aliars* or *merkalars*, there follows the ceremony called *marthk maj atpimi*. Early in the morning the *palikartmokh* brings *penmaj* (*i.e.*, butter and buttermilk) in an earthenware pot and two firebrands (*tütkuli*) to the front of the hut, puts the brands on the ground, lays the pot on them for a time, and then puts the pot on the raised platform in front of the hut. He then goes away, and a woman brings a brass vessel (*terg*) and transfers the butter and buttermilk to the *terg*, and gives it to the woman, who drinks and goes to the ordinary hut.

While the woman is in the *aliars* or *merkalars*, she is not confined to the dwelling as when in the *puzhars*, but may go about. She must not, however, do any household work, nor go to any other village, nor to the ordinary huts of her own village. If in the hinder part of the *merkalars*, she must not go to the fore part of the house.

Thus the ritual of the Tartharol differs greatly from that of the Teivaliol in these ceremonies. The rite of making an artificial dairy is entirely omitted by the Teivaliol, and, as we shall see later, it is also omitted in a similar ceremony performed after childbirth, though the pieces of reed used to pour water over the calf are named after dairy vessels in both cases. I could obtain no explanation of the difference of procedure, nor of the omission of the invocation of Pirn and Piri by the Teivali division. It is possible that this latter ceremony has been borrowed, but if so, there is no obvious reason why it should have been borrowed by one division, and not by the other.

In the ceremonies accompaning the return to ordinary life, it is perhaps natural that the Melgars man should only take part in the proceedings of his own division. The other chief difference in the procedure of the two divisions is that the return takes place in two stages among the Teivaliol, while the Tarthar woman goes directly from the *puzhars* to the ordinary hut. I was told that the difference was connected with the fact that the Tarthar women drank milk, whilst the Teivali women did not, but I could not discover why this should lead to a difference of procedure.

The Pursütpimi Ceremony

About the seventh month of pregnancy a ceremony is performed, which is called *pursütpimi*, "bow (and arrow) we touch." This ceremony begins on the evening before the day of the new moon. The pregnant woman goes into a wood about a furlong from the village at which she is living. She is accompanied by her husband, or if she has several, by the husband who is to give the bow and arrow. The husband cuts a triangular niche in a tree,[1] of which the Toda name is *kers*. The niche is large enough to contain a lamp, and is made a few feet above the ground, so that it is about on a level with the eyes of the woman when she is sitting on the ground. Ghi is then put in an earthenware lamp, which is lighted and placed in the niche. Some sort of arrangement is made on the tree to provide a covering under which the woman is later to sit, but I could not satisfy myself exactly how this is done. Husband and wife then go to find the wood called *puv*,[2] and the grass called *nark*.[3] A bow (*purs*) is made from the wood by stripping off a piece of bark and stretching it across the bent stick so as to

[1] *Eugenia Arnottiana.* [2] *Sophora glauca.*
[3] *Andropogon schœnanthus.*

form the string of the bow.[1] The grass is put in the little artificial bow so as to resemble an arrow.

The husband and wife return to the tree with the bow and arrow, and the relatives of the pair come to the spot. The father of the woman promises a young female calf, the off-spring of a given buffalo, which he names, saying after the the name *pòl todein*, or "calf I have given"; thus, *Kemars pòl todein* would mean, "I have given a calf, the daughter of Kemars."[2] Then husband and wife salute certain people by bowing before them and raising their feet to the forehead (*kalmelpudithti*). The wife salutes in this way all her male relatives and those of her husband older than herself—*i.e.*, she salutes those whom she would salute in this way under normal circumstances (see Chap. XXI). The husband salutes all the male[3] relatives of his wife, irrespective of their being older or younger than himself.

The wife then sits down beneath the tree in front of the lamp, and the husband gives her the imitation bow and arrow. In doing so he says the *kwarzam* of his village followed by the words "*Teikirzi Tirsk, pursvat!*"—*i.e.*, "To Teikirzi and Tirshti, hold the bow and arrow!" The wife replies, "*purs iveru?*"—"What is the name of the bow and arrow?"—and the husband then gives the name of the bow and arrow, which is different for each clan. The question and answer are each time repeated so that they are said three times. The formulæ repeated on this occasion differ for each clan in the *kwarzam* of the village and in the name of the bow. For the Kuudrol the latter was *pursgârûv*, so that a Kuudr man would first say, "*Atthkar Teikirzi Tirsk pursvat*," and in answer to his wife's question he would answer, "*Pursgârûv*." The only clan which does not say the *kwarzam* of the village is that of Nòdrs, where only the names of the gods are mentioned.

I only obtained the special names of the bow from three clans—those of Kuudr, Kars and Taradr. That of

[1] See the bow in the hand of the boy in Fig. 57. This bow is the same as that used in the *pursütpimi* ceremony.

[2] The buffalo given in this way is called *pulkwadr*, or bow and arrow gift.

[3] My notes do not make it absolutely clear as to whether he may not also salute the female relatives of his wife, but I do not think that he does so.

Kuudr has already been given; the name of the Kars bow is *pulkiükhm* and that of Taradr *pursüdsk*. When the husband gives the bow and arrow to his wife, she raises it to her forehead and then, holding it in her right hand, turns to gaze at the lamp in the tree. She looks for an hour or until the lamp goes out, and then all present[1] go to the village for food, except the husband and wife. The man makes a fireplace, lights a fire and cooks jaggery and rice in a new pot, using only ghi, and not butter, to mix the rice, and while he is doing this his wife ties up certain kinds of food in a cloth and puts the bundle under the tree. This food includes rice, ragi, barley, wheat, the grain (?) called *kirsi* (see p. 266), some jaggery and salt. Some pieces of honeycomb are also placed on leaves, which are then thrown away. When the food cooked by the man is ready both husband and wife eat together.

Later the relatives return from the village and all pass the night in the wood, the relatives keeping at some distance from the married pair. At daybreak on the following day, the day of the new moon, all return to the village and feast, food being given to all visitors.

Several of those who have described this ceremony have included in the description an account of "tying the *tali*."[2] So far as I could ascertain nothing of the kind is done. I inquired into the point many times and all agreed that it formed no part of the Toda ceremony and that its equivalent was the giving of the bow and arrow. More than one man spoke of the *pursütpimi* ceremony as "tying the *tali*," but the latter expression is merely the equivalent of "marriage ceremony," and the very man who used this expression denied vehemently that tying the *tali* or anything else round

[1] According to a recent account given to me by Mr. Thurston, the people leave the spot about six o'clock in the evening. The time is determined by the opening of the flowers of *Ænothera tetraptera*, which is called by the Todas *ār mani püv*, or six o'clock flower. This flower is a garden escape, so that this special practice must be recent, but it suggests that the general practice of telling the time of day by means of flowers may be an old Toda custom.

[2] Mr. Natesa Sastri (*Madras Mail*, August 28th, 1894) states that the bow and arrow are tied round the neck of the woman, so that they definitely take the place of the *tali*.

the neck of the woman formed any part of the Toda ceremony.

It seemed, however, that after *pursütpimi* the woman is allowed to resume her ornaments, which she has been prohibited from wearing up to this time, and it is possible that this resumption of her ornaments may have been mistaken for "tying the *tali.*" It seemed clear, however, that the ornaments were not put on by the husband, nor did the resumption of the ornaments partake in any way of a ceremonial character.

As I hoped to have a chance of witnessing this ceremony during my visit, I did not thresh out the details of *pursütpimi* as thoroughly as those of most other ceremonies and my account is not as complete as I could wish.

The ceremony of *pursütpimi* is of the greatest importance from the social point of view and, as we shall see later, the fatherhood of the child depends entirely upon it. The man who gives the bow and arrow is the father of the child for all social purposes, and is regarded as such even if he has had nothing to do with the woman before the ceremony.

The ceremony must always be performed during the first pregnancy of a woman and it takes place in any succeeding pregnancy only when it is desired for any reason to alter the fatherhood of the children. One of the most serious scandals in Toda society is the birth of a child when the mother has not been through this ceremony.

Both the pregnancy ceremonies are performed at the first funeral of an unmarried or barren woman. In the case of an unmarried girl the bow and arrow are given at the *pursütpimi* ceremony by a *matchuni* of the deceased—*i.e.*, by a relative whom the deceased girl might herself have married. The hand-burning of the *urvatpimi* ceremony is usually performed by a woman of the same clan as the deceased.

Since the ceremonies are only performed at the first pregnancy, or when it is desired to change the fatherhood of a child, it seems clear that they closely resemble marriage ceremonies. They would seem to be either marriage ceremonies which have been postponed till shortly before the birth of the first child,[1] or, what is more probable, pregnancy ceremonies resembling those customary in India, which have acquired social significance and have come to resemble marriage ceremonies. But the numerous ceremonies which are performed during pregnancy by the Hindus take place during every pregnancy and are, therefore, sharply differentiated from the Toda rites.

CHILDBIRTH

When the woman returns from the seclusion-hut after the *urvatpimi* ceremony she lives in her usual home with the rest of the family and does her usual work, and she is delivered there. It seemed that any one might be present, and that there was no special ceremony connected with delivery.

During delivery, the woman kneels with her head resting on the breast of a man, usually her husband, who clasps his hands behind her neck. She is tended by a woman, usually by one noted for skill in these matters. If there is much delay, all men and women present lay their hands on the head of the woman and say:

"*Swâmi maz vûrmâ; swâmi pûdikan termâ.*"

If this is not efficacious a man brings water in a vessel and prays, stirring the water with a piece of grass of the kind called *kakar*. When the prayer is finished, the man sprinkles the water over the woman.

The cord (*pekû*) is cut with a knife, being held down with a stick while it is being cut.

The afterbirth is called *naj* or *pekûkûdri*. If there is delay in its delivery, a medicine called *najmad* is given which is procured from the Badagas. The afterbirth is buried on the day on which the woman goes to the seclusion-hut, a few days

[1] This seems to have occurred in a similar ceremony practised by the Badagas, among whom it is said that a woman is not fully considered a wife till about the seventh month of the first pregnancy, when a cord is put round her neck by the husband and the legal marriage becomes complete. (See Thurston, *Bull.* IV., p. 167.)

after delivery. If the child is still-born its body is buried at the same time.

A caul is named *kwadri* (umbrella), but no importance is attached to it, nor is it kept.

Seclusion after Childbirth

Two or three days after childbirth the mother and child go to the seclusion-hut, or *puzhars*, the same structure being used as after the hand-burning ceremony. Various rites are performed, both when going to and leaving the seclusion-hut, and these have many points in common with those which take place before and after the hand-burning. As in that case, the procedure for the Tartharol differs considerably from that of the Teivaliol.

The general name for the ceremony of going to the *puzhars* is *pòlk pòtha nir utpimi*—"to the calf back (or hind quarters) water we pour," from one of the chief features of the proceedings. The ceremony takes place either in the early morning or in the evening.

The woman who is to be secluded, whether she be Tarthar or Teivali, rubs ashes on her head and face (*pûthi adipimi*, ashes we rub), and comes out of the ordinary hut in which she has been living since the delivery. She holds over her head a branch of the 'Nilgiri holly,'[1] which has spreading leaves so that it resembles an umbrella; this leafy umbrella is called *tòrikwadr*, and the act is called *tòrikwadr patipimi*, "we hold the umbrella." The head is also covered with the *putkuli*. From the moment she leaves the hut the woman is very careful to keep her face turned away from the sun, not on account of its noxious influence, but in order to avoid the star or other body called Keirt, which is supposed to be near the sun. The child is carried in front of the mother by another woman, who also holds a *tòrikwadr* to shelter the infant from the evil influence of Keirt. Among the Tartharol a small artificial dairy is made, exactly as in the *urvatpimi* ceremony, and four reeds are cut to represent dairy vessels.

[1] Called by the Todas *tòri* or *tòrimul* (*Berberis nepalensis*); its leaves are used in the ordination of the *kugvalikartmokh*.

As the woman walks towards the place where the *pülpali* has been erected, another woman lays on the ground before her a leaf of *kakud* on which she puts some threads taken from a *madtuni*—*i.e.*, the garment worn by the *wursol*. These threads are called *tunikar*,[1] and they are taken up by the mother and put in the string round her waist on the right side.[2] Water

FIG. 46.—TERSVELI SITTING AT THE DOOR OF THE 'PUZHARS' AT KARIA WITH HER FACE TURNED FROM THE SUN.

is then poured by the husband from the imitation *patatpun* over the hind quarters (*pòtha*) of a calf, so that it falls into the *ertatpun* just as in the *urvatpimi* ceremony. Before the woman drinks this water, three drops of it are put into the mouth of the child and a four-anna piece (*panm*) into its hand. The mother then drinks three times

[1] Possibly this means "calf of *tuni*."

[2] It will be noticed that the woman puts the fragments of *tuni* in her waist-string on the right side, while the various dairymen who wear *petuni* put it on the left side.

and bows down at the threshold of the imitation dairy, after which she goes into the seclusion-hut. During the whole of the proceedings she is careful not to turn her face towards the sun.

Among the Teivaliol there is no imitation dairy and, as in the *urvatpimi* ceremony, only two reeds are used as *ertatpun*. A fire is made on an improvised fireplace of three stones, and lighted by means of thatch brought from the hut,[1] and food is put on a fragment of an earthenware vessel and placed over the fire.

After the woman has drunk of the water which has been poured over the back of the calf, she breaks the earthenware fragment over the fire, saying, *Namavku*, "to Namav," this rite being called *Namavtur kwudrtpimi*, "to Namav we give." The woman then goes to the seclusion-hut, being assisted by her husband, who now acquires the impurity which is called *ichchil*, and any one else who touches the woman after this ceremony also becomes *ichchil*.

I saw the ceremony of going to the *puzhars* on two occasions, the woman each time belonging to the Teivaliol. The most striking feature of each occasion was the obvious and intense dread of Keirt. In one case, soon after leaving the hut, the woman, Sintagars, called out for another umbrella as she feared that the *tòrikwadr* was not sufficient to shelter her from Keirt, and during the rest of the proceedings she held over herself both the leafy umbrella and one of the ordinary kind.

I was told that all the chief incidents of the ceremony—the rubbing on of ashes, the holding of the leaf umbrella, the pouring of water over the calf and the giving to Namav—were all designed to avert the evil influence of Keirt, which they call *Keirtpudrtvuti* (see p. 269).

After the woman has gone to the seclusion-hut she is visited by relatives and friends, who stand at a distance, just as they did after the hand-burning ceremony. They bring rice with them as a present and call out

Marsvut	*sivu*	*mikh*	*mokh*	(or *kugh*)	*udpatia?*
Confined	life	remaining	son	(or daughter)	had you?

[1] I am doubtful whether this is essential.

"Have you had a son (or daughter) and are yet alive?" The visitors then go to the huts of the village and are entertained.

The woman and child stay in the seclusion-hut, accompanied by the husband and by a woman who is usually the assistant at the birth. If the child is not the first, the mother remains in seclusion till a few days before the next new moon, this kind of seclusion being called *nâtersper*. If the child is the first-born, the stay in the seclusion-hut is longer and is called *kadrthersper*. In this case the woman stays in the hut till a month has elapsed after the new moon following the birth. Thus Sintagars went into seclusion on Sunday, October 19th, and came out on Thursday, November 27th, 1902, exactly four weeks after the new moon of October 31st.

The proceedings on leaving the seclusion-hut are like those which take place after the seclusion following the *urvatpimi* ceremony, but with a few additional rites.

Among the Tartharol there is only one ceremony, called *marthk maj atpimi*, in which a buffalo is milked on the morning of the day by a Melgars man. Before the woman drinks the milk in the evening, another woman lays threads of *tuni* on leaves of *kakud*, and puts them on the ground before the mother, who puts them in the right side of her waist-string as when going to the seclusion-hut. After returning to the hut the woman drinks Melgars buttermilk and eats food cooked in Melgars buttermilk in exactly the same way as after the hand-burning ceremony.

Among the Teivaliol the return to ordinary life takes place in two stages, as after the hand-burning ceremony. The woman first goes to the *aliars*, or to the hinder part of the *merkalars*, after drinking water, which has been supposed to be turned into milk by pretended milking from a pregnant buffalo. I saw this ceremony on one occasion (Fig. 47) when the pretended milking was done by a small boy, Pongudr (52), and the supposed milk was poured into the leaves and given to the mother by a woman who had not been present in the seclusion-hut with her. The person who pretends to milk the pregnant buffalo becomes *ichchil* by doing so, and the reason why a young boy was chosen for this office was that the adult members of the family might escape the disabilities attendant on this condition. On this occasion especial care was taken that the mother should sit facing the sun during the ceremony. She at first sat down with her face turned away from the sun, and she was made to turn round, so that

FIG. 47.—SINTAGARS DRINKING AT THE 'MARTHK MAJ ATPIMI' CEREMONY. THE BOY, PONGUDR, IS SITTING BEHIND HER.

she directly faced it. This was the exact opposite of the procedure followed when going to the seclusion-hut.

After being in the *aliars* or *merkalars* for a week there follows the ceremony of *marthk maj atpimi*, which is the same as that after the *urvatpimi* ceremony, with the addition that a representation of a hut is made with five or six sticks of the kind called *kwadrikurs*. A boy goes within the imitation hut with a brass vessel (*achok*), and coming out gives this to the woman, who bows down (*nersatiti*) with her child at the threshold of the imitation hut. She then takes butter and buttermilk which have been placed by the *palikartmokh* on fire-brands (see p. 318). After taking the mixture the woman goes to the dwelling-hut and resumes her ordinary duties.

It is the custom for everyone present on this occasion to give the child a four-anna piece (*panm*), and near relatives may often give more. A small loincloth (*tadrp*) provided with a pocket called *terigs* is put round the child, and into this pocket the money is put, this action receiving the name of *terigs katpimi*, or "we tie the *terigs*." I did not hear of this pocket in any other ceremonies, and, so far as I know, it is only made in the *tadrp* used on this occasion, or if a constant feature of the *tadrp*, it has no other ceremonial use. So far as I am aware, the representation of a house is only used by the Teivaliol, while the imitation dairy made on going to the seclusion-hut after hand-burning and childbirth is only made by the Tartharol.

It is tempting to suppose that the water poured in these ceremonies from an imitation dairy vessel over the back of a calf is regarded as milk, and if this is so, the drinking of milk, real or fictitious, would be the essential feature of all these ceremonies. Further, the conjecture is natural that the drinking is designed to promote the formation and flow of milk in the woman. It is perhaps in favour of this that in the ceremony after childbirth, when this motive would be especially important, the water is poured over the hind-quarters of the calf and not over the middle of its back, as in the earlier ceremony. But if the promotion of lactation is the leading motive of the ceremonies, it is difficult to see why a buffalo in full milk should not have been chosen instead of a two-year-old calf.

It is possible that there is some reason why an adult buffalo should not be used on such an occasion, and that a calf is used as a substitute, and, on the whole, the view that some features of the ceremonies had their origin in the motive suggested is the most probable one; but this can only be conjecture, for it is, I think, quite clear that the ceremonies have now become purely ritual, and are performed with no other reason than that they are prescribed by custom.

The use of an artificial dairy among the Tartharol, however, has almost certainly a deeper meaning. It is a striking fact that a pregnant woman and one soon after childbirth should have relations with a dairy, even if only artificial, when in ordinary life they have nothing to do with it or its ceremonial. Still more remarkable is the fact that a Tarthar woman after childbirth puts round her waist threads from the garment worn only by dairymen, a garment which has a distinctly sacred character. If this were done only in the case of a male child, it might be supposed that the idea is one of initiation into the life connected with the dairy, but the artificial dairy after the hand-burning ceremony is made when the sex of the child is unknown, and, so far as my information goes, the use of the dairy and the threads from the *tuni* occurs after the birth of either a boy or girl. It is possible that the ceremonial observances are relics of a time when women had more to do with the dairy and its ritual than they have at present; or it may be that contact with the sacred objects, real or fictitious, is held to neutralise in some way the dangerous nature of pregnant and parturient women.

There is some reason to believe that the material of which the *tuni* is made is the same as that of the ancient clothing of the Todas, the cloth called *än*. As we shall see later, the *än* is still used in the funeral ceremonies, and it is possible that the threads of *tuni* are used in these ceremonies as relics of the ancient clothing of the Todas, and that they are obtained from the *madtuni* because it is the most convenient way of obtaining the ancient material. If this had been the motive, however, I think the word *än* would almost certainly have been used, as it still is in the funeral ceremonies. Nevertheless, this remains as a possible alternative explanation of the use of a sacred dairy garment by a woman after childbirth.

A further mysterious feature of these ceremonies is that

the two rites which seem to bring women into special relation with the dairy are limited to the Tartharol. If these rites be regarded as relics of a time when women had more to do with dairy operations than at present, the possibility follows that this former function of women was limited to one division of the Todas.

I could obtain no explanation of the meaning of the word *pülpali*, used for the imitation dairy made in the Tarthar ceremonies. *Püli* means tamarind, and in a ceremony of the Nairs of Malabar called *pulikati*, performed in the ninth month of pregnancy, the woman drinks tamarind juice.[1] It is possible that the two ceremonies have a common origin, the only indication of which in the Toda ceremony lingers in the name of 'tamarind dairy.' It is, however, possible that the dairy is so called because it is made on the outskirts of the village, though I do not know definitely that the word *pül* would be used for outskirts in this special sense.

Uncovering the Child's Face

While in the seclusion-hut with its mother and for some time after, the child has its face covered, and no one except the mother is allowed to see it. At the end of the third month[2] the face of the child is uncovered, and this ceremony is called *mokh mûtâr terithti*, "child outside he opens," or, more shortly, *mûtâr terthpimi*. If the child is a boy, he is taken by his father early in the morning to the front of the dairy, and both father and child bow down at the threshold of the dairy (*pavnersatiti*), the child being put down by his father so that his forehead touches the threshold. The child is then taken to the place where the buffaloes are standing, and there the face is uncovered, the child being held so that he looks towards the sun when the covering is removed.

If the child is a girl, she is taken by her mother to the *majvatvaiidrn*, the place where the women go to receive

[1] Fawcett, *Bull. Madras Museum*, vol. iii. p. 242.

[2] According to one account the ceremony takes place on the fortieth day after birth.

buttermilk from the dairyman, and there the mother uncovers the child's face.

I was not told that the covering of the face is designed to protect the child from the influence of the evil eye, but this is the probable motive. The object of the ceremony is probably to minimise the danger incurred when the covering is removed by putting the child, if a boy, into relation with the three sacred objects, the dairy, the herd of buffaloes, and the sun. If a girl, the child is taken to the spot nearest to the dairy where women are allowed to go.

Naming the Child

The child is named after its face has been uncovered. The ceremony is called *per vasthpimi*, "name we give,'" and it may take place immediately after the ceremony of uncovering the face, or a few days later. In the former case, the child, if a boy, is taken by his father from the place where the buffaloes are standing to the front of the house, and there the father shaves the middle part of the head of the child. Then the boy's maternal uncle (*mun*) gives the name, and promises a calf, saying, *pòl ud todein*, "calf one I have given," followed by the name of the child,[1] and raises each foot to the head of the boy and touches his forehead, the salutation on this occasion being called *kalkartiti*. Three grains of barley are put into the mouth of the boy and three into his back-hair, and then the grains are thrown away.

There was some doubt as to the relative by whom a girl is named. It seemed clear that the name is given by a woman, and I was told definitely by some that it is given by the father's sister (*mumi*) of the child. The wife of the *mun* would also be the *mumi* of the child, and it is possible that this relative may give the name. No calf is given to a girl, this being only done when boys are named.

After the naming, the parents of the child may give a feast if they are rich, but this seems to be now exceptional. After receiving its name, the child is given food for the first time, having been suckled up to this day, but my notes do not

[1] For the nature of the name see Chapter XXVI.

make it clear whether the child is weaned at this time or continues to be suckled.

When the child is shaved, a bone of a bird called *mâtpül* and a stone procured from the bazaar called *kansutimani* are put round its wrist. The bone is cut into small pieces and strung alternately with pieces of the stone so as to form a kind of bangle. It was said that the child would become ill if this charm were not used, and the name of the stone (*kan*=eye) shows that it is intended to avert the evil eye.

THE TERSAMPTPIMI CEREMONY

This is a ceremony closely connected with the naming of a child, but only performed after the second funeral (*marvainolkedr*) of a Tarthar man. It seemed probable that at one time the name was actually given during the *tersamptpimi* ceremony, but as the *marvainolkedr* of Tartharol now occur only at considerable intervals, it has become the custom to bestow the name in connexion with the ceremony of uncovering the face.

The ceremony of *tersamptpimi* is performed on the day after the funeral, this day being called *karvnol*, and as in the ceremony of naming, the chief part is taken by the child's maternal uncle. The uncle comes to the village where the child is living, bringing a stake of wood of the wild rose[1] called *kadakmän*. He splits the piece of wood into two pieces, each of which is called *ketkark*, and putting the hair of the child between the two *ketkark*, he cuts off a lock. If the child is of the Tarthar division, the hair is cut with a piece of sharpened iron called *kanab*,[2] while the hair of a Teivali child is cut with an ordinary knife (*turi*), but both *kanab* and *turi* on this occasion receive the special name of *tersampki*. After cutting the lock of hair, the uncle puts it on one side together with the *ketkark* and the *tersampki*, and if the boy has not already been named, the name is now given by the uncle and a calf promised.

Before this ceremony, the bangle of bone and stone, put

[1] *Rosa Leschenaultiana.*

[2] Lit. 'eye arrow.'

round the wrist of the child when it was shaved, is taken off and replaced by a piece of creeper called *peival*.[1] After the ceremony the *peival* is removed.

There was some doubt as to what was done with the lock of hair. Mr. Natesa Sastri states[2] that the hair is carefully preserved, but my informants did not confirm this, and it seemed as if they did not even adopt the precaution of hiding the hair, which is generally practised (see p. 268).

The Ear-piercing Ceremony

The ceremony of piercing the ears is called *kevi kûtiti*, and may be done at any time from infancy up to even twenty years of age. The ceremony is often delayed until it can be performed for several members of a family at the same time in order to avoid the considerable expense connected with it. The ceremony must be done on a Sunday or Wednesday, and there must be no *kedr* in the clan, *i.e.*, it must not be performed if the funeral ceremonies of a member of the clan are still unfinished.

On the day appointed for the ceremony many guests assemble at the village, and the boys whose ears are to be pierced are dressed in their best clothing. The piercing is performed by two men, one for each ear. One is the mother's brother (*mun*) of the boy, while the other is a man of the division to which the boy does not belong—a Teivali man if the boy is one of the Tartharol and *vice versa*.

The piercing is done with a piece of a small ring, so fine that it is like a needle. The ring used in this way may be of silver or gold, the latter only being used by the richer members of the community.

Each boy then salutes (*kalmelpudithti*) all those present older than himself, both male and female. Each man as he raises his foot to the head of the boy says:—

Tânenmâ,	*târmâmâ,*	*pathk mâ,*	*peda mâ,*
May it be well,	may it be well,	may he prosper,	may he prosper,

ïr	*anâr*	*ôl mâ,*	*âr mokh pai mâ.*
buffaloes	100	may he rule,	six sons may he have.

[1] Probably here *pei* = demon (see p. 180).

[2] *Loc. cit.*

Each man also gives four annas to the boy and each chief Toda may give one rupee.

The salutation of their elders seems to be conditional on this gift of money. One of the most recent cases in which the ceremony has been performed was when the ears of six of the sons of Tikievan of Kuudr and his brothers (56) were pierced. On this occasion Tikievan refused to take any money from those present, and the boys only saluted those men who had celebrated the occasion by giving buffaloes to their father.

As the *kalmelpudithti* salutation was omitted, the words given above as usually said by each person were on this occasion said collectively by all present while the six boys bowed down their heads to the ground. The ears of these boys were pierced by Teikudr (63), the first cousin of Sulnir, the mother of the boys, but regarded according to the Toda system as elder brother of the mother.

The representative of the Tartharol who pierced the other ear was Pidrvan (9), probably chosen because he was one of the oldest and most influential of the Todas who lived at Pakhalkudr, not far from Peivòrs, the home of the boys.

After the ceremony all those present receive two balls of the food called *ashkkartpimi*, even a young child receiving his two balls of food. Each person then makes a hole in his food, into which ghi is poured, and all eat, washing their hands afterwards in water brought from the *ars nipa*.

Only the ears of boys are pierced, and a boy may not enter upon the more sacred offices of the dairy till this ceremony has been performed. Among the Teivaliol, he cannot become *palol*, *wursol*, or *kaltmokh*, but he may be *palikartmokh*. Among the Tartharol, a boy cannot become *palikartmokh* at any kind of dairy till the ear-piercing ceremony has taken place.

In the case of the ceremony for the sons of Tikievan I inquired into the actual expenses of the day. These were as follows :—

grain	17 rupees
jaggery	10 ,,
rice	7 ,,
10½ *kudi* of ghi . .	21 ,,
tobacco and salt . .	2 ,,

amounting to 57 rupees.

On the other hand, six buffaloes were given to Tikievan; two by the Badaga Monegar of Tuneri; one each from Perner and Tebner (68), whose daughter Sinmokh had married Piliagar, one of the boys. The other two buffaloes were given by Teikudr, the uncle of the boys who had taken part in the ear-piercing.

Several of these buffaloes were either given in return for buffaloes which Tikievan had previously given, or Tikievan would be expected to give buffaloes in return when any suitable occasion arose in the families of the donors.

CHAPTER XV

FUNERAL CEREMONIES

THE funeral ceremonies of a Toda may be prolonged over many months. Soon after death the body is burnt and the general name for the ceremony on this occasion is *etvainolkedr*, the first day funeral (literally, "first which day funeral"). After an interval which may vary greatly in length, a second ceremony is performed connected with certain relics of the deceased which have been preserved from the first occasion. The rites on this occasion are more elaborate than at the *etvainolkedr*. The Toda name for this second funeral ceremony is *marvainolkedr*, the second day funeral, or "again which day funeral." The final scene, in which the relics are burnt and the ashes buried, takes place before daybreak on the morning following the *marvainolkedr*, and this part of the ceremony is known as *azaramkedr*, the name being derived from the *azaram*, or circle of stones within which the final cremation takes place.

The funeral ceremonies are open to all and visitors are often invited by the Todas. In consequence, the funeral rites are better known, and have been more frequently described than any other features of Toda ceremonial. Like nearly every institution of the Todas, however, they have become known to Europeans under their Badaga names. The first funeral is called by the Badagas *hase kedu*, the fresh or green funeral, and the term 'green funeral' has not only become the generally recognised name among the European inhabitants of the Nilgiri Hills, but has been widely adopted in anthropological literature. The second funeral is called by the Badagas *bara kedu*, the 'dry funeral,' and this term also has been generally adopted. I never heard these terms used by the Todas themselves, who always spoke of the *etvainolkedr* and the *marvainolkedr*, though it seemed that the first funeral might sometimes be called *karchokedr*, which probably means fresh or green funeral.

The funeral ceremonies have undergone some modification in recent times owing to the intervention of the Government. Formerly it was the custom to slaughter many buffaloes at every funeral. This impoverished the people and was prohibited by the Government about forty years ago, and since that time the number of buffaloes killed at each ceremony has been limited to two for each person. This has had most influence on the second funeral ceremonies, which, largely owing to this prohibition, are now much less elaborate and prolonged than in former times.

The funeral ceremonies are held at certain appointed places called *kertnòdr*, different for each clan. Sometimes these places are at, or close to, villages where the people are now living; sometimes they are at places which were formerly inhabited; while in other cases, again, there is no evidence that the funeral places have ever been inhabited. In every case, whether inhabited or not, the place where a funeral is held is called a *mad*, the same name as is used for a village.

Each clan has at least two funeral places, one for males and the other for females, and in several cases a clan has more than one funeral place for each sex. Some clans have different places for the two funeral ceremonies, and the Piedrol, who have one outlying branch of their clan at Kavidi in the Wainad, have special funeral places for the first funeral of members of this branch, the second funeral, or *marvainolkedr*, being held at the chief funeral place of the clan. Others, again, have a special place for boys who have not passed through the ear-piercing ceremony.

In general, a funeral hut (see Fig. 48) is specially built for the reception of the dead body, this hut being usually erected within a stone circle found at the funeral place. At the funeral of a male, this hut is called *kertnòdrpali* or *neilpali*. It is left standing after the funeral and may be used on a second occasion if it has not fallen into too great disorder.

Five clans of the Tartharol possess special dairies, each with three rooms which are used as funeral huts. These buildings are habitually or occasionally used as dairies; but when a man of the clan dies his body is laid in the outermost of the three rooms, either on the day of the funeral or for two or

FIG. 48.—FUNERAL HUT ROUND WHICH WOMEN ARE LAMENTING. SEVERAL PAIRS ARE PRESSING THEIR FOREHEADS TOGETHER. THE HUT IS NOT WITHIN A STONE CIRCLE, SHOWING THAT THE FUNERAL IS NOT BEING HELD AT AN OLD FUNERAL PLACE.

three days before it. While a dead body is lying in the dairy, women are allowed to enter the outermost room just as they may go into any other funeral hut, but they may not pass beyond. Men are allowed to enter the middle room, but the innermost room is only entered by the dairyman, who carries on his dairy work as usual.

The five villages at which these three-roomed dairies now exist are Nòdrs, Taradrkirsi (Kars), Keradr, Tim (Pan), and Akirsikòdri (Nidrsi). At Taradr a temporary funeral hut with three rooms is constructed within a circle of stones near the village. In the outermost room of this hut the corpse is placed, and women may only enter this room, while men may enter both outer and middle rooms as in the three-roomed dairies. In the innermost room the *palikartmokh* of the village places a vessel of the kind called *mu*, and he only is allowed to enter this room.

This temporary building is almost certainly the representative of a three-roomed dairy which at one time existed at this village; and it is probable that at other male Tarthar funeral places the funeral hut should be made with three rooms, though at present this is not done.

In every case the funeral hut which receives the body of a man is called *pali*, or dairy, and it is probable that at one time among the Tartharol it was the universal custom to place the body of a man in a dairy before the last rites. It is possible that the stone circle within which the funeral hut is built is the representative of the wall surrounding a dairy which formerly existed on the spot. Among the Teivaliol the funeral hut is also called *pali*, but there is no instance among them of an actual dairy being used to receive the dead.

At the funeral place of women a hut is specially built for the reception of the body, but it is always burnt down after each funeral. This hut is called *ars*, or house, and has a different name for each ceremony, being called *nersars* for the first funeral, and *kursars* for the second. Each kind of hut is constructed within a circle of stones, and the name seems to indicate that at one time the body of a woman was placed in the house of the village. Here again the stone circle may possibly be the representative of an actual house which once existed at the funeral place.

If, for any reason, the funeral of a person is not being held at the proper place, the funeral hut is not constructed within the circle of stones; thus at the funeral of a girl, Sinerani (see p. 392), the hut was placed by the side of the stone circle because her funeral was being held at the *kertnòdr* of her father and not at that of her husband.

At every funeral place there should be a second circle of stones forming a *tu*, or buffalo-pen. These pens are now rarely, if ever, used, and are a relic of the time when the ceremonies of the *marvainolkedr* were prolonged over two days, the buffaloes being caught and penned on the first day, and killed on the second. A third ring of stones is the *azaram*, at the opening of which the ashes are buried at the final scene of the funeral rites.

There are specially appointed days for the funeral ceremonies. These days differ to some extent for different clans and for the two sexes. Sunday, Tuesday, and Thursday are the most general days for the funerals of males, only two clans having Saturday as a funeral day for men. For females Thursday and Saturday are most frequently chosen, two clans only holding the funerals of women on Tuesdays. In no case could I find that funerals are performed on Monday, Wednesday, or Friday. These days are, on the other hand, the most usual days set apart as *madnol* or *palinol*,[1] and villages which have their *madnol* or *palinol* on Sunday or Tuesday do not appear to have their funerals on these days. The general rule is that a funeral must not take place on a *madnol* or *palinol*. In several cases I was told that if the *mani*, or sacred bell, were used, the funeral must be on one day of the week; thus for the Karsol, it must take place on Sunday; for the Kwòdrdoni people, on Tuesday. These obligatory days of the funeral ceremonies often involve the necessity of keeping the corpse for several days.

I did not make special inquiries into ceremonies of the deathbed, but Marshall states (p. 171) that a man who is not expected to recover is dressed in the ornaments and jewellery of his house, which he will wear till he dies or recovers; and Marshall mentions an instance of a man who had revived from what was thought to be his deathbed who paraded about, wearing the finery with which he had

[1] The *madnol* and the *palinol* are sacred days on which certain activities are prohibited (see Chap. XVII).

been bedecked. In this case, it was said that he would be permitted to carry the ornaments till his death. Marshall also states that the relatives give the dying man milk to drink when on the point of death.

After death the body should be wrapped in a dark cloth called *än*, which is of the same material as the *tuni* worn by the *palol* and other dairymen, and, like the *tuni*, is procured from the Badagas of Jakaneri. It is doubtful, however, whether this custom of enwrapping the body in the *än* is now kept up with any regularity. Outside the *än* should be an ornamented mantle (*pukuruputkuli*) and then a mantle of the ordinary kind.

The body of a woman is kept in the hut in which she has died till the day of the funeral, and, with special exceptions, this is also done with the bodies of men.

When a man dies at the village of Nòdrs, his body is taken into the three roomed *tarvali* and placed on the right-hand bed (*meitün*) of the outermost room. While the body is lying here, the building is still used as a dairy, but women are allowed to enter the outermost room except when the *palikartmokh* is actually engaged in the business of the dairy. It is only when it is being used as a funeral hut that women are ever allowed to enter a dairy, and then they may only sit on the left-hand bed—the *kitün*.

On the day appointed for the *etvainolkedr*, the body is carried to the funeral place. In some cases certain ceremonies are performed at the village at which the death has taken place; thus, at Kars, the body of a man is first laid in front of the *kudrpali* and then on one of the two eminences called *imudrikars* (see Fig. 21), which stand near the dairy, and from this it is taken to the other *imudrikars*, and after lying here for a while it is borne to the special funeral village of Taradrkirsi. At Kuzhu, another village of the Karsol, the body is taken from the hut and laid by the side of the stone called *menkars*; then it is taken to a stone called *imudrikars* in front of the *kudrpali*, and laid with the head at the stone and the feet towards the dairy. A buffalo of the ordinary kind (*putiir*) is then milked; the milk is put into a vessel and from this poured into a leaf cup of *kakud* leaves, and from this cup milk is poured three times into the mouth of the dead man.

In other villages at which there is no *imudrikars*, the body is laid in front of the dairy and fed with milk in the same way.

The body is borne from the village to the funeral place on a wooden bier, called *mänpedrkudr* (wood bier). It is taken by a specially appointed route, and in some cases certain ceremonies are performed by the way. Thus, when the body of a man is taken from Kars to Taradrkirsi, earth is thrown at two places. We shall see shortly that one of the most important features of the funeral of a man is that earth is dug at the entrance of a buffalo pen at the funeral place and thrown on the corpse and into the pen. On the way to Taradrkirsi this is also done at two places, which are probably the situations of the old buffalo pens of villages which have now disappeared. I did not hear of any similar practices for any other clan, but Kars is probably not exceptional in this respect.

Before the body arrives at the funeral place the people will have begun to assemble, and when the funeral procession reaches its destination all those present go one by one to the corpse, bow down by the side of the bier, and touch the body with their foreheads. Those older than the deceased and those related in certain ways (see Chap. XXI) bow down at the head of the corpse. Those younger and those related in certain other ways bow down at the foot. When all those present have saluted, the body is placed in the funeral hut, or in the dairy if the funeral is being held at one of the places where funeral dairies still exist, and late-comers enter the hut or dairy to perform their salutations. As soon as the body is placed in the hut or dairy, the female relatives and friends of the dead person collect round the hut and lament together in the characteristic Toda manner, arranging themselves in pairs and pressing their foreheads together while they wail and weep (Fig. 48).

While this is going on the men are busied in making preparations for the cremation. A place is cleared in a wood near the funeral place—the *methkudi*—and here a pyre is built of wood, some of which has been brought by the funeral party, while the rest is found near the burning ground. The wood used on this occasion must be of the kind called *kers*[1] and the pyre is built of an oblong shape, rising about three feet above the ground.

The first of the funeral ceremonies is different for the two sexes. At the funeral of a male the ceremony of *puzhutpimi*, "earth we throw," or *kedrpuzhutpimi*, "funeral earth we throw," is performed, while the corresponding ceremony for a woman is to place certain leaves in the armlet on the right arm of the corpse.

THE PUZHUTPIMI CEREMONY

In the *puzhutpimi* ceremony a man digs up a little earth in front of the entrance to the buffalo pen. The digger must belong to the Tartharol, if the dead man is one of the Teivaliol, and *vice versâ*; thus, at the funeral of Pursevan (53)[2] of Kuudr, the earth was dug by Kedjeri (6) of Nòdrs. In this case the Tartharol were told to send someone to dig, and they selected Kedjeri.

At the funeral of a Tarthar man the earth is first thrown by the *wursol*, who must be, on this occasion, one of the Teivaliol. A Melgars *wursol* may not perform this office. After the *wursol* has thrown earth, it is thrown by certain relatives of the deceased who are present. At a Teivali funeral only the relatives perform this ceremony, no one corresponding to the *wursol* taking part.

Before the people begin to throw earth, one of the dead man's division asks "*Puzhutkina?*"—"Shall I throw earth?" and a man of the other division replies, "*Puzhut!*"—"Throw earth!" At the funeral of Pursevan a Teivali man asked the Tartharol in this way, and the Tartharol responded. At this funeral earth was thrown by the following: Punatvan (53), a younger brother of the dead man; Kuriolv and Piliar (52), Pöteners (54); Targners, Pungusivan and Tevò, the sons of the

[1] *Eugenia Arnottiana*. This is the tree in which the hole is cut at the *pursütpimi* ceremony.

[2] This was a *marvainolkedr*, but the rules for the earth-throwing are the same at the first funeral.

dead man, and Pòl, the son of Punatvan. In this case all who threw earth were not only Kuudrol—*i.e.*, of the same clan as the dead man—but were also of the same family, so that their relation to one another can be traced in the genealogies. Kuriolv, Piliar and Pöteners would all have called Pursevan "*aia*," or father, and were first cousins once removed according to our system of kinship. I do not know whether the earth-throwing is usually limited to the nearer relatives in the same clan. The family to which Pursevan belonged was unusually numerous, and it is probable that in most cases other families of the clan are called upon to take a part.

At a funeral seen by Mr. Walhouse[1] the earth was thrown into a circle made of rough stones laid upon the grass with an opening on one side, and Mr. Thurston[2] records a similar case in which the earth was thrown into a circle of stones about a yard and a half in diameter, which had been constructed for the occasion. This is probably done when the funeral is held at a place where there is no *tu*, and it is possible that these funerals were not being held at regular funeral places of the clan, and that the circles of stones were intended to represent buffalo pens. At the funeral seen by Mr. Walhouse the 'priest' handed a bag to the nearest relatives, who tied it to the stick with which they turned up the earth.

Each man, as he throws, kneels down, facing the opening of the pen, and then bows down so that he touches the earth with his forehead, many saying "*Swami*" as they do this. Three handfuls of earth are thrown into the pen, and then three handfuls are thrown backwards on the corpse, the man standing up as soon as he has done this. Each man covers his head with his cloak before he throws, as shown in Figs. 49 and 50.[3]

[1] *Ind. Antiq.*, 1874, vol. iii., p. 274.

[2] *Bull.*, 1901, iv., p. 12.

[3] These photographs were obtained from Messrs. Wiele and Klein, and I do not know the place or nature of the funeral which they illustrate, but there is no indication of a pen in the picture; they probably represent throwing earth at the entrance of a former pen. There is such a place at Taradrkirsi, the male funeral place of the Kars clan. Here earth is thrown by the side of a wood where the forest has grown over the site of an old *tu*.

Fig. 50 shows the special action employed in throwing backwards, the hand being turned inward.

The earth-throwing ceremony is one of several funeral rites, in which men of one division take part in funerals belonging to the other division. Thus, at a Tarthar funeral

FIG. 49.—THE 'PUZHUTPIMI' CEREMONY. IN THE CENTRE IS THE CORPSE. THE FOREMOST MAN ON THE LEFT IS KNEELING DOWN PREPARATORY TO THROWING EARTH.

the earth is dug by one of the Teivaliol; the Tartharol then ask for permission to throw the earth, and the permission (or order) is given by the Teivaliol—*i.e.*, those who have dug the earth have to give the word that the earth may be thrown.

The Tiveri Tûr Ceremony

At the funeral of a woman no earth is thrown, but a ceremony is performed which is said to correspond to it. A woman goes in search of the leaves of the *tiveri* plant,[1] the leaves being called *tiveri tûr*. The woman who plucks the leaves must be the *motvilth* (daughter-in-law) of the dead

FIG. 50.—THE 'PUZHUTPIMI' CEREMONY. THROWING EARTH BACKWARDS ON THE CORPSE.

woman, but if it is a child who is dead the leaves are plucked by the mother-in-law or potential mother-in-law. If a dead woman has no daughter-in-law, it was said that her daughter might pluck the leaves, but at the funeral of Kiuneimi (3), a childless woman, the leaves were sought and plucked by Naburveli, the wife of Mushkers (28), who would have called the husband of Kiuneimi "brother," being of the same family and generation, although only his second cousin according to

[1] *Atylosia Candollei.*

our system of kinship. In this case, therefore, the leaves were plucked by a sister-in-law, or, more strictly, by the wife of the 'brother' of the dead woman's husband. In this case both Kiuneimi and Naburveli were daughters of Nòdrs men, but this was probably only a coincidence.

At the funeral of Kiuneimi, Naburveli was accompanied by a man and by another woman, but it was quite clear that they would on no account be allowed to touch the leaves, which must be plucked by the daughter-in-law or other relative who is performing the ceremony. When found, the *tiveri* leaves are put by the woman in the armlet on the right arm of the dead woman. Then the men present say to the woman :—

"*Parthûl*	*ûtchka,*	*tiveri*	*tûr*	*parch*	*pudthka!*"
In the armlet	is it put,	*tiveri*	leaves	plucking	have you come ?

and the woman replies :—

"*Tiveri*	*tûr*	*parch*	*pudthpimi,*	*parthûl*	*ûtchpimi,*
Tiveri	leaves	plucking	we have come,	in the armlet	we have put,

ir	*patz!*"
the buffalo	catch !

The woman thus announces that this ceremony has been completed, and that they may proceed to the next event of the funeral rites, that of catching the buffalo.

The *tiveri tûr* ceremony of a woman's funeral was said to correspond to the earth-throwing ceremony of a man's funeral, but this correspondence may only mean that each is the first of the actual funeral ceremonies. Since, however, a woman belongs to the clan of her husband, the leaves are always put into the armlet by a woman of the same clan as the deceased. In this respect the ceremony resembles that of earth-throwing, but my informants laid stress on the fact that the ceremony should be performed by a *motvilth* or other relative-in-law, and no reference was made to the fact that they would be of the same clan. This makes it probable that there is no real correspondence between the two ceremonies.

THE SLAUGHTER OF THE BUFFALOES.

The next stage in the proceedings is the catching and killing of the buffalo or buffaloes. At the present time the Todas are only permitted by the Government to kill two of these animals, and if the family of the dead person is poor only one may be killed. At the funeral of a man it is customary that one of the animals killed shall be an ordinary buffalo (*putiir*) and the other a sacred buffalo; one of the *pasthir* in the case of the Teivaliol, and usually one of the *wursulir* in the case of the Tartharol. At least one sacred buffalo must be killed at one or other funeral ceremony for every man, but this may be done either at the *etvainol-* or the *marvainolkedr*. Sacred buffaloes are only killed at the funerals of men, never at those of women.

When it was the custom to slaughter more than two buffaloes, there was often a rule that these should be of certain kinds; thus, at Nòdrs, it was once the custom to kill seven buffaloes at a man's funeral—viz., two *wursulir*, two *putiir*, and one each of the following kinds: *nashperthir*, *pineipir*, and *persasir*.

If the family possess no sacred buffalo, they must procure one by exchange, and it is customary to give two ordinary buffaloes for one of the sacred kind.

There is a definite spot appointed for the slaughter of each kind of buffalo. The ordinary buffalo is usually killed near the funeral hut, and sometimes there is a stone marking the spot at which the animal is to die. The *wursulir* are killed at a place usually marked by a stone called *teiks*. In cases where there is no stone the spot is marked by a wooden post (see Fig. 51), which has the same name, and I was told that it should be made of teak.[1]

In some cases there are other appointed stones or unmarked spots where buffaloes of other kinds are slaughtered; thus, at Nòdrs there are seven stones, at each of which a

[1] If the word *teiks* is the same as that of teak wood it would make it probable that the buffalo was formerly killed by the side of a wooden post and that the use of a stone is secondary.

buffalo used to be killed, and the people of Pan have two stones called *teiks*, one for each division of the clan.

The catching of the buffalo is one of the most exciting incidents of a Toda funeral. When only one or two buffaloes are to be killed it is usual to take about four buffaloes from the village of the dead person to the neighbourhood of the funeral place. When the preliminary ceremonies are over, all those who are attending the funeral move towards the place

FIG. 51.—THE WOODEN 'TEIKS' AT INIKITJ.

at which the buffaloes are standing, while several of their number are chosen to catch the appointed animal or animals. At the same time, the buffaloes, which are usually standing in some hollow so that they cannot be seen from the funeral place, are driven towards the people. As soon as they appear the appointed men drop their cloaks and race to meet the buffaloes. The buffaloes are driven on from behind in a more vigorous manner than that to which they are accustomed, are more or less infuriated, and often rush wildly about in their efforts to avoid the racing Todas, one of whom succeeds in catching the appointed animal, seizing it by the horns, and then hangs round its neck with one hand and seizes the cartilage of the nose with the other. Another of the men seizes a horn and also hangs round the neck of the animal, and both men put their whole weight on the neck of the buffalo and bear it to the ground. Often they are carried many yards before they succeed in getting the infuriated animal under control, and when catching the horns they are sometimes severely gored, though this rarely happens now, and I could hear of no case in which there had been fatal consequences.

The men who are appointed to catch the buffalo belong to the Tartharol at a Teivali funeral and to the Teivaliol at a Tarthar funeral. They are usually chosen from among the younger and more agile of the community, but at an important funeral the older and more experienced men may undertake the duty. The catching of the buffalo is critically watched, and some men have acquired great reputations for the adroitness with which they perform the feat.

I have some reason to think that it is the custom to catch the buffaloes at different places at the funerals of males and females (see p. 393), but my information on this point is not satisfactory.

The captured buffalo has next to be led to the spot appointed for its slaughter. The people of both divisions drive the animal, beating it with sticks, while the course taken by the animal is directed by the two men hanging on its horns and round its neck. The buffalo is beaten much more vigorously than ever happens on ordinary occasions, and it has seemed to many who have watched a Toda funeral that this vigorous beating must have some significance, and the idea of vicarious punishment is naturally suggested. I could obtain no information from the people on this point, and I am doubtful whether the beating means more than that, under the exceptional conditions, the animal requires much more vigorous driving than usual. Ordinarily the buffalo follows out its daily routine with little interference; it goes to its usual pasture, and, as I have seen myself, it may return to the dairy of its own accord at the proper time.

At one funeral at which I was present the buffalo was so alarmed or so infuriated by the proceedings that it lay down and absolutely refused to move, and the efforts of all present were insufficient to drag the animal to the slaughtering place. This incident will be described more fully later, but I mention it here to show that it may often be difficult to drive the buffalo, and that the unaccustomed vigour with which the animal is beaten may have a natural and not a ceremonial reason.

Before the buffalo is killed two things have still to be done. A bell or its substitute has to be hung on the neck of the buffalo, and butter rubbed on its back, head and horns.

If one of the *wursulir* is to be killed there is hung on its neck the sacred bell called *mani*, while the ordinary buffalo or *putiir* is given only the *kwungg* or household bell. A *mani* may also be used for the varieties of sacred buffalo called *nashperthir*, *persasir*, &c. Probably at one time there was a *mani* for each kind, but some of the sacred bells have been lost, and it is only in some clans that a bell can now be used. Those clans which have no *mani* do not use an ordinary bell, but they tie the sacred buffalo to the *teiks* by means of a piece of the creeper called *kakhudri*, about two yards in length. This is the case with all the Teivaliol except the people of Piedr and with the Melgarsol among the Tartharol. The *kakhudri* is said to be used in place of the *mani*.

The details as to the use of the *mani* differ somewhat in different clans. The Nòdrs people have two *mani*, called Kòdj and Kagur, which are now kept at Òdr. When a Nòdrs man dies these bells are fetched from Òdr by the *wursol* and one is hung on the neck of one of the *mersgursir* and the other on the neck of one of the *nashperthir*.[1] After the *etvainolkedr* these bells are kept outside the conical dairy at Nòdrs in a special hole in a stone called *karsalb*. The people of Kars similarly take their *mani* to Taradrkirsi for the

[1] Owing to the fact that the Nòdrs people do not kill both of these kinds of buffalo at one funeral at the present time, they now only bring one of the two bells from Òdr.

FIG. 52.—LEADING THE BUFFALO TO BE KILLED.

first funeral and keep it there till the funeral ceremonies are completed.

Among the Teivaliol the Piedrol are the only clan to possess a *mani*, which is called Kerâni. It is kept in a wood or *shola* near the funeral place and lies in an earthenware pot buried in the ground. At the funeral of a Piedr man the bell is hung on the neck of a buffalo belonging to the *kudeipir* (the special name for the *pasthir* of this clan). It is dug up by the Teivali *palikartpol* and given by him to a Nòdrs man, who ties it on the neck of the buffalo. The Nòdrs man chosen for this office must bathe on the morning of this day and must go without food till after the funeral.

Just before the buffalo is killed butter is smeared on the back of the animal, on the horns and on the part of the head between the horns. This should be done by a man of the same clan as the dead person.

The killing of the buffalo is called *irkîpti*. It is done by striking the animal on the head with the back of an axe (*masth*). The animal is usually killed by one blow, though in some cases more are necessary. The *wursulir* are killed by the *wursol* and the ordinary buffaloes by men of the same division as the deceased, but of a different clan. Certain clans appear to have a prescriptive right to kill the buffalo; thus, among the Teivaliol, a Kuudr man kills at the funerals of members of all other clans, while at the funeral of a Kuudr man a member of one of the other clans performs this function. Among the Tartharol, the members of the Nòdrs and Kars clans appear to occupy the most privileged position, but the relations are more complicated than among the Teivaliol. At a Kars funeral the ordinary buffalo is killed by a man of Nòdrs, Taradr or Pan. At a funeral of a member of any of these three clans, a Kars man kills. At funerals in other clans, the buffalo is usually killed by men either of Kars or Nòdrs, but in the case of a Kwòdrdoni funeral, it seemed that the killing might also be done by a man of Päm or Nidrsi. Each buffalo is killed at the appointed stone or post, and the *teiks* at which the *wursulir* are killed is at some distance from the funeral hut, and a woman is not allowed to approach the spot lest she should see the sacred bell.

Though there is no definite landmark for the killing of the *putiir*, each buffalo is killed at an appointed spot; thus, at the funeral of Sinerani (see p. 392), the buffalo at the *etvainolkedr* was killed on the left-hand side of the funeral hut.

As soon as the buffalo is felled, the corpse is brought up and placed by the head of the dying animal (Fig. 53). At the funeral of a man, the covering of the body is unfolded and the right hand of the dead man is made to clasp one of the horns. At the funeral of a woman, the body is laid with its feet by the

FIG. 53.—THE CORPSE BY THE HEAD OF THE DYING BUFFALO.

mouth of the buffalo.[1] At the funeral of a Pan man, Kwoten's ring is placed on the finger of the deceased before his hand is made to clasp the horn. Then the men present come to the buffalo and salute it by bowing down and placing their foreheads on the horns and on the head between the horns.

The people then group themselves round the buffalo and corpse and cry together by placing forehead to forehead so that their tears and cries mingle. In the case of the sacred

[1] Some observers have stated that the feet of the corpse are placed within the mouth of the buffalo, but I could not confirm this.

buffalo, wearing the *mani*, this circle is composed of men only. The lament[1] usually consists in calling first the name of the buffalo and then speaking of the dead person, not by his name, but by the term expressing the bond of kinship between the lamenter and the dead. Thus at a funeral at which the buffalo killed was called Pundrs, one man would cry:

"*Pundrsia,*	*en potch aia*	*ivanersia,*	*en potch aia*
O Pundrs,	O my father.		

I could not ascertain the meaning of *ivanersia*, except that its latter part is the word for buffalo with the vocative termination '*ia*.'

For a son, a man would cry after the name of the buffalo, "*en mokh ŭpa*"; for an elder brother, "*en potch anna*"; and similarly for other relatives. For a wife a man would cry "*iza kughia*," and for a husband a woman cries "*iza mokhia*" (*iza* is merely exclamatory).

It might appear from the form of lamentation that the buffalo itself was regarded as the father, son, &c., of the lamenter, and I could not satisfy myself as to what the people really had in their minds when they were lamenting in this way. It has been supposed that the lamentation is for the slaughtered buffalo, and I am unable positively to say that this is not the case. It is probable that the people grieve for the departure of one of their much-loved buffaloes, but I do not think that there is any decisive evidence that they are lamenting for the buffalo rather than for the dead person.

Within the group of mourners there is much going hither and thither. After two people have mourned together for a while they separate, and each seeks a new partner with whom to lament. When separating, the salutation of *kalmelpudithti* often takes place, and, as in general, it is the younger of each pair who bows down his head and raises each foot of the other so that it touches his forehead. It seemed to be the duty of everyone to salute certain of the older men in this way; and round these men there would be a continual coming and going, each person saluting by placing his head beneath the feet of the elder. At times the band of mourners would

[1] More elaborate laments are given on pp. 385-8.

FIG. 54. —SALUTING THE DEAD BUFFALO.

form a confused mass of struggling people, some crying forehead to forehead, others saluting head to foot, while others would be struggling through the mass to seek partners with whom to mourn (Fig. 55).

The Cloth-giving Ceremony

During or after the lamentation a ceremony is performed which is known as *kachüttthti*[1] (*kach*, cloth, *ütthti* or *ütiti*, he

FIG. 55—THE MOURNERS ROUND THE BODY.

puts). The essential feature of this ceremony is that a cloth is given by a near relative of the dead person to those who have married into his family, and the cloth is placed on the dead body by the wives of those to whom it is given. This ceremony takes place at the funerals of both sexes and for members of all clans. It is an inconspicuous ceremony, and with one exception[2] has escaped the observation of all those who have previously witnessed and recorded the procedure of

[1] This ceremony is also called *kachpütchpimi*.

[2] Natesa Sastri, *Madras Mail*, Aug. 28th, 1894.

Toda funerals. It takes place in the middle of a crowd, who gather round the corpse possibly while the lamentation is still going on or while other ceremonies are in progress. In the first funeral I witnessed the ceremony took place while dancing was going on, and I missed it entirely, though I was told afterwards that it had taken place as usual, and was able to obtain the names of the chief actors.

In the ceremony of *kachütthti*, a man belonging to the clan of the deceased gives a cloth to one of his *paiol*, or brothers-in-law. The latter gives the cloth to his wife or wife's sister, or to some woman whom he would be allowed to marry, and the woman places the cloth on the corpse. The man who originally gave the cloth then takes it from the body and gives it to another *paiol*, and the ceremony is repeated till the cloth has been given to all the *paiol* present.

The man who gives the cloth should belong to the same clan as the dead person. At the funeral of a male, the proper person is the father of the deceased, if he is alive, or some other elder of the clan. At the funeral of a woman, a man of the clan of the woman's husband is chosen. Thus, at the funeral of Kiuneimi (3 and 28), a widow of Ḳanòdrs, the cloth was given by Neratkutan (28), who was of the same family as the husbands of the dead woman and the eldest representative of their generation. At the funeral of Sinerani (52), the cloth was given by Tebkudr (68), who was the younger brother of the father of Keinba, the husband of the dead child.

The men called *paiol*, to whom the cloth is given, seem to include all those who have married women of the same clan as the giver of the cloth. Thus, at the funeral of Kiuneimi the cloth was given to Pepob (44) of Melgars, and to Nelkush and Tevò (3) of Nòdrs, who had all married women of Kanòdrs.

At the funeral of Sinerani, the cloth was given to Kuriolv (52), who was the father of the dead child, not, however, for this reason, but because he was the husband of Sintharap, Tebkudr's sister. At this funeral the only other man to whom the cloth was given was Piliag (52), who received it in the place of his brother, Piliar (52), who was not present. The latter, like Kuriolv, was the brother-in-law of Tebkudr (68).

If there is no *paiol* present the cloth may be given to a *matchuni*,[1] and this may also happen even when *paiol* are present. Thus at one funeral at which I was present, the *marvainolkedr* of Pursevan (53), the cloth was given by Piliar (52) to Teikudr (63), his *matchuni*. Piliar was the son of Mutevan and Teikudr was the son of Kavani, the sister of Mutevan.

If neither *paiol* nor *matchuni* be present, it was said that the cloth might be given to a brother, *i.e.*, a man of the same clan, but this probably never happens and the statement is possibly an error.

The man who receives the cloth hands it to his wife, if she is present; if she is not present, he may put it on the corpse himself, and I saw this done more than once. On one occasion a man gave it to a woman who was not his wife, but in this case he was acting as a substitute for the husband of the woman.

This ceremony is one in which a man of the same clan as the deceased person gives a cloth to a man who has married into his family. The latter hands on the cloth to his wife, who was, before her marriage, of the same clan as the giver of the cloth, and it is this woman who places the cloth on the dead body.

The father of each woman who places the cloth on the body receives a fee of one rupee called *kachkars*, or cloth-rupee, but the sum is not paid till the woman has attended twenty funerals. An account is kept and twenty rupees are paid when the number is completed. The money is paid by the husband of the woman.

In the ceremony of *kachüithti*, the men who have married into the family of the dead person have to perform this ceremony and have to pay a fee to the family of the dead person. As we shall see later, the chief mourner at a funeral should receive a buffalo from each of his sons-in-law, and we see here that this tribute is supplemented by an addition to the account kept of the times the cloth is given. The cloth-giving ceremony involves a payment to the family of the dead

[1] The *matchuni* of a person is the child of his mother's brother, or of his father's sister (see Chapter XXI).

man of certain fees from those members of other clans who have married into the family.

The cloth used is a red loincloth of a kind which is never worn by the Todas, but, so far as I could ascertain, it is only an ordinary cloth procured in the bazaar.

THE CREMATION

After the *kachütthti* ceremony the body is replaced on the wooden bier and borne to the *methkudi*, where the funeral pyre has been erected within the wood, usually at no great distance from the funeral hut.

The bier is laid by the side of the pyre, and the dead person is then supplied with the various necessaries for the other world. Many of the things are placed in the large pocket, or *kudsh*, between the two folds of the cloak in which the body is enclosed.

The things supplied are chiefly food, ornaments, and money. The food includes grain, rice, jaggery, limes, and honey. Some of the food is put directly into the *kudsh*, while some of the grain, rice, and honey are mixed together and put in a metal bowl. Tobacco, coconuts, ghi, or articles of food from the bazaar may be added.

A number of square boxes made of rattan and called *pettei*[1] are also placed on the bier. They are procured from Mitur in the Wainad, and are often called *miturpettei* or *mitudpettei*. Jaggery and other things are put into each of the boxes, and they are covered with cloth, tied with thread, and adorned with cowries.

The ornaments placed on the corpse included rings for the fingers, armlets, necklaces, and earrings.

The money is collected from all present and put in rolls into long purses, called *tinkani*. Most of the money used for this occasion is old with Arabic inscriptions and is known by the Todas as *irajkars*, the more recent coinage being called *englishkars*. In one collection of coins which

[1] At the *azaramkedr* (see p. 381) these boxes are only burnt at a woman's funeral, their place at a man's funeral being taken by bamboo vessels called *wak*. This is probably also true of the *etvainolkedr*.

I was allowed to inspect many bore the date 1780, and among the more recent coins were included two Japanese yen. The rolls of coins are placed within the cloak, often near the feet of the dead person.

Meanwhile the pyre has been lighted. At the funeral of a man this must be done by means of fire made by friction. I have not recorded whether the fire is made by any special relative of the deceased or other special person. At the funeral of a woman, the fire is started by means of a lighted rag which has been soaked in ghi. The rag is lighted by a man, who at present uses matches for the purpose. Though lighted by a man the fire is applied to the funeral pyre by a woman, usually of the same clan as the dead person. The pyre is lighted on the top, where small pieces of wood have been placed, and butter is poured on the fire which gradually spreads downwards. The progress of the fire is very slow, and at every funeral at which I was present the fire was far from strong when the body was placed upon it.

At the funeral of a male, imitation buffalo horns of wood (*tebkuter* or *petkuter*, see Fig. 35) are placed on the fire and burnt. This was also done at the funeral of the girl Sinerani, but it seemed clear that this was unorthodox and was done by Kuriolv, the father of the dead girl, on account of his great sorrow at her death.

The body on the bier is now taken up and swung three times over the fire, while a small wooden framework resembling a miniature bier is held under the larger bier. As the body is swung over the fire in this way the bearers say:—

"*Kedr*	*tüth*	*tâzâr*	*mud*	*tirk*	*tâkitth*	*tâthi.*"
Funeral	fire	over	three	times	lifted	must.

These words seem to be connected with the small wooden framework held under the body, for this is called *tüth tâzâr tâkitth kârs*, or "fire over lifted (or lifting) stick."

The bier is then replaced on the ground and nearly all the objects of value are removed from the bier or from the pocket of the cloak. In one case I observed that the bangles were taken from the arms, all the rings except one were taken from the fingers, and the coins were removed and redistributed to those who had given them. The people told me that when the body was swung over the fire, the dead person went to Amnòdr with all the ornaments and objects then on the bier, and that the removal of the things afterwards would not deprive the dead person of their use in the next world.

It would seem as if this ceremony of swinging the body over the fire was directly connected with the removal of the objects of value. The swinging over the fire would be symbolic of its destruction by fire, and this symbolic burning has the great advantage that the objects of value are not consumed and are available for use another time.

This is probably the real explanation of the ceremony, but it is not the explanation given by the Todas themselves. They say that long ago, about 400 years, a man supposed to be dead was put on the funeral pyre, and, revived by the heat, he was found to be alive and was able to walk away from the funeral place. In consequence of this the rule was made that the body shall always be swung three times over the fire before it is finally placed thereon. I could not discover the significance of the small wooden framework held under the body. Its appearance suggests that it is a miniature bier.

The objects of value having been removed, the body is now burnt. Formerly it was put on the pyre face downwards, and in the accounts of funerals given by Marshall[1] and Walhouse[2] thirty years ago, this was done, but it is no longer the custom, and in recent funerals attended by Mr. Thurston and myself the body was put on the fire with the face upwards. I was told that Teikirzi ordained that the body should be consumed face downwards, and it was believed that if this were not done, the dead person would have to make the journey to Amnòdr backwards. This seems to imply that the world of Amnòdr is below this world and that the dead person should be burnt in such a way that his face is set towards his future abode.

[1] *Loc. cit.*, p. 176.

[2] *Ind. Antiq.*, 1874, iii. 274.

At some time during the day, Kotas will have arrived, some to act as musicians (Fig. 56), others to take the flesh of the slaughtered buffaloes. The musicians play on their instruments, which may include a clarionet, a drum, tambourine, and brass horn, though usually I saw only the clarionet and drum. The musicians become especially active while the body is consuming. The other Kotas, who carry sharp sticks on which to carry away the flesh, begin to cut up the

FIG. 56.—KOTAS PLAYING MUSIC AT A TODA FUNERAL.

buffaloes as soon as the people have left the neighbourhood of the funeral hut. On more than one occasion I noticed Tamil women sitting not far from the funeral scene, and was told that they had come to buy some of the flesh from the Kotas, and I believe that it is not unknown for the flesh to find its way to the bazaar at Ootacamund.

Before the body is finally placed on the fire, a lock of hair is cut from the head to serve as one of the relics for the second funeral. It is cut by a near relative of the dead person; in the case of Sinerani, it was cut off by her boy-husband. According to Breeks,[1] one of the nails should also be removed, but I could not hear of this being done at the present time, and similarly I heard nothing of the practice of keeping the knee-cap bone, which is said by Hough[2] to have been preserved. When the burning is over, a piece of the skull is sought from among the ashes, and this, together with the hair, is put within two pieces of bark and wrapped in a cloak to be kept for the *marvainolkedr*.

The remainder of the ashes are left on the burning-ground till they are dispersed by wind and rain.

SOME SPECIAL FUNERAL CEREMONIES

In the previous account certain ceremonies which may be performed by special individuals have been omitted. In general, at the funeral of a man, the part of chief mourner and director of the ceremonies is taken by a brother or son of the deceased. At the funeral of a woman the husband takes the chief place.

While the mourning is going on, a ceremony will have been performed if the dead person should be a man or woman whose spouse is still alive. The husband of a dead woman goes to one of his *paiol*, most commonly to his father-in-law, if he is living, and the *paiol* draws up the cloak of the widower so that it covers his head. The man who has his head covered in this way is called *mad ár mitch nidvai*, "head on covered who stands" (see Fig. 61). The widower keeps his head covered in this way as a sign of mourning and does not take off the cloak till the end of the second funeral. When the *paiol* has arranged the cloak of the mourner, the two men cry together with forehead to forehead.

Similarly the wife of a dead man has her cloak drawn over her head as a sign of mourning, and this is done for her by her own father or someone of his clan who takes his place. This ceremony is performed by a relative of the woman, whether it is husband or wife who is dead.

It is the duty of the widower or widow to mix the grain and honey which is put into a bowl on the bier.

[1] P. 21.

[2] Letters on the Neilgherries, 1829, p. 81.

Other special ceremonies fall to the lot of the *mokhthodvaiol* or *sedvaitazmokh* of the dead person if there should be such. The *mokhthodvaiol* of a woman is the recognised lover whom she may have in addition to her husband or husbands. The *sedvaitazmokh* is the name of the woman in this Toda institution. The *mokhthodvaiol* of a dead woman goes to the funeral wearing his ring on the ring finger of the left hand. Before the buffalo is caught he pays the *kalmelpudithti* salutation to the father of the woman; bows down before him and raises each foot to his head. He then puts into the pocket of the cloak of the woman some limes, three handfuls (*mudteir*) of *patcherski* and one large piece of jaggery. He also puts a piece of the dark cloth called *än* into the pocket of the cloak, this act being called *än kudshk it pudithti*. The *mokhthodvaiol* asks the husband of the woman three times "*än kudsh idukina?*" ("Shall I put *än* into the *kudsh?*") and the husband answers each time "*idu!*" In putting the various things into the pocket, the *mokhthodvaiol* has to use his left hand throughout.

When a man dies his *sedvaitazmokh*, if there be one, goes to the funeral ceremony wearing a ring on the ring finger of her left hand, and similarly puts limes, grain, jaggery, and a piece of *än* into the pocket of the dead man's mantle. Before doing this the brothers of the dead man do *kalmelpudithti* to the father of the woman, and this was said to be done in order to obtain permission from him for his daughter to put things into the cloak.

At the funeral of a girl, or of a childless woman, there are performed the ceremonies of *urvatpimi* and *pursütpimi* which are usually performed during pregnancy. In life the *urvatpimi*, or hand-burning ceremony, is performed before that of *pursütpimi*, but after death the order may be reversed. These ceremonies are most frequently performed at the funerals of children, and a full description may be reserved till a later section (see p. 391).

In the case of an adult the ceremony is only performed if it has not been performed in life. If a woman dies in the later months of pregnancy after these ceremonies have taken place, they would not be performed at the funeral.

If an unmarried boy dies, a girl who should be the *matchuni* of the dead boy, is chosen to act as his wife. It seemed that the girl might be of any age, but she must be unmarried, and therefore must nearly always be young. One of the elder brothers of the dead boy performs the salutation of *kalmelpudithti* to the girl's father, or if there are no brothers this will be done by the boy's father. The head of the girl is then covered with her mantle by her father and the girl puts food into the pocket of the mantle of the dead boy. Thus, there is no *pursütpimi* ceremony in the case of an unmarried boy, but a girl is chosen to act as his widow would have done if he had been married.

At the funeral of a Teivali or Melgars male who has not held any dairy office, a piece of *tudr* bark is placed in the right hand of the deceased by a man of the Tartharol. Every male of the Teivaliol or Melgarsol who has been a dairyman of any grade will have been purified with *tudr* bark during the ordination ceremonies, and the piece of bark is only given after death to those who have not been so purified.

The Interval between the two Funerals

As soon as the body is consumed at the *etvainolkedr*, the people go home, the near relatives taking with them the relics of the deceased. These relics are enclosed in two pieces of bark called *pitûdri*, taken from the tree called *mûtmän*. I was once told that *tudr* bark was used, but this is unlikely. The relics and bark are covered with plain cloth, and the whole is enclosed in a mantle of the kind ordinarily worn.

The relics, which are known as the *kedr*, are not taken to the chief village (*etudmad*) of the clan, but to other villages, usually to a definitely appointed village for each clan. If the clan should only have one village, or if the appointed village should be inconveniently distant, a small hut may be especially built in which to keep the relics till the second funeral. The near relatives of the dead person may not go to the chief village in the interval between the first and second funerals. If they are living at the chief village at the time of the death, they must leave it and live elsewhere till the second funeral is over.

The term *kedr* is not only applied to the relics of the dead person, but also to the period between the two funerals, or rather the people say, "There is *kedr* in his family," or "So and so, or such and such a clan, has *kedr*," so that the same word is used for the funeral, for the body of a dead person, for the relics, and for the condition of persons or clans while funeral ceremonies are uncompleted.

All those who go near the corpse at a Teivali funeral become *ichchiloivichi*, usually abbreviated to *ichchil*, and the same is true of anyone who goes to a Teivali village where the relics are being kept. The whole family in which the death has occurred is spoken of as being *ichchil*. If anyone wishes to attend a funeral and yet avoid becoming *ichchil*, he must sit at some distance and take no part in the funeral proceedings. At several funerals I have seen people sitting apart from the rest in order that they might not incur the disabilities associated with the condition of *ichchil*, the chief of which is that it is forbidden to approach or salute a *palol*.

A person who has incurred *ichchil* remains so till the next new moon. Those in the family of the dead person remain *ichchil* till the new moon after the *marvainolkedr*, owing to the fact that between the two funerals they probably either live at or visit the village where the relics are kept.

The condition of *ichchil* arising from attendance at a funeral is regarded as of the same nature as that incurred by a visit to the seclusion-hut after childbirth.

Both Teivaliol and Tartharol may become *ichchil* at a funeral of one of the Teivaliol, but there is no *ichchil* due to attendance at a Tarthar funeral. All those who throw earth at a Tarthar funeral, however, are called *puzhut*, and incur the same disability as those who are *ichchil*—*i.e.*, they may not approach or salute a *palol*.

Melgars people incur the same disabilities as other Tartharol, and it is probably for them that the restrictions are of most importance, for they lose their special privileges as *mòrol* while they are in the condition of *ichchil* or *puzhut*.

During the condition called '*kedr*,' all the men of the

clan in which the death has occurred must tie their hair in a knot in front, as is shown in the case of the second man in Fig. 61. This method of wearing the hair is called *mad tutvai*, or "head (or hair) who rolls." When the people of a clan are in this condition they must not hold any of the feasts in which the food called *ashkkarthpimi* is used, but they may attend as guests at feasts held in the villages of other clans.

A person who is keeping the funeral ceremonies should not traverse the path by which the *ti* buffaloes go from one grazing ground to another. The ostensible reason why the buffaloes of the Nòdrs *ti* did not journey to Anto at their usual time in 1902 (see p. 131) was that Teitnir, whose wife had died, had passed over the road. The *ti* buffaloes, also, may not pass a place where the relics of a dead person are being kept between the two funerals. In 1902 the relics of the dead wife of Teitnir were removed from the village of Karia in order that they should not be in the way of the buffaloes. On this occasion the relics were followed by a procession of people and Teitnir gave a feast. This was said to be very unorthodox, and on cross-examination it was found that the procession and the feast were not connected with one another, the latter being part of another ceremony which was being performed on the same day.[1]

There are special regulations for widowers and widows—*i.e.*, for those who have their heads covered at the *etvainolkedr*. While they wear the mantle over the head they must never put out their hand or arm from above the mantle, but always from below. When they salute by raising the hand to the forehead (*kaimukhti*), they must do so by putting out their hand below the cloak, and in eating and all other acts they must do the same. When the mantle is over the head, it is probably most convenient to put the hand out of the mantle from below rather than from above, but it was quite clear that it was now regarded as wrong to do the latter.

[1] This experience gave me a very striking object-lesson, showing how easy it is to make mistakes in anthropological investigation. The first account given to me seemed to make it absolutely clear that the removal of the relics was made the occasion of a feast.

When a man crosses the Paikara or Avalanche rivers he must usually do so *kevenarut*, with his right arm outside his mantle, but if he has the mantle over his head as a sign of mourning he merely protrudes his right hand, so that it can be seen below the mantle. Similarly, the throwing of water done by *matchuni* (see p. 501), when they cross these rivers on certain days, is not done by people of a family in which there has been a death—*i.e.*, not between the two funerals—but they only chew the grass, which is the preliminary act of the ceremony.

The mourner who has his head covered has certain restrictions in regard to his food. A widower is not allowed to eat rice nor drink milk, and on every return of the day of the week on which his wife died he takes no food in the morning and only has his evening meal. The same holds good for a widow. This fasting on each weekly return of the day of death suggests that some rite is, or used to be, performed on this day, but I did not obtain an account of any such ceremony. The day of the week on which a man dies is always observed by his children, and is called *arpatznol*.

The *wursol* who attends to kill the sacred buffalo loses his office by so doing, and becomes a *perol*. Similarly, if a *palol*, *wursol*, or *kaltmokh* wish to attend the funeral of a relative, he can only do so by giving up his office, and this is a common cause of change in the various dairies. The dairyman who has thus given up his office often resumes it when the funeral ceremonies are completed, and if he expresses his intention of returning, the temporary occupant is often said to be doing the work for the other.

Between the two funerals it is the duty of every Toda who was not present at the *etvainolkedr* to salute the remains. When anyone visits the village where the remains are kept for this purpose the cloth containing the relics is brought out and the visitor bows down and touches the cloth with his forehead, just as is done with the body at the funeral. When I visited the village at which the *kedr* of Olidjeimi was being kept my Toda guide took the opportunity of performing his duty to the remains, and I was able to witness the reverent way in which the duty is performed. While I was on the hills, Tersveli, the wife of Teitnir, died while Sintagars was in the seclusion-hut after the birth of her first child, and on the morning on which Sintagars went from the *puzhars* to the *aliars* (see p. 327), she visited Karia to salute the *kedr* of Tersveli. Her first act after her period of seclusion was to show her respect to the remains of her dead relative. If any-one is too ill or feeble to visit the village the remains may be taken to them for salutation.

CHAPTER XVI

FUNERAL CEREMONIES—*continued*

THE MARVAINOLKEDR

THE second funeral may be held little more than a month after the *etvainolkedr*, or there may be an interval of a year or more, and in the case of a child both funeral ceremonies may be performed on one day. In the old days the *marvainolkedr* was a great occasion. The proceedings lasted for two whole days, and were prolonged till daybreak of the third. Many buffaloes were slaughtered; they were caught on the first day, when they were shut up in the circular pen and bells put on their necks. On the second day they were taken from the pen to the slaughtering place, and various ceremonies took place in connexion with and after their deaths. This kind of funeral was called *tuütthkedr*, meaning "the putting in buffalo-pen funeral." In the old days this putting into the pen was sometimes omitted, especially in the case of poor or unimportant people, and the catching and killing of the buffaloes were both carried out on one day, and this kind of funeral was known as *marppitkedr*. At the present time the Todas only have the *marppitkedr*, owing to the restrictions on the number of buffaloes killed. The Todas seem now to believe that the Government have actually prohibited them from putting the buffaloes into the pen at the funerals, but I could not find that this was the case.

It is now the custom, and seems long to have been so, to hold the *marvainolkedr* of several people at the same time. The Government allows two buffaloes to be killed for each person, and if two or more funerals are held simultaneously it gives an appearance of the olden times. So far as I could ascertain, however, the funerals of two or more people only take place together when they belong to the same clan.

In some cases, however, the funeral places of two or more clans are very near one another. In such a case there might be a certain amount of combination of the different ceremonies, but some of the rites would be carried out at different spots for each clan. Something of this kind appears to have happened at the funeral ceremonies recorded by Mr. Thurston (*Bull.* i., p. 176). Similarly the *marvainolkedr* of a man or woman of the same clan may be held simultaneously owing to the fact that the funeral places for the two sexes are usually close to one another. The buffaloes would, however, be killed at different places, and the remains would not be burnt and buried at the same *azaram*.

Owing to the custom of having the *marvainolkedr* of several people simultaneously, it has often been supposed that the Todas have a kind of anniversary ceremony for all those who have died during the year, but there is no doubt that this is wrong. There was a large *marvainolkedr* soon after I left the hills (in January, 1903), but it was a ceremony for two women only, Narskuti (63 and 56), and Tersveli (63 and 52), both belonging to the Kuudrol, and it was held at Kurkalmut, the proper funeral place for the women of Kuudr. It is quite possible that owing to the restrictions on the slaughter of buffaloes it may become more and more the custom to hold several *marvainolkedr* simultaneously, and that this custom may develop into an anniversary ceremony. This could only come about, however, by throwing over the custom that the funerals of each clan should be held at a definitely appointed place, and there is no doubt that this has not yet happened.

At the second funeral ceremony the relics are placed in a special hut, and at a man's funeral the hut has the same name as at the *etvainolkedr*, and apparently it may sometimes happen that the same hut is used at both ceremonies. The second funeral is not always held, however, at the same place as the first, and the interval between the two ceremonies may be so great that it may have become necessary to rebuild the hut. At the only *marvainolkedr* at which I was present a new hut had been built for the occasion.

The hut at the second funeral of a woman differs in name from that of the first funeral, being called *kursars* instead of *nersars*. After the second funeral the *kursars* is burnt down, but my notes do not make it clear whether the *nersars* is always burnt down after the first funeral, or whether it may not sometimes be kept for the second ceremony. The difference of name, however, makes this improbable.

If the *marvainolkedr* of two or more people are held simultaneously, a hut is built for the remains of each; thus, at the ceremony in January, 1903, there were two huts, one for Narskuti and the other for Tersveli.

The relics, now called the *narskedr*, are brought to the funeral place on a bier made of bamboo, and called *kailpedrkudr* instead of *mänpedrkudr* (wood bier) as at the first funeral. The *narskedr* is wrapped in an embroidered mantle (*pukuruputkuli*) and placed in the hut, and then all the women of the dead person's division who are present cry together, forehead to forehead, in the usual manner. The chief things to be burnt with the remains are also placed within the hut.

At a funeral witnessed by Mr. Thurston the relics were taken from a hole cut at the base of a tree, and the hair was unwrapped from off the skull, burnt in an iron ladle, and anointed with clarified butter before being placed in its cloth. This was probably a ceremony which should have been performed on the following morning at the *azaramkedr* (see p. 379).

As on the former occasion, a man's funeral begins with the ceremony of earth-throwing, which is carried out in the same way as at the *etvainolkedr*. The *narskedr* is laid at the entrance of the buffalo pen, and earth is thrown into the pen and on the remains in the manner already described. There is nothing corresponding to the *tiveri tur* ceremony of the woman's first funeral.

At the present time the driving, catching, and killing of the buffaloes are carried out in very much the same way as at the *etvainolkedr*. At the funerals of Teivaliol the buffaloes are caught by Tartharol and killed by Teivaliol of a clan different to that of the deceased. At the funerals of the Tartharol the buffaloes are caught by Teivaliol, and killed by the *wursol* or by a Tarthar man of a different clan, according as they are of the sacred or ordinary kind.

As the buffalo dies, the *narskedr* is brought up and laid by the head of the animal, and the lamenting and saluting take place around the buffalo and the remains, exactly as at the first funeral.

Sometimes a ceremony occurs immediately before the buffalo is caught. A man takes a ring of the creeper called *kakhudri* and throws it at one of the driven buffaloes. It should fall on the horns or neck of one of the buffaloes, but it does not matter whether on a buffalo which is to be killed or on another.

This throwing of the creeper, which is called *kakhudri erspimi*, or *kudri erspimi*,[1] "we throw the creeper," is done by the *wursol* at a Tarthar funeral, while at the funeral of the Teivaliol it is done by a *palikartmokh* of the same clan as the deceased. This ceremony used not to be performed at those funerals which lasted two days, when the buffaloes were shut into a pen on one day and killed on the next, but it should always be performed when the funeral ceremonies are limited to one day. It seems possible that the circular ring of creeper may be intended to represent the act of putting the animals in the circular pen, but the Todas could give me no information on this point. It seemed clear that it is only done at those funerals in which the buffaloes are not put into the pen.

THE KOÒTITI CEREMONY

Among the Tartharol, with the exception of the people of Melgars, a ceremony is performed at the funeral of a male which is called *koòtiti*. In this ceremony blood is used which in the present day is drawn from one of the slaughtered buffaloes, but formerly a special buffalo was killed for this purpose.

[1] *Kudri* is the generic word for creeper.

According to the old custom the buffaloes were killed about four o'clock in the afternoon. About an hour later another buffalo of the ordinary kind was brought to the funeral place and killed by striking it on the head with a stone, and not with the back of an axe, as in the case of the other buffaloes. It might be killed by any Tarthar man, and then the *wursol* made a cut in the right side of the animal at the part called *kegampkwꝺdr* (over the ribs near the forelegs). The blood which ran from the wound was received into a cup made of *tudr* leaves, and powdered *tudr* bark was mixed with the blood in the cup. It is to this part of the ceremony that the name *koꝺtiti* ("blood he takes") is properly applied. At the present time the blood is drawn from one of the buffaloes killed in the ordinary course of the ceremony. However the blood may be obtained, the next step is to bring a female buffalo calf less than one year old. The mantle with which the remains have been covered is taken off, and is worn by a Teivali man who has adorned himself with many ornaments, including those ordinarily worn by women, such as the chain (*tagars*), necklace (*keiveli*), earrings (*kevthveli*), and bracelet (*pulthi*). He also holds a long pole called *tadri*. The remains, which are now covered with a loincloth (*tadrp*) only, are carried by two women to the place where the calf is standing.

The *wursol* and Teivali man then walk to the calf, the former throwing before and behind him as he walks the mixed blood and *tudr* bark from the cup. When the *wursol* comes to the calf he throws down the leaf cup, and the Teivali man then hangs on the neck of the calf a bell of the kind called *tukulir mani*, and, taking a bow and arrow in his hand, he says three times to the Tartharol, "*purs adikina?*"—"Shall I touch with the bow?" Each time the Tartharol reply, "*Purs ad!*" The Teivali man then touches the remains with the bow and arrow. He puts down the *tadri* on the ground, and the calf is driven away from the spot on which it had been standing. As soon as it begins to move all present, Tartharol and Teivaliol, cry out, "*ua! ua!*" and fall down and touch the earth with their foreheads. The bell is then removed from the calf, which is not killed, but is allowed to go free. The bell (*tukulir mani*) is kept by the Kotas or Badagas till it is required by the Todas for another funeral.

The assumption of the cloak covering the remains by the Teivali man is called *ártûrverutiti*, and the throwing of the mixed blood and bark by the *wursol* is called *kedrkarchiti*—*i.e.*, funeral (or remains) purifying. Either at this stage or later the blood and *tudr* bark are rubbed on the piece of skull and hair which form the *narskedr*.

One of the most important features of this *kòbtiti* ceremony is that the sacred *tudr* bark is used The ceremony is not performed at the funerals of the Teivaliol or of the Melgarsol, because they may use *tudr* in the ordination ceremonies for the offices of *palol*, *wursol*, or *kaltmokh*.

The object of the ceremony appears to be that members of those clans who have no chance of being purified with *tudr* during life shall be purified with this substance before they go finally to Amnòdr. A Teivali or Melgars man, however, has only used *tudr* if he has been ordained to one of the three offices above mentioned. If the dead man has not been through an ordination ceremony, however, the purification does not take place at his second funeral, but a Tarthar man puts a piece of *tudr* bark into his right hand at the first funeral (see p. 367).

In the account which Breeks gives of this ceremony he states that certain formulæ are said, including "*Karma odi pona*," "May the sin run away." I could not confirm this, and I do not believe that *karma* is a Toda word. It is probable that the use of these or other formulæ is an innovation.

The Badagas of the Nilgiris let loose a calf at a funeral to bear the sins of the deceased.[1] It is possible that the calf in this Toda ceremony may have the same significance. If so, the practice has not improbably been borrowed, and the fact that the bell which is hung on the neck of the calf is kept by Kotas or Badagas suggests that the whole incident may have been borrowed by the Todas from one or other of these races.

[1] See Thurston, *Bull.*, ii. p. 4.

After the buffalo is killed dancing takes place at the funeral of a male. The men only dance and they may begin soon after the killing of the buffalo, while other ceremonies are still in progress. In the dancing the same tall pole (*tadri* or *tadrsi*) is used as is carried by the Teivali man who wears the cloak of the *narskedr*. It is a tall pole which, it was said, might sometimes be as much as 39 feet in length. I only saw a *tadri* at one funeral, when it was much smaller. It is decorated with rings of cowries, which are called *nîrpul*, the ornaments in general being called *tadri asteram* (see Fig. 67).

The pole is procured from Malabar through the Kurumbas. It is used at the funeral of males only of both the Teivaliol and Tartharol, and is burnt at the end of the *azaramkedr*.

In the only dance which I had the opportunity of seeing the men danced within the circular wall surrounding the funeral hut. In this case the floor of the enclosure was below the general level of the ground. The men formed a circle and danced round in slow step; one man said the name of the slaughtered buffalo—in this case, Purkirsi—and another repeated this name; then the first man said "*hau! hau!*" which was repeated by the second man.

After a time one of the men took the *tadri* and they danced round in a similar way, taking the pole with them as they danced (*i.e.*, they did not dance round the pole).

After the dancing is over, food is distributed to all the people present and most return to their homes, while the remainder wait at the funeral place till the following morning, when are held the final ceremonies, which are known as the *azaramkedr*.

THE AZARAMKEDR

This is the name applied to the ceremonies connected with the final burning of the remains and burial of the ashes. After food has been distributed at the *marvainolkedr*, many of those attending the funeral return home. The remainder stay at the spot during the evening, those nearly related to the deceased lamenting in the usual fashion almost continuously. At a funeral attended by Samuel, the people took the setting of Kadsht and the appearance of Keirt [1] as the indications that the final ceremonies were to begin, and this was about two o'clock on the following morning.

At every funeral place used for the *marvainolkedr*, there is a circle of stones, smaller than that in which the hut is built, with an opening which in some cases faces the east. This circle of stones is the *azaram*, and before the ceremonies begin, a man digs a hole by the opening in its side. The various objects to be burnt with the remains are now brought from the hut in which they had been placed on the previous day, and are laid outside the *azaram* and the *narskedr* is laid by their side. As the remains are removed from the hut, the wailing becomes louder and the people cry bitterly. Outside the stone circle a fire is made of the wood called *kidmän*,[2] upon which clarified butter is poured. This fire, which is known as the *puntüt*, is lighted by a man of the same clan as the deceased. At the funeral of a male, there is burnt on this fire the dairy vessel called *ertatpun* which had belonged to the dead man, and the imitation buffalo horns called *petkuter*, about ten in number for a man and five for a boy. At the funeral of a woman, I think that a *majpatitthpun* is burnt, viz., a vessel used for fetching buttermilk from the dairy, but I am not certain of this.

There now follows the ceremony called *narsatipimi*, *i.e.*, "the *nars* we rub," in which the leading part is taken by a person of the same sex as the deceased. I only have a full record of this ceremony at a woman's funeral, and in this case a woman took the relics out of their covering, and threw away the pieces of bark in which they had been enclosed. She rubbed butter on the pieces of skull and the hair, put the hair between two pieces of skull, tied them together with thread, and replaced them in the ornamented cloak (*pukuruputkuli*). She then bowed down and touched the remains with her forehead, and then this salutation was performed by all those present.

At a funeral seen by Mr. Thurston,[3] this ceremony was performed on the previous day at the *marvainolkedr*, and in

[1] See Chap. XXV.

[2] Probably *Olea robusta*.

[3] *Bull.*, i. 176.

this case the hair was burnt in an iron ladle before the clarified butter was applied.

This ceremony of *narsatipimi* is performed by the daughter-in-law of a woman, or by the mother-in-law of a girl or woman who has no daughter-in-law. At the funeral of Narskuti (56 and 63) it was performed by Piliurs, the wife of Tüliners (56), the son of the dead woman. At the funeral of Tersveli (52 and 63), a much younger woman, who had no daughter-in-law, the relics were anointed by Muteimi (52 and 69), the mother of Teitnir, Tersveli's husband. I have no record of the person who performs this ceremony at the funeral of a man.

The next step in the proceedings is to light a fire within the circle of stones, this fire being called the *azaramtüt*. Firewood is put within the *azaram* and the *narskedr* in its covering is placed on the wood. If the *azaramkedr* is being held for two or more people simultaneously, the remains of all are put on the wood together.[1] In the pockets of the mantles forming the coverings are placed grain, jaggery, and coins. The *azaramtüt* is then lighted by taking three firebrands in succession from the *puntüt*. The firebrands are placed on the firewood and on the remains by the daughter-in-law or mother-in-law of a female as in the last ceremony.[2] Then all the people take up the burning wood from the *puntüt* and place it within the *azaram* over the remains. The various objects previously brought from the funeral hut are now placed on the fire and burnt, and the special food known as *ashkkarthpimi* may be thrown into the fire. Then all the people cry together, forehead to forehead.

The following are the objects burnt with the remains on the *azaramtüt*, at the funeral of a male :—

(*a*) In the pocket of the cloak, jaggery, the husked grain called *patcherski*, husked barley (*kodjerski*), and rupees in two

[1] As I have already pointed out, this would only happen if the people were of the same clan and sex.

[2] My notes do not make it absolutely clear who lights the fire at the funeral of a male. The *puntüt* is lighted by a man of the same clan, and this is probably also the case with the *azaramtüt*. Owing to the fact that a woman becomes a member of her husband's clan, the daughter-in-law who lights the fire at a woman's funeral will also be of the same clan as the deceased.

bags, one called *tinkani*, made by the Todas themselves, and the other called *katshiram*, procured from Hindus.

(*b*) Sticks of the following kinds of wood: *pars*, *karneizi tavat*, *kali*, *toarsmitch*, *kar*.

(*c*) A *nanmakud*, a club or stick cut from the *pars* tree (Fig. 67).

(*d*) A *tadri*, or long pole used in the dance and in the *koòtiti* ceremony of the previous day.

(*e*) Several *wak*, bamboo vessels filled with grain, butter, ghi, honey, &c., usually ten in number for adults and five for children.

(*f*) A *tek*, a basket made by the Kotas in which barley or poppy heads are put.

(*g*) A bow (*purs*) and three arrows (*ab*) (Fig. 67).

(*h*) A *kafkati*, or knife, called on ordinary occasions *kudrval*.

(*i*) A *masth*, the axe used to kill the buffaloes on the previous day, called on this occasion *ŕrkŕpmasth*.

(*j*) A *miturkwadr*, the palm-leaf umbrella, so called because procured from Mitur in the Wainad.

(*k*) A *kudshmurn*, a special kind of sieve made by the Kotas and not used in ordinary life.

At the funeral of a woman boxes called *pettei* or *miturpettei* are burnt instead of the *wak*. These are small boxes made of rattan, covered with cloth and adorned with cowries. There are also burnt the three objects especially connected with women, the pounder (*wask*), sieve (*murn*), and broom (*kip*), but the pounder is only burnt after the following ceremony has taken place.

As soon as the things have been placed on the fire, there follows the ceremony[1] called *ŕrsankâti*. At the funeral of a male, the *matchuni*, or cousin, of the dead man puts on the woman's ornaments known as *tagars*, *keiveli*, and *pulthi*, and stands at the opening in the circle of stones with his right arm outside his cloak (*kevenarut*). He is joined there by the man who has lighted the fire, and they cry together, both standing at the entrance of the *azaram*, where they

[1] There was some question as to whether the ceremony did not begin as soon as the fire was lighted.

remain till the fire is extinguished. Owing to the fact that the fire is lighted by a man of the same clan as the deceased, the two men who cry together will also be *matchuni*—thus, at the funeral of Karspisti (12), the fire was lighted by his half-brother Karzo. Pakhwar (16), who performed the *irsankati* ceremony, was the *matchuni* of both Karzo and Karspisti, being the son of the brother of Tedjveli, the mother of Karzo and stepmother of Karspisti.

At the funeral of a female, the woman who stands at the entrance should also be a *matchuni* of the deceased. She is decorated with ornaments, in this case proper to her own sex, and she stands at the entrance of the *azaram* holding the pounder. She is joined by a woman closely related to the deceased and the two women cry together. After crying together for a while, they go round the circle and then put the pounder on the fire, after which they take off their ornaments.

At the funeral of Narskuti (56 and 63), Mutkadrk (56 and 72) stood in front of the circle holding the pounder, and was joined by Munat, the daughter of the dead woman.

At the funeral of Tersveli (52 and 63), Edjog (56) stood at the entrance; she was the *matchuni* of the dead woman, being the daughter of Tüliners, the brother of Tersveli's mother. She was joined by Teimidz (52), the sister of the dead woman's husbands.

The fire is now extinguished by pouring on water (*kêdr tüt ârs kudrchi*). Some of the food put into the pocket of the *putkuli* and in the various vessels may now be taken out[1] and given to the Kotas, who up to this time have been playing the special funeral tunes called *sagerthkwelv*.

The ashes are now swept into the hole which had been dug at the opening in the stone circle. They are covered with earth dug from elsewhere and the spot is covered with a stone.

At the funeral of a male, a man of the same clan as the deceased then brings a bell (*kwungg*) and goes round the

[1] This would seem to indicate that when the fire is extinguished, the objects burnt with the relics are far from being consumed by the fire.

burial-place three times ringing the bell, while another man goes with him holding him by the waist. The man who rings the bell then takes a new pot, ordinarily used for carrying water, and, raising it over his head, brings it down and breaks it on the stone covering the ashes. He bows down and touches the stone with his forehead, gets up, and goes away to the funeral hut without looking back toward the *azaram*. All the others present bow down to the stone in the same way and go away from the spot without looking back. The ceremony of bell-ringing and stone-saluting is called *kwungg tûki kârs nersatiti*, "bell lift, stone he salutes."

At the funeral of a woman, the bell is rung and the pot broken by her husband or by one of his brothers if he be dead. If it is the husband, he will have been wearing the cloak over his head[1] up to this time, and he takes it off just before he bows down to salute the stone. At the funeral of her husband, a widow will similarly remove the cloak from her head before she salutes the stone.

After saluting at the *azaram*, all go to the funeral hut, where they take food, having fasted during the night. Each person cuts a lock of hair from the head as a sign of mourning and then all return home.

At the funeral of a woman, the funeral hut is burnt before the people leave, this being called *ars pon atipimi*, "house up we send." It is the duty of the woman who first lighted the *azaramtüt* to set fire to the hut.

The foregoing account of the second funeral ceremonies is that of the proceedings at the present time. When the *marvainolkedr* was prolonged over two days, the proceedings of the first day opened with the capture of the buffaloes, which were put in the pen, and then followed a scene in which the Todas entered the pen, flourishing heavy clubs. The animals were belaboured and driven round and round the pen, and at intervals several men would catch and hold down a buffalo. According to some accounts the bells were hung round the necks of the buffaloes during this performance, but at a funeral witnessed by Mr. Walhouse[2] this was not done, and he believed that the

[1] See p. 365.

[2] *Ind. Antiq.*, 1874, vol. iii. p 35.

object of the fray was that the men might exhibit their agility and skill. There is little doubt, however, that the bells were put on the buffaloes at some time on this day. The remainder of the first day was occupied with dancing, singing, and feasting. On the second day, the proceedings began again in the middle of the day with more dances and with a repetition of the driving and catching within the pen. In the afternoon, after the earth-throwing ceremony, the buffaloes, now wearied and subdued, were dragged from the pen and killed, and then followed the ceremonies which have already been described.

At the funeral witnessed by Mr. Walhouse, part of the second day was occupied by the proceedings of a diviner, and divination seems to be a frequent feature of funerals, having been also seen both by Mr. Thurston and myself. In the latter case, the occasion of the divination arose directly out of the proceedings, but it is probable that the gatherings are used as opportunities of consulting the gods on other matters. A funeral may also be used as an occasion for settling disputes, especially those which concern the people especially connected with the funeral.

FUNERAL LAMENTS

At some stage in both funeral ceremonies laments for the dead may be sung or said which consist of sentences praising the virtues of the deceased and recounting incidents of his or her life. To these sentences the same term *kwarzam* is applied which is used for the words and clauses of the prayers. I am not certain at what stage of the proceedings the recital of these laments takes place, but it is certainly after the killing of the buffaloes, probably in many cases during the general wailing round the buffalo and the remains. At the second funeral of a male, however, I believe that the lament is recited during the dancing.

I did not succeed in obtaining any examples during my visit, but soon after my departure Samuel sent me two laments, one composed by Teitnir (52) and uttered by him at the second funeral ceremony for his wife Tersveli. The other was also composed by Teitnir for the first funeral ceremony of Pidrvan (9) of Kars.

The Toda name for these laments is *kunedstkin* or *kunedsti*, and certain men have great reputations as composers both for funerals and on other occasions, and Teitnir was one of these. The following is the lament for Tersveli:—

Iza kûgh ia,[1] *iza kutei, atûth*
O woman oh ! O woman, not born before

atia, pervoth perpia, pûv frsimitch ia
you were born, renowned you were born, flower lime oh !

pûv elet ia, kavath kud katethik,
flower (a bush) oh ! proper husband (?) found you married,

patath kud patiathenk, tevukhk nurs
proper wife found I married, (*kwarzam* of Piedr) to beautiful

ir notei kadrthenk, ûtthkark nurs mokh
buffalo looked I gave, (*kwarzam* of Kuudr) to beautiful woman

notei patiathenk, kuteia mun kutenathuk, kokiji[2]
looked I married, built house we built, imitation bracelets

kis narsiathûk kûter kis narsiathûk,
made we played, imitation buffalo horns made we played,

ûr mokh puchiathûk, ûr ir tû
six children we would produce, six buffalo pen

odethûk, orppasan (?) oithik pudrkwadr ners
we would enjoy, liberal you were, umbrella tree shade

oithik, irom ed ithothûk, pukhom
you were, we will live that we thought, we will go together

ed peithûk, kalav ir kadathûk, pûa tadri
that we went, strong buffalo we bought, ? pole

pusiathûk tudm athi ed kadrtethûk, udi athi ed
we beat, fine it is that we gave, have it is that

kadrt thûk, kutei ath kotei peithûk, keirtith keir
we gave, built bungalow we went, running waters reservoir

peithûk, ö katcheri peithûk, ö kapel
we went, seven courts (law) we went, seven ships

peithûk pedrk muri ituthûk, pash it
we went, Tamil to complaints we spoke, words spoke

[1] This is also the usual vocative termination.

[2] *Kokoji* is the Kota name for a toe-ring worn on the second toe of the right foot by Kota women (see Breeks, p. 123). A similar word is used for bracelets of vine made by the Todas as a game.

pudth	*kisthûk*	*pudth*	*it*	*pudth*	*kisthûk,*
prize	we won (made),	prize	spoke	prize	we won,

ûkudrem	*ed*	*thûk,*	*kan*	*udjem*
we will not be shaken	that	we said,	eye	we will not fear

ed	*thûk,*	*mûn*	*ânem*	*ed*	*thûk,*	*en*	*it*
that	we said,	face	?	that	we said,	me	here

puchvînia,	*en*	*it*	*pîshvînia,*	*purs*	*kan*	*nîr*
keep you went,	me	here	leave you went,	right	eye	water

pîrevînen,	*purs*	*metûvi*	*kurseivînen,*	*patnenk*	*kanânen,*
I shed,	right	nostril	I smart,	I bewailed	I could not find,

pesoduthenk	*kanânen,*	*enk*	*ud*	*swâmi*	*aivînen.*[1]
I called out	I could not find,	to me	one	god	I have.

The free translation of this is as follows :—

"O woman of wonderful birth, renowned were you born, O flower, lime, O flower, tree. Having found a proper husband you married; having found a proper wife I married. I gave my best buffalo to Piedr for you. I took you as a beauty to Kuudr. A house we built, bracelets and buffalo horns we made in sport. I thought we should have had many children and many buffaloes should we have enjoyed. Liberal you were and refreshing like the shade of the umbrella tree. We thought that we should live long. We went together as we willed. We bought strong buffaloes and we prevailed over injustice. Peacefully we paid our fine. We lent to those that had not. We went to see the bungalows and the reservoir. Many courts we visited and ships also. We laid complaints before the native magistrate; we made bets and we won. We said that we would not be shaken and would fear the eye of no one. We thought to live together, but you have left me alone, you have forsaken me. My right eye sheds tears, my right nostril smarts with sorrow. I bewailed but could not find you. I called out for you and could not find you. There is one God for me."

This translation is based partly on the literal meanings of the *kwarzam*, partly on explanations and renderings given to Samuel by Teitnir. The dead wife was a Piedr woman and the husband a Kuudr man. The mention of injustice refers

[1] In some cases Samuel could not give the literal meanings, and has only given the general sense of the *kwarzam*.

to trouble which arose when other men wished to take his wife from Teitnir. The visits to bungalows, &c., probably refers to a time when Teitnir and his wife lived in Ootacamund under the protection of the Zenana Mission. The ships must be purely imaginary on Teitnir's part, unless he is referring to boats on the lake at Ootacamund. The numbers six and seven are those generally used for 'many' under ordinary conditions, and there is a clause towards the end which probably refers to the evil eye. Teitnir was under, or pretended to be under, missionary influence, and his reference to "one God" at the end is certainly due to this.

The following is the lament composed by Teitnir for Pidrvan :—

Epukers *ia !* *elipukers* *ia !* *Pedth* *tedshk*
Kwarzam of *maiir* oh ! *kwarzam* of *maiir* oh ! rattan ring

ír *ia !* *Pekh* *kudeik* *kinim* *ia !* *peivalei* *muk* *ia !*
buffalo oh ! ? ? plate oh ! ? ? oh !

keiveli *mûdr* *ia !* *kapasth* *kal* *ia !* *kûdukatith* *kûdr* *ia !*
necklace neck oh ! trousers leg oh ! car horn oh !

âna *metu* *ia !* *arshan* *mudr* *ia !* *etamâv* *ia !*
elephant foot oh ! European walk oh ! sambhar oh !

nurs *írk* *kan* *âkithenk,* *kalochikum* *ed*
beautiful buffalo to eye I kept, old woman to (?) that

thînk, *kalôlkum* *ed* *thînk* *inâtvidshti* *inâtvan,*
they said, old man to (?) that they said, *kwarzam* of Kars clan,

iza *kâra* *ö* *vûr* *kada,* *pûrvunkâra !*
O chief seven village chief, conqueror oh !

pudrvantol[1] *ia !* *kavalkâra !* *Kavanadi* *pali* *put*
peace-loving man oh ! strong man oh ! Kavanadi dairy carried

oia ! *tû* *vut* *tüli* *ia !* *atâth* *ud*
oh ! pen carried posts oh ! not born before one

atithîk, *pervoth* *ud* *pertithîk,* *pûa* *kûtm*
you were born, renowned one you were born, ? council

paneithîk *saver* *ôkithîk,* *ter* *ud* *ôlk*
you held, money fine you imposed, buffalo fine one man to

edstethîk *mokh* *ud* *ôlk* *kisethîk,* *maiîr*
you told, girl one to man you made, barren buffaloes

kodik *peithîk,* *pîrer* *nôdik* *peithîk*
in the midst you went, buffalo to the neck you went,

[1] A play on Pidrvan's name.

pudr *ödichi* *peithīk,* *pan* *ertevīthīk,*
chosen number beat you went, chosen number you ran before,

kal *öt* *öditkīk* *peiveli pileidik* *ninth* *ud* *kalvi*
leg dance you danced ? ? your one new things

kisethīk, *ninth* *ud* *kek* *kisethīk,* *id* *kan*
you made, your one invention you made, to-day eye

mûn *âvini,* *Kars* *kazun* *podstha?* *parsners*
face I saw, Kars *kazun* has it come? *kwarzam* of *kazun*

podstha? *methkûdis* *mai* *kooisivini* *âzâratrs* *kargh*
has it come? burning-place at ashes heaped, *azaram* at grass

patevini.[1]
grew up.

The first part of this lament begins with the *kwarzam* of the *maiir*, or barren buffalo, slaughtered at the funeral. It is not quite clear which of the clauses at the beginning refer to the buffalo and which to the man. I do not know the meaning of the second clause. The free rendering of the third and fourth was said to be, "Your horns crept so well; your horns crept well to the front." The general sense of the other clauses was said to be as follows: "O, your leg like trousers, your horns like a car, your foot is like that of an elephant, you walk with a step like a European soldier, your appearance is like that of a sambhar. I saw you were the most beautiful buffalo of all." It seems probable that the lament so far refers altogether to the buffalo. Then follows, "They said that you would be the parent of the dead, but now you are dead yourself"; or, "When old people are yet alive, why are young ones taken?" Then follows the *kwarzam* of the Kars clan, and the rest obviously refers to Pidrvan himself: "O chief of many villages, conqueror, peace-loving and yet strong man. You were like Kavanadi, who carried the posts of the buffalo-pen.[2] O man of wonderful birth, renowned you were born; you held councils; you fined some by money and some by buffaloes; you settled who should marry the women. In

[1] As both these funeral laments were obtained from Samuel, I cannot guarantee that the method of spelling adopted is the same as that used elsewhere in the book; this is especially the case with the sign 'th,' which, in agreement with the practice customary in South India, was used by Samuel for the lingual 'ṭ,' and sometimes for a sound for which I have used the letter d.

[2] For the story to which this refers, see Chapter XXVIII.

the midst of barren buffaloes you went; you caught the throats of the buffaloes; you ran first and caught the buffaloes before the chosen men; well you danced and shouted finely; you invented new things. To-day for the last time I saw your face. Has the angel of death come to you? I see nothing but ashes in your burning-place. In your *azaram* place I see nothing but grass growing."

Purification Ceremonies

Certain further ceremonies are performed about the time of the first new moon after the *marvainolkedr.*

At one or both of the funerals of a Tarthar man a sacred buffalo will have been killed by the *wursol* and the sacred bell (*mani*) will have been used. By his acts at the funeral the *wursol* loses his office, and by its use on the same occasion the *mani* is defiled. On the day before the new moon following the funeral all the things in the dairy of the *wursol* are thrown away. Either a new dairyman is appointed and goes through the usual rites, or the old *wursol* is re-appointed and has to repeat his ordination ceremonies. This is done on the Sunday after the new moon, which is the proper day for the ordination of a *wursol*, exactly the same ceremonies being performed as those described in Chapter VII. The old *wursol* puts the *mani* in the dairy stream (*pali nipa*), and if he is not re-appointed, his duties then cease. The new *wursol*, or the old *wursol* who has undergone new ordination ceremonies, takes the *mani* from the stream and purifies it by rubbing it all over with pounded *tudr* bark and water. He then takes the bell to the dairy, which is now empty, finds a new stick on which to hang it, and puts both stick and bell in their proper place on the *patatmar*. Then the new dairy vessels are purified and put in their places in the usual manner.

This purification of the dairy is not done by the Teivaliol, and seems to be only necessary when the *mani* and the dairyman who looks after it have been defiled by the funeral ceremonies. In the case of the Nòdrsol, the *mani* between the two funeral ceremonies is kept at Nòdrs, and is taken back to Òdr on the Sunday after the new moon following the second funeral, and it is at Òdr that the purification takes place.

Similarly the Kars *mani* is returned from Taradrkirsi to Kars on this day. I was told that the *pepkaricha* ceremony of making new *pep* is performed after the funeral of a man among the Tartharol, and it seems as if this new appointment of a dairyman and this use and purification of new dairy vessels are regarded as a form of the *pepkaricha* ceremony.

Another ceremony which takes place after the *marvainolkedr* is designed to purify the places used during the funeral rites and especially the *azaram*. This ceremony is called *kertnòdrkarchpimi*, "funeral place we purify," or *mutnolnòdrvusthpimi*, "new moon day place (or ceremony) we keep." On the day of the new moon following the second funeral two men of the same clan as the deceased take a buffalo in the early morning from the pen to a spot about half a mile from the village. They wait there till about eleven o'clock, and then kill the buffalo by striking it on the head with a stone. They draw blood from one side of the animal and mix the blood with earth in a basket. The Teivaliol and Melgarsol add *tudr* bark to the earth and blood. The mixture is then taken to the funeral places and scattered over the spots where the buffalo was caught and killed, where the dead body or the *narskedr* had lain at the two funerals, at the *methkudi* and the *azaram*. If the places for the *etvainol-* and *marvainol-kedr* are different and far distant from one another, the spots used at the former may be omitted, but the most important place which must always be purified in this way is the *azaram*. In any case this place is the last to be purified, and the men then throw away the basket and go straight back to their village, where they bathe and take food, having fasted till this time.

This ceremony is only performed after the funerals of males. The buffalo killed is called the *nòdrvusthpir*. The Teivaliol and Melgarsol use a male buffalo calf for the purpose; the Tartharol, other than the Melgarsol, use an adult female buffalo.

No use is made of the flesh of the animal; the body is left where it falls and is not given to the Kotas.

After a funeral, the members of the Tarthar clans, except the Melgarsol, shave their heads, but this is not done either by the Melgarsol or Teivaliol. I did not inquire fully into this matter, and do not know what regulations there are in connexion with the practice, or whether it is regarded as purificatory.

THE FUNERALS OF CHILDREN

The body of a still-born child is buried at the same time as, and together with, the afterbirth, without any ceremonial. In one case which occurred during my visit, this was done by the woman who assisted at the delivery. The body was buried in the early morning on the day on which the mother underwent the ceremonies attending removal to the seclusion-hut.

If a child less than two years of age dies, both funerals are held on one day. The *etvainolkedr* takes place in the morning, the *marvainolkedr* in the afternoon; a buffalo is killed at each, and the *azaramkedr* is held on the following morning as usual. If the child is very young, less than a month old, a male buffalo only may be killed, but if the father chooses, two buffaloes may be killed as at the funeral of an adult.

Thus, the child of Piliag and Sintagars (52) died while the mother was in the seclusion-hut, and two ordinary buffaloes were killed. On this occasion, the two funerals were held on the same day as that on which the child died, owing to the death having taken place on one of the appointed days for a funeral of the clan. When the youngest child of Podners (47) died, only one male buffalo was killed for both ceremonies.

When a male child dies who has not cut his teeth nor been through the ear-piercing ceremony, the funeral is not held at the usual funeral place for males, but at another. Thus the Karsol do not take the body of such a child to Taradrkirsi but to a place called Punpali.

When I attended the funeral of a girl named Sinerani (52), the daughter of Kuriolv of Kuudr, both ceremonies were performed on the same day, and a number of incidents occurred which were very interesting as illustrations of many of the practices which have been described throughout this chapter. The child was about two years old and had not yet been betrothed, but as soon as she was dead it was arranged that she should marry her *matchuni*, Keinba (68), a little boy about four years of age, the son of her mother's brother, and this boy occupied a prominent position among those taking part in the funeral rites. Owing to the marriage of the dead child to this boy, the dead child would come to be one of his clan, the Keadrol, and there seemed to be no doubt that, according to strict custom, the funeral should have been held at the funeral place of this clan. Kuriolv, however, arranged that the funeral should take place at Kurkalmut, the funeral place for women of the Kuudrol, but as the girl did not properly belong to this clan the funeral hut was not erected within the circle of stones at this place, but outside it.

The beginning of the funeral ceremonies was delayed for some time because the little boy, Keinba (Fig. 57), had to be taken by his father, Perpakh, in search of the wood and grass out of which to make the bow and arrow to be used in the *pursütpimi* ceremony, and they had to go far to find the proper plants for the manufacture of the mimic weapon.

After this delay the ceremonial took its natural course till the buffalo which had been caught by the Taradr men was being taken to the place appointed for its slaughter by the side of the funeral hut. The people had great difficulty in making the buffalo move, and at last it lay down on a boggy piece of ground, and the efforts of all failed to make it go further. The diviners, Midjkudr and Mongudrvan, were then called upon to ascertain the cause of the obstinacy of the buffalo, and then followed the performance which I have already described (see p. 252).

The reasons given by Midjkudr were not very clear, and there seemed to be a good deal of doubt as to what he had really said, but the following appeared to be the chief reasons given :—

The buffalo, Kursi, which had delayed the proceedings, was the property of Kuriolv and was descended from a buffalo which had belonged to Teitchi, Kuriolv's grandfather. Since this buffalo was thus family property, it should go to the sons, and ought not to be killed for a daughter, and especially for one who now belonged to another clan. Kuriolv ought to have used a buffalo which he had acquired in his own lifetime. Midjkudr went on to say that Kuriolv, having done wrong, must pay compensation to the dead, and told him to give the buffalo named Perov. As a sign that he would do

FIG. 57.—KEINBA AND PERPAKH; THE FORMER IS HOLDING IN HIS HAND THE IMITATION BOW AND ARROW AND HAS HIS CLOAK OVER HIS HEAD.

so, Kuriolv performed the *kalmelpudithti* salutation to Perner, the grandfather of Keinba and also through Sintharap, of the dead girl.

Another reason given was that the buffalo had been caught at the wrong place—viz., at the place where it ought to be caught at the funeral of a male. I only heard of this reason a few days later, and I do not know whether it was one of the reasons given by Midjkudr or whether it was a later surmise. A third reason was that Perner and Tebner, his brother, had been on bad terms; and to put this right Tebner, the younger, performed the *kalmelpudithti* salutation to Perner.

The next special feature of the ceremony took place after the buffalo had been killed and before the *kachütthti* ceremony. Keinba knelt down before Kuriolv and Piliag and the two men touched the head of the boy with their feet, thus accepting him as the husband of Sinerani. Then followed the *pursütpimi* ceremony. The mantle covering the dead child was opened, her right hand unclenched, and Keinba placed the little bow and arrow in the hand, and the fingers of the dead child were closed over the bow so that they held it as they would have done in life. Then the bow was taken out of the hand, placed on the breast of the child, and the mantle was again folded over her. Teitnir, the half-brother of Kuriolv, who had now become the *paiol* of Keinba, came up and covered the head of the boy with his *putkuli* as a sign that he was a widower, and then Teitnir and Keinba put their foreheads together and cried. After crying together for a while, Teitnir touched Keinba's head with his foot. Then Sintharap, the mother of Sinerani, gave grain and jaggery and limes to Keinba, who put them in the pocket of the mantle of the dead child. Sintharap and Keinba then cried together, and Sintharap touched Keinba's head with her foot.

After the cloth-giving ceremony, the body was taken to the burning place, and Keinba mixed honey and grain in a metal bowl; when Keinba began to stir the grain and honey he put his right arm out from above his cloak as usual, but was speedily corrected and made to put out his hand from below the cloak in the manner proper for a widower.

The wrists of the girl were burnt as in the *urvatpimi* ceremony, the burning being done by Silkidz (53), the wife of a younger brother of Perpakh, Keinba's father, and, before her marriage, like Sinerani, one of the Kuudrol. Silkidz also lighted the pyre.

In spite of the results of his previous infringement of funeral law, Kuriolv made a further departure from orthodox custom in burning on the pyre imitation buffalo horns, which should only be burnt at the funerals of males. Then after being swung over the flames as usual, the body was placed on the pyre.

Less than half an hour later, and long before the body could have been consumed, the *marvainolkedr* began, and passed off without any special incident. Another buffalo was caught and killed and laid by the side of a mantle containing hair which had been cut from the head of the dead child by Keinba. The mantle should also have contained a piece of skull, but the body had not been sufficiently consumed to procure this, and so the hair alone was held to be sufficient.

Later a distribution of grain took place, and those who were to take no part in the *azaramkedr* on the following morning went to their homes.

At another funeral of an unmarried girl, Olidzeimi (21), the ceremony of *pursütpimi* was performed by the boy Pulgudr (38), who had been married in infancy to the girl. He was her *matchuni*, being the son of Teijer, the sister of Parkeidi, Olidzeimi's father. On this occasion Pulgudr said to his father-in-law, Parkeidi, three times, "*pursadikina ?*"—"Shall I touch (with the) bow?" and Parkeidi replied each time, "*Pursad!*"—"Touch with the bow!" Then Pulgudr put the bow and arrow into the hand of the dead girl, and Parkeidi covered Pulgudr's head with the cloak, and the boy put grain, jaggery, and limes into the pocket of the cloak of Olidzeimi. At the funeral of Sinerani, Keinba did not say the proper formula, probably because he was too young.

Funeral Contributions

In the old days, when a large number of buffaloes were slaughtered at the funerals, and especially at the *marvainolkedr*, it was the rule that every *manmokh*, or sister's son, should supply a buffalo, while in the case of a child it seemed that buffaloes were sometimes given by the *mun*, or mother's brother.

Buffaloes were also given by the husbands of the daughters of a man, whether they were the *manmokh* of the man or not. They might be given by other relatives, but it seemed that the gift was especially a duty of the *manmokh* and *paiol*. The *mokhthodvaiol* of a woman should also contribute a buffalo for her second funeral.

At the present time the limitation of the number of buffaloes which may be slaughtered has removed the necessity for these gifts, but it still remains the custom for one of the buffaloes to be supplied by the *manmokh* or some corresponding relative, or, at any rate, it seems to be usual for one buffalo to be supplied by relatives of a man on the male side, and the other by relatives on the female side; thus, at the funeral of Sinerani (52) one buffalo was given by Kuriolv, the father of the dead child, and the other by Perner (68), the father of the child's mother, and also the grandfather of her husband.

Contributions in money may be made by any relative, and all those who have married into the family of the deceased, even if only boys, should contribute eight annas or a rupee towards the general expenses, this custom being called *tinkanik panm ätpimi*. The *mokhthodvaiol* of a woman should contribute at least five rupees to the expenses of the second funeral.

The ceremony of *kachütthti* (see p. 358) also involves a payment from his sons-in-law to a man of the same clan as the dead man. The money is not paid, however, till the woman who places the cloths on the body has attended twenty funerals and is, therefore, probably not paid at all in many cases, but it may be regarded as tribute from those who have married into a family at each death in the family.

The contributions of buffaloes and money from a man to the relatives of his wife are called *pöürl*.

Contributions of food are received from various relatives, who also contribute certain of the objects used for the adornment of the body. Each relative gives a waist-string called *pennar*, made of black and white thread, which is put round the body of the corpse. That given by a *manmokh* is exceptionally honoured in that it is tied round the body inside the mantle together with that given by the son of the deceased, those given by other relatives being put outside the mantle.

Many of the necessaries for the funerals are provided by the Kotas. The part they take as the musicians has been already mentioned. In addition they provide for the first funeral the cloak (*putkuli*) in which the body is wrapped, and grain (*patm* or *samai*) to the amount of five to ten *kwa*. They give one or two rupees towards the expenses, and if they should have no grain their contribution of money is increased.

At the *marvainolkedr* their contributions are more extensive. They provide the *putkuli*, together with a sum of eight annas for the decoration of the cloak by the Toda women. They give two to five rupees towards the general expenses and provide the bow and arrow, basket (*tek*), knife (*kafkati*), and the sieve called *kudshmurn*. The Kotas receive at each funeral the bodies of the slaughtered buffaloes, and are also usually given food. The method by which these contributions from the Kotas to the Todas are regulated will be considered in Chapter XXVII.

AMNÒDR

Amnòdr[1] is the other world of the Todas to which the dead go. It lies to the west and is lighted by the same sun as this world. The sun goes there when it sinks to the west so that when it is dark on the Nilgiris it is light in Amnòdr, and when it is dark in Amnòdr it is light on the Nilgiris. When Kwoto tied down the sun it was dark in both worlds and the people of Amnòdr complained (see p. 206) and joined with those of this world in the request that the sun should be restored to its proper place. Amnòdr is considered to be below this world,

[1] This may possibly be the world of Yama, the Todas rarely, if ever, using the the letter y. The word was often pronounced Amanòdr.

and this was given as the reason why the dead used to be burnt face downwards. It will be remembered also that Ön was looking downwards when he saw his son Püv in Amnòdr (see p. 185).

Amnòdr is presided over by the god Ön, who went there after the death of his son Püv, and it is often called Önnòdr after him, while this world, presided over by the goddess Teikirzi, is known as Inanòdr or Eikirzinòdr.[1] The people of Amnòdr or Önnòdr are known as the Amatol. Formerly the Todas used to go freely to and fro between Amnòdr and Eikirzinòdr, but this was stopped owing to the behaviour of Kwoto, and since his time only the dead go to Amnòdr and they do not return.

The Amatol live in much the same way as the inhabitants of this world. They have their buffaloes and their dairies, and the daily life of the people appears to be much like that of the living Todas. As the people walk about, however, they wear down their legs. They have to walk every day, and when a man has worn down his legs as far as the knees Ön sends him back to this world as another man.

Ön will not allow any pigs or rats to enter Amnòdr, as they would root up and spoil the country.

Dead people travel to Amnòdr by well-defined routes, which are different for Tartharol and Teivaliol, while the Taradrol have a separate Amnòdr for their clan.

The dead do not set out for Amnòdr till after the second funeral, taking with them the things burnt at the *azaramkedr*. Both Tartharol and Teivaliol journey westwards towards the Kundahs and cross the Pakhwar or Avalanche river at the same spot.

The paths for the two divisions then diverge. The Tartharol go by a place called Katchâr, while the Teivaliol go by Kusheigûdr, situated by the bridle path now leading from Avalanche Bungalow to Avalanche Top. Whenever a Teivali man passes this spot for the first time he throws three stones called *oviônikârs*. Similarly, a Tarthar man passing Katchâr for the first time throws three stones in

[1] This is one of several instances in which the initial *t* of a word is omitted in compound forms.

the same way. At the top of the hill there is a spot at which every Toda salutes (*kaimukhti*) in all directions.

The two paths meet again at a stone called Nidzmûtkârs (hot knock stone). When the dead Todas reach this stone they knock on it, and in so doing lose all their love of this world. They proceed and reach the stone called Panîpikârs, on which also they knock, and by so doing lose all their diseases and become strong again, so that they are sound and vigorous when they reach Amnòdr.

After knocking on Panîpikârs, the dead pass a wood called Katiârnpül, in which there is a tree called *main*, and as they go they make a cut on this tree with the *kafkati* or knife burnt with them, and Todas who pass by Katiârnpül on the day after a funeral have often seen the newly made cut on the *main* tree. For women there is another place in the wood called Patkadipem, and here the woman pounds with the *wask* burnt at her *azaramkedr*.

On proceeding the dead Todas come to a ravine and river called Püvûrkin, near Sisapara. Across this river there is a thread bridge, and those who have been bad Todas during life fall into the river and are bitten by leeches (*püv* or *püf*). The people who cross the thread bridge successfully go straight to Amnòdr, but those who fall are helped out of the river by the people of Padrmukhteir (crowd plain swamp), who belong to all tribes and live on the further bank of Püvûrkin. The people of Padrmukhteir may keep the offending Todas in their country for some time. The greater their offences, the longer are they kept, but all, however bad, reach Amnòdr sooner or later.

The following are the people who fall into Püvûrkin:—(*a*) the *karainol*, selfish people; (*b*) the *kashtvainol*, jealous and grudging people; (*c*) the *kaspivainol*, those who have committed any offences against the dairy, whether *pali* or *poh*.

The danger of falling into Püvûrkin does not seem to have much influence on the people. It has been spoken of as the Toda Hell, but it is rather a mild variety of Purgatory, and only involves some discomfort and delay on the journey to the next world. The people of Kavidi in the Wainad may travel direct to Amnòdr without going over Püvûrkin at all, and they run no danger from this source, however bad they may have been.

The people of Taradr are said to have a separate Amnòdr near Külvari or Perithi, and they do not travel by Nidzmûtkârs or by Panîpikârs, nor do they cross Püvûrkin. They have no dangers by the way, and however wicked they may have been they go to their Amnòdr in security. Men, women and buffaloes all follow the same path.

Origin of Funeral Customs

The various funeral customs are said to have been partly ordained by Teikirzi. The following story is given as the account of their origin :—

At first no Toda died. After a time a Piedr man died at the village of Erparskòdr. He died in his hut and the Todas took his body to the funeral place, but on the way they laid it by a heap of stones between Erparskòdr and Umgas. The stones are still to be seen, and are called Möditikars.[1] While the body lay by these stones, some of the people were weeping bitterly; others were dancing and singing, and others were going to drive buffaloes. Teikirzi, who saw the people weeping, took pity and came to bring the dead man back to life. When she came to the place she found that though some of the people were crying, others seemed quite happy. She liked what she saw, and decided not to raise the dead man, so she went away and ordained that in the future some should cry at funerals and others should be happy, and her laws as to the conduct of the funeral ceremonies have been followed ever since.

Then the people took up the dead body and went on to Kûrûvòrs, near Umgas, where they performed the funeral ceremonies.

In the various complicated ceremonies described in this chapter there are certain features which may be briefly discussed.

[1] *Möditi* is the name applied to all the women of other tribes. It is perhaps suggestive that this name should be used for a stone connected with the goddess Teikirzi.

There is no doubt that the buffaloes killed at the funeral are supposed to go to Amnòdr with the dead person. Sacred buffaloes are only killed at the funerals of men, for they would be useless to women, who, in the next world as in this, have nothing to do with dairies at which the sacred buffaloes must be tended. There is no evidence that the slaughter of buffaloes is in any way a propitiatory sacrifice, and there seems to be a very marked absence of anything resembling prayer or other forms of appeal to higher powers in the funeral ceremonies.[1]

Dairymen take part in the funeral ceremonies, but chiefly in connexion with the sacred buffaloes. The highest kind of dairyman, the *palol*, has no duties whatever, and loses his office if he takes part merely as a visitor. At Tarthar funerals the *wursol* has important duties, chiefly connected with the sacred buffaloes and with the *mani*, which is hung round their necks. He also takes the chief part in the *koòtiti* and accompanying ceremonies of the second funeral, probably because the sacred *tudr* bark is used. In one rite there is no obvious reason why the *wursol* should play a part—viz., in that of throwing earth. As this ceremony, however, is of especial importance, it suggests that formerly dairymen may have had more to do with funeral ceremonies than is the case at present.

Among the Teivaliol, the *palikartmokh* has less important functions. He probably kills the sacred buffaloes, though on this point I am not certain. Only one Teivali clan possesses a *mani* which is used at a funeral, and it is noteworthy that, though the bell is removed from its hiding place (see p. 354) by the *palikartmokh*, it is taken to the funeral and hung on the neck of the buffalo by a Tarthar man belonging to the Nòdrs clan.

The facts that the *wursol* takes part in the funerals of men; that sacred buffaloes are killed; that dairies are used in these funerals, and that the funeral hut of a man is always

[1] Several of those who have witnessed Toda funerals have noticed that barren buffaloes are killed on these occasions, and I believe that it is a recognised custom to use such animals. Pidrvan's funeral lament begins with a reference to barren buffaloes, and the clause, "in the midst of barren buffaloes you went," evidently refers to Pidrvan's skill in catching buffaloes at the funeral ceremonies.

called *pali* or dairy, even when built for the occasion, all bring the funeral ceremonies of men into connexion with the religious dairy ceremonial of the Todas. On the other hand, even in those cases in which a daïry is used as a funeral hut, the dairyman of that dairy has nothing to do with the funeral ceremonies; thus, at Nòdrs the dairy in which the body of a dead man is laid is the *tarvali*, but the *tarvalikartmokh* has no duties in connexion with the funeral, and does his dairy work as usual, while it is the dairyman of the conical *poh*, the *wursol*, who takes an active part in the funeral rites.

The earth-throwing ceremony is of especial interest, because it would seem to be a relic of burial. Earth is thrown three times on the corpse before it is burnt. In connexion with the idea that the ceremony is a relic of a previous stage, in which the Todas buried their dead, it may be mentioned that a ceremony with some points of similarity is performed at the funerals of the Hill Arrians of the Western Ghats,[1] who bury their dead. A man of the same clan as the deceased takes a new cloth and tears from it a narrow strip which he fastens upon himself. He then goes backwards to the place fixed for the grave and digs with a hoe, removing three hoes full of earth. In this ceremony he is said to be calling on the earth to give up six feet for the dead. There is a suggestive resemblance between the ceremonies performed by these two hill tribes of South-west India, which lends some support to the view that the earth-throwing ceremony of the Todas is a relic of inhumation.

It perhaps may be regarded as a fact inconsistent with this view that the earth-throwing ceremony is performed at both funerals, and again the throwing of earth into a buffalo pen is so essential a feature that it is possible the whole ceremony may have some other meaning.

It is tempting to extend the conjecture by supposing that the dead were at one time buried in the *tu* or buffalo pen, but there is, as far as I know, no evidence that this was ever done by the Todas or by any other Indian tribe. Unless, indeed, the *azaram* is the representative of a *tu*, in which case the burial of the ashes at the entrance of the *azaram* may be

[1] See Fawcett, *Journ. Anthrop. Soc. Bombay*, 1890, vol. ii., p. 146.

a survival of a time when the body was buried at the entrance of a pen.

The custom of burning the hut at a woman's funeral is probably a survival of the common custom of burning the house of a dead person, but it is possible that in the case of the Todas this may have been associated with the belief that the hut would be useful in the next world. The funeral hut of a man is not burnt, and this is almost certainly because it is, or represents, a dairy. The motive for the burning of the house of a dead person is probably to remove a place which the ghost may haunt, and the sanctity of the dairy was probably such as to render this precaution unnecessary after the death of a man.

The Toda custom of cremating their dead is accompanied by a belief that the dead go to a distant spirit-world. It seems quite certain that the Todas believe that the dead do not set out on their journey to the next world till after the second funeral ceremonies, but I am not at all clear what is supposed to become of the spirits of the dead in the interval between the two ceremonies. The spirit of a Melgars man during the interval is said to be a *kazun* or malignant spirit, but I was unable to obtain a full account of the Toda belief about the *kazun*, nor was I able to find out whether there is any belief in the malignity of the spirits of the dead of other clans.[1] That such spirits are impure is, I think, shown conclusively by the impurity of the relics of the dead and of all those who have been in contact with them. The intense objection to the sacred *ti* buffaloes or their guardians coming into relation, however indirectly, with the relics is evidence of the belief in the impurity, if not in the malignity, of the spirits of the dead between the two funeral ceremonies.

There is one rite which seems to point to the influence of the spirits of the dead on the living, and this is the obscure ceremony of *tersamptpimi*, which is performed on the day after the *marvainolkedr* of a Tarthar man (see p. 333). The ceremony consists in cutting a lock of hair from a young child. One obvious explanation would be

[1] In Teitnir's lament for Pidrvan (see p. 387) he speaks of a Kars *kazun*, which suggests that each clan has its own *kazun*.

furnished if we supposed that the spirits of the dead are malignant and that the ceremony was postponed till after the spirit had set out on his journey to Amnòdr, but there are two objections to this explanation. If the Todas had had this in their minds, they would have said that the ceremony might not be performed while there was *kedr* among the Tartharol, *i.e.*, while the funeral ceremonies of a Tarthar man were still incomplete. For the *tersamptpimi* ceremony, however, it seems that a child has to wait till after a *marvainolkedr* even if there has been no recent death among the Tartharol. Further, if the proposed explanation had been correct, there is no reason why the *karvnɔl*, or day immediately after the funeral, should have been appointed for the ceremony. The fact that this day is prescribed points rather to some beneficial influence which it is hoped may emanate from the dead.

CHAPTER XVII

SACRED DAYS AND NUMBERS

WE have seen that nearly every Toda ceremony has its appointed day or days, and that the choice of these is often dependent on another Toda institution, the sacred day, either of the village or of the dairy. Every clan has certain days of the week on which people are restricted from following many of their ordinary occupations, although they are not the occasions of any special ceremonies. These sacred days are the *madnol* or village day, and the *palinol* or dairy day. Another occasion to which the same kinds of restriction apply is the *arpatznol*, the day of the week corresponding to that on which the father of a man has died.

THE MADNOL AND PALINOL

The *madnol* is literally the village day. Each village has its *madnol*, and in some cases it would seem that different villages of a clan might have different *madnol*, but in general the *madnol* is the same for the whole clan.

Certain things may not be done on the *madnol*:—

(i) *ponkisthògadi*, a feast may not be given (lit. feast may not divide, *i.e.*, food must not be shared out).

(ii) *kêdrvîtògadi*, funeral ceremonies may not be performed.

(iii) *kwadrtògadi*, nothing may be given (from the village). Since buying implies the departure of money from the village, a secondary consequence is that nothing may be bought on the *madnol*, but if anything is given to an inhabitant of the village, he may bring it into the village on this day.

(iv) Women may not leave the village, nor may women from other places come to the village.

(v) The people may not bathe nor cut their nails on the *madnol*, and the men may not shave. Clothes may not be washed, nor may the usual cleansing of the house with buffalo-dung be done. The ordinary meals may be prepared, but the people must not cook rice with milk.

(vi) The stone called *tukitthkars* may not be touched.

(vii) The dairyman may not leave the village, and the ordination ceremonies of a dairyman may not take place on this day.

(viii) The people may not migrate from one village to another, nor may the buffaloes be taken from one place to another.

Among the Teivaliol the *madnol* is the only sacred day of the week, but among the Tartharol there is also a dairy day or *palinol*, and if there is more than one dairy there may be one such holy day for each kind of dairy, each named after the dairy, the *wursulinol*, the *kudrpalinol*, or the *tarvalinol*. Similarly, Taradr has a *kugvalinol* and Kanòdrs a *pohnol*.

On these days milk and ghi may not be given out from the dairy, nor may they be sold. Butter and buttermilk may be distributed, but only to the people of the village. Buffaloes may not be driven on these days. Women may not leave the village, though women of other villages are allowed to come. Cleansing with buffalo-dung must not be done. There was some difference of opinion as to whether money might leave the village on these days. Some said not, but it seemed clear that at Kars money might be taken from the village on the *palinol*. The rules were said to be the same for the holy days of all kinds of dairy.

There are various recognised methods of evading the rules for the holy days, and of avoiding the inconvenience which the regulations might entail on a village.

Money may be taken out of the village on the day before the *madnol* and buried or left in some spot where it can be found on the following day, so that if there is an urgent reason why a purchase should be completed on the holy day this can be done.

Similarly, women who wish to leave the village on a holy day do so before daybreak. They wait outside the village till the sun is up, then return to the village, have their meals and do any necessary work, and may then leave. Having left the village before daybreak, a woman is apparently regarded as ceremonially absent during her return to the village, and by making this false start she is held to be keeping the law.

If there is an urgent reason why a woman from another village should come on a *madnol*, she must arrive after sunset.

If any of these rules are broken, the culprit may have to perform the ceremony of *irnörtiti* or one of the other allied rites. It seemed quite clear, however, that this only happened if some misfortune should befall the offender, his family, or his buffaloes. It would seem that a man might habitually and notoriously desecrate the *madnol*, but no steps would be taken by himself or the community so long as things went well with the man. If he should become ill or if his buffaloes should suffer in any way, he would consult the diviners and they would then certainly find that his misfortunes were due to his infringement of the laws connected with the sacred days.

As a matter of fact, it does not happen, so far as I could find, that anyone habitually infringes the laws, and breaking the *madnol* or *palinol* rarely forms an occasion for the *irnörtiti* ceremony.

THE ARPATZNOL.

Another sacred day is the *arpatznol* or *arpasnol*. This is the day of the week on which the father of a man has died. The father of Kutadri and Kòdrner died on a Friday, and every Friday is the *arpatznol* of these men. I could not learn definitely what are the restrictions for this day, but they seem to be of the same kind as those for the *madnol*, though I am doubtful whether they are very strictly kept. Kutadri and Kòdrner once drove their buffaloes from Kars to Isharadr on a Friday; the buffaloes were sick, and they moved them without thinking that it was their *arpatznol*,

Soon after Kòdrner fell ill and one of the buffaloes died, and the *teuol* found that the desecration of the *arpatznol* was one of the causes, though they had also bought things on a Monday, the *madnol* of Kars.

There is much variety in the days appointed as the *madnol* or *palinol* of different villages and clans. My records are very incomplete, but they show the most frequent days to be Wednesday and Friday, which are sacred in six clans. Sunday is sacred in five clans, Monday and Tuesday in three, and Thursday in two, while in no clan, so far as my records go, is Saturday a holy day.

It will have been noticed that funeral ceremonies may not be held on a *madnol*, and it seems to be exceptional that funeral ceremonies should take place on one of the dairy days. There is very little doubt that it is the prohibition of funerals on village and dairy days which chiefly determines the choice of funeral days. Thus, at Nidrsi, Wednesday is the *madnol*, Monday is the *wursulinol*, Friday is the *tarvalinol*, while the funeral of a male is held on Saturday or Sunday and that of a female on Tuesday or Thursday. Similarly, the village and dairy days of Melgars are Monday and Friday, while the funeral days for males are Sunday and Tuesday, for females Thursday and Saturday. At Kwòdrdoni, the village and dairy days are Wednesday, Friday, and Sunday, the funeral days Tuesday, Thursday and Saturday.

In a few cases, it would seem that funerals may be held on dairy days ; thus, at Kars Monday is the *madnol*, Tuesday the *wursulinol*, and Thursday the *kudrpalinol*, while the funeral days for males are Sundays and Tuesdays, for females Thursdays and Saturdays. If a *mani* is used, however, a male funeral must be held on Sunday, and I suspect that the holding of a male funeral on Tuesday is an innovation, and probably the same holds good for the choice of Thursday as a funeral day for females.

The funeral rites are not the only ceremonies which have their appointed days. Nearly every ceremonial occasion among the Todas has its prescribed day, and of these ceremonial days Sunday seems to occupy an especially favoured position. As many ceremonies are appointed for this day as for nearly all the other days of the week put together. It is also the most frequent day for the funerals of males, and it seemed to me that whenever it was possible this day was chosen.

Several clans, however, have Sunday as the *madnol*, and if the laws of this day are observed ceremonies of which feasts form a part could not be performed on this day in these clans; thus, though I have no definite information on the point, I have no doubt that the *irpalvusthi* ceremony could not be performed.

It so happens that the clans which have Sunday as their *madnol* or *palinol* are Pan, Kanòdrs, Päm, Kwòdrdoni, and Pedrkars, all clans seated in outlying parts of the hills about which my information is less complete than in other cases. None of the larger and more important central clans about whose customs I obtained the fullest information had either *madnol* or *palinol* on a Sunday, and I have very little doubt that in those clans which have Sunday as a *madnol*, ceremonies, at any rate of a festive nature, would not be performed on this day. There is little doubt that the great prominence of Sunday as a feast day would have come out less strongly if my information about the outlying clans had been more complete.

I must leave this point uncertain, but I have little doubt that with fuller information about the customs of different clans we should find that the choice of days for ceremonies is chiefly, if not entirely, determined by the necessity of holding these on some day other than the *madnol* or *palinol*.

At the same time, there can be no doubt that Sunday is one of the days appointed for a festival or ceremony very frequently, and this is especially the case at the *ti*, the procedure of which is to a large extent uninfluenced by considerations concerned with the *madnol* and *palinol*. Even here, however, these days are not altogether without influence, for certain ceremonial days at the *ti* are feast days for the clan to which the *ti* belongs, and this would make it necessary that the ceremonies should not be held on the *madnol* of the clan. Certain days were said to be feast-days throughout the whole Toda community, but I have no knowledge as to how these days would be kept by those clans on whose *madnol* they might fall.

Several previous writers, when recording the choice of certain days for the funeral ceremonies, have ascribed to the Todas a belief in lucky and unlucky days, in days of good or evil omen. One man, when telling me that Sunday, Wednesday, and Saturday were days on which the *irpalvusthi* ceremony might be performed at the *tarvali*, referred to them as lucky days.

I think it is extremely doubtful whether the Toda in general has any such belief, and if he has, it is probable that the idea is a recent importation borrowed from the Hindus, among whom the belief in lucky or unlucky days is of course very prevalent. The distinction among the Todas is rather into feast and fast days, using the latter term in a wide sense.

It is possible that the institutions of *madnol* and *palinol* have grown out of the belief in unlucky days; that certain things were not done on these days because they were unlucky days, and that so there came into existence a code of rules prescribing what might and what might not be done.

The chief difficulty in the way of this view is the fact that the different clans of the Todas have different sacred days. One would expect lucky and unlucky days to be the same for the whole community. The sacred days place very definite restrictions on the intercourse between different clans, and this inconvenience must be increased by the fact that the different clans have different *madnol*, and there is no obvious reason why this difference in the choice of sacred days should have come about.

The distinction between *madnol* and *palinol* is, again, one which can hardly have grown out of the belief in unlucky days, though perhaps, given a village day, it is not an unnatural step for the Todas to have decided that they would have a dairy day also.

Whatever the origin of the laws regulating Toda custom in this respect, I think there is little doubt that when at the present time a given act is done or not done on a given day, the action is not based on a belief in lucky or unlucky days, but, as nearly always among the Todas, on custom prescribing that the act shall or shall not be done on that day.

There are, however, other restrictions or relaxations connected with certain days of the week which have probably arisen out of a belief in lucky and unlucky days.

There is a regulation (now almost a dead letter) that the Todas must not cross the Paikara and Avalanche rivers on Tuesdays, Fridays, or Saturdays. Sundays and Wednesdays, on the other hand, are the days on which the *wursol* is allowed to sleep in the hut with ordinary people, and Mondays and Thursdays are the days on which the *palol* is visited by Todas other than the *mòrol*. Such facts suggest that the three days on which the rivers should not be crossed are unlucky days, but, on the other hand, the days which I was once told were lucky days included Saturday. The evidence at our command is conflicting, and does no more than suggest that the restrictions or relaxations common to the whole community may be connected with the belief in lucky and unlucky days.

Attention may here be called to the fact that the Todas evidently regard the first half of the month as most auspicious for their ceremonies, and it would seem that in most cases the first appropriate day of the week after the new moon is the proper day for nearly every Toda ceremonial. I met with no case in which any ceremony was appointed for the period of the full moon or for the second half of the moon's period. At the present, it seems that such ceremonies as those connected with the migrations of the buffaloes may take place in the second half of the month, but I have no doubt that this is only a result of modern laxity.

The definite values assigned to different days of the week is a very special feature of Toda custom, and in the *madnol* we have an institution very closely resembling that of the Sabbath. In a busier community than that of the Todas, the existence of different *madnol* for different clans of the community would soon become a serious obstacle to carrying on the business of life, and such a community would probably agree that all clans should have the same holy day. At present the *madnol* is undoubtedly more sacred than the other sacred days, and if the latter were then to be neglected, we should have a community in which various activities were prohibited on one day of the week, and the institution so arising would differ very little from the Hebrew Sabbath. It is possible that the Todas show in an early stage the institution of a Sabbath in which the whole community has not yet settled on a single and joint holy day.

Sacred Numbers

Certain numbers recur with great frequency in the dairy ceremonial, and may be regarded as having a special sanctity on this account. There seems to be a general preference for uneven numbers, and this preference comes out very strongly in the *tesherst* ceremony, in which an uneven number of men must take part on any one occasion. The number of men performing this ceremony together must be three, five, seven, nine, &c.

In the dairy ritual the numbers which occur chiefly are three, seven and nine, but other numbers have also been singled out in other branches of Toda lore. The numbers which occur in ceremonial may now be considered in detail.

Three.—A large proportion of the ritual acts of the dairy are performed three times, usually with the accompaniment of the sacred syllable *Oñ* uttered thrice, once with each performance of the act. This three-fold performance is especially marked in the ceremony of putting milk or curds on the sacred bells and in the ceremonial drinking of buttermilk. In the ordination ceremonies, the number occurs less frequently. The purificatory drinking is always done seven times or some multiple of seven, but after drinking, the candidate rubs himself three times with the shoots or bark, and, at the ordination of a *palol*, the candidate drinks three times seven on several occasions. Other acts during the ordination of the *palol* are also performed thrice, and the same number occurs in the ordination of the *kaltmokh*.

Acts are performed thrice with special frequency in the ceremonial of the *ti*, and, at the ordinary dairy, this number is especially connected with the 'feeding' of the sacred bell, and there is no doubt that it is a number regarded as especially sacred. Whenever the sacred syllable *Oñ* is used, it is nearly always uttered thrice, and there seems to be a special association between the number three and this word.

In the *erkumptthpimi* ceremony three branches of *tudr* leaves are used, and they and the log with which the calf is killed are passed round the body of the animal thrice. Later in the ceremony three pieces of wood are thrown over the fire.

In the ceremonies connected with childbirth, the woman drinks thrice on various occasions, in the *pursütpimi* ceremony the name of the bow is asked and the answer given three times, and in the ceremony of name-giving three grains of barley are put into the mouth of the child and three into his hair.

At the funeral ceremonies, earth is thrown three times on the corpse and three times into the pen, the body is swung on the fire three times, and at the final scene of the *azaramkedr* the man who rings the bell goes round the burial place of the ashes thrice. Three *oviônikârs* are thrown by the man who crosses the pathway of the dead. The number three is not limited to the dairy ritual, but is of frequent occurrence in the whole of Toda ceremonial.

The number three also appears in connexion with magical or semi-magical practices. The various methods of treatment used by the *utkòren* are carried out three times and never more frequently than this, and the sufferer who drinks hot water to allay the effects of fright also does this thrice. A remedy is probably held to be more potent if repeated the same number of times as in the case of so many sacred acts.

Five.—This number does not occur in the dairy ceremonial except in certain ceremonies at the Nòdrs *ti* which are repeated five times because there are five groups of buffaloes belonging to this dairy. The number in this case has, however, no ceremonial significance, and is merely a consequence of the fact that one *palol* at this *ti* has three groups and the other two groups of buffaloes. The only other occurrence of the number is at the Kars *ti*, where the ancient lamp probably had five cavities, but even this is doubtful.

The number five comes in one place into Toda magic. The

sorcerer, who wishes to injure one who has not granted his request, hides five stones tied together with hair in the thatch of his enemy's hut.

Six.—This number does not occur in the dairy ceremonial, but it seems to be regarded as an auspicious number in some ways. In Teitnir's lament for his wife, reference is made to the hope that they might have had six children and six buffaloes, and in the prayer on the occasion of the ear-piercing ceremony, one clause runs "may he have six sons."

Six sticks are used to make the artificial dairy of the hand-burning ceremony, but this is an obvious result of the fact that the dairy has to have two rooms.

Seven.—This number is especially prominent in the ordination ceremonies. The purificatory drinking out of leaf-cups is always done seven times or some multiple of seven, the *palikartmokh* drinking seven times only, the *wursol* seven times seven, and the *palol* three times seven, seven times seven and nine times seven at different periods of his prolonged ordination ceremonies. At the dairies of Taradr and Kanòdrs, the number occurs in a different form, seven different kinds of leaf being used in the purificatory ceremonies.

The number occurs again in connexion with the lamp. At the Nòdrs *ti* and at the Pan *ti*, and possibly at other dairies, there used to be lamps, each of which had seven cavities and seven wicks. Some of these lamps have been lost, but two remain at the dairies mentioned. I have already referred to the fact that some of the ancient lamps were said to have had five wicks, but it seems clear that in the only two examples which survive there are seven wicks, and it is possible that this was the number in all.

Another occurrence of the number seven is in the old dairies of the Nòdrs clan which had seven rooms. The funeral dairies, which are undoubtedly very ancient institutions, have three rooms, and the Nòdrs dairies, also undoubtedly ancient, had seven, but I heard of no case in which a dairy had four, five, or six rooms.

Outside the dairy ceremonial, the only occurrence of this number is in the lament of Teitnir for his wife, in which he speaks of their visiting seven courts and seven ships.

It is perhaps significant that the number seven should be a sacred number to a people who have so highly developed the cult of different days of the week. It is possible that the purificatory drinkings of the ordination ceremonies were at one time performed seven times with the idea that the candidate was sanctifying himself for each day of the week, but at the present time it is clear that the act is performed seven times because this number is prescribed by custom. It would be interesting to ascertain whether the sanctity of the number seven occurs predominantly in the religious cults of peoples who have a seven-day week.

Nine.—This number only occurs in the dairy ceremonial during the ordination of the *palol* when the seven-fold purification with *tudr* is performed nine times.

Twelve.—I only met with this number once, in the prayer at the *pilinörtiti* ceremony, when the expression "12 years" is used as if it were equivalent to "for ever."

Sixteen and *Eighteen.*—The chief interest of these numbers is that they are used in connexion with the gods. There are said to be 1600, 1800 gods, and these numbers are mentioned in the prayer of the Kanòdrs dairy and in the legends. The numbers are probably used in the way in which we should use the word 'infinite,' but there must be some reason why they should have been chosen.

The number 18 occurs in another connexion in the rule that the *palol* should perform a certain ceremony after eighteen years of continuous office.

I have one possible clue to the choice of the number eighteen. The Todas say that a species of Strobilanth growing on the Nilgiris as a shrub only flowers once in eighteen years. They call this shrub *püvkat*, and it was in flower during the year of my visit. Albert, my interpreter, had only seen it in flower once or twice, but had not paid special attention to the duration of the flowering period. The number of times that several Todas had seen the flowers agreed approximately with their probable ages. Thus, Kutadri saw the flowers in 1902 for the third time, having seen them for the first time when he was twelve years old. This would make his age forty-eight, which seemed from other sources of information to be approximately correct. The Todas use the flower as a record of age, and some Todas are reputed to have seen the flowers seven times, which, taking five years as the age when they were first seen, would make them over 110 years.

There is another Strobilanth called *tirparikat* which is said to flower every twelve years, and another every six. I do not know of any confirmation of the flowering periods of these plants except the last, which probably refers to *Strobilanthes sexennis*.

Whether the Toda belief in the eighteen-year period of the plant they call *püvkat* is correct or not, it seems probable that it may have furnished the suggestion for the special position taken by the number eighteen in Toda lore.

CHAPTER XVIII

SACRED PLACES AND OBJECTS

THE Todas show undoubted signs of reverence to various material objects. Many of the objects so reverenced have been mentioned incidentally in the account of the dairy ritual and in other places, and in this chapter I propose to consider how far these objects are regarded as sacred, and to give an account of some sacred objects not hitherto noticed.

Of the various objects of reverence the following are the most important: hills and rivers; villages, dairies, their thresholds and contents; bells; the buffalo and its milk; trees and plants; the sun, fire and light; and stones.

HILLS AND OTHER PLACES.

Any place connected with the gods is reverenced by the the Todas, and this is especially the case with the hills where they dwell. Only some hills, however, are shown reverence by means of the *kaimukhti* salutation. One of these is the hill of Nòtirzi (Snowdon), and every Toda visiting this hill salutes with hand to forehead in all directions. Another place where a similar salutation is performed is a spot at Avalanche Top. When I visited this place with Kutadri he saluted in all directions with both hands to his face, and told me that a man who once omitted to do this was killed soon after by a tiger. In this case I could not learn that Kutadri was saluting any particular hill or other spot. He seemed to be saluting the region of the Kundahs on which he was about to enter.

There are doubtless other places where the same sign of reverence is used.

The sanctity of the hills will be further considered in the next chapter, when discussing in what sense at the present time the gods are believed to dwell on their summits.

RIVERS

There are two sacred rivers, the Teipakh (Paikara) and the Pakhwar (Avalanche), both identified with or inhabited by gods. They are the two largest streams on the Nilgiris, and there are numerous indications of their sanctity. Every Toda crossing either of these streams must put his right arm outside his cloak (*kevenarut*) while he is doing so. The only exception to this rule is in the case of a widower who is wearing his cloak over his head, and he shows his respect by putting out his right hand below the cloak. On cold days the Todas wrap their cloaks closely around them, and I have often seen them put out their right arms just before they stepped on the bridge near the Paikara bungalow, and put them in again with obvious relief the moment they had reached the other side.

At one time these rivers might only be crossed on certain days of the week. The Toda believed that if they crossed on a Tuesday, Friday, or Saturday, consequences might ensue which could only be set right by the *irnörtiti* ceremony. This prohibition is no longer in force, but its influence is still shown in another way.

When two *matchuni* cross either of these rivers in company they usually perform a ceremony to be described on p. 501, but this ceremony is omitted on the three days above mentioned, probably because the people should not properly be there at all.

The *palol* may not cross either of the rivers except at certain spots which are not the places used by ordinary people. In the old days there were certain fords, and the *palol* had his own ford. At the present time, when the Todas habitually cross the Paikara by means of a bridge, the restriction is put in the form that "the *palol* may not cross the river by the bridge." The *kaltmokh* also may not cross the river by the bridge except when he is degraded to the rank of *perkursol.*

There is a small stream near Nòdrs which may not be crossed at a given spot, this being the place where Teikirzi is reputed to have shared out the buffaloes among the Todas.

The only other restriction on crossing water was of a different kind. One who had been bitten by a snake might not cross a stream, and this applied to any stream and not only to the two sacred rivers of Teipakh and Pakhwar.

VILLAGES

It is difficult to distinguish how far the sanctity of a village is due to its dairy. No village without a dairy is regarded as sacred, but there is no doubt that the village itself may have some sanctity, and it is probable that the chief village of a clan which no longer had a dairy might nevertheless continue to be treated with some degree of reverence.

Reverence is shown to every village which is called an *etudmad*, but this word is used in two senses. The chief village of the clan from which the people of the clan take their name is the *etudmad* of the clan or *madol*, but the same name is also given to any village to which any special idea of sanctity attaches, and this is especially marked if its dairy should possess a *mani*. The sign of reverence paid to an *etudmad* is the salutation called *kaimukhti* or *kaburlti.* Whenever a man comes within sight of one of these villages he purifies his mouth by chewing some grass, and then salutes the village by placing his hand in front of his face in the way shown in Fig. 10. The salutation is performed with the right hand outside the cloak (*kevenarut*), and if a man is wearing a turban he will take it off, as is shown in the figure.

When a man salutes in this way he may be two or three miles from the village, the salutation being made, according to some accounts, directly the man sees the village, and according to others, not until he sees the dairy. When my guide Kòdrner was saluting the sacred village of Kiudr, I could see neither the hut nor the dairy of this village, though I could see the grove in which I knew them to be. When going from Ootacamund to Paikara by the bridle path the village of Taradr is saluted at a spot about two miles from the village in a straight line.

When a man leaves an *etudmad* he turns towards the village when it is about to pass out of view, chews some grass, and salutes in the same way as on first viewing it. On all the chief routes over the hills the Todas know the exact spots at which different villages become visible, and I have noticed that the salutation to a given village has been made by different Todas and on different occasions from exactly the same spot.

In a few cases there was some doubt as to whether a given village should receive the *kaimukhti* salutation or not. It seemed that there were certain *etudmad* more sacred than the rest, and they would be saluted by every Toda, irrespective of the division or clan to which he belonged, while in other cases the salutation was only obligatory on the members of the clan to which the village belonged, though these villages were often saluted by others who were scrupulous in following the observances of their people. The villages which must be saluted by every one are the seventeen chief villages of the clans (excluding Kidmad and Karsh), and two others, Kiudr and Miuni, the former because it is a *satimad* (see p. 421) and the latter because formerly the Toda gods used to hold their *naim* or council there. I made a list of the villages of each clan to which the salutation is paid by the members of the clan, and found that they were villages with dairies of sanctity, and in every case, so far as I could tell, villages of great antiquity. Many of the villages so honoured are mentioned in legend, and I believe this salutation to be a useful indication that a village is ancient. I shall have to discuss later whether Kavidi, near Gudalur, in the Wainad, is an ancient village or one of modern growth, and I attach importance to the fact that it does not receive the *kaimukhti* salutation even from the members of the clan to which it belongs.

Certain villages are called *kalolmad*, or "old man villages," where only buffaloes and men may live. They are usually villages where there is plenty of grass for the buffaloes, and are in general visited for short periods. The only explanation which could be given was that owing to the short time they are occupied it is not worth while to transfer the whole family to the place. It seemed, however, certain that women were definitely forbidden to live at these villages—a village where a woman may live being distinguished as *ishnidvaimad*—and this suggests that the institution is based on something more than mere convenience, and that the villages have some kind of sanctity which makes it undesirable that women should live in them.

The following are the only existing villages of this kind:—Taradrkirsi, the male funeral village of Kars; Kúdrmas and Telgudr, belonging to Taradr; Perg, belonging to the Panol; and Pirsush, belonging to Kuudr.

Three of these, Taradrkirsi, Kudrmas, and Pirsush, receive the *kaimukhti* salutation, and are certainly ancient and sacred villages, while there was some doubt as to whether Telgudr should not also be saluted. The only *kalolmad* I visited was Taradrkirsi, where there is now only a dairy, so that there is a clear reason why women cannot live there, but this did not appear to be the reason at other places.

Again, I could not ascertain why they should be called "old man villages," and their existence must, I am afraid, remain a mystery, though I think we may be confident that there is, or has been in the past, some ceremonial reason to explain their existence.

Two Todas villages are known as *satimad*. If a dispute arises between two men they are taken to the front of the dairy of the *satimad*, and are made to state what has happened, and anything a man says under these conditions will be believed. It is thought that if a man does not speak the truth, he will fall sick and his buffaloes will die.

According to some accounts there is only one true *satimad*, the village of Kiudr, which we have already seen has several signs of especial sanctity, such as the mention of its house in the prayer, the severe restrictions on its women during pregnancy, and the homage rendered to it by Todas of every clan.

According to other accounts the village of Kanòdrs[1] is also a *satimad*, and Todas of all clans may be brought there to make statements. It seems most probable that both places are *satimad*, but that the custom of using Kanòdrs as a touchstone of truth is now no longer followed, Kiudr only being used for this purpose. It will be remembered that both Kiudr and Kanòdrs have features of dairy ritual peculiar to themselves, and that in some respects there is a close resemblance between the ritual of the two places.

In his book written in 1832,[2] Captain Harkness says that the Todas have a temple dedicated to Truth, but identifies this with a *ti* dairy (*teriri*). It is probable, however, that his statement was based on what he was told of the *satimad*, either of Kiudr or Kanòdrs.

The Dairy

As we have already seen, there is some doubt whether the reverence paid to a village is paid to the village as a whole or to the dairy. There is no doubt, however, that the dairy draws to itself most of the veneration which a village excites.

Whenever a devout Toda visits a strange village, he goes to the dairy, and prostrating himself at its threshold, utters a prayer. My ordinary guide, Kòdrner, was not devout and did not pay this reverence, but his brother, Kutadri, was very scrupulous in performing these duties, especially when he went with me to the Kundahs. I could not obtain from him the prayer that he employed on these occasions.

The contents of the dairy are regarded as sacred, and, as we have seen, definite means are taken to prevent these objects from contamination by the gaze or touch of ordinary mortals. Of the objects kept in the dairy the bells are undoubtedly the most sacred. The most sacred of the vessels is the *mu*, which is not kept in the dairy but is buried in the buffalo-pen, and is only used on certain ceremonial occasions.

[1] At this place there is now only a dairy.

[2] Pp. 18 and 67.

This *mu* is closely associated with the general sanctity of the dairy. The prosperity of the dairy is dependent on its condition, and it would seem to have very much the same ideas attached to it as we meet in the life-token. It may also be regarded as the emblem of a dairy, and in the case of the funeral hut of Taradr, we have seen that a building becomes a dairy when a *mu* is placed in its inner room.

In his account of the Todas, Breeks identifies the special name of the dairy with that of the presiding god of the dairy or village. If he is right, it would seem to follow that the Todas personify the dairy in some degree. The use of the name of dairies in such a formula as that used at the end of the *irnörtiti* ceremony (see p. 303) might be regarded as evidence of this personification of the dairy. I do not believe, however, in this personification, and if the dairy has attained in some measure to the dignity of a god, there is no doubt that this god belongs to a category very different from that of the true Toda gods of the hill-tops.

THE THRESHOLD

As we have just seen, a man in paying reverence to the dairy bows down and touches the threshold with his forehead, and the threshold also frequently plays a part in the dairy ceremonial. The dairyman bows down and touches the threshold of his dairy before entering upon his work, and this is also one of the acts performed on his entrance into office on ordination.

The Teivaliol at an ordination also sweep the threshold with the grass called *kakar*, and the same grass is used to sweep the threshold of the dairy by the young girl who performs this office on reaching the new village during the migration ceremony (see p. 128). In the *tuninörtiti* and *pilinörtiti* ceremonies the offering is laid on the threshold of the dairy, and in the ceremony of uncovering for the first time the face of a boy, the child is put down by his father so that his forehead touches the threshold.

Bells

These are the most sacred of the sacred objects of the Todas. It is necessary, however, to distinguish three kinds of bells, the *mani*, the *tukulir mani*, and the *kwungg*, and it is only the first of these which has any great sanctity.

The *tukulir mani* is only used in the *koòtiti* ceremony of the second funeral (p. 376), and between these occasions is kept by the Badagas or Kotas. I am doubtful whether it is a true Toda object, and suspect that it is a Badaga or Kota bell which is used in a ceremony borrowed by the Todas from one or other of these peoples.

The *kwungg* is the household bell and is kept in the hut. It is used in the funeral ceremonies on two occasions, being hung on the neck of one of the ordinary buffaloes before the animal is killed, and it is also the bell which is rung in the final scene of the *azaramkedr*. The bell may be touched or carried by women, and I have seen a *kwungg* removed from the neck of a slaughtered buffalo by a Kota who handed it to a woman. Though the bell is used in ceremonial, the fact that it may be touched by both Kotas and women shows clearly that it is not regarded as possessing any sanctity whatever. In general appearance, however, the *kwungg* probably differs little from the *mani*, being a large bell of the same oblong shape which is characteristic of cattle-bells.

The *mani* is a bell which, so far as I could ascertain, never has a tongue, though this loss may be nothing more than a sign of its antiquity.

There are several kinds of *mani*. At the *ti* dairy there are two distinct varieties: the *mani* proper which is kept in the inner room and is hung on the neck of a chosen calf of the *persinir* on the occasion of the migration ceremonies, and the *kudrsmani* which is kept outside the door of the dairy. The latter appear to have little sanctity, but the former are probably the most sacred of Toda objects of veneration. They are said to be extremely ancient; some are reputed to have come from Amnòdr, and others are believed to have had miraculous origins, one having been born in a vessel of milk while the buffaloes were on their way from Amnòdr, while another came from the sea. The Todas believe that some of these bells are of gold, and one was reputed to be made of three metals—gold, silver, and iron. The bell born in milk is said to be of iron.

It seems probable that each of the more sacred herds at the village had at one time its own *mani*, and that a clan which possessed both *wursuli* and *kudrpali* would have had two bells of this kind or two sets of such bells.

At the present time, many of the clans have lost their sacred bells, and those which possess *mani* have only one or two of them. My most definite account for the Tartharol comes from Kars, where it is clear that the *wursuli* has two bells, the same as those reputed to have been hung on the neck of Enmon in the legend of Kwoto.[1] The *kudrpali* also had two bells which have now been lost, but the place where they used to hang still shares in the dairy ritual and is fed with milk just as the bells would have been if they had been there.

Since it is the *wursol* who takes the prominent part in the funeral ceremonies of a male, it seems also clear that the bells which are hung on the necks of the slaughtered buffaloes are those of the *wursuli*, but I did not definitely ascertain whether the bells of a *kudrpali* might not be used for this purpose, and indeed I am not altogether certain that any rigorous distinction is made between *wursuli mani* and *kudrpali mani*.

One striking distinction between the dairies of the Teivaliol and Tartharol was said to be the absence of *mani* among the former, except in the Piedr clan, and here there was something exceptional, for when this bell is used at a funeral it is hung on the neck of the buffalo by a Tarthar man belonging to Nòdrs. I was often told that, with this exception, the Teivaliol had no *mani*, and it was only towards the end of my visit that I became aware of the existence in the dairy of Kiudr of six bells called *mani*, two distinguished as *patatmani* and four as *ertatmani*.

[1] According to another account, these bells are kept at the *wursuli* of Nasmiòdr, and the *wursuli* of Kars has three *mani* in addition to these.

Among the Tartharol there was no distinction of this kind, and it seemed that these bells were looked on by the Todas in a different light to other bells, and were not thought of when they told me that the Teivaliol had no *mani*. It was quite clear that they were not used at funerals. The suggestion which I have made in the chapter on the dairy ritual would provide an explanation of this apparently exceptional position of the Kiudr *mani*. If Kiudr is the relic of an old *ti* dairy and the bells are the old *mani* of the *ti*, it becomes clear why the bells have their exceptional character, and why they are not used at a funeral, for the bells of a *ti* would never be allowed to suffer the defilement to which this ceremonial use subjects them.

Most of the *mani* have milk, curds, or buttermilk offered to them during the dairy ceremonial. The only exceptions of which I heard were some of the bells of the *ti* dairy, the bell called Keu at the Nòdrs *ti*, and that called Pongg at the Pan *ti*, which are not 'fed,' to use the common Toda expression.

At the village dairy the 'feeding' is a regular part of the dairy ritual, curds being put on the bells in the earlier, and some of the milk from that first brought into the dairy, in the later part of the proceedings. I only heard of one instance in which bells were given buttermilk. This was done with the *ertatmani* of the Kiudr dairy, and if the supposition given above is correct, this should, therefore, also be the procedure with the *kudrs mani* of the *ti* dairy. It is quite possible that this is one of the details of the dairy ritual which escaped me, or it may be that it was a special custom of the *ti* dairy from which I suppose the Kiudr dairy to have been derived.

Some writers on the Todas have regarded the bells as the Toda gods, and there certainly is some evidence which would justify one in regarding them as idols. The 'feeding' is a definite indication that the bells are, to a certain extent, regarded by the Todas as living beings, and in the legendary accounts of the origin of certain bells, belief in their activity is obvious. One bell is born and another comes from the sea and sits on the side of a milking vessel. It is quite clear, however, that the bell belongs to a different category in the religion of the Todas from that occupied by the gods.

Possibly the Todas may have some clear ideas about the connexion between their bells, gods, and dairies, but I could not discover them, and am inclined to believe that the people are now very hazy about the exact place of the bell and the god in their theology.

It was quite clear that they believed an offence against the dairy was punished by the gods, and I cannot say definitely that in this case the bell may not have been personified as a god, but I do not think that this was so.

It seems to me probable that the present sanctity of the bell has come about by a process of transference[1] from the buffalo to the object worn by it. Probably at one time the buffaloes were more directly venerated than they appear to be at present. There is evidence that even in recent times the bell-cow or buffalo which carried the bell was an object of especial veneration. In such books as those of Harkness and Marshall, the bell-cow seems to occupy a more prominent position than, so far as I could tell, it occupies at present.

In the present day the *mani* of the *ti* is only hung on the neck of a buffalo at the migration from one *ti mad* to another and at the Nòdrs *ti*, only for a few minutes even then. At the village dairy, the *mani* is never, so far as I could tell, put on the neck of a buffalo except at the funeral ceremonies. The idea in the latter case seems to be that a sacred buffalo should wear its bell, and in order that the buffalo slaughtered at a funeral should go to Amnòdr with its bell, the *mani* is hung on its neck while it is being killed. The legend of Kwoto and Punatvan shows that the bells are believed to travel to Amnòdr with the buffaloes.

The following may be suggested as a sketch of the probable evolution of the sanctity of the bell. At one time the buffaloes were the chief sacred objects of the Todas. Then this sanctity was concentrated in the persons of the bell-buffaloes, and later became partially attached to the bells, and the Todas then probably reached a stage in which it was doubtful how far the sanctity of the bell-buffalo was due to its position

[1] As we have already seen (p. 243) there is some reason to think that there has been example of such transference of sanctity to an object in the case of the *mu* or buried dairy vessel.

as chief of the herd, and how far to the bell it carried. It is possible that this was the stage of evolution of the idea in which the earliest visitors to the Nilgiris found the Todas. We may suppose that gradually the sanctity became more and more attached to the bell, less and less to its possessor, until now the Todas seem to have reached a position in which the bell-buffalo has little or no sanctity above its fellows, and the sanctity resides almost wholly in the bell. The original use of the bell now only survives in the ritual accompanying the migration of the *ti* buffaloes and in the funeral ceremonies.

There is one small fact which may perhaps be taken to indicate that the word *mani* is now applied to any object of a sacred or magical nature. The armlet put on the wrist of a child at the naming ceremony is called *kansutimani*. If the last part of this word is the same as the name of the bell, it would seem to indicate that the word may be used for an object the significance of which is magical rather than religious, and in connexion with a practice which has probably been borrowed.

RELICS

The Todas have a few relics of heroes which are regarded as objects of veneration, and are kept in the dairies. One of these, which is believed to be the armlet of the Kars man who went with the *ti* buffaloes in the story of Kwoto, is kept at Kuzhu, and has milk put on it during the dairy ritual in the same way as if it were a bell.

Another object is the ring of Kwoten which was found on the sambhar skin after the disappearance of this god. I saw this ring, which is of silver and far more massive than the rings worn by the Todas at the present time. Breeks states that in his time the Todas also claimed to have had in their possession the spear of Kwoten.

THE BUFFALO AND ITS MILK

In discussing the sanctity of the bells of the Toda dairies we have seen that there is some reason to think that these objects have attained their sacred character, at any rate in part, by a process of transference of sanctity from the buffaloes by which they were borne.

It is in favour of this view that the buffaloes seem at one time to have been more sacred, or to have received more definite signs of reverence than at the present time. The evidence of the legends points to a time when buffaloes were regarded as having anthropomorphic characters, and they probably indicate a belief in the sacred nature of these animals. When the buffaloes of the Nòdrs *ti* first came from Amnòdr, they talked like men, and the buffalo who founded the *ti mad* at Makars was a very human animal.

In his book, Captain Harkness (p. 16) states that as the buffaloes of the village are about to be penned for the night, the whole family, male and female, salute them by bringing the hand to the face. So far as I could ascertain, this is no longer done, and the only definite sign of reverence paid to the buffaloes, so far as I could learn, is the salutation made, partly to them and partly to the sun, by the *palol* when he leaves his dairy. Whenever in my journeys about the hills we came across herds of sacred buffaloes, even those of the *ti*, no salutation or sign of respect was made by the Todas who were with me, though a dairy, especially if it contained a *mani*, would receive obvious signs of veneration. Except in connexion with ceremonial there was nothing in the behaviour of the Todas towards their buffaloes to indicate that they were sacred animals, and it seems probable that the sanctity of the buffaloes has been to a great extent transferred, partly to the *mani* and partly to the milk given by the animals.

The milk is undoubtedly regarded as a sacred substance. There are distinct restrictions on its use which become more onerous as one ascends in the scale of dairies, and we have seen that there is reason to believe that the whole complicated daily ritual of the dairy may be designed to neutralise the dangers attendant on the conversion of the milk into substances which may be used by the outside world.

Throughout this book I have spoken of sacred buffaloes to distinguish them from those which take no part in the dairy ritual, but it is a question whether the sanctity does not attach much more closely to the objects connected with the buffaloes than to the buffaloes themselves.

I think it is clear that at the present time none of the Toda buffaloes are so sacred that their milk in the form of ghi may not be used. Some writers have supposed that no profit is made from the sacred buffaloes of the *ti*, but at present this is certainly not so, and the ghi made from the milk of the sacred buffaloes is sold with the rest and may be used by all.

In earlier days, when the Todas led simpler lives than at present, when the bazaars of Ootacamund and Coonoor were not in existence to act as incentives to the acquirement of gain, it is possible that the Todas did not sell the ghi made from the milk of their more sacred buffaloes, and, as I have already suggested, it is even possible that at one time they were content to allow these animals to suckle their calves and made no use of their milk. Even at the present time a sacred buffalo will not be milked unless it is provided with the appropriate dairy and dairyman. The buffaloes of a *ti* which has no *palol*, or of a *wursuli* which has no *wursol*, are not allowed to be milked though they may be looked after by other men. With this exception, however, I believe that, at the present time, every buffalo, even of the most sacred herds, is a source of profit by the sale of the ghi which is made from its milk.

The various offerings of buffaloes made in connexion with ceremonial are also not allowed to interfere with the economic value of the animals. In the *irnörtiti* ceremony of the village, the offered buffalo simply passes from one division of a clan to another, and when a buffalo is said to be devoted to the gods, it does not mean that the owner profits a whit the less on account of the oblation, but only that he may not kill it at a funeral, and must allow it to die a natural death.

Even the slaughter of animals at the funeral ceremonies appears to be managed so as to interfere as little as possible with the profits obtained from the sale of the milk. I think there is little doubt that it is an established custom to kill old and barren buffaloes on these occasions. An animal is not sent to the next world till its owner has got the utmost out of it in this.

Only on one point is it clear that the Todas make no direct gain from their buffaloes. When once a buffalo is dead, the Todas seek no further profit, and the carcases become the property of the Kotas. But even here there is an indirect gain, for the bodies of the buffaloes form a large part of the equivalent received by the Kotas for the many services they render to the Todas.

OTHER ANIMALS

The Todas have so highly developed the cult of one animal that they show few traces of belief in the sanctity of others. I will put together here the whole of the scanty evidence which I possess concerning their relations with animals in general.

The Tiger.—The Todas have a legend that at one time the tiger used to watch over the buffaloes for them during the day and hand over his charge in the evening. One day the tiger was very hungry and its hunger made it angry. When it brought the buffaloes back to the village it saw a cat catching a rat. Then the tiger asked the cat for some of the flesh, but the cat said, "There is no fool like you; why don't you eat some of the buffaloes you look after?" At that time the tiger usually slept at the village, but on this evening it went into the wood and at midnight came slowly back and took one of the buffaloes out of the pen, and since then it has always done this.

According to another legend (see p. 185), buffaloes have been killed by tigers ever since the *arsaiir* of the Kwòdrdoni *ti* failed to come to the general gathering which assembled to bid farewell to Ön when he went to rule over Amnòdr.

Jervis[1] states that the natives of the hills salaam to the tiger. He does not say definitely that it is the Todas who do this, but it is probable that he is referring to them. He also states that the women of the village throw themselves on their knees before a tiger which has been killed, and touch his bristles with their foreheads. I do not know whether these practices are still followed.

[1] Falls of the Cavery, 1834, p. 49.

As we have seen (p. 417), there is a belief that a man who fails in the performance of certain sacred duties may be killed by a tiger, but the Todas do not appear to fear this animal except on behalf of their buffaloes, and I could only learn of one case in which a Toda had been killed, and as his name was not known it must have occurred very long ago, or may have been altogether mythical.

The Jackal.—I was told by my interpreter that he had seen the Todas saluting a jackal, but I did not hear of any beliefs associated with the practice.

The Sambhar.—The most interesting point in connexion with this animal is the fact that the Todas are undoubtedly permitted to eat its flesh. Kutadri, who was most scrupulous in his obedience to the customs of his people, had no reluctance in eating sambhar flesh, and when he had fallen ill soon after, he never thought of ascribing his illness to what was probably its real cause, which shows clearly that there could have been no idea that he had done anything forbidden or unorthodox.

The fact that the Todas may eat the flesh of the sambhar while taking that of no other animal, except ceremonially, might well be looked upon as an indication that there may at one time have been totemic restrictions on food. In their earlier homes, before they reached the Nilgiri Hills, it is probable that the sambhar was an unknown animal, and could not therefore have been a totem. Consequently, when they came to the Nilgiris, they would have found there an animal on the eating of the flesh of which there were no restrictions, and the absence of restriction would, on this hypothesis, have continued to the present day. The eating of sambhar flesh would be the proverbial exception that proves the rule.

It seems to me possible, however, that there is a different reason for the absence of any prohibition. The Todas have no weapons with which they could kill a sambhar, and if this animal is ever killed by Kotas or Kurumbas, the mere fact that it had been killed by these people would probably be a sufficient reason why the Todas should not eat its flesh.

It is possible that it is only since the advent of Europeans to the Nilgiris, and the extensive slaughter of sambhar which followed it, that the Todas have thought of eating the flesh of this animal, and as no prohibition against the eating of its flesh has been handed down to them, they have no reluctance in satisfying in this way the liking for animal food which the *erkumptthpimi* ceremony keeps in existence, if it does not actually stimulate it.

The Cat.—This animal, which is called *koti* or *kwoti*, is domesticated by the Todas. The cat is mentioned in the legend of the tiger recorded in this section, and the earliest writers on the Todas speak of them as keeping these animals. I have seen them on the walls of the dairies, and believe that they are allowed to go wherever they please. The only occasion on which they come into ceremonial is at the *erkumptthpimi* sacrifice, where the spleen is specially put aside to be given to the cat, and is on this account called *kwotinerñf.*

The dog occurs in the story of Kwoten and several other animals are mentioned in the prayers and incantations, chiefly as sources of danger to the buffaloes. In the incantation for the relief of headache given on p. 265, the names of many animals are uttered, probably with the intention that their heads may acquire the pain which is being charmed away from the head of the sufferer.

TREES AND PLANTS

The most sacred tree of the Todas is undoubtedly the *tudr* (Fig. 58). This name is given by the Todas to two species, *Meliosma pungens* and *M. wightii*, the two trees resembling one another closely.

The bark is largely used in the dairy ceremonial, and especially in the ordination ceremonies of the *palol* and other dairymen drawn from the Teivaliol and Melgarsol. Its use is especially connected with the people of these sections of the Toda community, but the rest of the Tartharol undergo a ceremony at the second funeral in which *tudr* is used, and this was said to have the purpose that every Toda should be purified with *tudr* before he enters on the future life.

A log and leaves of *tudr* are also used in the ceremony of

erkumptthpimi, and here it is used by both Teivaliol and Tartharol alike.

The leaves of *tudr* used in any of these ceremonies must be perfect, and the bark must be knocked off the tree by means of

FIG. 58.—BOUGH OF THE 'TUDR' TREE. (From Marshall.)

a stone, this being one of the Toda practices which show the persistence of stone implements in ceremonial. The identity of this sacred tree is important, for it may furnish a clue to the home of the Todas. So sacred a tree would almost certainly have been already known to the Todas when they reached the Nilgiris, though it is, of course, possible that it might have been chosen on account of its resemblance to some tree sacred in their past history. The tree has, however, a wide distribution in India.

Pope has suggested that *tudr* is connected with *tulasi*, *Ocymum sanctum* or holy basil. This is a small flowering plant, and it is improbable that there is any connexion between the two plants except a resemblance in name.

Another tree which appears to be especially sacred is the *kiaz* tree (*Litsæa Wightiana*). Whenever a tree is used to mark the spot where the *mani* is laid during purificatory and other ceremonies, the tree must be of this kind. The wood of this tree is used when making fire for most sacred purposes.

The leaves of trees and shrubs are used in various branches of the dairy ritual. Those in most frequent use are various kinds called generically by the Todas *muli*, three of which belong to the genus Rubus. The young shoots of the same plants are used in the ordination ceremonies.

Grasses are also used in Toda ceremonial, and one of these, a slender grass called *kakar* (*Eragrostica nigra*) is used on several occasions, those of especial importance being the ordination of the Teivali *palikartmokh* and the sweeping of the threshold of the dairy by a girl at the migration ceremony. The same grass is also used in one of the methods adopted to promote speedy delivery in childbirth.

Of the various kinds of grain used by the Todas, that called *patm* or *samai* (*Panicum miliare*) seems to be in most frequent use in connexion with ceremonial, but it cannot be said to be sacred in any way. Barley (*kodj*) seems to have a peculiar place in Toda belief. The *tòratthadi* or cooking-vessel of the dairy may not be used for this grain, although any other kind may be boiled in it. On the other hand, three grains of barley are put into the mouth and three into the hair of a boy at the naming ceremony. In explanation I can only offer the surmise that barley is not cooked in the dairy vessel because its use by the Todas is an innovation, and that similarly the use of barley in the naming ceremony is also an innovation borrowed from the Badagas or some other tribe.

The Sun, Light, and Fire

There is no doubt that the sun is an object of reverence to the Todas. It is the duty of every man when first he leaves his hut in the morning to salute the sun by raising his hand to his face in the *kaimukhti* salutation. The sun is also saluted by the *palol* as he comes out of his dairy to milk the buffaloes. All my informants were unanimous in saying that the salutation of the *palol* was both to the buffaloes and to the sun. The doors of the great majority of the dairies faced more or less in an easterly direction, so that the dairyman, on coming out of his dairy in the morning, would see the sun, and when the dairy had a different orientation, as at Mòdr, the *palol* had to turn so that he would perform the salutation looking eastward. At the afternoon ceremonial the salutation was performed in the same direction as in the morning, so that, so far as the salutation is performed to the sun, it would appear that it is to the place of the sun-rise rather than to the sun itself.

The sun plays a part in the ceremony which takes place when a woman goes to the seclusion-hut after childbirth, but there was some reason to think that this was due to the belief in the noxious influence of the mysterious body, Keirt, which is near the sun, and not to the influence of the sun itself. When performing the ceremony on leaving the seclusion-hut the woman faces the sun, and this may be an act of reverence, since now Keirt is no longer feared. It seemed quite clear that the moon is not saluted in the same way as the sun with the *kaimukhti* salutation. No salutation is paid at all to the new moon when it is first seen, but after a day or two, usually on the third day, it is the custom to bow down the head, so that the forehead rests on the corner of the *putkuli* lying on the ground. The salutation is that called *nersatiti* shown in Fig. 44. I only heard of one custom indicating reverence to the full moon. When the Todas throw away water on the day of the full moon, they do not throw it towards the moon, but away from it. Thus, if the moon is opposite the door of the hut, the people will go round to the back in order to throw the water there. Light is undoubtedly an object of reverence to the Todas. Captain Harkness states that when the household lamp is lighted in the evening, obeisance is paid to it by bringing the right hand to the face, and this sign of reverence is still shown. In the dairy ceremonial the lamp and the light it gives are also undoubtedly reverenced, and lighting the lamp is, as we have seen, an act of a ceremonial character.

In some cases the lamps used in the dairies are certainly very ancient and are believed to have come from Amnòdr, but it is clear that they are not reverenced merely on this account, for a lamp of modern origin would, when once consecrated, be treated with as much reverence as those which had come down from antiquity.

I did not learn that any sign of reverence is paid to fire, but the fire of the dairy may undoubtedly be said to have a sacred character. Whenever a new dairy is visited or an old dairy is reconsecrated in connexion with the *pepkaricha* ceremony, fire is made afresh by friction. Once made, it was, so far as I could learn, kept continuously alight; if on any occasion the fire should go out, it would have to be made again by friction. In the *ti* dairy there are two fireplaces, one in which fire burns continuously, while the other is lighted by brands transferred to it from the other, and the lamp is lighted by a brand taken from this sacred fire. Here it would almost appear as if the former fire had a profane character, so that it would be regarded as desecration to light the sacred lamp directly from it.

The fire of the *tòratthwaskal* is used to cook food which has come from outside, and the use of an intermediate fire to light the lamp is in keeping with the general law of the procedure of the *ti* dairy, according to which the sacred objects are prevented from all possible contamination from the outer world by employing vessels or other objects as intermediaries.

Fire has also to be made by friction in other ceremonies, and especially at those called *teutütusthchi* and *erkumptthpimi* and at the funerals of males. At the first ceremony the fire is made by the *palol*, and at the second by the dairyman conducting the ceremony. At the *azaramkedr* of a man the fire is made by a man of the same clan as the deceased, and this is probably also the case at the first funeral ceremony. I did not definitely ask whether fire by friction is ever made by a woman, but I am fairly confident that this would never happen.

I only heard of one case in which men were prohibited from making fire. The Kidmadol and Karshol, who suffer under several disabilities, are not allowed to make fire by friction, and this is due to a quarrel with their parent-clan many years ago.

Whenever fire is made for a sacred purpose[1] the fire-sticks must be of the wood which the Todas call *kiaz* or *keadj*, except in the *tesherst* ceremony, in which the wood of *muli* is used.

There are also definite regulations as to the kind of wood which is to be burnt in the fires of all ceremonial occasions. In various ceremonies I have recorded the Toda names of the woods prescribed, and if more were known about their identity, it is possible that some light might be thrown on the original home of the Todas, in the same way as has been suggested in the case of the sacred *tudr* tree.

STONES

The Todas have many stones which may be held to have some degree of sanctity; certainly many have their place in the religious ceremonial. All these stones have names, either general or individual, but two stones with the same name need not necessarily have the same function.

At the *ti* there are stones marking the spots where the dairy vessels are taken up and put down during the migration ceremonies, but the most interesting stones at these dairies are those called *neurzülnkars*. At several dairies these stones are anointed, and their appearance indicates that they have undergone the process for very long periods of time; at other places they are so weathered and worn away that they must obviously be of great antiquity. At some dairies of the Nòdrs *ti* these stones take the place of the head of the *kaltmokh* in the ceremonies accompanying migration, but at other places they are said to have different uses.

[1] For the special method employed see p. 581.

At an ordinary village the stones usually belong to one of the following classes:—

(*a*) Stones to mark off boundaries or places, such as the *majvatvaikars*, marking the path or spot used by the women in fetching buttermilk from the dairy.

(*b*) Stones used in the ceremonies in which offerings are made, the *irnörtkars* and the *pilinörtkars*.

(*c*) Funeral stones, at which the buffaloes are killed. These are, of course, only found at funeral villages, but there are certain other stones, such as the *imudrikars*, which may be found in any village. Such a stone may mark the spot where the body is laid, or may even, as in the case of the *imudrikars* of Kars, form a mound on which the body is laid.

(*d*) Stones in or near the *tu* or buffalo pen, such as the *mutchudkars* and *pudothkars*. I do not know the origin or use of these, but in some villages there are stones in the pen marking the places where the *mu* or dairy vessels are buried, and it is possible that the above stones are in some way connected with the buried dairy-vessels.

(*e*) The lifting stone or *tukitthkars*. This is usually a large round stone which sometimes resembles in appearance stones of a ceremonial character.[1]

(*f*) Commemorative stones. The *teidrtolkars* of Nòdrs (see Fig. 13), and certain stones with the same name lying between Nòdrs and Teidr, had their origin in events connected with the death of a man belonging to the village of Teidr who was once *wursol* at Nòdrs. When he was told to milk one of the buffaloes, he replied, "If I milk it, the milk will not fill this place," pointing to a small depression on his thumb. Still the people told him to milk, and when he did so the milking-vessel was completely filled. Then the *palikartmokh* was very angry, and, taking the wand which the *wursol* was carrying, he struck him so that he flew in the air and fell down midway between Nòdrs and Teidr. When the people came to the place they found that the man was dead, and they tried to take up his body and carry it to the funeral place. But

[1] Burton (*Goa and the Blue Mountains*, p. 316) brands the Todas as inveterate liars, because, evidently owing to some misunderstanding, he was told that a "putting stone" was the "grandfather of the gods."

the body would not move and so they held the funeral on the spot and made a *tu*. At the entrance of the *tu* they placed two women carrying pounders[1] in place of the posts or *tüli*, and these women were changed into stones and their pounders became the *tasth* of the entrance of the pen. The stones which are now found on the spot are the remains of the pen and the *teidrtolkars* of Nòdrs marks the spot where the *wursol* milked the buffalo.

In the village of Tovalkan there is a mound shown in Fig.

FIG. 59.—THE MEMORIAL OF KEIREVAN.

59 which is much like the *imudrikars* of Kars, but it is of modern origin, having been made to mark the spot where Keirevan (26) fell out of a tree and was killed.

(*g*) Stones connected with special features of the dairy ceremonial. I only know of one stone of this kind at a village, the *pârsatthkars* of Nidrsi, on which the *palikartmokh* puts milk every morning and evening.

Stones are often used for more than one purpose; thus, the

[1] It will be remembered that at the *azaramkedr* of a woman, two women stand at the entrance of the *azaram* one of whom holds a pounder in her hands.

irnörtkars of Umgas (see Fig. 72) is also a boundary stone, and the *menkars* of Nòdrs (see Fig. 12) used for the game called *narthpimi*, and the *teidrtolkars* at the same village are also funeral stones at which buffaloes are killed.

I have given a brief list of the chief stones which may be called sacred owing to their coming in one way or another into Toda ceremonial, but I should like to make it clear that no great idea of sanctity attaches to these stones, and in no case are they shown any definite signs of veneration or worship. They, and many of the other objects described in this chapter, are not sacred in the same sense in which the *etudmad* or the *mani* are sacred.

CHAPTER XIX

THE TODA RELIGION

THE last seventeen chapters have been almost entirely devoted to the religious institutions and ceremonies of the Todas. In the earlier chapters I have described the ritual of the dairy and have discussed some of the problems of general interest which this ritual suggests. In later chapters I have described the ceremonies which are associated with the chief incidents of life: birth, growth, and death. In these and in the chapter dealing with sacrifice I have described many details of Toda ceremonial which clearly establish its religious character, and Chapter X is especially devoted to the formulæ which bring the ceremonial into definite relation with the Toda gods. In Chapter XI I have described practices and beliefs all of which stand in some relation to religion, though most of them must be regarded as belonging to a different category. In the last two chapters I have collected a number of special features of the Toda religion, the existence of sacred days and the part played by numbers, places and material objects in the various religious observances, and I have discussed how far the attitude of the Todas towards these objects can be described as one of worship.

There remains the general nexus which binds all these beliefs and practices into a whole so that they constitute the Toda religion. I have given in Chapter IX the stories of the Toda gods, giving them in this place because they were necessary for the proper understanding of the dairy formulæ, and I can now discuss more fully than was then possible the essential nature of these deities.

The Gods

The Toda gods are definitely anthropomorphic beings, who are believed to have lived in this world before man existed. Both man and buffalo were created by the gods, and the Todas seem to picture a time when gods, men, and buffaloes lived together on the Nilgiri Hills, and the gods ruled the men. At this time the gods seem to have lived much the same kind of life as the Todas themselves. Ön was *palol* to the buffaloes of the Nòdrs *ti*, his son Püv was *palikartmokh* at Kuudr, and other gods are believed to have filled dairy offices. From the earliest times, however, the gods were connected with the hills—*i. e.*, they were believed to dwell on the summits of the hills of the Nilgiri plateau. At first they seem to have mixed at times in human society and at other times to have retired to their hill-tops. The earliest of the gods was Pithi, who was born in a cave, and the Todas and many of their buffaloes were created by his son Ön and his wife. Later death came to the gods in the person of Püv, the son of Ön and Ön followed Püv to the world of the dead, called Amnòdr, of which he has since been the ruler. He left behind him as predominant among the deities Teikirzi, a goddess, who ruled over the Todas. It is to her that the origin of most of the Toda institutions is ascribed, and there is some reason to think that she was predominant among the gods even before Ön went to Amnòdr.

The Todas seem to believe that Teikirzi was at one time a person living among them, giving laws and regulating the affairs of the people. At the present time she is believed to be all-pervading; and, though she has her special hill, she does not dwell there only, as in the case of all but one of the other Toda deities.

There seem to have been many other gods contemporaneous with Ön and Teikirzi, and certain of these are believed to have been related to these deities and especially to Teikirzi. The gods are believed to be very numerous: the Todas speak of the 1,600 gods, the 1,800 gods, but it would seem that these expressions are used in the sense of "an infinite number." The gods are believed to have held their councils, meeting on some special hill, to which each god came from his own hill-top. The hill of Pòlkab, near Kanòdrs, and the village of Miuni are both renowned as meeting places of the gods.

There is a very definite association between the Toda gods and the hills of the Nilgiri plateau. Nearly every one of the gods has his hill where he dwells, and often when speaking of the gods the Todas seem to identify the god with the hill. There are two river gods, Teipakh and Pakhwar, associated with the two chief streams of the district, but there is some reason to believe that even these gods have their hills where they sometimes live, while at other times they inhabit or are identified with their streams. In the case of Teipakh, the god and the natural object seem to be very closely identified, and Kuzkarv, growing up in the river Teipakh, is said to be sitting in the lap of his maternal uncle. Again, one god is associated with a bubbling pool, but he also has his hill-top and is believed only to visit the pool on certain occasions. There can be little doubt that most of the Toda gods are hill-deities and that the association of the gods with hills is so strong that even the gods of streams and pools may be assigned their hills in general belief.

There is one important feature which is said to be common to all the hills inhabited by deities. They all have on their summits the stone circles which the Todas call *pun*. My informants were very definite about this and fully understood that these stone circles corresponded to the cairns and barrows opened by Breeks and others.

I was not able to examine into the question for myself and ascertain whether the circles called *pun* were actually present on the god-inhabited hills, but I have no reason to doubt that this was usually the case. Most writers on the Todas have been inclined to suppose that the cairns and barrows, with their contents, were in no way connected with the Todas, and they have based this opinion largely on the indifference of the Todas to these monuments. The people who are so jealous of their dairies that they will not allow anyone to enter or even view their contents, will allow any stranger to open the cairns and take their contents, and will even assist in the demolition. When I asked the Todas what they thought of the rifling of the *pun* they showed just the same indifference. They did not seem to think the matter any concern of theirs, and yet they believe in a definite association between the presence of a *pun* and the abode of a deity.

There seem to be three chief possibilities. One, that the cairns are Toda remains and that the association of the stone circles above them with the presence of a god is the last surviving relic of the fact. The second is that when the Todas came to the Nilgiri hills they found mysterious stone circles on certain hills, which marked out these hills as possessing features out of the common, and that this gave them a sanctity which led to the idea that they were inhabited by gods. A third possibility is that the same peculiarities which led the original builders of the circles to choose certain hills also led the Todas to choose them as the abodes of their deities, and that it was only later that they came to recognise the association between the circle and the presence of a god.

Whichever possibility may give the true explanation, one would have thought that the Todas would have objected to the disturbance and excavation of the cairns. There is little doubt that they were ignorant of the fact that objects were buried beneath the stone circles, but they are quite intelligent enough to know that there is a connexion between the stones and the objects beneath them when once these have been found.

I have very little doubt that the true explanation of the indifference of the Todas towards these monuments is that they have no definite traditional injunction against interfering with the circles. The Todas are the slaves of their traditions and of the laws and regulations which have been handed down to them by their ancestors. Till the Europeans came to the hills, it had never occurred to anyone to meddle with these stones or explore the soil beneath and around them. In consequence there was no reason why injunctions against interference should be handed down, and when the European arrived with his spade and pickaxe the Todas found nothing in their traditional laws telling them that it was wrong to interfere with these places, and they exhibited the indifference which led the explorers to suppose that there was no connexion of any kind between the Todas and the monuments.[1]

Although the Toda deities seem to be in general a development of hill-spirits, there can be little doubt that some of the gods are deified men. In the case of Kwoten, the account of his life is so circumstantial as to leave little doubt that he was a real man who was deified after a mysterious disappearance, believed to have been due to intercourse with a female deity, and around whose life there have clustered certain miraculous incidents. Similarly, his servant Erten, and his relatives Teikuteidi and Elnakhum are probably deified men.

Another possible instance of a deified man is Kwoto or Meilitars. The account of his life is again so circumstantial that it seems most likely that he was an exceptional man who was deified while various incidents in his life acquired a miraculous setting. It is perhaps in favour of the comparatively recent origin of these gods that objects belonging to them, or which come into their lives in some way, are still preserved, and perhaps a still more cogent argument in favour of the recent deification of Kwoten is the fact that the prohibition against marriage between the clans of Pan and Kanòdrs, believed to be due to the murder of Parden by Kwoten, still persists.

Of these deified mortals one became associated with a definite hill while the other was not assigned any special hill, but it was believed that all places should form his province.

There is little doubt that these mortals were deified as heroes and not as ancestors, and there is little to indicate that ancestor-worship has played any part in the evolution of the Toda religion. When a person dedicated a buffalo on account of some fault committed, it seemed that the action might be spoken of indifferently as dedication to the gods or to the ancestors of the dedicator. Thus, when Teitnir gave a

[1] I do not intend by this to indicate my belief that these cairns are ancient Toda monuments. I only wish to point out that one of the arguments which has been directed against this view is probably not valid. I shall return to this point in a future chapter.

buffalo after the death of his wife, some said it was given to the gods, while others said it was given to Teitnir's grandfathers, and when I tried to inquire more definitely into this point the two things were said to be the same. The ideas of the Todas seemed to me, however, to be so indefinite and vague on this point that I am inclined to attach little importance to this one piece of evidence.

Against the identification of gods with ancestors is the fact that the dead go to another world, and are believed to return to this world after a long interval as ordinary mortals, while most of the gods belong to this world and are believed to have belonged to this world before death came to either gods or men.

There is little to support the idea that the gods are personifications of the forces of nature. There is no evidence whatever that any of the gods are personifications of the sun, of other heavenly bodies, of thunder, lightning, or other elemental forces.

We have already seen that there is evidence that light is reverenced, and that this reverence extends to the sun, and it is probable that definite worship of the sun may at one time have formed a prominent part of the religion of the Todas. But there is not the slightest evidence which would lead to the identification of any one of the Toda deities with the sun.

There is no evidence of phallic worship among the Todas. One of the *ti* villages in the Kundahs is known to the European inhabitants of the Nilgiris as "Ling mand," but the supposed Ling stone at this place is evidently a *neurzülnkars*.[1]

In the last chapter we have seen that it has been supposed that divinity attaches to some of the sacred objects of the Todas, and especially to the dairy and the *mani* or bell. I cannot say definitely that the dairy and the bell are not regarded as gods, but I do not believe that they are so, and, as I have endeavoured to show in the last chapter, I think it probable that the sanctity of the bell has arisen by a gradual

[1] I had no Toda with me when I visited the place, so cannot speak with absolute certainty on the point.

process of transference of sanctity from the buffalo to the object worn by it, and I think it not unlikely that this transference may have reached its full development in comparatively recent times.

If my view be accepted, it would still leave open the religious status of the buffalo, and especially of the bell-buffalo, and here, scanty as the evidence is, it seems to me probable that the buffalo was never regarded as a god in the same sense in which this word is used for the anthropomorphic beings of the hill-tops. In the oldest legends, in which the buffaloes spoke like men, it is clear that they were in subjection to the gods, and were in no way regarded as themselves divine.

Some writers on the Todas have supposed that the *palol* is regarded as a god, but at the present time it is certain that he is in no way divine. He is treated with respect, but nothing of the nature of worship or adoration is paid to him. His position among the Todas is exactly that of a priest upon whom it is incumbent to maintain a very high degree of ceremonial purity. That his isolation is not a sign of divinity is, I think, shown by the results of infringement of his isolation. If the *palol* is touched by an ordinary man he loses his office and at once ceases to be a sacred personage, but the person who touches incurs no penalty. The sacrilege, according to Toda ideas, would attach not to him, but to the *palol* who, in spite of being touched, should persist in performing the duties of his office.

Whether the *palol* may ever have been more sacred in the past I cannot say. An indication that he may at one time have been regarded as divine is to be found in the special clauses of the Kiudr prayer which are uttered on the occasion of the migration of the buffaloes of the Nòdrs *ti*. Here the *kwarzam* of the *palol* is *eupalol*, which stands for *teupalol*, or "god palol," but in the next *kwarzam* the same prefix is given to his garment, the *tuni*, and I have little doubt that these *kwarzam* simply refer to the sanctity which attaches to the *palol* and his garment as part of the sacred institution of the *ti*. There is no doubt, however, that, according to tradition, the gods held the office of *palol* and that the *palol* of the

Nòdrs *ti* is the direct successor of the god Ön, but to whatever extent Ön may have passed on his divine character to his immediate successors, there is little doubt that at present the *palol* has lost any divinity which may at one time have been ascribed to him.

It is very difficult to ascertain how far at the present time, according to Toda belief, the gods intervene in human affairs. Each clan is believed to have its *nòdrodchi*, or ruling deity, but I could not learn what he is supposed to do. In general the *nòdrodchi* of a clan is a god dwelling on a hill near the chief village of the clan, and two clans living near one another may have the same ruler. Thus Teipakh is connected with both Piedr and Kusharf, Atioto with both Kwòdrdoni and Pedrkars, while Etepi, who is the *nòdrodchi* of Keradr, and Kuzkarv, the *nòdrodchi* of Keadr, are almost certainly one and the same deity. In the two latter cases a Tarthar clan has the same god as a clan of the Teivaliol.

Little can be said about the nature of these connexions between gods and clans, but it is possible that when a clan or a member of a clan is said to incur the anger of the gods it is the *nòdrodchi* who is chiefly offended and inflicts punishment in the form of death or disease to man or buffalo. The Todas certainly believe that misfortunes are due to the anger of the gods. It is clear that the various offerings described in Chapter XIII are piacular and propitiatory. They are designed to atone for wrong done and to avert any future evil consequences of the offence which has been committed.

The power of the gods is believed to show itself in various ways. In several cases dairies have been disused because the dairymen have died in office, and this was said to have happened because the gods of those places were severe. It was apparently believed that they had visited infringements of the laws regulating dairy ritual with death.

The various misfortunes which befell different members of the community as the result of my visit were all ascribed to the anger of the gods. Again, the untoward incidents of the funeral of Sinerani (see p. 391) were ascribed to the anger of the gods because there had been an infringement of funeral custom. These and other cases show clearly that the gods are held to be the source of punishment for sins committed by the Todas, and that they may be appeased by offerings.

Each of the *ti* dairies has connected with it many deities whose names are especially mentioned in the prayers, and it is probable that for infringements of their ritual these gods are the avenging deities.

The attitude towards the gods shown by the formulæ used in the dairy ceremonial has already been considered. Though there is no direct evidence in these formulæ that there is actual supplication to the deities, it is almost certain that this supplication is implied. The formulæ used in other Toda ceremonies have the same general form as those used in the dairy ritual; and here, again, though there is no direct appeal to deities in the words of the formula, such appeal is almost certainly implied. The formulæ of the various ceremonies of the Todas are almost certainly of the nature of prayers in which the gods are asked to give blessings and avert evils. Apart from the formulæ of the definite ritual, there seems to be no doubt that the Todas offer supplications to their gods for help and protection.

In the formulæ used in Toda sorcery appeal to the gods is even more definite than in the prayers of the dairy ritual. In them the names of four most important gods are mentioned, and it seems quite clear that the sorcerer believes that he is effecting his purpose through the power of the gods.

Another definite way in which the gods of the Todas are believed to intervene in human affairs is in divination. During the frenzy into which the *teuol* or diviners fall they are believed to be inspired by the gods. The diviners are chiefly consulted in the case of misfortune, and they are believed to reveal the reasons for the divine displeasure which has been the cause of the misfortune, and to communicate the ways in which the gods may be appeased. The diviners are believed to be directly inspired by the gods, and their name, *teuol*, or "god men," shows how definitely this belief is present in the Toda mind. In this case each diviner is believed to be inspired by a special deity, though sometimes more than one deity may reveal himself by the same man.

In the process of divination men are possessed by gods; and another example of possession by the gods may be mentioned here, as I have not found a suitable place for it elsewhere. If any of the gods should sit on the back of a buffalo, the animal will go to the hill called Kûrâtvan, near Neduvattam, and this is said to have happened to two buffaloes in recent times. A buffalo which goes to this hill is allowed to find its own way back, and, provided the buffalo goes only to *etudmad*, its course will not be interfered with. One of the two buffaloes above-mentioned travelled back by way of Taradr, a place called Panmtu, Nòdrs, Miuni, and then went to its own village.

In the chapter on divination I have pointed out that many of the deities who inspire the diviners are not true Toda gods, and this suggests that the practice of divination may have been borrowed from surrounding peoples, in which case caution would be needed in drawing conclusions from the beliefs associated with the practice. I believe, however, that the information given to me on this point is based on recent utterances of the *teuol* themselves when in a state of frenzy. Each *teuol* was asked by whom he was inspired, and I think it not unlikely that the answers were influenced by the recent associations of the Todas.

At the present time none of the gods are ever seen by mortals. As we have already found, the hills where they are supposed to dwell are, in some cases, regarded with reverence; but I obtained no evidence that the Todas avoid the summits even of those hills where the most important deities are supposed to be, though unfortunately I omitted to put this to the test by asking any of the more scrupulous Todas to accompany me to these places. The god-inhabited hills, however, are, in most cases, the sites of cairns and barrows, and the whole experience of those who have excavated these sites seems to show that the Todas exhibit no special reluctance to visit these dwelling-places of the gods.

I think that there can be little doubt that most of the individual gods of the Todas are becoming very unreal beings to those who talk of them. The stories of the earlier gods are now being forgotten, and the ideas of the Todas about them are very vague. On the other hand, certain gods of obviously more recent origin seem to be replacing, to some extent, the older gods. The lives of Kwoten and Meilitars can be related by many in great detail, but though they seem to inspire more interest among the Todas I cannot say that I observed anything to show that they receive any special worship or reverence. Meilitars is especially mentioned in the Kanòdrs prayer, but this would only put him on a level with many objects of no great amount of sanctity. The attitude of the Todas towards these two beings seemed to me to be rather that of people towards heroes than towards gods, though the mythology has raised them to the level of the gods.

Nevertheless, the idea of "god" is highly developed among the Todas and I am inclined to believe that the most satisfactory explanation of the Toda deities is that the people came to the Nilgiri Hills with a body of highly developed gods; that round these gods have clustered various legends connected with the Toda institutions; that these old gods have gradually through long ages lost their reality; that certain heroes have been raised to the ranks of the gods and that the lives of these heroes, founded to some extent on actual fact, have more interest to the Todas and are remembered and passed on while the legends of the older gods are gradually becoming vaguer in the progress towards complete obliviscence; that the gods as a whole, however, are still regarded as the authors of punishment and that there is a tendency to make an abstraction of the power of the gods.

The Todas, then, show us a stage of religious belief in which gods once believed to be real, living among men and intervening actively in their affairs, have become shadowy beings, apparently less real, invisible and intervening in the affairs of men in a mysterious manner and chiefly in the case of infraction of the laws which they are still believed to have given.

The present state of the Toda religion seems to be one in which ritual has persisted while the beliefs at the bottom of the ritual have largely disappeared. The Todas are an example of a people whose lives are altogether dominated by custom and tradition, and on the religious side this domination has taken a form in which ritual has become all-important, while the religious ideas which underlie the ritual have become blurred and unreal or have disappeared altogether. It seems to me that the Todas have had a religion of a comparatively high order for people living in such simple circumstances. During a long period of isolation there has come about an over-development of the ritual aspect of this religion. Year after year, and century after century, the priests have handed on the details of the ceremonial from one to another. The performance of the prescribed rites in their due order has become the all-essential of the religion and the ideas connected with it have suffered. This is shown most clearly in the prayers, in which we have seen that the prayer proper has gradually come to take a relatively subordinate position, and is even in danger of disappearing altogether, while the importance of the ***kwarzam*** by which the sacred objects of the dairy are mentioned has been magnified. The dairy utterances, which were probably at one time definite prayers calling on the gods for help and protection, are now on their way to become barren and meaningless formulæ.

Just as the prayer of the Todas seems to have almost degenerated into the utterance of barren formulæ, so is there reason to believe that the attitude of worship which is undoubtedly present in the Toda mind is becoming transferred from the gods themselves to the material objects used in the service of the gods. I acknowledge that I am here on less sure ground than in the case of the dairy formulæ, but the general impression left on my mind by the study of the beliefs and sacred institutions of the Todas is that the religious attitude of worship is being transferred from the gods themselves to the objects round which centres the ritual of the dairy. If I am right in these surmises, we find the Todas to possess a religion in process of degeneration. I do not suppose that this degeneration has been in progress only during the short time that the Todas have been exposed to the injurious contact of the outer world. The study of the Toda religion makes it seem to me most probable that the Todas came to the Nilgiri Hills with a religion of a higher order than they possess at present, with a developed system of gods who were believed to direct and govern the affairs of men, and that by a long and slow process these gods have become unreal, the supplications of the people for their guidance and assistance have become mechanical, and worship has been transferred from gods, not to stocks and stones, but to bells and dairy vessels.

At the present time it would seem that even the ritual of the Toda religion is often carried out less carefully than of old. Among the former occupants of dairy offices of whom I made inquiries, I found some who gave accounts so full of inaccuracies and omissions that it seemed unlikely that they could have performed the duties of their offices in a satisfactory manner, and when I had the opportunity of observing parts of the dairy ritual it seemed to me that the ceremonial acts were performed by some of the dairymen in a very perfunctory and slovenly fashion. We have already seen that some of the features of Toda ritual have entirely disappeared, and it seems not unlikely that the same fate may overtake the whole at no great distance of time.

In the case of both custom and ritual, the Todas are now often content if they keep the letter of the law, and several examples of the evasion of ceremonial laws have been recorded. We have seen that several of the laws concerning the *madnol* are certainly not kept in the spirit, and only by a stretch of imagination, in the letter. A woman evades the law that she may not leave the village on the *madnol* by leaving it before daybreak and returning after daybreak till her work is done. A man takes money out on the day before the *madnol* and, burying it elsewhere, is able to carry out business which the spirit of the law forbids. In ceremonies, ritual duties which involve discomfort or restraint are assigned to young boys, to whom the restraint is no restraint. A man goes near the *palol* whom properly he should not approach, but since he does not speak nor is spoken to, he is regarded as ceremonially absent.

Objects of value which should be burnt for the use of the dead are sent to the next world ceremonially by swinging them over the fire, and are then removed. The emblems of womanhood are taken out of the hut when the *wursol* goes there to sleep, but the women themselves remain. Probably the behaviour of the *kaltmokh* in the sleeping hut during the ceremony after migration (p. 142) is a sign that he should not be there, and is evading an uncomfortable and perhaps dangerous custom.

The Todas seem to show us how the over-development of the ritual aspect of religion may lead to atrophy of those ideas and beliefs through which the religion has been built up and then how, in its turn, the ritual may suffer and acts which are performed mechanically, with no living ideas behind them, may come to be performed carelessly and incompletely, while religious observances which involve trouble or discomfort may be evaded or completely neglected. The Todas, in fact, show us, in little, the general traits characteristic of the degeneration of religion.

To people living in the simple surroundings and with the simple life of the Todas we might well look for material to help us to understand the evolution of religion, but, if I am right, we must look for this in vain. If the religion of the Todas is a product of degeneration, it is hopeless to seek among the customs of this people for evidence of the mode of growth of religious ideas and practices. Thus, it is natural that we find among the Todas no clear trace of totemism, or of those ideas connected with animals which are probably allied to totemism. There are several reasons why the Todas should not furnish any clear evidence of this frequent starting-point of religion. In the first place, they are people to whom one animal has become so predominantly sacred that it might be expected that any other relations with animals of a sacred character would have disappeared ; the cult of animals in general would have been swamped in the cult of the buffalo. Secondly, if I am right in the supposition I have advanced in this chapter, it is probable that the Todas came to the Nilgiri Hills with the cult of the buffalo or other milk-giving animal already to some extent developed, and if at this time they had customs and beliefs connected with other animals, these would naturally soon disappear if these animals were absent in the new country. At the same time, it is perhaps not without significance that the Todas are allowed to eat the flesh of the sambhar. In their former home, in the low country, it is almost certain that this animal would not have been a totem, and therefore it would be natural that on their reaching the Nilgiris they might be permitted to eat it.[1]

It is doubtful how far the Todas have an idea of a supreme god. At the present time they speak of and constantly appeal to Swami, and they will say that Swami is above all the gods, but I have very little doubt that this is a recent idea. Swami was chiefly spoken of and reverenced by the younger men, and it is quite clear that the name should not properly occur in the formulæ of any Toda ritual. Nevertheless, the possibility cannot be excluded that the idea is old. It is probable that at one time there existed direct appeal to gods in the Toda prayer, and this direct appeal may have been to some supreme being who was addressed as Swami.

Apart from this question of the meaning of Swami, two deities stand out from the remainder of the Toda gods. One of these is Meilitars, whose cunning was able to deceive the gods, and who was able to perform miracles which were regarded as beyond the powers of the other gods. His story seems to show one way in which a god might rise above his fellows, and might become a supreme god, but this has certainly not happened in his case. There is not the slightest evidence to show that Meilitars is in any way worshipped as a supreme god. There is a much stronger case for the supremacy of the goddess Teikirzi. Teikirzi is said to be the foundress of many of the Toda institutions; the final explanation of all things in the Toda mind is that "it is the will of Teikirzi." She is said to be all-pervading, and

[1] I do not wish to lay any stress on this argument, for, as I have already indicated, it is possible that the eating of sambhar is a recent innovation, which has arisen since the advent of Europeans to the Nilgiris. Also I do not wish to indicate by the above that I commit myself to a belief in the universality of totemism as a stage in religious development. I only wish to point out that if this has been so, the Todas furnish a good case in which we might expect all traces of this descent to have disappeared or to have become so blurred and scanty as to be of little value.

is regarded as the ruler of this world; she is mentioned in many of the sacred formulæ, and of the occasional *kwarzam* uttered by the Todas on various occasions by far the most frequent are those of Teikirzi Tirshti.

Teikirzi is undoubtedly the most important Toda deity, and yet she is not so pre-eminent that she can be said to be in any way a supreme god. Though she is the ruler of this world, it is Ön who rules the world of the dead.

INFLUENCE OF OTHER RELIGIOUS SYSTEMS

The Todas show undoubted signs of the influence of Hinduism on their religion. It would be quite easy for a visitor to the Todas to talk to some of the younger and more sophisticated men and to go away believing that the Todas differed little from the surrounding tribes in their religious beliefs. In my first conversation with the Todas on religious matters I was told that they worshipped the following six gods:—Nanjandisparan, whose temple is at Nanjankudi in Mysore; Petkon or Betakarasami, whose temple is at Gudalur; Punilibagewan, whose temple is called Punilikudi and is near Cheirambadi; Mari, a female deity, with a temple called Marikudi near Pokapparam; Magòli, another female deity, with a temple near Kodanad on the Nilgiris, and Karmudrangan,[1] whose temple is near Mettapollayam.

Four or five of these gods are probably Hindu deities, while Magòli may be a deity of the Kurumbas or Irulas. At the present time there is no doubt that their temples are visited by the Todas and offerings made to them. The most frequent motive for these offerings appears to be the desire for children. The Todas now pray to these gods, most commonly for this purpose to Nanjandisparan, Magòli or Karmudrangan, and if a child is born it is taken when one year old to the temple, its head is shaved, and an offering, usually in the form of an image of the child, given to the priest. Rice is also given, sufficient, it is said, to feed 101 men, and the proceedings are said to cost the Todas

[1] These were the names given to me by the Todas, and their spelling may not correspond with that in ordinary use.

from 40 to 100 rupees. They have a rule that, however much money they take away with them from their villages, all must be spent and none brought back.

If the Todas wish to obtain more buffaloes they offer silver images of these animals to the temples.

I do not know how long these Hindu gods have been worshipped by the Todas, but my informants were emphatic that Nanjandisparan and Petkon had been worshipped by the Todas for very long, and that annual offerings of small sums were made to them by every Toda family.

This worship and appeal to Hindu deities appears to me to have gone on side by side with the proper religion of the Todas, but to have influenced it little. It shows how people of low culture make use of the gods of other races as well as of their own, and in the same way I believe that the Todas reverence the gods of Badagas, Kurumbas, or any other of the tribes with which they have dealings, and if asked point-blank if the gods of these people are their gods they will assent.

It is probable that Hinduism is now having more influence on the Todas than ever before, and, as I have already pointed out, I believe that the reverence to Swami and the frequent utterance of his name is a sign of the increasing influence of Hinduism, perhaps combined with that of Christianity.

Christianity has so far had no appreciable influence. The Church Missionary Zenana Society has for some years employed two catechists to work among the Todas, and one of them, Samuel, who by the kindness of the Society was allowed to act as my interpreter for a large part of my stay, ought to have been successful if earnestness and honesty are of any avail, but his efforts, carried on for ten years, had borne very little fruit.

In the whole of the mythology and ceremonial there are few features which suggest the probability of Christian influence, and the chief of these is the incident in the legend of the origin of mankind where woman is created from a rib taken from the right side of a man. It is very unlikely that this is a recent accretion to the legend, and, if it is due to Christian influence, I think it must have arisen long ago. We know that, three centuries ago, priests visited the Todas and preached to them, and it is stated (see p. 720) that one chose the Hebrew story of the creation for his lesson, and it may be that the incident, striking the fancy of the people, was incorporated into their own tradition of the origin of man. The resemblance between the Toda *madnol* and the Sabbath may also excite the suspicion that the former institution is founded on ideas borrowed from Christians or Jews. I think we may be confident that, if this has been the case, the borrowing took place very long ago. I hope to show in the last chapter that it is probable the Todas came from Malabar, and it is possible that their migration to the hills took place after the settlement of Christians or Jews in that district. If Christianity has affected the religious beliefs or practices of the general body of the Todas, I think it is certain that this influence has not been recent.

Magic and Religion

A word may be added, at the end of this chapter, on the relation between the magic and the religion of the Todas. I have already pointed out reasons for believing that the Toda religion is one in process of degeneration, and we must not therefore expect to find among this people material for the study of the evolution of religion from magic or for the method of divergence of the two from some original stem which was neither magic nor religion.

The chief interest of the Todas from this point of view is that they show how side by side with a relatively high form of religion there may exist a body of beliefs crystallised in magical formulæ which bear a very close resemblance to the formulæ of the religious ritual. Their aim and their general nature leave no doubt that the formulæ given in the later part of Chap. XII are magical in nature, and yet they show more distinct evidence of appeal to deities than is to be found in the definitely religious formulæ of the dairy. These magical formulæ of the Todas seem to show us a stage of magic in which religion has been called to its aid. The sorcerer does not endeavour to effect his purpose merely by the belief in the efficiency of like producing like, or other ideas which dominate the lower forms of magic, but has called to his aid the power of the gods and uses a form of words almost identical with that used in the religious ritual. Magic and religion are here closely allied, but it is possible that this alliance is but one of the products of the degeneration to which I believe the Toda religion is subject. It is possible that we have here evidence that during the process of degeneration of religion, religion and magic may approach one another—an approach which recalls their common origin from those low beliefs and ideas of the savage to which the name of neither magic nor religion should perhaps be properly applied.

CHAPTER XX

GENEALOGIES AND POPULATION

THE preceding chapters have dealt with the ceremonies and religious aspect of the life of the Todas. This and succeeding chapters will deal with the social organisation and the more secular side of the life of the people.

The social organisation has been studied largely by means of the genealogical record which is given in Appendix V. Before going to India I had worked out the details of the system of kinship, of the regulation of marriage, and of the social organisation generally of two Papuan communities on the basis of the pedigrees preserved by those communities.

It is a familiar fact that, both in ancient writings and in the memories of peoples to whom writing is unknown, long lists of ancestors may be preserved, going back in some cases to mythical times. Among existing peoples good examples of such genealogies are found in Polynesia and Uganda, but such a genealogical record is of little value for the investigation of social organisation.

The records which I obtained in Torres Straits were of a different kind; they only extended back for three or four generations, but included all collateral lines, so that a man was able to tell me all the descendants of his great-grandfather or great-great-grandfather, and knew the descent of his mother, his father's mother, his mother's mother, and his wife as fully as that of his father. By this means I was able to collect[1] a record of the great majority of marriages which had taken place in the community for the last three or four

[1] See *Reports of the Cambridge Anthropological Expedition to Torres Straits*, vol. v, p. 122.

generations, was able to work out the laws which had regulated these marriages and to study in detail the system of kinship.

On going to the Todas, one of my first objects was to discover if their pedigrees were preserved with the same completeness and fidelity as among the Papuans of Torres Straits.

It seemed at first as if I was to be disappointed. Those to whom I first broached the subject professed not to know the names of their own fathers and mothers. Some said they had forgotten them, but their demeanour excited the suspicion that reticence, and not ignorance, was the cause of the failure, and it soon became clear that this suspicion was correct.

There was a taboo on the names of the dead, and especially on those of dead ancestors. No Toda liked to speak of the dead by name, but to utter the name of a dead elder relative was strictly forbidden, and to the end of my visit I never heard the name of a dead man from one of his descendants. Thus the last piece of genealogical information which I collected was that of the names of the father and mother of Kòdrner, my constant attendant. The fact that he was always with me had prevented my inquiries into his parentage.

Having discovered the cause of failure it soon became evident that the Todas preserved their pedigrees almost, if not quite, as fully as the natives of Torres Straits. As in the islands, certain men had especial reputations as repositories of genealogical lore, and I began my investigations with the aid of one of the most famous of these, Parkurs (8), an old man almost blind as the result of cataract and so feeble that he had to be carried when he came to see me. With his aid and that of many others I compiled the records given in Appendix V.

Throughout my visit, the collection of this genealogical material was regarded as something which should not be done. I never carried on this branch of my work during what I may call my public hours when I was visited by anyone who chose to come. At these times I sometimes obtained from a man the names of his wife and children, but always left any further inquiries till the time reserved for my investigations into more esoteric matters, when only one man was alone with me and was not subject to the restraints imposed by auditors who might disapprove of the utterance of the names of the dead.

One result of the taboo on the names of dead ancestors was that the record of a man's family was never obtained from one of that family; but this was no disadvantage, for the genealogical knowledge of those from whom I obtained my data was so wide that it covered the families of the whole or nearly the whole of the Toda community. I have no doubt that I could have obtained the whole of the material given in the tables from two men, one of whom would have given me the genealogies of the Tartharol, and the other those of the Teivaliol, and if I had chosen my informants wisely, I believe that their information would have been as full and accurate as that obtained from my many sources of information. Further, I found that the Teivaliol had a wide knowledge of Tarthar genealogies, and *vice versâ*, though a man of one division usually refused to guarantee the accuracy of anything he told me about the other division, and would often disclaim knowledge which some chance observation later showed that he possessed, at any rate in some measure.

Although certain Todas had special reputations for their knowledge of pedigrees and were undoubtedly more proficient in this respect than the general mass of the community, I believe that the knowledge was very widely spread throughout the people. My guide Kòdrner never professed to any special knowledge of genealogies, and yet chance observations would often show that his acquaintance with the pedigrees of the community was far more extensive and accurate than his professions would have led one to expect.

The results of the inquiry are given in Tables 1–72. This large accumulation of genealogical material was obtained from people who professed at first not to know the names of their own fathers and mothers. It would have been quite easy for me to have come away from the Todas and reported them as a people who did not preserve their genealogies.

The pedigrees are recorded in exactly the same manner as those which I have published in the *Reports of the Torres*

Straits Expedition, with the modifications rendered necessary by the presence of polyandry and infant marriage among the Todas. In any one table the descendants in the male line only are given, descendants in the female line being recorded in the genealogies of the husbands. Thus, if one wishes to ascertain the descendants of Pilivurch in Table 1, it is necessary to turn to Table 20 recording the genealogy of Teithi, the husband of this woman. The names of males are in capital letters, those of females in ordinary type, and the name of a wife always follows the name of her husband or husbands. Under the name of each individual is placed, in italics, the name of the clan to which the individual belongs, or, in the case of a married woman, of the clan to which she had belonged before marriage. The names of those now living are given in Clarendon type, of which Mudrigeidi and Savdur in Table 1 are examples. The abbreviation i.m. stands for "infant marriage." The abbreviations d.y. and d.n.n. stand for "died young" and "died before being named" respectively. The latter implies that the child died within a few weeks of birth.

When the names of men are enclosed in square brackets, polyandry, and when the names of women are so enclosed, polygyny, is indicated.

In the *Torres Straits Reports* I have shown that there are definite reasons why the people should have preserved their pedigrees so fully. The pedigrees are not preserved for amusement nor out of idle interest in the doings of ancestors or neighbours. In Torres Straits the complex and far-reaching nature of the marriage regulations form the chief motive for the preservation of the pedigrees, while the transmission of property is perhaps of almost equal importance.

Among the Todas we shall see that the marriage regulations are far simpler than among the Papuans of Torres Straits, and in their case the chief motive is probably connected with the inheritance of buffaloes, the only form of property in which the Toda takes much interest. In the succeeding chapters we shall find several examples of social transactions in which the knowledge derived from the genealogical record has determined the issue.

THE VALUE OF THE GENEALOGICAL RECORD

In the succeeding chapters I shall show the value of the genealogies in working out the nature of the system of kinship and in providing statistical material for the study of the marriage regulations. The greater part of my work on the social aspect of the life of the Todas is based on material derived from the genealogies; or perhaps I should rather say that most of the information I give has been checked, if not entirely obtained, by means of the genealogies.

I wish, however, to draw attention here to a far wider use of the genealogies in anthropological investigation. They bring a concrete element into anthropological work which greatly facilitates inquiry. The lower one goes in the social or intellectual scale in mankind, the greater difficulty is there in dealing with abstractions. The savage mind is almost wholly occupied with the concrete. Discuss his laws of inheritance with him, and you probably soon become hopelessly entangled in misunderstanding. Take a number of concrete cases, and his memory will enable him to heap instance upon instance showing how property was inherited in given cases. Similarly, in ceremonies, ask the savage to give an account of a given ceremony, and he probably omits many essential points, not because he forgets them, but because they are so familiar to him that he thinks you, like himself, take them for granted. Ask him to tell you exactly what A and B did when they performed a given ceremony, and he forms a mental picture of A and B going through the ceremony, and tells you exactly what they did and how they did it. When another individual comes into the ceremony, he too comes in as a concrete personage, and his sayings and doings are faithfully recorded.

The Todas are so intelligent that the genealogies were not so essential an instrument of investigation as was the case in Torres Straits, but they were nevertheless of enormous value in giving concreteness to the accounts of the Toda ceremonies. The Todas certainly gave fuller and more faithful accounts of their ceremonies when they described actual events, but such descriptions would have been of little value to me if I had not had my pedigrees as a guide. An account of a Toda funeral, for instance, with its many *dramatis personæ* would probably have baffled my powers of comprehension if I had not had my book of genealogies for reference.

I always worked with this book by my side whenever I was investigating any ceremonial in which the social side of life was concerned. I asked for a description of some ceremony recently performed of which the memories were fresh. The chief actors in the ceremony were always mentioned by name; and whenever a name occurred, I looked up the clan and family of the person in question and noticed his relationship to other persons who had taken part in the ceremony. The actors in the ceremony were thus real people to me as well as to my informants, and the account of the ceremony proceeded with the maximum of interest and the minimum of fatigue both to myself and to my informants.

The method had the further advantage that it afforded me the means of checking the accounts which I was given. An informant inclined to be careless soon found that I had the means of checking his narrative on many points; and some of the people, not knowing the source of my information, credited me with more knowledge than I really possessed, and were in consequence extremely careful not to wander from the truth, or perhaps I should rather say, not to tell me anything of which they were not absolutely certain. I have already stated my belief that the Todas are very truthful and that they err far more often from carelessness than intention, but the fact that I had a fund of knowledge of which the source was somewhat mysterious probably saved me from having much of my time wasted by careless or inaccurate information.

I think that my familiarity with the names and circumstances of the people helped me to acquire their confidence. Among the more simple people of Torres Straits, I used sometimes to let a man know, much to his astonishment, that I was acquainted with some of the affairs of his family. Among the more reticent Todas, it seemed to me unwise to do this, but, on meeting for the first time a man with whom I was already acquainted through the genealogies, I often referred to something I knew he had done, perhaps to the skilful way he had caught the buffalo at such and such a funeral, and the fact that I knew something of him and his doings often helped to put us at once on friendly terms, and at the same time put him on his mettle to give me the best of the knowledge at his command.

THE TRUSTWORTHINESS OF THE GENEALOGIES

Before using the genealogical record as a means of studying the details of the social organisation, it may be well to consider what guarantee we have that the genealogies form a truthful record of the past. In Torres Straits, where I gained my first experience in these matters, I was so incredulous of the accuracy of the record that I obtained almost every particle of information from two or three different and independent sources, and it was only when I had finished that I found the whole mass of material to furnish a record so consistent in itself that it could hardly have been other than veracious.

Further, on investigating kinship and the regulation of marriage, both on the basis of the genealogical record, it was found that the results of one investigation closely corroborated the results of the other, and that the combined investigations gave so consistent and coherent a result that it was incredible that the genealogies on which the investigations were based should have been other than faithful and accurate records.

The Toda community is considerably larger than either of those with which I worked in the islands of Torres Straits, and when I found that the memories of the people extended back as far or nearly as far as in those islands, it became obvious that I was confronted with a task of considerable magnitude, and the question arose whether it was necessary to obtain separate accounts of every family from independent witnesses, as I had done previously, or whether I might not rely on the account of a family given by one witness and only seek corroboration occasionally. I began by following the same procedure as in Torres Straits, but soon found that the accounts obtained independently showed a close agreement, and I therefore contented myself in my later work with one account, though every now and again I went over a piece of a pedigree with a second witness. When I had finished, the consistency of all the parts of the record with one another seemed to afford conclusive evidence that I had obtained what is, on the whole, a veracious record.

Of course, in so large a mass of material there are mistakes.[1] In one family no doubt a child has been omitted, especially when it died young and had no posterity to make its name important; in another case perhaps a child has been added to a family who was really the offspring of another mother. That there are such mistakes is certain, but they are probably few in number, and I have no doubt that, with one exception to be presently considered, such mistakes as have crept in do not appreciably impair the value of the genealogies as a record of the working of social regulations.

There is one deficiency of the record, however, of the existence of which I have little doubt—a deficiency entirely due to my own carelessness. To me the chief interest of the genealogies is that they are a record of the past—a record of the working of social regulations which at the present time may be already affected by the new influences coming into the lives of primitive people all over the world. In my absorption in the records of the past, I have often neglected the present and have omitted to ascertain carefully the children of families at present in process of growth. In several cases I have failed to obtain the names of children of people now living, and I have very little doubt that I have in several or many cases omitted the names of other children of growing families. I had one excuse for this in the fact already mentioned, that I had to obtain my information about a given family from people of some other family. A man would often know all about the members of the given family in the past, but, living perhaps at some distance from the family in question, he was often hazy as to the exact number and names of the children recently born, and it is the record of

[1] For a few cases in which an individual is entered as the child of a man who is known not to be his real father, see p. 534. In such a case I have assigned the child to the parent who is regarded as the legal father by the Todas.

children under five years of age which I know to be deficient.

If the number of the Todas now living and recorded in the genealogies be counted, it will be found that there are 736 individuals, 419 males and 317 females. In the census of 1901 the total population is given as 805, 451 males and 354 females. My record falls short of that of the census by 69 individuals, 32 males and 37 females.

Further, when I arrange the people now living according to age, it is found that there is a distinct deficiency in children under five years of age. Thus, my records of age come out as follows :—

	Males.	Females.
Above 65 years.	9	3
61—65 ,,	4	7
56—60 ,,	19	9
51—55 ,,	20	17
46—50 ,,	26	21
41—45 ,,	26	18
36—40 ,,	26	27
31—35 ,,	40	25
26—30 ,,	40	33
21—25 ,,	38	28
16—20 ,,	32	31
11—15 ,,	41	20
6—10 ,,	54	33
5 and under	44	45
Total	419	317

The ages upon which this table is based could only be obtained very roughly, and the figures must be taken merely as rough approximations to the truth. The irregularities of the table may be due partly to this defect, but it is very improbable that there are about the same number of children of five and under as of children between six and ten, and we may be fairly confident that but for omissions the numbers of the youngest group, especially of boys, would have been larger.

I have reason to believe, further, that I have not omitted any appreciable number of adults or children over five years of age. I tested 320 males and 183 females for colour-blindness, and as I was anxious to test every member of the community who was old enough, I obtained towards the end of my visit the names of all those who had not been tested. I only attempted to test children when over five years of age, and I have therefore an independent record of the living Todas above this age, so that it is fairly certain that the greater part of the deficiency in the genealogical record is of children about or below the age of five, though it is possible that I may also have missed a certain number of women.

This deficiency does not in the slightest degree affect the value of the pedigrees as a record of marriages or of the working of social regulations, but it does impair the value of the statistics concerning the average size of a family and other matters of biological interest, though only for the last generation.

On looking through my genealogical tables, it will be seen that different clans and families differ very greatly in the fulness of their record. In some cases I have pedigrees going back to the great-grandfathers of men now in middle life; in other cases I have only the names of the fathers of such men. The briefness of the record is especially marked in the case of the outlying clans, such as Kwòdrdoni, Pedrkars, and Päm, which I only visited for short periods. During these visits there was so much to be done that something had to suffer and the genealogies were usually the victims. If I had had more time, I have little doubt that I could have obtained much fuller records in many cases.

Buffalo Pedigrees

Marshall has stated that the Todas preserve the pedigrees of their buffaloes in the female line, and when I had found how carefully the Todas preserved their own pedigrees my next step was to endeavour to ascertain if the pedigrees of their buffaloes were preserved with the same amount of care and completeness. I returned to this subject again and again, but with very imperfect success. The Todas always treated my inquiries on this subject as if they were trifling and ridiculous. It is possible that this was one of the points on which they were reticent, but I am inclined to think that I was told all there was to tell.

To a certain extent it is correct to say that the pedigrees of the buffaloes are preserved, and in the female line only. If any given buffalo were taken as the starting-point, the owner could usually tell me the names of the mother of the buffalo and of the mother's mother, and occasionally I obtained the names of the immediate ancestors in the female line for four generations. Thus, Nertiners of Taradr (24) had a buffalo named Kârstum who was the daughter of Idrsh. Idrsh was the daughter of Persud, who was the daughter of Nerûv, who was the daughter of Kiûd. Another of his buffaloes, Keien, was descended from Koisi, Nerûv, and Kâsimi in the order named.

I could not ascertain that the Todas kept any record of the collateral lines of descent, nor was there, so far as I could find, any idea of kinship between buffaloes descended from the same recent ancestor. Two buffaloes born of the same mother would be known, of course, to be sisters, but no importance seemed to be attached to the relationship.

An obvious reason for the limitation of the pedigrees of the buffaloes to the female line is the fact that only female buffaloes are named, so that there are no means of recording male parentage. We shall see later that among themselves the Todas attach little importance to paternity, and the same indifference is found in their attitude towards their buffaloes. The essential reason for the nature of the record of buffalo-descent is the complete absence of desire to maintain the purity of the breed, even of the most sacred herds, and the complete lack of attention to ties of consanguinity between buffaloes mated together.

THE TODA POPULATION

The chapters on kinship and marriage will furnish object-lessons on the method of application of the knowledge derived from the genealogies to the study of social regulations. In the remainder of this chapter I propose to consider various problems connected with population, of biological as well as of sociological interest. The data derived from the genealogies are here of distinct service, though, for reasons already considered, their value is not so great as in the investigation of social regulations.

Records of the numbers of the Todas have been taken at various times, beginning with what must have been a very rough estimate made by Keys[1] in 1812, in which the number of the Todas or Thothavurs was placed at 179. In 1821, Ward[2] estimated the numbers of men and women at 140 and 82 respectively, of whom the great majority lived in the Todanad district of the hills.

Hough[3] in 1825 found the population to consist of 145 men, 100 women, 45 boys, and 36 girls, altogether 326.

In 1838, Birch[4] gives the population as consisting of 294 men and 184 women, amounting to 478, but elsewhere in his paper he says that the number of the Todas was computed at about 800.

In 1847, Ouchterlony[5] found the number of the Todas to be 337, made up of 86 adult males, 87 male children, 70 adult females, and 94 female children. The proportion of males to females is only 173 to 164, showing a very much smaller preponderance of males than in any other estimate before or since.

In 1856, Grigg[6] gives 185 males and 131 females, altogether 316.

In 1866, Grigg gives the population as 704. If the estimates of this year and that of 1856 were correct, it would show that the population had more than doubled in ten years. It is evident that the census of 1866 is the first which gives anything approaching an accurate record of the Toda population. Even in this year there is one obvious source of error, for it would seem that those living at the foot of the hills, near Gudalur were not included, and probably twenty or thirty, if not more, would have to be added on this account.

[1] Grigg's *Manual of the Nilagiri District*, 1880, Appendix No. 17, p. xlviii.

[2] *Ibid.* App. No. 20, p. lx.

[3] *Letters on the Neilgherries*, London, 1829, p. 75.

[4] *Madras Journ. of Lit. and Science*, 1836, vol. viii, p. 86.

[5] *Ibid.*, 1848, vol. xv, p. 1.

[6] *Manual*, p. 27.

For the census of 1871 the records are conflicting. On p. 29 of the *Manual*, Grigg gives the numbers as 693, 405 males and 288 females. On p. 187 he gives instead of these numbers 376 males and 263 females, making a total of 639. Breeks gives the latter numbers and also a revised result which brings out the total population as 683. This figure, or the earlier of Grigg's figures, evidently approximates to the correct population, which shows a slight falling off as compared with five years earlier.

In the census of 1881, the numbers would appear to have continued to diminish, the population being put at only 675; 382 males and 293 females.

In 1891, the number had risen to 736; 424 males and 312 females.

In the census of 1901, which was taken with especial care to record all the Todas, there were found to be 451 males and 354 females, making together 805.

The population as recorded in my genealogical tables compiled in 1902 was only 736; 419 males and 317 females. My numbers fall far short of those of the census taken a year previously. As I have already pointed out, my genealogies are untrustworthy as a record of the young children of the community now living, and it is possible also that I have omitted a certain number of women. The excess of men over women is distinctly greater in my figures than in the census of 1901, and this may be due to the fact that I failed to hear of a certain number of widows or unmarried women or girls. If so, it is probable that these defects are in the genealogies of the Teivaliol, and it is in them that the excess of men is greatest.

The earlier records of the population are certainly far below the mark. Captain Harkness, writing in 1832, estimates the attendance at a funeral at 300 men, nearly half that number of women, and about as many boys and girls. Those seen by Harkness may not have been all Todas, since Badagas and Kotas undoubtedly attend Toda funerals, but we may safely call this a total attendance of 500, which would show that the records of Hough in 1825 and of Birch in 1838 are far below the mark, and that Birch's rough estimate of 800 is probably far more nearly correct, and may even have been too small.

The records have probably been fairly complete since 1866, and if so, they show a falling off in population from this date till the 1881 census. It is, however, possible that the gradual increase in numbers during recent censuses has been due to the greater care taken at each succeeding census. Unsatisfactory as the records are, they seem to point to a diminution of population about the middle of the last century, which ceased between 1880 and 1890, since which time the population has probably increased.

Mr. R. C. Punnett[1] has analysed the data furnished by my genealogical records to ascertain the average size of the Toda family. He divided the families recorded in the genealogies into four groups: (A) those where the eldest child would in 1903 be over 90 years of age; (B) those where he would be between 60 and 90; (C) and (D) those where he would be between 30 and 60 and between 0 and 30 respectively. He has recorded the results for Tartharol and Teivaliol separately in the following table.

Group.	Tartharol.			Teivaliol.		
	No. of families.	Average size of family.	♂s per 100 ♀s.	No. of families.	Average size of family.	♂s per 100 ♀s.
A	9	3·0 [4·2]	237·5	4	4·5 [6·0]	200
B	49	4·1 [5·0]	159·7	21	3·8 [5·4]	259
C	87	3·3 [3·7]	131·4	40	3·8 [5·0]	202
D	104	2·5 [2·8]	129·2	45	2·3 [2·9]	171

The figures in square brackets give the average size of the family for each generation, making allowance for cases of female infanticide, which we shall see presently to be a Toda custom which is almost certainly diminishing in frequency.

The conclusion Mr. Punnett draws from this table is that there has been a marked decrease in fertility during the period covered by the genealogies.

The defects in my record as regards young children make

[1] *Proc. Camb. Philos. Soc.*, 1904, vol. xii, p. 481.

any conclusions about the last generation very inconclusive, but since the record for very young children is certainly defective, and since many families now existing will certainly increase in size, it is probable that any progressive decrease in the size of a family has now been arrested, and the details of the genealogical record would therefore agree with the Census Reports in showing the presence of a distinct tendency of the Toda population to increase.

None of the previous records have given any indication of the numbers of the two chief divisions of the Toda people. According to my genealogical records, there were living, in 1902, 528 Tartharol and 208 Teivaliol. The defects in my record are probably somewhat greater for the Teivaliol than for the Tartharol, but any difference there may be is certainly not great, and I think we may conclude that, though these figures are not accurate, they represent approximately the true proportion of the numbers of the two divisions. It is quite certain that the Tartharol are more than twice as numerous as the Teivaliol. Mr. Punnett's table does not show any great difference between the two divisions in the average size of the family, so that the proportion between the numbers of the two divisions has probably not altered during the period covered by the genealogical record. It is probable that the Teivaliol have always or for a very long time been the smaller division.

The Census Reports and the genealogical record then agree in pointing to a diminution of the Toda population about the middle of last century which has now ceased, the probability being that the Todas are increasing slightly in numbers.

There can be little doubt that any decrease in the Toda population about the middle of last century was the direct result of the changes brought about by the advent of Europeans to the Nilgiri Hills. The adverse influences which came into the lives of the Todas probably owe their origin to the large immigration of native servants and to the development of the bazaar. Though Europeans first began to come to the Nilgiri Hills about 1820, it was not till twenty or thirty years later that they arrived in any considerable numbers, so that it was probably the middle of the century before the injurious influences made their effects felt to any great effect.

The especial influences injurious to fertility have probably been syphilis and sexual immorality, for the Todas do not appear to have fallen to any very great extent under the influence of alcohol or opium. They certainly take both, and especially after the market day at the Ootacamund bazaar, I have seen Todas obviously under the influence of drink; but I believe this to have been only an influence of minor importance on the health of the people. Syphilis, on the other hand, has undoubtedly affected them to a considerable extent. At the present time its ravages are not very obvious, though, without looking for it especially, I saw several examples of its effects. There can be little doubt, however, that it has been a potent factor in the past. In a note in a book by A. C. Burnell,[1] it is mentioned that in 1871 thirty-one Todas were treated at Ootacamund for venereal disease, and of these thirty were syphilitic. This means that in one year over 4 per cent. of the total Toda population were treated for syphilis at one place, and we may be fairly confident that all those suffering from the disease did not apply for treatment.

Another factor working towards the diminution of the population has probably been sexual immorality. I shall have to return to this subject again later, and must be content here to point out that the Toda women have a very bad reputation, though perhaps their laxity is not as great as is usually supposed. Still, there can be little doubt that the women of some villages are extremely immoral, and it is probable that this has distinctly tended to produce sterility.

If the diminution in the size of the Toda family is due to these adverse influences, it should be found to be greatest in those sections of the Toda community which have been most subject to these influences. The best way of throwing light on this question is to compare the fertility of the different clans of the Tartharol. Some of these, such as Nòdrs, Pan, Taradr, and Kanòdrs, either live in outlying parts of the hills or are sufficiently remote from the chief centres of the European population not to have been influenced very greatly.

[1] *Specimens of South Indian Dialects*, Mangalore, 1873.

The chief village of the Kars clan is situated close to Ootacamund and has suffered greatly from its neighbours, but many of the villages of the clan are more remote, so that the clan may be put down as one partly influenced. The people of Päm and Nidrsi, on the other hand, are more influenced than any other of the Toda clans, as is shown by the alterations in their villages and the neglect of the ritual of their religion. The villages of the Pämol are, or were, near to Wellington Barracks, and it is certainly the most degenerated of all the Toda clans. The following table, taken from Mr. Punnett's paper, shows the average size of the family in each case, and though the figures are somewhat irregular, they bear out the view that sterility is greater the more the people have come into contact with Europeans and their followers.

Name of clan.	No. of families.	No. of offspring.	Average size of family.	Average size of family for group.
Nòdrs (uninfluenced)	14	54	3·84	3·59
Pan (uninfluenced)	8	21	2·37	
Taradr (uninfluenced)	9	43	4·77	
Kanòdrs (uninfluenced)	11	33	3·00	
Kars (partly influenced)	25	76	3·04	3·04
Päm (much influenced)	10	22	2·20	2·60
Nidrsi (much influenced)	10	30	3·00	

Proportion of the Sexes

The records of the Toda population in the past all show an excess of men over women, and with the exception of the record of Ouchterlony, which is certainly untrustworthy, the excess is considerable. In view of their untrustworthiness no importance can be attached to the records taken earlier than that of 1866, and in the report for that year I have been unable to ascertain the proportions of the sexes. In 1871 there were 140·6 men for every 100 women; in 1881, 130·4 for every 100; in 1891, 135·9, and in the census of 1901, 127·4 men for every 100 women. My figures, derived from the genealogical record, give for 1902, 132·2 men for every 100 women, a proportion distinctly greater than that of the census, which suggests that it is in the female portion of the community that my records are most defective.

In the table on p. 474 taken from Mr. Punnett's paper, it is seen that the data derived from the genealogical record agree with those of the Census Reports in showing on the whole a progressive decrease in the excess of men over women. The number of families in the first group is too small to give them much importance, but for the three succeeding generations of the Tartharol, the numbers of males for every 100 females are 159·7, 131·4, and 129·2, while for the Teivaliol the figures are 259, 202, and 171 respectively.

The Census Reports and the genealogical record thus agree in showing a progressive diminution in the excess of men over women.

There can be little doubt as to the cause of this. All accounts of the Todas agree in attributing to them the practice of female infanticide, though, at the present time, the Todas are very chary of acknowledging the existence of the practice. They deny it absolutely for the present, and they are reluctant to speak about it for the past.

I do not think that there is the slightest doubt that it was at one time very prevalent, and that it has greatly diminished in frequency, but that it is still practised to some extent. The chance remarks of children to my interpreter, Samuel, had shown him that the practice is still followed occasionally, and I think it far from unlikely that it is even now not a very rare occurrence.

In Mr. Punnett's table, it will be seen that the genealogical data show that the excess of men is far greater in the Teivaliol than in the Tartharol, and the excess in the former is so great as to leave little doubt that the practice is still followed in this division not infrequently. If this is so, it is probably due to the fact that the Teivaliol chiefly inhabit the more outlying parts of the hills, so that, on the whole, they have been less affected than the Tartharol by the various influences which have come into the lives of the Todas. An accessory factor may have been the priestly functions of the Teivaliol, which have probably tended to make them more conservative.

Previous writers on the Todas have differed considerably in their accounts of the method of infanticide, and I regret very much that I cannot contribute any facts towards the settlement of the question. The subject was one about which the Todas talked so unwillingly that I made no great endeavours to arrive at the truth. A method which has been commonly attributed to the Todas is that of placing the infant at the gate of the buffalo-pen before this is opened in the morning, the herd rushing out and trampling on the child. Another less likely method has been said to be that the infant is drowned in buffalo milk.

The most probable account is that given to Marshall[1] by an aged Toda, who stated that the child is suffocated by an old woman, who receives a fee of four annas, and that the child is then buried, which, as we have seen, is the method of disposing of the bodies of still-born children.

There is little reason to connect the practice of female infanticide among the Todas with any deficiency in the necessaries for existence. It seems clear that at one time the Todas supplemented their food of milk with berries, roots, &c., but it is improbable that they were ever in such straits for food that they would have resorted to infanticide on this account. Marshall's informant ascribed infanticide to the poverty of his people, but this was probably said in order to excuse the practice.

In an earlier part of this chapter we saw that there is evidence of a former diminution of the Toda population. At the same time we see that there is evidence of a diminution of the practice of female infanticide, which would, of course, tend to increase the population. It would thus seem that there have existed among the Todas, during the last fifty years, certain factors tending to diminish the population and one factor tending to increase it. We may conclude that, but for the diminution of infanticide, the falling off in numbers would have been greater, and that the tendency to increase which

[1] Pp. 194-5.

seems at present to exist may be due, wholly or in part, to the diminution of infanticide.

There is one indication that female infanticide has almost entirely ceased during the last five years, and even that there may now be an excess of female births. In the table of ages given on page 469, it will be seen that the pedigrees record more girls than boys of five years and under. There is no reason why my record of such young children should have been more defective for one sex than for the other, and the proportion here may be approximately correct.

TWINS

Twins are called *ömumokh*, and it is the custom to kill one of them, even when both are boys. If they should be girls, it is probable that both would be killed, or, at any rate, would have been killed in the past.

There is one case of twins in the genealogies. Iraveli, the wife of Kwötuli and Nudriki (8), gave birth to twins about twelve years ago. Both were boys, and I was first told that one had died shortly after birth, but later inquiries made it almost certain that the boy had been killed. Some time after the birth of the twins, one of the buffaloes of Kwötuli and Nudriki is said to have had a calf with one body, two heads, and four legs. The buffalo died before the calf was born, and the monstrosity was found by the Kotas, to whom the body was given. It was generally expected that something would happen to Kwötuli or Nudriki, but they have since been very prosperous.

THE DETERMINATION OF AGE

This is a suitable place to say a word about the method I adopted to ascertain the ages of the Todas. Like all people at a low stage of culture, the Todas are very uncertain about their ages, though their knowledge is more accurate than that of many peoples. Every Toda knows, however, whether he is older or younger than another, this fact determining the names and salutations they give to one another, as we shall see in the next chapter. A few of the younger men seemed to have accurate knowledge of their ages, and building up on this basis, and with a knowledge of the relative ages of the different members of the community, it became possible to arrive at estimates which probably do not deviate very widely from the correct ages; even in the case of the older people, I do not believe that my estimated ages are likely to be more than five years out in any case. As already mentioned (see p. 416), the Todas make use, in the estimation of age, of their belief in the eighteen-year period of a flower, and the ages so estimated in a few cases agreed fairly with those arrived at in other ways.

Among those now alive, it seemed that the usual time which separates the birth of two children of the same mother is about three years, and I have taken this time as the rule in estimating the ages of all those whose names are included in the genealogies. Similarly, so far as I could tell, women begin to bear children when about eighteen to twenty years of age.

The ages of the four groups given in the table on p. 474 were calculated on the assumptions that a woman had her first child when twenty years old, and that the interval between the births of two children was three years.

The oldest Toda now living is Kiugi (57). He looks an extremely old man, and is said by the Todas to be nearly a hundred years of age. There is evidence which makes it probable that he is at least eighty or ninety. Kòrs, the father of Kiugi, performed the *pursütpimi* ceremony before the birth of Teitchi (52) (see p. 564). Teitchi's grandson, Kuriolv, is now about fifty-four years of age. When Kòrs gave the bow and arrow he may have been only a young boy, and if we assume that he was fifteen years old, that Teitchi and Pareivan had their first children when twenty years old, and that the interval between the birth of Pilzink and that of Pareivan was six years, it would make the age of Kòrs, if he were still alive, 115. If Kiugi was born when his father was twenty years old, it would make his age ninety-five. If, on the other hand, we assume that Kòrs gave the bow and arrow when only ten years of age, and that he did not have his first child till he was thirty, it would make Kiugi's age eighty. Kiugi's eldest child, if alive, would now probably be about sixty, and this supports the view that the lowest possible estimate of Kiugi's age is eighty, and he is not improbably a good deal older.

CHAPTER XXI

KINSHIP

THE system of kinship was studied chiefly by means of the genealogies. The Todas are sufficiently intelligent to be able to give satisfactory definitions of their terms expressing different kinds of relationship, but the genealogies were very useful in checking these definitions and in working out several points in detail.

The Toda system of kinship is of the kind known as classificatory with several interesting special features. Perhaps the most important of these is the use of the same terms for mother's brother and father-in-law on the one hand, and for father's sister and mother-in-law on the other hand. This is a natural consequence of the regulation which ordains that the proper marriage for a man is one with the daughter either of his mother's brother or father's sister.

Another important feature of the Toda system is the existence of two well-marked groups of terms expressing bonds of kinship; one used when speaking of relatives, and the other when speaking to relatives and in exclamations. The latter, which may be regarded as vocative cases of the former, are fewer in number and used in a much more general sense; and if the two are not distinguished, it is easy to understand that one may find only "inextricable confusion in Toda ideas as to relationship."[1] I will first give a list of kinship terms, together with the forms used in direct address, and the approximate definitions, and these will be followed by a

[1] See Marshall, p. 213.

discussion of the exact meaning of each term. The vocative forms are enclosed in brackets.

Pevian, great-grandfather.
Peviav, great-grandmother.
Pian (*pia*), grandfather.
Piav (*piava*), grandmother.
In (*aia*), father.
Av (*ava*), mother.
Mokh (*ena*), son.
Kugh (*ena*), daughter.
Mokh pedvai mokh (*ena*), grandson.
Mokh pedvai kugh (*ena*), granddaughter.
An (*anna*), elder brother.
Egal (*egala*), brother of same age.
Nòdrved (*enda*), younger brother.
Akkan (*akka*), elder sister.
Nòdrvedkugh (*enda*), younger sister.
Mun (*mama*), mother's brother and wife's father.
Mumi (*mimia*), father's sister and wife's mother.
Manmokh (*ena*), sister's son.
Mankugh (*ena*), sister's daughter.
Matchuni, child of a mother's brother or father's sister.
Òl (*òl* or *òlia*), husband.
Kotvai or *tazmokh* (*tazmokh* or *tazmokhia*), wife.
Paiol, general name for male relatives of wife.
Motvilth (*ena*), son's wife.

A general name for those of the same clan is *annatam*, but I am not sure that this is not properly a borrowed word.

In giving a more detailed account of these terms of kinship, it will perhaps be convenient to begin with the relationship of *in*, or father.

In. A person speaks of his father as "*en in*," "my father," while "his father" would be "*tan in*." An *in* is addressed as *aia*. These names are applied not only to the father, but also to the father's brothers, whether they are husbands of the mother or not.

The names *in* or *aia* are also given to all the males of the clan (*madol*) who are of the same generation as the father;

also to the husbands of the sisters of the mother, sisters here including both own sisters and clan-sisters, *i.e.*, to the husbands of all those who are of the same clan and generation as the mother. Elder brothers of the father (either own brothers or clan-brothers) are often addressed as *perudaia*, while younger brothers are called *karudaia*, and in speaking of such men the expressions "*en in perud*" and "*en in karud*" would be used. When a man speaks of one of his more remote fathers, and it may be doubtful of whom he is speaking, he may add the name of the man; thus Siriar (20) would speak of Paniolv (26), the husband of his mother's sister, as "*Pani in.*"

Av. A mother is spoken of as *en av* or *tan av*, and addressed as *ava*. These names are also applied to the wife of a father other than the actual mother, to the sisters of the mother, to the wives of the father's brothers, and to the sisters of the wife's father. Every woman of the same clan and generation as the mother is an *av*. In general the wife of an *in* is an *av*. As in the case of the *in*, a distinction is made between the elder and younger sisters of the mother, the former being addressed as *perudava* and the latter *karudava*. Similarly the wife of an elder brother of the father is *perudava* and of a younger *karudava*. Such relatives may be spoken of as "*en av perud*" and "*en av karud.*"

Mokh and *Kugh*. Every one whom a man calls *in* or *av* calls the man *mokh*, and every one to whom a woman gives these names calls the woman *kugh*. In direct address, both *mokh* and *kugh* are called *ena* (? *enna*).

In speaking of his brother's children, a man may make clear whether he is speaking of the child of an elder or younger brother; thus he may say "*en nödrvedvain mokh*," "my younger brother's son." *Mokh* is often used as a general term for "child" and may be applied to persons of either sex.

Pian. This name is given to both paternal and maternal grandfathers and to their brothers, certainly in the narrow sense and probably in the wider. Every male of the speaker's clan of the same generation as the father's father would certainly be called "*en pian.*" The brother of the father's mother is also called *pian*, but I am doubtful whether the term is used for all the clan-brothers of the father's mother

Similarly I am uncertain how far the clan-brothers of the mother's father and mother's mother receive this name. A *pian* is addressed as *pia*.

Piav. This is the name of both paternal and maternal grandmothers, and in general the wife of a *pian* is a *piav*. A *piav* is addressed as *piava*.

All those addressed as *pian* or *piav* will address the speaker as *ena*. When speaking of his grandson, a man will say "*en mokh pedvai*" or "*en mokh pedvai mokh*," literally "my born to my son" or "my son born to my son," and there were no less elaborate terms.

The son of a daughter is called *en kugh pedvai mokh*, "my daughter who born to son," taking the words in order, or "my son born to my daughter." A daughter of a son is called *en mokh pedvai kugh*, and the daughter of a daughter, *en kugh pedvai kugh*. Since, however, *mokh* is often used as a general name for "child," I believe that this word usually takes the place of *kugh*, and that in consequence a grandchild of either sex is called *en mokh pedvai mokh*.

Pevian and *peviav*. These words for great-grandfather and great-grandmother have a similar wide connotation. The word *pef* is an ancient term for "great" which is used in some of the magical incantations (see p. 267).

An. This is the name for elder brother and for all members of the clan of a man or woman who are of the same generation as, and older than, the man or woman. An *an* is addressed as *anna*.

Nòdrved. This is the name for younger brother and for all members of the clan of the same generation as, and younger than, the speaker. *En nòdrved* or *nòdrped* means literally "my born with." A *nòdrved* is addressed as *enda*.

Egal. A corresponding relative who is of the same age is called *en egal* and is addressed as *egala*.

These terms are used both by men and women of and to men.

Akkan. This term is applied by both men and women to an elder sister, and is also given to all female members of the same clan who are of the same generation as, and older than, the speaker. An *akkan* is addressed as *akka*.

Nòdrvedkugh. A younger sister is spoken of by this name, which is also given to all the female members of the same clan and generation, but younger than the speaker. Such a relative is addressed by the same term as is applied to a younger brother, viz., *enda.* Two sisters of the same age are *egal* and *egala* to one another.

These terms for "brother" and "sister" are also applied to one another by the children of two sisters. Thus a man would call the son of his mother's sister *an*, and address him as *anna* if the latter were older than himself, and would be spoken of by the latter as *en nòdrved* and addressed as *enda.* If of the same age they would be *egal* or *egala* to one another. Similarly a man addresses the daughter of his mother's sister as *akka* or *enda* according to age. I am doubtful how widely the terms for brotherhood and sisterhood are applied in this case. I do not know whether the children of two women of the same generation in a large clan like that of Kars would call one another brother and sister.

Thus the children of two brothers are brothers and sisters, and the children of two sisters are also brothers and sisters, while, as we shall see shortly, the children of brother and sister receive another name. The children of two sisters belong to different clans except in those cases in which the sisters have married men of the same clan. Thus a man may have brothers and sisters in several different clans.

Mun. This is the name of the mother's brother, of the father's sister's husband, and of the wife's father. The last is also spoken of as *paiol* together with other relatives of the wife. In the case of the orthodox Toda marriage, in which a man marries the daughter of his mother's brother, or of his father's sister, the *mun* is at the same time both wife's father and either mother's brother or father's sister's husband, but the wife's father is still called *mun* even when a man marries a woman to whom he is unrelated.

The term *mun* is not only applied by a man to the own brothers of his mother, but also to her clan-brothers. When a man has many *mun*, he may show to which he is referring by mentioning his name; thus Siriar (20) would say "*Karsüln mun*" if he referred to this relative, the husband of his father's sister, and he might speak in the same way of a clan-brother of his mother.

A distinction is often made between older and younger *mun*; thus, if a man's mother had two brothers, the elder would be called *en mun perud* and the younger *en mun karud*. A *mun* is addressed as *mama*.

Mumi. This is the name of the father's sister, of the wife of a mother's brother, and of the wife's mother, the terms brother and sister being again used in a wide sense. In general, the wife of a *mun* is a *mumi*. A *mumi* is addressed as *mimia*.

Manmokh. A person would apply the term *manmokh* to his sister's son and his wife's brother's son. It is a term reciprocal to *mun* in so far as this term is one for mother's brother and father's sister's husband. I am not quite certain whether it would be used for a son-in-law who was not also a sister's son, but I am almost certain that this would be done.

The term is also applied to the sons of clan-sisters, and when used in this more distant way a distinction is sometimes made. *En manmokh* would mean "my (own) sister's son," *Em manmokh*, literally "our sister's son," would be used for children of a more distant sister.

Mankugh is used in exactly the same way as *manmokh* for sister's daughter, &c.

Matchuni. This is the term applied to one another by the children, both male and female, of brother and sister. While the children of two brothers are brothers or sisters (*an*, *egal*, *akka* or *nòdrved*) and the children of two sisters are also brothers and sisters, the children of a brother and sister are *matchuni*. In other words, the children of an individual's mother's brother or of his father's sister are the *matchuni* of the individual.

When a man addresses his male *matchuni* he calls him *anna*, *egala* or *enda*, according to their relative ages. Similarly when a woman addresses her female *matchuni*, she calls her *akka*, *egala* or *enda*, according to age.

When a man addresses his female *matchuni*, he calls her either *tazmokhia* or *kughia* (see below). He gives her the former name because he is allowed to marry her; she is a woman who might normally be his wife and he therefore addresses her as wife.

Similarly a woman addresses her male *matchuni* as *òlia*; she calls him husband because he may become her husband.

As in the case of other relationships, a man may define more exactly of whom he is speaking when he refers to a *matchuni*, and may say instead *en munkugh*, the daughter of my *mun*. Two kinship terms are thus used which resemble one another closely, but have very different meanings:—*en munkugh*, my uncle's daughter, and *en mankugh*, my sister's daughter.

Òl, husband. A woman speaks of her husband as *en òl* and addresses him as *òlia*.

Kotvai and *tazmokh*, wife. A man speaks of his wife as *en kotvai*, and addresses her as *tazmokhia*.

Paiol. This is a general term for the male relatives of the wife. It is applied especially to the wife's father, the wife's brothers, and the brothers of the wife's father.

It seemed that this term should only properly be applied to the near relatives of the wife. Those whom the wife would address as *aia*, *anna*, or *enda*, because members of her clan, need not be called *paiol* by the husband.

Paiol is a reciprocal term, and it is therefore applied by a man to the daughter's husband, the sister's husband, and to the husband of the brother's daughter.

A *paiol* is addressed as *anna*, *egala*, or *enda*, according to age.

Motvilth. This term is the equivalent of daughter-in-law and is applied by a man to his son's wife. A woman is also the *motvilth* of the brothers of her husband's father. A *motvilth* is addressed as *ena*.

There did not seem to be any brief term for the sister of a wife, and a man would speak of her as *en kotvai akkan* if older, or as *en kotvai nòdrved* if younger than the wife.

Sometimes the Todas add to some of the kinship names

the word *potch*, which is said to have the meanings "begetting" or "begotten." I met with this especially in the lamentations used at funerals. A man would say, "*en potch aia*"—"O my father which begot me"; "*en potch anna*"—"O my elder brother begotten with me." For a younger brother, however, this word would not be used; a man would not say, "*en potch nòdrved ia*," because *ved* has the same significance as *potch*, *nòdrved* meaning also "born with" or "begotten with."

Every male of a man's own clan is either his *pian*; his *in*; his *an*, *egal*, or *nòdrved*; his *mokh*, or his *mokh pedvai mokh*. In most cases a clan consists of several families, and these families may be unrelated to one another so far as the evidence from the genealogical record goes. Nevertheless, every Toda knows exactly the proper kinship terms to apply to all the members of his clan. I inquired in detail into the basis of this knowledge in the case of the Taradrol, consisting of six *pòlm* or divisions. All the members of each *pòlm* trace their descent from a man whose name is known, and the pedigrees of the six *pòlm* are given in the genealogical tables 20 to 25.

It was known that three of these *pòlm* were closely related to one another, and that the other three were also closely related. The following table expresses the relationship in the first case:—

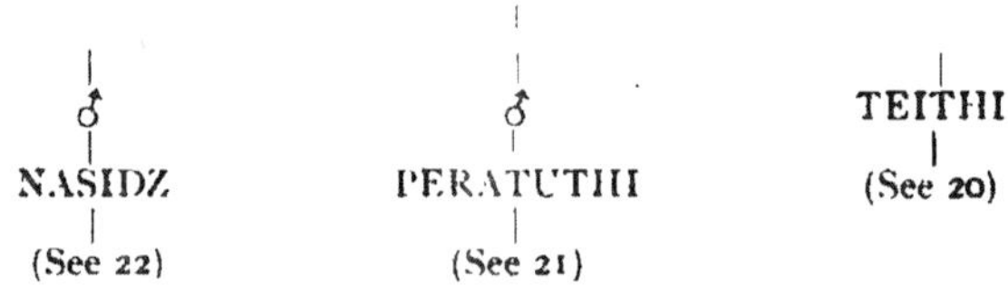

It was not perfectly certain whether Teithi and the two men whose names were not remembered were own brothers, but it was known that they were closely related and of the same generation. They were certainly clan-brothers and possibly own brothers. The kinship names applied by members of the three *pòlm* to one another were all in accordance with this scheme; thus, there was no one living in these three *pòlm* whom Siriar (20) called *aia*; he would have given this name to Nasidz or Peratuthi if they had been alive. He calls Arthothi and Parkeidi *anna*; they are the sons of Peratuthi, who was of the same generation as Siriar's father. The following are called *mokh* or *ena*:—Püldenir, Keinodz, Idrshkwòdr (21), Polgar, Pundu, Keinmuv, and Pushtikudr (22), although at least one of these men is older than Siriar, and several others are approximately of the same age. Similarly, Muners (21) is the *mokh pedvai mokh*, or grandson of Siriar.

The other three *pòlm* of the Taradr clan are known to be related in a similar way: Kiusthvan (23), Pachievan (24), and Pungut (25) being either own brothers or men closely related and of the same generation. I was thus able to ascertain definitely how each member of the first three *pòlm* knew the appropriate name to be given to members of these families, and similarly how members of the other three *pòlm* knew the exact terms of kinship to apply to one another.

Each member of the first three *pòlm* also knew, however, the proper kinship terms to apply to members of the other three *pòlm*, although I could not obtain, and there seemed to be no record of, the way in which the two groups of families were connected. Thus Siriar addresses as *aia* Paners and his brothers (23) and Irkiolv (24). He addresses as *anna*: Teitukhen, Idjkudr and Kandu (23), Tòleidi, Nertiners, Mogai, Teimad and Orguln (24), and Kudeners and his brother (25). The children of these men are the *mokh* of Siriar, and are addressed by him as *ena*.

The explanation seems to be that the mode of relationship is handed down from generation to generation; thus Teithi, the grandfather of Siriar, called Kiusthvan (23) brother, and in consequence Ircheidi and Paners, their sons, also call one another brother, and so Siriar, the son of Ircheidi, knows that he has to call Paners father. In this way a man would know the correct term to apply to every member of his clan, though the links by which their pedigrees are connected may have been completely forgotten.

I also worked out the relationship of the different divisions of the Kuudr clan in the same way, and may perhaps give the record briefly.

Teitnir (52) calls the following Kuudr men *aia*:—Mutevan (52), Punatvan (53), Keitas (55), Tüliners (56), Kiugi (57), Tütners, Etamudri, Madsu, and Koboners (58), Ishkievan (60).

He calls the following *anna*:—Kuriolv and Ivievan (52), Targners (53), Keinkursi (54), and Mudriners (57). The following are his *nòdrved*, and are called by him *enda*:—Kwelthipush and his brothers, Piliar and Piliag (52), Pungusivan, Tevò, Karov and Pòl (53), Pöteners (54), Sinar and Katsog (55), Erai, Kil, Kanokh (56), Onadj and Kwòdrthotz (57), Kishkar and Tormungudr (59). All the sons of these brothers are the *mokh* of Teitnir.

In the above list Teitnir omitted Tikievan and Tushtkudr (56), who according to the genealogies are his *pia* or grandfathers, while their sons, though much younger than Teitnir, are his fathers, and are addressed by him as *aia*.

The other kinship terms are used in the same wide way. If a man's mother belonged to Kuudr all those Kuudr men would be his *mun* who were the *an*, *egal*, or *nòdrved* of his mother; and all the children of those men would be his *matchuni*.

The terms used for the relatives of a wife are also used for the corresponding relatives of a *sedvaitazmokh*. This is the name of the woman in the Toda institution according to which a woman consorts with one or more men in addition to her husband or husbands (see p. 526). The man, or *mokhthodvaiol*, calls the fathers and brothers of the woman *paiol*, and calls her father *mun* and her mother *mumi*.

Relatives are often spoken of by the Todas in a way that defines their relation to the speaker more exactly than is usual in the classificatory system. Thus, a man may call his brother's son "*en nodrvedvain mokh*"—"my younger brother's son"; or he may speak of his wife's elder sister as "*en kotvai akka*," an abbreviation of *en kotvai tan akka*—"my wife her elder sister." Similarly, a wife's younger sister may be called "*en kotvai nòdrved*."

It seemed to me that the Todas afford an interesting example of a people who are beginning to modify the classificatory system of kinship in a direction which distinctly approaches the descriptive system. The essential features of the system of kinship are those known as classificatory, but the Todas have various means of distinguishing between the near and distant relatives to whom the same kinship term is applied. Two examples of this have already been given; the son of an own sister may be called "my sister's son," while the son of a clan sister is called "our sister's son," and the own brother of a mother is simply called *mun*, while in the case of a clan brother of the mother, the name of the man is added. Further, a term which is definitely descriptive may be used in the examples quoted above.

The Todas have reached a stage of mental development in which it seems that they are no longer satisfied with the nomenclature of a purely classificatory system, and have begun to make distinctions in their terminology for near and distant relatives.

Another point of interest about the Toda system is that the two sets of kinship terms—those used in direct address and those used when speaking of a relative—do not correspond closely with one another.

The terms used in direct address are few in number compared with the kinship terms used when speaking of a relative. Brothers of all kinds, *matchuni* and some *paiol* (brothers-in-law) are all addressed as *anna*, *egala* or *enda*, according to age. Children, grandchildren, sisters' sons and sons-in-law are all addressed as *ena*. If exclusive attention were paid to the kinship terms used in address we should seem to have a kinship system which is almost wholly based on relative ages and generations, all other distinctions being ignored.

The Toda system distinguishes widely between elder and younger members of the family and clan. This feature, which is of very general occurrence in connexion with the classificatory system, has been highly developed by the Todas, and their system differs from any other with which I am acquainted in having a special term for relatives of the same age.

When two members of a clan or two men related in other ways address one another as brother, the terms employed depend altogether on their relative ages, and are not influenced by the relative seniority of the branches of the family or clan to which they belong.

The Toda system appears to be closely related to that of the Dravidians of Southern India. In several cases the names for certain kin are identical with or closely resemble those of other South Indian languages.

The three most characteristic features of the Toda system are (i.) the use of the same term for mother's brother and father-in-law, &c.; (ii.) the marked development of vocative forms of the kinship terms; (iii.) the marked development of distinctions according to age. These three features are also found in Tamil, and as far as my information goes in Telugu and Canarese. The Toda system appears to be a simplified form of the Tamil system with many points of identity. The resemblance between the Toda and the Tamil names seems certainly to be closer than that between the Toda names and those of the Telugus and Canarese.

I do not wish here to consider these resemblances and differences in any detail, but in the Table on the opposite page I have given a list of those kinship terms in which the Todas resemble other inhabitants of Southern India. The Tamil terms I owe to Mr. K. Rangachari of Madras; the others I have taken from Morgan's *System of Consanguinity and Affinity of the Human Race.*

Kinship Taboos

A man never mentions the name of his *mun*. If he wishes to make clear of whom he is speaking he will give the name of the place at which his *mun* lives, as "*Tedshteiri ithvai en mun podchi*," "My uncle who lives at Tedshteiri." This restriction only applies to the own brothers of his mother. Other more distant *mun* may be spoken of by name, and as we have already seen, if a man wishes to make it clear of whom he is speaking, he mentions the name in addition to the kinship term.

A man is also prohibited from uttering the name of the man from whom he has received his wife—*i.e.*, to whom he has done *kalmelpudithti* (see p. 502). This man, who is called the *mokhudrtvaiol*, is usually the father of the wife and would normally be also a *mun*, but sometimes the place of the *mokhudrtvaiol* is usurped by somebody else and in such a case there might be no restriction on the name of the wife's real father. In the only case of this kind of which I have a record, the marriage of Siriar (20) and Pupidz, the place of *mokhudrtvaiol* was taken by Kuriolv, who was living with Pilimurg (7), the girl's mother, and though he was no real

	Toda.	Tamil.	Telegu.	Canarese.
Son........	mokh	maghan		
Elder brother ...	an (anna)	aṉṉan (aṉṉa)	anna	anna
Elder sister	akkan (akka)	akkal (akka)	akka	akka
Mother's brother.	mun (mâmâ)	amman or maman (mama)	mena mama	mava
Father-in-law ...	mun (mama)	mamaner (mama)	mama	mava
Father's sister ...	mumi (mimia)	attai		
Wife of mother's brother	mumi (mimia)	ammami		
Wife's mother ...	mumi (mimia)	mamiyar (ammami)		
Sister's son	manmokh	maruman or marumakan		
Mother's brother's son	matchuni	maittunan (?)		
Father's sister's son	matchuni	attan or maittunan		
Wife's brother ...	matchuni or paiol	machchinan or maittunan		

relative of the wife, Siriar might not mention his name. In spite of the fact, however, that Kuriolv had become his *mokhudrtvaiol*, Siriar went privately to Patirsh (35), the real father of his wife, and did *kalmelpudithi* and would also refrain from saying the name of this man.

A man is prohibited from saying the name of his wife's mother (*mumi*), but my notes do not make clear whether he is also prohibited from saying the names of other *mumi*—*i.e.*, father's sisters, but probably this is so. In any case this restriction only applies to near relatives.

A man may not utter the name of his *pian* or *piav*.

There seemed to be some reluctance to say the name of a wife, but there did not appear to be any definite prohibition against it. It was probably part of a reluctance to utter personal names in general of which the Todas show some traces, though it is less marked among them than in the case of many uncultured people.

The taboo on names was far wider in the case of dead relatives. No one was allowed to utter the name of a dead relative, and this rule appeared to be especially stringent in the case of relatives who had been older than the speaker. As I have already mentioned, this taboo was for some time a great obstacle in my way when trying to obtain the pedigrees of the people. If a man had to refer to a dead relative, he did so by mentioning the name of the village at which he had died; thus, if the father of a Taradr man had died at Taradr, the man would say, "*en in Taradr pon*," while, if he had died away from home, say at Kuudr, he would refer to his father as "*en in Kuudr odthavai*," "my father who died at Kuudr."

In the funeral lamentations, each mourner mentions the deceased by the name indicating the bond of kinship between himself and the dead, and does not utter the personal name.

Kinship Salutations

There are certain well-defined salutations which are regulated by kinship.

The characteristic Toda salutation is called *kalmelpudithti*, in which salutation one person kneels or bows down before another, while the latter raises each foot and touches the forehead of the other. In general this salutation is only paid by women to their elder male relatives; a woman places her head beneath the foot of her *pian*, *in*, *an*, or *mun*, using these terms in their widest sense. The salutation seems to be very largely one connected with kinship. In everyday life the salutation is only paid by women to men, but under special circumstances, men may bow down before men, and women before women, and men even may bow down before women (see p. 502).

Since, owing to the *mokhthodvaiol* connexion, a Tarthar woman may have a Teivali *mun* and *vice versa*, the *kalmelpudithti* salutation takes place between people of the two divisions, and I have often seen a woman of one division placing her head beneath the foot of a man of the other division.

When a person meets one of his kin, he uses a form of greeting which depends on the nature of the relationship. Most of these greetings consist of some form of the word *iti* or *itvi*, which was said to mean "blessing" or "bless," together with the kinship term.

A man would greet an elder brother or anyone whom he would call *anna* by the word "*tioñ*," cut very short so as to sound like a single syllable. This is a corruption of *iti anna*. A person greets a younger brother or one whom he would call *enda* by uttering his name followed by the word *ers*, as in "*Sakari ers*," "*Pakhwar ers*." A father is greeted as *itiai*, a mother as *itiava*. An elder sister as *itiakka*; a younger sister as *itvena*, and this latter form is used for any female relative younger than the speaker. It is the duty of younger female relatives to perform the *kalmelpudithti* salutation, and as soon as a man says *itvena*, the woman at once bows down and places her head beneath the raised foot of the man, helping him to raise it at the same time.

A mother's brother or father-in law (*mun*) is greeted by *itimoñ* and a *mumi* is greeted by *itimimia*, but so slurred as to be hardly recognisable. The grandfather and grandmother are greeted in the words *itin pia* and *itin piava*.

Whenever a new Toda came to join people who were with me, there would be a chorus of greetings, and the newcomer would look round carefully to see who was present, giving to each his proper salutation and obviously taking the greatest care that no one was overlooked. Since the relationship of brother is the most frequent, the greetings heard most often on these occasions were "*tioñ*" and ". . . . *ers*."

The regulation of salutation by kinship applies also to

the salutation of the dead. When the body first reaches the funeral place it is saluted by all present, and in the case of kin, the mode of salutation varies with the bond of kinship. Those related to the deceased as *in*, *av*, *pian*, *piav*, *mun*, *mumi*, *an*, or *akkan*, bow down at the head of the corpse and touch the body with their foreheads, while all those whom the deceased would have called *enda* or *ena* bow down at the feet. The place saluted by those who are not kin is determined by age, but in the case of kin, the bond of kinship is more important than the age, so that the former condition determines the mode of salutation. Thus at the funeral of Kiuneimi (3), Kòdrner (7) saluted at the head of the dead woman. He was the younger, but was her *mun* owing to the fact that Kiuneimi's step-mother Kureimi, was a Kars woman whom Kòdrner called sister.

The Duties of Kin

The funeral ceremonies provide the greatest number of examples of kinship duties, the parts taken by many of the mourners being determined largely by their bonds of kinship to the deceased. The place of chief mourner is taken by the brother or son of a dead man, by the husband of a dead woman, and by the father of a dead child, though, at the funeral of a girl, the husband plays the most important *rôle*.

Various duties fall to relatives of the same clan or of the same family of the clan. The earth-throwing at the funeral of a male, the smearing of butter on the buffalo, lighting the pyre at the first funeral and the two fires at the *azaramkedr*, and ringing the bell at the final scene, are all performed by near relatives of the same clan and family as the deceased.

Cutting off a lock of hair and mixing food are acts performed by the chief mourner, who is of the same clan as the deceased, whether brother, son, husband, or father.

The *manmokh*, or sister's son (who may be also son-in-law), has certain definite duties. Formerly, when many buffaloes were killed, one was always given by the sister's son, and he still gives a thread cord, called *pennar*. Many other relatives give these cords, but that given by the *manmokh* is especially honoured in that it is put round the body of the dead man inside his cloak, and not merely laid on the covering of the body as are the others.

The *mun* does not appear to have any duties at a funeral, though in old days he contributed a buffalo, and, at the present time, one of the two buffaloes slaughtered may be given by the *mun* or other representative of the mother's family.

The *matchuni* (child of a maternal uncle or of a paternal aunt) has several duties, of which the most important are those at the *irsankati* ceremony of the *azaramkedr*. The other duties are the secondary result of the marriage regulation which makes the *matchuni* the natural bridegroom or bride, and, in consequence, it is the *matchuni* who performs the *pursütpimi* ceremony at the funeral of an unmarried girl. Similarly, the *matchuni* may take the place of a *paiol* at the cloth-giving ceremony.

The duties which have, however, the greatest social interest are those performed by the relatives by marriage. At the funeral of a woman certain ceremonies, such as that in which leaves of the *tiveri* plant are put in the dead woman's armlet, the *urvatpimi* ceremony for an unmarried girl, rubbing the relics, lighting the fire at the *azaramkedr*, and burning the funeral hut, should be performed by the daughter-in-law of a woman or the mother-in-law of a girl. These relatives are, however, of the same clan as the deceased, owing to the fact that a woman becomes a member of the same clan as her husband; and I am therefore doubtful how far these relatives perform the duties in question as members of the same clan, and how far as relatives by marriage. Some of the duties, such as lighting the funeral fires, are done by men of the same clan at the funeral of men; and I am therefore inclined to believe that they are performed by a woman for this reason and not because she is mother-in-law or daughter-in-law, but this point is one which must remain indefinite with our present information.

Similarly the duty of covering the head is a little difficult to understand. The head of a widower is covered (see p. 365) by one of his *paiol*—his father-in-law or his brother-in-law—and in this case it is clearly a duty which falls to a relative by marriage, but the head of a widow is covered by her own father or by someone of his clan who takes his place. The plausible explanation appears to be that the covering is performed by the father of the woman, not as father of the widow, but as father-in-law of the dead man.

Those who have married into the family of the deceased, the *paiol*, have to make certain contributions towards the outlay for the funeral, and it is in connexion with one of these contributions that the interesting ceremony of cloth-giving occurs.

The essential feature of the ceremony seems to be that a cloth passes between a relative or representative of the dead person and those who have married into the family of the dead person, and the ceremony involves a money payment to the family of the dead person from those who have married into the family. The ceremony is one which links the funeral ceremonies to those of marriage.

In other ceremonies of the Todas the parts played by different kin are far less conspicuous. The *mun* or mother's brother has, however, several important functions. To him falls the duty of naming a child, on which occasion he has also to give a calf. He takes the chief part in the *tersamptpimi* ceremony, in which he cuts the hair of the child with a special ritual. In the ear-piercing ceremony the maternal uncle pierces one ear, and in the special case of which I have a record, he gave two buffaloes towards the expenses attendant on the ceremony.

It is probable that a girl is named by her *mumi*, or father's sister, but this is a point on which I am not quite sure.

Under certain conditions *matchuni*, when associated together, have to perform certain ceremonial acts. When two male *matchuni* eat rice and milk together, they must first ask each other, "*pa tòr tinkina?*" "Milk food shall I eat?" and if they eat honey together, they must say "*tein tinkina?*" Two female *matchuni* eating together must also use these formulæ, but they are not said when a man is eating in company with his female *matchuni*, though possibly the two would never actually eat at the same time.

Male *matchuni* have also to go through a ceremony when

they pass in company over either of the two sacred rivers of the Todas, the Paikara (Teipakh) and the Avalanche (Pakhwar). As the two men approach the river, they pluck and chew some grass, and each man says to the other "*pò tûdrikina, pò kudrikina?*"—"Shall I throw the river (water), shall I cross the river?" or, instead of the second sentence, they may say "*pò pûkhkina?*"—"Shall I enter the river?" They then go to the side of the river and each man dips his hand in the water and throws a handful away from him three times and then they cross the river, each with the right arm outside the cloak as is usual when crossing these sacred streams.

If the *matchuni* cross on a Tuesday, Friday or Saturday[1] they do not throw water, but are content with chewing the grass, and if the funeral ceremonies of a person belonging to the clan of either are not complete the water will not be thrown.

This ceremony performed by *matchuni* when crossing a sacred river was said to be connected with the legend given on p. 592, in which two *matchuni* are concerned.

[1] Properly the river should not be crossed at all on these days (see p. 418).

CHAPTER XXII

MARRIAGE

THE custom of infant marriage is well established among the Todas, and a child is often married when only two or three years of age. When a man wishes to arrange a marriage for his son, he chooses a suitable girl, who should be, and very often is, the *matchuni* of the boy, the daughter of his mother's brother or of his father's sister. The father visits the parents of the girl, and if the marriage is satisfactorily arranged he returns home after staying for the night at the village. A few days later the father takes the boy to the home of his intended wife. They take with them the loin-cloth called *tadrp* as a wedding gift and the boy performs the *kalmelpudithti* salutation to the father and mother of the girl, and also to her brothers, both older and younger than himself, and then gives the *tadrp* to the girl. Father and son stay for one night at the girl's village and return home on the following morning. Sometimes the girl returns with them to the village of her future husband, but, much more commonly, she remains at her own home till she is fifteen or sixteen years of age.

If a man has not been married in childhood he may undertake the arrangement of his marriage himself, and visit the parents of the girl unaccompanied by his father; and in this case the girl may at once join her husband if she is old enough.

From the time of the child-marriage the boy has to give a *tadrp* twice a year until the girl is ten years old, when its place is taken by a *putkuli*. The *tadrp* which is given at first is very small, worth perhaps only four annas, but as the girl becomes older it is expected that the garment shall become larger and more valuable.

If any member of the girl's family should die it is expected that the boy's family shall on each occasion give a sum of eight annas or a rupee. This gift is called *tinkanik paum ätpimi*, or "we give a piece of money to the purse."

Formerly the boy's family had also to contribute one of the buffaloes killed at the funeral, but this custom is now obsolete. The contribution of buffaloes and money from the boy to his parents-in-law is called *pödri*. The boy has to take part in a ceremony at the funeral in which a cloth is laid on the dead body, and with this ceremony there is associated a further gift of one rupee, paid to the relatives of the dead person by the family of the boy who has married into the family of the deceased (see p. 358).

Certain ceremonies are performed shortly before the girl reaches the age of puberty. One is called *putkuli tâzâr ütiti*, or "mantle over he puts," in which a man belonging to the Tartharol if the girl is Teivali, and to the Teivaliol if she is Tarthar, comes in the day-time to the village of the girl and lying down beside her puts his mantle over her so that it covers both and remains there for a few minutes.

Fourteen or fifteen days later a man of strong physique, who may belong to either division and to any clan, except that of the girl, comes and stays in the village for one night and has intercourse with the girl. This must take place before puberty, and it seemed that there were few things regarded as more disgraceful than that this ceremony should be delayed till after this period. It might be a subject of reproach and abuse for the remainder of the woman's life, and it was even said that men might refuse to marry her if this ceremony had not been performed at the proper time.

It is usually some years later, when the girl is about fifteen or sixteen, that she joins her husband and goes to live with him at his village. The parents of the husband announce that they will fetch the girl on a certain day, which must be one of two or three days of the week,[1] different for each clan. The husband, accompanied by his father and a male

[1] The probable rule is that the day must not be a *madnol* or *palinol*.

relative of the same clan, goes to the village of the girl, and the three are feasted with rice and jaggery. The husband puts five rupees into the pocket of the girl's mantle and then takes her home. There is no ceremony of any kind, not even the salutation such as was performed at the original ceremony.

If the youth does not wish to live with the girl when the time arrives, he may annul the marriage by giving one buffalo as a fine (*kwadr*) to the girl's parents ; but, on the other hand, the parents of the girl have to return as many buffaloes as he may have given as *pödri* at funeral ceremonies.

If the girl refuses to join her husband the fine is heavier, and at the present time usually amounts to five or ten buffaloes, the number being settled by a council according to the circumstances of the people. The girl's family must also return any buffaloes given as *pödri*. According to Harkness the fines were in his day much heavier ; three buffaloes when the man annulled the marriage, and as many as fifty when this was done by the woman (see p. 538), and the Todas acknowledge that the fine for refusing to fulfil the marriage contract is now lighter than it used to be.

When a girl goes to join her husband she may be given clothing or ornaments by her parents or brothers, and their gifts are known as *adrparn* or dowry, but I could not learn that there were any definite regulations prescribing what should be given. It seemed also that occasionally buffaloes might be given as *adrparn*.

THE REGULATION OF MARRIAGE

The Todas have very definite restrictions on the freedom of individuals to marry. One of the most important of these is that which prevents intermarriage between the Tartharol and the Teivaliol. These groups are endogamous divisions of the Toda people. Although a Teivali man is strictly prohibited from marrying a Tarthar woman, he may take a woman of this division to live with him at his village, the man being known as the *mokhthodvaiol* of the woman. This connexion, which will be more fully considered at the end of this chapter, may be regarded as a recognised form of marriage, but it differs from the orthodox form in that the children of the union belong to the division of the mother. They do not, however, belong to her clan, but to that of her legal husband. Similarly, the same kind of connexion may be formed between a Tarthar man and a Teivali woman, but in this case the woman is not allowed to live at the village of the *mokhthodvaiol*, who may either visit her occasionally or go to live at her village.

It has already been mentioned that each of the two divisions of the Toda community is divided into a number of septs or clans, and these are definite exogamous groups. No man or woman may marry a member of his or her own clan, but must marry into another clan. This restriction applies even to the members of clans which are known to have separated from one another in recent times. Thus, among the Tartharol certain members of the Melgarsol separated from the main group, and their descendants have formed a separate group or groups known as the Kidmadol and Karshol (see p. 664), but although the separation took place many years ago there still remains a definite prohibition against a marriage of members of these clans with the Melgars people. The clans of Pedrkars and Kulhem among the Teivaliol are offshoots of the Kuudrol, but here the separation seems to have occurred so long ago that the common origin is not regarded as a bar to marriage.

In the whole of the genealogical record given in the tables at the end of the volume there is not a single case in which marriage has occurred between two members of the same clan.

Among many races at or below the stage of culture of the Todas prohibition of marriage within the clan is usually accompanied by prohibition of sexual intercourse, and such intercourse is regarded as incest and often as the greatest of crimes. It is doubtful whether there is any such strict prohibition among the Todas. In the qualifying ceremony for the office of *palol* known as *tesherst*, it is ordained that the woman who takes part in the ceremony shall be one who has never had intercourse with one of her own clan, and I was told that it was far from easy to find such a woman. The fact, however, that this restriction should exist in connexion with a ceremony suggests that even to the Todas there is something reprehensible in intercourse between man and woman of the same clan (see also p. 530).

There are certain special prohibitions against marriage between members of certain clans. Among the Tartharol the Panol are not allowed to marry the Kanòdrsol, a prohibition said to be due to the murder of Parden by Kwoten, and it is said that since that day no marriage has ever taken place between the clans of the two men. In the genealogical record there is no case in which these two clans have intermarried.

I was also told that the people of Melgars and Kwòdrdoni might not intermarry, but there are three examples of such marriages in the genealogies. I could not obtain any reason for the restriction, and the information is probably incorrect. The restrictions on marriage between the people of Melgars and those of Kidmad and Karsh have already been considered.

Among the Teivaliol there are also prohibitions against intermarriage between certain clans. The people of Piedr may not marry those of Kusharf. Judging from the genealogical record, the prohibition is not strictly followed, for three such marriages have taken place in recent times. In one of these cases, however, in which a Piedr man married a Kusharf woman, the woman soon became seriously ill, and the marriage was annulled. I could obtain no reason for the prohibition of marriage between these two clans. Marriage was also prohibited between the Piedrol and the Pedrkarsol, this being due to a comparatively recent quarrel between members of the two clans, of which an account is given in Chapter XXVIII.

I have analysed the genealogical records with the view of ascertaining whether certain clans intermarry with any special frequency. Among the Tartharol, I find that the people of Nòdrs marry most frequently those of Kars and Taradr. The Karsol, the largest of the Tarthar clans, distribute their marriages widely over the whole Tarthar division. The Panol chiefly marry with Kars and Melgars.

The Taradrol have married most often with Nòdrs, Kars and Melgars. Keradr, a very small clan, shows no special predilection. The people of Kanòdrs have intermarried most often with Kwòdrdoni, Päm, Kars and Melgars. The people of Kwòdrdoni marry most often people of Kanòdrs, Kars and Nidrsi. The Pämol have married chiefly with Kanòdrs, Kars and Melgars. Most of the Nidrsi marriages have been with Kars. The Melgarsol have married in fairly equal proportions people of Nòdrs, Kars, Taradr and Päm.

These facts are interesting in that they show that there is a tendency for the three clans of Nòdrs, Kars and Taradr to intermarry. These are not only the most important Tarthar clans, but they occupy the same district of the hills, in the centre and towards the north and north-west. Similarly, the clans of Kanòdrs, Kwòdrdoni and Päm, situated towards the north-east and east, show a distinct tendency to intermarry. Further, the Melgarsol, who form a special group standing somewhat apart from the rest, distribute their marriages fairly equally, but have often married with Päm, a clan seated near them geographically.

The analysis of the genealogies shows that the geographical distribution of the Tartharol on the hills has had a definite influence on the intermarriage of the different clans.

Among the Teivaliol, intermarriage has been greatly influenced by the enormous size of the Kuudrol as compared with the other clans of the division. In order to marry outside their own clan, the people of Kuudr have married nearly all the available members of the other clans of the Teivaliol, leaving very few to intermarry with one another. Thus the genealogies record 161 marriages between Kuudrol and members of the other five Teivali clans, leaving only sixteen marriages between the members of those five clans. Owing to the enormous development of one clan, the Teivali division has almost come to be in the position of a community with a dual marrying organisation in which every member of one group must marry a member of the other group, but there is no reason whatever to think that this is due to any other reason than the excessive development of one clan in numbers.

On studying the marriages in detail, it is found that the Kuudrol have married members of the Piedr clan most frequently, but this is chiefly because the Piedrol stand second to the Kuudrol in point of numbers, although it is also furthered by the restriction in marriage between Piedr and Kusharf. The marriages of the Kuudrol with other clans seem to be determined more by the numbers available than by any predilection for special clans.

Both Pedrkars and Kulhem are said to be offshoots of the Kuudrol, but apparently the separation is so remote that the common origin is not regarded as a bar to marriage. It is possible that the necessity of providing spouses for the Kuudrol has tended to break down a restriction which probably once existed.

The Todas have never married people outside their own community, and a strong prejudice against such marriages still exists. This may be illustrated by two recent cases.

A woman, married in the usual way, was divorced by her husband because she became ill. She returned to her own home, where she was visited by a Tamil blacksmith. The latter was very anxious to marry the woman and on one occasion took her away to the plains, but she was followed by her relatives and brought back to her home. Later she married two Toda brothers and was taken by them to their village, but she was followed by the blacksmith, who brought her back to the village of her parents. The Todas seem to have no strong objection to her relations with the stranger so long as she remains among themselves.

In the other case a woman about twelve years ago was visited by a rich Mohammedan who gave money to her husbands, and it was said also that he bribed the chief Toda people, *i.e.*, the members of the council. The Mohammedan wished very much to marry the woman and for a sum of money the Todas consented. After the woman had lived for a few days in the bazaar with her new husband, her relatives came and took her away, and I was told that the Mohammedan took the loss so much to heart that he died of grief, but my informants were doubtful whether his grief was due to the loss of his wife or whether it was because he had impoverished himself by the bribes which he had given. Here again the people appear to have had no objection to the relations of the woman with the Mohammedan so long as she remained in the community.

Kinship and Marriage

The members of his own clan are not the only kin whom a man is not allowed to marry. The Todas have a general term, *püliol*, for those relatives whose intermarriage is prohibited. The term is applied by a man not only to the women whom he may not marry, but also to the families in general into which he may not marry; thus a man may speak of other men as his *püliol*, meaning by this that he may not marry their sisters. This, however, is only a loose way of using the word, and, putting on one side this sense in which the word may be used, the following are the *püliol* of a man:—

(i.) The daughters of his father's brothers, whom he would call *akka* or *enda*, according to age.

(ii.) The daughters of his mother's sisters, also *akka* or *enda*.

(iii.) The sisters of his father and conversely the daughters of his sisters, *i.e.*, his *mumi* and his *mankugh*.

(iv.) The daughters of the sisters of his father's father, *i.e.*, of the sisters of his *pian*.

The relatives under the first head will be members of the same clan as the man, and the prohibition of marriage between *püliol* under this head may be regarded as a restriction dependent on either clanship or kinship.

There seemed to be no doubt, however, that in connexion with marriage, a man always thought of these relatives as *püliol*, a term which denotes certain kin, to whatever clan they may belong. So far as I could ascertain, if a man thought of a given woman, he thought of her as one, or not one, of his *püliol*, and it seemed to me in several cases as if it came almost as a new idea to some of the Todas that his *püliol* included all the people of his own clan.

If I am right in this, it means that it is the bond of blood-kinship which a Toda has chiefly in his mind when he considers whether he may or may not marry a given woman. He has not two kinds of prohibited affinity, one depending on clan relations, and another on relations of blood-kinship, but he has only one kind of prohibited affinity, to which he gives the general term *püliol*, including certain kin through the father and certain kin through the mother, and there is no evidence that he considers the bond of kinship in one case as different from the other as regards restriction on marriage.

The fact that the Toda includes all those kin whom he may not marry under one general term, and that the kin in question include members both of his own and other clans, goes to show that the Todas recognise the blood-kinship as the restrictive agency rather than the bond produced by membership of the same clan.

The analysis of the genealogical record has shown that these restrictions on marriage are enforced. I have already stated that the genealogies show no single case in which marriage has occurred between members of the same clan. *i.e.*, between *püliol* who come under the first head in the list given above.

I have also failed to find a single case in which marriage has taken place between the children of two own sisters, or of marriage between the children of two women who would call each other "sister" whose names occur in the same genealogical table. Thus I have found no case in which a marriage has taken place between the children of two women so closely related to one another as Punzucleimi and Nasturs, of Table 3, these women being first cousins according to our system of kinship.

It would be a prolonged task to ascertain whether marriage ever takes place among the Tartharol between the children of two clan-sisters in the widest sense, and I do not know whether such marriage may not sometimes occur.

Among the Teivaliol marriages between clan-sisters even in the widest sense must be very rare owing to the fact that nearly all marriages take place between people of Kuudr on the one hand and members of the five other Teivali clans on the other. Since in most cases two women of any one of these five clans marry men of Kuudr, marriage between their children would be restricted under the first prohibition, and similarly the children of two Kuudr women could only intermarry in those cases in which members of the other five clans have married one another. Among the Teivaliol, I do not believe that marriages take place between the children of sisters in the widest sense, and I have little doubt that they are very exceptional among the Tartharol.

There is no case in the genealogies in which the third restriction has been broken, in which a man has married his father's sister or his sister's daughter, his *mumi* or his *mankugh*.

There is at least one case in the genealogies in which there has been an infringement of the fourth restriction given on page 509. The marriage of Nargudr (62) with Tolveli (58) is an example of the marriage of a man with the daughter of his grandfather's sister. I believe that this restriction is part of a wider regulation. Using Toda terms of kinship the law would run: a person must not marry the child of his *matchuni*. The marriage of a man with the daughter of his grandfather's sister, such as that of Nargudr with Tolveli, would be an infringement of this law. I have only found one other case in the genealogies in which this law would have been broken, *i.e.*, in the marriage of Teitnir (52) and Tersveli (63). Tersveli's father, Teikudr, is the son of Kavani, the sister of Pareivan, Teitnir's father. Teikudr is therefore the *matchuni* of Teitnir, who has married his daughter.

I was told that though a man might not marry the daughter of his sister, he might marry the children of this woman. I do not know of any such marriage and it is improbable that it would often come about, since it would involve the marriage of a woman with the brother of her grandfather. There is, however, at the present time an example of the marriage of a woman with her father's mother's brother, whom she would therefore call *pia*, or grandfather. This is the marriage of Kaners and his brother Kudrievan (63) with Edjog (56), the daughter of Tüliners, the son of the sister of the two men. I was told, however, that this marriage met with a good deal of disapproval among the Todas, but I could not learn that there was any definite prohibition against it.

The Marriage of Matchuni

While marriage with the daughter of a father's brother and a mother's sister is prohibited, the daughter of a father's sister or a mother's brother is the natural wife of a man. The orthodox marriage is marriage between *matchuni*, the children of brother and sister. Thus it is obviously not nearness of blood-kinship in itself which acts as a restriction on marriage, but nearness of blood-kinship of a certain kind.

I have analysed the genealogies to ascertain the frequency with which marriages between *matchuni* occur. The genealogical tables record about 550 marriages, of which 373 are Tarthar and 177 Teivali. Only a small proportion of these are marriages between children of own brother and sister. Among the Tartharol there are 40 and among the Teivaliol 25 such marriages, making together 65 or 11·8 per cent.

Since, however, the *matchuni* of a man include a much wider circle of relatives than the children of his mother's own brother and father's own sister, the number of marriages between *matchuni* is very much larger than this.

Nearly all the Teivali marriages are marriages between *matchuni* in this wider sense, while among the Tartharol there are also many other marriages of this kind.

One of the reasons why the orthodox marriage custom is not still more commonly followed is the existence of the practice called *terersthi*, to be considered later in this chapter. According to this practice wives are transferred from one man to another, and in this transference no attention appears to be paid to the kinship tie. The woman, or rather girl, originally married to a man may have been his *matchuni*, but the woman who finally becomes his wife by the working of the *terersthi* custom may not be and probably in most cases is not his *matchuni*. In many cases in the genealogies, the original infant marriage may have been forgotten, and the marriage recorded may be the result of the *terersthi* custom. If I had a complete record of all infant marriages, I have no doubt that the proportion of marriages between *matchuni* would have been larger.

In some families marriages between *matchuni* in the near sense occur much more frequently than in others. Thus out of the forty *matchuni* marriages among the Tartharol, the husband or wife belonged to the Taradrol in fifteen cases, and in one large Taradr family, that of Parkeidi (21), six out of eight children married their *matchuni* in the near sense. It is perhaps significant in this connexion that the Taradrol have been comparatively little affected by outside influences. They are a clan which might be expected to keep up the orthodox Toda custom.

Another example of a family in which the orthodox marriage custom has been frequently followed is that of Table 52, where there may be found eight cases of the marriage of *matchuni* in the near sense, and several others where the *matchuni* relationship is more distant.

In some cases marriages have taken place between the children of *matchuni*. Thus the marriage of Uvolthli (15) with Sinmundeivi (20) among the Tartharol, and of Pangudr (66) with Nelbur (54) and Kanokh (56) with Sanmidz (63) among the Teivaliol, are all cases in which marriages have taken place between the children of two men who called one another *matchuni*. There may be other cases, but these examples are perhaps sufficient to show that these marriages may be held to take the place of the orthodox *matchuni* union.

While marriages between *matchuni* are the rule and marriages between the children of *matchuni* certainly not unlawful, we have seen that marriage with the child of a *matchuni* is prohibited. From our point of view, this means that while marriage with a first cousin is orthodox, marriage with a first cousin once removed is unlawful, while again it seems that marriage with a first cousin twice removed may be lawful. The more distant tie of kinship from our point of view is unlawful, while the nearer is commanded.

Marriage with a *matchuni* may often involve considerable disproportion of age. In one case at the present time a boy of about two years of age is married to a woman of about twenty. The woman, Nulnir (10), was still unmarried when she reached this age, so she was married to her *matchuni*,

Kagerikutan (25), the son of her mother's brother. In this case the orthodox marriage was resorted to when the woman had failed to obtain a husband in any other way, although it involved marriage with a baby.

In another case, the marriage of Keitkarg (38) and Pötoveli (49), in which the woman is considerably older than her husband, the husband and wife are *matchuni*.

There is one ceremonial marriage in which the husband always stands in the relation of *matchuni* to the wife. This is in the performance of the *pursütpimi* ceremony at the funeral of a girl unmarried at the time of her death. The boy who is chosen to give the bow and arrow and to act as the husband is always, so far as I could discover, the *matchuni* of the dead girl.

Similarly, if an unmarried boy dies, the girl who is chosen to act as his widow should be his *matchuni*. In one case of which I have a record, the son of Tütners (58) died and Sotidz (66) was chosen to act as widow. None of the brothers of Puvizveli (65), the mother of the dead boy, had at that time a son, so the duty was undertaken by the daughter of Pangudr, of the same clan as Puvizveli, but belonging to a different family. In this case the *matchuni* was the daughter of a clan-brother because there was no nearer *matchuni* available.

Keinba, who acted as husband at the funeral of Sinerani (see p. 394), was the *matchuni* of the dead girl in two ways, as the son of her mother's brother and as the son of her father's half-sister.

A *matchuni* may be either the child of a mother's brother or of a father's sister, and I have examined the genealogies to see if a man marries the daughter of his mother's brother or of his father's sister the more frequently, and find that there is no great difference, though the former marriage is somewhat the more frequent. There are among the Tartharol twenty cases in which a man has married the daughter of his mother's brother, two of marriage with the daughter of a stepmother's brother, and one with the daughter of a stepmother's half-brother, making twenty-three cases in all. On the other hand, a man married the daughter of his father's sister in fourteen cases, twice he married the daughter of his father's half-sister, and once the stepdaughter of his father's sister, making seventeen cases in all.

Among the Teivaliol marriages with the daughter of a father's sister are the more frequent, there being fifteen of these as compared with ten cases of marriage with the daughter of a mother's brother. There is evidently no special preference for either kind of marriage.

POLYANDRY

The Todas have a completely organised and definite system of polyandry. When a woman marries a man, it is understood that she becomes the wife of his brothers at the same time. When a boy is married to a girl, not only are his brothers usually regarded as also the husbands of the girl, but any brother born later will similarly be regarded as sharing his older brothers' rights.

In the vast majority of polyandrous marriages at the present time, the husbands are own brothers. A glance through the genealogies will show the great frequency of polyandry,[1] and that in nearly every case the husbands are own brothers. In a few cases in which the husbands are not own brothers, they are clan-brothers, *i.e.*, they belong to the same clan and are of the same generation. Instances of such marriages are those of Toridz (65) with Kulpakh (52) and Kiladrvan (60), and of Sintharap (68) with Kuriolv (52) and Ònadj (57).

There is only one instance recorded in the genealogies in which a woman had at the same time husbands belonging to different clans, viz., the marriage of Kwelvtars (60) with Nidshtevan of Piedr (64) and Tütners of Kusharf (67), and in this case the men were half-brothers by the same mother, the fathers being of different clans. While I was on the hills, there was a project on foot that three unmarried youths belonging to three different clans should have a wife in common, but the project was frustrated and the marriage did not take place.

[1] In cases of polyandry the names of the husbands are enclosed in square brackets.

It is possible that at one time the polyandry of the Todas was not so strictly 'fraternal' as it is at present, and it is perhaps in favour of this possibility that in the instance of polyandry given by Harkness[1] the husbands were obviously not own brothers. It must be remembered, however, that this case came to the notice of Captain Harkness because the polyandry had led to disputes, and, as we shall see shortly, it is in those cases of polyandry in which the husbands are not own brothers that disputes arise.

The arrangement of family life in the case of a polyandrous marriage differs according as the husbands are, or are not, own brothers.

In the former case it seemed that there is never any difficulty, and that disputes never arise. The brothers live together, and my informants seemed to regard it as a ridiculous idea that there should ever be disputes or jealousies of the kind that might be expected in such a household. When the wife becomes pregnant, the eldest brother performs the ceremony of giving the bow and arrow, but the brothers are all equally regarded as the fathers of the child. If one of the brothers leaves the rest and sets up an establishment of his own, it appeared, however, that he might lose his right to be regarded as the father of the children.

If a man is asked the name of his father, he usually gives the name of one man only, even when he is the offspring of a polyandrous marriage. I endeavoured to ascertain why the name of one father only should so often be given, and it seemed to me that there is no one reason for the preference. Often one of the fathers is more prominent and influential than the others, and it is natural in such cases that the son should speak of himself as the son of the more important member of the community. Again, if only one of the fathers of a man is alive, the man will always speak of the living person as his father; thus Siriar (20) always spoke of Ircheidi as his father, and even after Ircheidi is dead, it seems probable that he will so have fallen into the custom of speaking of the latter as his father that he will continue to do so, and it will only be when his attention is especially directed

[1] See his account at the end of this chapter.

to the point that he will say that Madbeithi was also his father.

In most of the genealogies, the descent is traced from some one man, but there can be no doubt whatever that this man was usually only one of several brothers, and the probable reason why one name only is remembered is that this name was that of an important member of the community, or of the last surviving of the brother-husbands.

When the husbands are not own brothers, the arrangements become more complicated. When the husbands live together as if they were own brothers there is rarely any difficulty. If, on the other hand, the husbands live at different villages, the usual rule is that the wife shall live with each husband in turn, usually for a month at a time, but there is very considerable elasticity in the arrangement.

It is in respect of the 'fatherhood'[1] of the children in these cases of non-fraternal polyandry that we meet with the most interesting feature of Toda social regulations. When the wife of two or more husbands (not own brothers) becomes pregnant, it is arranged that one of the husbands shall perform the ceremony of giving the bow and arrow. The husband who carries out this ceremony is the father of the child for all social purposes; the child belongs to the clan of this husband if the clans of the husbands differ and to the family of this husband if the families only differ. When the wife again becomes pregnant, another husband may perform the *pursütpimi* ceremony, and if so, this husband becomes the father of the child; but more commonly the *pursütpimi* ceremony is not performed at all during the second pregnancy, and in this case the second child belongs to the first husband, *i.e.*, to the husband who has already given the bow and arrow. Usually it is arranged that the first two or three children shall belong to the first husband, and that at a succeeding pregnancy (third or fourth), another husband shall give the bow and arrow, and, in consequence, become the father not only of that child, but of all succeeding children till some one else gives the bow and arrow.

[1] I use the term 'fatherhood' instead of 'paternity' because the latter term seems to imply a meaning which does not belong to the Toda notion of 'father.'

The fatherhood of a child depends entirely on the *pursütpimi* ceremony, so much so that a dead man is regarded as the father of a child if no other man has performed the essential ceremony.[1]

In the only case in the genealogies in which the husbands of a woman were of different clans, it happened there were only two children, and that one father gave the bow and arrow for the first child and the other for the second.

If the husbands separate, each husband takes with him those children who are his by virtue of the *pursütpimi* ceremony.

There is no doubt whatever as to the close association of the polyandry of the Todas with female infanticide. As we have seen, the Todas now profess to have completely given up the practice of killing their female children, but it is highly probable that the practice is still in vogue to some extent. It has certainly, however, diminished in frequency, and the consequent increase in the proportion of women is leading to some modification in the associated polyandry.

It has been stated by most of those who have written about the Todas that the custom of polyandry is dying out, but a glance at the genealogies will show that the institution is in full working order even in the case of the infant marriages which are being contracted at the present time. There is, however, some reason to believe that it is now less frequent for all the brothers of a family to have one wife only in common. A study of the genealogies shows that often each brother has his own wife, or that several brothers have more than one wife between them. It seemed to me, however, almost certain that in these cases the brothers have the wives in common. In compiling the genealogies, one informant would give me the names of two or more brothers each with one wife, while another would give me the name of one brother with two or three wives, and would say that the other brothers had the same wives. When I pointed out the discrepancy and asked which was the true account, they usually said it made no difference and were almost contemptuous because I seemed to think that there was any disagreement

[1] For an instance, see p. 535.

between the two versions. I think it probable that it has become less frequent for several brothers to have only one wife in common, but I am very doubtful whether this indicates any real decrease in the prevalence of polyandry.

It seems to me that the correct way of describing the present condition of Toda society is to say that polyandry is as prevalent as ever, but that, owing to the greater number of women, it is becoming associated with polygyny. When there are two brothers it does not seem that each takes a wife for himself, but rather that they take two wives in common.

It is probable that this will lead in time to a state of society in which each brother will come to regard one wife as his own; and in a few cases it seemed to me that there was already a tendency in this direction. If this forecast should be fulfilled, the custom of monogamy among the Todas will have been developed out of polyandry through a stage of combined polyandry and polygyny.

One case happened during my visit which seemed to indicate that though several brothers might be regarded as husbands of a woman, the part of husband for ceremonial purposes might be taken only by one or two of them. In this case I was told that four brothers had one wife, but when the wife died only two of the brothers acted as widowers and performed the ceremonies associated with that condition. When I asked for an explanation of this, I was then told that the other two brothers were not husbands, but I strongly suspected that this was a mere device to enable two of the brothers to avoid the disabilities attendant on the condition of widowerhood. I have very little doubt that while the woman was alive, all the four brothers were her husbands, but after her death it became convenient to assume that only two had been husbands, leaving the others free from the restrictions of widowerhood.

Many writers have believed that the widely spread custom of the Levirate is a relic of polyandry. If it were true that the custom of polyandry is dying out among the Todas, this people might have provided material for the study of the relations of polyandry and the Levirate. It will be obvious, however, from the account already given, that polyandry is still strongly established among the Todas. Still, there are a few cases in the genealogies which seem to show that when two brothers had different wives, and one brother died, the widow might be taken by the surviving brother. Thus, in Table 34, two brothers, Matovan and Kemners, had one wife, Sargveli, while Atcharap had his own wife, Puners. When Matovan died, Sargveli was regarded as the wife of both Atcharap and Kemners.[1] Again, after the deaths of Mulpolivan and Peigvan (3), the widow of Nersveli was married by Perol, the clan-brother (first cousin) of the husband.

In other cases, the widow of one brother has not become the wife of her husband's brothers, but has married elsewhere; and though the evidence is necessarily very unsatisfactory, it seems on the whole probable that the Todas show no special relation between polyandry and the Levirate custom.

If the widow marries a man who is not one of the brothers of her dead husband, the new husband has to pay a certain number of buffaloes. He does not, however, give these buffaloes to the brothers of the dead man, but to his children; thus, when Karnisi of Päm (37) died, his widow, Nersaveli, married Mutthuvan (34) of Kanòdrs, who paid fourteen buffaloes to Pungievan, the son of Karnisi. This payment of buffaloes is known as *terkudrichti*, "compensation he gives," and it is the custom for the number of buffaloes in this case to be twice the number given by the dead man for his wife; in this case Karnisi had taken Nersaveli from another man for seven buffaloes.

In relation to the Levirate, the important point here is that the buffaloes are paid to the sons of the dead husbands, not to his brothers.

I do not think that the Todas provide any definite evidence towards the solution of the vexed question of the relation between polyandry and infanticide. It is possible that at their first arrival in the Nilgiri Hills, the Todas had few sources of food, and had a severe struggle for existence; that

[1] It will be noticed that I am using the term 'Levirate' in a wider sense than that in which it is sometimes employed, for Sargveli was not a childless widow.

they therefore adopted the practice of female infanticide, and that polyandry followed as a consequence. At the present and during recent times there has certainly been no economical motive for infanticide, and I am very doubtful whether it has ever existed. I think it far more probable that the Todas brought the practice of polyandry with them when they came to the Nilgiris; but if this view should be adopted, there is still no evidence to show whether they also brought infanticide with them, or whether this custom developed owing to the fact that polyandry diminished the need for female children.

POLYGYNY

In the last section we have seen that there is a tendency for the polyandry of the Todas to become combined with polygyny. Two brothers, who in former times would have had one wife between them, may now take two wives, but as a general rule the two men have the two wives in common. In addition, polygyny of the more ordinary kind exists among the Todas, and is probably now increasing in frequency, as one of the results of the diminished female infanticide.

One example of polygyny is the marriage of Kuriolv (56) with two wives, one of about the same age as himself, the other a young wife whom he shares with Onadj (57). In another case Odrkurs (1), has two wives, the second wife being a young girl recently married in the hope of obtaining a son (see p. 550).

There is one example of polygyny in the genealogies in which a young boy, Mokudr of Nidrsi (42), has two wives, both young girls. He has been doubly married in order that he may get rid of one of his wives by the *tererstthi* custom and so become rich. He has been married to two wives in order that he may sell one.

When a man or a group of men have more than one wife, the two wives usually live together at the same village, but sometimes they live at different villages, the husband or husbands moving about from one village to the other.

EXCHANGE OF BROTHER AND SISTER

Although I was not told that it was the custom for a brother and sister of one clan to marry a sister and brother of another, examination of the genealogies makes it clear that this frequently happens. A good example which may be cited is the marriage of Kuriolv (52) with Punaveli (65), while Sinkòrs, the sister of Kuriolv, married the three brothers of Punaveli. Two other similar instances may be found in Table 52, and they are of general occurrence throughout the genealogies.

In some communities this custom of exchange is definitely connected with the bride-price, which may be so large as almost to compel a man to give his sister in exchange for the wife he takes from another clan. In the case of the Todas the bride-price is so inconsiderable that it is unlikely that it would form a motive for exchange, and I think it improbable that in such marriages as those cited above, the idea of exchange is even definitely formulated, but that the combination of marriages comes about for such obvious reasons as may occur in any community. The marriage of *matchuni*, if widely practised, would obviously lead to an appearance of exchange, and it may be that among the Todas this is the chief cause of its occurrence.

Similarly, instances will be found in the genealogies of two brothers (or two groups of brothers) marrying sisters. An example may be given from Table 53, where Orzevan marries one woman and his two brothers marry her sister. Another instance may be found in Table 58.

In several cases in which a man or group of men have had two wives the wives have been related. Thus, Kutthurs (12) and his brothers first married Tedjveli (16). After her death, Kutthurs, the only surviving brother, married Sabnir (34), the daughter of Arsner, Tedjveli's sister. Again, Paners (23) and his brothers first married Pergveli, and when she died they married her brother's daughter. Pungusivan (53) married his *matchuni*, Sinodz (68), and when she was taken from him by the *tererstthi* custom, he married Sintharap, her sister.

There is often very great disproportion of age in Toda marriages. I have already given two cases in which the woman is the older, in each of which the disproportion of age is due to the custom of marrying a *matchuni*. More commonly the man is much the older, and there are at the present time many cases in which elderly men are married to young girls. This is partly due to the practice of infant marriage. Unless a widower can take advantage of the *terersthi* custom, which is always expensive, he may have to marry a child and wait till she has reached a marriageable age. Thus, Kòdrner, my guide, lost his wife some years ago, and then married a girl whose present[1] age is only thirteen, Kòdrner being forty-two. The girl is still living with her parents, and will probably not go to her husband for another three or four years.

The Custom of 'Terersthi'

The marriage tie among the Todas at the present time has become very loose. Wives are constantly transferred from one husband, or group of husbands, to another, the new husband or husbands paying a certain number of buffaloes to the old. The amount of the compensation or *ter* is settled by a council, and from this the transaction has received its name of *terersthi*, or "compensation he tells (decides)."[2]

There is much reason to believe that this custom has altered its character in recent times. I was told that formerly the custom only applied to cases in which a man had lost his wife by death. If he wished to marry a woman who was already the wife of another or others, he went to the father of the woman and asked for his consent. The father would consult with two other elders, and if they were in favour of the proposed transaction the three elders would go to the woman, and if they obtained her consent they then went to her husband for his. If husband or wife were unwilling to be parted nothing was done, but if both consented, the new and

[1] In 1902.

[2] *Ter* is also used in the sense of 'fine,' but is only used when the fine takes the form of a buffalo or buffaloes. A money fine is called *saver*.

the old husband, the father of the woman, and the two elders met and decided on the number of buffaloes to be given as *ter* or compensation. This meeting was called *terersthi.* The *ter* had to be paid within a month, and all the buffaloes given had to be females. The man who was giving up the woman went to the village of the new husband and received his buffaloes, of which he was allowed to choose a certain number. If he had been awarded more than four buffaloes, he might choose three, if four or less, he might only choose two. Among the Tartharol, a man would usually choose *wursulir*, and among the Teivaliol, *pasthir.*

At the present time the number of buffaloes given as *ter* varies very greatly; the most frequent number is three, but often more are given, and in one case, about ten years ago, a man had to give twenty-five. The number seems to depend largely on the size of the herd possessed by the man taking a new wife. The more buffaloes he has, the more he has to pay.

When the buffaloes are given, the new husband has to give a feast, after which the old husband drives away his buffaloes. In a recent case Teigudr of Nòdrs (4) had taken Uwer from Nertolvan and Palpa of Pan (16) for nine buffaloes. These two men went to the village of Tedshteiri, where Teigudr was living, and were feasted, the food being cooked on nine ovens, corresponding to the number of the buffaloes. This correspondence between the number of the ovens and of the buffaloes given as *ter*, suggests that there may have been some definite ceremonial in connexion with this feast of which I failed to obtain an account.

The custom of *terersthi* has some reason on its side. Wherever infant marriage exists in a small community, it must often happen that a widower finds all the women of his community married, and without some machinery by which he is allowed to take the wife of another, he must remain unmarried or be content with marriage to a mere child. Even at the present time, we have seen that an adult man who has lost his wife may marry a girl only a few years of age.[1]

[1] For an instance in the past see p. 538.

At the present time the custom of *terersthi* has a far wider range. It is obvious that when a widower takes the wife of another he is simply transferring his difficulty, and the man whose wife he has taken will have to seek a new partner. It often happens that a man takes the wife of a boy married, perhaps, to a girl of about the same age as himself, and when this boy reaches manhood he will have to seek a wife and will naturally try to obtain the wife of another rather than be content with a child perhaps only three or four years of age. It would be impossible that such a custom as that of *terersthi* should remain limited in scope, but there is no doubt that at the present day it has become the custom for any man who takes a fancy for the wife of another to endeavour to obtain her for himself, and I was told that he would give large bribes to the elders of the Todas to attain his object. It seems quite clear that, at the present time, it is not considered necessary to obtain the consent either of the wife or of the husband, and in some cases the wife has been taken from her husband by force.[1]

In some recent cases the aggrieved parties in such disputes have appealed to the Government, and during my visit a petition was being drawn up for presentation to the Governor of Madras, asking that the abuses of the *terersthi* custom should be remedied.

DIVORCE

Divorce exists among the Todas quite apart from the transference of wives just considered.

I was told that a man divorces his wife for two reasons, and for two only, the first reason being that the wife is a fool and the second that she will not work. Barrenness is not generally regarded as a reason for divorce, though I was told of one case in which a man had sent away his wife on this account. It seemed more usual in such a case to take a second wife. In some cases the illness of the husband has been regarded as a ground for divorce. Intercourse between

[1] For an instance see p. 535.

a wife and another man is not regarded as a reason for divorce but rather as a perfectly natural occurrence.

When a man divorces his wife, the woman's people usually complain to the *naim* or council, but if it is decided that the man shall take his wife back, there appears to be no way of compelling him to do so. In any case the husband pays a fine (*kwadr*) of one buffalo to the wife's people, just as he would have done if he had refused to take her when she reached the marriageable age, but he receives back any buffaloes he may have given as *pòdri*. Even if the council decides that the man ought to take his wife back and he refuses, a fine greater than one buffalo cannot be inflicted.

If the divorced woman re-marries, the previous husband does not receive anything, and any buffaloes given become the property of the woman's family.

The Mokhthoditi Institution

In addition to the regular marriage, there is another recognised mode of union between men and women, which is called *mokhthoditi*. The man who becomes the consort of a woman in this way is called her *mokhthodvaiol*—viz., "man who keeps *mokh*,"[1] and the woman is called *sedvaitazmokh*—viz., "woman who joins." The *mokhthoditi* union differs from the regular marriage in one important respect. It may be, and usually is, formed between Tarthar men and Teivali women, or between Teivali men and Tarthar women. The great majority of instances of which I heard were of this kind. One woman might have more than one *mokhthodvaiol*, the largest number of which I heard being three. Similarly, a man might have more than one *sedvaitazmokh*, but as the custom entailed considerable expenses on the man, this was not common, and I did not hear of any instance in which a man had more than two.

The *mokhthodvaiol* has no rights over any children who might be supposed to be his; they are regarded as the children of the regular marriage. This would be the case

[1] *Mokh* here means 'child' in general, not son.

even if the husband were dead or separated from his wife. If a Teivali man took a Tarthar widow as *sedvaitazmokh*, and a child were born, the child would belong to the Tartharol, and would be regarded as the son of the dead husband of the woman, and would belong to his clan. The child might live with the *mokhthodvaiol*, and be spoken of ordinarily as the child of this man, but yet for all social and legal purposes, the child would be a member of its mother's husband's clan. The dead husband is regarded as the father because it was he who last performed the *pursütpimi* ceremony.

There are two forms of the *mokhthoditi* union. In one the woman lives with the man just as if she were his real wife, almost the only difference being that any children would be legally the children of the legal husband of the woman or of some man of her division called upon to perform the *pursütpimi* ceremony. In the other and more usual form the man visits the woman at the house of her husband.

Owing to the restriction on the visits of Teivali women to Tarthar villages, there is a difference in the nature of the *mokhthoditi* union in the two divisions. A Teivali *mokhthodvaiol* may take his wife to live with him at one of the Teivali villages, but in those cases in which Tarthar men live permanently with Teivali women, the *mokhthodvaiol* must live at the woman's village. There are two examples of this practice at the present time in which Tarthar men live altogether at Teivali villages.

When a man wishes to have a given woman as his *sedvaitazmokh* he goes to the husband or husbands of the woman and asks for his or their consent. As a sample of the kind of negotiations which ensue, I will give a definite instance. A Tarthar man wished to become *mokhthodvaiol* to the wife of two Teivali brothers. He went to them and asked for their consent, which they gave, but said they should like to have the agreement confirmed by a third party (*nedrvol*), and they settled on a *nedrvol* to whom all went. The *nedrvol* asked each if he consented to the arrangement, and it was decided that the Tarthar man should give a *putkuli* worth three rupees annually to the woman's husbands, and the former became *mokhthodvaiol* to the woman on that day.

A few days later the two husbands and the *mokhthodvaiol* went to the woman's father and brothers (called collectively *paiol*), and the *mokhthodvaiol* promised that he would give the woman either a *keivali* (necklace) or a *sin* (gold earrings), each worth about thirty rupees. [A poorer man might only give a *pulthi* (bracelet), worth about twelve rupees]. He also promised that he would give a three-year-old buffalo to the son of the woman, this being called *mokh ir kwadrti*, *i.e.*, "son buffalo he gives." After making these promises, the *mokhthodvaiol* performed the salutation of *kalmelpudithti* to all the *paiol*, *i.e.*, he bowed down before each, and placed his head beneath their feet.

As we have seen earlier, not only are the relatives of the *sedvaitazmokh* called *paiol*, the term in use for the relatives of a real wife, but the father of the woman is called *mun* and her mother *mumi*, names which are also terms of blood-relationship.

When a man or woman dies, the *mokhthodvaiol* of the woman and the *sedvaitazmokh* of the man have definitely assigned duties at the funeral ceremonies. Each wears a ring on the ring finger of the left hand and has to put various things with the left hand into the pocket of the *putkuli* of the dead person.[1]

The *mokhthoditi* institution was first described by Ward in 1821,[2] the man being called by Ward the *coombhal* (the *kumbliol*, cloak or blanket man). This is the Badaga name, and it has usually been adopted by those who have since referred to the institution.

The custom is said to have originated with the god Kulinkars, who was the *mokhthodvaiol* of the goddess Nòtirzi, but I could obtain no details of the way in which the custom is supposed to have arisen.

The ceremonial connected with the process of becoming a *mokhthodvaiol* is very much like that of the real marriage. A garment is given or promised and the salutation of *kalmelpudithti* is paid to the woman's relatives. The chief difference is that the gifts are more numerous

[1] For a full account see p. 366.

[2] Grigg's *Nilgiri Manual*, Appendix, p. lxxiv.

and expensive for the *mokhthodvaiol* than for the husband. Further, in some cases the *sedvaitazmokh* of a Teivali man may live with him exactly in the same way as a wife. Except for the prohibition against Teivali women living at Tarthar villages, and the important difference in the mode of descent of the children there seems to be little essential difference in some cases between the *mokhthoditi* union and marriage. In describing the institution, one of my informants laid great stress on the disability of a man of one division to perform the *pursütpimi* ceremony for a woman of the other division and treated this as the essential point of difference. He seemed to regard this ceremonial disability as primary and the other differences as the secondary results, but I do not know how far this is the general Toda view.

Sexual Morality

From the foregoing account it appears that a woman may have one or more recognised lovers as well as several husbands. From the account given of the dairy ritual, it appears that she may also have sexual relations with dairymen of various grades—that, for instance, the *wursol*, on the nights when he sleeps in the hut, may be the lover of any Tarthar girl. Further, there seems to be no doubt that there is little restriction of any kind on sexual intercourse. I was assured by several Todas not only that adultery was no motive for divorce, but that it was in no way regarded as wrong. It seemed clear that there is no word for adultery in the Toda language. My interpreter, Samuel, had translated the Commandments shortly before my visit, and only discovered while working with me that the expression he had used in translating the seventh Commandment really bore a very different meaning.

When a word for a concept is absent in any language it by no means follows that the concept has not been developed, but in this case I have little doubt that there is no definite idea in the mind of the Toda corresponding to that denoted by our word 'adultery.' Instead of adultery being regarded as immoral, I rather suspected,[1] though I could not satisfy myself on the point, that, according to the Toda idea, immorality attaches rather to the man who grudges his wife to another. One group of those who experience difficulty in getting to the next world after death are the *kashtvainol*, or grudging people, and I believe this term includes those who would in a more civilised community be plaintiffs in the divorce court.

In nearly every known community, whether savage, barbarous or civilised, there is found to exist a deeply rooted antipathy to sexual intercourse between brother and sister. In savage communities where kinship is of the classificatory kind, this antipathy extends not only to the children of one mother, but to all those who are regarded as brothers and sisters because they are members of the same clan or other social unit. In some communities, such as those of Torres Straits, this antipathy may extend to relatives as remote as those we call second and third cousins, so long as descent through the male line from a common ancestor and membership of the same clan lead people to regard one another as brother and sister.

It is very doubtful whether this widespread, almost universal abhorrence is shared by the Todas. I was told that members of the same clan might have intercourse with one another, and in the preliminary ceremony for the office of *palol*, a special part was taken by a woman who possessed the qualification that she had never had intercourse with a man of her own clan, and it was said it was far from easy to find such a woman. When I collected this information, it seemed clear that this meant that a woman who, before marriage had belonged to a given clan, had never had intercourse with a man of that clan. But since a woman joins the clan of her husband, and since, marriage taking place at an early age, the woman belongs to her husband's clan from this early age, it has since occurred to me that an alternative explanation of the restriction is possible, though it does not seem to me to be likely. It is possible that what is meant is that the woman

[1] The definite appearance of jealousy in the history of Kwoten must, however, be noted in this connexion.

should never have had intercourse with any of her husband's clan except those who are properly her husbands. If this explanation were the correct one, the prohibition would seem to be directed against practices resembling communal marriage, and would be interesting evidence in favour of the existence of this type of marriage, since there are no prohibitions against what does not exist nor has ever existed. As I have said, however, I think it very unlikely that the prohibition is to be interpreted in this way, but I regret very greatly that it did not occur to me to inquire carefully into this point on the spot.

So far as I could tell, the laxity in sexual matters is equally great before and after marriage. If a girl who has been married in infancy, but has not yet joined her husband, should become pregnant, the husband would be called upon to give the bow and arrow at the *pursütpimi* ceremony and would be the father of the child, even if he were still a young boy, or if it were known that he was not the father of the child. I only heard of one case in recent times in which an unmarried girl had become pregnant. In this case a man who was a *matchuni* of the woman was called in to give the bow and arrow, but he did not regard himself as married to the woman and did not live with her. That some stigma was attached to the occurrence may possibly be shown by the fact that this woman remained unmarried for some years, and then only married a man who was certainly below the general standard of the Todas in intelligence. The child, a daughter, of the woman died soon after birth, so that I had no chance of ascertaining whether the irregularity of her birth would have had any influence on her position in Toda society. If, however, a child is born without the *pursütpimi* ceremony having been performed, it is called *padmokh* and an indelible disgrace attaches to it throughout life.

From any point of view, and certainly from the point of view of the savage, the sexual morality of the Todas among themselves is very low. It is an interesting subject of speculation how far this laxity is the result of the practice of polyandry, for since low sexual morality brings in its train various factors which tend to sterility, we may have here, as

Mr. Punnett has suggested elsewhere,[1] a reason why polyandry is so rare a form of marriage. The practice of polyandry must almost inevitably weaken the sentiment of possession on the part of the man which does so much to maintain the more ordinary forms of marriage.

The low sexual morality of the Todas is not, however, limited in its scope to the relations within the Toda community. Conflicting views are held by those who know the Nilgiri Hills as to the relations of the Todas with the other inhabitants, and especially with the train of natives which the European immigration to the hills has brought in its wake. The general opinion on the hills is that in this respect the morality of the Todas is as low as it well could be, but it is a question whether this opinion is not too much based on the behaviour of the inhabitants of one or two villages near the European settlements, and I think it is probable that the larger part of the Todas remain more uncontaminated than is generally supposed.

That the Todas are perhaps not so black as they are painted is suggested by two considerations. There is little evidence of the existence of many half-breeds. I examined in one way or another over 500 Todas and must have seen nearly the whole of the 800 people who form the Toda population. I saw few who suggested Tamil or Badaga intermixture and only one boy whose appearance suggested European parentage. A more careful examination than I gave might, however, have revealed other suspicious cases, and perhaps in a race which practices infanticide the absence or paucity of half-breeds may not carry much weight.

The other consideration is of a different kind and tends to show not only that the Todas are not so black as they are painted, but that they are not so black as they paint themselves.

By means of the genealogical record I was able to work out the relationship to one another of forty-three individuals suffering from colour-blindness. Since this condition runs mainly in the female line, it does not afford very cogent evidence of paternity; but a full examination of my records

[1] *Loc. cit.*

seems to show that colour-blind men, or rather males of colour-blind families, had colour-blind descendants more often than perhaps might have been expected if the Todas are in practice quite as promiscuous as their social regulations allow them to be. The record of the affinity of the colour-blind suggests that in spite of the theoretical promiscuity, the husbands are, in practice, very often the fathers of their children.

A few histories of individuals may be given as examples of the various marriage customs which have been described in this chapter. One of the most married of Toda women is Puvizveli of Kusharf (65). She was married in infancy to Singudr (55), of the same clan as Sinkòrs, the mother of Puvizveli, and the two were probably the *matchuni* of one another, though only in a distant way. Puvizveli was taken from Singudr by Madsu and Koboners (58), who gave for her three buffaloes. From them she was transferred to Kangudr of Piedr (62), it being arranged that he should pay eleven buffaloes. Soon after joining Kangudr, Puvizveli became ill, and since there is a prohibition of marriages between the clans of Piedr and Kusharf, it was agreed that the pair should separate, and the woman was taken by Tütners and Etamudri (58). The eleven buffaloes had never been paid by Kangudr, so Tütners and his brother gave their buffaloes directly to Madsu and Koboners, but only four instead of eleven. All these transactions took place while Puvizveli was still young, but by her new husbands she had a son who died soon after birth. During her second pregnancy, she was taken by Perpakh and Tebkudr (68), who gave six buffaloes. The transference took place before the *pursütpimi* ceremony had been performed. Perpakh gave the bow and arrow, and the daughter since born is regarded as the child of Perpakh and Tebkudr. Puvizveli has also a Tarthar *mokhthodvaiol*.

Edjog of Kuudr (56) was married in infancy to Nargudr (62), the son of her mother's brothers, and therefore her *matchuni* in the nearest sense. From him Kiudners (70) and his two brothers took her for five buffaloes. Kiudners died before the buffaloes had been paid, and Edjog was taken by Mavòdriners (65), who arranged to pay the five buffaloes to Nargudr. He did not do so, but after having a son by Edjog, he sent her back to the father, paying a *kwadr* of one buffalo. So far, Nargudr had not received his five buffaloes, but he now obtained them from Kaners and Kudrievan (63), who took the woman although she was the granddaughter of their sister Narskuti. The marriage met with disapproval among the Todas on this account, though there does not appear to be any definite regulation against such a marriage; and at the time of my visit Edjog, a young woman of about twenty-seven, was still the wife of the two old men, aged about seventy and sixty-seven respectively.

Kuriolv of Kuudr (52) first married Punaveli (65), by whom he had two children. He then took to live with him Pilimurg (7), a Tarthar woman, giving to Pepners (44), the husband of the woman, fifteen buffaloes. Though Pilimurg is only legally his *sedvaitazmokh*, Kuriolv treats her as a wife She lives at one of the Kuudr villages, while Punaveli lives at another. Pilimurg has had one son, Meilitars, since she has been living with Kuriolv, and Kuriolv always speaks of the boy as his son, though legally he is the son of Pepners, and his name will be found in the genealogies among the children of this man.

Recently Kuriolv has also married Sintharap (68), sharing her with Ònadj (57), of the same clan as Kuriolv, but belonging to a different family. Sintharap has had three children, for the first of whom Kuriolv performed the *pursütpimi* ceremony, and since no one has performed this ceremony for the succeeding children, they are also regarded as the children of Kuriolv. One of these children was Sinerani, whose funeral ceremonies have been described.

Kuriolv's son, Kulpakh (52), married Toridz (65), sharing her with Kiladrvan (60), of the same clan as Kulpakh, but of a different family. At the first pregnancy Kulpakh gave the bow and arrow, and was regarded as the father of that child and of two succeeding children who were born while Kulpakh was alive. After the birth of the third child Kulpakh died, and Toridz has since continued to live with Kiladrvan and has had two more children. Kuriolv, the father of the dead man, succeeded in preventing Kiladrvan from performing the *pursütpimi* ceremony before the birth of either of these children, and consequently they are regarded as the children of the dead Kulpakh and belong to Kuriolv's division (*pòlm*) of the clan and not to that of Kiladrvan. Here, by virtue of the *pursütpimi* ceremony, a dead man is the legal father of two children who are known to be really the sons of his fellow-husband.

In the preceding cases the people belong to the Teivaliol. Among the Tartharol there are similar histories.

Pupidz of Kwòdrdoni (35) was married in infancy to two brothers, Kalgeners and Kinagudr, belonging to the same clan as the mother of Pupidz, so that she would probably have called them *matchuni*, though they were not nearly related. From these boys Pupidz was taken by Patser (26), who gave for her three buffaloes. From Patser she was taken by Siriar (20) for five buffaloes. Some time later Pepob (44) wished to marry Pupidz, but both she and Siriar were unwilling to be separated. Pepob, however, persuaded the council to arrange that he should have the woman for three buffaloes, and soon after five or six men carried off the woman by force, entering Siriar's hut at night. Two of the men held Siriar while the others carried off his wife, who became pregnant by Pepob, but Siriar, who had been trying to get back his wife, succeeded when she was about at the sixth month. The hand-burning ceremony had already been performed, but Siriar gave the bow and arrow, and is therefore the legal father of the boy born afterwards, although Pepob is known to have been the real father. Siriar had to give Pepob eleven buffaloes, though he had only received three, and had given five to the previous husband.

Nanbarvan of Kars (7) first married Pothenir (47), by whom he had one son. Nanbarvan went to England with a party of Todas, and Pothenir then married Kutadri, Nanbarvan's first cousin. On his return from England, Nanbarvan married Sindod (38), by whom he had a second son. Then he fell ill, and in consequence sent Sindod away, and since that time he has had no wife, though he claims that Iraveli, his brother's wife, is also his. There seems to be no doubt, however, that he does not live with his brother in the same way as in most cases of polyandry, and is a wanderer with no regular home of his own, but I could not discover the cause of this.

A dispute about a marriage was in progress while I was on the Hills, which I did not understand completely, but it appeared that Oselig (24), who had been first married to Teigudr (4), was then taken by Punog (14). Punog was said to have treated his wife badly, and to have failed to perform his duties when there was a funeral in the family of Nertiners, the brother of Oselig. He had not given the proper *pödri*, nor had he taken part in the cloth-giving ceremony, so Oselig ran away from him and took refuge with her brother. After a month Punog demanded back his wife and also twelve buffaloes which he had left with Nertiners for grazing purposes. Nertiners refused to send back his wife, and returned only eight of the buffaloes. He also proceeded to arrange that Oselig should marry Udrchovan (36), and Punog accused Nertiners of having got up the whole quarrel in order that Oselig should make this marriage. The matter was referred to the council, and it was decided that Oselig should become the wife of Udrchovan, but I did not hear for how many buffaloes, nor how the other disputes about buffaloes and *pödri* were settled.

At this time Udrchovan had another wife, Pandut (45). She had been the wife of Udrchovan and his brother Popners from infancy, and after having three children, who died young, she had been sent away and Udrchovan married Kavener (3), while his brother married Silkot (10). Later Kavener was taken from Udrchovan by Kudrvas (11), and Udrchovan remarried Pandut, who in the meantime had had two other husbands.

To the foregoing accounts, which I give as exceptional and not as typical examples of the uncertainty of Toda married life, I add one taken from the book published by Captain Harkness in 1832, p. 121. The notes are added by myself.

The History of Pinpurz Kutan

"I was not seven years old, when my father, taking a child's garment, in value about a quarter of a rupee, and selecting one of the best of our herd, desired me to accompany him to the morrt[1] of Kinōri. This Kinōri had, a month or two before, a daughter born to him. Soon after we had arrived at the morrt, it being understood that Kinōri gladly consented to the propositions which had been made by my father, I was directed to bow myself down, and in the presence of the whole family to ask his foot. This I did; and touching it with my forehead, the buffalo and the garment were presented him, and I was considered to be affianced to his daughter. We remained there for some days, during which period it was agreed upon, what number of kine I was to receive in dower, on my intended spouse coming of age, and we again set out to return to our own morrt. I had no brothers, or they also would have been affianced to my intended, as this was part of the agreement, in case of my father having any more sons born to him. In this case Kinōri's daughter would have been wife to us in succession as we arrived at manhood, and we should have formed one united family—the supreme authority, however, still resting with me. The next year, my father presented to my intended bride a garment, double in value to the first which he had presented, and in each succeeding year, one proportionately increasing in value. We also sacrificed a buffalo, and presented a kutch[2] on every occasion of a death among any of the relations of my intended's family, and one also at their obsequies. In case of any accident of the kind in our family, we expected the same to be observed towards us, except the presenting of the kutch, from which my bride's father was exempted on account of the dower he had to give with her, which would greatly exceed in amount any expense which I could be

[1] This is evidently the same word as *marth*, which occurs in Chapter XIV as a word for village.

[2] This is the *kach*. Harkness states that it was generally a piece of dyed or printed cotton as at present.

to my father. My father died, and when I had attained man's estate, I was not pleased with my betrothed; and presenting her father with three kine, the contract was by mutual consent dissolved. Had the reverse been the case, and the bride or her father had declined to allow of consummation, I could have claimed of the latter a fine equal to fifty kine, and till this fine was paid the former could not marry any other. Freed from my contract with my first bride, I sought to affiance myself in a manner more to my own inclinations, and wishing to be connected with the family of my present wife, Pilluvāni, who was then only six years of age, I spoke to her father, and, obtaining his consent, presented her with a garment in value, according to her age, of about a rupee and a half, and a milch buffalo. I continued to present her with a garment every succeeding year; and on the occurrence of a death among any of the relations of her family, and at the obsequies, I always sacrificed a buffalo, and presented the kutch. Pilluvāni was afterwards betrothed to two others, Khakhood and Tūmbŭt. When she had arrived at a certain age, and had for eight days been living with one of her female friends in a dwelling separate from those of the family,[1] intimation was sent to me, and I went to her father's morrt, that is, Kerjwan's, her second father, the first one being dead. I was feasted and bedded; and after a few days, Kerjwan, laying on his hands, gave us his blessing, and I returned with my wife to my own morrt, receiving with her in dower four buffalo kine; her father also presented to her on this occasion a pair of ear-rings, a pair of armlets, a necklace, a brazen salver, and five rupees.

"Now, according to our customs, Pilluvāni was to pass the first month with me, the second with Khakhood, and the third with Tūmbŭt; and the two latter, waiting in succession on the father-in-law, were to ask his blessing and claim their privilege in right. I was to give her raiment the first year, Khakhood the second, and Tūmbŭt the third. I had the option of claiming the first three children, Khakhood the second three, and Tūmbŭt the third three; when the option again revolved to me. It was my place to go to her father

[1] This is a custom of which I failed to obtain any account.

two or three months prior to the birth of a child, and, delivering to him a small piece of wood, which we call a billu,[1] to claim the forthcoming infant, whether male or female, and acknowledge before him and his relations that I would protect and nourish it; and that, whatever might happen, I allowed this to be in satisfaction of one of my claims. On this occasion, also, I was to present him either five or ten rupees, and in return he was to allow me to select, if I presented him five rupees, three; if ten rupees, six of the best kine of his herd. If the child proved a boy he would have to present me with a heifer, and another one also on the birth of each son, but not on the birth of a daughter, as it is supposed that she will soon be betrothed, and that a fortune will accrue to her in that way.

"After the third birth the same observance and privilege would have fallen to Khakhood and Tūmbŭt successively, or if I chose to give up any of my rights the two latter would successively have had choice of adoption, &c., &c. We all three should have been equally bound to protect the whole of the children, to marry, and to give them in marriage; but the superior authority would always have rested with me.

"The case of Pilluvāni and myself, however, was at variance with this custom. We were very fond of one another and determined not to separate. I offered to pay the usual fines, but the other party would not accept of them. I had been unfortunate. A murrain had attacked my herd; the greater part of Korrorr,[2] and which belonged to my fathers, had been forsaken by the Marvs and Cūvs,[3] from the oppression of some of their rulers, and from being a leading man among my own people I was now reduced, but principally by the oppressions of my wife's relations, to comparative poverty."

[1] This is evidently due to misunderstanding of the *pursütpimi* ceremony. The Tamil word for 'bow' is *vil.*

[2] Probably Keradr.

[3] Badagas and Kotas.

CHAPTER XXIII

SOCIAL ORGANISATION

IN this chapter I propose to bring together a number of matters connected with the social organisation; to consider the various sections into which the clan is divided for social or ceremonial purposes, the method of government, the laws concerning property and inheritance, and the position of women.

We have already seen that the primary fact in the social organisation of the Todas is the existence of two divisions, the Tartharol and the Teivaliol,[1] and the last chapter has shown that these divisions form endogamous groups, each of which is divided into a number of exogamous septs or clans. In some respects the clan is a definite unit in the social organisation with a certain amount of power in regulating its own affairs, owning property and having in many cases social or religious usages peculiar to itself.

THE CLAN

The clan system is territorial, and I could discover no trace of its ever having been totemic. The clan owns a number of villages and takes its name from the chief of these, the *etudmad*. The connexion of the clan with the village is so generally recognised that in some cases in which the *etudmad* of the clan has disappeared, or is rarely visited, there is a tendency to name the clan after the chief village

[1] A full account of the two divisions and of their relation to one another will be given in Chapter XXIX.

still in use. Thus the people of Pirspurs have now become the Pämol and the Kusharfol are often named after Umgas, a village in more frequent use than Kusharf. In general the villages belonging to a clan are situated in the same part of the hills, but a clan often possesses outlying villages at a considerable distance from the chief group. Sometimes these outlying villages are of comparatively recent origin, and in other cases they have been established on account of grazing necessities; thus several clans which have their chief seats near Ootacamund have villages in the Kundahs or in the district near Makurti Peak, which are visited in the dry season.

The members of a clan have many common rights and privileges which bind them together, so that the clan-tie has a very real meaning. Property, however, as we shall see shortly, is largely centred in the family or the individual, and the Todas are in a state of social evolution in which the common bond constituted by membership of the clan has been largely replaced by the bond constituted by the family. They are in an intermediate condition between the state of society in which the clan is the social unit and that in which the family has taken this position.

Nearly all who have previously written about the Todas have described them as divided into five clans—viz., the Peiki, Pekkan, Kenna, Todi, or Tothi, and Kuttan. These are the five divisions recognised by the Badagas, and a Badaga knows each Toda as belonging to one of them. The Todas are also perfectly acquainted with these divisions, and they could always say, if asked, to which of them a given village or a given man belonged. If a Toda is asked by a European to which clan or division he belongs, he will probably give one of these names, but I do not believe that they are in use among themselves, being reserved for their intercourse with Badagas and other Indian castes and with Europeans.

The Peiki of the Badaga classification are the Teivaliol; the Pekkan correspond to the Melgarsol, the people of Kidmad and Karsh being also usually included in this group. Kenna is the Badaga name of the Karsol; the Todi or Tothi include two clans, the Nódrsol and the Panol, while the Kuttan comprise the remainder of the Tarthar clans—viz., those of Taradr, Keradr, Kanòdrs, Kwòdrdoni, Päm and Nidrsi. I could obtain no direct information from the Todas which would explain why the Badaga classification should differ from their own. It is possible that it is an old classification of the Todas, but this is unlikely, since it is probable that the intercourse with the Badagas is not very ancient. It seems to me possible that it may have arisen out of the constitution of the *naim* or council. This has four Toda representatives belonging to Kuudr (representing the Teivaliol), Kars, Nòdrs and Taradr. This would correspond to four of the Badaga divisions, and the fifth, the Melgarsol or Pekkan, would certainly be well known to the Badagas through their privileges as *mòrol*. It is possible that the Nòdrs representative used also to represent Pan, and that the Taradr member represented the remaining clans, and, if so, it would point to there having been some old five-fold division of the kind believed in by the Badagas. It is quite clear that the five-fold division has no influence on the marriage regulations and Peiki, Todi and Kuttan all marry freely within their divisions. Except in connexion with the *naim*, I could learn of nothing which would show that the five-fold division has any social significance, and I know of no other way in which the Panol are associated with the Nòdrsol nor of any other way in which the six clans included in the Kuttan are associated together. It is possible that the five-fold division is connected with some customs regulating the payment of the Badaga tribute to the Todas, but I could learn nothing of such customs.

Each clan has divisions of two kinds called *kudr* and *pòlm*. The *kudr* is a division of ceremonial, the *pòlm* of practical, importance.

THE KUDR

Normally each clan has two *kudr* and two only, and, as we have seen in Chapter XIII, these divisions become of the greatest importance in connexion with the *irnörtiti* ceremony, the whole regulation of which is dominated by the division into *kudr*. So far as I could ascertain, the *kudr* has now no other significance, and I do not know whether the division is one which formerly possessed a social significance which it has now lost, so that the *kudr* only persists in ceremony, or whether it is a mode of division of the clan which has arisen purely in connexion with the *irnörtiti* and other allied ceremonies.

In one or two cases there was some doubt as to whether a certain division of the people was a clan or a *kudr*. This was especially the case with the Kwaradrol, now extinct, who were said by some of my informants to have been a clan, but it seemed clear that they only formed a *kudr* of the Keadrol, and were not properly a distinct clan. This is one case in which a *kudr* has a distinctive name, and another example occurs in the Panol where the *kudr* have separate names, one the Panol or Pandar, the other the Kuirsiol or Peshteidimokh. In general, each *kudr* is named after its leading man, thus the two *kudr* of the Nòdrsol are spoken of as the *kudr* of Mudrigeidi (1) and Kerkadr (2). The man who gives his name to the *kudr* is probably responsible for the general management of the ceremonies in which the *kudr* is concerned.

In a few cases a clan was said to have more than two *kudr*, but on cross-examination it turned out in each case that the statement was due to the fact that the clan contained a section which had no part, or only a subordinate part, in the *irnörtiti* ceremony and that this section might sometimes be spoken of as a *kudr*. Thus, in the Kuudr̀ clan there are three sections, two which have reciprocal relations in the *irnörtiti* ceremony, and a third consisting of the family of Tövoniners (61) which lost certain privileges owing to a dispute many generations ago (see p. 675). This family could perform the *irnörtiti* ceremony, but in such a case the buffalo would go to the members of the two other divisions and Tövoniners would receive nothing if either of the other divisions performed the ceremony. Another example of a clan said to have three *kudr* is that of Piedr, where the family of Nongarsivan (62) stands in the same relation to the other divisions as is the case with the family of Tövoniners in the Kuudrol. In this case Nongarsivan's exceptional position is probably due to the fact that his family lives at Kavidi in the Wainad.

When a *kudr* becomes extinct a new division of the remaining *kudr* may take place, but, as a rule, this is not done till an occasion for the *irnörtiti* ceremony arises. There are several cases in which one *kudr* of a clan has now been extinct for several years, but though the re-division is often a subject for discussion, it is not probable that a new *kudr* will be instituted till the necessity arises. Occasionally, however, it would seem that a new *kudr* may be decided on apart from an occasion for the *irnörtiti* ceremony, for about the time of my visit the people of Keadr, who had lost one *kudr* by the dying out of the Kwaradrol, decided that the family of Karem (69), of which the sole living representatives are three boys, should form a new *kudr*. I could not learn what had been the motives for the decision. Some unimportant clans which have arisen by fusion from other clans, such as those of Kidmad and Kulhem, have no *kudr*, and do not appear ever to have possessed these divisions.

THE PÒLM

The word *pòlm* means 'portion,' and is the name of the section of the clan by means of which is regulated the sharing of any expenses which fall on the clan as a whole. Any expenses which the clan may incur as a whole are not equally divided among the individual members of the clan, but are equally divided among the *pòlm*. The chief occasion on which such expenses arise is in the repair or rebuilding of a dairy.

When a clan owns a *ti* and a dairy of the *ti* needs to be rebuilt or repaired, the expense also falls on the clan, and is equally divided among the *pòlm*, as in the case of the village dairy.

The outlay is equally divided among the *pòlm*, however much they may vary in size. Thus in the Kars clan one *pòlm* has sixteen adult male members, while another has only one, but this one man would contribute exactly the same amount as the other sixteen.

Occasionally a *pòlm* is so poor that it cannot pay its share, and in one such case at the present time the *pòlm*, in this case consisting of two boys only, has been incorporated into another.

The number of *pòlm* in a clan varies greatly, from ten in the case of Kars to one only in the Pedrkars clan. There is no definite relation between the *kudr* and the *pòlm* as regards numbers; thus, one *kudr* of a clan may consist of one *pòlm* only, when the other *kudr* is divided into many *pòlm*. When there is a great degree of inequality in the sizes of different *pòlm*, a redistribution may take place, and this is probably the more likely to happen the more influential are the members of the smaller *pòlm*.

I believe that redistribution in the case of both *pòlm* and *kudr* is usually decided by the members of the clan itself, but in cases of doubt it is probable that the general council may have a voice in the matter.

Each *pòlm* has a headman and is spoken of as the *pòlm* of this man. He is responsible for collecting the amount due from it, but as the *pòlm* often consists of a number of brothers, who hold much of their property in common, the collection is not usually a matter of difficulty, and I never heard of any disputes arising from this source.

The Todas recognise the existence of the family (*kudupel* or *kudubel*) within the clan, meaning by this a group of people bound together by near blood kinship. As a general rule, the family corresponds with the *pòlm*, but sometimes there may be more than one *pòlm* in the same family. It seemed to me that the term *kudupel* had not the same clear meaning as the *pòlm*. The family has no important function in the social organisation except in so far as it corresponds with the *pòlm*, but it is taken into account when the *pòlm* and *kudr* are readjusted.

The term was chiefly used when the Todas were speaking of certain families as being noted in certain ways or as having certain privileges. Thus, some families are noted for their powers as sorcerers, and these are called *pilikudupel*; others are known as *manikudupel*, or chief families, whose members are important in government and can hold the office of *monegar* and serve on the *naim*. Other families important in government whose members can serve on the *naim* or council are called *tinkaniputitth kudupel* or *tinkani kudupel* and *palutth kudupel*. The members of certain other families have certain duties of a lower order in connexion with the *naim*. They take messages and act generally as servants at the meetings, and the families with these functions are called *kavòdiputipol kudupel*, or servant families. They are also sometimes called *armanol* or palace people, because at one time the Rajah of Nelambur in the Wainad put his buffaloes into their charge.

LAWS OF DESCENT

Descent among the Todas is always reckoned in the male line. A man is always of the same clan as his father, if by his "father" we understand the man who has given the bow and arrow to his mother at the *pursütpimi* ceremony. In the case of the offspring of a *mokhthoditi* union, there is at first sight an appearance of female descent. The child of a Teivali mother and a Tarthar father belongs to the Teivaliol and *vice versâ*, but on further inquiry it is found that the child does not belong to his mother's clan, but to that of her legal husband. The child of a Teivali mother in such a case is not Teivali because his mother is of this division, but because a Teivali man only is allowed to perform the *pursütpimi* ceremony with a Teivali woman and become the legal father of her child. If, in such a case, the *pursütpimi* ceremony had not been performed, the child would belong to the division and clan of neither father nor mother, but would be a *padmokh*, of no division and of no clan.[1] I did not definitely inquire into the point, but from my general knowledge of the position of such an individual, I have little doubt that he would not be allowed to perform the *pursütpimi* ceremony, and could therefore never become the legal father of a child.

In this as in all cases the clan to which a child belongs

[1] Another name for a man of no clan is *pazuli*, but I do not know whether this is merely a synonym of *padmokh* or whether a man can lose the right of belonging to a clan for any other reason than that described above.

is determined entirely by the *pursütpimi* ceremony. If in a polyandrous marriage the husbands belong to different clans, a child belongs to the clan of the husband who has last performed this ceremony, and, as we have already seen, in the case of the death of one of the husbands, the dead man may become the legal father of several children, if the surviving husband does not perform the ceremony of giving a bow and arrow to the wife.

Again, in the case of a woman becoming pregnant while still unmarried, the father of the child is the man who is called in to give the bow and arrow, although he may have had nothing to do with the woman before the ceremony. Further, if for any reason the husband of a woman should be prevented from performing the *pursütpimi* ceremony, some other man is called upon to give the bow and arrow and he becomes the father of the child. Lastly, in the numerous cases of transference of wives from one man to another by the *tererstki* custom, one man may be the real father of a child, but another will become the legal father if the transference should take place in time for him to perform the essential ceremony.

The Todas show few traces of mother-right. In some communities there is little reason to doubt that such acts as are performed by a Toda towards his sister's son are survivals of a condition of society in which the mother's brother was responsible, largely or altogether, for the welfare of the child. Among the Todas, however, the *mun* stands in two relations to a child. He is the mother's brother, and he is also the prospective or actual father-in-law, and we have no means of telling in which of these two *rôles* he performs his duties. If the duties of a man towards his sister's son among the Todas be a relic of mother-right, there can be little doubt that this condition must have been very remote.

The Todas have a special name for the village of a man's mother—viz., *karuvnòdr*, or "honoured place," and when a *manmokh* gives a buffalo or other contribution on the occasion of a funeral, he speaks of it as a gift to his *karuvnòdr*. When a man visits his *karuvnòdr*, he goes to the door of the dairy and bows down with his head to the ground at its threshold, and then goes to the huts, where he is greeted with the appropriate greeting, but this differs in no way from the procedure of a visitor to any *etudmad.*

Marshall in his book[1] on the Todas has suggested that the existence of female succession among the buffaloes of the Todas may be a relic of female descent among the people themselves. He suggests that at one time the scheme of descent and kinship was the same for the Todas and for their buffaloes, and that with the introduction of polyandry there came in inheritance through males among themselves, while they continued to reckon the descent of the buffaloes in the female line.

We have seen (see p. 471) that the method of reckoning descent among the buffaloes is due superficially to the absence of names for male buffaloes and more deeply to the lack of interest in paternity. Nevertheless, Marshall's suggestion, wild as it may seem, should not be utterly scouted. The Todas regard their buffaloes so much as fellow creatures that any of their ideas concerning the relations of their buffaloes to one another should not be without interest to the student of social regulations.

If one may speak of social organisation among buffaloes—and in the case of the Toda herds we are justified in doing so—we have a state of society in some ways analogous to that which many sociologists suppose to have existed at one time in the early stages of human society. We have various groups of buffaloes, and each buffalo—certainly each female buffalo—belongs to the same group as its mother. There is complete promiscuity, and the buffalo belongs to its mother's group because paternity is unknown or disregarded.

It is true that this condition is artificial, but it is this very artificiality which gives it its interest, for it shows that people like the Todas, whose whole lives are devoted to the buffalo, to whom the breeding of the buffalo should have the deepest interest, have allowed this state of things to come about. If they had attached importance to paternity nothing would have been easier than to regulate breeding, to record paternity,

[1] P. 132.

and even to have developed a system of male descent among their buffaloes such as exists among themselves.

The nature of what may be called the social regulations of the buffaloes shows that the Todas take little interest in the part played by the male in the process of mating, and, as we have seen, this lack of interest is almost as great among themselves. Side by side with the strictest regulation of marriage as a social institution, such great laxity prevails in regard to sexual relations that the Todas may almost be said to live in a condition of promiscuity, though, as I have endeavoured to show, the degree of promiscuity is in practice perhaps hardly as great as their statements would lead one to expect.

ADOPTION

It is clear that the custom of adoption of children is not practised by the Todas. They denied its existence emphatically, and I met with no instance which led me to suspect its presence in compiling the genealogies.

If a child is left an orphan, it is looked after by the people of its clan, but it is always clearly recognised that the child retains the father's property, and belongs to the *madol* and *pòlm* of the father.

There is, so far as I could ascertain, no religious custom which makes it necessary that a man should have children. The duties of a child at the funeral ceremonies can quite well be performed by some other member of the clan.

There is a social reason which makes it inconvenient in some cases that a man should die without male issue. If a man is the only representative of his *kudr*, and has no children, the *kudr* will become extinct, and the clan will be put to the trouble of rearranging the families of which it is constituted. If such a man is childless he may take another wife in the hope of having a son to carry on the *kudr*, but the adoption of a child for the purpose is never thought of. A good case is that of the two brothers Mudrigeidi and Odrkurs in Table I. They are the last two representatives of one *kudr* of the Nòdrsol. They have had two wives, one of whom has had a daughter and a boy who died, and in the hope of having a son, one of the brothers had recently married a young girl, Obalidz, as his third wife, the others being still alive, though one had been taken by another man.

GOVERNMENT

The most important feature of Toda government is the *naim*, or *noim*,[1] a council having a definite constitution. The *naim* proper has to do with the affairs of the Todas in general, and, in addition, more informal councils,[2] consisting of the chief members of a clan, may be held to settle matters arising within the clan. It seems, however, that the supreme *naim* may sometimes be called upon to settle the internal affairs of a clan.

The *naim* of the general body of Todas should have five members, or, if more than five members, they should be drawn from five sources. Four of these sources are the Tarthar clans of Kars, Nòdrs, and Taradr, and the Teivali clan of Kuudr. The fifth source is the Badaga village of Tuneri, from which a Badaga man may be sent to take part in the *naim*. He is only called upon to sit, however, on special occasions; and in the many councils which I saw during my visit a Badaga was rarely present. He probably only sits, as a rule, when questions arise which involve the relations between the Todas and Badagas.

The Toda representatives should be drawn from certain families of their respective clans. The Kuudr representative should belong to the family known as the *manikudupel*, and the representatives of Kars, Nòdrs, and Taradr to the families known as *tinkanikudupel*. A few years ago the Toda representatives were Kuriolv of Kuudr (52), Parkurs (8) and Piutolvan (10) of Kars, Kudòdrsvan (3) of Nòdrs, and Ircheidi (20) of Taradr, though there was some question whether Ircheidi was on the *naim*, or whether his place had not been taken by Piutolvan, the second Kars representative. All these men are at present living, but, with the exception of

[1] A meeting of the council is often spoken of as *kûtkûdriti*, "the assembly assembles," or *kûtpuniti*, "the assembly makes."

[2] It seemed clear that the term *naim* is also applied to these clan councils.

Kuriolv, they are too old or infirm to serve. Kuriolv is still on the *naim*, and his influence is entirely predominant, and it appears that he has been instrumental in altering the constitution of the council very largely. The number of representatives has been increased, and the following were the members in 1902: —Kuriolv and Ivievan (52) of Kuudr, Perner and Tebner (68), of Keadr, Parkeidi (21), Paners (23) and Siriar (20) of Taradr and Pidrvan (9) of Kars. Thus several members of the Kuudrol and Taradrol are serving, while there appears to be no representative of the Nòdrsol; and I was told by several Todas that Perner and Tebner are on the council because they are friends of Kuriolv, though, as members of the Keadr clan, they have no right whatever to the position.

On the slopes below the hill called Mirson, near Paikara, there are the remains of ruined walls marking a place where the *naim* used to meet. This place is called Idrgûdipem, and seems to have been at one time the chief meeting-place.

At the present time the *naim* meets anywhere. I have seen the council sitting in the compound of the bungalow at Paikara and on one occasion, when I was working in a bungalow at the Ooty Club, the *naim* sat in the grounds of the club. In general, they now meet at the places which happen to be most convenient for the chief members.

The members usually sit in a semicircular row. If they are considering a dispute between two parties, representatives of the parties take part in the sitting, and in these cases the members of the *naim* sit in the middle of the row while the representatives sit on either wing.

During my visit the council was chiefly occupied with the various complicated transactions which are always arising out of the custom of transferring wives from one man to another. This custom is the chief source of disputes among the Todas, and at times the *naim* may sit for several days before one case is settled.

I am doubtful whether the *naim* should have a definite head, but at the present time it certainly has such in the person of Kuriolv of Kuudr. He is the senior representative of the *manikudupel* of Kuudr, and is therefore the natural representative of this clan on the *naim*. He is highly intelligent, and gave me the impression that he might have risen to a high place in any community. He has the reputation among the Todas of being very eloquent and of having great persuasive powers. When persuasion fails, there is very little doubt that he resorts to intimidation of some kind, though I could not discover what his means of intimidation are.

FIG. 60.—KURIOLV AND PILIMURG.

On one occasion the *naim* spent a whole day discussing a marriage case in the compound at Paikara. On the following day they met in a distant part of the hills to continue the discussion of the case, and I was told that this was arranged by Kuriolv because he hoped to enforce his wishes in some secluded spot more effectively than in the publicity of Paikara where the evidences of the 'government' probably lent moral support to his opponents.

However Kuriolv effects his purpose, there is no doubt that

he almost entirely dominated the Toda people at the time of my visit. We have already seen that he has succeeded in altering the constitution of the *naim*, and several examples are given in this book of his interference in the normal course of Toda affairs; interference usually in favour of his own family or friends. In at least one case (see Chap. XVI) during my visit he considered himself superior to ceremonial laws.

He seemed to me to afford an excellent example of the process by which one man may bring about considerable changes in the laws and regulations of a community; though I was told in several instances that the Todas would revert to their old customs as soon as Kuriolv died.

I did not obtain a full account of the duties of the *naim* and of the affairs which come under its jurisdiction. There is no doubt, however, that it is largely concerned with the settlement of civil disputes arising between individuals, families, and clans. As I have already mentioned, it seemed to me that it was almost exclusively engaged during my visit in the regulation of the disputes arising out of the *tererstli* custom. In one such case the question of funeral contributions was involved, and I have no doubt that the settlement of any dispute arising from this source would come within the province of the *naim*, and probably any doubtful point in the working of the social regulations would be submitted to it.

In addition to its functions in disputes between individuals, the *naim* has wide functions in connexion with Toda ceremonial. It decides when many ceremonies take place, and has the chief word in regulating the affairs of the *ti* dairies. Thus it appeared that the various arrangements and alterations of arrangements in connexion with the migration of the buffaloes of the Nòdrs *ti* which were made during my visit were the work of the *naim*, or, at any rate, of its chief members.

Crime

I have no knowledge about the power of the *naim* in criminal as opposed to civil matters. I never heard of inquiry by the *naim* into any criminal offence committed by one man against another or against the community. It is, however, doubtful whether crime can be said to exist among the Todas.

Acts such as infanticide are committed which would be regarded as crimes by others, but since these are the outcome of custom they are not crimes from the Toda point of view. Again, we have seen that the Todas have a code of offences against the dairy, but these must be regarded as sins rather than as crimes, for they are neither investigated nor punished by the civil authority, the *naim*, but are punished directly by the gods, and the various ceremonies described in Chapter XIII are expiatory and not punitive.

The list of offences given on p. 295 includes quarrelling between people of the same clan at a festival and quarrelling in the dairy. In both cases the quarrelling is an offence against the dairy, and I have no information to show whether quarrels ever lead to acts of violence which might in other places become the subject of criminal investigation. So far as I could learn, any investigation by the *naim* would only deal with the causes which had led to the quarrel; it would deal only with the civil and not with the criminal aspect of the case.

Again, the custom of *tererstthi*, or transference of wives, which is the chief subject of the deliberations of the *naim*, sometimes leads to acts of violence. A woman who has been transferred by the *naim* from one man to another may be carried off by force from the home of the former, but, however such an act may be regarded from our standpoint, it is not a crime from the Toda point of view, but merely the carrying out of the decision of the judicial authority. So many Todas are, however, discovering that such an act is regarded as a crime by Europeans that there will probably soon come about a state of public opinion which will regard such abduction as a crime, and possibly the same idea may become attached to the whole custom of transference of a woman from one man to another unwillingly. It seemed not unlikely at the time of my visit that this conversion of a custom into a crime might be assisted by the action of the Government.

In the legend of Kwoten, this hero kills Parden, but so far

as I know this is the only example of murder, either legendary or historical, among the Todas. The Todas may take part in the murder of a Kurumba who has been working magic, but this is of course no crime from the Toda point of view, but an obvious method of self-defence, for it is believed that the only way of stopping Kurumba sorcery is to kill the sorcerer.

With the exception of the occurrences accompanying the transference of wives, which I have already considered, I heard of no case of assault by one Toda on another.

Similarly, I heard of no offence against property except in connexion with the dairy. So far as I know, ornaments or clothing are never stolen. In the list of offences against the dairy, stealing ghi is included, but it was clear that this is regarded as sacrilege, as an offence against the dairy and not as an offence committed against the individual.

SUICIDE

In the legend of Kwoten there is a record of suicide by strangling, and since the suicide of Erten and his confederates this is said to have been a recognised custom among the Todas. Several instances have occurred in recent times; thus, about four generations ago, at a village called Podzkwar, near Taradrkirsi, a woman and her husband had a dispute and the woman strangled herself. About three generations ago a man strangled himself in the dairy at Melgars, and when a Toda is very angry he will threaten to commit suicide, saying "*on mëdr kati këdraividikin*"—"my neck tying, I will die."

Another way of committing suicide, said to have been borrowed from the Badagas, is that of taking opium. There has been a recent case of suicide, by this means, and when angry, a Toda sometimes says, "*mud tid këdraividikin*"—"Opium eating, I will die."

THE MONEGAR

The Todas have a *monegar*, or headman, who is responsible for the assessment which the Todas pay to Government for their grazing rights, &c. (see below).

The earliest *monegar* whom the Todas remember is Teitchi or Teiti (52). He was succeeded by his fourth son, Mutevan, who is still alive. The two eldest sons had died before their father, and Persevan, the third son, was said to be weak-minded, and Mutevan was therefore chosen to succeed.

Mutevan is now a very old man, probably about eighty years of age, and his office was taken over some years ago by his eldest son, Ivievan. Though Ivievan is the *monegar* he is not the chief representative of his family on the *naim*, this position belonging to Kuriolv, the son of Parcivan and Persevan. Ivievan is helped in collecting the assessment by an assistant *monegar*, and till lately this place belonged to Parkurs of Kars.

It does not appear that the monegarship is a real Toda office, but that the earliest *monegar* was appointed by Mr. Sullivan, the first British official of the Nilgiris. The family, however, to which the *monegar* belongs is called the *manikudupel*, which may mean the *monegar* family, but I could not discover definitely whether this title is older than the institution of the monegarship. It is possible that Teitchi was one of the chief men of the *naim* when the Europeans first came to the hills and that he was therefore appointed as *monegar*.

It is quite clear that at the present time the *monegar*, Ivievan, is not the most important man among the Todas, but that the predominant position belongs to his cousin, Kuriolv, the representative of the family on the *naim*.

HEADMEN

Though it is very doubtful whether the institution of *monegar* is not an innovation, and whether the Todas as a whole have properly any true chief, it is fairly clear that the clan and its divisions have definite leaders.

Each clan has a headman or *etudol*; usually, it seemed to me, one who had come to the top by virtue of his character and ability. I did not learn how far his position was generally recognised nor by what means he was chosen. It was quite clear, however, that the leading man of a clan might lose his position in old age or as the result of illness, and at the time of my visit there were several men who had been the heads of their clans but no longer occupied those positions.

Similarly, as we have seen, both *kudr* and *pòlm* have their leading men, who give their names to the divisions and are probably responsible for the conduct of their business.

Property

Among the Todas, property may be held by the clan, the family or the individual. I am not clear whether there is any case in which property is held to belong to the Todas as a whole, or to either of the two divisions. There were two villages, Padegar and Ki Perththo, said to be common property, so that any one might live at them. At the time of my visit both were occupied by Melgars people, and I could not satisfy myself as to what was meant by saying that they were common property.

In general, land, the dairies of the chief villages, and some buffaloes may be said to be the property of the clan. The house, and probably also some villages, are the property of a family, and most buffaloes, household goods and ornaments are the property of the individual.

Land.—The relation of the Todas to the land has been a much discussed theme, and for many years after the first settlement of the hills by Europeans it was a subject of controversy. The fact that the Badagas paid what seemed to be a tribute of grain to the Todas was held to show that the latter were regarded as the "lords of the soil," and the view was strongly upheld that they should be so regarded by the Indian Government. The other view taken of the matter was that permanent rights in the soil throughout India belong to the State. The controversy[1] was not settled till 1843, when it was decided that the Todas should have the privilege of pasturing their herds on the State lands on payment of a small tax. At the present time the Todas receive an annual

[1] For a full account of this controversy see the *Manual of the Nilagiri District*, by H. B. Grigg, Madras, 1880. See also Thurston, Bull. i. 182.

sum from the Government as compensation for land taken from them in Ootacamund and elsewhere.

Although the Todas have thus had much difficulty with the Government in relation to the ownership of land, it does not seem that they have trouble in this matter among themselves, and I heard of no disputes between members of different clans or different villages about grazing rights.

In the account of the marriage dispute between Punog and Nertiners (see p. 536) the former had evidently put many of his buffaloes in the charge of his brother-in-law for grazing purposes, but it was quite clear that no question of grazing rights came into this dispute. The buffaloes only came into the quarrel because Nertiners happened to have them in his charge when the marriage dispute arose.

I did not ascertain definitely how grazing rights between two clans or families are regulated, but I think it is quite clear that there is no individual ownership in land.

Certain dairies, and probably all the chief villages (*etudmad*), are regarded more or less as the property of the whole clan. There probably never arises any real question of ownership, but as regards the dairies, it was clear that any expenses incurred in the repair or rebuilding of a dairy fall on the whole clan, each *pòlm* of the clan contributing an equal share.[1]

The buffalo herds of the *ti* are also regarded as the property of the whole clan, but the rights of ownership are in these cases very shadowy. It does not appear that the owning clan derives any pecuniary benefit from its possession of the herd, while, on the other hand, the possession involves considerable expense, chiefly owing to certain feasts which have to be provided, and these expenses are given as the reason why certain of the sacred dairies are unoccupied. The people of the owning clan have, it is true, the right of choosing the *palol*, but as the choice is limited, and there is, in most cases, little competition for the office, this is a very empty honour.

Houses. Each house belongs to a certain family. The normal Toda family consists of a number of brothers with

[1] I am not clear on whom the expense of rebuilding and repairing a dairy would fall when the dairy is situated at a village occupied by one family only, and used exclusively for buffaloes which are the private property of that family.

one wife, and each house belongs to a family of this kind, and is handed on to the children of the brothers.

If the brothers quarrel, the affair is settled by the *naim*, and it is usually decided that one brother or more than one of the brothers shall occupy the house for a certain period, usually a year, and that at the end of this period he (or they) shall move to another village, when another brother or brothers will occupy the house.

Such disputes do not seem to be frequent, but one was in existence during my visit. The two younger of three brothers had taken a wife without the knowledge of the eldest. The latter did not approve of the choice, and wished his brothers to send the wife away, which they refused to do. As the dispute had not yet been settled, the eldest brother at the time of my visit was living in the house, while the other brothers were living at the village of their newly chosen wife.

If a family dies out, it seems that the house is not, as a rule, taken on by another family. It falls into disuse, and in time disappears. As a village may sometimes consist of one house only, villages may disappear in this way, and the ruins of some villages were pointed out to me which had fallen into disuse owing to the dying out of the families which formerly occupied them. A really important village, *i.e.*, one with an important dairy, would of course never disappear in this way, but it is possible that the reason why some villages, such as Nasmiòdr and Kanòdrs, now consist of a dairy only, is that the families which possessed the houses at these villages became extinct. I do not, however, know positively that a house at such an important village may not, in some cases, be taken over by another family.

Breeks has stated that the Toda custom is that the house shall pass to the youngest son. It seems quite clear that this is wrong, and that this custom is absolutely unknown among the Todas. It is, however, a Badaga custom, and among them I was told that it is due to the fact that as the sons of a family grow up and marry, they leave the house of the parents and build houses elsewhere. It is the duty of the youngest son to dwell with his parents and support them as long as they live, and when they die he continues to live in the parental home, of which he becomes the owner.

Buffaloes. These are to a very large extent individual property. In practice, owing to the fact that brothers usually live together, a herd of buffaloes is treated as the property of a family of brothers, but whenever the occasion arises there are definite rules for the division of the buffaloes among them.

I have already referred to the fact that certain herds of buffaloes, such as the *ti* herds and the *kugvalir* of Taradr, are the common property of a clan, but the great majority of both sacred and ordinary buffaloes belong to families or individuals.[1] When a man who owns a certain number of buffaloes dies, the buffaloes are not necessarily divided among his sons. If the sons are all living together, the buffaloes may be treated as if they were common property. The milk of the ordinary buffaloes is churned in the dwelling-hut, and that of the sacred buffaloes in the dairy, and the produce in each case is regarded as the property of the whole family. It is only when dissensions arise, or when some reason makes it desirable that the brothers should separate and live in different villages, that the laws regulating the partition of buffaloes come into force.

When such an occasion arises the buffaloes are equally divided among the brothers, with the exception that the eldest son and the youngest son each receive one buffalo in excess of the rest. This custom is known as *ĭrvâkhtuŭdr meilkŭdr*, or "if divide buffaloes, superior portion."

If there are only two sons, each will get *meilkudr*, and the buffaloes are equally divided; but if there should be an unequal number of buffaloes, the odd buffalo is taken by the elder son.

If there are more than two sons, the buffaloes are equally divided with *meilkudr* to the eldest and youngest, and any odd buffaloes are in this case sold and the proceeds equally divided, or, more commonly, one of the brothers takes the odd buffaloes and gives the right proportion of their value to the other brothers.

[1] On p. 70 I have given an example of the ownership of sacred buffaloes in the Kars clan.

Thus, if sixteen buffaloes are to be divided among four brothers, the eldest and youngest would each take four, the second and third brothers would each take three, and the remaining two buffaloes would either be sold and the purchase money equally divided, or taken by one of the brothers, who would divide three-quarters of the value of the buffaloes between the other three men. If there should be only fourteen buffaloes, the eldest and youngest sons would each take four buffaloes and the others three.

The *meilkudr* is also operative if a man divides his buffaloes among his sons in his lifetime. In this case a man usually keeps some buffaloes for himself; thus I was told that a man who had sixteen buffaloes and three sons might give four buffaloes to the eldest, three to the next, and four to the youngest son, keeping five for himself.

The Todas told me of one apparent exception to the law of *meilkudr*. If, in a family of four brothers, the two elder brothers marry one wife and the two younger marry another and the two groups separate, the buffaloes would be equally divided, but this is because each would receive a *meilkudr*. If, on the other hand, the eldest and youngest son married one wife, and the other two sons married another woman, the first group would receive two buffaloes in excess of the second. The former example is, of course, an obvious consequence of the law of *meilkudr*. I only mention it because the Todas told me of it especially, and seemed to regard it as a case which might be thought to be a departure from custom.

I gave the Todas a number of hypothetical problems of buffalo division, and all were solved in accordance with the law of *meilkudr*. I have not been able to learn of any exact parallel in other parts of the world, and it seems possible that it is an independent invention of the Todas. The division is called *kudr*, or horn, and it seems to me quite possible that at some time it occurred to an ingenious Toda that the two extremities of the family should be regarded as the two horns of the family, and that this fact should be recognised in the division of property, or, it may be, that the custom of endowing the eldest of the family above his fellows existed among the Todas as among so many other races, till it was pointed out that this was like a buffalo with one horn, and the youngest son was therefore similarly endowed to restore the symmetry of the family. The buffalo influences the Toda mind so much that I do not think this is a far-fetched explanation of a custom which appears to be the unique possession of this people.

The word *kudr* is also the name of one of the divisions of the clan, and it seemed clear in this case that the proper number of *kudr* in each clan is two.

There is much transference of buffaloes from one man to another, or from one family to another. Many ceremonies involve gifts of buffaloes, and these are usually presented by a member of one clan to a member of another. Marriage is one of the chief occasions of such gifts. Refusal to fulfil the marriage contract and divorce involve the payment of buffaloes, and the *tererstthi* custom is a great source of the passing of buffaloes from one clan to another. Similarly, buffaloes are given at the ceremonies of naming, ear-piercing, &c., and as I have already pointed out, these transferences have led to great confusion in the classification of the different kinds of sacred buffaloes, as a man may have in his possession animals belonging to several named groups.

In the case of ordinary buffaloes, or *putiir*, it seemed that a distinction is made between buffaloes which have been acquired by a man and those descended from animals which had been in the possession of his father and grandfather. My attention was drawn to this point by the occurrence at the funeral of Sinerani. The recalcitrant buffalo on this occasion was one of the latter kind, and I was told that it should not have been killed at the funeral of a girl because, being descended from a buffalo which belonged to Kuriolv's grandfather, Kuriolv's heirs had a right to it of which they were deprived by its slaughter for a girl. If the dead child had been a boy the slaughter of this buffalo would have been proper, for the dead child in this case would have been one of the heirs.

Transferences of buffaloes also take place between Todas and Badagas, as we have seen in connexion with the ear-piercing ceremony described in Chapter XIV. In this case the gift appeared to be nothing more than a friendly compliment, but it is possible that transferences of buffaloes may in some cases be connected with the other complicated relations between the two tribes.

Household Goods. These are equally divided among the sons, though, as in the case of the buffaloes, they are used in common so long as the sons live together. If household goods have to be divided among the members of a family they are shared as equally as possible, and this is also the case with any ornaments. If the man had only one ring, it was said that this ring would either be broken up and shared equally, or its value would be divided. Money is shared equally among the sons.

If one of several brothers who has his own wife should die and leave children, the sons would take their father's share at any division of property. Thus, at the time of my visit, Piutolvan and Püljcidi (10), two very old men, were thinking of dividing their buffaloes among their descendants. In this case Menkars would receive the number which his father Tagners would have received if he had been alive. If Tagners had left two sons, the portion which their father would have received would be divided between the two boys or devoted to their common use.

Daughters inherit nothing. They only receive from their parents what they are given as dowry (*adrparn*).

Any property given to a woman as dowry goes with her if she changes husbands, but any ornaments or other property given to a wife by her husband are kept by the husband if the wife is transferred to another man or group of men.

Harkness records a case in which a dispute about property arose. In this case a woman bore two children to three husbands. One of the husbands died and the other two husbands married other wives. The two children claimed one-third of the property of the mother and her first husband, and Harkness was told that this was generally recognised to be a just claim. I did not inquire into this special case but according to the laws of inheritance of property which I have given, it would seem that the children were entitled to one-third of the whole of the property of the three brothers. If the property had been divided among the three brothers, the man who died would have received one-third, and the children should have received his share.

In all cases of distribution of property, inheritance depends on descent as determined by the *pursütpimi* ceremony, and not on the real descent, even if this should be well known. Thus the boy Meilitars (44), who is really the son of Kuriolv, but is legally the son of Pepners, should not inherit any of Kuriolv's buffaloes, but will receive those of his legal father, Pepners, of whom at present he is the only son.

If the whole of a family, such as is given in one of the genealogical tables, should die out, the inheritance of the buffaloes and other property is determined by the nearest links of descent, of which a tradition may be preserved, even if the actual relationship cannot be definitely traced.

Several interesting features of Toda law are illustrated by a case out of which a lawsuit may one day arise. If the family of Kiugi (57) should become extinct, there would arise a dispute about the succession to the property, which would turn largely on a case in which the *pursütpimi* ceremony was performed several generations ago. When the eldest child of Tudrvan (52) was about to be born, Tudrvan was away from home, and had not performed the *pursütpimi* ceremony. There was a danger that the delivery might take place before the ceremony could be performed, and Kòrs (57) was therefore called in to give the bow and arrow, and Teitchi, who was born soon afterwards, was, according to Toda custom, the child of Kòrs. When Teitchi grew up, however, he decided to regard himself as the son of his real father, Tudrvan, and being a powerful and influential person like his grandson Kuriolv, he appears to have had his way, and his descendants have been regarded as the descendants of Tudrvan. Tudrvan himself gave the bow and arrow in the succeeding pregnancy, and there is therefore no doubt about the legitimacy of Pusheiri and his younger brothers and sisters.

Owing, however, to the part played by Kòrs before the birth of his grandfather, Kuriolv has lately directed that Kiugi, the son of Kòrs, should belong to the same *pòlm* as himself in order that he or his family may succeed to the buffaloes of Kiugi's *pòlm* if this should die out. It is known, however, that Kiugi's *pòlm* is closely related to that of Tüliners (56), so that should the *pòlm* of Kiugi become extinct, there would arise a lawsuit between Kuriolv and Tüliners or their representatives for the possession of Kiugi's buffaloes.

The essential point of the situation is that Kuriolv is trying to make use of his double position as the descendant of Tudrvan by real paternity and of Kòrs by virtue of the *pursütpimi* ceremony. According to the latter he is of the same *pòlm* as Kiugi, but if equity prevails in the decision of the *naim* which may have to settle the dispute, Kuriolv or his representative will have to decide whether he is descended from Tudrvan or Kòrs, and will not be allowed to take advantage of both lines of descent.

As a matter of fact, I was assured by several Todas that though they have apparently fallen in with Kuriolv's wishes, they still regard Kiugi's *pòlm* as most closely allied to that of Tüliners, and if Kuriolv should die before the extinction of Kiugi's family, I have little doubt that the *naim* would decide that the buffaloes of Kiugi should go to the family of Tüliners.

This potential lawsuit is important as showing the *rôle* played by the genealogies in the social regulations of the Toda community. We see that an eventuality which may never arise and probably will not arise for many years to come is already the subject of consideration and discussion, that the crucial point upon which the lawsuit will turn is an event which occurred probably about 120 years ago, and that the ties of kinship which will be involved in the dispute are carefully preserved in the memories of the people.

The history is also very interesting in showing that a century ago a man of force was able to set aside a fundamental regulation of Toda society, and that his grandson, who has apparently inherited the powerful character of his ancestor, is following in his footsteps, and, as we have seen frequently during this volume, is able to put on one side Toda customs or laws when they conflict with his interests or desires.

Debt and Servitude

It seems to be not uncommon for a Toda to die in debt, and it is the duty of the sons to pay off the debts of their father. If there are no children, the payment of the debt is regarded as the duty of the brothers of the dead man.

When children have to pay the debts of their father, they may give their services to others, receiving in return money and other recompense. The usual pay is six rupees a year, two cloaks, and food. To this is often added the loan of a milking buffalo.

This custom of working for another is called *kâlvatkerthchi* or *kâlvatkerthiti*. Several of the eight sons of Pushteidi and Keitan (6) are now working to pay their father's debts. Two of the sons are married to one woman and live at one of their own villages, where they look after the buffaloes of the family. Another brother is unmarried, but lives with a Teivali woman. The other five sons are unmarried and work for various people. One is employed on a tea estate, and the others are working for different Todas, who reward them in the manner already described. The milking buffaloes lent to them are handed over to the charge of the brothers who are married.

It is very exceptional to find a family in which so many of the men are unmarried, and this was said to be due to the necessity of paying off their father's debt. In this case the two eldest brothers have remained unmarried, but this was said to have been due to their own choice. It seems that it is left to the family to decide which of them shall marry and which shall undertake the duty of paying the debt. As soon as the debt is paid off, all the sons are allowed to marry.

The Position of Women

There is no doubt that women have a subordinate position in the Toda community. The ceremonial of the dairy has a predominant place in the lives and thoughts of the people, and the exclusion of women from any share in this ceremonial must have influenced the attitude of the community towards the sex. The laws regulating the relations of the dairymen with women also can hardly have contributed to raise the esteem in which they are held. The special ceremonies in which women are concerned involve various disabilities due to the ideas of impurity connected with these ceremonies. The seclusion-hut of a woman has attached to it the same ideas of impurity which attach to a corpse or its relics.

Not only are women excluded from any share in the work of the dairies connected with the sacred buffaloes, but they are also prohibited from any part in the milking of the ordinary buffaloes or in the churning of their milk, which is performed solely by males in a part of the hut with which women have nothing to do. It seems that at one time women had the one function of tending the buffaloes at the time of calving, but even this is no longer allowed them.

In other household matters, the duties of women are very limited in scope. Their chief work is the pounding and sifting of grain, the cleaning of the hut, and the decoration of clothing. I am doubtful whether they are allowed to cook, at any rate to cook food in which milk forms one of the ingredients. With such occupations as divining and sorcery they have nothing to do, but one woman has the reputation of possessing the powers of healing which belong to the *utkòren*.

I could not learn of any matters of social importance in which women are consulted. When collecting genealogies in Torres Straits, I found that women were often repositories of this important branch of knowledge, but I received no indication that this was the case with the Toda women, though I cannot say definitely that they may not have possessed some knowledge of this and cognate subjects.

Though thus unimportant in ceremonial and of little influence in the regulation of social affairs, women have nevertheless much freedom. In general social intercourse the two sexes always seemed to be on the best of terms, and I never saw or heard anything to indicate that women are treated harshly or contemptuously.

In my psychological tests it certainly seemed to me the general intelligence of the women was very much lower than that of the men. Some of the younger women were as acute and intelligent as the men, but the older women seemed to me hopelessly stupid. They did not try to give their minds to the tasks I set them with anything approaching the keenness and interest shown by the men, and again and again I failed to obtain results of any value in tests which men understood readily.

It seems probable that the intelligence of the two sexes is not appreciably different in youth, but that the social life of the women does nothing to develop this intelligence and everything to force its exercise into the narrowest channels.

It might, I think, be expected that polyandry would be associated with a subordinate position of woman, and there can be no doubt that the Todas show the association of the two conditions.

When a woman marries she becomes of the same clan as her husband, and this is a matter of some importance in connexion with religious and social ceremonial. Thus, in the funeral ceremonies of a woman, the choice of appropriate day and place, of the people who are to take part in the funeral rites and other features of the ceremonial are determined, not by the clan of the woman's father, but by that of her husband, and this even when the marriage itself forms part of the funeral ceremonies.

While I was on the hills, the widow, Kiuneimi (3), who had been living with her father at Nòdrs, died. Her husbands had belonged to Kanòdrs, and as a member of this clan she should have been taken to its burning-ground. This was, however, so far from Nòdrs that it was decided not to go there, but to hold the funeral ceremonies near the place where she had died. The proper funeral place for Nòdrs women could not, however, be used, for she belonged to another clan, and the body was therefore taken to a village which was not a true funeral place, and so no laws were infringed.

The funeral of Sinerani (p. 391) is an excellent example which shows how all the details of a funeral ceremony are dependent on the transference of a young girl to the clan of a boy who acts as husband to the corpse. By her marriage to Keinba, the dead girl became a member of the Keadrol, and her funeral should have been held at the burning-ground of this clan. Many of the features of the ceremonies were in accordance with this change of clan, and since all were not so, the various mishaps which occurred at the funeral were ascribed by the Todas to the departure from prescribed custom.

CHAPTER XXIV

ARTS AND AMUSEMENTS.

THE arts of life among the Todas are extremely simple. The fact that their agriculture is done for them by the Badagas and that all the objects they use in their daily life are made for them by the Kotas leaves them free to devote their whole attention to the care of the buffalo and the dairy. This employment has acquired so ceremonial a character that, having dealt with the ceremonies of the Todas, we find little left to consider in connexion with the regulation of the affairs of daily life.

The artistic side of life among the Todas is but little developed. Their interest is so much absorbed in ceremony that little is left for the development of art, even of a primitive kind. The decorative arts are of the simplest and are directed only to the adornment of the clothing or the person, and even here we shall find that the methods of wearing the clothes or the hair are quite as much influenced by ceremonial as by æsthetic considerations. In their amusements again we shall find that the influence of ceremonial is so great, that many of the games are merely imitations of ceremonial occupations.

I have included in this chapter an account of the ideas which are held about the heavenly bodies, the primitive astronomy of the people. To the Todas, though in a less degree than to many people of low culture, it is the sun, moon, and stars which are the chief objects of those observations and speculations which are the beginnings of science.

CLOTHING

The clothing of the men consists of a large cloak called the *putkuli*, a loincloth called *tadrp*, and a small perineal cloth called *kuvn*, kept in its place by a string round the waist called *pennar*.

The *putkuli* is made of a large piece of double cloth, which is usually worn by placing one side over the left shoulder and then throwing the whole garment round the back and over the right shoulder and across to the left shoulder, so that it completely envelops the body. This method of wearing the cloak, which is shown by the third man of Fig. 61, is called *kai ulk üt nidvai*, "hand into laid who stands," or "who stands with hand placed within the cloak."

The double layer of cloth of which the cloak is made is sewn together at the edges except at the upper part of one side, leaving the opening of a large pocket which is bounded by lines where the two layers of the cloak are again sewn together. This pocket is called *kudsh* and is very capacious, so that a Toda may produce a surprising number of articles from it. As we have seen, many of the articles given to the dead are placed in this pocket.

There are two methods of wearing the cloak adopted on special occasions. One of these is that called *kevenarut* (adopted by the second man in Fig. 61), with which we have already often met. The right arm is put out of the cloak, so that the arm and shoulder are bare whenever a Toda approaches certain sacred personages or objects. The cloak is worn *kevenarut* whenever the wearer is engaged in prayer or employed in any way at the dairy. It is also worn in this way when approaching a *palol*, when performing the *kaimukhti* salutation, and when crossing either of the sacred streams.

The other method is that shown by the fourth man in Fig. 61 and is called *mad âr mitch nidvai*, "head on covered who stands." The cloak is worn in this fashion by a widower between the middle of the first funeral ceremony and the final scene of the *azaramkedr*. It is also worn in this way by those who throw earth in the *puzhutpimi* ceremony of each funeral.

The *tadrp* is a loincloth worn in the ordinary way, as shown by the first man in Fig. 61. The *tadrp* of a young child has a pocket called *terigs*, but I do not know whether this pocket also exists in the *tadrp* of an adult.

Both *putkuli* and *tadrp* are manufactured by Hindus, probably in the Coimbatore district. Thirty years ago, according to Breeks, the cloth was procured from weavers who came from Serumuge in Coimbatore, but at the present time the garments are bought by the Todas at the bazaar. When obtained by the Todas they have certain red and blue lines, and sometimes the Todas supplement this decoration by embroidery called *pukuru*, which is the work of the women, and a cloak so decorated is called *pukuruputkuli*. The decoration is shown in Figs. 1 and 9. Some women are especially expert at this work, and one woman who has recently had to change her name is now called Pukuruveli on account of her special skill.

The chief point of interest in connexion with the *kuvn* is the string by which it is supported. This string is called *pennar*, or "butter string," and forms a special contribution made by relatives, and especially the sister's son, at a funeral. Further, the string is of especial significance in the dairy ceremonial, where it is sometimes called *kerk*.

Both *putkuli* and *tadrp* are also worn by women. The garments are of the same kind as those of the men and are worn in the same ways.

The higher grades of dairymen wear garments called *tuni*, made of a different material, a grey cloth, which has been said to be manufactured by the Badagas of Jakaneri, but is probably only procured by their help. A cloak of similar material called *än* is, or should be, used to enwrap the bodies of the dead; and, as we have already seen, there is some reason to believe that garments of this material may have been the original clothing of the Todas, for in the legend of Kwoten, the wife of this hero wore a cloak of this kind.

The Todas themselves manufacture a special kind of

FIG. 51. SHOWING METHODS OF WEARING THE TODA GARMENTS AND OF DOING THE HAIR.

material called *twadrinar* from the bark of a plant, and this is largely used in the ordination ceremonies. In the ordination of a Teivali *palikartmokh*, it may take the place of the *petuni*; at that of a *wursol*, *twadrinar* may be used as a girdle; and on the fourth day of the ordination ceremonies of the *palol*, the candidate manufactures and wears a rough *kuvn* made of this material. Its use in ceremony appears to be limited to the Teivaliol, and it is possible that it also is a survival in ceremony of clothing once in general use by this or both divisions of the Toda people.

Many of the older and more important Todas now wear the turban called *madpâri*, but there is no doubt that this is an innovation. The Todas themselves sometimes speak of the Badagas as "they who wear the turban," and it seemed clear that the custom has been adopted in imitation of these people. Harkness and other of the earliest writers state that the Todas never wear any covering to the head, and there is little doubt that the practice has been adopted during the last century.

At the present time a man always removes his turban when performing any act of reverence (see Fig. 10) and when crossing one of the sacred rivers.

Mr. Thurston mentions that on his first visit, the man whom he chose as his guide adopted the turban in honour of his appointment, and my guide, Kòdrner, although much younger than most of those who wore turbans, also adopted this custom when he was with me.

Methods of Wearing the Hair

There are various methods of wearing the hair, each of which has its special significance. The ordinary method for men is to allow it to grow to a certain length, so that it forms a compact mass, as shown by the first man of Fig. 61, or as in Fig. 15.

When a member of a clan dies, all the men of the clan tie their hair in knots in front till the funeral ceremonies are completed. This is called *mad tutvai*, "head (or hair) who rolls," and the second man in Fig. 61 is wearing his hair in this fashion, a girl of his clan having died not long before, whose second funeral ceremonies had not yet taken place.

Another method of wearing the hair is shown by the third man in Fig. 61. This method is called *mad nadrk vai*, "head (or hair) long to who." It is adopted by anyone who

FIG. 62.—TILIPA (12) WEARING HIS HAIR LONG ON ACCOUNT OF A VOW MADE AT A HINDU TEMPLE.

has made a vow. In Fig. 62 another man is shown in the same condition, but his head has a different appearance owing to the fact that he has tied two locks behind in order to keep the long hair away from his face. This tying back has no other significance.

Women wear their hair as shown in Figs. 3 and 11, in long ringlets, and there do not appear to be any differences in the method of wearing the hair under different conditions corresponding to those of males.

After a funeral the Tarthar division of the Todas except the Melgarsol shave their heads, and this may also happen in connexion with vows made at the Hindu temple at Nanjankudi or elsewhere.

The hair of a child is shaved about the third month of life (see p. 332), so that the head has the appearance shown in Figs. 63 and 64. The head is shaved on the top and sides, and in a strip from the top to the forehead, so that three locks are left, two in front, called the *mîkuti* (*? meikuti*), and one behind, called the *kut*.

In the case of a girl, there is some difference in the method of shaving according to the position of the child in the family. If a girl is the eldest of the family, she wears three locks like a boy, but younger girls and the eldest girl, if she should have an elder brother, wear only the two front locks, the *mîkuti*.

SKIN-MARKS

The only kind of skin-mark made on males takes the form of a cicatrix on the right shoulder and, less commonly, on the elbow. It is produced by means of a stick made hot by the drill method of producing fire, exactly as in the production of fire for ceremonial purposes. The operation is not, however, accompanied by any ceremonial and may be performed by anyone. The marks are made when a boy is about twelve years old, at which age he begins to milk the buffaloes. The object of the marking is to cure the pain arising from the fatigue of milking. If the operation has not the desired result and the boy still feels the fatiguing effect of milking, a second mark is made, and occasionally a third or fourth may be necessary. In one case, in which a man had three marks one on the shoulder and two on the elbow, the third mark was not made till he was fifteen or sixteen years of age, three or four years after the first mark had been produced. This was done because, even after this lapse of time, he still suffered from aching in his arm after milking the buffaloes. Another

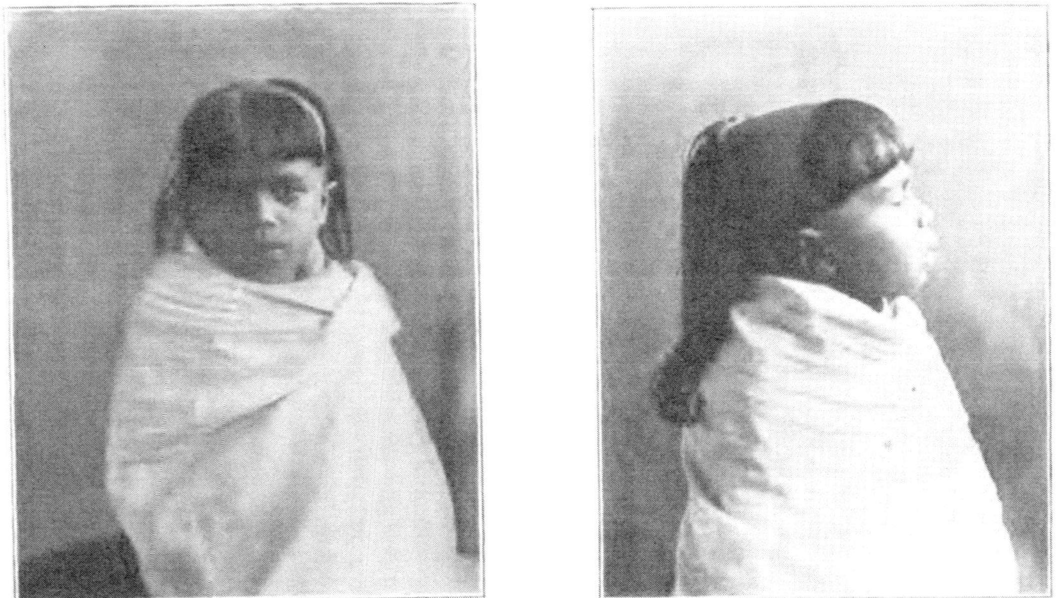

FIGS. 63 AND 64.—TO SHOW METHOD OF SHAVING THE HEAD OF A CHILD.

man had four scars on the shoulder, this being the largest number I observed.

Occasionally I observed a man without any of these scars, and, in more than one of these cases, the reason given was that the man had been one of a large family and had not had to do much milking. The cicatrices are usually raised well above the surrounding skin and are often distinct lumps of scar tissue (keloid). This appears to be the result of special treatment of the burn. A leaf called *kudiers* is put on the wound with butter, and this keeps it open for a considerable time. If the wound remains open too long, another leaf, called *pöturers*, is used to hasten the healing.

Similar, but less raised, marks are occasionally seen on the wrist or elsewhere. In men these are always the result of treatment for pain or illness and are made in the same way by means of a hot stick. Sometimes a metal instrument called *sunurkudi* is now used for this purpose.

The ceremonial burns made on the wrists of women during the first pregnancy have already been fully considered.

Tattooing is only practised by women. The patterns consist of rings and dots arranged in straight lines, and they are most commonly to be seen on the chest, shoulders, and upper parts of the arms.[1]

I believe that there is some kind of ceremonial connected with tattooing, but unfortunately I failed to obtain satisfactory information about it. When I began the subject one day, I received an intimation that it was not a matter to be discussed in public, and later the subject slipped my attention and was never properly investigated.

The tattooing is performed by certain women, but it seemed that any woman who had learned how to tattoo might undertake the business. The following are at present recognised as experts: Achaveli (43), Sinpurs and Edjog (20), Sinpurs being probably the same woman who acts as one of the *utkòren*. The woman who tattoos is given eight or twelve annas and she also receives food.

The tattooing must not take place before puberty, but it may be done either before or after childbirth.

[1] Some patterns are given by Mr. Thurston, *Bulletin*, i. 1896, pl. xii.

Little use is made by the Todas of pigments. The juice of a fruit called *tlpom*, which has a red colour, is sometimes used to adorn the forehead, and another reddish juice from a fruit called *puthimulpom*[1] is used for the same purpose. The yellowish juice of the *pelkurthpom* is rubbed on the face, but this was said to be done in frosty weather only, as a protection against the cold. Ashes are now occasionally rubbed on the face and head, especially by women at the ceremony of going to the seclusion-hut after childbirth. The last is certainly a recently borrowed custom, and I suspect the other adornments just mentioned to be modern imitations of the forehead marks of the Hindus.

Ornaments

The men usually wear silver rings on the fourth digit of one or other hand. Often earrings are worn by the men and these are not uncommonly of gold. Harkness says that men sometimes wore chains of silver round the neck, but it is doubtful whether these are ever worn now. Formerly it seems that men used to wear far more solid rings, and one such ring is preserved which is said to have belonged to the hero or god Kwoten.

The ornaments of the women are more numerous and take the form of bracelets or bangles; armlets, often adorned with bunches of cowries; necklaces, sometimes made of silver coins; earrings; and a brass circlet worn round the waist. These ornaments are usually of brass or silver. At one time they seem to have been very massive, Breeks recording that a pair of brass armlets worn on one arm weighed six pounds. Formerly gold ornaments seem to have been commonly worn, and, so far as one can judge from older accounts and illustrations, it seems that Toda jewellery has greatly degenerated and is of a very paltry kind compared with that worn in the past.

[1] This is the fruit of one of the plants (*Rubus lasiocarpus*) of which the leaves are used in the ordination ceremonies of the dairymen of Taradr and Kanòdrs.

Food

The chief foods are milk, buttermilk, ghi, grain, rice, and sugar. The chief drink is buttermilk, and milk is used chiefly when boiled with rice or grain.

In clarifying their butter the Todas add some grain or rice, and this forms a sediment on the bottom of the cooking vessel which is called *al*, which is the chief food of the dairymen, and it is probably also used largely as a food in ordinary life.

A list of various herbs, fruits, &c., eaten by the Todas is given by Mr. Thurston.[1] There is very little doubt that at one time these were used much more largely than at present, when the grain provided by the Badagas is supplemented by rice and grain bought in the bazaar. The Todas have a tradition of a time when they lived chiefly on roots, herbs, fruits and honey, and the importance of honey comes out in several of their legends.

A much prized substance called *patcherski* is made from *samai* grain (*Panicum miliare*), which is roasted and pounded so as to get rid of the husk. It is used in the preparation of a food which is eaten on all the chief ceremonial occasions. When they prepare it the Todas say "*ashkkartpimi*," and this verbal form is used as the name of the food. In making *ashkkartpimi*, *patcherski* is put into a basket (*tòdri*) which has been carefully cleansed by rubbing it all over with dried buffalo-dung. Buttermilk and jaggery are added and the whole mixed together and rolled into balls, each about as large as a cricket ball. When eating, a hole is made in the ball into which ghi and butter, sometimes honey, are poured, and then the hole is covered with rice.[2] A man will usually eat two of these balls at a feast, but a greedy man may manage three or four.

The Todas do not like others to see them eating, and if this happens, the same consequences may ensue as are

[1] *Bulletin*, vol. iv., p. 16.

[2] *Ashk* is one of the Toda words for rice, and the name of the food is therefore derived from this substance.

produced by the evil eye. Their natural politeness also makes the Todas uncomfortable when they see others eating, and in the early part of my visit I sometimes dispersed a group surrounding me by taking sandwiches out of my pocket and beginning to eat.

I did not ascertain definitely who cooks among the Todas. I had some reason to suppose that all the cooking is done by the men and that the women have nothing to do with this part of domestic economy, but I am not clear about this. It is possible that it is only food containing milk which must be cooked by the men.

The Todas are an example of a people who have no native intoxicant, but they have now taken to alcoholic drinks, though I do not believe that they indulge in these habitually. The only occasions on which I saw Todas under the influence of alcohol were when they were returning from the bazaar on market days. I was only once asked by a Toda for alcohol and then by a woman. Tobacco is now largely used and opium is certainly also used, though I do not believe that it is taken in excess. It may be employed, however, as a means of committing suicide.

FIRE-MAKING

We have already seen that the fire used for several sacred purposes must be made by friction with the fire-sticks. The method employed is a variety of the drill method shown in Figs. 65 and 37. In the former the *wursol* of Taradr is making fire in order to enable me to procure a photograph; the latter is the result of a snapshot taken when the fire was being produced during a ceremony. In the horizontal stick, which is held firmly by the foot, a hole is made for the insertion of the vertical stick, and in this a little charcoal is placed. A small groove is cut on one side to assist the falling of the spark on the tinder beneath. The vertical stick is inserted into the hole and twirled between the two hands. In the only case in which I saw fire produced by friction in a ceremony (Fig. 37), the continued efforts of the two old men were unavailing, and a third younger man was called upon, and with a few powerful manipulations he was rapidly successful.

Several kinds of wood are used for the fire-sticks, the Toda names of these being *kiaz* or *keadj*, *mòrs*, *parskuti*, and *main*. Only the first of these, however, may be used if fire is being

FIG. 65.—KAROL (64), THE 'WURSOL' OF TARADR, MAKING FIRE.

made for sacred purposes, and I was told that it was much easier to make fire with this than with any other.

In some Toda villages a stone is kept called *tütmükal*, which was used at one time for making fire by striking it with a piece of iron. Probably this method was employed for non-sacred purposes in the period between giving up the fire-sticks for ordinary purposes and the introduction of matches.

The Todas have two kinds of fireplace, the *waskal*, consisting of three stones, and the *kudrvars*, with four stones. The former is found in the dwelling-hut, in the *wursuli*, and in the *ti* dairy, and the latter in the *tarvali* and *kudrpali*; but I did not discover why the more sacred dairies should have the same kind of fireplace as the house. According to one account *waskal* is the name used by the Teivaliol and *kudrvars* by the Tartharol, and it may be that this is the explanation of the apparent anomaly.

THE HOUSE

Various parts of the house have definite names, and may only be used for certain purposes. As we have already seen, there are raised seats both outside and inside the house, the latter being used as beds. These are made of earth, the upper surface of which is made level, and the whole is usually well coated with a layer of dried buffalo-dung, sometimes nearly half an inch thick. The general name for these raised parts is *tün*, the seats outside the building on either side of the door being called *kwottün*, while the bed on the right side of the interior is the *meitün*, and that on the left side the *kitün*. The part of the hut where the bed or beds stand is called the *idrtul*.

The floor is called *kuter*, and this is divided into two parts by the hole in which the women pound the grain. The part near the door is called *kikuter*, and it is in this part only that dairy operations may be carried on. The part behind the pounding hole is especially assigned to the women and is called *meilkuter*.[1]

The end wall, on which various objects, such as sticks, are kept is called *tashten*, and the fireplace, usually on one side, is called *waskal*. The part above the fireplace where firewood is kept is called *waskalkûbi*, and the place of the cooking vessels is called *adikudi*. The western side of the hut is sometimes called the *meilmakol*, and the eastern side the

[1] It might have been expected that the part of the floor near the door used for the dairy operations would be the *meilkuter*, but it is not so. *Meil* also means 'west' and the explanation may be connected with this.

kimakol, but I do not know if this implies any rule as to the orientation of the houses.

The method of building is illustrated by Fig. 66, which shows a hut only partially built. Certain Todas have special reputations as architects, and the most famous of these at the present time is Kijievan (50), who superintended the building of the hut at Kiudr shown in Fig. 7, the most spacious and artistic of the strictly Toda dwellings which I saw on the

FIG. 66.—TO SHOW A STAGE IN THE CONSTRUCTION OF A HUT.

hills. Especial care is often taken with the arrangement of the rattan on the front of the hut, which is shown in Fig. 20. This is a picture of a dairy, but it shows the arrangement which is also found in the best of the houses.

The hut used for the seclusion of women before and after childbirth is a rough structure of wood and thatch, but its name, *puzhars*, means "mud house," which suggests that huts made of earth may at one time have been used by the Todas.

IMPLEMENTS AND UTENSILS

The most important objects in the economic life of the Todas are their dairy vessels, which have been already amply considered. Cooking vessels and implements used for cutting wood or for any other purpose are, like the vessels of the village dairy, procured chiefly from the Kotas, though at the present time the source of supply is probably supplemented by purchases in the bazaar.

As the Todas practise few arts, their need of implements is very small. At one time they used thorns as needles, but now steel needles have taken their place. Thorns are also used for tattooing. Leaves are used as plates and cups, and the fingers take the place of forks. The only definite implements used are knives and axes, the latter being especially needed for procuring firewood.

In some of their ceremonies, the Todas have preserved practices which may possibly be survivals of the use of stone implements. In the funeral ceremonies the buffaloes destined for the next world are killed with the back of an axe, but the buffaloes killed at the *koòtiti* ceremony and at the ceremony of purifying the funeral places must be killed with a stone. Further, the bark of the *tudr* tree used in so many ceremonies must always be knocked off the tree by means of a stone. The latter of these practices must certainly be very ancient, and may well be a relic of an age in which implements were made of stone.

THE POUNDER, SIEVE, AND BROOM

The interest of these articles lies in the fact that they are evidently regarded as the emblems of woman. When the *wursol* sleeps in the village hut, these articles are removed from the hut, and when the *ti* buffaloes pass the village of Kiudr, the women who leave this village take with them the pounder, sieve, and broom.

In the case of the *wursol*, this sacred personage may associate with the women themselves if the three objects which seem to be emblematic of womanhood are removed.

The pounder, sieve, and broom are burnt at the funerals of women, who use the pounder on their journey to the other world. A special kind of sieve called *kudshmurn* is also burnt at the *azaramkedr*, but I believe that this is burnt at all funerals, both of males and females.

The pounder, sieve, and broom are widely endowed with magical properties, and this is especially the case in India,[1] but I do not know of any other instance in which they are especially regarded as the emblems of woman.

WEAPONS

At the present time it cannot be said that the Todas use any weapons, but they retain in their ceremonies weapons which were, no doubt, formerly in use. These are the club and the bow and arrow.

The club only remains in the funeral ceremonies, in which it is called *nanmakud* (see Fig. 67), and is burnt at the *azaramkedr*, and several other special sticks are also burnt, which may have been of the nature of clubs.

The bow and arrow have left more traces of their former importance. They are burnt at the *azaramkedr* of a man, and the weapons for this purpose are provided by the Kotas. The bow and arrow are also used in the *koðtiti* ceremony of a Tarthar funeral. In the *pursütpimi* ceremony the husband gives an imitation bow and arrow to his wife. The bow gives its name to the ceremony and its gift forms the essential incident of the ceremony. Further, the bow has a special name different for each clan. The use of an arrow lingers in name in other ceremonies. In the *erkumptthpimi* ceremony, the knife used for cutting up the sacrificed calf is called *ab*, or arrow. In the ceremony of *tersamptpimi* a lock of hair is cut from a young child with a piece of sharpened iron called *kanab*, or "eye arrow," but this name is only in use among the Tartharol. The use of these words seems to point to a time when iron-tipped arrows were used as cutting instruments, and it is even possible that this is a survival of a time when

[1] See Crooke's *Popular Religion and Folk-Lore of Northern India*, 1896, vol. ii. pp. 187–191.

the Todas were so much isolated that their only iron was that of the tips of their arrows.

The bow and arrow are also mentioned in the legend of

FIG. 67 (FROM BREEKS).—THE FIRST MAN ON THE LEFT IS HOLDING A BOW AND ARROW; THE SECOND A CLUB (PROBABLY THE 'NANMAKUD') IN HIS RIGHT HAND, AND THE 'TADRI' IN HIS LEFT; THE THIRD MAN IS CARRYING A CLUB, AND THE FOURTH MAN IS PLAYING THE 'BUGURI.'

Kwoten. Teikuteidi was killed by an arrow shot by a lame man who lay down when he shot. It is possible that this legend points to an ancient custom of shooting the bow and arrow by means of the legs.

Measures and Numerals

The Toda measure of length is the *mogai* or *mogoi*, which corresponds to the cubit, being the length from the elbow to the tips of the fingers. The word is probably related to *mogal*, the term for fore-arm.

The usual measure of capacity for liquids is the *kudi*, said to be equal to about four pints. Another measure is the *kòni*, two of which make one *kudi*. The *kòni* probably corresponds to the milking vessel, or *pun*.

For measuring out grain, the Todas use a special table of measures consisting of *âk* and *kwâ*, eleven *âk* making one *kwâ*. When measuring out grain, modifications of the ordinary numerals are used.

In the following lines I give these on the right-hand side of the page, those on the left being the ordinary numerals. *Urâk* is the equivalent of *ud âk*, or one measure.

ud	one	*ûrâk*
erd	two	*îrâk*
mûd	three	*mûk*
nonk	four	*oponi*
udz	five	*oiâk*
âr	six	*ârâk*
ö or *eu*	seven	*öâk* or *euâk*
öt	eight	*ötâk*
unpoth	nine	*unpâk*
poth	ten	*pothâk*
ponud	eleven	*ukwâ*
ponerd	twelve	*ponerdâk*
ponmûd	thirteen	*ponmûdâk*
ponnonk or *pânk*	fourteen	*ponnonkâk*
ponudz or *podz*	fifteen	*ponudzâk*
pâr	sixteen	*pârâk*
pö or *pör*	seventeen	*pöâk*
pût	eighteen	*pûtâk*
ponpoth	nineteen	*ponpothâk*
evoth	twenty	*evothâk*
evoth ud	twenty-one	*evothudâk* (doubtful)
evoth erd	twenty-two	*ikwâ*
evoth mûd	twenty-three	*ikwâ ûrâk*
:	:	:
:	:	:

mopoth	thirty	*ikwâ ötâk*
:	:	:
:	:	:
mopoth mûd	thirty-three	*mûkhwâ*
:	:	:
:	:	:
nâpoth	forty	*mûkhwâ öâk*
:	:	:
:	:	:
nâpoth nmk	forty-four	*nâkhwâ*
:	:	:
:	:	:
epoth	fifty	*nâkhwâ ârâk*
:	:	:
:	:	:
epoth udz	fifty-five	*aiiwâ*
:	:	:
:	:	:
âroth	sixty	*aiiwâ oiâk*
:	:	:
:	:	:
âroth âr	sixty-six	*ârwâ*
:	:	:
:	:	:
övoth	seventy	*ârwâ oponi*
:	:	:
:	:	:
övoth ö	seventy-seven	*ökwâ*
:	:	:
:	:	:
ötvoth	eighty	*ökwâ mâk*
:	:	:
:	:	:
ötvoth öt	eighty-eight	*ötkwâ*
:	:	:
:	:	:
unvoth	ninety	*ötkwâ ârâk*
:	:	:
:	:	:
unvoth unpoth	ninety-nine	*unpawâ*
:	:	:
:	:	:
anâr	hundred	*unpawâ ud*

Above a hundred the numbers of *kwâ* are continued to *potkwâ*, *ponudkwâ*, &c., up to twenty *kwâ*, which make one *siligh*, and then the people begin again at the beginning.

This occurrence of the number eleven is probably a consequence of the transactions between Todas and Badagas.

There was some reason to believe that the true Toda measure is the *âk* (probably a contraction of *achok*) and that the Badagas brought their grain to the Todas in vessels called *kwâ*. The *kwâ* contained eleven of the Toda *âk*, and hence came about the very unusual proportion between two measures.

In giving ages or any other period of time, the word for year, *kwòdr*, is often abbreviated to *wâ*; thus *nâpoth kwòdr*, forty years, becomes *nâpothwâ*.

In counting the Todas use their fingers largely and have a special method of indicating the numbers. To signify one, the thumb is placed against the tip of the little finger; for two, against the tip of the ring finger; for three, against the middle finger; for four, against the forefinger; for five, the tip of the index finger is placed over the nail of the thumb; the same position is used for six, while that for seven is the same as for four, and so on, so that when ten is reached the thumb is resting again on the tip of the little finger.

Money

The Todas use the ordinary Indian currency. In their legends and ceremonies there is frequent reference to the *panm*, or four-anna piece.

Among the coins used by the Todas at the funeral ceremonies there are many of considerable age with Arabic inscriptions, and the earlier visitors to the hills describe the Todas as possessing old Venetian gold pieces. In the legend telling how the *kaltmokh* of the Nòdrs *ti* dispersed the invading Coorgs (p. 114), the boy made use of a small gold coin called *pirpanm*, which he had in his possession.

The Calendar

The Todas have twelve months, each of which begins with the new moon. The first month of the Toda year is *Tai*, which begins with the new moon in October, so that this month usually includes part of October and part of November. Some of the chief Toda ceremonies, such as that of *teutüt-*

usthchi and the more important ceremonies of *erkumptthpimi*, take place soon after the new moon marking the commencement of this month, and these ceremonies were sometimes said to signalise the beginning of a new year. The following are the names of the Toda months, with the periods of our year to which they approximately correspond:—

Tai	October—November
Emioti	November—December
Kûdrl	December—January
Alâni	January—February
Nalâni	February—March
Âni	March—April
Âtheri	April—May
Âdi	May—June
Ovâni	June—July
Peritâthi	July—August
Tudeivi	August—September
Kirdivi	September—October.

Each month has thirty days. A record is kept of the number of days from one new moon to the full moon, and from that to the next new moon. The full moon is counted as being on the fifteenth day after the new moon, and the new moon as being on the sixteenth day after the full moon.

The Week

The names for the days of the week are as follows:—

Âsvom	Sunday
Tûvom	Monday
Òm	Tuesday
Pûthvom	Wednesday
Tâm	Thursday
Pîlivom	Friday
Thanivom or *Tanivom*	Saturday.

According to Schmid, who wrote in 1837, *Òm* is regarded as the first day of the week. Schmid also notes that the names for Wednesday, Friday, and Saturday agree in etymology with Tamil, Wednesday being Buddha's day and Friday the day of Venus. He gives *Etnat* as an alternative name for Saturday.

Astronomical Ideas

We have already seen that the Todas reverence the sun, and that the period of the moon is of the greatest importance in the regulation of the times for their ceremonies. In this chapter we have to deal with their views as to the nature of these bodies and of the stars.

The Sun

The Todas believe that when the sun goes down in the west, it goes to Amnòdr. The same sun illuminates both worlds, and this is shown very well in the story of Kwoto; when this demi-god tied down the sun, there was darkness both in this world and in the other, and the people of Amnòdr joined with those of this world in imploring that the sun should be restored to its proper place.

When the Todas know that there is going to be an eclipse of the sun, they abstain from food, but they do not shout out during the eclipse as we shall see they do in the case of the moon. When the eclipse is over, they have a feast with *ashkkartpimi*.

The Moon

The new moon is called *mut* and the full moon *nërv*. We have already seen the enormous influence of the period of the moon in Toda ceremonial and I have given above the method of counting between the periods of new and full moon so as to know the correct day of the new moon if for any reason it should not be visible.

The Todas see a figure in the moon which they call *mürs*, the hare.[1] The following story not only shows how the hare comes to be there, but also furnishes the explanation of eclipses of the moon and the origin of the Paikara river.[2]

Two men who were *matchuni* (see p. 501) went out one day to fetch honey. After a time they separated, and one

[1] In India the marks on the moon are frequently supposed to represent a hare.

[2] For another version of this story obtained by Mr. Thurston, see *Bulletin*, iv. p. 1.

found honey, while the other found none. The man who found the honey put it into a dairy vessel called *pun*, which he hid in a tree, and when he met the other did not tell him of his good fortune. After a time the *pun* containing honey which had been put in the tree suddenly broke, and the vessel became a snake, while the honey became the Paikara river. The snake ran after the man who had hidden the honey, and when the man saw the snake coming after him, he ran away. As he was being pursued, a hare came between the man and the snake. Then the man threw his cloak over the hare and hid himself, and the snake ran after the hare. The hare ran to the sky followed by the snake, and they came near the sun, which said, "Don't come near me because I am very hot. Go to the moon!" So the hare went to the moon, and the moon said, "Do not be afraid; I will protect you till the end of the world." The snake still goes sometimes to catch the hare in the moon, and when he goes the moon becomes dark and some people fire guns and send up rockets and the Todas shout. When it is known that there is going to be an eclipse the Todas abstain from food, and when they see the moon being eclipsed they shout out.

I was told that there was another incident of the story connected with shooting stars, but I was unable to obtain an account of it.

Planets

The Todas know Venus, which they call *Pili*, and they also speak of the "morning star."

Constellations and Stars

The Todas have names for several stars or constellations. The Pleiades are called *Kadsht* and the constellation is believed to be composed of six stars.

Another heavenly body which I could not identify is called *Keirt*. *Keirt* has already been mentioned in Chap. XIV., and it is the evil influence of this body which is chiefly feared after childbirth. It is said to be a star which is never present in the same part of the sky as *Kadsht*. The reason for this is that once *Keirt* and *Kadsht* fought together. *Kadsht* had six men and *Keirt* only one. *Keirt* broke the leg of one of the six men, so that now there are five stars close together in the Pleiades and one lags behind. On account of this quarrel Swami ruled that *Kadsht* and *Keirt* must never be together, but that when *Kadsht* is on one side of the sky, *Keirt* must always be on the other.

When talking about *Keirt* in connexion with the ceremony of going to the seclusion-hut, it was said that *Keirt* was near the sun and that the sun was dangerous because *Keirt* was near it. It seemed that *Keirt* was always near the sun, which led me to suspect at first that it was Venus. It was quite clear, however, that this was not so. No one could show me *Keirt*, nor was anyone clear as to the part of the sky in which it was to be seen at any time in the night, and I think it most probable that this mysterious inhabitant of the sky is not a star at all, but a being allied to the Hindu *Ketu*. On the other hand, at a funeral attended by Samuel, the setting of *Kadsht* and the appearance of *Keirt* was taken as the sign that the proceedings of the *azaramkedr* might begin, which looks as if *Keirt* was a real heavenly body. I think it is most probable that the whole idea of the injurious influence of *Keirt* is borrowed from the Badagas, and, if this is the case, the Toda word is probably merely an altered form of *Ketu*. I was told that *Keirt* was a Badaga word and that the Badagas feared its influence on women after childbirth.

A group of stars called *Pòdimin*, or porcupine star, corresponds to the stars in the sword of Orion. They are regarded as a porcupine from which the three stars of the belt are trying to escape.

A constellation of seven stars is called *Katikâlmin*. From the description it appeared to be the Great Bear. This constellation was not visible, but when I made a drawing of its seven chief stars, it was at once recognised as *Katikâlmin*.

A single star called *Ishtkati* is almost certainly Sirius.

This star was not visible in the evenings during my visit, and at first Jupiter was pointed out to me as *Ishtkati*, but this was certainly wrong. *Ishtkati* appeared to correspond to the Badaga *etukaḍichi*, which means "bull deceiving." The origin of the name is that one night a Badaga went out from his house and saw a very bright star, so bright that he thought it was the morning star. So he let his bulls out from the enclosure in which he had put them for the night. When a long time passed and it did not become day, the man said, "Let the star be called *etukaḍichi*."

A pair of stars to which the Todas give the names of *Tüdrvalmokh* and *Tidiishti* are near Aldebaran, forming part of the Hyades (probably γ and ϵ Tauri). The following story tells how these stars come to be in the sky.

Once on the hills there was a bird with young. The mother went away to get food and a snake came to eat the young ones. When the young birds saw the snake climbing up the tree, they called out to Kudursami, who is above. He heard their cry and took them to the sky. The name of the bird was *tüdrval*, and so one star is called *tüdrvalmokh*. The *tüdrval* still sings "*Kudursami trrrrrr*."

According to another version, the bird *tüdrval* had offended Swami, and as a punishment Swami took its young and they became the two stars.

This story appears to be a well-known Indian folk-tale, and it has certainly been a recent acquisition of the Todas.

It will be seen that there is much reason to believe that the greater part, if not all of the ideas of the Todas about the stars have been borrowed. In their own folk-lore there seems to be very little concerning the heavenly bodies except in the story of the man and the honey, and I even suspect this to be a borrowed legend which has been somewhat modified by Toda ideas.

It is interesting, and I think important, that references to Swami occur in these stars-myths. In an earlier chapter I have given it as my opinion that the idea of Swami has only recently been acquired by the Todas, and I attach importance to the occurrence of the name in legends which have certainly been borrowed from another race.

GAMES

It is not altogether easy to draw the line between Toda games and Toda ceremonies. The sport which is practised with the greatest zest is undoubtedly the catching of the buffaloes at the funeral ceremonies, and in the old days when the *marvainolkedr* lasted two days, the first day, devoted to catching the buffaloes and putting them in the pen, must have been largely of a sportive character. Even now it is evident that the catching of the buffaloes is a spectacle which is much enjoyed by all in spite of the sad event which has led to its taking place.

The Todas have, however, pure games, though it is doubtful whether some of them have not acquired in a certain degree a ceremonial character.

In one of these games called *narthpimi*, a boy squeezes through a narrow tunnel formed by a flat slab of stone over two upright slabs. Two boys start from different distances, and the object of the nearer boy is to squeeze through the tunnel before the other can touch his feet. I did not have an opportunity of seeing this game, and I only saw the stones with which it is played at one village. This was at Nòdrs, where the three stones are called *menkars* and mark the spot at which one of the ordinary buffaloes is killed at the funeral ceremonies. The *menkars* is shown in Fig. 12 in front of and a little to the right of the entrance to the dairy.

Another game resembling tip-cat is called *eln*, and at some villages there is a special stone where the game is played. A piece of wood pointed at both ends is propped against the stone and struck with a stick, and should be caught by some-one at a distance. The name for this game is probably Badaga,[1] and this suggests that the game has been borrowed from this people.

According to Breeks another game called *kàriàlapimi*, resembling 'puss in the corner,' is played by the Todas. The name suggests a true Toda game and I regret that I know nothing about it.

[1] The game is described by Breeks and Thurston under the name of *ilata*, but this again is certainly not Toda.

One day I observed a stone near the village of Pakhalkudr, and, asking whether it was for tip-cat, was told of a different game. If a man jumped high enough at the stone, he could see the top of a certain hill. On jumping at the stone I could not see the hill, but by going a little way back, I found that it became visible, and as far as I could judge, the jump necessary at the stone would be a possible though a good performance.

At many villages there is a large globular stone called *tukitthkars* (lifted stone) and in another of the Toda games this stone is lifted. A man should be able to lift it to the shoulder, but this can now rarely, if ever, be done, and some of the stones can only be lifted a little way from the ground. Mr. Thurston saw the stone at Nòdrs lifted as high as the pit of the stomach. These stones seem to afford clear evidence of the degeneration of the Todas in physical strength. There is little doubt that they could be lifted much better by the Todas of a generation or two ago. Thus there is a stone at Nidrsi which was brought by the grandfather of Kudrmaskutan (43) in the pocket of his *putkùli* from a place called Attibadi at a considerable distance from Nidrsi. At the present time no Toda can do more than lift the stone a little way from the ground. The *tukitthkars* may not be lifted either on the *madnol* or the *palinol*. Feasts are prohibited on these days, and it is probable that the stone was often lifted on festive occasions. There is evidence that, in some places at any rate, the stone has acquired in some degree a sacred character. Thus, at the village of Kiudr, one of the most sacred of Toda dairies, the *tukitthkars* lies on a raised wall surrounding the dairy and in this situation would most certainly acquire some of the sanctity of its surroundings.

The Todas are very interested in athletic feats performed by any of their number and sometimes put up memorials of such feats. Thus, at Pishkwosht there are two stones marking the distance once jumped by a Toda. Such an athletic feat may be made the subject of a bet. Thus, four generations ago, one of the ancestors of Kudrmaskutan (43) jumped a stream called Kavageir, winning eighteen *nakh* (three-year-old buffaloes) from a Badaga by doing so. Bets of this kind are probably only made with Badagas, and betting is almost certainly not properly a Toda custom.

In addition to developed games, the Todas, and especially the children, often play with mimic representations of objects from practical life. Near the villages I have seen small artificial buffalo-pens and fireplaces made by the children in sport. On the hill of Mirson, where the chief council used to be held, I found a small pen, well built and with a gate, and was assured that it was made in sport by the children only a few years ago. This hill is one on which there are many cairns and such mimic representations may possibly mystify some future archæologist.

The commonest toys with which the children play are little imitation buffalo horns made of wood (see Fig. 35). In the legend, the boy Kuzkarv played with such horns, and even little children in arms may be seen fondling these play-things. The horns are burnt with the body at the funeral ceremonies, but only at those of males, though this rule was infringed at the funeral of Sinerani. In the funeral lament for his wife Teitnir speaks of their playing with imitation horns and imitation bracelets, so that adults evidently amuse themselves in this way as well as children.

Another imitation sport I have often seen is that of boys or youths hanging on the horns and round the necks of buffaloes exactly as is done when catching the animals at the funeral ceremonies. The skill shown at these ceremonies is probably the result of long practice in play of this kind.

Nearly all thes mes are connected in some way with the buffalo or the dairy, in some cases only remotely, as when the *menkars* of Nòdrs is used for the *narthpimi* game, while the *tukitthkars* may be kept by the dairy. Only one of the games so far described is wholly unconnected with the dairy, and this, the *eln* game, has a name which suggests that it has been borrowed.

Though the Todas have, as we see, a fair number of games, they are not much given to playing them. I never saw one of the more developed games in progress, and this formed a great contrast to my previous ethnological experience in Torres Straits, where hardly a day would pass without seeing games being played.

The chief interest in the case of the Todas is the clear evidence they give of games arising owing to the sportive imitation by children of the more serious occupations of their elders. In some of these cases the games so arising are useful in providing the younger members of the community with practice in feats which they will in later life be called upon to perform.

RIDDLES

The Todas are very fond of riddles, which they call ***werat***. The following are examples :—

Mers	*illâth*	*karthti,*	*poi*	*illâth*	*âdti?*	*Mâ,*	*neln.*
Udder	without	milks,	mouth	without	drinks?	Rain,	earth.

I.e., What is it that gives milk without an udder, what is it that drinks without a mouth? Rain, earth.

Urk	*mers*	*illâth,*	*kâdak*	*kal*	*illâth,*	*athinu?*	*Kûdi,*	*pob.*
In (or to) village	udder	without,	in forest	leg	without,	what is it?	Hen,	snake.

Kerûd	*mokh*	*perûd*	*aiu,*	*perûd*	*mokh*	*kerûd*	*aiu?*	*Kûdr,*	*kevi.*
Little	son	big	becomes,	big	son	little	becomes?	Horn,	ear.

This riddle depends on a comparison of the horn and ear of the buffalo. The horn of the calf is very small, the ear is relatively large.

Pûv	*pûvadi,*	*kaim*	*kaimadi?*	*Tâf.*
Flower	does not blossom,	berry	does not ripen?	Fern.

Wûrûdr	*nolm,*	*mokh*	*pachtam,*	*pîr ârchtam,*	*ithithanithi*	*ank?*	*Pishkimän.*
Whole year	days,	son	begetting,	pregnant,	this is custom	to it?	

Pishkimän is a tree which bears flowers or is giving fruit the whole year round.

Puzhârḍuûdr	*adetpoloḍthi?*	*Kûdi*	*kûgiti.*
Calls out if	why that says no?	Cock	crows.

What is it that calls out and no one replies? The cock.

Nelu	*tiri*	*kai,*	*pon*	*tiri*	*pûv?*	*Eln.*
Earth	goes round	fruit,	sky	goes round	flower?	The tip-cat game.

Mudâl	*pir*	*vatvai,*	*pin*	*marsvati;*	*pin*	*pir*
First	pregnant	who becomes,	later	is delivered;	later	pregnant

vatvai,	*mudâl*	*marsvati?*	*Tâmi,*	*kodj.*
who becomes,	first	is delivered?	A grain,	barley.

Tami or *samai* (*patm*) is the grain from which *patcherski*, one of the chief Toda foods, is made. It shows above the ground later than barley, but is reaped earlier.

I did not hear of any mechanical puzzles or tricks used by the Todas, and it was quite clear that they had no knowledge of cat's-cradle.

Poetry and Music

I have given two samples of Toda poetry in the chapter on funeral ceremonies. These are the chief occasions on which songs are composed, but they are also made when a new dairy is being built, and may be composed and sung on any festive occasion. The general name for compositions of this kind is *kunedsti*, and certain men have special reputations as composers. The most noted of recent times was a man named Mervoin belonging to the family of Kiugi.

Of those now living, Teitnir, whose two funeral songs I have given, is a noted composer, and I was told of six other men who were especially gifted in this way.

Though I have called these compositions songs, they should, perhaps, rather be called recitations. They are certainly not songs with any musical accompaniment. I understood, though I am not clear about this, that the clauses, or *kwarzam*, of the funeral poems are said in a low voice "in the throat," so that they are not understood by the people who hear them. If this is correct, the funeral *kwarzam* resemble in this respect those of which the prayers consist.

The Toda poets also compose songs on any festive

occasion, and Mr. Thurston[1] has recorded examples of several such compositions.

Dancing takes place at the funeral ceremonies, and exhibitions of these or other dances are sometimes given by the Todas. The only dancing I saw was at a funeral and it was of the simplest possible description, the men who took part forming a circle and moving slowly round and round.

The only musical instrument of the Todas is a simple flute, called the *buguri*. It is shown in Fig. 68, where it is being played by the man on the right. The instrument is not much used by the Todas and is not, so far as I know played on any ceremonial occasion. The music at the funeral ceremonies is always performed by Kotas.

[1] *Bull.* iv. p. 7.

CHAPTER XXV

LANGUAGE

My chief purpose in writing this chapter is to give information which, I hope, may increase the value of the linguistic material which is scattered throughout this book, and especially to describe some of the doubts and difficulties which I encountered in my attempts to reduce the Toda language to writing.

At the end of the chapter I give some new facts relating to the sacred and secret languages of the Todas, and I will begin with a brief sketch of the views commonly held on the linguistic position of the Toda language.

The Nilgiri Hills are situated at the point of junction of three of the chief linguistic districts of Southern India. In the country on the South and East, Tamil is spoken ; on the West, the language is Malayalam, and the people of Mysore to the North speak chiefly Canarese. The Todas live at this meeting-place of three languages, but owing to their isolated position their language is not a blend of these, but has very definite and distinctive characters of its own, as might, indeed, be expected from the character of the people. The Badagas with whom the Todas have much intercourse speak a corrupt form of Canarese, and the Todas have undoubtedly borrowed many words from their language.

Previous writers have differed in their views on the special affinities of the Toda language. No one has now, I think, any doubt that the language is Dravidian. Bernhard Schmid,[1] who wrote in 1837, appears to me to have known more of

[1] *Madras Journ. Lit. and Sci.*, 1837, vol. v. p. 155.

the true Toda language than anyone who has written since, and he ascribed two-thirds of the Toda vocabulary to Tamil and was unable to trace the remaining third to any other language. Caldwell[1] believed the language of the Todas to be most closely allied to Tamil. According to Pope[2] the language was originally old Canarese with the addition of a few Tamil forms, but he has included in his vocabulary words which have probably been borrowed from the Badagas.

The linguistic material which I have collected is far more extensive than that which was available at the time Pope wrote his sketch, and though the material is in one way less satisfactory since it has been collected after thirty more years of Toda intercourse with the outside world, it is in another way more satisfactory than any previous material in that by far the larger part of it is derived from the formulæ used in the religious ceremonies and in magic. It is, of course, well known that an ancient language may linger on in religious and magical formulæ long after it has disappeared from ordinary speech, and when I discovered how many of these formulæ were preserved by the Todas, I made a point of collecting as many as possible in the hope that they might preserve relics of the ancient speech of the Todas.

In collecting this material I suffered under grave disadvantages; firstly in not being a phonologist, and secondly, in my ignorance of any Dravidian language. I had had, however, a fairly large experience in taking down unwritten languages phonetically, and, whatever the errors into which I have fallen, I hope that they are consistent throughout my record. As a matter of fact, I find my spelling to be fairly constant, words taken down from different individuals and on different occasions being written in the same way.

From one point of view my ignorance of Dravidian languages is not an unmixed evil. When anyone hears a language which is allied to one he knows, it is almost impossible to avoid being influenced by this knowledge. This

[1] *A Comparative Grammar of the Dravidian Languages*, 2nd ed., London, 1875, p. 557.

[2] *Outlines of the Tuḍa Grammar* appended to Marshall's *Phrenologist among the Todas.*

influence has not been escaped by some of those who have previously recorded words from the Toda language. Thus in his *Comparative Dictionary of non-Aryan Languages of India and Higher Asia*,[1] Hunter gives two vocabularies from different sources which he calls Toḍuva and Toḍa, and from the differences between these he thought they might be different dialects. According to Breeks these differences are due to the fact that the compiler of one vocabulary paid exclusive attention to the sounds he heard, while the compiler of the other was influenced by his knowledge of the derivation of the words. I have very little doubt that many of those who have recorded Toda words have not written them down exactly as the Todas said them, but as they ought to have said them according to the usual rules of Dravidian pronunciation.

We find, in consequence, very great diversity in the spelling of Toda words, and when there is agreement, it is of very little value, for many of those who have written on the Todas have evidently adopted the spellings of previous writers, even when they quite misrepresent the real sounds.

Another difficulty which besets the investigation of the Toda language is the presence of dialectical differences even in the small community of only eight hundred people. Metz[2] noted such differences, and I found undoubted variations in the vocabularies of the two divisions of the Todas (see p. 687) and suspected variations in pronunciation.

Still another difficulty is the large use of sounds, chiefly *sh*, *ch*, and *th*,[3] euphonically inserted in words. Pope notes this as quite a Toda peculiarity, and it adds greatly to the formidable character of this language, though a word of the most appalling complexity may become quite simple when these euphonic (!) sounds are eliminated.

Another of the sources of discrepancies in Toda vocabularies is the influence of the Badagas to which I have already referred. The Todas are a bilingual people speaking Badaga in their intercourse with other races and keeping Toda for

[1] London, 1868.

[2] *Madras Journ. Lit. and Sci.*, 1857, N.S., vol. i., p. 104.

[3] These sounds have usually been omitted in the Toda words as written in this book.

themselves. I have already pointed out that the great majority of the names of Toda places and institutions which have been recorded by previous writers are the Badaga names and not the Toda names, and, as might have been expected, many Badaga words have found their way into previously published Toda vocabularies.

In my own work my procedure was to take down a sentence first through the interpreter, then to go through the words of the sentence one by one asking the Toda to say each word carefully, and often he had to repeat it many times before I could satisfy myself about the nature of the sounds. Often I would get a second or third Toda to say the word, and I have frequently spent many minutes over one word, and have perhaps then been baffled in my attempts to write the word satisfactorily.

I noticed continually that the Toda words as pronounced by my interpreters were quite different in sound from those which came from the mouths of the Todas themselves. This was especially the case with the vowels, and in the addition of the initial *y*, so well known in the Tamil pronunciation of English. So far as I could detect, there was no trace of this initial *y* in Toda, although it occurs occasionally in some of the previously recorded Toda vocabularies.

These differences between the pronunciation of my interpreter and that of the Todas may often be the source of inconsistencies in my record, for on some occasions, owing to lack of time, I was unable to listen carefully to the Todas themselves, and had to content myself with the words given to me by the interpreter.

PHONETICS

In order to indicate the sounds of the Toda language, I have kept as closely as possible to the generally recognised system in use in India, but have been obliged to adopt many more signs than those usually employed.

The vowel sounds which I distinguished were very numerous. The following vowels and diphthongs certainly occurred :

â, a, ä, ê, e, î, i, ô, o, ö, ò, û, u, ü, ai, au, ei, eu, oi.[1] I am doubtful, however, whether in some cases a distinction between two sounds was not due to individual differences of pronunciation or to dialectical differences. This is almost certainly the case with the distinction between *ai* and *oi*. Some other cases which are more complex may be considered in detail.

Â, *ò*, and *o*. The first two sounds are often interchanged with one another. There is no doubt that the usual *â* of some Dravidian languages becomes *ò* in Toda, as in the change from *nâḍ* to *nòḍr*, and most previous writers have regarded this change as constant, and have used the sign *â* for the sound which the Todas undoubtedly pronounce like the *aw* of the English word 'law.' I should much have liked to follow their example, and by so doing could have avoided the introduction of a new sign for the Toda sound, a sound for which there appears to be no generally recognised symbol in the phonetic systems used by anthropologists. I could not do so, however, because the Todas sometimes use the true *â* sound. There are certain words which are always pronounced with exactly the same sound as in the English word 'father,' and I never heard these words pronounced otherwise. In some cases there is a definite reason why this should be so. Thus the Toda word for 'again' is *mâr*, and I never heard this word uttered otherwise than as I have written it. If it had undergone the common transformation it would have become *mòr*, the *ti* word for buttermilk, and in one case at least there would have been occasion for misunderstanding, for one of the salt-giving ceremonies is called *mârup* or 'again salt,' while another is called *mòrup* or 'buttermilk salt.' The syllable also occurs in the words *pâtatmâr* and *ertatmâr*, and is never pronounced in these words otherwise than as I have written it. On the other hand, there are certain words in which the sound is always that of *ò*, and in other cases the two sounds are undoubtedly interchanged, and in the latter case I have usually adopted the spelling in *â*. A good example of this is *pârs* or *pòrs*, milk, for which

[1] For equivalents of these signs in English words see the Phonetic System at the beginning of the book.

I have throughout adopted the former spelling, though it is quite as often called *pòrs*.

The *ò* is often shortened into *o*, and this is especially the case with the word for 'man.' The general Dravidian form of this word is *âḷ*, but in Toda it becomes *ò̤ḷ* or *oḷ* (which I write as *ol*), and in compound words, such as *palol* and *wursol*, it is always, or nearly always, pronounced so as to be indistinguishable from the *o* of the English word 'olive.' The long *ô* is not a very frequent sound in Toda.

A and ä. The sign *a* is used, in accordance with the general Indian practice, for the sound of the English word 'hut,' one of the commonest of Toda sounds. It is undoubtedly interchanged sometimes with the sound of the English word 'hat,' for which I use the sign *ä*. In such cases of interchange, I use the sign *a* in preference, but when I always heard the *ä* sound, I have used it. It seemed to me that this sound was especially frequent in proper names, as in that of the village Päm and in such words as Kän.

Û and u. These are used for the sounds of the words 'moon' and 'full,' and both are of frequent occurrence. The short form seems occasionally to be changed into *a*; thus, the word *mun* means 'maternal uncle,' but the word for 'sister's son' is *manmokh*. This is a good instance of the value of vowel sounds in Toda; the *mankugh* is the sister's daughter, but the *munkugh* is the name of the daughter of a maternal uncle. The two words which resemble one another so closely have two very different meanings, those of niece and cousin.

Ê and ei. I use *ê* for the sound of the *ei* in the English word 'their.' *Ei* is the sign which I use for the long *ä* of the English word 'date.' A sound for which I often use this sign is one which gave me a great deal of trouble. In it the vowel sound is prolonged so as to form almost a dissyllable, and in my earlier records I wrote it *êe*, the first *ê* having the sound of the *ei* in 'their.' I decided later to use *ei*, though I acknowledge it is not at all a satisfactory representation of the sound I heard.

Î. The only point on which I have to remark about this sound is that it is sometimes prolonged so as to become a dissyllable as in the example already mentioned. In one case, the word *mīis*, used in the *erkumptthpimi* ceremony, this prolongation of the sound is so marked and so constant that I have preserved a record of it in the spelling, but in most cases I have been content to indicate it by *ī* only.

Eu and ö. I use the former sign for a sound which seemed to me very much like the French *eu*. It often resembled very closely the German *ö*, and in some cases, as in that of the word for the numeral 7, I was doubtful which was the right sign. The sound for which I use *eu* is, however, more prolonged, and approaches a dissyllable. It occurs in the most definite form in the word for god, *teu*. This is undoubtedly derived from the Sanscrit '*deva*' in general use in Southern India, and it is therefore very interesting that this word, which has become '*Dieu*' in French, should have become the very similar *teu* in the Toda language.

U, *ü*, and *i*. The *ü* sound, almost exactly like that of the German language, was common, though in many cases I was doubtful whether to write *u*, *ü*, or *i*. Thus it was difficult to say whether the word for bow was *purs*, *pürs*, or *pirs*; the last named would bring it in line with general Dravidian orthography, but the first seemed to me the most frequent, and I have therefore adopted it.

Ai and *oi*. The sound *ai* is not very frequent in Toda, and when it occurs is often on the way to *oi*. Thus the *naim* or council was often *noim*, and *mogai* and *mogoi* were said indifferently.

I had very much difficulty in writing the consonants, being especially troubled by my lack of familiarity with linguals. The following were those which I heard:—*b*, *ch*, *d*, *ḍ*, *f*, *g*, *gg*, *gh*, *h*, *j*, *k*, *kh*, *l* and *ḷ*, *m*, *n*, *ñ*, *p*, *r*, *s*, *sh*, *t*, *th*, *v*, *w*, *z*, *zh*.

In the text of the book I have not attempted to distinguish the lingual consonants, and I have also omitted the very common euphonic insertions, especially of *ch*, *sh*, and *th*.

B, *p*, *v*, *w*, and *f*. The sound expressed by *b* was heard very rarely, and I am doubtful whether it really occurs in true Toda. It is a common letter in Badaga, but when a Badaga word is pronounced by the Todas, the letter usually becomes *p*. In a few words I had much difficulty in making up my mind whether a given sound was *b* or *p*, and this was especially the case with the word *kudupel* or *kudubel*, which is probably a Badaga word.

One of the most frequent consonants in Toda is *p*, which often changes into *v*, especially when *p* is the initial letter of the latter part of a compound word; thus the word *pet* or wand in *pôhpet* became *pôhvet*, *kugpali* became *kugvali*, and *nedrpol*, *nedrvol*. Occasionally *p* would become a distinct *w*, as in the name of the flower *kargwâv* for *kargpâv*.

The letter *f* undoubtedly occurs in Toda, though not very frequently. It is sometimes changed into *v*, but in some cases, as in the name of the ancient village Kusharf, I never heard any sound other than a distinct *f*. I did not hear *f* and *p* interchanged.

As already mentioned, the letter *w* may occasionally occur as a variant of *p* or *v*, but it also occurs in words where it is never interchanged with either of these letters. The most frequent example of the occurrence of the letter is in the word *wursol*, and here the sound was so elusive that for a long time I hesitated whether to write the word as *wursol* or *ursol*. Breeks wrote this word *varzhol*, and we may take it that he distinctly recognised the initial letter as allied to *v* and *p*.

D, *ḍ*, *t*, *th*. I have used the sign *d* for two sounds in the text. One I could not distinguish from the English sound expressed by this letter. It is sometimes the representative of *nd* of Badaga, *mand* or village becoming *mad* in Toda,[1] while the Badaga form of Pidati is Benduti. The *d* of other Dravidian languages often becomes *t* in Toda; thus *pandava* becomes *pateva*, and the Teivaliol almost certainly derive their name from some form of the word *deva*.

More frequently, however, *d* is used for the lingual consonant *ḍ*, which is one of the commonest sounds in Toda. Very often this letter is immediately followed by the letter *r*, and the combination *ḍr* (which in the text of the book I have written *dr*) is an extremely frequent sound. Often to my ear it was quite indistinguishable from the simple *r*, and usually I had to refer to my interpreter to know whether a given sound was *ḍr* or *r*. Neither of my interpreters

[1] *Mad*, or more usually *madth*, is also the Toda word for churn, and this word is probably derived indirectly from the Sanscrit *mantha*.

seemed ever to be in any doubt, and they were so consistent on this point that wherever this spelling occurs it is probably correct. So far as I can tell the *ḍr* is the representative of *ḍ* in other Dravidian languages; thus, *nâḍ* of Canarese becomes *nòḍr*, and the *kêḍu* of Badaga becomes *kêḍr*. On reference to the list of Badaga and Toda names of villages given in Appendix III. it will be seen that the *ḍr* of the Todas is usually the equivalent of the Badaga *ḍ*, Telkodu becoming Telkudr, and Kudimal becoming Kudrmas.

The sound which I express by *dr* has been very variously spelt by previous writers; thus, the Toda future world has been written *Humanorr* or *Omnorr* by Harkness, *Amunâd* by Breeks, *Amnôr* by Marshall and Pope, and *Amnor* by Thurston, and the sacred plant *tudr* has been written *tûd*, *tûde*, *tiurr*, *tûre* and *tûr*.

When the sound *ḍ* occurs before letters other than *r*, I am afraid I may have often omitted it. Thus till nearly the end of my visit I wrote the word *teḍshk* as *teshk*, and the name of the village *Teḍshteiri* as *Teshteiri*, and I have little doubt that this letter, the presence of which I had so much difficulty in recognising, may have been omitted in other cases.

There seems to be no doubt that *ḍr* and *t* might sometimes be interchangeable. Thus the termination of personal names, *kûtan* seemed to be the same word as *kûḍr*. A horn is *kûḍr* and imitation-horns are *kûter*. An assembly is *kût*, and the corresponding verb is *kûḍriti* (3rd person singular). Sometimes *ḍr* becomes *rt*; thus the word *kêḍr* becomes *kêrt* in the compound word *kêrtnòḍr*, and the names of the clans Kuuḍr and Pieḍr often become Kuurt and Piert in the words Kuurtol and Piertol.

I failed to distinguish between *t* and *ṭ*, and it is probable that my *t* includes both letters. My interpreters used the sign *th* for *ṭ*, as is common in the transliteration of missionaries and others in India, and I am afraid that in a few cases my *th* should stand for the lingual *ṭ*. It is very unfortunate that *th* should be used for *ṭ*, for the true *th* not only occurs among the Todas but is a very frequent consonant. It is frequently inserted euphonically in words which are at other times pronounced without it, and this is especially the case in connexion with the letter *l*. The consonant *th* also occurs frequently apart from any other consonant, in such words as *pûthi*, *pathanmul*, &c.

I think it probable that under the sign *th* I have included two sounds, that of the English word 'though' and that of 'throw,' but I could not make up my mind whether the two sounds were definitely distinguished. The softer sound is undoubtedly the more common, and often it seemed to me to be even softer than this sound is ever heard in English.

K, *kw*, *g*, *kh*, *gh*, *h*. Perhaps the commonest Toda consonant is *k*, which often becomes *kw*, and it seemed to me that the two were sometimes interchanged, *kûḍr* becoming *kwûḍr*, &c.

The consonant *g* is less frequently heard, but *kûḍr*, especially as the termination of the names of men and places, is often pronounced *gûḍr*, and it seemed to me that this pronunciation is somewhat more common among the Teivaliol than among the Tartharol. The sound *g* occurs very definitely, sometimes at the ends of words as in the names of villages, as in Kwirg and Perg, and in the word *kug*, and in these cases there is no doubt that it is a true Toda consonant.

The sounds which I have expressed by *kh* and *gh* are fairly common, though I do not feel quite confident that the two sounds are definitely distinguished from one another. I heard them very frequently in the words *mokh* and *kûgh*, and it certainly seemed to me that the final sound of the latter was always softer than that of the word *mokh*. When one or other of these sounds occurs at the end of a word, it is probable that I have in some cases omitted to notice it. A man named Perpakh was called by me Perpa till nearly the end of my visit, and it is probable that I made similar errors which were not detected. Similarly *kh* in the middle of a word may easily escape attention, and this has probably happened in some cases.

I also had much trouble about a sound occurring at the end of a word for which I have used the sign *h*. Its chief occurrence is in the word *pôh*, and the same or a closely similar sound sometimes occurs in the middle of the word *pali*. The word *pôh* has usually been written *boath*, following Marshall, or *boa* (Breeks). The word certainly often sounded like a dissyllable, but I was doubtful whether this was anything more than the prolongation of vowels to which I have already referred in the case of *ei* and *ī*. There is some kind of consonantal sound at the end of the word, but it is certainly not the ordinary *th* nor is it *kh*, and I have adopted *h* as the nearest equivalent though I recognise that it is not the right sign.

R, *l*. I have already considered the letter *r* in connexion with *ḍ*, but it also occurs frequently by itself. At the end of a word it is sometimes distinctly rolled. When used after a short vowel, as in such a word as *persin*, it was sometimes not easy for me to detect its presence, and occasionally it is possible that I have omitted it from words in which it should occur.

The letter *l* is of fairly frequent occurrence, but has certainly often been lost in Toda in words which contain it in other Dravidian languages; thus the word *kīl*, lower, inferior, becomes *kī* in Toda, though the *l* has been retained in *meil* or *mel*, meaning upper or superior.

There are almost certainly two different *l* sounds in Toda which I failed to distinguish definitely. I have written the word for dairy *pali*, but the second consonant of the word is certainly a different sound from that of the *l* in *meil*, and is probably the representative of the *ḻ* of Tamil. It is in connexion with this letter that the euphonic *th* is so often inserted, and I believe that the proper name for a Toda dairy is *paḻthḻi*. When this *l* occurs at the end of a word, it is sometimes hardly audible, and to my ear bears a very close resemblance to the French *i*. The end of the word Kudreiil seemed to me to be pronounced almost exactly like the end of Auteuil.

It appears that *r* and *l* may sometimes pass into one another; thus, the name of the bow and arrow ceremony is *pursütpimi*, but the buffalo given on this occasion is called *pulkwadr*.

M and n. The letters *m* and *n*, indistinguishable to my

ear from the corresponding English letters, are of frequent occurrence. They are, however, often omitted in the Toda forms of Tamil or Canarese words; thus, as we have already seen, the word *mand*, village, becomes the Toda *mad*; the Tamil *ambu*, arrow, becomes *ab*; and the Toda form of Kurumba is *Kûrub*.

The *n* may also disappear from the Toda names of villages when it exists in their Badaga names; thus Tarnard becomes Taradr and Korangu, Kwirg. The omission of the letter *n* and other changes which words undergo in Toda are very well shown in the word *padjpateva*, which is the Toda form of the *Panchpandavas*. Although my ear failed to separate the *n* of the Todas from the English *n*, it is probably different and represents the *ṇ* of Tamil.

In addition to the ordinary *n* the Todas have another consonant which is extremely like the final French *n* for which I have used the sign *ñ*. The sound only occurs in certain exclamations or greetings; the *Oñ* which occurs so frequently in the dairy ritual is pronounced in this way, and so is *bañ*, which is uttered by the *palol* as a greeting to the Tartharol. The sound also occurs in the various kinship greetings. The commonest of these, *tioñ*, offered to an elder brother, is a corruption of *itian*, but I never heard the nasal pronunciation when the word *an* or *anna* was uttered in the ordinary way. In this case the sound I have expressed by *n* is undoubtedly the letter *ṇ* of Tamil, this word being *aṇṇa* in that language.

S, *sh*, *z*, *zh*, *dz*, *j*. The sound for which I have used the letter *s* is a somewhat harsh sound, harsher, I think, than is heard in English, but much like the sound which I have heard in English words pronounced by Scottish Highlanders. Breeks wrote *zh* for this sound, but I have used this sign for a different sound which was exactly like the *si* in the English word 'occasion.' It occurs not uncommonly in Toda in such words as *puzh*, earth, and in the verbal form *kaizhvat*.

The sound *z* occurs frequently. I was often doubtful whether to write *dz* or *z*, especially at the ends of personal names, and in other cases what was obviously the same termination was pronounced more like *dj*; thus I was often doubtful whether to write the name Piliodz in this way or as Pilioz or Piliodj (the three English equivalents would be the sounds of Dods, Boz and Dodge).

The sounds *s* and *sh* are often inserted euphonically; thus, the name Kuriolv is as often as not pronounced Kursiolv, and, more rarely, Kurshiolv.

SACRED LANGUAGE

There are three varieties of sacred language in use among the Todas. There is the *kwarzam*, the word or clause used in prayer and other sacred formulæ; secondly, there are certain words and phrases peculiar to the *ti* dairy, and thirdly, there are certain words called by the Todas, *teu* language, which are only used in the legends of the gods.

The *kwarzam* is used especially for the names of gods, persons or objects used in the first portions of the prayers. It is also used in the magical formulæ and in the funeral laments, but it may be that the last use is only due to an extension of the strict meaning of the term. When I began to collect the prayers, I hoped that the *kwarzam* might turn out to belong to some ancient and otherwise forgotten language, but their general nature is evidently the same as that of other Toda words. The *kwarzam* arises either by a slight modification of a name in ordinary use or as a phrase recording some historical or mythical incident.

I give here a short list of *kwarzam* which, with a few exceptions, have not occurred elsewhere. The following are the *kwarzam* of the Tarthar clans:—

The Nòdrsol, *Nòdrstharkûtthars*; the Karsol, *Kârstharkunnadrpêdr*; the Panol, *Pandârpeshdthvaimokh*; the Taradrol, *Püłkudutharpeithar*; the Keradrol, *Kerâdrtharkerâdrkûtan*; the Kanòdrsol, *Munantharpinnantho*; the Kwòdrdoniol, *Adutharathiars*; the Pämol, *Pämûtharkathar*; the Melgarsol, *Narzthar*. The *kwarzam* of the Kuudrol is *Ivikanmokhkûtmeilteu* (see p. 101), but the other Teivali clans have no such special names.

The only one of the above, of which the meaning is quite

clear, is that of Pan, in which case the *kwarzam* gives the names of the two *kudr* of the clan (see p. 652). The latter part of the *kwarzam* of the Keradrol means a horn or son of Keradr, and is also the name of a man, and with further knowledge there is little doubt that the other *kwarzam* would be found to have some meaning.

The following are the *kwarzam* of the buffaloes of the different clans:—

Nòdrs, *karûdchîrkünâkh*; Kars, *inâtvidshti inâtvan*;[1] Pan and Taradr, *Mutchôthvanmodethokvan*; Keradr, *miniapîr mâvelkar*; Kanòdrs, *Tîrztashkkarzikunp*; Kwòdrdoni and Nidrsi, *Keitankeikar*; Päm, *Arzomolkutchi*; Melgars, *Narzulnnatülnnâkh*; Kuudr and Pedrkars, *Kishvettarskvan*; Piedr, *Kûzherikwelvpurserthunm*; Kusharf, *Nulkarsîrnazhuv*; Keradr, *Nelppârsîrkudeipar*; Kulhem, *Pelthrîrkan.*

The *kwarzam* of the Keradr buffaloes refers to the tradition of their creation (see p. 192), and here again with further knowledge there is little doubt that most of the *kwarzam* would be found to have a definite meaning, probably derived from legends concerning the buffaloes or the villages to which they belong.

The second kind of sacred language, in use at the *ti* dairies, has been already considered. Every kind of dairy vessel or other object used in the dairy ceremonial has a name at the *ti* different from that used in the house or village dairy. These different names have been given in describing the dairy ceremonial, but I have not hitherto referred to certain other differences of language, especially in verbal forms. Different words are used in the two kinds of dairy for the verb 'to drink'; thus, when a village dairyman orders another to drink buttermilk, he says "*Maj ûn*!" while at the *ti* the *palol* says "*Kaizhvat!*" This latter formula is interesting in that *kaizh* is not the usual *ti* word for buttermilk (*mòr*) and only occurs, as far as I can ascertain, in conjunction with the verb *vat.* A village dairyman uses the verb *part*, pray, while at the *ti*, the verb *pôhvetnört* is used. Thus the question "have you prayed?" would be "*partikudricha?*" at the village and "*pôhvetnörtikudricha?*" at the *ti.* Similarly

[1] See story of Kwoto.

different forms of the verb 'to milk' are used. "We have milked" at the village would be "*ťrkartkudrvispimi*," often shortened into *ťrkartspimi*, while at the *ti* "*kaṛvukkudrivispimi*" would be said; "we have not milked" would be "*ťrkarami*" at the village and "*ťrkarpûkhami*" at the *ti*.

There are certain verbs used at the *ti* dairy which may only be pronounced by ordinary people in the third person. A good example is the verb *nört*, and it will be noticed that the names of ceremonies in which this verb is used have always been given in the third person, *irnörtiti*, and never in the first person plural as in the case of most other ceremonies.

About the third kind of sacred language, I know very little. It will have been noticed that the words and sentences which are used in the legends of Chapter IX are unlike those which occur elsewhere, and I was especially told that certain words only occurred in the stories of the gods. A special instance given was that of the words "*tar tûrzhoḍthrska*" (see p. 201), where *tar*[1] was said to be the *teu* word for 'man.' The words *kwudrpedrshai* and *kaipedrshai* in the same legend were given as other examples of *teu* language.

SECRET LANGUAGE

The Todas have a large number of expressions which they use in the presence of Badagas, Tamils and others when they wish to be understood only by themselves. Many of the Badagas and Tamils with whom the Todas associate no doubt pick up some knowledge of their language, and even if this were not the case, the Toda language is sufficiently like Tamil to enable a stranger to understand part of what is said. In consequence the Todas have adopted a secret code for use among themselves which they call *kalikatpimi*, literally "stolen we tie," while in distinction the ordinary language is called *itherkelv* or "front fact."

[1] The last syllable of the name Meilitars given to Kwoto is probably this word so that the name means 'superior man.'

The following are the chief instances of which I was told.

Ordinary Language.	Secret Language.
Pürshk nír at kwadr! Milk to water mix give. *i.e.*, give milk mixed with water!	*Nonk nür pudvaink* Four sides which came from *kagír pürs at kwadr!* old buffalo milk mix give! *i.e.*, give milk mixed with what comes from the four teats of an old buffalo.
Pürs üdr milk cook *i.e.*, cook food in milk!	*Nonk nür pud müdn tarsk* Four sides come three on up *idsht!* put *i.e.*, Put what comes from the four teats upon the three (stones of the oven).
Tör tidshia? Have you taken food?	*Kütö nörth kershia?* Teeth between did you throw?
At vokh! There (or away) go!	*At erd af!* There (or away) two (legs) get!
Iren akaik ud! The buffalo in the wood hide!	*küdr valvpoi törs ülür kí!* Horn crooked wood into go!
Kan odthi? Is he not blind?	*Küdren pom odthinü* Black fruit has he not?

When a man is thought to be dying, the Todas may ask "Is this man going from one place to another?"

Whenever a Toda first sees a man, he looks at his feet, and, correspondingly, when a Toda asks another his opinion of a man, he says "*Kal pel ilüdinü*, "What sort of leg and nail has he?" In secret language the leg may be called *metipol*, "walk thing," also used for footprints or *pümi ülür pí pol*, "thing that goes into the earth."

Many other things and persons have secret names; thus, a rupee, or money generally, is called *atchertvai*, that which is stamped; butter is called *pelthpol* or white thing; clarified butter (*nei*) is called *kürtpol* or melted thing; sugar and honey are called *tichedpol* or sweet thing; rice is called *peitpudvai*, that which comes from Peit, a place near Kavidi in the Wainad from which rice used to be procured; arrack (*saraim*) is called *írthpol* or *püshetpol*, each meaning "drink thing." The sun is called *etüdol*, "great man."

The various tribes on the hills have secret names; thus, both Badagas and Tamils are called *tutâr katvai*, he who wears or ties the turban; a Kota is called *kîmas ithvai*, he who is beneath; a Kurumba is called *âr kârthpol*, the man who watches the way; a European is called *pelthpol*, or white man. A forest guard is called *petuni ütvai*, *petuni* being here used as a term for uniform, so that if a forest guard has come, they will say, *petuni ütvai podvuchi*.

Several of the words used in the secret language do not appear to have any other meaning and are not ordinarily used. Thus the ordinary word for tooth is *pars*, but in secret language *kâtô* or *kâtû* is used. This word is the name of the wall of a buffalo-pen and it is possible that it may mean stones, but I could not ascertain whether this was the derivation, and could only learn that it was another word for tooth. Similarly the ear, of which the ordinary name is *kevi*, is called *pertars*, and the question "Did you wear gold earrings?" becomes *pertarsk ütshia?* "to ear did you wear?"

CHAPTER XXVI

PERSONAL NAMES

THE ceremonies of name-giving have already been considered, the chief point of interest being that the name of a boy is given to him by his maternal uncle, while that of a girl is probably given by her paternal aunt. In this chapter I wish to consider the general nature of the personal names of the Todas and some special customs connected with them.

The genealogies provide a large store of material, for it is exceptional for two Todas to have the same name, and no Toda should bear a name which has been borne by another for four generations, and certainly not one which has been borne by one of his own family.

The great majority of Toda names have distinctive terminations which are different for men and women.

The common terminations for males are *-van*, *-kûdr*, *-kût* or *-kûtan*, *-olv*, *-eidi*, and *-ners*. The first was said to be the same word as *pan* or *pun*, the Toda name for the stone circles found on the summits of the hills. The names of deities often receive the same termination; thus Nòtirzi is also called Nòtirzivan, and, in several cases, men received the names of gods or hills followed by the syllable *-van*. The same termination is also given to names which have other derivations.

The terminations, *-kûdr* or *-gûdr*, *-kût* or *-kûtan*, are different forms of the word *kûdr*, which means primarily 'horn,' and when it occurs in a name seems to mean 'child.' The termination in *-kûdr* or *-gûdr* seems to be much more frequently used by the Teivaliol than by the Tartharol, and in both divisions it is rare in older generations.

I do not know the meaning of the terminations in *-olv* and *-eidi*: it is noteworthy, however, that *-olv* is also a frequent ending of the names of dairies.

The termination *-ner* or *-ners* sometimes becomes *-nfr*, and it may be the word for water, possibly with the idea of 'spring.'

The usual terminations of female names are *-veli*, *-veni* or *-vani*, *-eimi*, and *-idj* or *-idz*. Of these, the first is by far the most frequent, being usually pronounced with a *th* sound, as in *-velthli* or *-vilthli*. It is possibly the same word as a frequent Indian name of Venus, which is also the Toda name for this planet. The word also means silver and in the form *pelthiti* is used for 'white.'

The termination *-veni* or *-vani* is probably derived from *pani*, which is said to be an ancient name for a Toda woman. Occasionally the latter form occurred, as in the name of Sinadapani (67), and one of the wives of Kwoten was named Kwaterpani. I know nothing of the derivation of the terminations *-eimi* and *-idz*.

The names of Todas are often derived from villages, dairies or dairy vessels, hills and their deities, and objects of various kinds. There seems to be no objection to use the names of deities or of such sacred objects as the *mani* as personal names, but only as those of men. Recently the Todas have begun to use words of Hindu or even English origin for the names of their children.

It is the names of men which are chiefly derived from villages, and at least twenty examples occur in the genealogies. In some cases the name of the village is used without any suffix, as in Ushadr (48) and Madsu (58); in other cases one or other of the customary terminations is used, as in Keradrkutan[1] (26), Nongarsivan (62), Kuirsiners (18), and Karseidi (8). The special point of interest here is that the names of villages which have now disappeared may be preserved as personal names; thus Harkness mentions the village of Kattaul as being near Ootacamund, and, though the

[1] This name also occurs in the story of Kwoten.

village has now disappeared, its memory is preserved in the name Katolvan (44), borne by one of the Melgarsol, to whom the village belonged. Again, the village of Kepurs, an extinct village mentioned in the legend of Kwoten, is preserved in the name of Kepursvan (18), borne by one of Kwoten's clan, the Panol.

In general, when a man receives a name derived from a village or other place, the village or place is one belonging to his own clan. Names may be derived from *ti* places as well as from ordinary villages, of which Makars (10) and Pursas (42) are examples.

The special feature of interest about these sources of nomenclature is that personal names may thus preserve records of the past, and a full investigation of the genealogies from this point of view might bring to light the names of many other villages now extinct.

Names are also derived from dairies, buffalo-pens, stones, and other objects of the village; thus Tarziolv, the special name of the *kudrpali* of Kars, is borne by a member of the Karsol (15), and Tilipa (12) is probably a corruption of Tilipoh. A boy of Nidrsi is named Punatu (43) after the buffalo-pen of his village, and the men called Agar (7), Pepners (44), and Persinkudr (16), have received names connected with the operations of the dairy.

The names of stones occur in the examples Menkars (10) and Mutchud (45). Several men are named after the sacred bells, or *mani*, of which examples are Nalani (35), Kerani (35), Pongg (47), while Mudriners (57) is named after Mudrani, one of the *patatmani* of Kiudr. The name of Eshkiaguln of Kars (8) is very much like that of one of the bells of Nidrsi, Eshkiakudr, and in one case a man is called Maniners (62).

The *kwarsam* of the prayers form a frequent source of personal names. Thus the name of Puthion (64) occurs in the last clause of the Kuudr prayer, and no less than six men take their names, either directly or with some modifications, from the Kiudr prayer; these are Kil, Erai, Etamudri, Kwelthipush from Kwelpushol, Kishkar from Arsvishkars, and Keikudr, who was also called Parvakudr, derived from another *kwarzam* of this prayer. In one of these cases the name is taken from the *kwarzam* with so much modification that I should not have guessed its derivation if I had not been told; and if this extensive modification is frequent, there may be many more names derived from *kwarzam* than appears to be the case at first sight.

The names of deities are not uncommonly adopted as personal names; the chief examples being Nòtirzi (47), Meilitars (44), Teipakh (20), Etepi (26), Karzo (12), Pòrzo (4), and Pakhwar (16). Two people are also called Tevò (3 and 53), which is a corruption of Teipakh, and a boy is called Kòdrthokutan (43). In many cases men are named after hills, of which Drugevan (40), Kòdrner (7), and Mopuvan[1] (16) are examples, and it is not improbable that these hills are also provided with deities. Two of the instances given above are the names of river-gods, and there is also a man, Palpa (16), named after the stream by which Kwoten met the goddess Terkosh. Punatvan (53) is named after one of the personages in the story of Kwoto. Among these names it is noteworthy that Nòtirzi, the name of a female deity, is borne by a man, and that there is no instance in which a man is named after one of the three ancient and important deities, Pithi, Ön, and Teikirzi.

This use of the names of deities as personal names seems to point to the absence of any high degree of reverence for the divine beings. The Todas are by no means free from the ideas of danger and disrespect connected with the utterance of names; and if their gods still received any great degree of veneration, I think it is improbable that their names would be allowed to be in everyone's mouth, as must be the case when used as personal names. It is possible that this use of the names of deities is recent; it is certainly more frequent at the present time than in the older generations recorded in the genealogies, and I strongly suspect that the practice adds another indication to those already given of the decay of the religious sentiment of the Todas.

It seems to be extremely rare for persons to have the same

[1] Mopuvan is named after the hill Mopuvthut, which is mentioned in the legend of Puzi (193).

names as buffaloes. There is only one doubtful example in the genealogies, Kerani (35). This is also the name of a bell, and I am doubtful whether it is really a buffalo-name. It is probable that the absence of the names of buffaloes is merely utilitarian and has no deeper significance. Buffaloes are generally referred to by name, and it would obviously be inconvenient that they should have the same names as people.

Many other names are derived from objects or from the language of everyday life. Examples of such are Nipa, stream; Perol, unsanctified man; Irsimitch, lime; Sakari, sweet; Kakar, a grass; Mogai, cubit; Kapur, camphor; and Pòl, a two-year-old calf. Sometimes such words become names by the addition of the terminations *-kûdr* or *-veli*, as in Panmkudr, the horn of a four-anna piece, and Nirveli and Kadakveli, derived from the words for water and for the wild rose. Probably with a wider knowledge of the Toda vocabulary, it would be found that a very large number of the names are formed in this way.

In one case a girl was called Mudukugh (72). She was the third girl in the family, and the name was no doubt given to commemorate the fact.

Often two or more children of a family are given names with a considerable degree of similarity to one another. In one case two brothers are called Mongeidrvan and Tergeidrvan (53); in another, Piliar and Piliag (52); and in a third, Singudr and Sinar (55); three sisters are called Teinesveli, Ternersveli, and Kenerveli (51), and in such cases it seems probable that new names are invented.

At the present time children are in many cases receiving Hindu names. Three young boys are called Arjun, Parvishki, and Sandisparan, and a young girl is called Natcham, which was said to represent Latchmi. Other Hindu names are Katcheri (Cutcherry), Sirkar, Kedjeri, and probably there are many others.

In a few cases names of English origin have probably been given, as in the case of Pensil, and the name Birkidj was said to be derived from Breeks.

The genealogical record shows clearly that this use of names derived from external sources is quite recent. There is a very striking difference in general character between the names of the present and those of older generations, and a foreign origin is especially frequent in the names of children less than ten or fifteen years of age. The evidence from names would seem to point to a rapid spread of outside influence during the last ten years.

Shortened forms of names are often used. The termination of a word may be dropped; thus Nurmaners is often called Nurman, Ultzkudr becomes Ultz, and Paniolv, Pani. Sometimes the contraction is of a different kind; thus the girls Astrap and Pumundeivi are usually called Asp and Pumidz, and the name of the boy Kulpakh often becomes Kulen.

In addition to his proper name nearly every Toda has a nickname, usually given to him by the Badagas. These names often refer to some personal peculiarity, and this is probably the reason why nicknames were usually given to me with great reluctance, there being a distinct reversal of the condition found in communities of lower culture, where the proper names are usually kept secret, while only nicknames are uttered. Arpurs (46) was nicknamed Suri (knife) on account of his sharp nose, and Nertolvan (16) is called Teinkan or 'Bee eye,' on account of the smallness of his eyes, like those of the honey bee. In other cases I do not know the origin of the Badaga names, but they have usually different forms from those of true Toda names, often terminating in *-oin* or *-üln*. Sometimes the Badaga name is merely a modification of the Toda name, as when Tudrvan becomes Utudiki. In a few cases I heard the Badaga name of a man more often than his Toda name; thus Tövoniners is usually called Aravoin, and a noted Toda of the last generation is always spoken of by his Badaga name, Mervoin. In a few cases, men long dead are remembered by their Badaga names, while their Toda names are forgotten.

As I have already indicated, nicknames are often used by people of low culture as a means of evading taboos, and though, as we shall see shortly, such taboos exist among the Todas, I met with no instance in which a Toda, who was unable to utter a name, gave a nickname in its stead.

From the foregoing account it is evident that in the names of the Todas we have a storehouse of words the investigation of which might lead to many discoveries in connexion with their half-forgotten folklore and past history. We have seen that the names of villages which have now entirely disappeared may still be preserved in the names of persons, and I have little doubt that a complete investigation of the names included in the genealogies would furnish a record of many more extinct villages and possibly provide clues to institutions which have now wholly disappeared.

Change of Name

There are three chief conditions which lead Todas to change their names. If two men have the same name, and one of the two should die, the other man would change his name, since the taboo on the name of the dead would prevent people from uttering the name of the living. The most recent example of this occurred about six years ago. There were two men named Matovan, one of Pan (19) and the other of Kwòdrdoni (34). The Kwòdrdoni man died and Matovan of Pan changed his name to Imokhvan, and it is this name which will be found in his pedigree.

This change of name may also be effected even when there is only a similarity between two names. Thus when Punbuthuvi, the wife of Parkurs (8), died, Sinbuthuvi of Kusharf (65) changed her name to Pukuruveli. Similarly when Òners of Kuudr (56) died, Einers of Piedr[1] (64) changed his name to Tokulvan.

A person may also change his name merely because it is the same as, or very similar to, that of another, this being done simply to avoid inconvenience and misunderstanding. It sometimes happens that a child is given the same name as some other child, and then one or other is renamed. Thus a boy was named Oblodj, but it was found later that there was a girl at Kars called Obalidz (12), and so the name

[1] It will be noticed that, in these two cases, the old names are those which occur in the genealogies. My informant probably remembered these better than the new names, which had been assumed only late in life.

of the boy was changed to Meilitars (44). A boy of Päm was called Kudeners, but it was found that there was another Kudeners at Taradr (25), so the name of the former was changed to Arparners, often shortened to Arpar (38).

When Kainir (3) married, his wife's name was Kanir, but she changed it since it was so like that of her husband. It was said to have been changed to Singub, but she was always known as Udz at the time of my visit.

Change of name of this kind is not obligatory, and there are several cases in which two people now living have the same name. When a change is made because two people have the same name or similar names, it is the younger of the two who changes. In most of the cases in which two people bear the same name it will be found that one belongs to the Tartharol and the other to the Teivaliol, and I am doubtful whether in this case names are changed except as the result of death.

A third reason for changing names is illness or other misfortune. When a man is ill, change of name is sometimes recommended by a diviner, but this is not often done. One of my guides, Kutadri (7), had changed his name twice. His original name had been Okeithi or Okvan, but as there was another Okvan of Keadr (68), he became Tagarsvan. Later he fell ill, and, on the recommendation of a diviner, Tagarsvan changed his name to Kutadri, and I never heard him spoken of or addressed by any but this name during my visit.

Taboos on Names

The only definite restrictions on the utterance of the names of living people are those connected with kinship which have already been considered in Chapter XXI. A man may not utter the names of his mother's brother, his grandfather and grandmother, his wife's mother, and of the man from whom he has received his wife, who is usually the wife's father. The names of the above are tabooed in life, while after death the restrictions are still wider, and it is forbidden to utter the name of any dead elder relative, while the names of the dead are in any case only said reluctantly.

It may seem strange that this reluctance should exist among a people who possess so full a genealogical record. The reluctance probably only extends to the public utterances of ordinary life and disappears when the people discuss affairs in which genealogical lore plays a part, or when they are transmitting this lore to others.

In addition to the definite taboos, there is often much reluctance in uttering personal names. The Todas dislike uttering their own names, and a Toda, when asked for his name, would often request another man to give it. Sometimes my guide was obviously reluctant to give me the names of the people who came to see me, and it seemed to me that this was especially so when the people were related to him by marriage, *i.e.*, men who had married into his clan; but I could not satisfy myself definitely that it made him more uncomfortable to utter the names of such relatives than those of other people.

In some parts of the world the taboo on the names of the dead involves also a taboo on the names of the objects which correspond to the names of the dead or to parts of these names. If such restrictions existed among the Todas, they would have on the death of Nirveli and Panmkudr to find other names for water and for a four-anna piece. It was quite clear, however, that there were no such restrictions, and that this frequent cause of change of vocabulary has not been at work in the case of the Toda language.

CHAPTER XXVII

RELATIONS WITH OTHER TRIBES

In this chapter I propose to put together the chief facts with which I am acquainted which throw light on the very difficult problem of the relations between the Todas and the other tribes of the Nilgiri Hills. The chapter could only be written with any degree of completeness by one who had studied the question from the point of view of each of the Nilgiri tribes separately. I have only been able to do so, and that incompletely, from the Toda point of view. My information is derived almost wholly from the Todas themselves, and gives their way of regarding the relations between themselves and the other tribes.

The five tribes inhabiting the Nilgiri Hills are shown in Fig. 68 (taken from Breeks), the Todas in the centre with the Badagas on their right and the Kotas on their left. Next to the Badagas are the Irulas, and next to the Kotas are the Kurumbas.

The tribes with which the Todas come into contact habitually are the Badagas and Kotas, while their points of contact with Kurumbas and Irulas are much less important. The Badagas are not only the agriculturists of the Todas, but are the constant intermediaries between the Todas and the extra-Nilgiri world. The two tribes regard each other more or less as social equals. The Kotas, on the other hand, who are the artisans of the Todas, are regarded by them as social inferiors. The relations with the former may be considered first.

Irulas. Badagas. Todas. Kotas. Kurumbas.

FIG. 68 (FROM BREEKS).—THE FIVE TRIBES OF THE NILGIRI HILLS.

TODAS AND BADAGAS

The Todas call a Badaga *Mav*,[1] which seems to be a form of the Canarese word for father-in-law or maternal uncle. The origin of this term is said to have been that when the Todas first met a Badaga, they asked his name and he answered "*Mav*." A Badaga who performs certain services for the *palol* is called *tikelfmav*. Certain elders of the Badagas are also called *madtin*.

Whenever a Toda meets a Badaga *monegar* (headman) or an old Badaga with whom he is acquainted, a salutation passes between the two which is represented in Fig. 69. The Toda stands before the Badaga, inclines his head slightly, and says "*Madtin pudia!*" ("*Madtin*, you have come.") The Badaga replies "*Buthuk! buthuk!*" ("Blessing, blessing") and rests his hand on top of the Toda's head. This greeting only takes place between Todas and the more important of the Badaga community. It would seem that every Badaga headman may be greeted in this way, but a Toda will only greet other Badaga elders if he is already acquainted with them. The salutation is made to members of all the various castes of the Badagas except the Torayas. It has been held to imply that the Todas regard the Badagas as their superiors, but it is doubtful how far this is the case. The Todas themselves say they follow the custom because the Badagas help to support them. It seems to be a mark of respect paid by the Todas to the elders of a tribe with which they have very close relations, and it is perhaps significant that no similar sign of respect is shown to Toda elders by the Badagas.

The Badagas perform definite services for the Todas and give what may be regarded as a tribute of grain at the harvest. The tribute is called *gudu*. I did not myself investigate the nature of the *gudu*, and there is some difference of opinion among previous writers[2] as to whether a definite amount of grain

[1] *Mav* is also the Toda word for sambhar.

[2] According to Harkness, "each burgher, hamlet, or village" gives about two quarts (p. 108), or (p. 135) half a bushel to the *ti* and half a bushel to the other Todas. According to Breeks (p. 9), the *gudu* is about one-tenth, one-eighth, or one-fifth of the gross produce.

or a given proportion of the crop is given. I have no information as to the way in which the giving of the tribute is regulated, and it is eminently one of those points on which evidence must be sought from both Todas and Badagas. In the case of the Kotas, we shall see that there is a definitely

FIG. 69.—A BADAGA GREETING A TODA.

organised system regulating the relations of certain Kota villages to certain Toda clans, and some such system probably exists to regulate the supply of Badaga grain to different clans, but I have no information on the point.[1]

[1] It is possible that the elucidation of this point might also help towards the explanation of the Badaga account of the Toda clans.

The contribution of grain from the Badagas has usually been regarded as given in return for the use of the land, the Todas being supposed to be the original owners of the soil. That this is not the whole explanation is shown by the fact that the Badagas also give a tribute of grain to two other Nilgiri tribes, the Kotas and Kurumbas. Harkness[1] was told by the Badagas that the portion given to the *ti* was in return for the prayers of the *palol*, and that they did not believe that "their crops or their cattle, themselves or their children, would prosper without his blessing." The Badagas also stated that they generally desisted from cultivating their fields when the *ti* was left without a *palol*. They looked on the tribute of grain to the Todas as given of their own good will, while a similar tribute to the Kurumbas was dictated by fear of the consequences of sorcery which might be employed if the duty were neglected.

It has been supposed that the fear of Toda sorcery is one reason for the maintenance of the tribute, and, since the Badagas undoubtedly fear the power of the Toda sorcerers, it is probable that this factor plays a part, though one less important than in the case of the Kurumbas.

Another view which has been taken is that the Todas maintain rights over old dairies in the middle of the Badaga fields, and that any recalcitrance on the part of the Badagas might be followed by the taking up of these old rights. It is possible that the Todas have at some time threatened to resume their rights over disused dairies, but, in the case of the more sacred dairies, the fear of defilement of the sacred buffaloes by approaching a Badaga village would prevent the Todas from putting such a threat into practice.

The grain is probably given, partly because it is an immemorial custom, partly because the Badagas believe that they receive benefits and avoid evils in consequence of the custom.

At the present time, the amount of grain supplied by the Badagas is not sufficient for the needs of the Todas, and both grain and rice are bought by the Todas in the bazaar. All the grain used by the *palol* must, however, be that supplied by

[1] P. 136.

the Badagas; but if more grain is required than the Badagas supply, it is possible that other grain may be used, though it is always in this case procured through the Badagas. The rice used at a *ti* dairy must also be procured through the Badagas.

The supply of grain is far from being the only duty of the Badagas to the *ti* dairies. Each *ti* has one or more special Badagas, each called *tikelfmav*, or "*ti* help Badaga," who acts as intermediary between the *palol* and the Hindus. The earthenware vessels used in the inner room, the various garments of the *palol*, and other objects are made by Hindus, from whom they are procured by the *tikelfmav*. I did not learn of any material recompense given to the Badagas for these services, and the motive is probably some such belief as that described by Harkness.

One of the most important parts played by the Badagas in the Toda community is in connexion with the *naim*, or council, of which one member is a Badaga belonging to the village of Tuneri. He is only called upon to sit, however, in cases of difficulty, and probably one of his functions is to assist in the settlement of any dispute which may arise in connexion with the tribute of grain, or other transactions between members of the two communities.

There is little evidence that the Badagas have had much influence on the more important customs and ceremonies of the Todas. Few traces of their influence are to be found in the dairy ceremonial, but it is possible that some of the rites accompanying birth and death may have been borrowed from this people. The practice of making cicatrices on the arm (p. 576) is common to both Badagas and Todas, and may have been borrowed by the latter from the former, but the practice is not in any way of a ceremonial character. The only part played by a Badaga at a Toda funeral is that the bell called *tukulir mani* may be kept by a Badaga or a Kota, and, as I have suggested on p. 377, the whole ceremony with the calf in which this bell is used may have been borrowed from the Badagas. The idea of a thread bridge between this world and the next is said to be common to Todas and Badagas, but I have no evidence to show which has borrowed from the other.

In the ordinary life of the people there is more evidence of influence. At many Toda villages there may now be seen huts like those of the Badagas which usually result from the practice of allowing Badagas to occupy a Toda village when the proper occupants have gone elsewhere. The visitors build a hut of their own kind in which to live, and sometimes the Todas on their return inhabit this hut, though in general they only use it as an appanage to the hut of the proper kind.

The fact that the Badagas will thus come to live at a Toda village seems to show that when the Todas move from one place to another the pasturage is not necessarily exhausted, for the Badagas would not bring their buffaloes in this case. It seems that the grazing-grounds for the Badaga buffaloes are not very extensive, and that the Badagas are always glad to use the more extensive pasturage of the Todas, even when the grass has been partly eaten off.

Transactions in buffaloes between Todas and Badagas seem now to be fairly frequent. I often heard of a buffalo as having been received from the Badagas, but I have no very definite information as to the reasons for the transference. On the occasion of the ceremony of the ear-piercing of Tikievan's sons (p. 336), Tikievan received a present of two buffaloes from the Badaga *monegar* of Tuneri, and this present was said to be in return for things which Tikievan had previously given to the *monegar*, but I did not learn the exact nature of this gift.

In two departments there is very clear evidence of Badaga influence. The astronomical ideas of the Todas are almost certainly borrowed from their neighbours (see Chap. XXIV), and in the closely allied practical question of the calendar I think Badaga influence may be suspected.

The other department is medicine. There is no special reason to suppose that the magical remedies of the *u꞉kòren* (Chap. XII) have been borrowed from the Badagas, but the more strictly medical remedies used by the Todas are largely borrowed, the actual leaves or other substances employed being obtained from the Badagas. The practice of suicide by opium, said to be very prevalent among the Badagas, has, in at least one recent case, been adopted by a Toda, and the threat of suicide by this means is said to be fairly common.

There is no doubt that the Badagas believe in the powers of the Toda sorcerers. I was told of several definite instances in which misfortunes were believed to have been brought upon the Badagas in this way, and there is little doubt that, in one case, the supposed author of the death of a child was murdered by the Badagas.

If a Badaga suspects magical influence of this kind he may consult one of the Toda diviners, showing that the Badagas believe in Toda divination as well as in Toda sorcery.

It is probable that the relations between the Todas and Badagas have existed for very long. It is generally held that the Badagas are comparatively recent immigrants to the Nilgiri Hills. Breeks[1] states that the Badagas are said to have come to the hills about three centuries ago in consequence of the troubles that followed the fall of Vijayanagar, but it is certain that they have been on the hills much longer than this, for the account of Finicio in 1602 (see App. I) shows that the relations between Todas and Badagas were much the same then as they are now. The close connexion of Badagas with the *ti* dairies, their intermediation between the *palol* and the Hindu, and the fact that the *palol* must eat Badaga grain, are all indications of very ancient relations between the two tribes.

There is one fact which may be held to show that the relation between Todas and Badagas is recent as compared with that between the Todas and other Nilgiri tribes. This is the fact that the Badagas are not mentioned in one of the legends of the Toda gods, while Kotas, Kurumbas, and Irulas each play a part in one or more of these stories.

TODAS AND KOTAS

The Toda name for a Kota is *Kuv.* The relation between the two people is very different from that between Toda and

[1] P. 4.

Badaga. While a Toda regards a Badaga as his equal, or perhaps even as his superior, he looks down on the Kota as inferior, as hardly to be classed as a man with himself. In their secret language, a Toda speaks of a Kota as *kimas ithvai*, "he that is beneath," and in the remedies for the evil eye (see p. 264) the Kotas are the only hill tribe which is not thought worthy of mention—they are not thought to be of sufficient importance to be able to cast the evil eye. When a Kota meets a Toda, he raises both hands to his face and salutes from a distance. The two people do not touch one another in general, though I do not know that contact is definitely prohibited. A Toda will not sleep or take food at a Kota village in general, but makes an exception in the case of Kulgadi in the Wainad (see p. 200). It is usually supposed that the contempt of the Toda for the Kota is due to the flesh-eating, or even carrion-eating, habits of the latter, and this is certainly one of the elements which influence the relations between the two peoples.

The Kotas supply the Todas with the larger part of their pottery and ironware.[1] All the earthenware vessels of the dairies, except those of the inner rooms of the *ti* dairies, are supplied by the Kotas, and the various knives and other metal objects of the Todas are chiefly obtained from these people. The Kotas supply most of the things burnt at Toda funerals and they supply the music on these occasions.

Just as the Badagas do not supply grain to the Todas only, so the Kotas do artisan work for Badagas, Kurumbas, and Irulas. The Kotas are the artisans, not of the Todas only, but of the whole hill district.

The relations between the Todas and Kotas are strictly regulated, each Kota village supplying certain Toda clans. There are seven Kota villages on the hills, of which the following are the Toda and Badaga names:—

In the Todanad district:—

Tizgudr, Tizgadr, or Tizgwadr (Badaga, Tirichigadi), between Ootacamund and Kanòdrs, near the Toda village of Ushadr.

[1] According to Breeks, the Kotas who supply the Todas are known as *muṯṯu* Kotas.

Kurguli (B. Padagula or Kuruvoje), near the Badaga village of Sholur.

In the Mekanad district :—

Kalmal (B. Kolamala or Kollimalai), not far from Kateri.

In the Peranganad district :—

Meilkukal (B. Melkotagiri or Perangada) in Kotagiri, one of the three chief European stations on the hills. Kikukal (B. Kilkotagiri or Kinnada), north-east of Kotagiri.

In the Kundanad district :—

Medrkukal (B. Menada).

The seventh is Kulgadi (B. Kalagasa) at Gudalur in the Wainad.

The village of Tizgudr is connected with the Toda clans of Kars, Melgars, Kanòdrs, and sometimes with the people of Kulhem. Kurguli supplies the clans of Nòdrs, Taradr, Kuudr, Piedr, and Kusharf, and occasionally Kulhem. Kalmal supplies Keradr, Nidrsi, Päm, Kidmad, and Keadr. Meilkukal and Kikukal are both connected with Kwòdrdoni and Pedrkars, and Medrkukal is the Kota village of the Panol. Kulgadi is connected only with the village of Kavidi, near Gudalur, which belongs to the Piedrol. When there were several Toda villages in the Wainad, it probably served them all.

The connexion between clans and villages seems to depend almost wholly on geographical distribution. The clans are supplied by the Kota villages which are nearest to their headquarters. An outlying village such as Kavidi has not the same Kota village as the rest of its clan. The Kidmadol, who are a branch of the Melgarsol, have not the same Kota village as the parent stock ; but, on the other hand, the Panol, who now live chiefly among other Todas near Governor Shola, are still connected with the Kundah Kotas.

Each Kota village is responsible for the supply of the clan or clans with which it is connected. Its inhabitants make the various utensils used in the household and in the less sacred dairy work of the Todas. At the funeral of any member of a clan with which they are connected, they provide the music and the following objects :—

At the *etvainolkedr*, a cloak in which the corpse is wrapped, five to ten measures (*kwa*) of the grain called *patm* (*samai*), and one or two rupees. If the Kotas do not possess the grain, they may give another one or two rupees in its stead.

At the *marvainolkedr*, they supply a cloak; eight annas to pay for the embroidery of the cloak, which is done by the Toda women; two to five rupees towards the funeral expenses; a bow and three arrows; a knife (*kafkati*); a sieve (*kudshmurn*) and a basket (*tek*).

In return, the Kotas receive the carcases of the buffaloes killed at the funeral, and on the occasion of a Kota funeral, the Todas supply one male calf from three to five years of age and one measure (*kudi*) of clarified butter. The Kotas also receive the bodies of any Toda buffaloes which die a natural death.

A Kota visiting a Toda village at any time is given clarified butter to take away with him. He is also given food consisting of jaggery and rice, which must be eaten on the outskirts of the village. A Kota is never given milk, buttermilk, or butter.

Once a year there is a definite ceremony in which the Todas go to the Kota village with which they are connected, taking an offering of clarified butter and receiving in return an offering of grain from the Kotas. I only obtained an account of this ceremony as performed between the people of Kars and the Kota village of Tizgudr, and I do not know whether the details would be the same in other cases.

In the Kars ceremony the Todas go on the appointed day to the Kota village, headed by a man carrying the clarified butter. Outside the village, they are met by two Kota priests whom the Todas called *teupuli*, who bring with them a dairy vessel of the kind the Todas call *mu*, which is filled with *patm* grain. Other Kotas follow with music. All stand outside the village, and one of the Kotas puts ten measures (*kwa*) of *patm* into the pocket of the cloak of the leading Toda, and the *teupuli* give the *mu* filled with the same grain.

The *teupuli* then go to their temple and return, each bringing a *mu*, and the clarified butter brought by the Todas is divided into two equal parts, and half is poured into each *mu*. The leading Toda then takes some of the butter and rubs it on the heads of the two Kota priests, who prostrate themselves, one at each foot of the Toda, and the Toda prays as follows:—

Ultamâ;	*Kôv*	*erdm*	*tâuenmâ;*	*kadr*	*pelumâ;*
May it be well;	Kotas	two	may it be well;	fields	flourish may;

mâ un mâ;	*ïr*	*kar*	*mâ,*	*nôv*	*pedr*	*mâ.*
rain may;	buffalo	milk	may,	disease	go	may.

The Toda then gives the two *mu* containing the clarified butter to the Kota priests, and he and his companions return home.

This ceremony is obviously one in which the Todas are believed to promote the prosperity of the Kotas, their crops, and their buffaloes.[1]

In another ceremonial relation between Todas and Kotas, the Kwòdrdoni *ti* is especially concerned. The chief annual ceremony of the Kotas is held about January in honour of the Kota god Kambataraya. This ceremony lasts about a fortnight, and, during part of the time, the proceedings are attended by Todas and other of the hill tribes. In order that this ceremony may take place, it is essential that there should be a *palol* at the Kwòdrdoni *ti*, and at the present time this *ti* is only occupied every year shortly before and during the ceremony. The *palol* gives clarified butter to the Kotas, which should be made from the milk of the *arsaiir*, the buffaloes of the *ti*. Some Kotas of Kotagiri whom I interviewed claimed that these buffaloes belonged to them, and that something was done by the *palol* at the Kwòdrdoni *ti* in connexion with the Kambataraya ceremony, but they could not or would not tell me what it was.

The relations between Todas and Kotas are probably of very old standing. The fact that the Kotas supply the bow and arrows burnt at a Toda funeral suggests that the connexion goes back to the time when the Todas used these weapons, while the special sieve supplied by the Kotas for a funeral is of a different pattern from that in use at the present

[1] The Kotas are agriculturists as well as mechanics, and, according to Breeks, they are quite as efficient as the Badagas in this occupation. They also keep buffaloes, though chiefly or entirely for their own use.

time. The Kotas are mentioned in Toda legend. The people of Tizgudr play a prominent part in the story of Kwoten (p. 195), and this deity is said to have been the first Toda who stayed at a Kota village, viz., at the village of Kulgadi (or Gudalur). He sat and slept on the Kota *tün* and since that time the Todas have stayed at this village, though they will not stay at any other. The relation between Kwoten and the Kotas seems to have been especially close. The old woman, Muturach, from whom the present people of Kanòdrs are descended, according to the legend, may have been a Kota. The Kotas who give tribute to the Todas are known as their *muttu* Kotas, and the first part of the old woman's name may have been this word.

Our acquaintance with Kota mythology is too scanty to contribute much to our knowledge of the relations between the two peoples. Breeks states that Kurguli (Padagula) is the oldest of the Kota villages, and that the Badagas believe that the Kotas of this village were made by the Todas. At Kurguli there is a temple of the same form as the Toda dairy, and this is said to be the only temple of the kind at any Kota village.

Breeks gives a legend which records the origin of the different foods of the Nilgiri tribes. Kambataraya, perspiring profusely, wiped from his forehead three drops of perspiration, and out of these formed the Todas, Kurumbas, and Kotas. The Todas were told to live principally upon milk, the Kurumbas were permitted to eat the flesh of buffalo calves, and the Kotas were allowed perfect liberty, being informed that they might eat carrion if they could get nothing better. My interpreter, Albert, was told a different version of this legend, according to which Kambataraya gave to each people a pot. In the Toda pot was calf-flesh, and so the Todas eat the flesh of calves (*i.e.*, at the *erkumptthpimi* ceremony); the Kurumba pot contained the flesh of a male buffalo, so this is eaten by the Kurumbas. The pot of the Kotas contained the flesh of a cow-buffalo, which may, therefore, be eaten by this people.

TODAS AND KURUMBAS

The Toda name for a Kurumba is *Kurub*, which often sounds like *Kurb*. In the secret language, a Kurumba is called *ár kârthpol*, "the man who watches the way." Mr. Thurston states that when a Kurumba meets a Toda, he bends forward and the Toda places his hand on the Kurumba's head. The Todas may visit Kurumba villages and take food in them.

Two ceremonial objects are obtained by the Todas from the Kurumbas. One is the tall pole called *tadrsi* or *tadri*, which is used in the dance at the second funeral ceremonies and afterwards burnt. Poles of the proper length are said to grow only on the Malabar side of the Nilgiris and are probably most easily obtained from the Kurumbas. The other is the *teiks*, or funeral post at which the buffalo is killed, which is probably made of teak wood.

The most striking feature of the relations between Todas and Kurumbas is the belief of the former in the magical powers of the latter, a belief which is shared by both Kotas and Badagas. The sorcery of the Toda is dangerous, but can be remedied, while for *kurubudrchiti*, or Kurumba sorcery, there is no remedy, and all that can be done is to kill the Kurumba, apparently to avoid further evil consequences to the community rather than from motives of revenge.

The Kurumbas play no part in the social life of the Todas. With the one exception of providing the funeral pole, I could not learn that they had any functions at Toda ceremonies. It was said that the *teuol*, Pangudr, who was believed to be inspired by Kwoto, must dance, *i.e.*, divine, to the Kurumbas before he dances to the Todas, and when so doing, must dance like a lame man, this behaviour owing its origin to the god Kwoto (see p. 209). It is possible that this shows that the Kurumbas believe in Toda divination and consult the diviners.

The Kurumbas are mentioned in several Toda legends. According to one account, it was this people whom Kwoto deceived, making them eat the flesh of a buffalo calf;

according to another, it was the Panins or Panyas who were deceived by the god.

Kwoten is said to have initiated the practice of allowing Todas to visit Kurumba villages, and he appears to have been closely connected, in some way, with the Kurumbas, who still offer plantains to Terkosh and light lamps in her honour, Terkosh being the goddess who was connected with his disappearance and deification.

In the story of Kuzkarv, the Kurumbas, together with the Irulas, collect honey for the Todas from nests in a tree,[1] and this seems to point to a time when these tribes took an active part in the social life of the Todas. It seems possible that the Kurumbas and Irulas were the huntsmen of the Todas, and sought roots and honey for them, just as the Badagas were the agriculturists and the Kotas the mechanics.

TODAS AND IRULAS

The Irulas live on the lower slopes of the Nilgiri Hills and have few relations with the Todas. They are called *Erl* by the Todas, and, according to Mr. Thurston, they are saluted in the same way as the Kurumbas. The Irulas are among the people mentioned in the remedial formula used against the effects of the evil eye, and are evidently regarded as having some magical power, though they are not feared in the same measure as the Kurumbas.

The name of the Irulas only occurs once in my collection of Toda legends, in the story of Kuzkarv, where they are associated with the Kurumbas. Atioto, who is the special deity of Kwòdrdoni and Pedrkars, is said to have a temple of which the priest is an Irula. This is probably an Irula temple to which the Todas make offerings.

[1] It is perhaps noteworthy that some of the Kurumbas of Malabar are still noted for their cleverness in collecting honey, and are known as *Tēn* or honey Kurumbas (Fawcett, *Bull. Madras Museum*, iii, p. 9).

CHAPTER XXVIII

THE CLANS OF THE TODAS

IN this chapter I propose to give a short account of each of the Toda clans with any special features which characterise its ceremonial and social organisation. The chapter will consist largely of detail, much of which may be thought to have no great interest, but it seems desirable to put on record as full an account as possible of the condition of the people at the time of my visit. A certain amount of folklore will be included, those tales being given which are specially connected with the history of a clan.

THE TARTHAR CLANS

NÒDRS

The people of Nòdrs owe their special importance to their connexion with the goddess Teikirzi, who was the *nòdrodchi*, or first ruler of the clan, and according to tradition bestowed certain special favours on her people. Chief among these is the possession of the Nòdrs *ti*. This is undoubtedly the most sacred and important of the five *ti* institutions, and its herds are much larger than those of any other. The fact that the Nòdrs people own this *ti* and have the power of appointing to the office of *palol* gives them great distinction in the eyes of the Todas, and this is emphasised when the *palol* is undergoing his ordination ceremonies, for several of these take place in villages of the Nòdrsol. The preliminary ceremony for those who wish to become *palol*, which is called *tesherst*, is also usually performed at a Nòdrs village.

Another title to fame is the possession of the *poh*, or conical dairy temple at Nòdrs, which is known to the European inhabitants of the Nilgiri Hills as the "Toda Cathedral." It is certainly not the most sacred of Toda dairies, but it is the most accessible of the few dairies of this kind now remaining.

The Nòdrsol are one of the clans represented in the *naim*. They now stand second among the Tarthar clans in point of numbers, having forty-three males and thirty females.[1] It has two *kudr*, one of which, consisting of the family given in the first of the genealogical tables, has now only two male members; as these have at present no son, it is possible that it may shortly become extinct. The other *kudr* has five *pòlm*, of which the chief men are Kerkadr (2), Kudòdrsvan (3), Teigudr (4), Mondothi (5), and Keitan (6). If any of the members of these five *pòlm* should perform the *irnörtiti* ceremony, the buffalo would go to Mudrigeidi and Odrkurs, while, if either of these men had to give a buffalo, its value would be divided among the other five *pòlm*. Kerkadr is regarded as the head of the second *kudr*.

The *madnol* of the Nòdrs people are Tuesday and Friday, and they hold the funerals of men on Sunday, and of women on Thursday. The special features of their funeral ceremonies are that the body of a man lies in the *tarvali* of Nòdrs for some days before the *etvainolkedr* and that a special bell (*mani*) is used at male funerals which has to be brought from Òdr. Male funerals are held at Nòdrs, and female funerals at Külthpuli. The clan used also to have another funeral place close to the Paikara road, which is not now used.

The Nòdrsol have many villages, of which fourteen are still inhabited, and I obtained the names of five others now in ruins.

The following are the chief villages.

Nòdrs (Muttanadmand). In addition to the conical *poh*, this village has the distinguishing feature of a long wall which passes between this dairy and the huts where the

[1] By this I mean that there are now living thirty females who were born members of the Nòdrsol, but since a woman becomes a member of her husband's clan, most of these are now members of other clans. I give the numbers of each clan in this form because it brings out several features of interest in relation to the relative fertility of different clans, the proportions of the sexes, &c.

people live. The wall then passes at the back of the *poh* and runs for some distance northward. The *tarvali* (in Fig. 12) is situated in an enclosure of the wall near the dwelling-huts, so that the women can go to it for buttermilk without crossing the wall and entering the enclosure in which the *poh* stands. In the south part of the wall is the gap through which the calf is driven at the *irnörtiti* ceremony (see Fig. 43). The wall is reputed to have been built by Elnakhum.

Close to the *poh*, between it and the *tarvali*, are the ruins of another dairy, the former *kudrpali*, which is said to have had seven rooms. It was disused on account of the difficulty in obtaining the services of a *kudrpalikartmokh*. It will be remembered that this grade of dairyman has to do his work without any covering, and in the bleak exposed position of Nòdrs, it seems that this was so great a hardship that the office went begging. The Nòdrs people are said to have ceased to use this dairy about four generations ago, and the condition of the ruins is about what might be expected if this statement were correct.

There are a large number of important stones at Nòdrs. Formerly seven kinds of buffalo were killed at the funeral of a male, and each was killed at a different stone. Now only two buffaloes may be killed, but the stones remain to show what was formerly done. Two *wursulir* were killed, one at the stone called *uteiks* and another at the stone *nerovkars*, both of which are shown in Fig. 70. One *nashperthir* was killed at the *nashperthkars*. The two sacred *mani* were hung on the necks of one of the *wursulir* and the *nashperthir*. One *pineipir* was killed at the stone called *tukervòrskars*. One *persasir* was killed at the *persaskars*, and two *putiir* were killed, one at the *teidrtolkars* and the other at the *menkars*. The *teidrtolkars*, shown in Fig. 13, also marks the spot where the unfortunate *wursol* milked his buffaloes (see p. 439). The *menkars*, shown in Fig. 12, is the stone used in the game of *narthpimi*, in which a boy creeps under a stone. It is on the village side of the wall, close to the entrance to the *tarvali*. All the other stones are on the same side of the wall as the *poh*.

Òdr (Aganadmand). This is second in importance among

the villages of the Nòdrsol, and it was a question whether the *wursuli* dairy, though of the ordinary form, had not even a greater sanctity than the *poh* of Nòdrs. More difficulty was made when I wished to go close to it than at any other place during the whole of my visit (except, of course, at the *ti* dairy), but, unfortunately, the affair was complicated by the fact that on this day my usual attendant, Kòdrner, was not with me, and the difficulty may have been partly due to this. When I was allowed to approach the building, only

FIG. 70.—A VIEW OF NÒDRS. THE STONE IN THE FOREGROUND ON THE LEFT IS THE 'NEROVKARS'; THAT ON THE RIGHT IS THE 'UTEIKS.' IN THE BACKGROUND IN THE CENTRE IS AN OLD 'TU.' THE LOWER PART OF THE CONICAL DAIRY CAN BE SEEN BETWEEN THE BOY AND THE 'UTEIKS.'

one man came with me and he would not go within several yards of the dairy, while allowing me to go on. The special sanctity of this dairy is due to the fact that the two *mani* of the Nòdrsol are kept here. Both this dairy and a smaller *tarvali* are at a much greater distance from the village than usual, but with that exception there is nothing to distinguish them from the dairies of other villages. The *wursuli* is one of those which has two rooms. It is at the village of Òdr that the *palol* passes one night during his ordination ceremonies, and I was shown the spot under a tree where he has to sleep, the same spot being also used by the *wursol* and *kaltmokh* when they undergo any part of their ordination ceremonies at Odr.

Another feature of interest is the connexion of this village with Kuudr. An Òdr man must be present at the *irpalvusthi* and salt-giving ceremonies of Kuudr, and a Kuudr man must attend when these ceremonies are performed at Òdr. Further, the *kwarzam* of Òdr are said in the prayer of the *erkumptthpimi* ceremony at Kuudr and the *Kwarzam* of Kuudr are said at Òdr.

The following legend records the origin of these customs:—

Soon after Teikirzi had given the buffaloes to the different villages, the buffaloes of Kuudr and Òdr were grazing together, and when evening came they could not be separated and both herds went together to the funeral place called Keikars. The *wursol* of Òdr and the *palikartmokh* of Kuudr brought their milking-vessels, each to milk his own buffaloes, and they also brought their churning-vessels (*patat*) and cooking-vessels. After they had milked, the *wursol* of Òdr went to pour his milk into his *patat*, and when doing so some of the milk splashed into the vessel of the *palikartmokh*. They then cooked some food with the milk, and as the food was boiling strongly, some of it went from one cooking-pot to the other. Then the people of the two villages met and decided that, as the two kinds of buffalo had been milked in one place and the two kinds of milk had been mixed with one another, each of the villages should mention the *kwarzam* of the other in its prayer, and people of one village should attend the ceremonies of the other.

Tedshteiri (Talapattaraimand). This is another important Nòdrs village. It was vacant at the time of my visit, but is still often occupied. It had at one time a dairy called *Okurshapali* with seven rooms, which was, like that of Nòdrs, a *kudrpali*. It fell into disuse at the same time as the Nòdrs dairy, and its site is still quite distinct; but though it seemed larger than usual, I could discover no indication of the number of rooms it had had. When I visited the village there were nine ovens standing in a row, which had been used to cook the food when Teigudr (4) took his wife Uwer from Nertolvan of Pan (16). On this occasion Nertolvan came to Tedshteiri to receive nine buffaloes from Teigudr, and the number of ovens corresponded with the number of the buffaloes.

Kudrnakhum (Kudinagamand). The chief point of interest about this village is that it is the place where the ceremony of *tesherst* often takes place. It is an outlying village to the west which I was unable to visit.

Perththo (Perattitalmand). This is a village which is shared by two clans. The part occupied by the Nòdrsol is called Meil Perththo, or Upper Perththo. The other part of the village was said to be general property, but it is at present occupied by Melgars people.

Kozhtudi or *Kozhteidi*. The special feature of this village is that it has a *wursuli* in which everything has to be carried out *kabkaditi*, *i.e.*, the dairyman is not allowed to turn his back to the contents of the dairy. This certainly points to the village having been at one time of importance.

KARS

This is at present the largest of the Tarthar clans, having sixty-seven male and fifty female members. It is represented in the *naim*, and there was some reason to think that it occupies a more important position in this body than the other Tarthar clans. The family of Parkurs (8) is called *tinkanikudupel*, ranking next to a *manikudupel*, and Parkurs was till lately a second or assistant *monegar*.

There seems to be no doubt that the Karsol have always been an important clan, and its members are often mentioned in the stories, though they do not appear to have had any legendary hero such as those of Melgars and Pan. Their *nòdrodchi* (ruler or presiding deity) is Kulinkars, now believed to live on a hill near Makurti Peak. The Kars people possess a *ti* which in importance and wealth is second only to that of Nòdrs.

Kars resembles Nòdrs in having two *kudr* differing greatly in size. Kutadri is the head of one, which comprises all the members of the family given in Table 7. It has two *pòlm*, headed by Kutadri and Peithol. The other *kudr* has eight *pòlm*, of which the chief men are Parkurs (8), Pidrvan (9)[1], Piutolvan (10), Kudrvas (11), Kutthurs (12), Mongudrvan (13), Kiunervan (14), and Keitazvan (15). Till recently there appear to have been only five *pòlm* in the Kars clan, each of which has lately been divided into two. There is a very marked disproportion in the number of members of some of these divisions; thus the *pòlm* of Parkurs has sixteen males in five more or less distinct families, while others have only three or four males. Nevertheless each of the latter would contribute the same amount towards joint expenses of the clan as the sixteen males of the *pòlm* of Parkurs.

The chief villages of the Karsol are in or near Ootacamund, and this clan formerly had several other villages on sites now occupied by modern buildings.

The following are the chief places:—

Kars (Kandalmand). This village is one of the best known of Toda villages, being just on the outskirts of Ootacamund. It is a very typical example of a Toda village; there is a small group of houses, with a large dairy, the *kudrpali* (Fig. 21), called *Tarziolv*, close to them; just above the houses on the rising ground is a smaller dairy, the *wursuli* called *Karziolv*, shown in the background of Fig. 42 and partly shown in Figs. 23 and 44. Opposite the *kudrpali* are two raised circular mounds with flat tops called the *imudrikars* (seen in the foreground in Fig. 21), on which the body of a dead man is laid before being taken to the funeral hut at Taradrkirsi. Above the *kudrpali* is the hut for calves.

In the middle of the enclosure within which the village lies, is a row of stones (shown in Fig. 42) which are the *irnörtkars*, and in the ceremony of *irnörtiti* the calf is driven across these stones.

Behind the houses there is a small circular enclosure which is now used as a *tu* and is called *Althftu*. The entrance to this enclosure is shown in Fig. 29 just in front of the boy carrying the dairy vessels. Formerly there was a dairy of the conical kind within this circle, of which the name was *Ishpoh*. About five generations ago, this dairy still existed

[1] Pidrvan died soon after my visit.

and was tended by a *wursol*; but several dairymen died in succession, and this so alarmed the Todas that it became impossible to obtain anyone to fill the office, and when the dairy decayed its remains were removed and the circular enclosure within which it stood has since been used as a pen. In size and appearance the enclosure is quite unlike other pens, and resembles much more nearly the circular walls round the conical dairies of Nòdrs and Kanòdrs.

Kuzhu (Kunditolmand). This, the second in importance of the villages of the Karsol, is a very picturesque place south of Ootacamund. There is a *kudrpali* called *Tudrpoh*, in front of which is a stone called *imudrikars*. The gold bracelet mentioned in the story of Kwoto is kept in this dairy. In front of the dwelling-huts is another stone called *menkars* (see p. 342). The *menkars* at Kuzhu and that at Nòdrs are the only stones of this name, but they do not resemble one another, and the Kuzhu stone is not adapted for the *narthpimi* game as is that of Nòdrs.

Keshker (Kakerimand). This is a large village near Ootacamund at which there is a *kudrpali*, but little else of interest. It is probably the Kishkeijar mentioned by Harkness.

Nasmiòdr (Aganadmand). This is a very old village which was probably at one time much more important than at present. It is situated about a quarter of a mile from the road leading from Ootacamund to Ebanad, not far from the Badaga village of Tuneri. There is now only a small dairy (*wursuli*) situated in the middle of a wood. When I visited Nasmiòdr, this dairy was unoccupied, and, as is usual in such cases, my Toda guide refused to go to the dairy with me, and remained outside the wood. Soon after I left the hills, it was to be occupied by the *wursol* of Kars, who would take his buffaloes there for a month.

This village is mentioned in two Toda legends, in both of which it seems to have been a village at which people were living. The dairy is called *Tilipoh* or *Pohtilipoh*, and it still contains the two *mani*, Karzod and Kòni, which were hung on the neck of Enmon (see p. 208). It is one of the few *wursuli* which have two rooms.

Pakhalkudr (Bagalkodumand). This village, not far from

Paikara, is one of the most outlying villages of the Karsol. There is a very small dairy here resembling the *merkalars* which serves both as *kudrpali* and *wursuli*, the former being in front, while the latter is behind, with the door on one side. The *wursuli* is so small that there can scarcely be room for a fully grown man to do the churning.

Isharadr and *Peletkwur*. These are outlying villages of no special interest. The former was only built in the time of the grandfather of Parkurs (8), and has a dairy resembling that of Pakhalkudr.

Taradrkirsi (Kavaikkadmand). This is the funeral place for men of the Kars clan, and is also a *kalolmad*. There is a *kudrpali* with three rooms called *Paliven keirsi*, and a pen called *Tuoks*. There are two stones where the *wursulir* and *nashperthir* are killed, and close to them there is a spot by the side of a wood where earth is thrown at a funeral. There is a slight break in the edge of the wood here, and this is probably the position of an old pen which has been completely overgrown.

There is a long wall at this village passing near the dairy and the funeral stones, and then extending a long way towards the east. It resembles the Nòdrs wall, and these seem to be the only two examples of walls of this kind at Toda villages. The wall at Taradrkirsi is said to have been built by Kwoten, but it seems unlikely, for this hero had no special connexion with the Karsol.

Several villages which have now wholly disappeared are still mentioned in the prayer which the Kars people use at the *erkumptthpimi* ceremony. One of these, Tashtars, stood where the Masonic Hall at Ootacamund now stands. The site of another, Turskidt, is occupied by a private house. Two, Tüli and Keitaz, were situated on Elk Hill, and two others, Sing and Kurkars, were near Nasmiòdr.

Pan

The Pan clan have their headquarters in the Kundahs and are often called the Medrol, or people of Medr, the Toda name for the Kundahs. The chief villages of this clan are in the

Kundahs, but they are only visited during the dry season, and for the greater part of the year the Panol live at the comparatively new village of Naters in the most thickly populated part of the hills. The legendary hero, Kwoten, belonged to Pan.

The clan is small, having now about twenty-seven male and nine female members. It is not represented on the *naim*, and in the Badaga grouping of the Todas this clan is joined with that of Nòdrs.

The Panol have two *kudr*, and provide the only example among the Tartharol in which the *kudr* have special names. The formation of the *kudr* is said to have been due to Kwoten, who divided the people into Panol and Kuirsiol, named after the two chief villages of the clan. The two divisions are also called Pandar and Peshteidimokh.

The Pandar or Panol have three *pòlm*, headed by Timurvan (16), Todars (16), and Nòrtiners (17). The Peshteidimokh or Kuirsiol have two *pòlm*, headed by Timners (18) and Imokhvan (19).

The *irnörtiti* and *tuninörtiti* ceremonies are performed in front of the *wursuli* at Pan or Kuirsi. The spots on which the ceremonies take place are not marked by any stones, and the ceremonies are spoken of as *paliknörtiti*, *i.e.*, "he gives to the dairy," though, as a matter of fact, the calf passes from the men of one *kudr* to the men of the other *kudr* as in other clans.

The *madnol* of Pan are said to be Sunday and Wednesday, and the funerals of men take place on Sunday or Tuesday, and those of women on Thursday or Saturday. It is probable that Tuesday is the proper day for the funerals of men, but that they are now sometimes held on Sunday.

The following are the chief villages of the Panol:—

Pan (Onnamand) is commonly known to Europeans as "One mand." It is a large village in the south-west corner of the Kundahs, with two houses of the long variety, with a door at each end and a partition in the middle. There is a *wursuli* called *Keinulv*, and a *kudrpali* called *Nersolv*, and outside the pen there is a stone called *mutchudkars*.

Kuirsi (Kolimand). This village is near Pan. It has a

wursuli and *kudrpali*, the former being called *Marsolv* and the latter *Keinulv*. Outside the pen, called *Tu matu*, there is a large stone called *keinkars*, and inside it there are two stones called *mutchudkars* and *pudrthkars*. I could learn little of the history or functions of these stones, but they were said to have been "played with" by Kwoten and Terkosh.

Perg (Yeragimand) is a small village near Avalanche Bungalow and is an example of a *kalolmad*.

Naters (Natanerimand) is a large village near Governor Shola, where most of the Panol live for the greater part of the year. This village has a *wursuli* and *tarvali*, but nothing else of interest.

Near Avalanche Bungalow there is the site of a village called *Pathmars*. Little remains of it, but the fireplace of a hut can still be seen.

Kabudri (Tebbekudumand). This is the male funeral village of the Panol. Here there are two stones called *teiks* where the *wursulir* are killed, and they are reputed to have been set up by Kwoten; one, called *parsteiks*, is for the Panol, and the other, called *kirshteiks*, for the Kuirsiol. Another place given as the male funeral place of Pan was Tim, where there is a three-roomed dairy of the same kind as that at Taradrkirsi, in the outermost room of which the body is placed. It is probable that Tim and Kabudri are two names for the same place.

TARADR

All the villages of this clan are situated in the north-west corner of the hills and the clan appears to have no villages far removed from the *etudmad*. The clan is a large one having now at least thirty-seven male and thirty-nine female members.

The Taradrol appear to have in several ways a special position among the Tarthar clans. They possess the special institution of the *kugvali*, which, though resembling in some respects a *ti*, is situated by the other dairies of the village and is tended by dairymen belonging to the clan. The Taradrol are also unique in having their future world (Amnòdr) near Perithi.

The Taradrol are divided into two *kudr*, each of which has three *pòlm*. The chief men of the *pòlm* of one *kudr* are Ircheidi (20), Parkeidi (21), and Polgar (22); of the second, Paners (23), Irkiolv (24), and Kudeners (25). About the time of my visit the place of Ircheidi, who was ill, was taken by his son, Siriar.

The six *pòlm* of the clan take it in turn to look after the *kugvalir*, each having charge of the dairies and herd for a period of three years. Shortly before my visit, the charge had been taken over by the *pòlm* of Ircheidi and Siriar.

The following are the chief villages:—

Taradr (Tarnardmand). This is one of the most characteristic Toda villages, situated near the road leading to the Paikara falls. It is shown in Figs. 5 and 6, and has three dairies, situated at some distance from the dwelling-huts. The two dairies shown in Fig. 5 are the *tarvali* and *kugvali*, the former on the left-hand side and the latter on the right. The third dairy of the village is a *wursuli*, situated to the right of the *kugvali*.

Near the *kugvali* is a stone (shown in Fig. 24) at which the *wursulir* is killed at a Taradr funeral. The stone is called *püdrshtikars* after the name of the buffaloes (*püdrshtipir*). At a little distance from the three dairies are the remains of another *pali*, which was only used at the funeral of a male. This *pali*, like those at other funeral places had three rooms, and in the ruins at the time of my visit it was easy to make out the three divisions. When the occasion arises, the dairy is rebuilt on the day of the funeral, and the *tarpalikartmokh* takes the *mu* into the innermost room after purifying it with *tudr* bark. The body of the dead man is then laid in the outermost room and kept there till it is taken out after the slaughter of the buffaloes. If this temporary building is the representative of a former dairy with three rooms, it would seem that the village of Taradr once had four dairies.

Kudrmas (Kudimalmand). This is a *kalolmad* on the western side of the Paikara. The *kugvalir* were here during the greater part of my visit.

Telgudr (Telkodumand). This is another *kalolmad*.

Pushtar (Pattaraimand). This village is one at which the *tesherst* ceremony (see p. 154) is sometimes performed.

Kudimad (Kulimand). This is a large village near Taradr at which many of the people live, but it is not an important village ceremonially, having only one dairy, a *tarvali*.

Near Paikara there can still be seen the remains of a village called *Pevar* which was deserted because the family which lived there became extinct.

KERADR

This is one of the smallest of the Tarthar clans, all its members being included in Table 26. There are at present sixteen male and nine female members.

There is at present only one *kudr*, the other having become extinct about three generations ago. As there has been no occasion for *irnörtiti*, no fresh division has been made. The *kudr* has two *pòlm*, one headed by Paniolv, and the other by Teikner.

The chief village, Keradr (Kannagimand), is situated in the south-west part of the hills near the Teivali village of Keadr. Keradr is also the male funeral place of the clan and was not occupied at the time of my visit. At this time most of the Keradrol were living at Tovalkan, near Paikara, a recent village at which there is a dairy of the ordinary kind (*tarvali*). Near the houses there is a raised mound shown in Fig. 59, erected to mark the spot on which Keirevan (26) was killed by falling from a tree into which he had climbed to cut wood.

KANÒDRS

This is one of the outlying Toda clans, and its people were said to have been less influenced by the altered conditions on the hills than any other clan, but they seem nevertheless to have given up several of their institutions. The sacred *poh* is only occasionally occupied, and I am doubtful whether they can be said to be in a more untouched condition than several other clans. The people are often called the Kererol, but I could not find that there was any village of Kerer from which this name is derived, and it is possibly the name of a district of the hills. The clan is distinguished by its possession of the conical *poh* at Kanòdrs, and by the fact that many of the adventures of Kwoto or Meilitars took place in the region it inhabits. Although Kwoto was a Melgars man, he is regarded as having a close connexion with the Kanòdrs people, and various features of the ritual of the Kanòdrs *poh* are said to be derived from him.

The clan is at present a small one, with a distinct majority of females. In fact, it seems so usual for members of this clan to have no children or only female children that there is some likelihood that the Kanòdrsol may become extinct. The present numbers are about thirteen males and twenty-three females.

There was some doubt as to the number of *kudr*. I was told that there are three, headed by Arsolv (27), Kineri (29), and Pòlkab (30) respectively, but at an *irnörtiti* ceremony both Arsolv and Kineri would give to Pòlkab, while the latter would give to both, so that it seems probable that there are properly only two *kudr*, as in other clans. One of these has only one *pòlm*, that of Pòlkab. The other has three *pòlm*, headed by Arsolv, Neratkutan (28), and Kineri.

The following are the chief villages of the Kanòdrsol :—

Kanòdrs (Devarmand). This village now consists of the *poh* only. There are still two *mani* at this village, one of which is called *Pünkòghlag*, a name closely resembling the name of the churning-stick at the *ti*. There are at present no dwelling-huts at the place, nor any remains of such huts, though it would appear from the legend of Kwoten that the village was inhabited at one time.

Pishkwosht (Bikkapatimand). This is a large village where most of the Kanòdrsol now live. The only dairy is in ruins. Close to the village there are a number of flat stones almost level with the ground (Fig. 71) which are called *Teuâr*, "the god way," and are said to mark the spot where the gods (*teu*) used to meet. Just above these is a large buffalo pen, which is reputed not to have been made by man. Whenever the gods went this way they used to deposit pieces of dried buffalo-dung on this spot and these became the stones of the *tu*.

Near the village is a forest hut, and opposite this are two stones called *pedrkars*. The Todas once had a large gathering here, and a man jumped a long distance which was recorded by means of these stones.

The other villages of the Kanòdrsol, *Taknin*, *Kuzhu* or

FIG. 71.—THE STONES AT PISHKWOSHT CALLED 'TEUAR.'

Kushu, &c., are in the same neighbourhood, but I was unable to visit them, and do not know whether they have any objects of interest.

KWÒDRDONI

This is the most outlying of Toda clans, but numerous tea estates have been established in its neighbourhood, and the people appear to have been a good deal influenced by the altered conditions. I was unable to visit any of the villages, and I know less about this clan than any other.

All the villages of the clan are situated in the district of the hills called by the Todas Purgòdr, and the people of the clan are, therefore, often called the Purgòdrol.

At present there appear to be seventeen males and fourteen females, but it is probable that these numbers are not complete. There are two *kudr*, headed by Kiurvan (32) and Atcharap (34). The former has three *pòlm*, of which the chief men are Puner (31), Kiurvan (32), and Òrudz (33), and the latter has two *pòlm*, headed by Atcharap (34) and Kudar (35).

This clan seems now to occupy only two villages. One is Kwòdrdoni (Kodudonnemand), where there is only a *tarvali*, though there was formerly a *wursuli*, now ruined, in which was kept a *mani* called *Kirsongg* which has disappeared. The other village is *Katikar* (Kodanadmand). The male funeral place is *Iudi*, and the female, *Punmud*.

PÄM

This is a clan which formerly occupied the site of Coonoor and Wellington. Its numbers are small, probably only seventeen males and thirteen females. There are two *kudr*, headed by Udrchovan (36) and Pungievan (37). Udrchovan's *kudr* has only one *pòlm*. Pungievan's *kudr* has three *pòlm*, of which the chief men are Pungievan (37), Arparners (38) and Seili (39).

The original *etudmad* of the clan was *Pirspurs*, the site of which was used for the Coonoor racecourse. *Päm* was then adopted as the chief village, but it has been allowed to fall into ruins, though still giving its name to the clan. The dairy at Päm was called *Palikñdrbedz* and the buffalo-pen, *Tñgñdron*. *Inikitj*, where the people now live, is an uninteresting village at which there are the ruins of a *tarvali*. There is a building in which the four or five sacred buffaloes (*nashperthir*) are kept, but they are not milked as there is no *palikartmokh*.

The male funeral place of this clan was *Puvi*, and the female, *Kwatkash*. These were situated where the Wellington barracks now stand, and the funerals are now held near Inikitj. Fig. 51 shows the wooden *teiks* at which the sacred buffalo would be killed at the funeral of a male.

There are several stories about Karnisi (37), a member of this clan. He is said to have been an exceptionally strong man, and the Todas tell how on one occasion two English soldiers came to Päm and insulted the women and how Karnisi took the two men unaided to the barracks at Wellington.

Karnisi also spent a fortune which had been stored in the dairy of Päm for many generations. A vessel (*pun*) full of rupees had been deposited in the dairy by an ancestor of Karnisi called Kiuten. It remained there till Karnisi spent it in buying buffaloes, ornaments for his many wives and household goods. He gave some of the rupees away and spent others in travelling to Coimbatore, and in a short time the money had disappeared.

NIDRSI

The headquarters of the Nidrsi clan are to the south of Coonoor. The people are closely surrounded by tea estates and have been much influenced. It is not now a large clan, having about sixteen male and twenty-five female members.

There are two *kudr*, headed by Todrigars (41) and Kudrmaskutan (43) respectively, each *kudr* having two *pòlm*. The chief men of the *pòlm* of one *kudr* are Puveners (40) and Todrigars, and of the other *kudr*, Kadrkutan (42) and Kudrmaskutan.

This clan affords a very good example of the degeneration which has in some cases befallen the dairy organisation. The people have only one *wursulir* left. The dairy (*wursuli*) has fallen into ruins, and they have no *wursol* and, therefore, the one buffalo is not milked. At a funeral of a male they will have to procure a *wursol* from another clan to kill this buffalo.

There are two *mani*, called *Eshkiakudr* and *Eikudr*, each with an iron chain, but as they have no *wursuli* these bells are kept under a stone at Akirsikòdri, the male funeral village. The other sacred buffaloes, *pineipir*, &c., are milked at a *tarvali*.

There are now only four inhabited villages, and only one of these seems to be of any importance.

Nidrsi. This is near the Badaga village of Hulikal. It

consists chiefly of huts obviously of recent construction and not of the proper Toda form. There is a small dairy (*tarvali*) and the situation of the former *wursuli*, almost completely overgrown, can still be seen. There is a buffalo enclosure called *Punatu*. The *irnörtkars* is a stone of ordinary appearance with other smaller stones round it, and there is also a *pilinörtkars* of which only a small piece now shows above the ground. There is a very large *tukitthkars* at this village (see pp. 252 and 597).

Another stone here is called *imudrikars* or *parsatthkars*. Milk is put on it every morning and evening by the *palikartmokh*, but it is not used in any way in connexion with a funeral. The Todas relate that an Englishman shot at and splintered this stone some years ago. Soon after he was bitten by his horse, and he asked the Todas, with whom he was on very good terms, what ought to be done. He was told that he should perform the *irnörtiti* ceremony, and a few days later he brought a three-year-old calf to the *irnörtkars* at Nidrsi and gave it to the people. It was taken by both *kudr* and the Englishman was soon well again. The whole affair was regarded as a good joke, and is interesting as showing that the Todas do not object to making sport of one of their sacred ceremonies, especially when they gain an addition to their stock of buffaloes.

Akirsikòdri. This is the male funeral village, at which there is a dairy with three rooms, in which the body of a dead man is placed on the day of the *etvainolkedr*.

MELGARS

The Tarthar clan which takes its name from the village of Melgars occupies a very special position in the Toda social organisation and in the dairy ceremonial. Although a Tarthar clan, the Melgarsol in many respects resemble the Teivaliol much more closely than they resemble the other clans of their own division.

In former times the Melgarsòl are said to have held the office of *palol* at the Kars *ti* and at the Pan *ti*, and to have lost this privilege owing to misbehaviour of a *palol*, of which an account has been already given. They are still capable of holding the offices of *wursol* and *kaltmokh*, for which otherwise only Teivaliol are eligible, and they have privileges and duties in connexion with various kinds of Toda ceremonial which are wholly unshared by other clans.

Though they may still hold the offices of *wursol* and *kaltmokh*, they are not allowed to carry out certain of the duties; thus, a Melgars *wursol* may not kill the sacred buffalo at a funeral, nor may he perform any of the other duties which fall to the part of a *wursol* on this occasion.

Although a Melgars man may no longer be *palol*, the Melgars people have a large number of privileges and duties connected with the *ti*. An account of these has already been given, but they may shortly be recapitulated here with the names given to them by the Todas.

(i.) *Mòr vatiti, tòr tititi.* "Buttermilk he drinks, food he takes." The Melgars men may take buttermilk and food at the dwelling-hut of any *ti*, and they alone have this privilege at the dairies of the Nòdrs *ti*.

(ii.) *Teirpülk mad oiiti.* "He goes at the head (of the procession) to (the place called) *teirpül*."

(iii.) *Ti alugpur putiti.* "The *alug* things of the *ti* he carries."

(iv.) *Alug puts nitz ithtothi.* "*Alug* come, stand he must." The Melgars man must stand by a certain tree with the *alug* when he comes to the new place during the migration of the *ti* buffaloes.

(v.) *Erd pünrs ithtothi.* "Two *pünrs* (four days) he must be." He stays at Anto from the Sunday on which the buffaloes migrate till the following Wednesday.

In addition to these privileges, it is also the duty of the Melgarsol to carry out rebuilding or repairing operations at a *ti mad*, and he has also to assist in carrying the body of a dead *palol*.

The special duties of the Melgarsol are not limited to the ceremonial of the *ti*, but in certain other ceremonies it is essential that a Melgars man shall be present or take part. He must milk a buffalo to provide milk for Tarthar women coming out of the seclusion-hut both after the hand-burning ceremony of pregnancy and after childbirth. He does this for women of his own clan and for those of all other Tarthar clans except that of Kwòdrdoni. A Melgars man must be present on the second day of the *irpalvusthi* ceremony of the *kugvalir* of Taradr, and the ceremony of this day, which is called *irpataduthti*, cannot take place if a Melgars man is not present.

It was also said that a Melgars man must be present whenever a feast is given at the end of a period called *pon* in any clan, but I am very doubtful as to the necessity of this. I think it is probable that no feast ever occurs at which a Melgars man fails to put in an appearance, and that my informants had come to regard his presence as necessary, but it seemed very doubtful whether his presence was an essential condition for the occurrence of this, as it certainly was in the case of certain other ceremonies.

There was some difference of opinion as to the reasons why the Melgarsol enjoyed these exceptional privileges. The Melgars people themselves believed that their exceptional position was due to the connexion of Kwoto with their clan. They said that when Kwoto became superior to all the gods, and was called Meilitars, these privileges were given to the clan to which he belonged. According to another account, the position of a Melgars man at the head of the procession of the Nòdrs *ti* was settled by Anto in order to appease the buffalo Enmars when two of its bells were taken away and given to the Pan *ti*. Others, again, said that the privileges of the Melgarsol were given as a recompense when this clan was deprived of its privilege of becoming *palol*. There is little doubt that the real reason for the Melgars privileges has been lost and that different reasons have been sought in the Toda legends. The Melgars people have chosen a reason which gratifies their pride in claiming Kwoto as one of themselves, while other Todas have reasons which serve to add to the importance of the sacred institution of the *ti*, of which they are so proud.

There are other special features in which the Melgars people differ from the rest of the Tarthar clans. They have no *wursulir*, though they can become *wursol* to other clans, so that, in this respect, they resemble the Teivaliol in being able to tend buffaloes which they do not themselves possess. Another difference is that the *palikartmokh* of the Melgarsol uses *tudr* bark in his ordination ceremonies, and this gives him a higher rank than other *tarpalikartmokh*. It is on this account that a Melgars *palikartmokh* may not visit the *tarvali* of another clan (see p. 66).

The Melgarsol again resemble the Teivaliol in not shaving the head after a funeral, as is done by Tarthar clans other than that of Melgars.

The Melgarsol resemble the Teivaliol in so many respects that it is tempting to suppose that this clan must at one time have formed part of the Teivali division and for some reason was transferred to the Tartharol. Every Toda whom I questioned on the point was, however, certain that the Melgars people had always been members of the Tartharol.

There are two facts which show that there is some special relation between the people of Melgars and those of Kwòdrdoni. One is that intermarriage is said to be prohibited between members of these two clans; the other is that the milking by a Melgars man when a Tarthar woman is leaving the seclusion-hut does not take place in the case of a Kwòdrdoni woman. These facts point to some relation between the two clans of which I was unable to obtain any account.

The Melgarsol form a fairly large clan, having at the present time about thirty-one male and twenty female representatives. They have at present only one *kudr*, the other having become extinct about eight years ago on the death of Tikon (49). A half-sister of this man is still living, but the *kudr* has no male representative. During the last eight years, the Melgarsol have had no trouble (*kaspel*) which has made it necessary to perform the *irnörtiti* ceremony, but should the occasion arise, a *naim* would decide on a re-division of the other *kudr*. I was told that the matter was continually the subject of discussion, and it seemed probable that the nature of the re-division was already more or less arranged, but would not be definitely settled till the occasion arose.

The one *kudr* has four *pòlm*, of which the chief men are Kiunievan (44), Artholvan (45), Nòtirzi (46) and Ilgeivan (48). Tergudrvan (47) belonged to the same *pòlm* as Artholvan. The families included in Table 49 are all extinct in the male line, and, with the exception of Tikon, I am doubtful to which *kudr* or *pòlm* they belonged.

Melgars, the chief village, is situated behind the gardens of Government House at Ootacamund. It has few features of interest, and there is little to be seen at the other villages of the clan. *Nüln* (Narigulimand) is situated in the Kundahs.

Two Toda villages, Ki Perththo and Padegar, are said to be the general property of the Tartharol, but at the time of my visit both were inhabited by the Melgarsol.

The village of *Katol*, which is now ruined, is mentioned by Harkness as one of the villages near Ootacamund.

The chief funeral place is *Ushadr*, mentioned in the story of Kwoto. There is another funeral place called *Mirzoti* common to Melgars and Kidmad.

Kidmad and Karsh

These are two sub-divisions of the Melgarsol which separated from the main body, probably about seven or eight generations ago. At first I heard only of Kidmad, and it was only when working over the Nidrsiol that I found there were people living with this clan who did not belong to it, but were an offshoot of the Melgars people and were called Karshol.

According to one account, both Kidmadol and Karshol separated from the main body at the same time, but, according to another, the people who first separated belonged to Karsh and then split some generations later into the two groups.

The separation was due to a quarrel between father and son. The Melgars people were holding a council and one of the chief men of the clan was late in coming. When he appeared in the distance, he was recognised by nobody but his own son, who, when asked who was coming, said "*pazuli padmokh pöti àtham nòtthred? Kùtm it vòrs!*—*i.e.*,

"A wanderer and bastard comes, why do you look at him? Let the council go forward!" (*Pazuli* is a name applied to a man who belongs to no clan, and *padmokh* is the name of the child of a woman with whom no man has performed the *pursütpimi* ceremony.)

The *manmokh* (sister's son) of the father was present at the council, and when his uncle arrived, the *manmokh* told him what had been said by his son in the council, and the father said, "I am no *pazuli*, it is you who are the *pazuli*: henceforward you must not live at Melgars; you will have nothing from me except what I give you to-day." The father gave the son a one-horned buffalo (*kwadrkutir*) and a portion of the Mirzoti funeral place.

Since that day descendants of the son have been separate from Melgarsol and they have held their funerals at Mirzoti, but not on the same spot as the Melgars people.

The Kidmadol and Karshol have lost certain privileges possessed by other Todas. The loss of these privileges is expressed by the Todas as follows:—

(i.) *Meitün kitht ògadi.* "He may not sit on the *meitün*." When a man of Kidmad or Karsh goes to any Tarthar dairy he is not allowed to sit on the raised bed on the right hand side of the door.

(ii.) *Nïrsi nest ògadi.* "He may not rub the fire-sticks." If fire has to be made at a male funeral, or on any other occasion, it must be done by a man of another clan.

(iii.) *Ertatpun pitth ògadi.* "He may not touch the *ertatpun*," a dairy vessel which may be touched by any other Toda man. The result of this restriction is that a man of these clans can never hold a dairy office.

Marriages are not allowed between Melgars people and those of either Kidmad or Karsh.

The village of Karsh no longer exists; it was near Akirzikòdri, but in the time of Kilpan (51) the people were so poor that they went to live with the Nidrsiol and have remained with them since. Though living at Nidrsi, they are still regarded as a separate people, and marriages may take place between the two clans. They have only three or four ordinary buffaloes. If a male dies they have to kill a *persasir*, which they obtain from Melgars. The only males living are one man and his son, the father having also two sisters.

The Kidmadol are more prosperous, and the men of the clan appear to be fairly prominent people among the Todas, in spite of their disadvantages. Kijievan (5) has the reputation of being one of the ablest people of the whole community. The clan numbers five males and three females.

THE TEIVALI CLANS

KUUDR

This is the most important of the Teivali clans, at any rate from the social point of view. It has supplied the *monegar* since the institution of this office, and it is the only Teivali clan represented on the Toda *naim* or council. From the religious point of view the Kuudrol are less important and have no exclusive rights to any sacred office,[1] though they are exceptional in being greeted by the *palol* with the *kwarzam* of their clan, *Ivikanmokhkûtmeilteu*, followed by *idith* as in the prayers. The origin of this custom is said to be that long ago strangers came to the hills and massacred all the people of the clan except one boy, who hid himself in the buffalo pen. The present people of Kuudr are descended from the boy and his escape is commemorated in the greeting of the *palol*. The Kuudrol also possess the very sacred dairy of Kiudr.

The Kuudr clan is the largest of the Teivali clans and stands second in point of numbers among all the Toda clans. It has at least sixty-three male and thirty-five female representatives. I omitted to obtain the children of two families, and these would raise the numbers slightly.

I had much difficulty in obtaining a correct account of the organisation of the Kuudrol, the difficulty proving to be due to certain anomalies in this clan. It has three chief divisions, headed by Kuriolv (52), Ishkievan (60) and Tövoniners (61),

[1] For the story how the Kuudr people came to lose the right of providing the *palol* for the Nòdrs *ti*, see p. 114.

and each of these divisions is sometimes called a *kudr*. From the point of view, however, of the *irnörtiti* ceremony it is clear that the division of Tövoniners is not a definite *kudr*, for the men of this division do not receive buffaloes from any other division, although they may themselves perform the *irnörtiti* ceremony, in which case the buffalo goes to the men of the other two divisions. The family of Tövoniners differs also from other families of the clan in having no place at the village of Kuudr. This anomalous position of the family is due to the part played by the men of the family in the quarrel which led to the separation of the Pedrkars people from Kuudr (see p. 675). The family of Tövoniners is probably not a *kudr* in the strict sense of the term, and if so, the Kuudr clan falls into line with other clans in being divided into two *kudr* only.

There was also some confusion about the *pòlm* of the Kuudr clan, one source of confusion being due to the trouble connected with the parentage of Teitchi (52), which has been already considered (see p. 564).

It was quite clear that the *kudr* of Ishkievan has two *pòlm* only, headed by Ishkievan and Tadrners (60).

Kuriolv's division was said to have eight *pòlm*, the head men being Kuriolv (52), Targners (53), Pöteners (54), Keitas (55), Tüliners and Tikievan (56), Mudriners (57), and Madsu (58). The men of the first four *pòlm* are known to be closely connected with one another, and, as may be seen in the genealogies, the first three claim common descent from Tudrvan. Similarly the *pòlm* of Tüliners, Tikievan and Madsu are known to be closely connected. About the position of the *pòlm* of Mudriners, as we have already seen, there is much doubt, the state of affairs being that it is really most closely connected with the *pòlm* of Tüliners and Tikievan, but that Kuriolv claims it as closely allied to his own through the relation of Teitchi to Kòrs. Formerly the family of Arsners (59) formed a separate *pòlm*, but owing to the fact that it now has only two young members, and is very poor, it has been joined to the *pòlm* of Madsu (58).

Including the families of Tövoniners and Arsners, there

would thus be twelve *pòlm*. This is not consistent with the information given in connexion with the *pepkaricha* ceremony (see p. 169), from which it appears that there are fifteen heads of families in the Kuudrol. It may be that the *pòlm* and family do not correspond with one another, or there may be some other explanation of the discrepancy.

The following are the chief villages of the Kuudrol :—

Kuudr (Kundakodumand). This is a large village with substantial huts in the Tamil style which have been built by Kuriolv. There is a large dairy, the *tudrpali*, and a smaller dairy, the *kidpali*, in front of it, with two buffalo enclosures (*tu*), one apparently for each dairy. In the large *tu* there are three stones called *keinkars*, *tashtikars* and *mutchudkars*, all of ceremonial importance (see p. 169). Growing in one side of the *tu* there is a tree called *teikhuwadiki*, under which the *mu* is buried.

As usual, water is taken from two sources, and at Kuudr that used for sacred purposes is drawn from a spring, called *kiznir*. The origin of this spring has been already given in connexion with the prayer of Kuudr, in which this and other events in the history of the village are commemorated. The special relations between Kuudr and Òdr have been already considered in the account of the latter village.

Kiudr (Kengodumand). This village has a somewhat anomalous position in that, though not the chief village of its clan from the social point of view, it is in many ways more sacred than Kuudr.

It is a very picturesque village, shown in Fig. 7, in which there are two dwelling-huts. That shown in the figure is one of the largest and best constructed of existing Toda huts, having been rebuilt recently under the direction of Kijievan (50), who has a special reputation as an architect. It was at this village that a pregnant woman was not allowed to come to the hut, but had to remain at some little distance, and the sacredness of the hut is also shown by the fact that the prayer of this village provides the only instance in which the *kwarzam* of a hut occurs.

The dairy is situated at some little distance from the huts, quite out of sight of people at the latter. On going from the huts to the dairy a shallow stream flowing over broad flat stones is crossed. This stream is called *Keikudr*, and is of some ceremonial importance (see p. 307).

The dairy which is called *Kilpoh* is shown in Figs. 20 and 31, and is a large, well-built structure of the ordinary shape. It is situated within a high wall, which is much thicker than usual, and in front it must be several yards across, so that it is possible to walk about on the top of it. On this wall, on the right hand side, are two old stones (shown in Fig. 31), called *neurzülnkars*. Close to the dairy there are two ancient and weatherworn stones, shown in Fig. 32, to which the same name is given.

There are six bells in the dairy. Two are kept on the *patatmar* and are called *patatmani*, the individual names of the bells being *Mudrani* and *Kerani*. The other four are called *ertatmani*, and are kept on the *ertatmar*; their individual names are *Pongg*, *Nongg*, *Pundrths*, and *Pan*.

Kiudr is one of the villages which was said to have been at one time a *ti mad*. In favour of this is the fact that its dairy is called *poh* and that there are stones called *neurzülnkars* which are usually found at a *ti mad*. The people have also to play a part during the procession of the buffaloes of the Nòdrs *ti*, and there seems to be little doubt that the village is in some way especially connected with the *ti* institution, though exactly how is uncertain.

Kiudr is certainly a village especially revered not only by the Kuudrol, but by all Todas. It is a *sati mad*, and any Toda will be believed if he speaks in front of its dairy. Another sign of the sanctity of the dairy is the fact that the ceremony of *pilinörtiti* may be performed here not only by members of the Kuudr clan, but also by any other Toda.

Molkush. This is a recently established village, little more than a quarter of a mile from Kiudr. The scenes shown in Figs. 16 and 17 were taken at this village. It has no dairy and the milk of the ordinary buffaloes is churned in the dwelling-hut. This village may be regarded as an adjunct to the sacred village of Kiudr, at which the ordinary buffaloes are tended. At the time of my visit the wife of one of the men who usually lived at Kiudr gave birth to a son and the seclusion-hut was at Molkush, and both before and after the birth the woman and those connected with her were living at this village. It seemed as if the restrictions connected with life at Kiudr are avoided by building at a little distance what is technically another village, at which the people live whenever for any reason they are not allowed to live at Kiudr. Its existence seemed to me to be one of the many devices by means of which the Todas keep the letter of the law with the minimum of inconvenience.

Miuni (Marlimand). This is a village of the Kuudrol which is reverenced by all Todas on account of the belief that it was formerly the meeting-place of the gods. It is a very picturesque village, situated near the Marlimand reservoir and has two dairies.

Kwirg is chiefly important as the place at which new *pep* is made for the Kuudr clan. Its prayer is given on p. 222.

Ars is an uninteresting village near Kuudr.

Peivòrs. This is a village near Paikara. It contains a double house, shown in Fig. 8, and has two dairies, one of which is now used as a calf-house. The second dairy was built when two families were living at the village, and the one dairy was not large enough for both.

Pirsush. This is a *kalolmad*.

Karia, a village near the Paikara road, from which a modern long house in the Tamil style is to be seen. Behind this are the old dwelling-hut and the dairy. At the time of my visit the new house was unoccupied and the people were living in the old hut.

PIEDR

The people of Piedr derive their special importance from the fact that they provide the *palol* for the sacred *ti* of Nòdrs. According to tradition, they had this privilege exclusively at one time; later, they shared it with the Kuudrol, and now they share with the people of Kusharf. They form a fairly large clan, having about twenty-eight male and fourteen female members.

As in the case of the Kuudrol, there was some doubt about

the divisions of the clan. There are said to be three *kudr*, of which the chief men are Teikudr (63), Eisòdr (64), and Nongarsivan (62). If a man of Teikudr's division has to perform the *irnörtiti* ceremony, the buffalo goes to Eisòdr's division, and *vice versa*. If a man of Nongarsivan's division performs the ceremony, the buffalo would go to both the other divisions. Thus Nongarsivan's *kudr* seems to form an extra division, like that of Tövoniners among the Kuudrol. I did not obtain any explanation of this, but it is probably due to the fact that the people of Nongarsivan's division live at Kavidi in the Wainad, and are, in consequence, regarded as being outside the regular affairs of the clan. I failed to obtain an account of the *pòlm*.

The chief village of the clan is now rarely visited. It is in the northern parts of the hills near the Badaga village of Hullatti. I had hoped to have visited it and the neighbouring village of Kusharf, but had not time. Some members of the clan visit the village of Piedr once a year, but I did not learn what was done on the occasion.

Kuudi. This is now one of the chief villages of the clan. It has a modern house, the largest and most highly ornamented Toda dwelling which I saw on the hills.

Tavatkudr is a village of one hut and a dairy. It was this dairy which was burnt during my visit as a consequence of the revelation of *ti* secrets to me by Kaners, who lived at this village.

Eparskòdr is an ancient village at which the first Toda died (see p. 400). At present the village consists of a dairy only.

Kavidi is situated in the Wainad, not far from Gudalur. I did not visit it, but, so far as I could gather, it contained no object of interest and there was no evidence that it was an ancient settlement.

The clan has several funeral places, partly owing to the fact that the Kavidi people are at too great a distance from the top of the hills to hold the *etvainolkedr* in the ordinary funeral place. The Kavidi people, therefore, have two special funeral places, called *Sudvaili* for males and *Mòmanothi* for females. The second funeral, or *marvainolkedr*, was, however, held at the regular places of *Meroln* and *Pamarkol.*

A disused village in the Wainad is called *Potvaili*. The termination *vaili* of this village and of the male funeral place only occurs here, and is probably borrowed from some other language, possibly from the Kurumbas.

One abandoned village of this clan, *Nongarsi*, seems to have been situated near Ootacamund. Its Badaga name is Kettarimand, and it is possibly one of the villages mentioned by Harkness.

KUSHARF

The people of this clan are called indifferently Kusharfol or Umgasol. There seemed to be no doubt that Kusharf is the chief village, but, like Piedr, it is little used, and Umgas is coming to be regarded as the *etudmad*.

The Kusharfol seem to be in some way related to the Piedrol. They share with the latter the privilege of providing the *palol* for the Nòdrs *ti*, and the two clans are not allowed to intermarry. They have the same *nòdrodchi*, Teipakh, and it seems possible that they were originally two sub-divisions of one clan.

At present the Kusharfol are not numerous, having only about thirteen male and thirteen female representatives. They have two *kudr*, headed by Nòdrners and Ongudr, each of which has two *pòlm*. The chief men of the *pòlm* of one *kudr* are Ongudr (65) and Pangudr (66); of the other, Nòdrners and Erkhud (67).

The chief village of Kusharf is near Hullàtti, and, like the neighbouring Piedr, is rarely visited.

Umgas. This is at present the most important village of the clan; it is shown in Fig. 72. There are two large dwelling-huts shown on the right-hand side of the figure. The building to the left of them is the chief dairy, which is called *Kwotòdrvoh*. It is a *poh* and not a *pali*, though of the ordinary form, and is exceptional in being situated so near the dwelling-huts. The *pali* is situated still more to the left, hidden by trees.

The two tall stones in the foreground are called *nadrkkars*. They serve as *irnörtkars* and also mark out the path by which women must go on their way to the huts, the women having to keep on the right-hand side of these stones. By the wall of the huts and close to the *poh* there are two stones, the *majvatitthkars*, at which women stand when they receive buttermilk (*maj*) from the dairy. About fifteen yards in front of the other dairy (*pali*) there is a stone called *imudrikars*. On one side of this there is a narrow well-worn track along which women must go on their way to the dairy.

FIG. 72.—THE VILLAGE OF UMGAS, SHOWING THE 'NADRKKARS' IN THE CENTRE. BEHIND THE STONES IS THE 'POH' OF THIS VILLAGE, AND ON ITS RIGHT ARE THE DWELLING-HUTS.

and nearer the *pali* there are two *majvatitthkars*, where they stand when receiving buttermilk.

Between the *poh* and the *pali* there is the *tu* and at the far end of this is a large stone, the *muütthkars*, marking the spot where the *mu* is buried.

Teidr is not far from Nòdrs. It has two huts and a dairy. The *teidrtolkars* of Nòdrs takes its name from this village, the *wursol* who gave the name to the stone being a Teidr man.

Teidr is one of the villages which is said to have been

formerly a *ti mad*, and in support of the statement I was taken to see two stones called *neurzülnkars* at some little distance from the village.

Pòln is close to the tree known in Ootacamund as "the umbrella tree." There are two huts and a dairy, which was in ruins at the time of my visit. Under the "umbrella tree" there are two stones. One of these has been overgrown by the tree so that it is now firmly imbedded. It is called *Korateu* and is said to have been thrown by Korateu from his hill. The other stone is deeply imbedded and only shows three small projections above the ground. This is the *Nòtirzikars* and was thrown to this spot by the goddess Nòtirzi from her hill.

In a wood near at hand overgrown by trees, there is another stone called *Känkars*, marking the spot where the *pasthir* were killed at the funeral place which formerly existed here.

KEADR

This clan had at one time the privilege of supplying the *palol* to the Pan *ti*, but its numbers are now small, and the *palol* of this *ti* at present belongs to the Piedrol. There are now only eleven males and ten females belonging to the clan.

Till recently there was a branch of the clan called Kwaradrol, taking their name from the village of Kwaradr. According to some, the Kwaradrol were a separate clan, but there seemed to be little doubt that they were part of the Keadrol and formed one *kudr* of the clan. The division only became extinct in the male line a few years ago, and the genealogical record of the family is given in Table 70.

The head man of the other *kudr* is Perner (68), and this division has three *pòlm*, two of which are headed by Perner and Pichievan (69), while the third has only three young boys, Karem (69) and his brothers, as members. Since the Kwaradrol died out, the clan has only had one *kudr*, but during my visit it was decided that a new *kudr* should be formed, and the *pòlm* of Karem was made the new division, so that in future the Keadrol will have one *kudr* consisting of one *pòlm*, and another of two *pòlm*. It was said that the original partition of the clan into Keadrol and Kwaradrol was due to Kwoten, who established the two divisions in order that there should be someone to take the place of a *palol* who left on account of a funeral in his clan.

Keadr. This, the chief village of the clan, is situated near Keradr. I was unable to visit it, and have no record of any features of interest it may possess.

Kwaradr, the village from which one division took its name, is near Avalanche, and is now falling into ruins owing to the dying out of the family which occupied it.

Pekhòdr is called by the Badagas Osamand, or "new village," and has only been in existence about ten years.

Kapthòri is now in ruins, but is mentioned in the story of Kwoten.

PEDRKARS

This clan is an offshoot of the Kuudrol, from which it has now for a long time been separated. The division arose out of a quarrel at a council which was once being held at Kuudr.[1] There were three parties in the *naim*, each wishing that a different ceremony should be performed. One party wished to give salt to the buffaloes, a second wanted to sacrifice a calf (*erkumptthpimi*), and a third were in favour of moving to another village (*irskidthtothi*). The three parties could not agree, and it was finally decided that those who wished to do *irskidthtothi* should separate from the rest. They did so and went to live near Kwòdrdoni, and have since been a separate clan, now known as the Pedrkarsol. The people who wished to do *erkumptthpimi* were the ancestors of Tövoniners, and it is in consequence of this quarrel that this family occupies its anomalous position and has no place at Kuudr.

At the same time the people of Pedrkars lost the privilege of being *palol* or *wursol*, but they may become eligible by performing the *irnörtiti* ceremony at Kuudr or Kiudr.

[1] This was evidently a council consisting of the members of the clan only.

For some time after the separation intermarriage was not allowed between Kuudr and Pedrkars, but recently such marriages have taken place, and several are recorded in the genealogies.

There are very few members of the clan, only seven males and five females. At present there is only one *kudr* and this has only one *pòlm*. Formerly there were two *kudr*, but one became extinct some time ago.

About three generations ago there was a quarrel between the people of Pedrkars and those of Piedr. A man of Pedrkars named Kavanadi had married a woman of Piedr and one day quarrelled with his wife's father. At Piedr there were at the entrance of the buffalo-pen two large wooden posts (*tüli*). After the quarrel Kavanadi went to Piedr and carried off both the posts with the wooden bars (*tasth*) by which the opening of the pen is closed. When Kavanadi had carried the posts and bars as far as a place called Kalin, near the Kota village of Tizgudr, a stone on the top of one of the *tüli* fell down. It may still be seen and is known as *Kalinkars*. Kavanadi went on, but he soon began to spit blood, and when he had gone some way further, he was obliged to drop the *tüli* at a place which is now called *Tülipudinpem*. He managed to reach his home at Pedrkars and then died. A council was held and it was decided that marriage should not be allowed in future between the Piedrol and Pedrkarsol, and no such marriages are recorded in the genealogies.

The stone called Kalinkars which fell by the way is now said to be able to move about and may be seen one day at one spot and on another day at another. The Kotas of Tizgụdr have several times taken the stone to their village, but it has always gone back again. In spite of his unfortunate end, Kavanadi is regarded, more or less, as a hero by the Todas and is mentioned in the funeral eulogy of Pidrvan (p. 387).

All the villages of the Pedrkarsol are in the part of the hills near Kwòdrdoni. Pedrkars itself is said to have been at one time a *ti mad*. Some Tamil people once came to the hills and found some of the buffaloes of the *ti* standing by a swamp. The Tamils fired at the buffaloes and one was killed. When the *palol* saw this, he cursed, saying "*pedr kars ama, kwòdr nòdr ama,*" "may the Tamil stone become; may the *ti* place an ordinay place become!" Then the people who had killed the buffalo became stones and the buffaloes were taken by the *palol* to the *ti mad* of Kakwai. The people who had separated from Kuudr had before this been living at Pongudr, but when the *ti mad* was deserted they went to live there, and the place was called Pedrkars in consequence of the curse of the *palol* and the clan has since taken its name from this village.

KULHEM

This clan appears to occupy the same kind of inferior position among the Teivaliol as that taken by the Kidmadol among the Tarthar clans. The Kulhemol are not allowed to sit on the *meitün* (right-hand side) of a dairy, and they are not allowed to perform the ordination ceremony with *tudr* bark, which cuts them off from holding the offices of *palol*, *kaltmokh*, or *wursol*.

There was some difference of opinion about the cause of the inferior position of Kulhem. According to one account the people separated from Kuudr at the same time as the Pedrkarsol and for the same reason. According to another account, when Teikirzi was dividing the buffaloes, she left Kulhem till last, intending to give them a good portion. When she was about to give the people of this clan their buffaloes, the invaders came who have been mentioned in the story of Teikirzi (p. 187). After the invaders had been turned to stone, Teikirzi returned to her task of giving buffaloes to Kulhem, but she came to the conclusion that the clan was in some way responsible for the misfortune which had happened, and she gave them no sacred buffaloes and only a few *putüir*, and she enjoined that they should not be ordained with *tudr*. It seems, however, that the Kulhemol resemble the Pedrkarsol in becoming eligible for the office of *palol* if they do *irnörtiti* to Kuudr.

The chief village, *Kulhem* or *Kulthlem*, is near Kanòdrs.

The only other village of importance is *Konikwòr*, near Paikara. At the time of my visit several of the clan were living at a place called *Kultu*. This is not properly a Toda village, the people living in a hut of the Badaga form near a tea plantation in order to sell the buffalo dung to the planters.

This clan now numbers only six males and three females, all belonging to one family (72). They have neither ***kudr*** nor ***pòlm***.

CHAPTER XXIX

TEIVALIOL AND TARTHAROL

THE existence of these two divisions of the Toda people raises one of the most interesting problems of their social organisation. The fact that the Todas are an Indian people at once suggests that we have to do here with some form of the institution of caste. Each division is endogamous, as is the caste, and each is divided into a number of exogamous septs resembling the gotras of a caste. Again, there is some amount of specialisation of function, the Teivaliol being the division from which the most sacred of the dairymen are chosen.

The names of the two divisions probably correspond with this differentiation of function. The Teivaliol evidently derive their name from the sacred office, *deva*, of Sanskrit origin, being in common use in South India for 'sacred,' while *devalayam* means a temple.[1] The origin of Tartharol[2] is more doubtful, but I believe that the word carries the idea of ordinary, *tár* being used sometimes in this sense.

There is little restriction on social intercourse between the two divisions. So far as I am aware, they can eat together, and a member of one division can receive food from any member of another.

Though intermarriage is forbidden, the irregular unions in which the man is the *mokhthodvaiol* of the woman (see Chap.

[1] There is also a place called Devali in the Wainad which may possibly be connected in some way with the Teivaliol.

[2] Grigg (*Manual*, p. 187) derives the word from *tasan*, a servant. *S* or *sh* is sometimes inserted into the word Tartharol, but it is purely euphonic, and I do not think that this derivation is at all probable.

XXII) are frequent, and, indeed, it seems to be the rule for connexions of this kind to be formed between members of the two divisions.

The only definite restriction on social intercourse is that a Teivali woman may not visit a Tarthar village, so that if a Tarthar man becomes the *mokhthodvaiol* of a Teivali woman, he has to visit her at her home, or may go to live at her village altogether or for long periods. There is no similar restriction on the visits of Tarthar women to Teivali villages, and at the time of my visit at least one Tarthar woman was living altogether at the village of her Teivali consort.

The prohibition of the visits of Teivali women to Tarthar villages is said to have had its origin in the misbehaviour of certain Teivali women who once visited the village of Nòdrs, but I did not learn in what their offence consisted.

The most obvious features which mark off the two divisions from one another occur in connexion with the dairy organisation. The most important dairy institutions of the Todas belong to the Tartharol, but their dairymen are Teivaliol. This applies not only to the *ti* dairies, but also to the *wursuli* dairies of the Tarthar villages. The highest dairy office, that of *palol*, can only be held by a Teivali man, while the lower offices of *kaltmokh* and *wursol* must be held by them or by one of the Melgars clan of the Tartharol. According to tradition, the members of the Melgarsol were also at one time capable of holding the office of *palol*, but lost the right owing to the misbehaviour of one of their number. As I have already suggested, the Melgarsol may have been formerly a Teivali clan, but on repeated inquiry, it seemed clear that they had always been Tartharol, so that at one time in Toda history certain Tartharol were permitted to hold the highest dairy office as well as the lower grades for which they are still eligible. The position of the Melgars clan is, however, so much of a mystery in itself that it can contribute little to the understanding of our present difficulties.

Although the Teivaliol hold the highest dairy offices, and while holding them have a very high degree of sanctity, it is quite clear that, apart from the holding of these offices, they have no sanctity whatever. A Teivali man who, while holding office as *palol*, is so sacred that he may not be touched by nor touch anyone, and may be visited even by his nearest relatives on two days of the week only, becomes an ordinary person, with absolutely no restrictions on intercourse, the moment he ceases to hold office.

Further, the fact that the Teivaliol hold these sacred offices does not lead to any respect being shown by Tartharol towards Teivaliol; there is not the slightest trace of the belief that their right to exert the highest priestly functions gives the Teivaliol any superiority, nor, it seemed clear to me, did the right inspire the Teivaliol themselves with any feeling of superiority. Indeed, it was distinctly the other way. The Tartharol always boasted that they were the superior people and that the Teivaliol were their servants, and the Teivaliol always seemed to me to acquiesce, though unwillingly, in this opinion. Whenever I asked a Tarthar man why he regarded his division as superior, he always answered, "We have the *ti* and we appoint the Teivaliol to act as our servants." In the case of the Teivali dairyman acting as *wursol* at the Tarthar villages, I had definite evidence in more than one instance that the priest was regarded as a paid servant, to be treated with scant respect except in the special points prescribed by custom. The fact that the Teivali dairyman living at a Tarthar village may not touch any of the Tartharol puts him very much at the mercy of the latter, and the dairyman has, so far as I know, no redress for any wrong, real or fancied, which he may receive.

The inferiority of the Teivaliol came out in one very striking point to which I shall return later. I learnt from the Tartharol that there were certain differences in language between the two divisions; that the Teivaliol used certain words as names of objects which were not used by the Tartharol. I obtained a list of these, and later approached a Teivali man on the matter. When I opened the subject he was very much taken aback, and then became very angry because I had been told of the difference, though its existence was not denied. His whole attitude was that of a man ashamed of his lowly origin. Far more indignation was shown by him and by other Teivaliol because I had been told of their peculiarities of language than was ever shown after the exposure of deeds distinctly immoral even from the Toda point of view. I shall return to this subject again shortly; I mention it here because it seemed to me to afford the clearest evidence that the Teivaliol were conscious of their own inferiority in the social scale.

In the story of Kwoten we find that the Tarthar hero is accompanied by Erten of Keadr, a Teivali man, and the latter was said to have been the servant of the former. This suggests the possibility that at one time the Teivaliol may have acted as servants to the Tartharol, even more definitely than at present.

At the present time there are some features of the social organisation and social life which might be held to weigh strongly against the idea that the Teivaliol are the inferior division. The *monegar* of the Todas is one of the Teivaliol, and the most influential member of the *naim*, or council, at the present time is a Teivali man. I believe the monegarship, however, to be a recent institution, possibly dating only from the advent of Europeans to the hills. The chief duty of the *monegar* is the collection of the assessment made by the Government, and it is quite consistent with Toda ideas that this troublesome, and from their point of view menial duty should be handed over to one of the Teivaliol. The great power of the Teivaliol in the *naim* is probably still more recent and due to the influence of one man. The Teivaliol should have only one representative on the *naim*, while the Tartharol should have three, and it is entirely owing to the powerful personality of Kuriolv that this balance has been disturbed, and that the influence of the Teivaliol is so predominant. It is possible that Kuriolv will do much to obliterate the social inequality of the two divisions, though I suspect from what the Todas told me that it is intended to revert to the old order as soon as he dies.

There is one custom which shows very clearly that it is only as dairymen that the Teivaliol have any sanctity. If the sacred buffaloes (*pasthir*) of the Teivaliol go to a Tarthar village, they may be milked either at a *wursuli* or a *tarvali*, and the

Tarthar people may use the milk. If Tarthar buffaloes, however, go to a Teivali village, the Teivaliol may neither milk them nor use their milk or its products. Thus buffaloes which are normally milked by a Teivali dairyman when at their own village may not be milked by Teivaliol at a Teivali village, while there is no restriction on the milking of Teivali buffaloes by the Tartharol.

Although the Tartharol are in the habit of speaking of the Teivali dairymen as their servants, they have no means of enforcing service. The post of dairyman of any kind is one of profit, and, as we have seen, when the post, even of *palol*, ceases to bring a sufficient income, the Tartharol fail to obtain people to occupy it.

In the ceremonial of the dairy, the relation between the two divisions is entirely one-sided. The Tartharol own the buffaloes and the dairies, and the Teivaliol do the work. In certain other ceremonies, there is more reciprocity in the relations of the two divisions to one another.

The Tartharol have certain definite duties at a Teivali funeral and the Teivaliol at a Tarthar funeral, and in most cases the duties are thoroughly reciprocal and the two divisions appear to act on equal terms. Thus, in the earth-throwing ceremony, the earth is dug by a Teivali man at a Tarthar funeral, and the Tarthar men before they throw ask the Teivaliol whether they may do so. At a Teivali funeral these positions are reversed. Similarly, the buffaloes are caught by Tartharol for Teivaliol and *vice versa*.

On the other hand, there are some ceremonies in which the Teivaliol have definite duties to perform at a Tarthar funeral which are not reciprocated. In the earth-throwing ceremony of the Tartharol, earth is first thrown by the Teivali *wursol*, but he does this as dairyman and not as one of the Teivaliol. The *kodtiti* ceremony of the second funeral is, however, only performed at a Tarthar funeral, and in it a Teivali man plays an important part, wearing the cloak which has been covering the relics and adorning himself with women's ornaments. He hangs on the neck of the calf the bell called *tukulir mani* and touches the relics with the bow and arrow after asking the Tartharol if he may do so. It is said that this ceremony is performed at a Tarthar funeral in order to purify the Tartharol with *tudr* before they go to Amnòdr, and the prominent position of the Teivaliol in this ceremony is evidently due to the use of this sacred substance.

After a funeral the Tartharol in general shave their heads, and this is not done by the Teivaliol, but it is also not done by the Melgarsol, which shows that the difference is connected with the different relations of the two divisions to the dairy ritual.

One important difference between the funeral ceremonies of the two divisions is that the *mani*, or sacred bell, is not used by the Teivaliol, except by the Piedr clan, and in this case the bell is hung on the neck of the buffalo about to be slaughtered by a Tarthar man belonging to the Nòdrs clan. The use of a *mani* at the funeral appears to be pre-eminently a Tarthar custom.

A further distinction between the two divisions is a consequence of the last difference. The Teivaliol do not purify the dairy after the funeral ceremonies because nothing has been taken from the dairy to be defiled. Similarly, the fact that the Teivaliol and Melgarsol use a male buffalo calf for the ceremony of purifying the various funeral places is connected in some way with the use of *tudr* by these divisions, while the general body of the Tartharol who are not purified with *tudr* use the blood of an adult female buffalo.

It will thus be seen that there is definite reciprocity between the two divisions as regards certain funeral duties, while the differences between the procedures of the two divisions are largely, if not altogether, connected with the use of the *mani* among the Tartharol and of the *tudr* tree among the Teivaliol, and each of these are points at which the funeral ceremonies come into relation with the dairy ritual. The differences in funeral rites would seem to be chiefly due to the different organisation of the dairy and its ritual in the two divisions.

There are other ceremonies in which the duties of the two divisions are reciprocal. In the ceremony of ear-piercing, a Tarthar man pierces one ear of a Teivali boy and a Teivali man performs the same service for a Tarthar boy, and in the ceremony called *putkuli tdzdr ïititi* (see p. 503), a man belonging to one division acts when the girl undergoing the ceremony belongs to the other.

One of the most obscure of Toda ceremonies is that called *tersamptpimi*, which is performed together with or later than the ceremony of name-giving when a child is about three months old. The chief feature of the ceremony is that a lock of the child's hair is cut by the maternal uncle of the child, the hair of a Tarthar child being cut with a piece of sharpened iron called *kanab*, while the hair of a Teivali child is cut with an ordinary knife. The special interest, however, for our present purpose lies in the fact that this ceremony must be performed on the day after the second funeral of a Tarthar man, and this whether the child be Tarthar or Teivali.

This ceremony points to the existence of a belief in the influence of the spirit of the dead man, and I have already (p. 404) given reasons why it is probable that this influence should be regarded as good rather than bad. But, whether good or bad, we are left wholly without a clue why this influence should be exerted by the ghosts of the Tartharol and not by those of the Teivaliol.

In the ceremonies connected with childbirth the ritual of one division differs from that of the other more widely than in any other case. The most striking difference is that the ceremonial of the artificial dairy is limited to the Tartharol, and here again it is possible that the difference is a secondary consequence of the difference in dairy organisation. In the chapter dealing with these ceremonies, I have thrown out the conjecture that the use of an artificial dairy, and of threads from the *madtuni*, or sacred dairy garment, may be a survival of a time when women had more to do with the dairy ritual than they have at present; and if there is anything in this conjecture, it would point to this connexion of women with the dairy having been limited to the Tartharol, or to its having persisted longer in this division.

The fact that a Tarthar woman drinks milk drawn by a Melgars man, while a Teivali woman drinks water which is assumed to be the milk of a pregnant buffalo, again brings the differences into relation with the dairy ritual, but another difference between the two divisions in the hand-burning ceremony is entirely foreign to this ritual. This is the ceremony of invoking Pirn and Piri, and there is no evident reason why this rite should be practised by the members of one division and not by those of the other. Similarly, the ceremony of offering to Namav by a Teivali woman when going to the seclusion-hut after childbirth stands entirely apart from the dairy ritual.

Both of these ceremonies are unlike the ordinary run of Toda ritual, and it is, on the whole, most probable that they have been borrowed.

We have thus seen that a large number of the ceremonial differences between the two divisions may be regarded as secondary consequences of the differences in the dairy ritual and that the few ceremonies which stand in no relation to the dairy ritual may have been borrowed.

Taking the differences of ceremonial as a whole, it is tempting to surmise that some of them may have arisen owing to differences of environment during some past stage of Toda history. The Todas now form so small a community, living in so small a space and knowing so much about each other, that it seems improbable that the differences can have come altogether into existence while they have been on the Nilgiri Hills. In so far as they can be explained as secondary consequences of the dairy organisation, it is possible that they may have arisen since the Todas have been on the Nilgiris, but when the practices have no relation to the dairy ritual it seems improbable that one division would have adopted a custom quite independently of the other.

Such a view would involve the consequence that at some time in their history the two divisions of the Toda people have had a different environment, and if the Todas are derived from one tribe or caste, this could only have come about if the two divisions came to the hills at different times, the interval having been sufficiently long to enable differences of ceremonial to have arisen. The differences would perhaps be still more readily explicable if we suppose the Tartharol and Teivaliol to have been derived from two different castes or tribes which reached the hills at different times, and I will now proceed to give some evidence which points to this having really happened.

Perhaps the strongest evidence in this direction is the existence of the differences of language to which I have already referred. The chief differences are as follows:—

	Tarthar.	Teivali.
Wooden spoon	*chudi* or *sudi*	*kîrstegi*
Basket	*tôdri*	*putukîri*
Food vessel	*paterkh*	*tôdriterkh*
Round metal vessel	*kûdikunm*	*kûdichakh*
Milking-vessel	*pun*	*kônipun*
A dairy vessel	*tat*	*kashtat*
Iron instrument	*pôditch*	*pôtch*
Comb	*tîrkôli*	*siekhkôli*
Small boy's cloak	*kuchâr*	*kupichâr*
Roof	*pôdri*	*idrnpôdri*
Western side of hut	*meilmerkal*	*meilkushkôni*
Eastern side of hut	*kîmerkal*	*kîkushkôni*
Mushroom	*kiân*	*âlabi*
A tree	*tipöti*	*ketak*
A black fruit	*kalpom*	*akatpom*
To-morrow morning	*telikhaski*	*pedrkhaski*

I was given one sentence as quite different in the two divisions. This was "Bring a piece of ragged cloth to the dairy!" By the Tartharol this would be rendered, ***Palivorsk pari evâ***! but by the Teivaliol, ***Kutanpari palivorsk panmeiliteivâ***! the chief difference here being in the verb.

Though these are all the differences in vocabulary of which I could obtain a record, I was told by the Tartharol that formerly there were many more, and that they were diminishing in number because "the Teivaliol were now learning to speak properly."

I think it possible that a phonologist might also detect many differences in pronunciation and accent in the two divisions. I thought that I detected such differences myself —that the Tartharol used a *k* when the Teivaliol used a *g*, for instance—but I am so uncertain about this that I do not feel entitled to lay any emphasis on it. In one case, however, the Todas themselves told me of a difference in pronunciation. They said that the usual word for dairy was pronounced as I have written it in this book but that by the Tartharol it was rather *püli*.

Scanty as the evidence is, there can be no doubt of the existence of dialectical differences between the two divisions of the Toda people.

Another indication that the Todas are two tribes or castes which have coalesced is of a different and more doubtful kind. There is some reason to believe that people sometimes preserve a relic of their migrations in the belief concerning the path taken by the dead in their journey to the next world. We have seen that the Todas believe that the dead journey to the west, but the special point of interest in the present connexion is that the dead Teivaliol are believed to travel by a path different from that traversed by the Tartharol.

I must reserve till the next chapter the full consideration of the path by which the Todas reached the hills, but I hope to show then that there is a great probability that the Todas came from Malabar. If this view be correct, it is not impossible that in the belief as to the different paths traversed by the dead, we may have a relic of two independent migrations.

A third indication is one about which I am still more doubtful, because I have no exact observations to support it. When on the hills I was struck at times by differences in the general appearance of the people of the two divisions. Towards the end of my visit I sometimes made a successful guess that an unknown village I was entering was a Teivali village, and this guess was founded, so far as I could tell, on a difference in the appearance of the people. The Teivaliol seemed to me to be, on the whole, darker, and to have a lower type of face. My surmises in this direction only took shape towards the end of my visit, when it was too late to make any exact observations. I know how dangerous such impressions are, and I do not wish to lay any stress on them, and I mention them hoping that more exact observations on the point may be made at some future time.

The idea that the two divisions of the Toda community reached the hills at different times is perhaps supported by their distribution on the Nilgiri plateau. In Fig. 73 I give a plan of the district, giving all the villages from which the Toda clans take their names, the Tarthar villages being in Roman type and those of the Teivaliol in italics. I have omitted the chief villages of those clans which I know to have arisen in recent times by splitting off from other clans, and I have included two villages of which I can only give the approximate positions. These are Piedr and Kusharf, which are now rarely occupied, and are situated off the main plateau, near the Badaga village of Hullatti. I also give

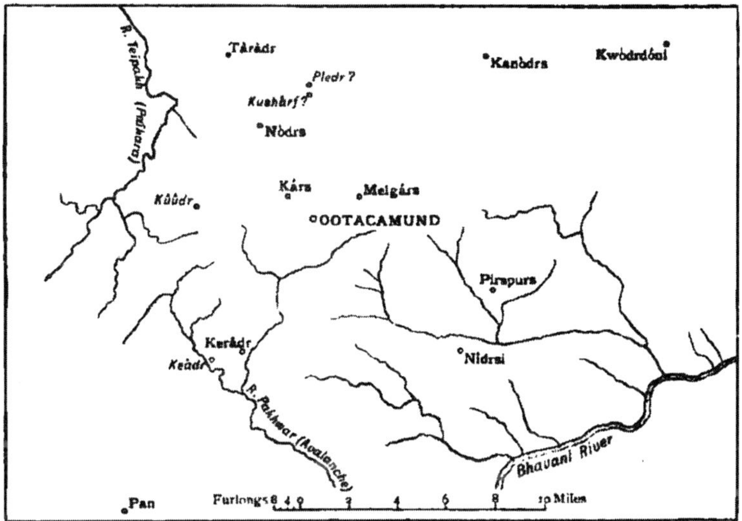

FIG. 73.

Pirspurs, the old *etudmad* of the Pämol. In Fig. 74 I give a second plan, showing the positions of all the villages which I know to be ancient, either because they possess sacred dairies or because they are mentioned in legend.

It will be seen that the greater part of the hills is occupied by the Tartharol, while the Teivali villages lie chiefly in the north-west part of the hills. The chief exception is the village of Keadr, which is situated some way south of the rest.

If, in coming to the hills, the Todas followed the routes now supposed to be traversed by the dead, the position of

Keadr would suggest that this clan was assigned a seat soon after the Teivaliol had crossed the Pakhwar, and that the others journeyed on northwards.

The plans certainly make it clear that there is a difference in the geographical distribution of the two divisions, and the nature of this distribution is consistent with the advent of the two divisions at different times. It will be noticed in both plans that one Tarthar clan has its seat in the middle

FIG. 74.

of what would otherwise be exclusively a Teivali district. This clan is that of Taradr, and it is perhaps significant that the Taradrol have many features which differentiate them from Tarthar clans in general, especially in their possession of the *kugvalir* and in the possession of their own Amnòdr, though, as we have seen, the latter feature may merely be a later consequence of their isolated position.

It is known that when two tribes coalesce to form a community, the inferior people may act as the sorcerers and wizards of the community. At the present time the majority of the *teuol*, or diviners, belong to the Teivaliol, but this branch of sacred function is not limited to that division. The magical powers of the sorcerer seem to be now almost equally divided among the two divisions, and there is no evidence that magical powers in the past have been attributed to one division more than to the other.

In the preceding pages I have put together the chief evidence which throws any light on the problem raised by the existence of the two divisions of the Toda people. It is far from conclusive, but I incline to the view that the present organisation of the Todas is due to the coalescence of two tribes or castes which came to the hills at different times. It seems probable that the Tartharol arrived first and occupied the hills widely. When later the Teivaliol came, it seems possible that they were placed by the Tartharol in those priestly offices which, though honourable, involved many hardships and restrictions, and were assigned dwelling-places and pastures in a comparatively limited district of the hills.

The analysis of the genealogical record has brought out some interesting differences between the two divisions. The data compiled from the genealogical tables by Mr. Punnett[1] would seem to show that the preponderance of males was and is still greater among the Teivaliol than among the Tartharol. The tables provide statistics roughly for four generations. In the second of these,[2] the number of males for every hundred females was 159·7 among the Tartharol, 259 among the Teivaliol. For the last generation, these numbers have sunk to 129·2 and 171 respectively. These figures almost certainly mean that female infanticide was more in vogue among the Teivaliol and is still practised by them to a greater extent than by the Tartharol.

This would seem to show that the Teivaliol have clung more closely to the old custom of infanticide and may be taken as an indication of the greater conservativeness of the priestly caste, but the Teivaliol chiefly occupy those parts of the hills furthest removed from the European settlements,

[1] *Proc. Camb. Philos. Soc.*, 1904, vol. xii, p. 481.

[2] I neglect the first generation on account of the small number of families for which there are data.

and the greater freedom from external influence is probably an important reason for the greater frequency of infanticide among them at present, though it will not explain the greater prevalence in the earlier generations.

The Teivaliol are now much the smaller of the two divisions, the numbers at the most liberal estimate being less than half of those of the Tartharol, and this difference is certainly of long standing. It may be due to original disproportion of numbers, but if female infanticide has long been more frequent among the Teivaliol, this might furnish a cause of their smaller population. It is perhaps significant in this connexion that the only extinct clan of which I have a record is a Teivali clan, the Kemenol, which is said to have become extinct about a hundred years ago, and the causes which led to its extinction may well have produced a great diminution of numbers in other branches of the Teivaliol.

CHAPTER XXX

THE ORIGIN AND HISTORY OF THE TODAS

I HAVE now given the whole of the material which I have collected on the institutions of the Todas. In describing these institutions I have discussed various general problems suggested by their nature, but I have said little about the points of resemblance or difference between the customs of the Todas and those of other peoples either in India or elsewhere. It remains in this last chapter to see how far the evidence which I have given throws any light on the very difficult questions: Who are the Todas? How do they come to be living on the Nilgiri Hills?

The evidence which might be available for our inquiry is of three kinds: records of the Todas in the past, traditions preserved by the Todas, and, lastly, evidence derived from the comparative study of physical and psychical characters, language, beliefs, and institutions.

The evidence coming under the first two heads is of the scantiest. Our earliest record of the Todas is contained in a Portuguese manuscript now in the British Museum. It records the visit of a Portuguese priest named Finicio to the Nilgiri Hills in 1602. This manuscript was partially translated and published by Thomas Whitehouse in a book dealing with the Syrian church of Malabar, under the title "Lingerings of Light in a Dark Land." As the translation given by Whitehouse is incomplete, I had the manuscript retranslated, and it was then found that several interesting details had been omitted, and that there were several errors in the translation, The new translation is given on pp. 721–730.

The account given by Finicio is very superficial, being the result of only two days' intercourse, but it is sufficient to show that there has probably been little change in the Todas and their surroundings in the three centuries which elapsed between his visit and mine. I have referred in the general body of the work to several of the points in which his account either corroborates or differs from my own. Perhaps the most important feature of his story is that it shows the relation between the Todas and Badagas three centuries ago to have been very much what it is at the present day, and shows clearly that this relation between the two tribes is of longer standing than has usually been supposed. Finicio's account is, however, so brief and superficial that it helps us little in our search for evidence on the evolution of Toda society. We know from it that the institution of the *ti* was in existence, and the scanty evidence goes to show that the life of the *palol* was much what it is now, but there is nothing to tell us whether the ritual had then reached the high pitch of development which it now shows, nothing to tell us whether since that time there has been development or degeneration.

From 1602 to 1812 we have, so far as I am aware, no record of the Todas. In the latter year William Keys, Assistant Revenue Surveyor, reported the existence of the Todas, or Thothavurs, and other tribes in a letter to the Collector of Coimbatore. His account gives little information about the Todas, except that they kept buffaloes and held it a sacred and inviolable custom to keep their heads uncovered. In 1819 "a Subscriber" wrote an account of the Nilgiri tribes which was published in the *Madras Courier*. Beyond a description of their appearance, the only information given about the Todas or Todevies is that it is against the custom to wear either turban or sandal, that they permit hair and beard to grow long, and that the Badagas pay a few handfuls of grain from each field as acknowledgment that they received their land from the Todas. In 1820 Lieutenant Macpherson reported the practices of polyandry and infanticide, and in the following year Captain B. S. Ward described the marriage customs more fully, and gave some account of the dairies and priesthood. In 1826 the Rev. James Hough addressed a number of letters to the Bengal Hurkaru, giving an account of the Nilgiris and their inhabitants, and these letters were republished in a book in 1829. A more elaborate and most excellent account of the Todas was given by Captain Harkness in 1832, in a work entitled *A Description of a Singular Aboriginal Race Inhabiting the Summit of the Neilgherry Hills*, and since that time very many of those who have visited the Nilgiri Hills have had something to say about the Todas and their ways. As I have already pointed out, these records from the earlier part of last century differ but little from my own, and do not furnish us with any evidence that Toda customs underwent any great change during that century.

As regards the evidence from Toda tradition, we are in no better case. Several writers have stated that the Todas believe that they came to the Nilgiris from elsewhere, but whenever I made any inquiries on this point I was assured that they had always been on the Nilgiri Hills, the first Toda having been created on the Kundahs in the manner already described.

It seems most probable that those who have ascribed such traditions to the Todas have been misled by the account of the Kamasòdrolam. These are the people who are believed to have been driven away from Kanòdrs by Kwoten (see p. 195). The Todas have a very sincere belief in the existence of these people, and when I showed one man the frontispiece in Marshall's book, representing a Toda village and its inhabitants, something unfamiliar in the arrangement of the scene made the man think that it must be a picture of the Kamasòdrolam. Any Toda who is asked whether there are other Todas and where they live will at once think of the Kamasòdrolam and will tell of these people, and the story might easily be mistaken for a tradition of their origin.

The Todas are also said to believe in their descent from Ravan, and I was told by one man that they were descended from the Pandavas, but I have little doubt that such beliefs are only recent additions to their mythology.

In studying the origin and history of the Todas we have

thus no record earlier than three centuries ago, and no traditions of any value, and we are altogether thrown back on the evidence furnished by the manners and customs of the people, their language, and their physical characteristics.

Though the manners and customs of the Todas are in many ways unique, or very exceptional, there is a general resemblance between them and those comprised under the general title of Hinduism, and especially with such more popular customs as are described by Mr. Crooke.[1] The great development of the ritual aspect of religion, the importance of ceremonies connected with birth and death, the sacredness of the milk-giving animal, the nature of the system of kinship, the marriage regulations and many other features bear a general, and in some cases a close, resemblance to institutions found in India generally, or in certain parts of India.

On the social side these resemblances are perhaps closer than on the religious side. The system of kinship is very similar to that of other parts of Southern India, and, so far as my knowledge goes, to that of India generally. The marriage regulation that the children of brother and sister should marry is found throughout Southern India and probably throughout the Dravidian population of India. The practice of polyandry probably exists scattered here and there throughout India, and has undoubtedly existed in recent times in Malabar. The practice of the *mokhthoditi* union between man and woman has also close analogies in Malabar.

On the religious side the high development of the dairy ritual, so far as I know, stands alone, but the customs connected with birth and death have many resemblances to practices followed in other parts of India, though this resemblance is general only and usually breaks down on going into detail.

Thus in Brahmanic ritual there are several ceremonies prescribed at different stages of pregnancy, and some Indian tribes or castes have pregnancy ceremonies peculiar to themselves, but I do not know of any tribe or caste except that

[1] *Popular Religion and Folklore of Northern India.* London, 1896.

of the Todas in which giving a bow and arrow forms the essential feature of a pregnancy ceremony, though it is not uncommon for this weapon to play a part in marriage rites, and in Coorg a little imitation bow and arrow is put into the hand of a newly born boy.

Similarly, seclusion after childbirth is common in India, and in the Brahmanic ceremony of Jatakarma water is poured over the heads of mother and child by the priest. In some cases from Mysore (see p. 705) there is a still closer resemblance to Toda custom, but there are some features of the Toda ceremonial for which I can find no parallel.

In many points, again, there are distinct resemblances between the practices of the Todas and the more popular customs of India; thus the pounder, sieve and broom frequently play a part in the popular magic of India,[1] as of other parts of the world, but I do not know of any parallel for their being regarded as especially the emblems of women, as they appear to be in Toda belief.

It is perhaps in the funeral ceremonies that we find the largest number of resemblances between Toda custom and that of other parts of India. Thus, among those who cremate their dead, it is usual to have ceremonies some time after the cremation, and some have regarded the second funeral ceremony of the Todas, the so-called dry funeral, as the representative of the Sapindi ceremony of orthodox Hinduism. Among several tribes fragments of bone are preserved after the cremation, which become the objects of further ceremonies. Thus, the Hos and Mundahs[2] preserve large fragments of bone, which are hung up in the house and are buried in an earthenware pot much later, after being taken in procession to every friend and relation of the deceased. Again, among the Saoras of Madras[3] fragments of bone are picked out from the ashes and covered over with a miniature hut.

Animals are frequently killed at funerals throughout India, and among the Saoras, just mentioned,[4] the animal is a

[1] Cf. Crooke, *loc. cit.*, vol. ii. pp. 187–191.

[2] Dalton, *Trans. Ethnol. Soc.*, London, N.S., 1868, vol. vi, p. 37.

[3] Fawcett, *Journ. Anthrop. Soc.*, Bombay, 1888, vol. i. p. 249.

[4] *Loc. cit.*

buffalo, which is killed close to the stone on which its blood is smeared. Again, among the Kois[1] a bullock is slain and the tail placed in the hand of the corpse.

A funeral practice which is very widely spread in India is the breaking of a pot, and in some cases the pot so broken is one which has contained the water used to quench the fire. Among the Naickers and the Reddies of South India[2] the body is bathed with water from an earthen pot, which is then dashed upon the ground, while in other places an earthen pot filled with water is carried round the body three times, after which the fire is lighted and later extinguished by water which runs from a perforation in the pot. The common Indian practice, according to Padfield,[3] is for the chief mourner to throw a pot over his head behind him so that it is dashed in pieces.

That the kindred should retire with averted faces from the place where the corpse is left is prescribed by Manu,[4] and the custom of burning or burying face downwards is practised by low caste people, the motive in this case being to prevent the evil spirit from escaping and troubling its neighbours.[5]

While there is thus a general resemblance between many of the manners and customs of the Todas and those existing in various parts of the Indian peninsula, there is one district which possesses customs and institutions which seem to stand in a much closer relation to those of the Todas than is the case elsewhere.

The social and religious customs of the west coast, and especially of Malabar, not only bear a general resemblance to the customs of the Todas, but this resemblance in some cases persists when followed into detail. The similarity would probably become still more obvious if we knew more of the customs of the less civilised inhabitants of this district of India.

In going over the resemblances I will begin with those on the social side. The most characteristic feature of the social

[1] Cain, *Ind. Antiq.*, 1876, vol. v, p. 357.
[2] Kearns, *Tribes of South India*, p. 51.
[3] *The Hindu at Home*, Madras, p. 234.
[4] IV. 240.
[5] Crooke, *loc. cit.*, vol. i. p. 269.

organisation of the Todas is the institution of fraternal polyandry. The Nairs of Malabar have given their name to a different type of polyandry, but it is extremely doubtful whether the relations existing in recent times between Nair women and their consorts should be regarded as examples of polyandry. Nevertheless, there is undoubted evidence that true polyandry has existed in Malabar, and in the most definite examples known this has been of the fraternal type. From the Report of the Malabar Marriage Commission, published in 1891, it is clear that, though polyandry is now extinct in North Malabar, it still persists in some districts of South Malabar. One witness before the Commission stated that at one time polyandry was very prevalent in South Malabar, and that it was still the practice for a woman of the Kammalar or artisan caste to have five or six brothers as husbands, and the witness had known personally a woman in Calicut who was the wife of five brothers, spending a month at a time with each. Another witness stated that polyandry existed in some parts of Cochin, and in a few places in South Malabar. Another said that among the Tiyans of North Malabar it was the custom for one man to marry a girl for all the brothers of the family. One of the names for marriage in Malabar is *uzham porukka*, which probably means "marriage by turns." The Kanisans or astrologers of Malabar proudly point out that, like the Pandavas, they used formerly to have one wife in common to several brothers, and that the custom is still observed by some.[1]

Polyandry is not the only marriage institution in which there is a resemblance between the Todas and the people of Malabar. The *mokhthodvaiol* of a Toda woman seems to be very much like the consort of a Nair woman, and when these consorts are, as they usually are, Nambutiris or Malabar Brahmans—*i.e.*, belong to a different caste—the resemblance to the *mokhthoditi* custom becomes very close.

More important is the custom of giving a cloth as the essential marriage ceremony. The two chief features of a Toda marriage are the giving of a loincloth to the girl and the salutation of the girl's relatives by the husband. Simi-

[1] Logan's *Malabar Manual*, vol. i. p. 141.

larly the essential feature of the irregular union between man and woman is that the *mokhthodvaiol* gives a cloak to the woman, and the Badaga name by which the relation has previously been known is derived from this fact—the man is called the "blanket man" of the woman. Throughout the greater part of the Malabar coast the essential feature of the marriage ceremony is that the man gives a cloth to the woman. The Nairs have two marriage ceremonies,[1] of which the later, or *sambandham*, forms the actual alliance between man and woman. The ceremony of this marriage consists in giving a cloth, and various names for the ceremony, such as *muntukotukkuka*, *vastradanam*, *putavakota* and *pudamuri*, all mean "cloth-giving." In South Malabar a marriage is dissolved by tearing up a cloth called *kachcha*,[2] and among the Izhavas,[3] the actual wedding ceremony consists of the gift of a cloth.

The act of giving clothing as part of the marriage ceremony is found generally throughout India, but it seems to be a much more prominent and essential feature of marriage in Malabar than elsewhere.

Among the funeral ceremonies of the Todas there is one in which a cloth is laid on the body of the deceased. The essential feature of this ceremony is that a cloth is given by a man belonging to the clan of the deceased to those who have married into the clan, the cloth being then placed on the corpse by the wives of these men. The whole ceremony seems to be essentially a transaction between clans which have intermarried and evidently stands in a close relation to the regulation of marriage, and it is therefore of great interest not only that a cloth should play so prominent a part, but also that the word used for the cloth which gives the name to the ceremony should be *kach*, the same word as is used sometimes in Malabar for the cloth so important in the marriage ceremonies.

The resemblance between the Todas and Nairs in this direction goes, however, one step further. Among the funeral

[1] See *Malabar Marriage Commission* and Wigram's *Malabar Law and Custom*, 2nd ed., Madras, 1900.

[2] *Census of India*, 1901, vol. i., Eth. App., p. 136.

[3] *Ibid.*, p. 142.

ceremonies of the Nairs there is one called *potavekkuka*, in which new cotton cloths are placed on the corpse by the senior members of the deceased's Tarawad (corresponding to clan), followed by all the other members, sons-in-law, daughters-in-law, and other relatives. The details of the ceremony differ in the two communities; among the Nairs the placing of cloths is the duty of a wide circle of relatives, but the resemblance between the customs is sufficiently close to make it highly probable that we have to do with two developments of one custom.

The ceremony just described is not the only point in which the funeral rites of the Todas resemble those of Malabar. The earthen pot which I have already mentioned plays a part in the rites of both Nairs and Nambutiris. By the Nairs[1] the pot is carried three times round the pyre while the water leaks out through the holes, and on completing the third round the pot is dashed on the ground close by the spot where the head of the corpse had lain. The Nambutiris burn their dead and bury the ashes three days later, and when the body is being burnt an earthen pot containing water is carried round the fire, and is then punctured and the water received into another vessel, from which it is thrown on the fire, and then the pot is smashed and thrown away.[2]

We have seen that according to Toda belief it is necessary that those who have not been through certain ceremonies in life must do so after death, and the same belief is entertained by the Nambutiris, who tie the *tali* at the funeral of an unmarried girl,[3] just as the Todas perform the *pursütpimi* ceremony.

The Nairs collect pieces of unburnt bones from the ashes fourteen days after the cremation, but they either throw them into the nearest river or take them to some sacred place, thus following a frequent Indian practice.

There is one feature of the *urvatpimi* ceremony of the Todas which also suggests a possible link with Malabar, and this is the name, *pülpali*, given to the artificial dairy

[1] *Madras Gov. Museum Bull.*, iii. p. 247. [2] *Ibid.*, p. 70.

[3] *Ibid.*, p. 61. See also Dubois, *Hindu Manners, Customs, and Ceremonies*, Oxford, 1899, p. 17.

used by the Tartharol. The Nairs of Malabar have a ceremony at the ninth month called *pulikuti*, in which the woman drinks tamarind (*puli*) juice which has been poured over a knife by her brother.[1] The Toda word for the sour taste is *pülchiti*, derived from tamarind, and I have suggested that the name *pülpali* may mean 'tamarind dairy,' and be a survival of community between the Toda ceremony and that of Malabar.

I have now enumerated a number of points in which there is a close resemblance between the customs of the Todas and those of the people of Malabar. In some cases, as in that of the cloth ceremony of the funeral, the resemblance is so close that we seem almost bound to seek its explanation either in identity of origin or in borrowing. We may be confident that if there has been any borrowing from the inhabitants of Malabar, it has not been recent, and we may also be fairly confident that the physical barrier in the past must have prevented any but the most infrequent intercourse between the inhabitants of the Nilgiri plateau and those of Malabar. If we attach any significance to the resemblances I have indicated, the conclusion seems almost inevitable that the Todas at some time lived in Malabar and migrated to the Nilgiri Hills, and it remains to inquire whether there are any other facts in favour of this view.

On one line of evidence I cannot speak with any authority, but I strongly suspect that there is a very close resemblance between the Toda language and Malayalam.

I think there is little doubt that the Toda language is much more nearly allied to Tamil than to Canarese, and I believe that the contrary opinion of Dr. Pope was due to the inclusion in his material of many words borrowed by the Todas from their Canarese-speaking neighbours, the Badagas. Malayalam is closely allied to Tamil, differing from it chiefly in its disuse of the personal terminations of the verbs and in the large number of Sanscrit derivatives,[2] and I should like to make the suggestion, for the consideration of Dravidian philologists,

[1] *Madras Museum Bull.*, iii. p. 242.

[2] Cf. Caldwell, *A Comparative Grammar of the Dravidian or South-Indian Family of Languages*, 2nd ed., London, 1875, p. 23.

that there is a close resemblance between the Toda language and Malayalam, minus its Sanscrit derivatives.

The Todas claim that their diviners, who, when in their frenzy, are believed to be inspired by the gods, speak the Malayalam language, some clans speaking a language which the Todas say is that of people they call Mondardsetipol, living in Malabar. I do not know whether the Toda claim is justified, but in any case the belief exists that the diviners speak the languages of Malabar, and that these are the languages of the gods. It is possible that in their beliefs concerning the language of the gods the Todas may be preserving a tradition of their mother-tongue, and if it could be proved that the diviners actually speak the Malayalam language the link with Malabar would be very materially strengthened.[1]

The Todas believe that their dead travel towards the West and are able to describe the paths by which they pass. Here, again, there is some reason to think that people may preserve in their beliefs about the passing to the next world a tradition of the route by which their ancestors travelled from a former home, and this may be so in the case of the Todas.

Another fact linking the Todas with Malabar is the use of the tall pole called *tadri* in the funeral ceremonies. This pole is procured for the Todas from the Malabar side of the hills by the Kurumbas, and I was told that suitable poles only grew in Malabar, and the pole is adorned with cowries which are also probably of Malabar origin. Other objects burnt at the funeral, such as the boxes called *pettei* and the umbrella called *miturkwadr*, are also procured from Malabar. The use of objects in funeral ceremonies which are procured from Malabar is suggestive, though, taken alone, it would have little significance.

A fact which would perhaps be regarded by most as more important is that there is now a settlement of the Todas at Gudalur in the Wainad, on one of the routes from Malabar to the Nilgiris. It seems clear that at one time the settlement

[1] It is perhaps worth noting that at present only Teivali diviners are reputed to speak Malayalam.

was larger than it is at present, and it is tempting to suppose that we have here evidence of the route of the Toda migration. There are, however, facts which make it improbable that this clue is of any value. If the villages about Gudalur had been survivals of the migration they would almost certainly have been sacred villages, but it was quite clear that they had no sanctity whatever and were not even saluted when seen from a distance. Unfortunately I did not visit Kavidi, the only village which remains, and if I had done so I might have discovered some evidence of sanctity and antiquity, but from what I was told it is very unlikely that any such evidence exists. This absence of sanctity is further in agreement with the traditions of the Todas, who say that the settlement at Gudalur is recent. There are, however, other facts which point to an ancient connexion of the Todas with this district. Some of the buffaloes of the most sacred and ancient Nòdrs *ti* are said to have come from Perithi in the Wainad, and the Taradrol, in many ways an exceptional Toda clan, are said to have their own future world or Amnòdr at this place.

It will thus be seen that, in addition to the points of similarity in custom and belief, there are definite facts pointing to connexion with Malabar, and if we suppose that the Todas migrated from this district we have next to conjecture the path by which they travelled. If any importance is attached to the belief in the paths taken by the dead, we should regard it as the most probable view that the Todas travelled over the Kundahs, the two divisions of the people travelling by slightly different routes. The Toda tradition that men were created on the Kundahs is perhaps in favour of this route, which would seem to correspond with the road to the Nilgiris known as the Sisipara Ghat. If, on the other hand, we attach importance to the settlement at Kavidi, the route followed would be that through Gudalur. At the present time the latter road is far the easier of the two, and, if the Todas had travelled during the last few years, it would have been the natural road by which to come, but it does not appear that there was any essential difference in the difficulties of the two routes before the roads were made. The evidence in favour of either route is very scanty, but if the Todas came from

Malabar it is probable that they came by one or other of these paths.

There are two other districts which have some claim to be considered as possible places from which the Todas may have migrated—*viz.*, Mysore and Coorg.

The Todas regard with some reverence a Hindu temple at Nanjankudi in Mysore, and visit it to pay vows, and there is little doubt that they have done this for a long time. Further, Nòdrs, one of the oldest and most sacred of the Toda villages, is close to the present road from Mysore and may have been near the most convenient route from Mysore in ancient times. I think, however, that, though not recent, the relations with the Hindu temple at Nanjankudi are not of very great antiquity, and I am inclined to ascribe the Toda reverence for it to their association with the Badagas, who almost certainly came from Mysore. I have not been able to find many parallels to Toda customs in Mysore. In one case, however, the resemblance is very close. Among the Gollavalu of Mysore[1] a woman after delivery is turned out into a leaf or mat hut, about 200 yards from the village, and on the fourth day a woman of the village pours water over her. In this case the woman lives in the hut for three months, her husband also living in a special hut. Again, among the Kadu (or forest) Gollas of Mysore[2] the mother and child remain in a small shed outside the village for seven to thirty days.

The other district which has customs especially resembling those of the Todas is Coorg. Among the people of Coorg cloth-giving appears at one time to have formed the essential marriage ceremony, and there still exist what are called 'cloth-marriages,' in which a man becomes the husband of a woman merely by giving her a cloth. There is also some evidence that polyandry has been practised in Coorg, and I have already referred to the resemblance between the *pursütpimi* ceremony of the Todas and the Coorg custom of giving a little bow and arrow to a newly born boy. The bow is made of a stick of the castor-oil plant and for the arrow

[1] *Journ. Anthrop. Soc.*, Bombay, 1889, vol. i. p. 535.
[2] *Mysore Census Report*, 1901, Pt. i. p. 521.

the leaf-stalk of the same plant is used. In Coorg the imitation bow and arrow is put into the hand of the newly born child, but this custom is not widely removed from that of the Todas in which the bow and arrow is put into the hand of the mother shortly before the child is born.

The Todas know the people of Coorg, which they call Kwûrg, and have a tradition of an invasion of their hills by these people, but it is very improbable that there has been any direct borrowing, and it seems more likely that some of the customs of the Todas and Coorgs have had a common source.

The resemblance with the customs of Coorg are perhaps more striking than with those of Mysore, and the former region is much more likely to have been influenced by Malabar than the latter. The links with Coorg do not weaken, and perhaps even strengthen, the conclusion that the Todas owe much to Malabar.

If we accept provisionally the view that the Todas migrated to the Nilgiris from Malabar, we are next confronted with the problem as to whether they are directly derived from any of the races now living in that district. The most diverse views have been held by those who have considered the racial affinities of the Todas. Leaving on one side the conjectures of those who have supposed them to be Scythians, Druids, Romans, or Jews, we find that the Todas have been supposed by several writers to be of Aryan or Caucasic origin. De Quatrefages[1] grouped the Todas with the Ainus of Northern Japan and Keane[2] follows him in putting the two peoples together, and regards both as witnesses to the widespread diffusion of Caucasic races in Asia. Deniker[3] suggests that they belong to the Indo-Afghan race, with perhaps an admixture of the Assyroid race.

Previous writers have found no special reason to link the customs of the Todas with those of Malabar, and, so far as I am aware, no one has considered how far the Todas may be of the same race as any of the inhabitants of

[1] *Histoire générale des Races Humaines*, Paris, 1889, Introduction, p. 469.
[2] *Ethnology*, Cambridge, 1896, p. 418.
[3] *The Races of Man*, London, 1900, p. 412.

this district.[1] In considering this matter, we may anticipate that even if the Todas and any of the tribes or castes of Malabar had the same origin, marked differences would have been produced by the long sojourn of the former on the Nilgiri plateau. How long the Todas have been on the Nilgiri Hills no one can say, but we may safely conclude that a very long time must have been necessary to produce the wide divergence in custom and belief which is found to separate them even from those other inhabitants of India whom they most closely resemble. If the Todas came from Malabar, they came from a country differing enormously in temperature and in general physical and climatic characters from the Nilgiri plateau. Life on the hills must almost certainly have altered the physical characters of the people, and it is perhaps now hopeless to expect that any exact resemblance would be found with the existing races of Malabar even if the Todas are an offshoot of one of them. Nevertheless, in comparing the physical measurements of the Todas, which we owe to Mr. Thurston, with those of various Malabar races taken by Mr. Fawcett, it would seem that the differences are not very great, and in the measurements to which anthropologists attach most importance, those of the head and nose, they are very slight.

In the table on the following page I give the chief measurements in centimeters for Todas, Nairs, and Nambutiris.

The average dimensions of the heads and noses of the Todas correspond very closely with those of the Nairs, and the differences from the Nambutiris are nowhere great. It must be remembered that the measurements on the Todas were taken by one observer, and those on the Nairs and Nambutiris by another,[2] and this may partly account for

[1] In a paper which I have only seen since the above was written (*C. R. de la Soc. de Biol.*, 1905, t. lix, p. 123) M. Louis Lapicque has called attention to the resemblance between Todas and Nairs. He regards the Todas as pure or almost pure examples of one of the two races of which he believes the Dravidian population of India to be composed, the Nairs being more mixed with the negroid element, which forms the other component of the population according to M. Lapicque.

[2] It must also be borne in mind that the figures of the Nambutiris and those of some of the Todas are based on the measurement of twenty-five individuals only in each case.

the large divergence in the case of the maxillo-zygomatic index, which is calculated from the bigoniac and bizygomatic measurements, in both of which there is considerable scope for differences between different observers. The only other measurements which show any decided divergence are the stature and the length from the middle finger to the patella, and the greater stature of the Todas may well be the result of their more healthy environment. The cubit of the Todas also differs very decidedly from that of the Nambutiris, though little longer than this dimension of the Nairs.

	Todas.[1]	186 Nairs.	25 Nambutiris.
Stature	169·8	165 6	162·3
Span	175·9	175·1	170·0
Chest	82·0	80·6	83·7
Middle finger to patella	12·0	10·1	10·5
Shoulders	39·3	40·0	40·7
Left cubit	47·0	46·2	44·2
Left hand, length	18·8	18·5	18·0
,, ,, width	8·1	8·3	7·8
Hips	25·7	26·0	26·2
Left foot, length	25·0	25·4	24·5
,, ,, width	9·2	8·8	
Cephalic length	19·4	19·2	19·2
,, width	14·2	14·1	14·6
,, index	73·3	73·1	76·3
Bigoniac	9·6	10·4	10·6
Bizygomatic	12·7	13·1	13·2
Maxillo-zygomatic index	75·7	80·1	80·4
Nasal height	4·7	4·8	4·9
,, width	3·6	3·6	3·7
,, index	76·6	76·8	75·5

We do not know the probable errors of these different groups of measurements, but the agreement between the Todas and the two castes of Malabar is so close as to suggest strongly a racial affinity between the three.[2]

The hairiness of the Toda is perhaps the feature in which he differs most obviously from the races of Malabar, while the robustness of his physique and general bearing are perhaps almost as striking. The latter qualities may be entirely due

[1] Some of these measurements are based on the examination of eighty-two men, others are derived from twenty-five men only.

[2] The relations existing between Nair women and Nambutiri men must have brought about an approximation of the two Malabar castes in physical characters, even if they were originally of different ethnical origin.

to his environment, to his free life in the comparatively bracing climate of the Nilgiris, and, so far as we know, the development of hair may have a similar cause. Of all the castes or tribes of Malabar, the Nambutiris perhaps shows the greatest number of resemblances to the customs of the Todas,[1] and it is therefore interesting to note that Mr. Fawcett describes these people as the hairiest of all the races of Malabar and especially notes that one individual he examined was like a Toda.

I am not competent to express a decided opinion on the amount of importance which is to be attached to the resemblance which is shown by the figures on p. 708, but it seems to me that the facts before us give no grounds[2] for separating the Todas racially from the two chief castes of Malabar.

The identification of the Todas with Nairs or Nambutiris would still leave their racial affinities somewhat indeterminate. The Nambutiris are often supposed to be Aryan invaders of Malabar, and, owing to the cause already mentioned, the Nairs are so largely of Nambutiri blood that, if the Nambutiris are Aryan, the Nairs must also be strongly Aryanised even if they were originally of pure Dravidian descent.

If future research should show that the Todas are an offshoot of one of the races now existing in Malabar, and if any definite conclusion can be drawn as to the time during which they have been on the Nilgiri Hills, physical anthropologists will be provided with a most interesting example of the influence of environment on the physical characters of a race. Few greater contrasts of environment could be found in a country than that existing between Malabar and the Nilgiris, and it is possible that the Todas may furnish a striking example of the influence of environment on physical characters.

[1] It is worth noting that they practise male descent, while the Nairs follow the Marumakkattayam system of inheritance.

[2] I should much like to know the ratios between the lengths of different limb bones, such as those shown by the radio-humeral or tibio-femoral indices. The observations on the cubit and the distance from the middle finger to the patella suggest that considerable differences might be found between the Todas and the Malabar castes in these ratios, which do not seem to me to have yet received from the physical anthropologist the attention they deserve.

In endeavouring to link the Todas with Malabar I have naturally dwelt on the points of resemblance rather than on the points of difference. The differences are, however, very great. The general manner of life of the two peoples is now wholly different, while on the religious side I may point to the wide prevalence of snake worship in Malabar, especially among the Nambutiris.

The hypothesis that the Todas are derived from one or more of the races of Malabar would not be tenable for a moment except on the assumption that the migration took place very long ago, and that the culture of Malabar has undergone great changes since the migration. As to the length of time during which the Todas have been on the Nilgiris, we can only offer the vaguest surmises. We know that three centuries ago the Todas were living on the Nilgiris, apparently in much the same state as at the present day. The appearance of some of their sacred stones suggests great antiquity, especially the well-worn polished appearance of the *neurzülnkars*, which, if the accounts are right, are only rubbed a few times in the year.

On the other hand, the history of Malabar is highly conjectural. The two great positive landmarks in its history are the beginning and end of the rule of the Perumal princes. The date of the first Perumal is put at about the time of Christ, or somewhat later, and it is tempting to surmise that the Todas may have been driven or have retired from Malabar in consequence of the political changes which took place at this time. The last Perumal probably reigned about a thousand years ago, but there does not appear to have been any political upheaval at the time, the last prince having his period of office prolonged beyond the usual twelve years, and having then divided his dominions among his family and retainers.

If we assume that the Todas came from Malabar, the date of their migration would be of great interest in relation to the possibility of Christian or Jewish influences on the Toda religion. There are ancient settlements of both Christians and Jews in Malabar. Tradition assigns the starting-point of the native Christian settlements in Malabar to St. Thomas;

but, leaving this on one side, there seems to be no doubt that both Christians and Jews were well established in Malabar more than a thousand years ago. An ancient document is still preserved by the Jews of Cochin, which was given to their leader by the Perumal of the day, and this document can be dated about 750 A.D. A similar document preserved by the Nestorian Christians can be dated 774 A.D.

If the Todas left Malabar at the beginning of the Perumal rule, Jewish or Christian influences can be excluded, but if at a

FIG. 75 (from Breeks).—A CAIRN ON THE NILGIRI HILLS.

later period such influences may have been present, though it is very improbable that they were important; for, unless the Todas have changed very much, they would have been very unlikely to have borrowed from religious settlers of an alien race. Still, in considering the strange resemblance between the Hebrew and Toda versions of the Creation, this possible influence should be borne in mind.

I have so far said nothing of the archæological evidence which may possibly help in the settlement of the vexed questions which I have raised in the preceding pages. Our knowledge of the history of the Todas would be very materially advanced if we knew whether the cairns, barrows and other ancient remains which are found on the Nilgiri Hills are Toda monuments. In the cairns and barrows there are found objects which suggest a Toda origin, such as figures of buffaloes with bells round their necks (see Fig. 76, 9), but the vast majority of the finds are utterly unlike anything now possessed by the Todas. They include pottery of many designs, the lids of the vessels being often adorned with the figures of animals. Many other animal figures have also been found, and though that of the buffalo often occurs, figures of the horse (see Fig. 76, 10), sheep, camel, elephant, leopard (?), pig (?), and low-country bullock with hump are all found. Such figures can only have been made by those well acquainted with the low country, and none of these animals are ever mentioned in Toda legends.

Metal work is also found in the cairns and barrows; bronze vases, basins and saucers (Fig. 76, 1, 2, 3), iron razors, styles or pins (?), and daggers (Fig. 76, 8), while iron spear-heads (Fig. 76, 4, 7, 13) are frequently met with.

In addition to the more elaborate cairns, cromlechs and barrows found on the Nilgiri Hills, Breeks, to whom we owe most of our knowledge on this subject, found what he took to be ancient examples of the *azaram* or circle of stones within which the Toda buries the ashes of his dead at the end of the second funeral. In such *azaram* in the district between Kotagiri and Kwòdrdoni, Breeks found bronze bracelets and rings, iron spear-heads, a chisel, a knife and an iron implement in something of the style found in Malabar and differing from those usually found in the cairns.

Breeks points out that the characteristic feature of the cairns and barrows of the Nilgiris is the circle of stones, and that some consist of an insignificant circle hardly to be distinguished from the Toda *azaram*. He often found it difficult to say whether a given monument was a cairn or an *azaram*, so that it would appear that there are intermediate gradations between the more elaborate cairns or barrows containing the pottery and metal work and the simple Toda *azaram*.

FIG. 76—VARIOUS OBJECTS FOUND IN THE NILGIRI CAIRNS, TAKEN FROM BREEKS.

From the amount of rust on the iron implements, however, Breeks concluded that there was a long interval of time between the most recent of the cairns and the oldest *azaram*, but he points out that if the latter are really *azaram*, they show that the Todas used at one time to bury such objects as iron spears.[1]

As regards the cairns, Breeks points out that though the figures of many animals occur in addition to that of the buffalo, most of the animals are so badly imitated that it is difficult to identify them, while the figures of the buffaloes are singularly characteristic and often very spirited.

The only implements found by Breeks which might be agricultural were shears and sickles (Fig. 76, 12, 5), and he recalls the *kafkati* burnt by the Todas with their dead, which is a curved knife, different, however, in shape from the sickles often found in the cairns.

On the other hand, very few of the human figures found in the cairns resemble the Todas in any way; the women have the low-country top-knot instead of the Toda curls, and they carry chatties on their heads, which would never be done by a Toda woman at the present time, whatever she may have done in the past.

Breeks himself inclined to the view that the cairns are Toda monuments. One objection which has been made to this view is that the Todas exhibit little or no interest in the cairns, and offer no objection to their excavation. I have already given reasons[2] why this cannot be regarded as a conclusive argument against the Toda origin of the monuments. The Todas certainly identify the hills which possess stone circles with the abodes of their gods, and the absence of objections to the excavation may merely be due to the fact that they have no traditional injunctions against interference with these circles.

In dealing with the religion of the Todas, I have advanced the view that the ritual and beliefs of the people furnish us with an example of a religion in a state of decadence. It seems probable that the Todas once had a religious cult of a

[1] It will be remembered that the Todas claim to have once possessed a spear which had belonged to their god, Kwoten.

[2] See p. 445.

distinctly higher order than that they now possess, and if I am right in supposing that the Todas came from Malabar, it might follow that they brought their highly developed religion with them, and that although certain features of the religion may have undergone great development, the general result of the long isolation has been to produce degeneration. The study of the religion suggests that we have in the Todas an example of a people who show us the remnants of a higher culture.

If we could accept the view that the cairns, barrows, and cromlechs of the Nilgiri Hills were the work of the ancestors of the Todas, we should have at once abundant further evidence that the Todas have degenerated from a higher culture. We should have an example of a people who once used, even if they did not make, pottery, showing artistic aptitudes of a fairly high order which they have now entirely lost. The Toda now procures his pottery from another race, and, so long as this is of the kind prescribed by custom, he is wholly indifferent to its æsthetic aspect. I doubt if there exists anywhere in the world a people so devoid of æsthetic arts, and if the Nilgiri monuments are the work of their ancestors, the movement backwards in this department of life must have been very great.

It is easy to see how the Todas may have lost such arts, supposing that they once possessed them. The Toda now regards nearly every kind of manual labour as beneath his dignity, and if a people showing artistic skill in the adornment of the articles they use in everyday life should hand over the making of these articles to another race, it is fairly certain that the artistic side would suffer, and this is especially likely to happen when the artisans whose services are employed are such people as the Kotas.[1] Assuming that such a transference took place, it is easy to understand the complete disappearance of art even higher than that which the contents of the monuments show.

The use of the bow and arrow and the club in ceremonial

[1] The argument will hold equally well if the Todas in their previous home had been accustomed to procure their pottery from others, but had when they reached the Nilgiris to rely solely on the Kotas for help in this direction.

furnishes us with another example of material objects which have wholly disappeared from the active life of the Todas, and here again it is easy to see why the disappearance has taken place, for on the Nilgiris the Todas have had no enemies, either human or feral. This disuse of weapons has indeed so obvious an explanation that it cannot be treated as an instance of degeneration; and while the origin of the cairns remains doubtful, the only evidence of degeneration of culture is shown by the religion; and though it seems to me that the evidence here, especially that derived from the nature of the prayers, is conclusive, it may not be so regarded by all.

In the preceding lines I have put forward for consideration the tentative hypothesis that the Todas may furnish us with an example of a people who once have possessed a higher culture of which some features have undergone degeneration. If we combine this hypothesis with that advanced earlier, that the Todas came from Malabar, we may suppose that the Todas brought the higher culture with them from this district, and if this were so, the original culture of the Todas may have been on much the same general level as that of the dominant castes of Malabar at the present day. On this hypothesis, it seems to me most likely that in their new home the religion of the Todas underwent a very special development, its ritual coming to centre more and more round the buffalo, because in their very simple environment this was the most accessible object of veneration. I think there is little doubt that the extraordinary development of the ritual of the dairy must have taken place since the Todas have been on the Nilgiris; and, as I have already pointed out, it seems to me most probable that the degeneration of the religion has been largely a consequence of the extreme development of this ritual aspect of their religion.

If we reject the view that the Todas are representatives of one or more of the castes of Malabar whose institutions have in some ways degenerated during a long period of isolation, the most likely alternative view is that the Todas are one of the hill tribes of the Western Ghats who have developed a higher culture than the rest in the very favourable environment provided by the Nilgiri plateau. I have already referred to the resemblance between certain Toda customs and those of one such tribe, the Hill Arrians, who live in the hills in Travancore and on the Travancore-Cochin boundary. These people are fair, about five feet six inches in height, and frequently have aquiline noses. They inherit in the male line, and have an early marriage ceremony, followed by another in which cloths are presented to the bridegroom. After childbirth the woman lives in a shed for sixteen days. They bury their dead, the earth being dug with the ceremony to which I have already alluded,[1] and though we are not told that a cloth is laid on the corpse at the funeral ceremonies, Fawcett[2] records the fact that a cloth is placed on the grave. There are thus several points of resemblance between their customs and those of the Todas, and this resemblance extends in some measure to the physical appearance and suggests, not only that they and the Todas have been influenced by the same culture, but even that they are people of the same race. We are here, however, plunged almost entirely in the region of conjecture, and we must wait for further information before we consider whether such tribes as the Hill Arrians are representatives of the same race as the Todas, both having been driven from the plains of Malabar into their mountain fastnesses, or whether the Todas and Arrians are two hill tribes of similar descent who have each been influenced by Malabar, of whom the Todas have advanced more in culture, owing to their exceptionally favourable environment on the Nilgiri plateau.

The whole of this last chapter is, I am afraid, open to the charge of being highly conjectural. It has, however, seemed to me desirable to raise some of the problems suggested by the existence of the Todas. In the settlement of these problems much further research is necessary, and I have somewhat reluctantly dealt so largely with the conjectural topics of the chapter, because they seem to point clearly to two lines of research in which further work is necessary. One is the archæology of the Nilgiris, which would, I believe, now well repay further investigation; the other is a detailed

[1] See p. 402.

[2] *Loc. cit.*

inquiry into the more popular customs of Malabar and especially of its less known peoples, such as the Hill Arrians, of whom I have just written. It is in the hope that further interest may be awakened in these lines of inquiry that I have devoted so much space to the hypotheses and surmises of this final chapter.

If further research should show that the Todas are derived from ancient races of Malabar, it is possible that the existence of this strange people may help to illuminate the many dark places which exist in our knowledge of the connexion between the Aryan and Dravidian cultures. It is even possible that the Todas may give us a glimpse of what the culture of Malabar may have been before the introduction of Brahmanism, a culture from which many features would have disappeared, while others would have undergone special development; and, if this were the case, the complex dairy ritual of the Todas would be the most striking instance of the development, a development, however, carrying with it the germs of that degeneration from which the Toda religion now seems to be suffering.

APPENDICES

APPENDIX I

I give here a translation of two extracts from Portuguese manuscripts preserved in the British Museum. The original spelling of the names of places and persons has been preserved and I have added some notes. I am indebted for the translation to Miss A. de Alberti.

The Mission of Todramala.[1]—This new mission of Todramala belongs to the college of Vaipicotta, and it seems necessary to give your Rev. an account thereof that you may be informed of what has been discovered, as well as of what still remains to be done. Vague rumours had reached the Lord Bishop Dom Frco. Ros that in the interior of this Malabar, among some mountains, there dwelt a race of men descended from the ancient Christians of S. Thomas; in order to discover and open the way to them he sent from our seminary a Cassanar[2] and a Chamas, which means a priest and a deacon, who after travelling for more than fifty miles reached the summit of the mountain of Todramala. Here they came upon a race which appeared, in accordance with the rumour, to be of those who were driven from the territory of S. Thome by the many wars in former times and scattered through these parts. They did not call it by that name, however, but pointing in the direction of S. Thomas, they said that certain men came thence, some of whom settled in those mountains, and others went further down, of whom they knew nothing. The Cassanar thereupon took occasion to ingratiate himself with them, saying that those who settled lower

[1] Add. MS. 9853, pp. 464–5, MS. 25–26 vol. [Translation].

[2] Or Cattanar, a native priest of the Syrian Church.

down were his ancestors, and therefore they were all of one race, and they had come solely to visit them as their brethren and relations. This moved them to such love and pity that men, women, and children embraced and welcomed them with tears. They found no trace of Christianity in them; they had neither crosses nor books, though they said they had some once, but they were lost as those who could read had died out. They have no pagoda worship nor pagan ceremonies. On being questioned concerning their god they spoke of a bird, a father, and a son, from which it may be presumed that they had some notion of the Blessed Trinity. They rejoiced to hear of the creation of the world and other discourses which the Cassamar and the Chamas held with them; and they were very eager that they should remain with them a long while, but they could not do so, as their guide was very pressing that they should return. They are a somewhat white-skinned race and tall of stature; they grow long beards and wear their hair after the ancient Portuguese fashion, bushy on the head and falling on the shoulders behind. They have necessaries in abundance, namely, rice, some wheat, vegetables, and meat in great variety, both fowls and wild game; quantities of cattle, and so much milk that they cannot use it all and give it to the very cattle to drink. Many other things were related of their customs which I leave until more is known of them. Upon this information the Father Vice-Provincial, at the instance of the Bishop, resolved to send thither a priest well acquainted with the Malabar tongue, and therefore he commissioned the father who was going to the residence of Calicut to inquire the easiest road and best season for this mission. He found that it was much nearer Calicut through the territory of the Samorim, and that the best time was the month of January, when, by the help of God, a father will set out with several Cassamars, and of what occurs your Rev. will be informed next year.

The Mission of Todamalâ.[1]—Last year your Rev. received a brief account of a new mission destined for Todamalâ to a certain race dwelling in the interior of this country of Malabar, among rugged mountains, at a distance of fifty leagues or thereabouts. These were supposed to be descendants of the Christians of S. Thomas who had somehow drifted to those parts. Though last year the Bishop of Angamale, Dom Frco. Ros, sent a priest belonging to the Christians

[1] Add. MS. 9853, p. 479, MS. 40 vol. [Translation].

of S. Thomas, accompanied by a deacon and a good guide, to explore the land and acquire information concerning this race, they did not bring back such full and certain intelligence as was desired. Therefore the Lord Bishop asked our Vice-Provincial to send one of our fathers, and the choice fell upon Father Yacomo Fenicio,[1] who has known the people of Malabar for many years and is well acquainted with their language. The father set out from Calicut, where he resides, and whence the road is easiest, and with the assistance of good guides reached the desired destination, though at the cost of great labour and risk. Having acquired ample information, he returned to Calicut from Thodomala, and on his arrival wrote a letter to the Vice-Provincial, dated the 1st of April, 1603, giving him an account of his discoveries, of which the following is a copy—

Copy of a letter from FATHER YACOME FINICIO *to the* VICE-PROVINCIAL OF CALICUT, *1st of April*, 1603

Thanks be to God, I am returned from Todamalâ, though with great labour and little satisfaction, for I did not find there what we hoped and were led to expect. And as the prosecution or abandonment of this mission depends upon it, I think it necessary to give you here a detailed account of all I discovered and endured. The road by Charti being impracticable on account of the wars which had broken out among the people, I was obliged to go by Manarechatem, and this was providential for us, it being the road taken by the Cacenar whom the bishop sent last year. It is thirteen leagues from the shore of Tanor. So far the way was safe and easy, this being the territory of the Samorim, and in every village we met people who knew our Christian Errari,[2] the nephew of the Samorim, who accompanied me. I was very glad of his company, because he offered it himself, and because he could speak Canara, the language of the Badegas, neighbours of the Todares. Before we reached Mararachate we had an interview with the chief ruler of the Samorim, who lives within two leagues. I gave him a palm-leaf from Carnor, chief ruler of the Samorim, in which he bade him give me the men and assistance necessary for my journey to Todamalâ, and to go with me himself if necessary. The ruler welcomed us with many

[1] In the translation given by Whitehouse the name of this priest is given as Ferreira.

[2] A member of the Errari or cowherd caste.

compliments, but as regards the journey he made many difficulties, and not only he, but many others of that place said that the way was very long and full of wild and rugged mountains; that there were elephants and tigers, that it was very cold up there, and finally that there was a risk that some of us would die. The ruler wished to send two Naires, who knew the way, with me, but they would not go for fear of falling sick, even though I would have paid them well. Finding that they made so many difficulties I pressed the Errari to return to Calicut with his people, as it was feared that they would fall sick upon the way, and I would go to Manaracathe and there provide myself with a guide and escort. This touched the Errari upon a point of honour, and he bade me not to speak of such a thing, for he was resolved to go, and his Naires had all bound themselves by an oath to go likewise. The Errari had with him a Varser,[1] which is little less than a Brahmin, and he said to me, "Father, if I die on the road, bury me where you will; it is of no consequence." I asked another young Naire if he wished to go, and he replied, "I will accompany your Reverence while I have breath." Upon this we took leave of the ruler and went to Manarecathe, where we found the very chatim who went with the Cacenar; however, the Errari thought it best to take another more trustworthy, who had relatives in the country. Here we were told that it was six Canara leagues to Todamalâ, which is twelve Malabar leagues, and that it would take two days and a half to get there. Everyone provided himself with clothes against the cold of Todamalâ, and with provisions for the journey; also with pots which the Naires carried on their heads, not for want of coolies, but because the Naires and Brahmins will not allow those of a different caste to touch the pots in which they cook their rice. The arms were left behind that the natives might not suppose that the people of Malabar had come to fight with them. Thus we set out cheerfully, and the first day, as we could not reach a village before night, we dined, and started between eight and nine in the morning, and marched quickly until evening that we might not be benighted in the thicket, for fear of the elephants, and yet our guide said we had only travelled two Canara leagues. That day we crossed a sandy mountain.

The second day we wished to start at dawn, but we met fifteen or sixteen men of that village coming by the road we were to pursue, all armed, and they told us that there were three elephants in the

[1] ? Vaishya.

way, so we waited until nine o'clock and in the meantime the elephants sought their pasture. This second day we supped at the foot of a very high mountain over which our road lay, and as there was no village and there were elephants about, after supper we climbed part of the mountain and slept there. After midnight we climbed nearly all the rest of the mountain by moonlight, with great labour and fatigue. On reaching the summit other great mountains appeared, and others beyond them, at which we were all astounded, for some of them were so steep that we were obliged to descend in a sitting posture. When the Errari found himself on these mountains, he said that God was punishing him for his sins, and that going up and down such mountains would shorten their lives by ten years. The chatim, our guide, looking down from a mountain, said that merely looking down dazzled his eyes, and so said the Naires on other occasions in similar circumstances. But I could not restrain my laughter, and began singing hymns in Malabar against pagodas, whereupon the others laughed too, and joined in the hymns. It was now noon, and we had still another mountain to climb before reaching the village of the Badagas, neighbours of the Thodares, but we were so tired that we could go no further. We wished to dine, and there was very good cold water flowing from a mountain, but we had no fire. The Errari offered to go up with the Brahmin and to send us down a light. I would not suffer him to take so much trouble, nor was it necessary, for the chatim, our guide, struck fire from two twigs, and thereupon everyone sat down to rest, cooking his rice meanwhile. When we had rested we climbed the mountain and reached the village of the Badegas. It is a village of 150 to 200 souls, called Meleuntaõ.[1] The Cacenar is reported to have visited it. Here we found the chief of the Todeos and spoke with him. He promised to go and assemble the rest, that we might speak to them. In this village they have fowls, cows, goats, rice, lentils, mustard seed, garlick, and honey. They brought me some wheat in the husk, which was very difficult to remove, and therefore it seemed to me more like barley or some other grain than wheat. The Badagos are like the Malabars, and they say there are two other villages like this in these mountains, four, five, and six leagues distant from each other. These trade with the Thodares and sell them rice, buying buffalo butter from them, which they carry to Manaracathe for sale. The next day I wished to discourse to these Badagas concerning our

[1] Whitehouse suggests that this is Melur.

law. I showed them the pictures of Our Lady of St. Luke, telling them that the child was God, who became man to teach us his law and save us. I showed them a gilt Bible and told them that it was the book of our law, and as they all surrounded me, I went up into a high place and the Errari with me. I spoke in Malabar and the Errari interpreted in Canara, which is their language. A Badaga who understood Malabar could not contain himself, but came up to where I was and spoke to me in Topas.[1] Then I taught him that the law given to us by the God made man was contained in ten commandments, &c., and they all rejoiced at the ten commandments and their explanation. Only at the sixth[2] commandment the Topas Badaga represented to me that the Malabars also had many wives. I told him that this law was not the law of the Malabars, but of God, and that they did wrong in having many wives, whereupon he was satisfied. Finally I told him that I had not come to teach the Thodares only, but them also if they would accept this law. They replied that the law was very good, but they did not dare adopt it, neither could I live in these barren mountains, &c. I make no doubt that if a priest were there they would all be converted. While I was in this village of Melentaõ the priest of the Thodares came thither, but he remained outside the village, for he may not touch a woman. I went to see him and found him seated on the ground with seven or eight others seated near him. He was a huge man, well proportioned, with a long beard and hair like a Nazarene falling on his shoulders, the front hair drawn back over his head, leaving his forehead uncovered. His dress was a shawl from the waist to the knees, and the rest of his body was naked; he held a sickle in his hand. When I had come up to him and sat down, he asked me how I was; I replied that I was well and all the better for meeting him, for it proved to me that God was my guide, since I had come from so far to see the Thodares and immediately met with their chief. He asked the purpose of my coming. I replied that I had come to see the Thodares, having heard that we were of the same race and laws, and that last year one of our people visited them and gave us a very good account of them. I asked him if they knew from whom they were descended. He said no, and thereupon would have taken leave of us. Then I said that it was not right to wish to leave us so soon, since we had come so far solely to visit them, and

[1] I do not know the meaning of this. One caste of the Badagas is called Torya.

[2] Seventh?

upon this he remained. Then I inquired of those around who he was, and what was his office. They replied that he was called Pallem and was like the Belicha Paro among the Malabars. Belichaparo is he who takes care of the pagoda, and sometimes the devil enters into him, and he trembles and rolls upon the ground, and answers questions put to him in the name of the pagoda. I asked if the Thodares had pagodas; they replied that they had a live buffalo cow for a pagoda, and they hung a bell round its neck, and the Pallem offered it milk every day, and then let it loose in the fields to graze with the rest. And every month or thereabouts, the Pallem seizes the buffalo by the horns and trembles, saying that the buffalo bids them change the pasture, and thereupon they change their place and pasture. By the milk and butter of this buffalo and that of its children and grandchildren, which already reach 120, this Pallem is maintained. On this mountain where I was there were 100 Thodares,[1] and they had three pallems between them, each having his buffalo for a pagoda. When the buffalo dies the Thodares assemble, choose one of these hundred, tie the bell round its neck, and it becomes a pagoda. Besides the buffalo they have 300 pagodas to whom they also make offerings of milk. I asked him why he carried the sickle in his hand, and he replied that God commanded him to carry no other arm or stick but only that sickle. He used it to scratch his head, which was swarming with lice, and they could be seen crawling among his hair. I asked if he was married; he answered that he and his younger brother were married to the same woman, but as he might not touch a woman in the house she always lived with his brother, but he sent for her into the bush every week or so, when it was a fine day. And when he liked he sent for any of the wives of the Thodares whom he chose, and the husbands allowed it so long as he paid them. I asked if they had books and he said no; none of them can read or write. He also told me that they had a father whom God took up to heaven, body and soul, and the buffaloes looked up to heaven after him, and that was why they made offerings to the buffaloes. At last I gave him one of the looking-glasses from Calicut, with which he was very pleased and said he would give it to his wife. Then I took leave of him, after showing him the pictures and Bible, at which he wondered. Besides this pallem they have another whom they call Ferral,[2] who is present

[1] By the context this should be 100 buffalo cows.

[2] Evidently the *wursol*.

when they give the buffaloes salt water, and he trembles, bidding them give them drink, and they will give much milk, and grow fat, and give butter in plenty, &c.

The next day we went to visit the villages of the Thodares. We climbed quite half a league above this village, and on reaching the summit nothing was visible on every side but mountains and valleys; all was desert without a single fruit or forest tree, excepting in an occasional damp place where there were a few forest trees. There are no palm trees or jacks in all these mountains, nor any fruit trees, as I have said. As we traversed these mountains and valleys, every now and then we saw a herd of buffaloes in the distance with a Thodar or two guarding them. In this way we met four or five Thodares and sent them to fetch the rest. As no women were visible, I promised one a looking-glass if he would go and fetch them. He hastened away up a mountain and brought back four women, who remained at a distance through timidity and would not join the rest. I sent them word that they must approach if they wanted looking-glasses, and then they came up. After this we went on for another half a league or more and came upon two Thodar huts at the foot of a mountain. They were like a large barrel half buried in the ground, or like a covered bier. They were nine spans in length and the same in breadth; and six spans in the highest part. The hoops of the barrel were of thick reeds like Indian cane, bent into a hoop with both ends fixed in the ground. Pieces of wood from the bush were laid across these reeds and covered with grass. The front was made of stakes set on end, like organ pipes, with no other filling whatever. The door was a span and four inches wide, and two spans and an inch high, so that the Errari and myself could scarcely enter, and inside we had to kneel. There were two beds with grass mattresses on each side, and a small pit in the middle of the hut which was the fireplace. There was a little window on one side, a finger's length high and a span wide. Beside these houses was a pen for buffaloes, and close by another little house where they make the butter. They said the other houses were half a league distant from each other. Thirty or forty Thodares assembled; they are clothed in a large sheet with no other covering but a small loincloth four or five fingers wide. Their arms are long sticks smeared with butter; when new they look like strips of white paper at a distance, but they cure them and they turn black. They wear long beards, and rather long hair, but not so long as the Pallem. It was two months since I had shaved or cut my hair, so that I looked like one of them, and they did not wonder at me as they did at the Cacenar, who went there with no hair or beard. They never shave except when one of them dies. At a death they kill half of the dead man's buffaloes, and the other half goes to his heirs. If he has no buffaloes each person gives one, and half of them are killed and the rest are left. They burn the dead body, but it must be wrapped in a veil of pure silk, which they call a toda-pata, worth five or six fanams; and if this is lacking they must wait for it, though it be for a year. In the meantime, in order to preserve the body they open it at the loins, take out the entrails, and cut off the occiput; then they place it in an arbour and dry it in the smoke. Two brothers marry the same woman; she lives with the eldest at night, and with the youngest by day. Others have two or three wives. They do not eat fowls, cow's flesh, nor goat, and so they breed none of these. They do not eat buffalo's flesh, but only wild boar and venison. They eat no salt. They have no crops of any kind, and no occupation but the breeding of buffaloes, on whose milk and butter they live. They have no vassals, as was reported; on the contrary, they are subject and pay tribute to the Badega chiefs. When they eat they hold the rice in their left hand, take a lump of butter in the right, mix it with the rice, and so eat it; when their meal is finished they rub their hands together and wipe them on their hair, and so they all smell of butter. In colour they resemble the Malabars, some whiter and some darker; they are generally moderately tall. Their ears are pierced or bored, not long like those of the Malabars, and some wear a silver circle in them like a ring. They wear black threads round their necks, and some have a large silver bead like a pater-noster in front. I had a skein of black thread in my pocket and drew it out; a Thodar seeing it begged it of me earnestly two or three times. I told him that I must give it to the women, and I divided it in four and gave it to the four women above mentioned, and I gave them a looking-glass each, with which they were very delighted. The women wear nothing but a long sheet like the men; they wrap it round them, throwing the right end over the left shoulder, and so cover themselves. Their hair hangs loose, but their faces are uncovered. I said that the women lower down wore bracelets, chains, and jewels on their arms and necks, and in their ears, and thereupon one of them uncovered her arm, on which she wore four large well-made copper bracelets. The sheet worn by both men and women is so filthy that it looks as if it would not burn if you put it on the fire, and if water were thrown on it, it would not penetrate. The men look after the house, cook the rice, do the milking, make the butter, and mind the buffaloes. The women do nothing but pound the rice, and sometimes mind the buffaloes in the absence of their husbands. In speaking with the Pallem I asked him whether he or his wife cooked the rice; he replied that it was a great disgrace among them to allow the wife to cook the rice. The Thodares being thus assembled, I told them that, hearing that we were of the same race and law, I had come to visit them, and as I knew they had neither priest, book, nor law, I being a priest had come to teach them. I asked if they were glad to have me with them, and they replied that they rejoiced greatly at it. I asked if they would follow all my instructions, and they said they would. Then I asked if they would leave off adoring the buffalo and the 300 pagodas. They replied that they feared the buffaloes and pagodas would do them some harm. I said I would be answerable for it, and that I had more power than the pagodas. Then they said that if I would defend them they would willingly leave off adoring them. I asked if they would give up the custom of two brothers marrying one woman, and they said they would. I asked if they thought it right to give their wives to the Pallem; an old man replied, "If it is the command of God, what can we do?" After this they asked me of their own accord to show them the pictures and the book; I did so, and they paid homage to them with great rejoicing. I also gave them a looking-glass each, and after discoursing and conversing with them for some time I asked them to give me two children to take away with me; they excused themselves, saying that they could not do so just then. I asked from whence they were descended, and one replied that he had heard that they came from the East, and some remained there while some settled lower down. They were amazed at seeing white men, and asked me to uncover my arms for them to look at. They were delighted with the Errari's red tunic and gold buttons, and velvet cap with the gold braid.

At last I took leave of them, promising to return at some time during the year and remain with them longer. It did not seem to me necessary to delay any longer, nor to lay any foundation of our faith, as I do not think that the present is a suitable time for the Company to undertake such out-of-the-way enterprises, since it cannot attend to others of greater importance which are close at hand, for want of workers. The Thodares only number a thousand, and these are scattered about four mountains, two belonging to the Malabar, where there are 300. I went to one of these which belongs to the Samorim, another belonging to the Naique, where there are another 300, or a little over; and another belonging to another king, near Charti, where there are another 300 or rather more; the whole distance being eight Canara leagues, which are sixteen in Malabar. And they live scattered about—every month or thereabouts they move their village. The whole district is uninhabited desert. The winds and climate are very cold; the water is excellent, but icy cold; it flows down from the mountains; it cannot be drunk at a draught because of the cold. One is obliged to pause, and after drinking one has to wait awhile for the gums and teeth to get warm. The journey there and back is very laborious and can only be undertaken in January and February. From Manarcate upwards it is impossible to travel in a litter. On the return journey I was very fatigued and asked if it were possible to find men to carry me. I was told that there were plenty of men, but that it was impossible to be carried over these mountains, where one person alone could only climb up and down with great difficulty. Besides this, the Errari and all the rest were very pressing that I should return before any of us fell ill; the Errari said he was himself indisposed, as well as some of the others. They could not tell me anything concerning the Blessed Trinity. I asked them why they wore their hair loose, and a Badaga replied that in the time of Charamparimatei they killed the father of the Thodares, and they asked, "Who killed our father?" and they answered that God killed him; whereupon they unbound their hair and said, "Never will we bind up our hair again until we have killed God, in revenge for our father [and] for the broken pots." On the return journey the Badegas showed us a shorter and less difficult road, which took us two days and a half, but saved going up and down the last steep mountains. However, there was no lack of mountains to climb, but they were not so difficult, though the first day we climbed down one which was very high and steep. We numbered fourteen with the guides. There was a Badega village at the foot of the mountain, and seeing us they took us for a hostile band and fled into the bush. Our guides called to them not to fly, for we were men of peace who had been to visit the Thodares, whereupon they returned, and coming down we found them armed with their little lances, but we saw the women and children still hidden in the bush. A little further on we came upon four or five more houses; these people also fled into the bush, the women carrying the children on their backs. The second day we slept in the bush two leagues from Manarecate. There were tigers and elephants about, but God preserved us and we all reached Calicut in safety, thanks be to Our Lord. Several afterwards fell sick, however, among whom was the Variel, who is still suffering. May God restore him, for he has promised me to become a Christian, and has already broken his own law as regards food, &c.

APPENDIX II

BIBLIOGRAPHY

1812. Keys, William. A Topographical Description of the Neelaghery Mountains (a letter printed in Grigg's Manual of the Nilagiri District, Appendix, p. xlviii).

1819. "A Subscriber." Letter to the Madras Courier, Feb. 23, 1819 (reprinted in Grigg's Manual, Appendix, p. lii).

1820. Macpherson, Evans. A Letter reprinted in Grigg's Manual, Appendix, p. lv.

1821. Ward, B. S. Geographical and Statistical Memoir of a Survey of the Neelgherry Mountains (printed in Grigg's Manual, Appendix, p. lx).

1829. Hough, James. Letters on the Climate, Inhabitants, Productions, etc., of the Neilgherries or Blue Mountains of Coimbatore, South India. London. (Letters previously published in the Bengal Hurkaru, 1826.)

1829. Young, D. S. An Account of the General and Medical Topography of the Neelgherries. Trans. Medical and Physical Soc. of Calcutta, vol. iv, p. 36.

1832. Harkness, Henry. A Description of a Singular Aboriginal Race inhabiting the Summit of the Neilgherry Hills. London.

1834. Jervis, H. Narrative of a Journey to the Falls of the Cavery; with an historical and descriptive Account of the Neilgherry Hills. London.

1834. Mignon, Capt. Notes extracted from a Private Journal written during a Tour through Malabar and among the Neilgherries. Bombay, American Mission Press (I have not been able to see a copy of this book).

1837. Schmid, Bernhard. An Essay on the Relationship of Language and Nations. Madras Journ. Lit. and Sci., vol. v, p. 133: on p. 155 is a section "On the Dialect of the Todavers, the Aborigines of the Neelgherries."

1837. Barron, Richard. Views in India. London. (Coloured plates of Toda man and woman, and of the village of Kars.)

1838. Birch, de Burgh. Topographical Report on the Neilgherries. Madras Journ. Lit. and Sci., vol. viii, p. 86.

1838. Schmid, Bernhard. Ueber Sprache- und Völkerverwandschaft, Halle. On S. 27 is a section on the dialect of the Todas.

1842. Stevenson, Rev. Dr. A Collection of Words from the Language of the Todas, the Chief Tribe of the Nilgiri Hills. Journ. Bombay Branch of Roy. Asiatic Soc., vol. i, p. 155.

1844. Muzzy, C. F. Account of the Neilgherry Hill Tribes. Madras Christian Instructor and Missionary Record, Madras, vol. ii, p. 358.

1844. Anon. Madras Spectator, Aug. 31, 1844, p. 559 (an account of a Toda funeral).

1844-5. Congreve, H. The Descent of the Thautawars. Madras Spectator, 1844, pp. 361, 655, 694, 768; 1845, pp. 29, 37, 63.

1847. Congreve, H. The Antiquities of the Neilgherry Hills, including an Inquiry into the Descent of the Thautawars or Todas. Madras Journ. Lit. and Sci., vol. xiv, p. 77.

1848. Ouchterlony. Geographical and Statistical Memoir of a Survey of the Neilgherry Mountains. Madras Journ. Lit. and Sci., 1848, vol. xv, p. 1.

1849. Schmid, B. Remarks on the Origin and Languages of the Aborigines of the Nilgiris, suggested by the papers of Captain Congreve and the Rev. W. Taylor on the supposed Celto-Scythic Antiquities in the South of India. Journ. Bombay Branch Roy. Asiatic Soc., vol. iii, Part I, p. 50.

1851. Ford, Sir Francis. Neilgherry Letters. Bombay, 1851.

1851. Burton, R. F. Goa and the Blue Mountains. London, 1851 (pp. 316–344).

1856. Caldwell, R. A Comparative Grammar of the Dravidian Languages. London; p. 503, "Are the Nilgherry Tudas Dravidians?" (2nd edition, 1875, p. 555).

1857. Metz, J. F. Die Volkstämme der Nilagiri's. Basel.

1857-8. Metz, F. A Vocabulary of the Dialect spoken by the Todas of the Nilagiri Mountains. Madras Journ. Lit. and Sci., N.S., vol. i, pp. 103, 131, and vol. ii, p. 1.

1864. Metz, F. The Tribes inhabiting the Neilgherry Hills: their Social Customs and Religious Rites; from the rough notes of a German Missionary. Second enlarged edition, Mangalore.

1868. Shortt, J. An Account of the Tribes on the Neilgherries. Madras (republishes part of Ouchterlony's Memoir).

1869. Shortt, J. An Account of the Hill Tribes of the Neilgherries. Trans. Ethnol. Soc., N.S., vol. vii, p. 230.

1870. King, W. Ross. The Aboriginal Tribes of the Nilgiri Hills. London (republished from Journal of Anthropology).

1873. Marshall, William E. A Phrenologist among the Todas. London (includes "a Brief Outline of the Grammar of the Tuda Language," by the Rev. G. U. Pope).

1873. Breeks, James Wilkinson. An Account of the Primitive Tribes and Monuments of the Nilagiris. London.

1873. Burnell, A. C. Specimens of South Indian Dialects. Mangalore.

1873–5. de Quatrefages. Étude sur les Todas. Journal des Savants, Paris, 1873, p. 729; 1874, pp. 5 and 96; 1875, p. 30.

1874. Walhouse, M. J. A Toda Dry Funeral. Indian Antiquary, vol. iii, p. 93. A Toda "Green Funeral." *Ibid.*, p. 274.

1874. Kittel. On some Dravidian Words. Indian Antiquary, vol. iii, p. 205.

1877. Walhouse, M. J. Archæological Notes. Indian Antiquary, vol. vi, p. 41.

1880. Grigg, H. B. A Manual of the Nilagiri District in the Madras Presidency. Madras.

1894. Natesa Sastri, S. M. A New Study of the Todas. Madras Mail, Aug. 28th, 1894.

1896. Thurston, Edgar. The Todas of the Nilgiris. Bull. Madras Government Museum, vol. i, p. 141.

1901. Thurston, Edgar. Todas of the Nilgiris. *Ibid.*, vol. iv, p. 1.

? Ling, Catharine F. The Todas. Publication of the Church of England Zenana Missionary Society: London.

1904. Shams-ul-Ulma Jivanji Jamshedji Modi. A few notes on the Todas. Journ. Anthrop. Soc., Bombay, vol. vii, p. 68.

APPENDIX III

LIST OF TODA VILLAGES (not including *ti mad*)

Village.	*Clan.*	*Badaga name.*	*Remarks.*
Akîrsikòdri	Nidrsi	Taranadmand	male funeral place.
Ârpâr	Päm		
Ârs	Kuudr	Anekkalmand	
Artol	Taradr	Aretalmand	
Âtimad	Taradr	Karadikottumand	
Eirgûdr	Nòdrs	Nerkodumand	
Erparskòdr	Piedr	Yeppakodumand	
Îdrtol	Kuudr	Edattalmand	
Inikitj	Päm	Bettumand	
Isharâdr	Kars	Kadimand	
Iûdi	Kwòdrdoni		male funeral place.
Îvigar	Kuudr	Kekidamand	in ruins.
Kabûdri	Pan	Tebbekudumand	male funeral place.
Kâkhûdri	Melgars	Kaggodumand	
Kalmathi	Kars	Kalmattimand	in ruins ten years.
Kalmad	Kars	Kulamand	in ruins.
Kanòdrs	Kanòdrs	Devarmand	*etudmad.*
Kapthòri	Keadr	Kunnapemand	in ruins.
Karars	Keradr		
Karia	Kuudr	Kariyamand	
Kârs	Kars	Kandalmand	*etudmad.*
Kârsh	Karsh		
Kashtkòdr	Kuudr	Kattikadumand	unoccupied.
Katerk	Nòdrs	Kaitarkemand	
Katikâr	Kwòdrdoni	Kodanadmand	
Katol	Melgars		in ruins.
Kâvâther	Nidrsi	Kabaiteraimand	
Kavîdi	Piedr		in the Wainad.
Keâdr	Keadr	Karrikadumand	*etudmad.*
Kebâr	Nidrsi		female funeral place.
Kedâr	Nòdrs	Kangatarmand	in ruins.
Keirod	Kuudr	Keradamand	
Kerâdr	Keradr	Kannagimand	*etudmad*, also male funeral place.
Kerkârs	Taradr	Karrakalmand	
Keshkar	Kanòdrs		

Village.	*Clan.*	*Badaga name.*	*Remarks*
Keshker	Kars	Kakerimand	also called Minikimand.
Kidmad	Kidmad		
Kîrsâs	Melgars		
Kiûdr	Kuudr	Kengodumand	*satimad.*
Kiûsh	Piedr	Karimulimand	
Kòdrers	Piedr	Hadamand	
Koers	Keradr	Kokimalmand	in ruins.
Kozhber	Kuudr	Kasubiramand	disused.
Kozhtûdi	Nòdrs		
Kûdimad	Taradr	Kulimand	
Kudòdrs	Nòdrs	Kombutukkimand	
Kûdrâdr	Keadr	Kudukkadumand	
Kûdrmâs	Taradr	Kudimalmand	*kalolmad.*
Kûdrnâkhum	Nòdrs	Kudinagamand	
Kugwuln	Kuudr		disused.
Kûirsi	Pan	Kolimand	
Kûlikâl	Kwòdrdoni	Kolikkalmand	in ruins.
Kulkòdri	Nòdrs	Kolakkadumand	in ruins.
Kûlmud	Kars	Malaividumand	female funeral place.
Kûlthpuli	Nòdrs		female funeral place.
Kûrkalmut	Kuudr		female funeral place.
Kurvâs	Nòdrs	Kurudamand	
Kushârf	Kusharf		*etudmad.*
Kûûdi	Piedr	Anaikundukulimand	(? Köûdi).
Kûûdr	Kuudr	Kundakodumand	*etudmad.*
Kuzhû	Kars	Kunditolmand	
Kuzhû	Kanòdrs		near Kanòdrs : disused.
Kwarâdr	Keadr	Kugadodmand	
Kwatkash	Päm	Marunallimand	female funeral place.
Kwîrg	Kuudr	Korangumand	
Kwòdrdôni	Kwòdrdoni	Kodudonnemand	*etudmad.*
Madôni	Pedrkars		
Madsû	Päm	Manjathalmand	
Madsû	Kuudr		disused.
Marsners	Päm		
Melgârs	Melgars	Manjakkalmand	*etudmaa.*
Melkòdr	Kuudr	Mekkodumand	
Melûr	Pedrkars	Madaliyurmand	
Merkwadrvalth	Kanòdrs		
Meroln	Piedr		male funeral place.
Mîrzôti	Melgars		male funeral place.
Miûni	Kuudr	Marlimand	
Molkush	Kuudr	Malkodmand	
Mòmanôthi	Piedr		female funeral place.
Mulòrs	Nòdrs		funeral place for boys.
Muthûkòr	Kuudr		disused.
Nasmiòdr	Kars	(Aganadmand)	
Nâtêrs	Pan	Natanerimand	
Nedrdol	Taradr	Kilmand	in ruins.

Village.	*Clan.*	*Badaga name.*	*Remarks.*
Nelkush	Nòdrs	Neykadimand	in ruins.
Nerigudi	Nòdrs	Nergulimand	
Nerngòdr	Kuudr		disused.
Nersvem	Kwòdrdoni	Nervenumand	in ruins.
Nersvem	Nidrsi	Nadumand	in ruins.
Neshkwòdr	Keadr	Nedikodumand	
Nidrsi	Nidrsi	Nidimand	*etudmad.*
Nîrkâtji	Kuudr	Nirkachimand	
Nîrsht	Piedr		
Nirsk	Päm		female funeral place.
Nòdrmad	Taradr	Nadumand	
Nòdrs	Nòdrs	Muttanadmand	*etudmad.*
Nongârsi	Kars	Kettarimand	in ruins (? belonged to Piedr).
Nüln	Melgars	Nerigulimand	
Òdr	Nòdrs	Aganadmand	
Òrs	Taradr	Alaikudalmand	
Padegâr	Melgars	Kottapolmand	also called Kotapol, see p. 664.
Pâkhalkûdr	Kars	Bagalkodumand	
Paliners	Kuudr		
Pām	Päm		in ruins.
Pamârkol	Piedr		female funeral place.
Pan	Pan	Onnamand	*etudmad*: often called "One mand."
Panmuti	Nidrsi	Banatimand	
Parzkadi	Nidrsi		in ruins.
Pathâdr	Nòdrs	Buddankodumand	
Pathmârs	Pan	Bettumand	
Pêdrkârs	Pedrkars	Bedakalmand	*etudmad.*
Pegârsi	Keradr	Attumand	in ruins.
Peivòrs	Kuudr		
Pekhòdr	Keadr	Osamand	"new mand."
Peletkwur	Kars	Attakoraimand	
Pêrg	Pan	Veragimand	*kalolmad.*
Perththo	Nòdrs	Perittitalmand	see p. 648.
Peshkimad	Pedrkars		female funeral place.
Pevar	Taradr	Pevarmand	in ruins.
Pidati	Nidrsi	Bendutimand	
Pîedr	Pîedr	Waragudumand	*etudmad.*
Pîitth	Kuudr		male funeral place, near Kuudr.
Pineiwars	Nòdrs	Pinnapolamand	in ruins.
Pirshti	Nòdrs	Baggulamand	
Pîrsûsh	Kuudr	Billanjikadumand	
Pishkwosht	Kanòdrs	Bikkapatimand	
Pòdzkwar	Kars	Narigulimand	or Pûzhkwar.
Poln	Kusharf	Pagulimand	
Pömad	Pemand	Kars	in ruins twenty years: near Peletkwur.
Pongûdr	Pedrkars		
Pòsh	Melgars	Onnekudimand	

Village.	*Clan.*	*Badaga name.*	*Remarks.*
Pòti	Piedr	Pattimand	
Potvaili	Piedr		disused.
Pülkwûdr	Taradr	Olakkodumand	
Pulthkûln	Keradr	Bikkolmand	
Punmud	Kwòdrdoni	Banukudumand	female funeral place.
Punumikâtuni	Kuudr		female funeral place.
Purati	Nòdrs	Portimand	
Puretimokh	Melgars		female funeral place.
Purskudiâr	Pan	Porikodiyoramand	
Pushtar	Taradr	Pattaraimand	
Putamad	Kuudr		disused.
Pûtol	Nòdrs	Puttalmand	
Püvars	Kars	Ammakoraimand	
Pûvi	Päm	Pudiyapalamand	male funeral place.
Sultar	Pedrkars		male funeral place.
Sudvaili	Piedr		male funeral place in the Wainad.
Tâktut	Päm		place for small male funerals.
Taknin	Kanòdrs		near Kanòdrs.
Tâmâkh	Kuudr	Tamogamand	
Târâdr	Taradr	Tarnardmand	*etudmad*, and male funeral place.
Târâdrkîrsi	Kars	Kavaikkadumand	male funeral place, also *kalolmad.*
Tarkòdr	Kuudr	Terkodmand	
Tavatkûdr	Piedr	Tavattakoraimand	
Tebmârs	Taradr	Urutharaimand	
Teḍshteiri	Nòdrs	Talapatharaimand	
Teidr	Kusharf	Denadmand	
Telgûdr	Taradr	Telhodumand	*kalolmad.*
Tigòir	Piedr	Tukkaramand	
Tîm	Pan		male funeral place: possibly another name of Kabûdri.
Tòthikeir	Nòdrs	Jegadevarmand	in ruins.
Tôvalkan	Keradr	Tuvalkandimand	
Tûdrkwur	Kusharf	Todakaraimand	
Tülchoven	Päm		male funeral place.
Umgâs	Kusharf	Yemmekalmand	
Ushâdr	Melgars	Kavaimand	male and female funeral place.
Wengûdr	Taradr	Yenakodumand	in ruins.

APPENDIX IV

In the following list I give the botanical names of the plants or kinds of wood used by the Todas in their ordinary life or in their ceremonial. I owe these names to the kindness of Mr. Thurston and Mr. K. Rangachari.

Ànmul	Rubus moluccanus, L.
Àvelashki	Hedyotis stylosa, Br.
Kabûdri	Euphorbia Rothiana, Sprengl.
K'adak or *kadakmul*	Rosa Leschenaultiana, W and A.
K'âkâr	Eragrostica nigra, Nees.
K'âkhûdri	Dregea volubilis, Benth.
K'âkkûdri	Gardneria ovata, Wall.
Kâkûd	Mappia foetida, Miers.
Kârkekoi	Rhamnus Wightii, W and A.
Karneizi	Acronychia laurifolia, Bl.
Kėrs	Eugenia Arnottiana, Wight.
Kîâz	Litsaea Wightiana, Benth. and Hk. f.
Kid	Probably Olea robusta.
K'îri or *K'îrsi*	Amaranthus (speciosus ?).
K'udi	Hydrocotyle asiatica, L.
Kûrêrs	Eugenia calophyllifolia, Wight.
Kurskat	Strobilanthes, ? species.
K'wadiki or *kwadriki*	Myrsine capitellata, Wall. var. lanceolata.
Kwagal	Polygonum rude, Meissn. and P. chinense, L.
Kwatimali	Coriandrum sativum, L.
Main	Cinnamomum Wightii, Meissn.
Melkûdri	Piper sp.
Mòrs	Michelia nilagirica, Zenk.
Nârk	Andropogon schoenanthus, L.
Pârs (wood)	? Sideroxylon.
Pârs (leaves)	Pentapanax Leschenaultii, Seem.
Parskuti	Eleagnus latifolia, L.
Pâsòr	Dodonaea viscosa, L.
Pathanmul	Solanum indicum, L.
Patm	Panicum miliare, Lamk.
Pelkkodsthmul	Rubus ellipticus, Sm.
Peshteinmul	? Phyllochlamys sp.

Pŏhvet	Pavetta creniflora, DC.
Pötûr	Anaphalis oblonga, DC.
Pûl	Ilex Wightiana, Wall.
Purs	Rhododendron arbŏreum, Sm. and Elaeagnus latifolia.
Pûthimul	Rubus lasiocarpus, Sm.
Pûv or *pûf*	Sophora glauca, Lesch.
Püvkat	Strobilanthes, ? species.
Takmul	Berberis aristata, DC.
Tavat	Rhodomyrtus tomentosus, Wight.
Teinkûdri	Senecio corymbosus, Wall.
Tib	Leucas zeylanica, Br., and L. aspera, Sprengl.
Tirparikat	Strobilanthes, ? species.
Tiveri	Atylosa candollei, W and A.
Tŏûrsmitch	Diospyros sp.
Tòri or *tòrimul*	Berberis nepalensis, Sprengl.
Tûdr	Meliosma pungens, Wall. and M. Wightii, Planch.
Twadri	Girardinia heterophylla DC.
Wâdr	Ochlandra sp.

GLOSSARY

Only the more important Toda words used in this book are included in the glossary. The words are arranged in alphabetical order, neglecting the quantity or other value of the first vowel. The numbers refer to the pages on which fuller descriptions of the terms are given.

Âdrpârs, coagulated milk, curd, p. 64.
agâr, a stand in the dairy, p. 60.
al, the deposit after the clarification of butter used as food, pp. 50, 242.
alug, a vessel of the *ti* dairy, p. 90.
Amnôdr, the world of the dead, p. 397.
an (*anna*), elder brother, p. 486.
än, ancient clothing of the Todas, pp. 196, 342, 572.
Anto, a dairy, p. 112; also a god, p. 188.
ârpatznol or *ârpasnol*, a sacred day, p. 407.
ârs, house, p. 583.
ârsaiîr, buffaloes of the Kwôdrdôni *ti*, p. 121.
ârsâp, a salt-giving ceremony, p. 175.
ashkkârtpimi, a food used on ceremonial occasions, p. 580.
âtîr, buffaloes of the Nôdrs *ti*, p. 112.
âv (*âvâ*), mother, p. 485.
âzâram, the circle of stones in which the ashes are buried at a funeral, pp. 337, 379.
âzâramkêdr, the last part of the second funeral ceremony, pp. 337, 378.
Epotirikhtârs, a double hut, p. 29.
êr, a male buffalo, p. 47.
êrkumptthpimi or *êrkumpttkiti*, the ceremony of sacrificing a calf, p. 274.
êrnkâr, sacrificial place at the *êrkumptthpimi* ceremony, p. 276.
êrs, leaf.
êrsteiti, the act of making a leaf-cup, pp. 75, 148.
ertatpun, a dairy vessel, p. 60.
ertatmâr, part of the dairy where the less sacred vessels stand, p. 58.
ertatpur, the less sacred objects of the dairy, p. 58
etûdpali, chief dairy, p. 40.

etûdmad, the chief village of a clan or other important village, pp. 24, 36, 419.
etvainolkêḍr, the first funeral ceremony, p. 337.
ichchil, a condition of impurity due to death or child-birth, pp. 102, 326, 368.
iḍith, "for the sake of," p. 216.
îḍrkwoi, a vessel used at a *tî* dairy, p. 90.
îḍrtul, part of a hut containing the sleeping-places, p. 583.
îmûḍrikârs, stones at certain villages, p. 439.
in, father, p. 484.
îr, a female buffalo, p. 47.
îrkarmus or *îrkarmüs*, the milking-place, p. 53.
îrkârtpun (*îrkârithtpun*), milking-vessel, p. 58.
îrnörtiti, the offering of a buffalo calf to the *tî*, p. 293; or to another division of the clan, p. 294.
îrnòḍrthnol, the day of migration, p. 124.
îrpâlvusthi, ceremony after the birth of a calf, p. 172.
îrsankâti, a funeral ceremony, p. 381.
îrskiḍithbûtnol, the day of migration, p. 124.
Kaban, iron.
kabkaḍiti, procedure in which the back is not turned to the contents of the dairy, p. 73.
kachütthti, the cloth-giving ceremony at a funeral, p. 358.
kaḍr, the calf-pen, p. 26.
kâfkati, knife burnt at the *âzâramkêḍr*, p. 381.
kagârs, the *tî* name of the *kâvn*, p. 103.
kaimûkhti, a salutation, p. 31.
kaizhvatiti, the rite of pouring out buttermilk for the *palol*, p. 97.
kâkûdêrs, leaves of the *kâkûd* plant, p. 79.
kâkûl, stick used in the *ponûp* ceremony, p. 178.
kalkani, part of the dairy, p. 58.
kalmelpuḍithti, a salutation, pp. 34, 496.
kalolmad, villages where women may not live, p. 420.
kâltmokh, the attendant on a *palol*, pp. 42, 105.
kalvol, a path, p. 26.
Kamasòḍrolam, legendary Todas, p. 195.
kanârvaznûḍr, the evil eye, p. 263.
kar, a young calf, p. 47.
karenpôh, the calf-house of a *tî*, p. 85.
kârpun, a milking-vessel of the *tî*, p. 90.
kârs, stone.
karûd, younger, p. 485.
karûvnòḍr, the mother's village, p. 547.
kârvnol or *kârivnol*, the day after a ceremony, pp. 105, 333.
kâtû, the wall surrounding a house or dairy, p. 24.
kavulpûv, a flower, p. 111.
kêḍr, funeral, relics, etc., p. 368.
keitankursîr, the *wârsulîr* of Niḍrsi and Kwòḍrdôni, p. 71.
kepun (*kaipun*), vessel to hold water, p. 57.

kerk, the name of the waist-string during the ordination ceremony, pp. 148, 572.
kêrtnòḍr, a funeral place, p. 338.
kevenârûl, mode of baring the right arm, pp. 31, 571.
kîp, the broom, p. 32.
kîtün, bed on left-hand side of dairy, p. 57.
kô, stake used at the *êrkumptthpimi* sacrifice, p. 276.
kòghlag, the name of the churning-stick at the *tî*, p. 89.
kòrûp, one of the salt-giving ceremonies, p. 175.
kubuntuni, the cloak of the *palol*, p. 103.
kudeipîr, the *wûrsulîr* of Pan, p. 71; also the sacred buffaloes of Pieḍr, p. 81.
kudi, a measure used for liquids corresponding to about four pints, p. 588.
kûḍr, horn, a division of a clan, pp. 37, 295, 542.
kûḍrpali, a Tarthar dairy, pp. 40, 66.
kûdrpalikârtmokh, the dairyman of the *kûḍrpali*, p. 66.
kûḍrs mani, the bells of the *punîr* of the *tî*, p. 91.
kûḍrvars, fireplace made of four stones, pp. 57, 583.
kudupel or *kudubel*, family, p. 545.
kûgh, daughter, p. 485.
kûghîr, a buffalo whose horns bend downwards, p. 47.
kugvali, a sacred dairy of Târâḍr, pp. 41, 76.
kugvalîr, the buffaloes of the *kugvali*, pp. 41, 77.
kugvalikârtmokh, the dairyman of the *kugvali*, pp. 41, 76.
kûlâtîr, buffaloes of the Nòḍrs *tî*, p. 113.
Kûlinkârs, a god, p. 188.
kunedsti, funeral laments, etc., pp. 385, 600.
Kûrub, a Kurumba, p. 641.
kûrubûḍrchiti, Kurumba sorcery, p. 262.
kush (? *kûḍsh*), structure for young calves, p. 26.
kuter, floor, pp. 62, 583.
kûvn, the perineal band, p. 30.
kûvun or *kûpun*, a vessel used at the *kugvali* of Târâḍr, p. 79.
kwainûr (*kwoinûr*), the *tî* name of the *pennâr*, p. 103.
kwarkûl, stick used at the *ponûp* ceremony, p. 178.
kwarzam, name used in prayer, etc., pp. 216, 384, 614.
kwoi, the milking-vessel of the *tî* dairy, p. 89.
kwoinîr spring supplying water for a *tî* dairy, p. 85.
kwoinörtpet, a wand used by the *palol* when milking, p. 90.
kwotârs, the calf-house, p. 26.
Kwoten, a *teu* or god, p. 193.
Kwoto, a god, p. 203.
kwottün, seat, p. 29.
kwungg, the ordinary bell, p. 424.
Kwûrg, Coorg, p. 114.
Mad, village, pp. 24, 338; head, p. 282.
madnol, sacred day of village, p. 405.
madol, village people or clan, p. 36.
madth, the churning-stick, p. 60.

maj, buttermilk.
majpariv, a dairy vessel, p. 60.
majvatitthkalvol, path reserved for women, p. 27.
majvatvaiïḍrn, spot on which women receive buttermilk, p. 28.
maiïr, a barren buffalo, p. 47.
mani, the sacred bell, pp. 40, 66, 424.
mankûgh, er's daughter, 488.
manmokh, sister's son, pp. 484, 488.
martïr, the sacred buffaloes of the Kârs clan, p. 68.
mârûp, one of the salt-giving ceremonies, p. 175.
mârvainolkêḍr, the second funeral ceremony, pp. 337, 372.
masth, axe, pp. 57, 585.
matchuni, children of brother and sister, pp. 488, 512.
Mâv, a Badaga, p. 630; also sambhar.
meilkûḍr, extra share, 560.
meitün, bed on right-hand side of dairy, p. 57.
merkalârs, double hut, pp. 29, 318.
mersgûrsïr, the *wârsulïr* of Nòḍrs, p. 71.
methkûdi, place of cremation, p. 343.
miniapïr, the *wârsulïr* of Kerâḍr, pp. 71, 192.
mogâl, forearm, also segment of forelimb of calf corresponding to metacarpus, p. 281.
mogoi, a cubit, p. 588.
mokh, son, child, p. 485.
mokhthoditi (*mokhthodvaiol*), mode of union between the sexes, p. 526.
mokhûḍrtvaiol, man who gives away a wife, p. 494.
Mondârdsetipol, Toda name of a tribe living in the Wainad.
mòr, the name of buttermilk at the *ti*, p. 107.
mòrkuḍriki, a ladle of the *ti* dairy, p. 90.
mòrol, privileged visitors to a *ti*, p. 107.
mòrpun, a dairy vessel used to hold buttermilk at the *ti*, p. 90.
mòrûp, the ordinary salt-giving ceremony at the *ti*, p. 175.
mû, a name given to several kinds of dairy vessels, pp. 58, 422.
muli or *mul*, a name for various plants, p. 145; also used for thorns, p. 194; and for the quills of a porcupine, p. 267.
mulinïròditi, the ordination ceremony of the *palikartmokh*, p. 148.
mun, mother's brother and wife's father, pp. 487, 492.
mûrn, the sieve, p. 32.
mûrthvichi, anger, p. 260.
Naim or *noim*, the council, pp. 32, 550.
nâkh, a three-year-old calf, p. 47.
nan, a young shoot, p. 145.
nânmakud, a club, pp. 381, 586.
nârthpimi, a game, p. 596.
nâshperthïr, sacred buffaloes originally given to Nòḍrs, p. 69.
nòḍrkursh, middle room of a three-roomed dairy, p. 57.
nêḍrvol, intermediary, pp. 258, 527.

nei, clarified butter or ghi, p. 50.
nersatiti, a salutation, p. 304.
neurzûtpol, name of the *kâltmokh* at the migration ceremony, p. 139.
neurzülnkârs, stones of ceremonial importance, pp. 129, 140, 438.
nîpâ, stream, p. 26.
nîr, water, spring.
nîròdibudnûdr, the initial stages of the ordination of the *kâltmokh*, p. 153.
nîròditi, the ordination ceremony, pp. 144, 157.
nîrsi, the fire-stick, p. 60.
nòdr, country, place; sometimes used for 'ceremony.'
nòdrkûtchi, ancestors of buffaloes, p. 112.
nòdrodchi, a ruler, pp. 183, 186.
nòdrved, younger brother, p. 486.
Nòtîrzi, a goddess, p. 189.
Ol or *òl*, man, husband, p. 489.
oñ, a sacred syllable uttered in the dairy ceremonial, p. 65.
Ön, a god, p. 184.
Paiol, male relations-in-law, pp. 489, 492.
Pâkhwâr, a river, 418; also a god.
pali or *palthli*, the dairy, p. 26.
palikârtmokh (? *pallikârithtmokh*), the dairyman, p. 39.
palinol, sacred day of dairy, p. 405.
pâlmän, staff used in churning, p. 52.
palol, the dairyman of a *tî*, pp. 42, 98.
paniûp, one of the salt-giving ceremonies, p. 175.
pâpun, a water-vessel at the *tî*, p. 92.
pârkûl, stick used at the *ponûp* ceremony, p. 178.
pârsêrs, milk-leaves, p. 317.
parsîr, buffaloes of the Kârs *tî*, p. 117.
pârskadrvenmû, vessel to hold butter, p. 58.
pasthîr, the sacred buffaloes of the Teivaliol, p. 39.
pâtat, vessel to hold milk, p. 58.
pâtatmâr, part of the dairy where the more sacred vessels stand, p. 58.
pâtatpur, the more sacred objects of the dairy, p. 58.
patcherski, the husked grain of *patm* (samai), p. 580.
pâtol, one who has held the office of *palol*, p. 104.
pâtun, screen separating the two rooms of a *tî* dairy, p. 86.
pâv, threshold.
pâvnersatiti, saluting the threshold, p. 65.
Pedr, a Tamil.
pelk, the lamp, p. 60.
pelkkodichiti, the ordination ceremony, p. 144.
pelkkatitthwaskal, fireplace at a *tî* dairy used in lighting the lamp, p. 92.
pem, a plateau or a gradual slope of a hill.
pen, butter, p. 58.
pennâr, the string supporting the *kâvn*, pp. 30, 572.
pep, buttermilk used ceremonially, pp. 64, 166.

pepeirthti, a rite at the *kûḍrpali*, p. 67.
pepkarichâ or *pepkarichti*, the ceremony of making new *pep*, p. 166.
pepkarmus, the milking-place of a *tî*, p. 85.
peptòrzum, a dairy vessel of the *tî*, p. 89.
pepûti, the rite of drinking buttermilk at the ordinary dairy, p. 78; also the ceremonial drinking of buttermilk by buffaloes, p. 135.
perithîr, buffaloes of the Nòḍrs *tî*, p. 113.
perkûrsol, the lower stage in the office of *kâltmokh*, p. 105.
perol, an ordinary person, not ordained to any dairy office, p. 39.
persâsîr, sacred buffaloes originally given to Melgârs, p. 69.
persin, the vessel in which milk is churned at the *tî*, p. 89.
persinîr, the sacred buffaloes of a *tî*, p. 84.
perûd, elder, p. 485.
petuni, a piece of *tuni*, p. 105.
pîan, grandfather, p. 485.
pîâv, grandmother, p. 486.
pîlikòren, sorcerers, p. 255.
pîlinörtiti, offering of a ring, pp. 294, 306.
pîliûtpol, a sorcerer, p. 255.
pîliûtvichi, sorcery, p. 255.
pineipîr, sacred buffaloes originally given to Pan, p. 69.
pöḍri, contributions from relatives by marriage, p. 396.
pòḍrshtuni, the loin-cloth of the *palol*, p. 103.
pôh, the conical and other sacred dairies, p. 45.
pôhkûrtpol, the dairyman at Kanòḍrs, p. 79.
pôhvelkârs, seat on which the *palol* sits, pp. 87, 96.
pôhvet (*pôhpet*), a wand used by the *palol* when praying, pp. 89, 96.
pòl, a calf of one to two years, p. 47.
pòlm, a portion, a division of a clan pp. 37, 544.
pòlmachok, a dairy vessel, p. 60.
pon, festival, pp. 85, 161; up, p. 383; see also p. 496.
ponkûrtvaimokh, boy who takes a leading part at the *îrnörtiti* ceremony, p. 302.
ponnol, festival day.
ponûp, a salt-giving ceremony at the *tî*, p. 177.
pòrmunkursh, outer room of dairy, p. 56.
püḍrshtipîr, the *wûrsulîr* of Kârs and Târâḍr, p. 71.
pûkûrûputkûli, the ornamented cloak, p. 572.
pül, surroundings or outskirts, p. 85.
püliol, relatives with whom marriage is prohibited, p. 509.
punetkalvol, path reserved for the dairyman, p. 27.
punîr, the ordinary buffaloes of a *tî*, p. 84.
punrs, a name for two days, p. 142.
pürsîr, buffaloes of the Kârs *tî*, p. 117.
pursütpimi, the ceremony of giving a bow and arrow during pregnancy, p. 319.
pût, a stirring-stick, p. 60.
pûthpep, the buttermilk obtained in the *pepkarichâ* ceremony, p. 169.
putiîr, ordinary buffaloes, p. 39.

putkûli, the cloak, pp. 30, 571.
puzhârs, seclusion-hut, p. 313.
puzhûtpimi, the ceremony of throwing earth at a funeral, p. 344.
Satimad, a village of especial sanctity, p. 421.
sedvaitazmokh, name of the woman in the *mokhthoditi* union, p. 526.
Tadri, pole used in funeral ceremonies, p. 376.
tadrp, the loin-cloth, p. 30.
tâf, fern.
tagârs, a chain.
tarsîr, buffaloes of the Pan *tî*, p. 119.
Târthârol, one of the two divisions of the Toda people, p. 34.
târûpunkudi, hole used at the salt-giving ceremony at a Tarthar village, p. 177.
târvali or *târpali*, the lowest grade of Tarthar dairy, pp. 40, 61.
târvalikârtmokh, the dairyman of the *târvali*, p. 461.
tasth, the bars in the opening of a pen, p. 153.
tazmokh, woman, wife, p. 489.
tedshk, a ring used in carrying dairy vessels, p. 60.
Teikîrzi, a goddess, p. 186.
teiks, stone or post at which a buffalo is killed at a funeral, p. 349.
Teipâkh, the Paikara river, p. 418; also a god, p. 187.
teirtîr, buffaloes of the Nòdrs *tî*, p. 112.
Teivaliol, one of the chief divisions of the Toda people, p. 34.
tek (*tekh*?), basket, p. 57.
têrersthi, custom of transferring wives, p. 523
tersamptpimi, a ceremony of childhood, p. 333.
terzantirikiti, the rite of putting curd or milk on the bell, p. 66.
tesherst, a qualifying ceremony for the office of *palol*, p. 154.
teshnîr, the first stage of the ordination ceremony of the *palol*, p. 157.
teu, god, p. 182.
teukwoi, clay vessel made at the *ponûp* ceremony, p. 179.
teuol, diviner, p. 249.
teutütusthchi, ceremony of lighting a fire on a hill, p. 290.
tî, the most sacred dairy institution of the Todas, pp. 42, 83.
tîîr, the buffaloes of the *tî*, p. 42; also used of a special group of these buffaloes at the Nòdrs *tî*, p. 112.
tîkelfmâv, Badaga associated with a *tî*, p. 98.
tî mad, a village or place belonging to a *tî*, p. 83.
tòratthwaskal, fireplace at a *tî* dairy used to cook food, p. 91.
tòrzum, the *tî* name of the *mû*, p. 89.
tû, the buffalo-pen, p. 26.
tûdr, a sacred tree, pp. 67, 433.
tûkitthkârs, stone lifted as a sport, p. 597.
tûkulîr mani, a bell used in the funeral ceremonies, pp. 376, 424.
tün, a seat or bed, p. 30.
tuni, the grey garment used by many dairymen, pp. 72, 572.
tuninörtiti, offering of a *tuni*, pp. 294, 305.
tunitusthkâltmokh, the full *kâltmokh*, pp. 105, 152.

tûrâvali, the cooking-pot of a *ti* dairy, p. 90.
tûri, knife.
twadrinûr, material made by the Todas, p. 574.
Ulûrwûrthkûrs, a wand, p. 60.
ulkkursh, inner room of dairy, p. 56.
unir, buffaloes of the Nòdrs *ti*, p. 112.
ûppun, a vessel of the *ti* dairy, p. 90.
ûpunkudi (? *ûppunkudi*), hole used at the salt-giving ceremonies, p. 176.
ûrvalpimi, ceremony during pregnancy, p. 313.
ûlkòren, people who apply certain magical or medical remedies, p. 263.
ûtpol, medicine man, p. 263.
Wâk, vessels burnt at the *âzâramkedr*, p. 381.
warsir, buffaloes of the Nòdrs *ti*, p. 112; and of the Pan *ti*, p. 119.
wask, grain-pounder, p. 32.
waskal, fireplace of three stones, pp. 57, 582.
wûrsol, the dairyman of the *wûrsuli*, pp. 40, 72, 74.
wûrsuli, a Tarthar dairy, pp. 40, 71.
wûrsulir, the buffaloes of a *wûrsuli*, p. 40.

INDEX

The numbers in Clarendon type refer to the most important places where the subject is considered.

E

F

G

H

1.

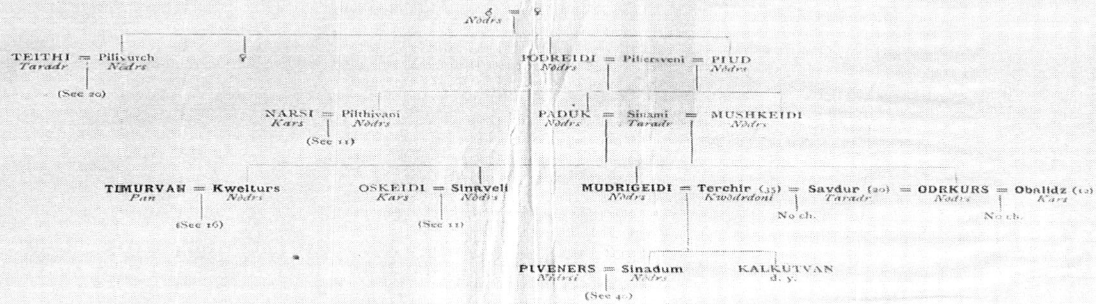
♂ = ♀
Nödrs
TEITHI = Pilivurch
Taradr Nödrs
(See 20)
♀
PODREIDI = Piliersveni = PIUD
Nödrs Nödrs
NARSI = Pilthivani
Kars Nödrs
(See 11)
PADUK = Sinami = MUSHKEIDI
Nödrs Taradr Nödrs
TIMURVAN = Kwelturs
Pan Nödrs
(See 16)
OSKEIDI = Sinaveli
Kars Nödrs
(See 11)
MUDRIGEIDI = Terchir (35) = Savdur (20) = ODRKURS = Obalidz (12)
Nödrs Kwödrdoni Taradr Nödrs Kars
No ch.
No ch.
PIVENERS = Sinadum
Nölvsi Nödrs
(See 40)
KALKUTVAN
d. y.

2.

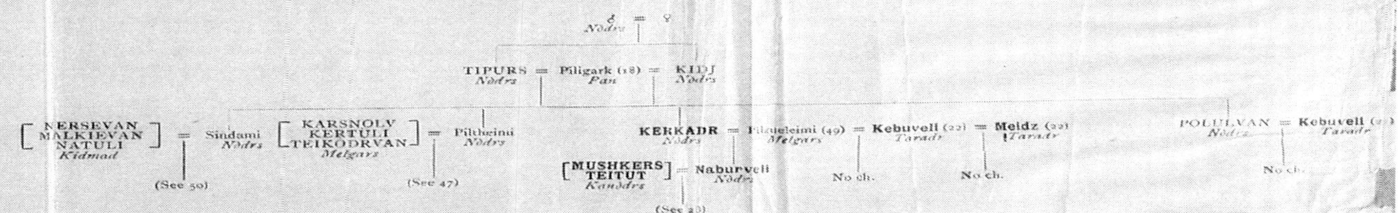
♂ = ♀
Nödrs
TIPURS = Piligark (18) = KIDJ
Nödrs Pan Nödrs
NERSEVAN
MALKIEVAN
NATULI
Kidmad
= Sindami
Nödrs
(See 50)
KARSNOLV
KERTULI
TEIKODRVAN
Melgars
= Piltheini
Nödrs
(See 47)
KERKADR = Pilzueleimi (49) = Kebuvell (22) = Meidz (22)
Nödrs Melgars Taradr Taradr
No ch.
No ch.
MUSHKERS
TEITUT
Kandörs
= Naburveli
Nödrs
(See 20)
POLULVAN = Kebuveli
Nödrs Taradr
No ch.

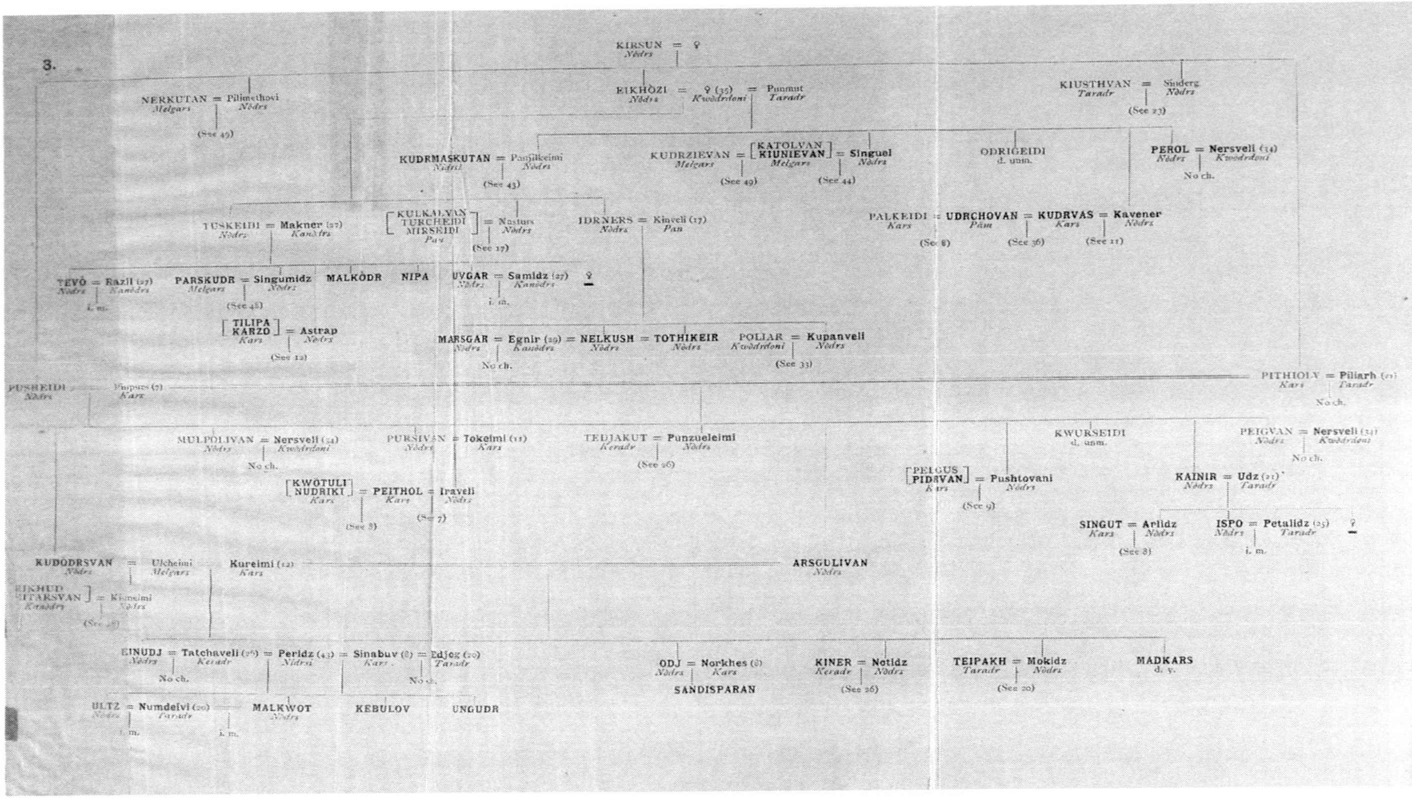
3.
KIRSUN = ♀
Nōdrs
NERKUTAN = Pilimethovi
Melgars Nōdrs
(See 49)
EIKHŌZI = ♀ (35) = Punmut
Nōdrs Kwōdrdoni Taradr
KIUSTHVAN = Sinderg
Taradr Nōdrs
(See 23)
KUDRMASKUTAN = Panjilkeimi
Nidrsl Nōdrs
(See 43)
KUDRZIEVAN = KATOLVAN KIUNIEVAN = Singuel
Melgars Melgars Nōdrs
(See 49) (See 44)
ODRIGEIDI
d. unm.
PEROL = Nersveli (34)
Nōdrs Kwōdrdoni
No ch.
TUSKEIDI = Makner (27)
Nōdrs Kanōdrs
KULKALVAN TURCHEIDI MIRSEIDI = Nasturs
Pan Nōdrs
(See 17)
IDRNERS = Kinveli (17)
Nōdrs Pan
PALKEIDI = UDRCHOVAN = KUDRVAS = Kavener
Kars Pām Kars Nōdrs
(See 8) (See 36) (See 11)
TEVŌ = Razil (27)
Nōdrs Kanōdrs
i. m.
PARSKUDR = Singumidz
Melgars Nōdrs
(See 48)
MALKŌDR
NIPA
UVGAR = Samidz (27)
Nōdrs Kanōdrs
i. m.
♀
TILIPA KARZO = Astrap
Kars Nōdrs
(See 12)
MARSGAR = Egnir (29) = NELKUSH = TOTHIKEIR
Nōdrs Kanōdrs Nōdrs Nōdrs
No ch.
POLIAR = Kupanveli
Kwōdrdoni Nōdrs
(See 33)
PUSHEIDI = Pinpurs (7)
Nōdrs Kars
PITHIOLY = Piliarh (21)
Kars Taradr
No ch.
MULPOLIVAN = Nersveli (34)
Nōdrs Kwōdrdoni
No ch.
PURSIVAN = Tokeimi (11)
Nōdrs Kars
TEDJAKUT = Punzueleimi
Keradr Nōdrs
(See 26)
KWURSEIDI
d. unm.
PEIGVAN = Nersveli (34)
Nōdrs Kwōdrdoni
No ch.
KWŌTULI NUDRIKI = PEITHOL = Iraveli
Kars Kars Nōdrs
(See 8) (See 7)
PEIGUS PIDRVAN = Pushtovani
Kars Nōdrs
(See 9)
KAINIR = Udz (21)
Nōdrs Taradr
SINGUT = Arlidz
Kars Nōdrs
(See 8)
ISPO = Petalidz (25)
Nōdrs Taradr
i. m.
♀
KUDODRSVAN = Ulcheimi
Nōdrs Melgars
Kureimi (12)
Kars
ARSGULIVAN
Nōdrs
EIKHUD ITARSVAN = Kiuneimi
Kanōdrs Nōdrs
EINUDJ = Tatchaveli (26) = Peridz (43) = Sinabuv (8) = Edjeg (20)
Nōdrs Keradr Nidrsi Kars Taradr
No ch.
No ch.
ODJ = Norkhes (8)
Nōdrs Kars
SANDISPARAN
KINER = Notidz
Keradr Nōdrs
(See 26)
TEIPAKH = Mokidz
Taradr Nōdrs
(See 20)
MADKARS
d. y.
ULTZ = Numdelvi (20)
Nōdrs Taradr
i. m.
i. m.
MALKWOT
Nōdrs
KEBULOV
UNGUDR

4.

OIKUTAN = [illegible]

ONEIDI = [Pilikodjveni = Pulinir]

[PUIGARSI PANIOLV] = Ungreimi [MADOITHI IRCHEIDI] = PARKURS = Katcheri TEIGUDR = Oselig = Uwer AGIEVAN = Perur TEITUKHEN = Navob

PORZO = Tivi PARSNUDJ KIDRNERS = Tichidz

[MONTE PUNIDZ KORNERS] = Singaveli KAUKORNERS = Sorpnir

5.

KERIEVAN = [illegible]

KADROEVAN = [illegible] MONDOTHI = Sinag = NOTEIDI KERVEIDI = Nelami

ARMAN Sinai KAIGUDR [NUDJEN ESHKIAGULN ARKNERS] = Prams KU

6.

MUNKU = [illegible]

PUSHITHI = [illegible] = KEITAN [KUNZERVAN KIDJKUTAN IRKIOLV] = Konaveli TUKEIDI = Panir UVUDI TOASNERS = Nersami

PUJON = Tulgeimi

PIRSNEFS = Sapnir OSHKIAK [illegible] = KERSKIDRVAN = Turchveli

KOSNERS KEINGEIDI KARDOL KARMARS = Siregi PEITMARS KEDJERI TIDJKUDR ARGWA

KATNARS [PEPNERS KODRENURS] = Singar

7.

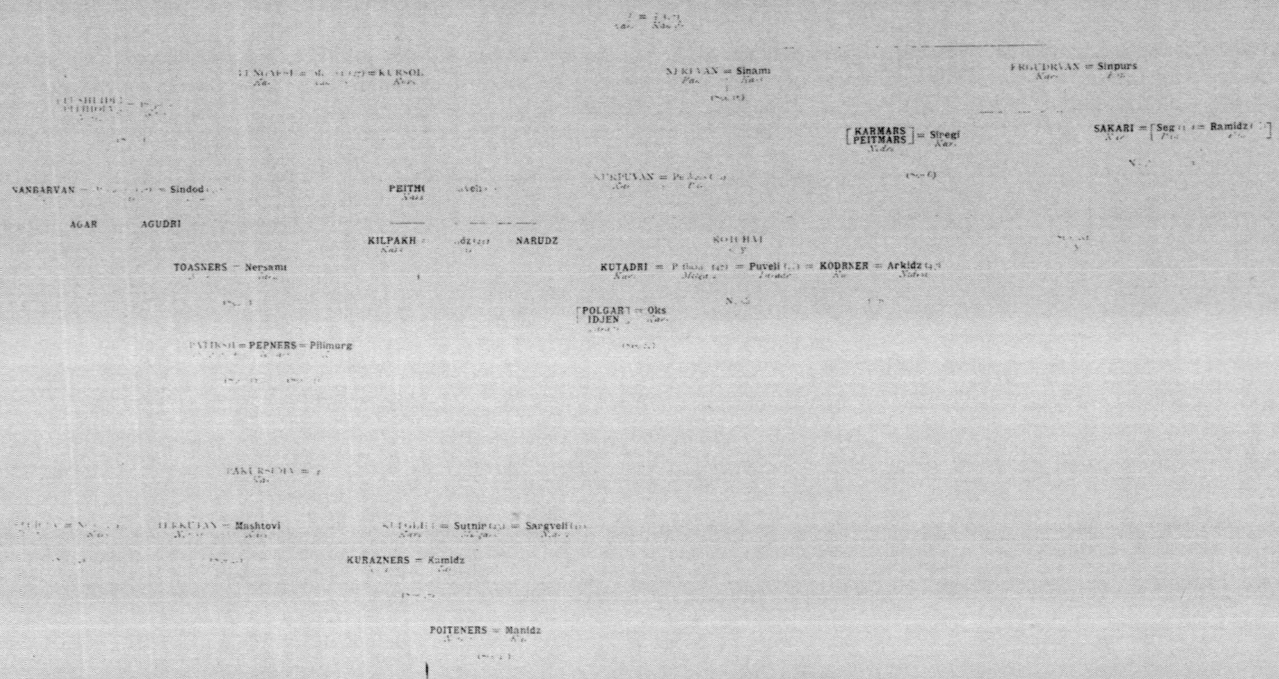
KURSOL
Sinam
Sinpurs
KARMARS
PEITMARS
Siregi
SAKARI
Ramidz
VANBARVAN
Sindod
AGAR
AGUDRI
KILPAKH
NARUDZ
TOASNERS
Nersami
KUTADRI
Puveli
KODRNER
Arkidz
POLGART
Oks
IDJEN
PEPNERS
Pilimurg
Mashtovi
Sutnir
Sargveli
KURAZNERS
Kamidz
POITENERS
Manidz

8.

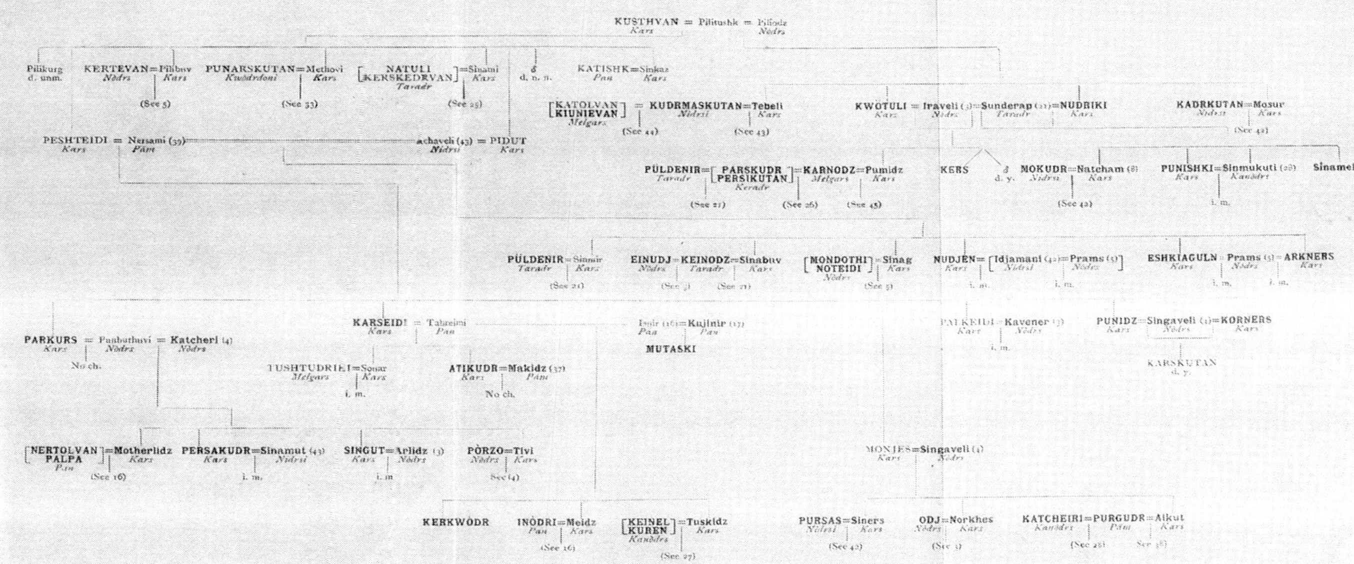
KUSTHVAN = Pilitushk = Pilitsiz
Kars Nödrs
Pilikurg d. unm.
KERTEVAN=Pilibuv
Nödrs Kars
(See 5)
PUNARSKUTAN=Methovi
Kuödrdoni Kars
(See 33)
NATULI
KERSKEDRVAN
Taradr
=Sinami
Kars
(See 25)
♂ d. n. n.
KATISHK=Sinkaz
Pan Kars
KATOLVAN
KIUNIEVAN
Melgars
= KUDRMASKUTAN=Tebeli
Nidrsi Kars
(See 44)
(See 43)
KWÓTULI = Iraveli (3)=Sunderap (21)=NUDRIKI
Kars Nödrs Taradr Kars
KADRKUTAN=Mosur
Nidrsi Kars
(See 42)
PESHTEIDI = Nersami (39)
Kars Pàm
achaveli (43) = PIDUT
Nidrsi Kars
PÜLDENIR=
Taradr
PARSKUDR
PERSIKUTAN
Keradr
=KARNODZ=Pumidz
Melgars Kars
(See 21)
(See 26)
(See 45)
KERS
♂ d. y.
MOKUDR=Natcham (6)
Nidrsi Kars
(See 42)
PUNISHKI=Sinmukuti (28)
Kars Kanödrs
i. m.
Sinameli
PÜLDENIR=Sinmir
Taradr Kars
(See 21)
EINUDJ=KEINODZ=Sinabuv
Nödrs Taradr Kars
(See 3)
(See 21)
MONDOTHI
NOTEIDI
Nödrs
=Sinag
Kars
(See 5)
NUDJEN=
Kars
i. m.
Idjamani (42)=Prams (5)
Nidrsi Nödrs
i. m.
ESHKIAGULN=Prams (5)=ARKNERS
Kars Nödrs Kars
i. m.
i. m.
KARSEIDI = Tabresimi
Kars Pan
Isnir (16)=Kujinir (17)
Pan Pan
MUTASKI
PALKEIDI=Kavener (3)
Kars Nödrs
i. m.
PUNIDZ=Singaveli (1)=KORNERS
Kars Nödrs Kars
KARSKUTAN
d. y.
PARKURS = Panbuthuvi = Katcheri (4)
Kars Nödrs Nödrs
No ch.
TUSHTUDRIEI=Sonar
Melgars Kars
i. m.
ATIKUDR=Makidz (37)
Kars Pàm
No ch.
NERTOLVAN
PALPA
Pan
=Motherlidz
Kars
(See 16)
PERSAKUDR=Sinamut (43)
Kars Nidrsi
i. m.
SINGUT=Arlidz (3)
Kars Nödrs
i. m
PÒRZO=Tivi
Nödrs Kars
See (4)
MONJES=Singaveli (4)
Kars Nödrs
KERKWÓDR
INÒDRI=Meidz
Pan Kars
(See 16)
KEINEL
KUREN
Kanödrs
=Tuskidz
Kars
(See 27)
PURSAS=Siners
Nilrsi Kars
(See 42)
ODJ=Norkhes
Nödrs Kars
(See 3)
KATCHEIRI=PURGUDR=Aikut
Kanödrs Pàm Kars
(See 28)
See 38)

9.

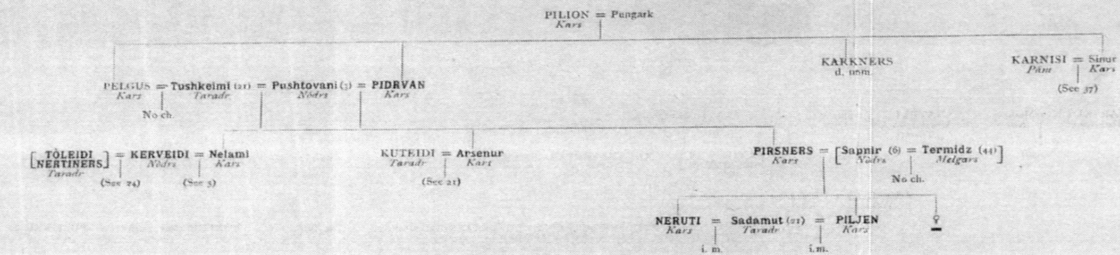
PILION = Pungark
Kars
PELGUS = Tushkeimi (21) = Pushtovani (3) = PIDRVAN
Kars Taradr Nödrs Kars
No ch.
KARKNERS
d. unm.
KARNISI = Sinur
Päm Kars
(See 37)
[TÒLEIDI NERTINERS] = KERVEIDI = Nelami
Taradr Nödrs Kars
(See 24) (See 3)
KUTEIDI = Arsenur
Taradr Kars
(See 21)
PIRSNERS = [Sapnir (6) = Termidz (44)]
Kars Nödrs Melgars
No ch.
NERUTI = Sadamut (21) = PILJEN
Kars Taradr Kars
i. m. i.m.
♀

10.

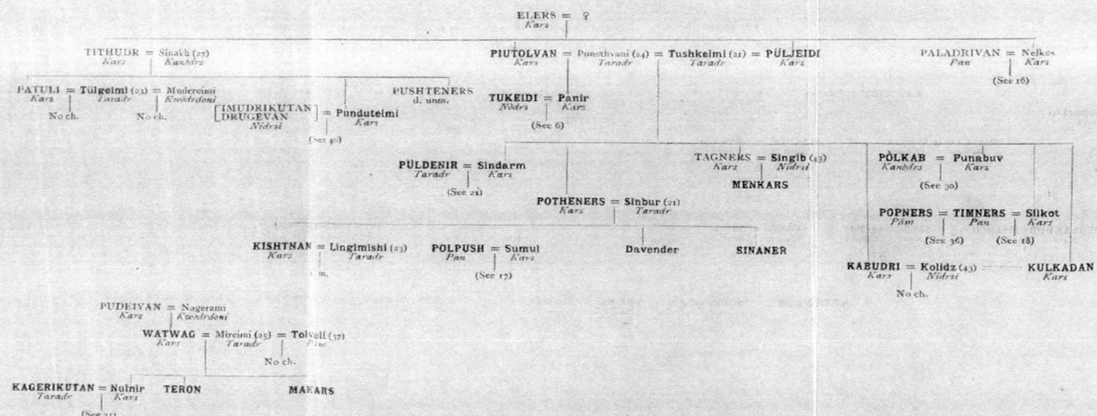
ELERS = ♀
Kars
TITHUDR = Sinakh (27)
Kars Kandrz
PIUTOLVAN = Punothvani (24) = Tushkeimi (21) = PÜLJEIDI
Kars Taradr Taradr Kars
PALADRIVAN = Nelkos
Pan Kars
(See 16)
PATULI = Tülgeimi (23) = Mudereimi
Kars Taradr Kwdrdoni
No ch. No ch.
[IMUDRIKUTAN DRUGEVAN] = Punduteimi
Nidrsi Kars
(See 40)
PUSHTENERS
d. unm.
TUKEIDI = Panir
Nödrs Kars
(See 6)
PÜLDENIR = Sindarm
Taradr Kars
(See 21)
TAGNERS = Singib (43)
Kars Nidrsi
MENKARS
PÒLKAB = Punabuv
Kandrs Kars
(See 30)
POTHENERS = Sinbur (21)
Kars Taradr
POPNERS = TIMNERS = Slikot
Päm Pan Kars
(See 36) (See 18)
KISHTNAN = Lingimishi (23)
Kars Taradr
i. m.
POLPUSH = Sumul
Pan Kars
(See 17)
Davender
SINANER
KABUDRI = Kolidz (43)
Kars Nidrsi
No ch.
KULKADAN
Kars
PUDEIYAN = Nagerami
Kars Kwdrdoni
WATWAG = Mireimi (25) = Tolveil (37)
Kars Taradr Päm
No ch.
KAGERIKUTAN = Nulnir
Taradr Kars
(See 25)
TERON
MAKARS

11.

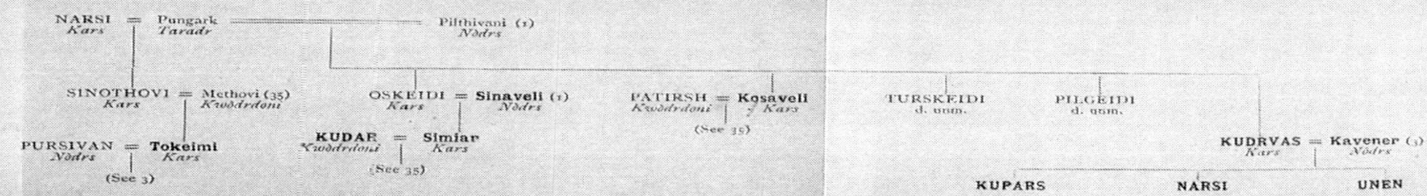
NARSI = Pungark
Kars Taradr
Pifthivani (1)
Nòdrs
SINOTHOVI = Methovi (35)
Kars Kwòdrdoni
PURSIVAN = Tokeimi
Nòdrs Kars
(See 3)
OSKEIDI = Sinaveli (1)
Kars Nòdrs
KUDAR = Simiar
Kwòdrdoni Kars
(See 35)
PATIRSH = Kosaveli
Kwòdrdoni Kars
(See 35)
TURSKEIDI
d. unm.
PILGEIDI
d. unm.
KUDRVAS = Kavener (3)
Kars Nòdrs
KUPARS
NARSI
UNEN

12.

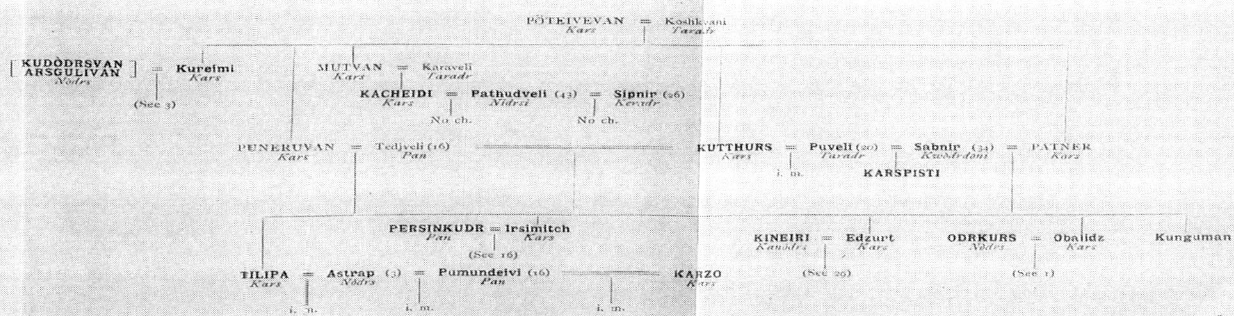
PÒTEIVEVAN = Koshkvani
Kars Taradr
KUDÒDRSVAN
ARSGULIVAN
Nòdrs
= Kureimi
Kars
(See 3)
MUTVAN = Karaveli
Kars Taradr
KACHEIDI = Pathudveli (43) = Sipnir (26)
Kars Nidrsi Kevadr
No ch.
No ch.
PUNERUVAN = Tedjveli (16)
Kars Pan
KUTTHURS = Puveli (20) = Sabnir (34) = PATNER
Kars Taradr Kwòdrdoni Kars
i. m.
KARSPISTI
PERSINKUDR = Irsimitch
Pan Kars
(See 16)
TILIPA = Astrap (3) = Pumundeivi (16) KARZO
Kars Nòdrs Pan Kars
i. m.
i. m.
i. m.
KINEIRI = Edzurt
Kanòdrs Kars
(See 29)
ODRKURS = Obalidz
Nòdrs Kars
(See 1)
Kunguman

13.

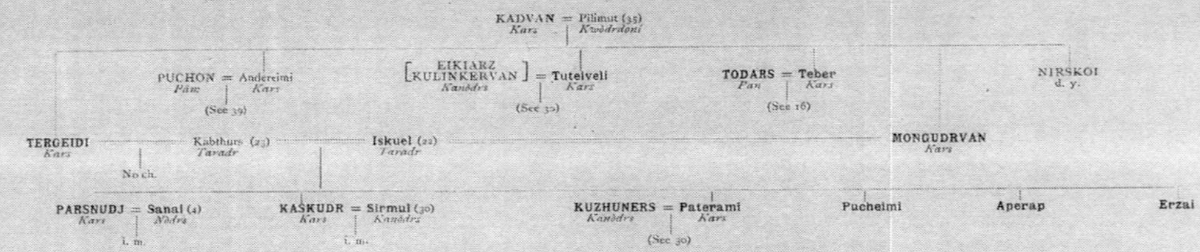
KADVAN = Pilimut (35)
Kars
Kwòdrdoni
PUCHON = Andereimi
Päm
Kars
(See 39)
EIKIARZ
KULINKERVAN = Tuteiveli
Kanödrs
Kars
(See 30)
TODARS = Teber
Pan
Kars
(See 16)
NIRSKOI
d. y.
TERGEIDI
Kars
Kabthurs (23)
Taradr
No ch.
Iskuel (22)
Taradr
MONGUDRVAN
Kars
PARSNUDJ = Sanal (4)
Kars
Nödrs
i. m.
KASKUDR = Sirmul (30)
Kars
Kanödrs
i. m.
KUZHUNERS = Paterami
Kanödrs
Kars
(See 30)
Pucheimi
Aperap
Erzai

14.

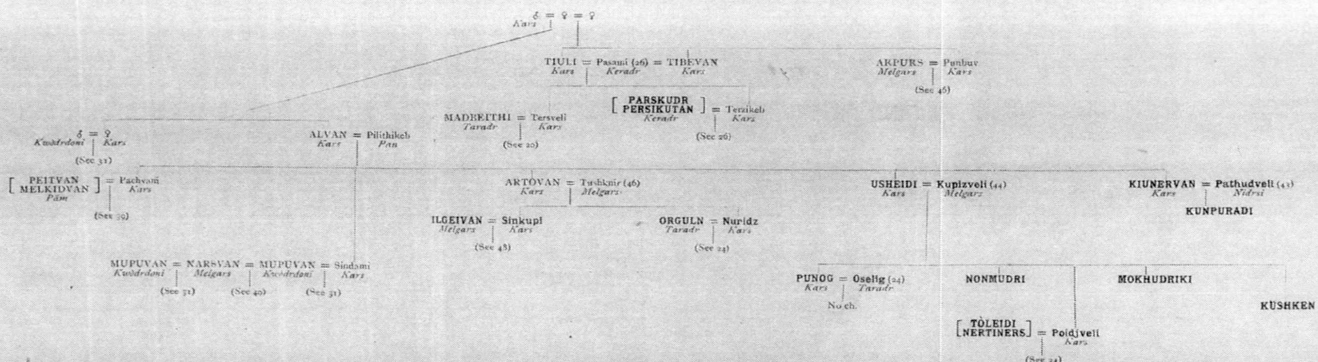
♂ = ♀ = ♀
Kars
TIULI = Pasami (26) = TIBEVAN
Kars
Keradr
Kars
ARPURS = Punbuv
Melgars
Kars
(See 46)
♂ = ♀
Kwòdrdoni
Kars
(See 31)
ALVAN = Pilithikeb
Kars
Pan
MADBEITHI = Tersveli
Taradr
Kars
(See 20)
PARSKUDR
PERSIKUTAN = Terzikeb
Keradr
Kars
(See 26)
PEITVAN
MELKIDVAN = Pachvani
Päm
Kars
(See 39)
ARTOVAN = Tushknir (46)
Kars
Melgars
USHEIDI = Kupizveli (44)
Kars
Melgars
KIUNERVAN = Pathudveli (43)
Kars
Nidrsi
KUNPURADI
ILGEIVAN = Sinkupi
Melgars
Kars
(See 48)
ORGULN = Nuridz
Taradr
Kars
(See 24)
MUPUVAN = NARSVAN = MUPUVAN = Sindami
Kwòdrdoni
Melgars
Kwòdrdoni
Kars
(See 31)
(See 40)
(See 31)
PUNOG = Oselig (24)
Kars
Taradr
No ch.
NONMUDRI
MOKHUDRIKI
KUSHKEN
TOLEIDI
NERTINERS = Poidjveli
Kars
(See 24)

15.

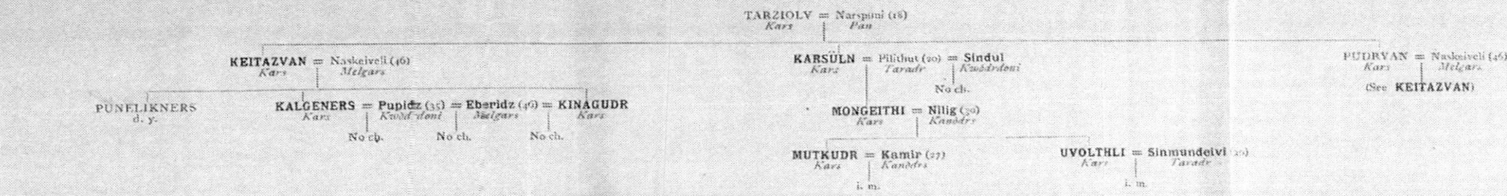

TARZIOLV = Narspini (18)
Kars Pan
KEITAZVAN = Naskeiveli (46)
Kars Melgars
PUNELIKNERS
d. y.
KALGENERS = Pupidz (35) = Eberidz (46) = KINAGUDR
Kars Kwŏdr doni Melgars Kars
No ch.
No ch.
No ch.
KARSULN = Pilithut (20) = Sindul
Kars Taradr Kwŏdrdoni
No ch.
MONGEITHI = Nilig (30)
Kars Kanŏdrs
MUTKUDR = Kamir (27)
Kars Kanŏdrs
i. m.
UVOLTHLI = Sinmundeivi (20)
Kars Taradr
i. m.
PUDRVAN = Naskeiveli (46)
Kars Melgars
(See KEITAZVAN)

16.

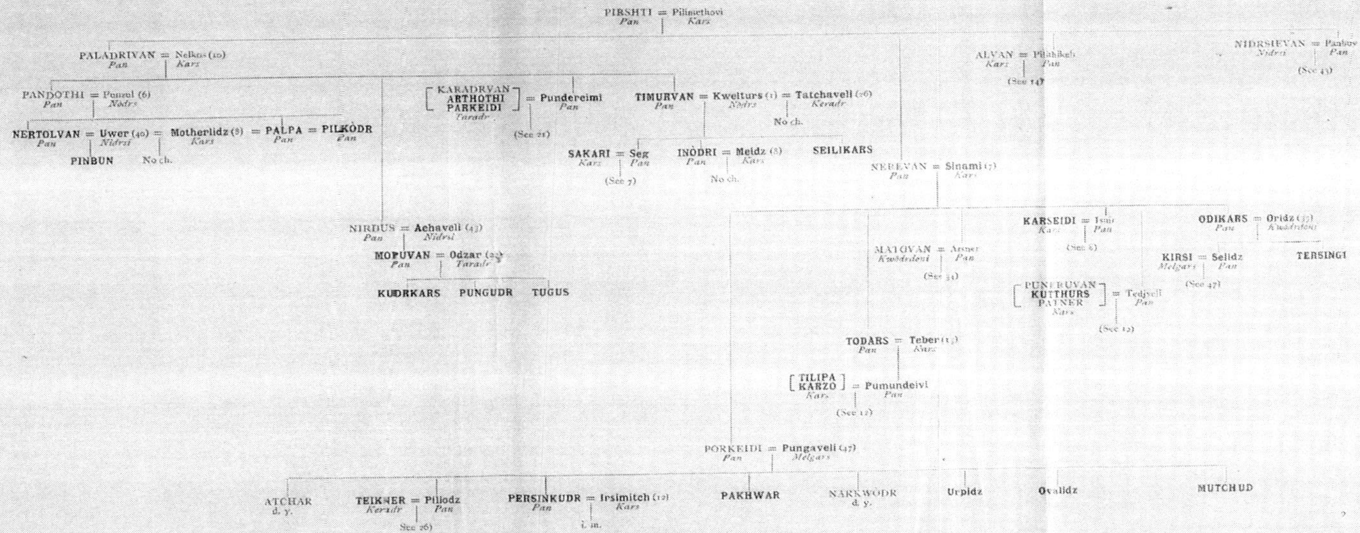

PIRSHTI = Pilimethovi
Pan Kars
PALADRIVAN = Nelkus (10)
Pan Kars
PANDOTHI = Punzel (6)
Pan Nŏdrs
NERTOLVAN = Uwer (40) = Motherlidz (8) = PALPA = PILKODR
Pan Nidrsi Kars Pan Pan
PINBUN
No ch.
KARADRVAN
ARTHOTHI
PARKEIDI
Taradr
= Pundereimi
Pan
(See 21)
TIMURVAN = Kwelturs (1) = Tatchaveli (26)
Pan Nŏdrs Keradr
No ch.
SAKARI = Seg
Kars Pan
(See 7)
INŎDRI = Meidz (8)
Pan Kars
No ch.
SEILIKARS
NIRDUS = Achaveli (43)
Pan Nidrsi
MOPUVAN = Odzar (22)
Pan Taradr
KUDRKARS
PUNGUDR
TUGUS
ALVAN = Pilahikeh
Kars Pan
(See 14)
NIDRSIEVAN = Panluv
Nidrsi Pan
(See 43)
NEBEVAN = Sinami (7)
Pan Kars
MATOVAN = Asner
Kwŏdrdoni Pan
(See 31)
KARSEIDI = Isni
Kars Pan
(See 6)
ODIKARS = Oridz (37)
Pan Kwŏdrdoni
KIRSI = Selidz
Melgars Pan
(See 47)
TERSINGI
PUNERUVAN
KUTTHURS
PATNER
Kars
= Tedjveli
Pan
(See 12)
TODARS = Teber (13)
Pan Kars
TILIPA
KARZO
Kars
= Pumundeivi
Pan
(See 12)
PORKEIDI = Pungaveli (47)
Pan Melgars
ATCHAR
d. y.
TEIKNER = Piliodz
Keradr Pan
See 26)
PERSINKUDR = Irsimitch (12)
Pan Kars
i. m.
PAKHWAR
NARKWODR
d. y.
Urpidz
Ovalidz
MUTCHUD

17.

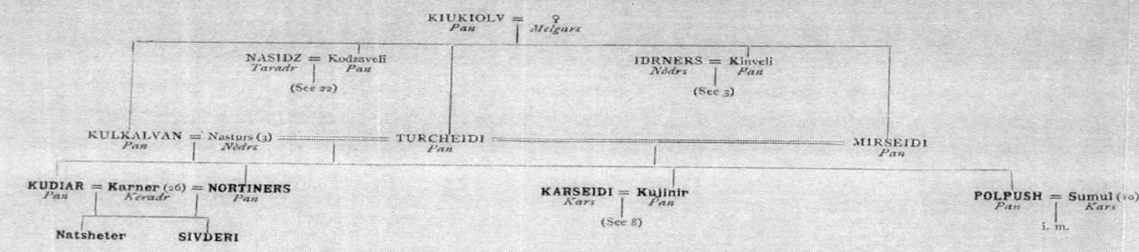
KIUKIOLV = ♀
Pan Melgars
NASIDZ = Kodzaveli
Taradr Pan
(See 22)
IDRNERS = Kinveli
Nödrs Pan
(See 3)
KULKALVAN = Nasturs (3) = TURCHEIDI = MIRSEIDI
Pan Nödrs Pan Pan
KUDIAR = Karner (26) = NORTINERS
Pan Keradr Pan
Natsheter
SIVDERI
KARSEIDI = Kujinir
Kars Pan
(See 8)
POLPUSH = Sumul (10)
Pan Kars
i. m.

18.

KEPURSVAN = ♀
Pan
[TIPURS KIDJ] = Piligark
Nödrs Pan
(See 2)
TARZIOLV = Nanpuni
Kars Pan
(See 15)
PAREIJIVAN = Piljeimi (48) = ENMUVAN = MIRJEIVAN
Pan Melgars Pan Pan
KUIRSINERS = Savtam (48)
Pan Melgars
No ch.
TIMNERS = [Silkot (10) = Peldz (44)]
Pan Kars Melgars
No ch.
No ch.

19.

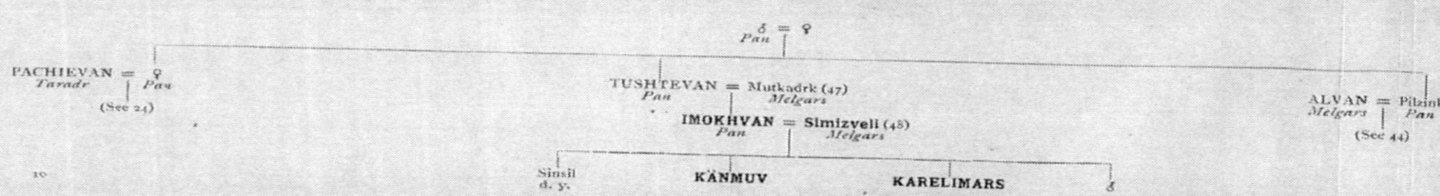
♂ = ♀
Pan
PACHIEVAN = ♀
Taradr Pan
(See 24)
TUSHTEVAN = Mutkadrk (47)
Pan Melgars
IMOKHVAN = Simizveli (48)
Pan Melgars
Sinsil
d. y.
KÄNMUV
KARELIMARS
♂
ALVAN = Pilzink
Melgars Pan
(See 44)

20.

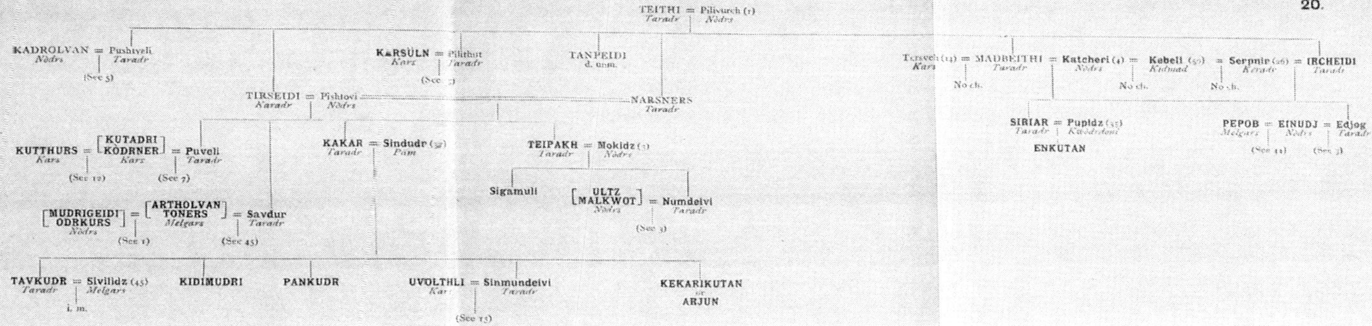
TEITHI = Pilivurch (1)
Taradr Nödrs
KADROLVAN = Pushtveli
Nödrs Taradr
(See 5)
KARSULN = Pilithut
Kars Taradr
TANPEIDI
d. unm.
TIRSEIDI = Pishtovi
Karadr Nödrs
NARSNERS
Taradr
KUTTHURS = [KUTADRI KODRNER] = Puveli
Kars Kars Taradr
(See 12)
(See 7)
KAKAR = Sindudr (32)
Taradr Pam
TEIPAKH = Mokidz (3)
Taradr Nödrs
Sigamuli
[ULTZ MALKWOT] = Numdeivi
Nödrs Taradr
(See 3)
[MUDRIGEIDI ODRKURS] = [ARTHOLVAN TONERS] = Savdur
Nödrs Melgars Taradr
(See 1)
(See 45)
TAVKUDR = Sivilidz (45)
Taradr Melgars
i. m.
KIDIMUDRI
PANKUDR
UVOLTHLI = Sinmundeivi
Kars Taradr
(See 15)
KEKARIKUTAN
or
ARJUN
MADBEITHI = Katcheri (4) = Kebeli (50) = Serpnir (26) = IRCHEIDI
Taradr Nödrs Kidmad Kerade Taradr
No ch.
No ch.
No ch.
SIRIAR = Pupidz (35)
Taradr Kwödrdoni
ENKUTAN
PEPOB = EINUDJ = Edjog
Melgars Nödrs Taradr
(See 11)
(See 3)

21

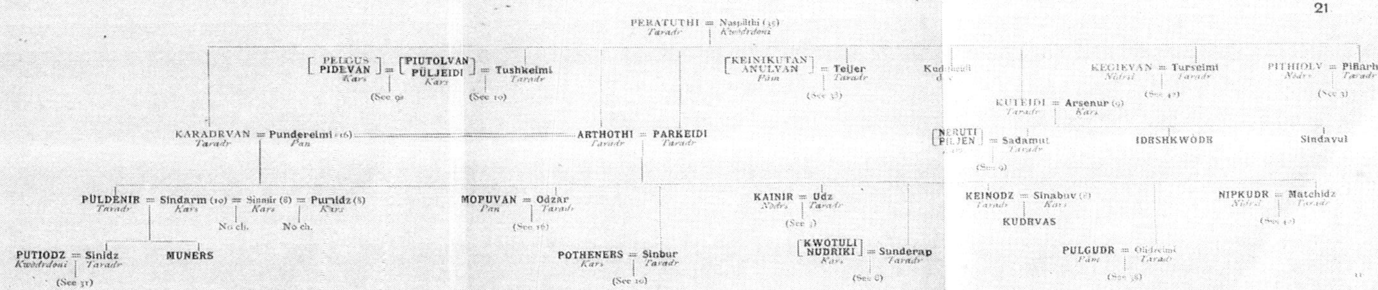
PERATUTHI = Naspilthi (35)
Taradr Kwödrdoni
[PELGUS PIDEVAN] = [PIUTOLVAN PULJEIDI] = Tushkeimi
Kars Kars Taradr
(See 9)
(See 10)
[KEINIKUTAN ANULVAN] = Teljer
Pam Taradr
(See 33)
KEGIEVAN = Turseimi
Nödrs Taradr
(See 42)
PITHIOLV = Piñarh
Nödrs Taradr
(See 3)
KUTEIDI = Arsenur (9)
Taradr Kars
KARADRVAN = Pundereimi (16)
Taradr Pan
ARTHOTHI = PARKEIDI
Taradr Taradr
[NERUTI PILJEN] = Sadamut
Taradr
(See 9)
IDRSHKWODR
Sindavul
PULDENIR = Sindarm (10) = Sinnir (8) = Puridz (8)
Taradr Kars Kars Kars
No ch.
No ch.
MOPUVAN = Odzar
Pan Taradr
(See 16)
KAINIR = Udz
Nödrs Taradr
(See 3)
KEINODZ = Sinabuv (7)
Taradr Kars
KUDRVAS
NIPKUDR = Matchidz
Nödrs Taradr
(See 42)
PUTIODZ = Sinidz
Kwödrdoni Taradr
(See 31)
MUNERS
POTHENERS = Sinbur
Kars Taradr
(See 10)
[KWOTULI NUDRIKI] = Sunderap
Kars Taradr
(See 6)
PULGUDR = Oidzeimi
Pam Taradr
(See 38)

22.

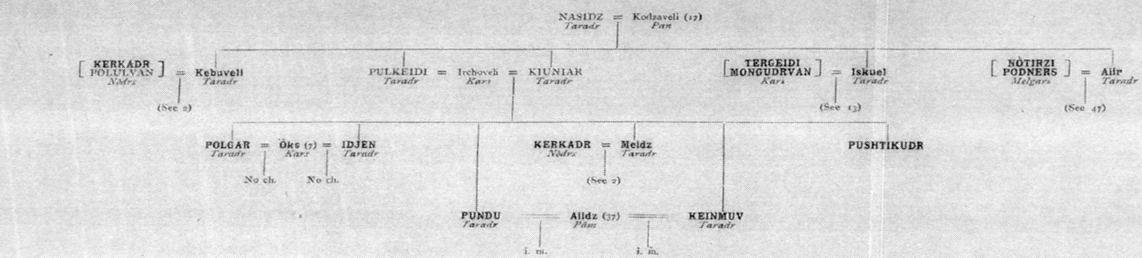
NASIDZ = Kodzaveli (17)
Taradr
Pan
KERKADR POLULVAN = Kebuveli
Nòdrs
Taradr
(See 2)
PULKEIDI = Ircboveli = KIUNIAR
Taradr
Kars
Taradr
TERGEIDI MONGUDRVAN = Iskuel
Kars
Taradr
(See 13)
NÒTIRZI PODNERS = Aiir
Melgars
Taradr
(See 47)
POLGAR = Öks (7) = IDJEN
Taradr
Kars
Taradr
No ch.
No ch.
KERKADR = Meldz
Nòdrs
Taradr
(See 2)
PUSHTIKUDR
PUNDU — Alldz (37) — KEINMUV
Taradr
Pâm
Taradr
i. m.
i. m.

23.

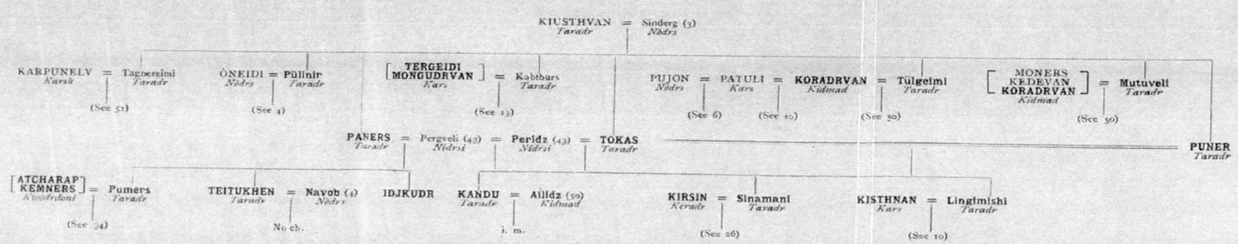
KIUSTHVAN = Sinderg (3)
Taradr
Nòdrs
KARPUNELV = Tagnerelmi
Karsh
Taradr
(See 51)
ÒNEIDI = Pülinir
Nòdrs
Taradr
(See 4)
TERGEIDI MONGUDRVAN = Kabthurs
Kars
Taradr
(See 13)
PUJON = PATULI = KORADRVAN = Tülgelmi
Nòdrs
Kars
Kidmad
Taradr
(See 6)
(See 10)
(See 50)
MONERS KEDEVAN KORADRVAN = Mutuveli
Kidmad
Taradr
(See 50)
PANERS = Pergveli (43) = Peridz (43) = TOKAS
Taradr
Nidrsi
Nidrsi
Taradr
PUNER
Taradr
ATCHARAP KEMNERS = Pumers
Kwodrdoni
Taradr
(See 54)
TEITUKHEN = Navob (4)
Taradr
Nòdrs
No ch.
IDJKUDR
KANDU = Alldz (50)
Taradr
Kidmad
i. m.
KIRSIN = Sinamani
Keradr
Taradr
(See 26)
KISTHNAN = Lingimishi
Kars
Taradr
(See 10)

24.

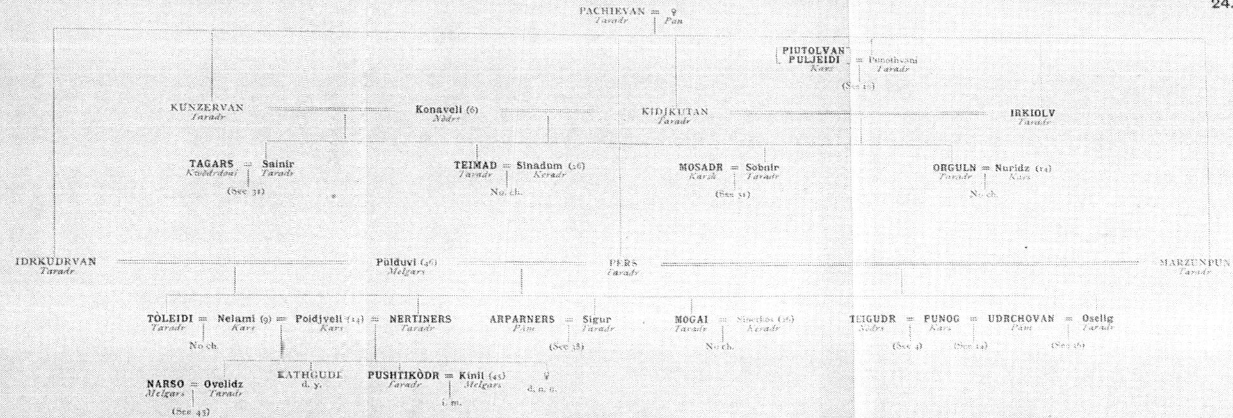
PACHIEVAN = ♀
Taradr
Pan
PIUTOLVAN
PULJEIDI
Kars
= Punothvani
Taradr
KUNZERVAN
Taradr
Konaveli (6)
Nödrs
KIDJKUTAN
Taradr
IRKIOLV
Taradr
TAGARS = Sainir
Kwödrdoni
Taradr
(See 31)
TEIMAD = Sinadum (26)
Taradr
Keradr
No ch.
MOSADR = Sobnir
Karzh
Taradr
(See 51)
ORGULN = Nuridz (14)
Taradr
Kars
No ch.
IDRKUDRVAN
Taradr
Pülduvi (46)
Melgars
PERS
Taradr
MARZUNPUN
Taradr
TÒLEIDI = Nelami (9) = Poidjveli (14) = NERTINERS
Taradr
Kars
Kars
Taradr
No ch.
ARPARNERS = Sigur
Pâm
Taradr
(See 38)
MOGAI = Sinerlos (26)
Taradr
Keradr
No ch.
TEIGUDR = PUNOG = UDRCHOVAN = Oselig
Nödrs
Kars
Pâm
Taradr
(See 4)
(See 14)
(See 36)
NARSO = Ovelidz
Melgars
Taradr
(See 43)
KATHGUDE
d. y.
PUSHTIKÒDR = Kinil (43)
Taradr
Melgars
i. m.
♀
d. n. n.

25.

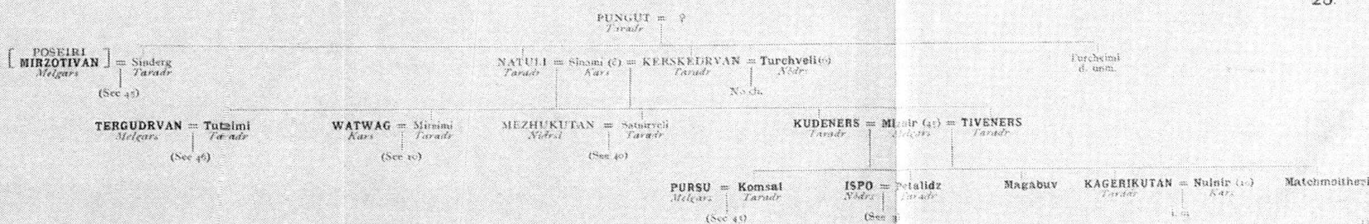
PUNGUT = ♀
Taradr
POSEIRI
MIRZOTIVAN
Melgars
= Sinderg
Taradr
(See 45)
NATULI = Sinomi (6) = KERSKEDRVAN = Turchveli (6)
Taradr
Kars
Taradr
Nödrs
No ch.
Turchsimi
d. unm.
TERGUDRVAN = Tutzimi
Melgars
Taradr
(See 46)
WATWAG = Mirnimi
Kars
Taradr
(See 10)
MEZHUKUTAN = Satnirveli
Nidrsi
Taradr
(See 40)
KUDENERS = Mlznir (45) = TIVENERS
Taradr
Melgars
Taradr
PURSU = Komsai
Melgars
Taradr
(See 43)
ISPO = Petalidz
Nödrs
Taradr
Magabuv
KAGERIKUTAN = Nulnir (10)
Taradr
Kars
i. m.
Matchmoitheri

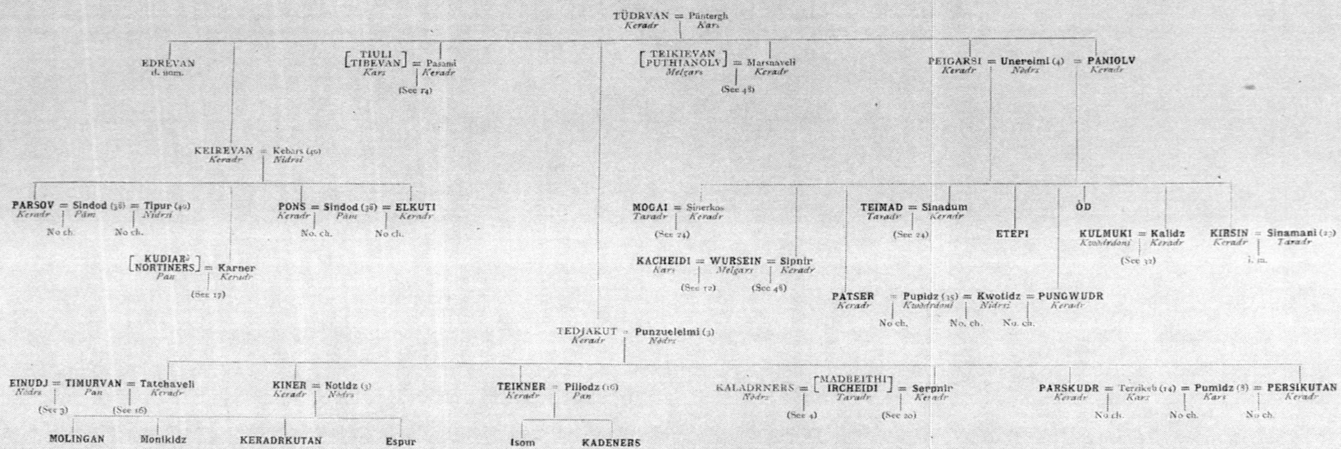
TÜDRVAN = Päntergh
Keradr Kars
EDREVAN
d. nom.
[TIULI TIBEVAN] = Pasami
Kars Keradr
(See 14)
[TEIKIEVAN PUTHIANOLV] = Marsnaveli
Melgars Keradr
(See 48)
PEIGARSI = Unereimi (4) = PANIOLV
Keradr Nödrs Keradr
KEIREVAN = Kebars (40)
Keradr Nidrsi
PARSOV = Sindod (38) = Tipur (40)
Keradr Päm Nidrsi
No ch.
No ch.
PONS = Sindod (38) = ELKUTI
Keradr Päm Keradr
No. ch.
No ch.
[KUDIAR? NORTINERS] = Karner
Pan Keradr
(See 17)
MOGAI = Sinerkos
Taradr Keradr
(See 24)
KACHEIDI = WURSEIN = Sipnir
Kars Melgars Keradr
(See 12)
(See 48)
TEIMAD = Sinadum
Taradr Keradr
(See 24)
ETEPI
ÖD
KULMUKI = Kalidz
Kwödrdoni Keradr
(See 32)
KIRSIN = Sinamani (23)
Keradr Taradr
i. m.
PATSER = Pupidz (35) = Kwotidz = PUNGWUDR
Keradr Kwödrdoni Nidrsi Keradr
No ch.
No. ch.
No. ch.
TEDJAKUT = Punzuelelmi (3)
Keradr Nödrs
EINUDJ = TIMURVAN = Tatchaveli
Nödrs Pan Keradr
(See 3)
(See 16)
MOLINGAN
Monikidz
KINER = Notidz (3)
Keradr Nödrs
KERADRKUTAN
Espur
TEIKNER = Piliodz (16)
Keradr Pan
Isom
KADENERS
KALADRNERS = [MADBEITHI IRCHEIDI] = Serpnir
Nödrs Taradr Keradr
(See 4)
(See 20)
PARSKUDR = Terzikeb (14) = Pumidz (8) = PERSIKUTAN
Keradr Kars Kars Keradr
No ch.
No ch.
No ch.

27.

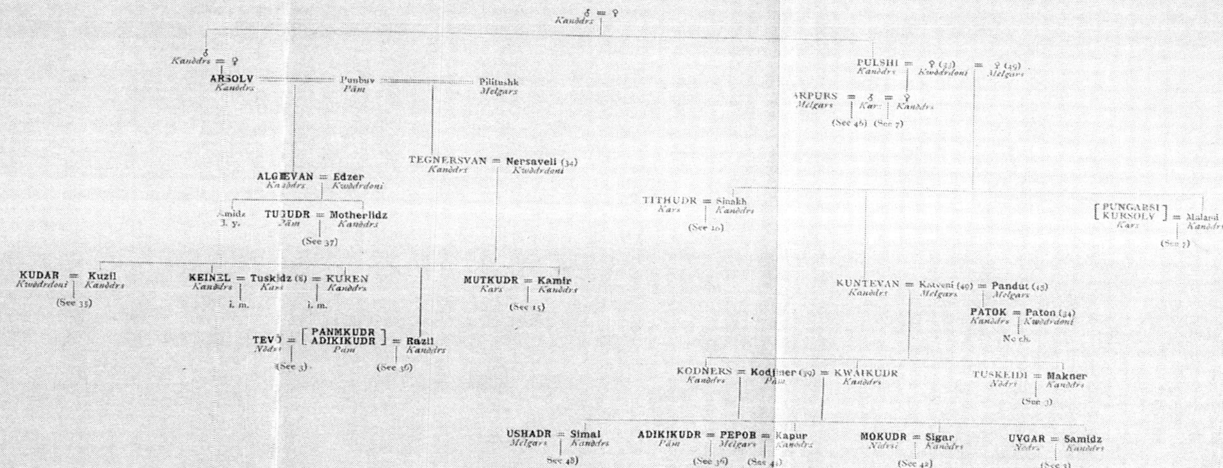
♂ = ♀
Kanðdrs
♂
Kanðdrs = ♀
ARSOLV
Kanðdrs
Punbuv
Pām
Pilitushk
Melgars
PULSHI = ♀ (33) = ♀ (49)
Kanðdrs Kwðdrdoni Melgars
ARPURS = ♂ = ♀
Melgars Kars Kanðdrs
(See 46) (See 7)
TEGNERSVAN = Nersaveli (34)
Kanðdrs Kwðdrdoni
ALGEVAN = Edzer
Kanðdrs Kwðdrdoni
Amidz
1. y.
TUJUDR = Motherlidz
Pām Kanðdrs
(See 37)
TITHUDR = Sinakh
Kars Kanðdrs
(See 10)
PUNGARSI
KURSOLV
Kars
= Malarsi
Kanðdrs
(See 7)
KUDAR = Kuzil
Kwðdrdoni Kanðdrs
(See 35)
KEINEL = Tuskidz (8) = KUREN
Kanðdrs Kars Kanðdrs
i. m.
i. m.
MUTKUDR = Kamir
Kars Kanðdrs
(See 15)
KUNTEVAN = Katveni (49) = Pandut (15)
Kanðdrs Melgars Melgars
PATOK = Paton (34)
Kanðdrs Kwðdrdoni
No ch.
TEVÐ = PANMKUDR
ADIKIKUDR
Pām
= Razil
Kanðdrs
Nðdrs
(See 3)
(See 36)
KODNERS = Kodjner (39) = KWAIKUDR
Kanðdrs Pām Kanðdrs
TUSKEIDI = Makner
Nðdrs Kanðdrs
(See 3)
USHADR = Simal
Melgars Kanðdrs
See 48)
ADIKIKUDR = PEPOB = Kapur
Pām Melgars Kanðdrs
(See 36) (See 41)
MOKUDR = Sigar
Nðdrs Kanðdrs
(See 42)
UVGAR = Samidz
Nðdrs Kanðdrs
(See 3)

28.

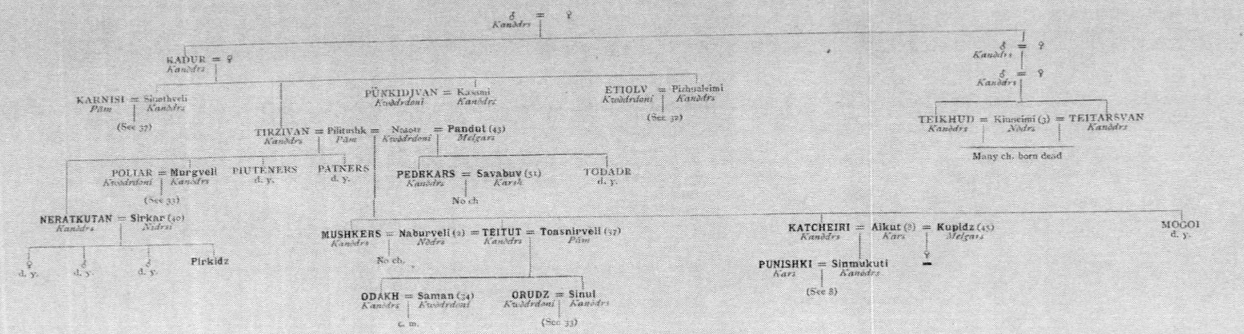
♂ = ♀
Kanðdrs
KADUR = ♀
Kanðdrs
♂ = ♀
Kanðdrs
♂ = ♀
Kanðdrs
KARNISI = Sinothveli
Pām Kanðdrs
(See 37)
PŪNKIDJVAN = Kasmi
Kwðdrdoni Kanðdrs
ETIOLV = Pizhualeimi
Kwðdrdoni Kanðdrs
(See 32)
TEIKHUD = Kiuneimi (3) = TEITARSVAN
Kanðdrs Nðdrs Kanðdrs
Many ch. born dead
TIRZIVAN = Pilitushk = Nsaotr = Pandut (43)
Kanðdrs Pām Kwðdrdoni Melgars
POLIAR = Murgveli
Kwðdrdoni Kanðdrs
(See 33)
PIUTENERS
d. y.
PATNERS
d. y.
PEDRKARS = Savabuv (51)
Kanðdrs Karsh
No ch.
TODADR
d. y.
NERATKUTAN = Sirkar (40)
Kanðdrs Nidrsi
♀ d. y.
♂ d. y.
♂ d. y.
Pirkidz
MUSHKERS = Naburveli (2) = TEITUT = Toasnirveli (37)
Kanðdrs Nðdrs Kanðdrs Pām
No ch.
ODAKH = Saman (34)
Kanðdrs Kwðdrdoni
c. m.
ORUDZ = Sinul
Kwðdrdoni Kanðdrs
(See 33)
KATCHEIRI = Aikut (8) = Kupidz (45)
Kanðdrs Kars Melgars
♀
PUNISHKI = Sinmukuti
Kars Kanðdrs
(See 8)
MOGOI
d. y.

29.

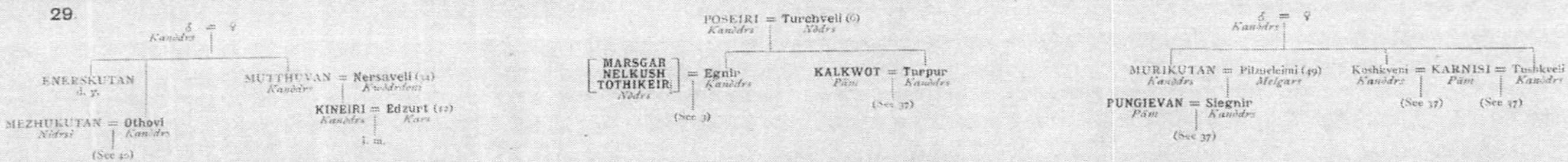
♂ = ♀
Kanðdrs
ENERSKUTAN
d. y.
MEZHUKUTAN = Othovi
Nidrsi Kanðdrs
(See 40)
MUTTHUVAN = Nersaveli (34)
Kanðdrs Kwðdrdoni
KINEIRI = Edzurt (12)
Kanðdrs Kars
i. m.
POSEIRI = Turchveli (6)
Kanðdrs Nðdrs
MARSGAR
NELKUSH
TOTHIKEIR
Nðdrs
= Egnir
Kanðdrs
(See 3)
KALKWOT = Turpur
Pām Kanðdrs
(See 37)
♂ = ♀
Kanðdrs
MURIKUTAN = Pilzueleimi (49)
Kanðdrs Melgars
PUNGIEVAN = Siegnir
Pām Kanðdrs
(See 37)
Koshkveni = KARNISI = Tushkveli
Kanðdrs Pām Kanðdrs
(See 37)
(See 37)

30.

NARTHOVAN = Tukaveli
Kanðdrs Pām
PÒLKAB = Komuleimi (32) = Punabuv (10)
Kanðdrs Kwðdrdoni Kars
♂ d. y.
Pernel
TUKUD
KUPINERS
Kwðdrdoni
= PERSGAS = Koizveli
Nidrsi Kanðdrs
(See 31)
(See 43)
PORZAN = ♀
Kanðdrs
EIKIARZ = Tuteiveli (13) = Salnir (35) = KULINKERVAN
Kanðdrs Kars Kwðdrdoni Kanðdrs
No ch.
KUZHUNERS = Paterami (13) = Pensil (45)
Kanðdrs Kars Melgars
i. m.
i. m.
KASKUDR = Sirmul
Kars Kanðdrs
(See 13)
MONGEITHI = Nilig
Kars Kanðdrs
(See 15)
PATIRSH = Sinkab
Kwðdrdoni Kanðdrs
(See 35)
PUNER = Pashtnirveli
Kwðdrdoni Kanðdrs
(See 31)

31.

♂ *Kwődrdoni* = ♀ (14) *Kars*

MUPUVAN *Kwődrdoni* = Sindami (14) *Kars*

Piliner d. unm.

PUNER *Kwődrdoni* = **Pashtnirveli** (30) *Kanődrs*

TAGARS *Kwődrdoni* = **Sainir** (24) *Taradr* — No ch.

PUTIODZ *Kwődrdoni* = **Sinidz** (21) *Taradr* — No ch.

TUKUD *Kwődrdoni* = **Kolzveli** (30) *Kanődrs* — No ch.

Kolzveli (30) = **KUPINERS** *Kwődrdoni* — No ch.

KUPINERS = [**Maildz** (43) *Nidrsi* — No ch. = **Singib** (43) *Nidrsi* — No ch.]

32.

KATVUN *Kwődrdoni* = Pilikadrk *Melgars*

ETIOLV *Kwődrdoni* = Pizhualeimi (28) *Kanődrs* — No ch.

TERVAN *Kwődrdoni* = **Tarselmi** (41) *Nidrsi* — No ch.

TEIDÜLVAN *Kwődrdoni* = **Sinur** (41) *Nidrsi* — No ch.

KIURVAN *Kwődrdoni* = **Tarselmi** (41) *Nidrsi* — No ch.

Tarselmi (41) = **Sinur** (41) *Nidrsi*

KULMUKI *Kwődrdoni* = **Kalidz** (26) *Keradr* — i. m.

Kalidz (26) = **Kapal** (41) *Nidrsi* — i. m.

PÔLKAB *Kanődrs* = Konorcini *Kwődrdoni* (See 30)

33.

♂ *Kwődrdoni* = ♀

PULSHI *Kanődrs* = ♀ *Kwődrdoni* (See 27)

♂ *Kwődrdoni* = ♀

PUNARSKUTAN *Kwődrdoni* = Methovi (8) *Kars*

POLIAR *Kwődrdoni* = **Murgveli** (26) *Kanődrs* — No ch.

Murgveli (26) = **Kupanveli** (3) *Nődrs*

ORUDZ *Kwődrdoni* = **Sinul** (28) *Kanődrs* — i. m.

34.

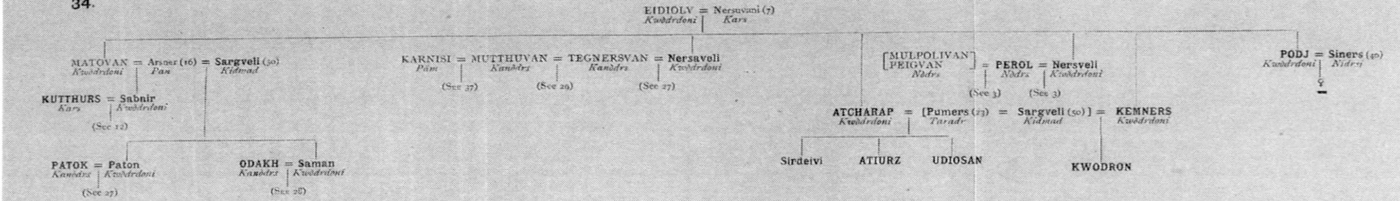
EIDIOLY = Nersuvani (7)
Kwòdrdoni | Kars
MATOVAN = Arsner (16) = Sargveli (50)
Kwòdrdoni | Pan | Kidmad
KUTTHURS = Sabnir
Kars | Kwòdrdoni
(See 12)
PATOK = Paton
Kanòdrs | Kwòdrdoni
(See 27)
ODAKH = Saman
Kanòdrs | Kwòdrdoni
(See 28)
KARNISI = MUTTHUVAN = TEGNERSVAN = Nersaveli
Pām | Kanòdrs | Kanòdrs | Kwòdrdoni
(See 37)
(See 29)
(See 27)
MULPOLIVAN
PEIGVAN
Nòdrs
= PEROL = Nersveli
Nòdrs | Kwòdrdoni
(See 3)
(See 3)
ATCHARAP = [Pumers (23) = Sargveli (50)] = KEMNERS
Kwòdrdoni | Taradr | Kidmad | Kwòdrdoni
Sirdeivi
ATIURZ
UDIOSAN
KWODRON
PODJ = Siners (40)
Kwòdrdoni | Nidrsi
♀

35.

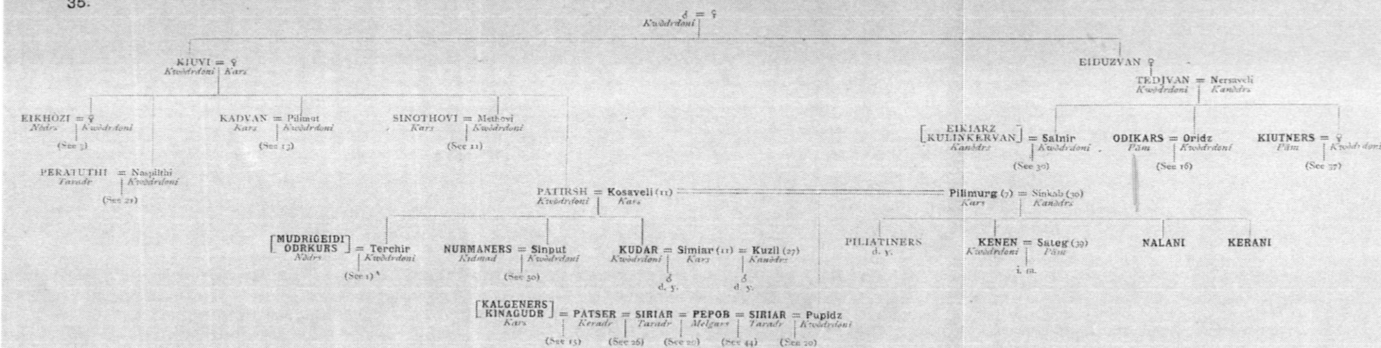
♂ = ♀
Kwòdrdoni
KIUVI = ♀
Kwòdrdoni | Kars
EIKHOZI = ♀
Nòdrs | Kwòdrdoni
(See 3)
PERATUTHI = Naspilthi
Taradr | Kwòdrdoni
(See 21)
KADVAN = Pilmut
Kars | Kwòdrdoni
(See 13)
SINOTHOVI = Methovi
Kars | Kwòdrdoni
(See 11)
PATIRSH = Kosaveli (11)
Kwòdrdoni | Kars
MUDRIGEIDI
ODRKURS
Nòdrs
= Terchir
Kwòdrdoni
(See 1)
NURMANERS = Sinput
Kidmad | Kwòdrdoni
(See 30)
KUDAR = Simiar (11) = Kuzil (27)
Kwòdrdoni | Kars | Kanòdrs
♂
d. y.
♂
d. y.
KALGENERS
KINAGUDR
Kars
= PATSER = SIRIAR = PEPOB = SIRIAR = Pupidz
Keradr | Taradr | Melgars | Taradr | Kwòdrdoni
(See 15)
(See 26)
(See 20)
(See 44)
(See 20)
EIDUZVAN ♀
TEDJVAN = Nersaveli
Kwòdrdoni | Kanòdrs
EIKIARZ
KULINKERVAN
Kanòdrs
= Salnir
Kwòdrdoni
(See 30)
ODIKARS = Oridz
Pām | Kwòdrdoni
(See 16)
KIUTNERS = ♀
Pām | Kwòdrdoni
(See 37)
Pilimurg (7) = Sinkab (30)
Kars | Kanòdrs
PILIATINERS
d. y.
KENEN = Sateg (39)
Kwòdrdoni | Pām
i. m.
NALANI
KERANI

36.

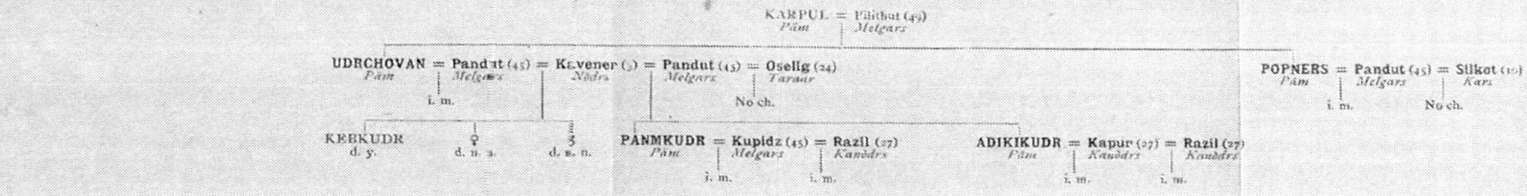
KARPUL = Pilithut (49)
Päm Melgars
UDRCHOVAN = Pandut (45) = Kavener (5) = Pandut (45) = Oselig (24)
Päm Melgars Nödrs Melgars Taradr
i. m.
No ch.
KEBKUDR d. y.
♀ d. n. s.
☿ d. n. n.
PANMKUDR = Kupidz (45) = Razil (27)
Päm Melgars Kanödrs
i. m. i. m.
ADIKIKUDR = Kapur (27) = Razil (27)
Päm Kanödrs Kanödrs
i. m. i. m.
POPNERS = Pandut (45) = Silkot (10)
Päm Melgars Kars
i. m. No ch.

37.

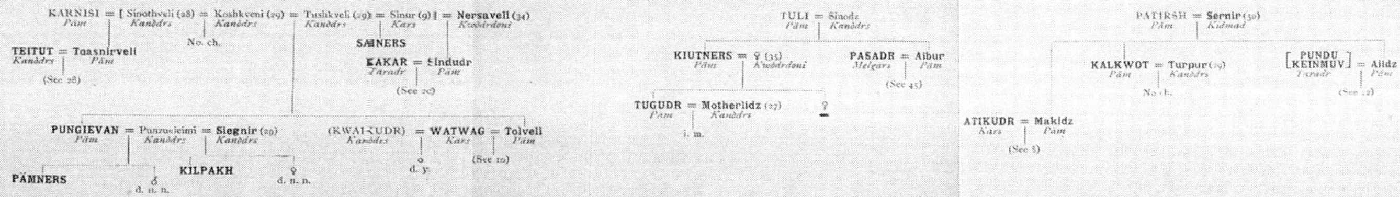
KARNISI = [Sinothveli (28) = Koshkveni (29) = Tushkveli (29) = Sinur (9)] = Nersaveli (34)
Päm Kanödrs Kanödrs Kanödrs Kars Kwödrdoni
No. ch.
SÄNERS
TEITUT = Toasnirveli
Kanödrs Päm
(See 28)
KAKAR = Sindudr
Taradr Päm
(See 20)
PUNGIEVAN = Punzosieimi = Siegnir (29)
Päm Kanödrs Kanödrs
PÄMNERS
♂ d. n. n.
KILPAKH
♀ d. n. n.
(KWAIKUDR) = WATWAG = Tolveli
Kanödrs Kars Päm
o d. y.
(See 10)
TULI = Sinodz
Päm Kanödrs
KIUTNERS = ♀ (35)
Päm Kwödrdoni
TUGUDR = Motherlidz (27)
Päm Kanödrs
i. m.
♀
PASADR = Aibur
Melgars Päm
(See 45)
PATIRSH = Sernir (30)
Päm Kidmad
KALKWOT = Turpur (29)
Päm Kanödrs
No ch.
[PUNDU KEINMUV] = Alidz
Taradr Päm
(See 22)
ATIKUDR = Makidz
Kars Päm
(See 8)

38.

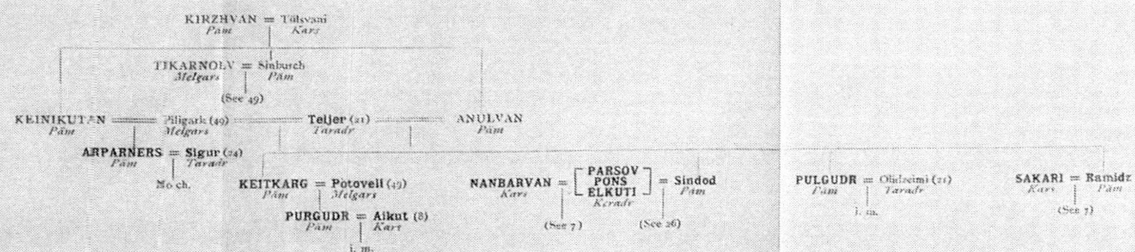
KIRZHVAN = Tölsvani
Päm Kars
TIKARNOLV = Sinburch
Melgars Päm
(See 49)
KEINIKUTAN = Piligark (49) = Teljer (21) = ANULVAN
Päm Melgars Taradr Päm
ARPARNERS = Sigur (24)
Päm Taradr
No ch.
KEITKARG = Potoveli (49)
Päm Melgars
PURGUDR = Aikut (8)
Päm Kars
i. m.
NANBARVAN = [PARSOV PONS ELKUTI] = Sindod
Kars Keradr Päm
(See 7) (See 26)
PULGUDR = Olidzeimi (21)
Päm Taradr
i. m.
SAKARI = Ramidz
Kars Päm
(See 7)

39.

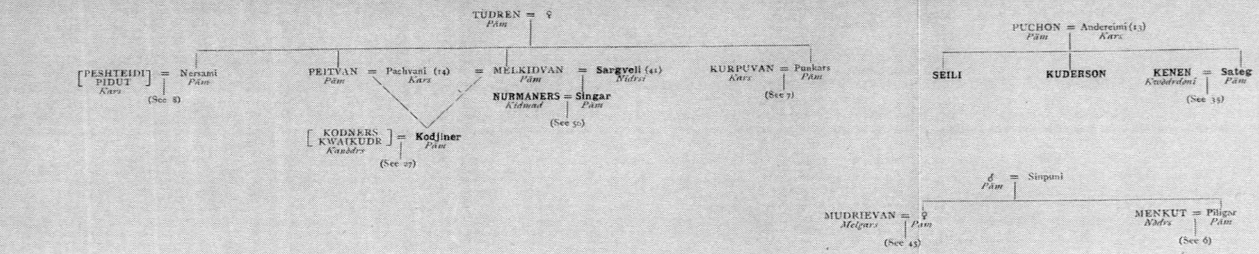
TUDREN = ♀
Pām
PESHTEIDI
PIDUT
Kars
= Nersami
Pām
(See 8)
PEITVAN = Pachvani (14) = MELKIDVAN = Sargveli (41)
Pām
Kars
Pām
Nidrsi
NURMANERS = Singar
Kidmad
Pām
(See 50)
KODNERS
KWAIKUDR
Kanödrs
= Kodjiner
Pām
(See 27)
KURPUVAN = Punkars
Kars
Pām
(See 7)
PUCHON = Andereimi (13)
Pām
Kars
SEILI
KUDERSON
KENEN = Sateg
Kwödrdoni
Pām
(See 35)
♂ = Sinpuni
Pām
MUDRIEVAN = ♀
Melgars
Pām
(See 45)
MENKUT = Piligar
Nödrs
Pām
(See 6)

40.

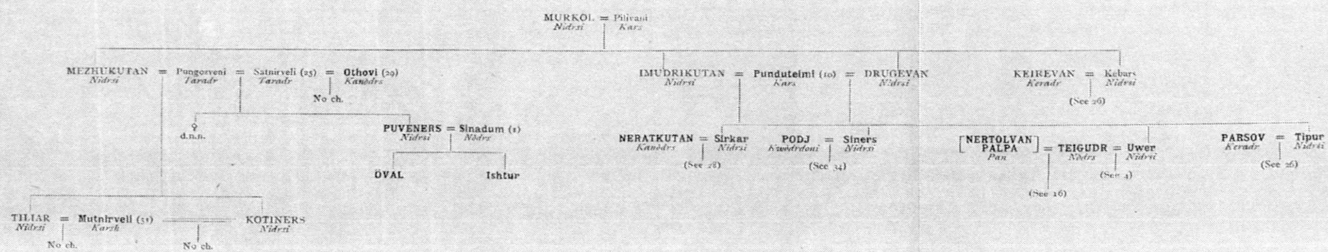
MURKOL = Pilivani
Nidrsi
Kars
MEZHUKUTAN = Pungozveni = Satnirveli (25) = Othovi (29)
Nidrsi
Taradr
Taradr
Kanödrs
No ch.
♀
d.n.n.
PUVENERS = Sinadum (1)
Nidrsi
Nödrs
OVAL
Ishtur
TILIAR = Mutnirveli (51) = KOTINERS
Nidrsi
Karsh
Nidrsi
No ch.
No ch.
IMUDRIKUTAN = Punduteimi (10) = DRUGEVAN
Nidrsi
Kars
Nidrsi
NERATKUTAN = Sirkar
Kanödrs
Nidrsi
(See 28)
PODJ = Siners
Kwödrdoni
Nidrsi
(See 34)
KEIREVAN = Kebars
Keradr
Nidrsi
(See 26)
NERTOLVAN
PALPA
Pan
= TEIGUDR = Uwer
Nödrs
Nidrsi
(See 16)
(See 4)
PARSOV = Tipur
Keradr
Nidrsi
(See 26)

41.

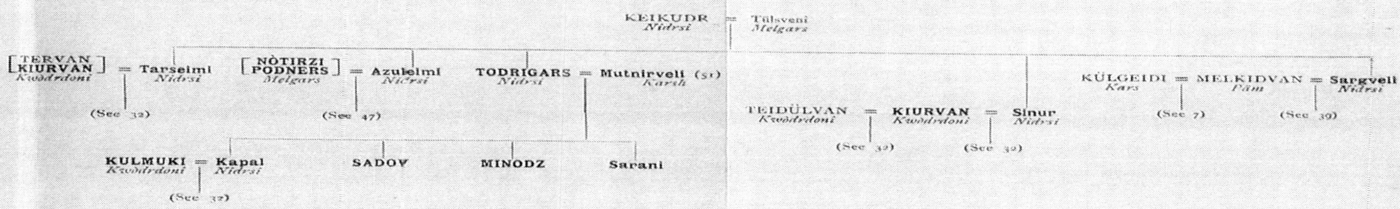
KEIKUDR = Tülsveni
Nidrsi Melgars
[TERVAN KIURVAN] = Tarseimi
Kwödrdoni Nidrsi
(See 32)
[NÒTIRZI PODNERS] = Azuleimi
Melgars Nidrsi
(See 47)
TODRIGARS = Mutnirveli (51)
Nidrsi Karsh
TEIDÜLVAN = KIURVAN = Sinur
Kwödrdoni Kwödrdoni Nidrsi
(See 32) (See 32)
KÜLGEIDI = MELKIDVAN = Sargveli
Kars Päm Nidrsi
(See 7) (See 39)
KULMUKI = Kapal
Kwödrdoni Nidrsi
(See 32)
SADOV
MINODZ
Sarani

42.

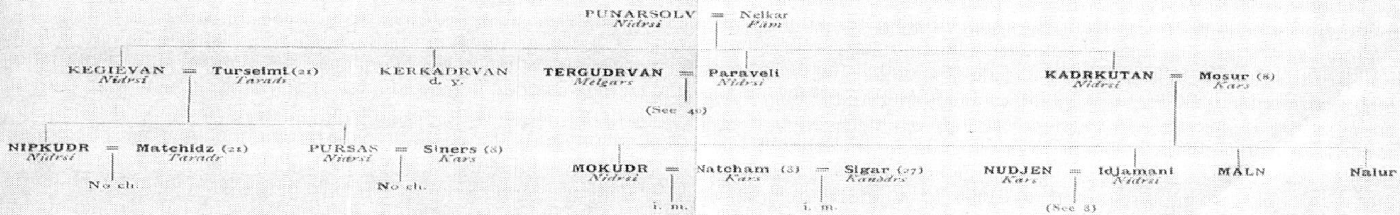
PUNARSOLV = Nelkar
Nidrsi Päm
KEGIEVAN = Turseimi (21)
Nidrsi Taradr
KERKADRVAN
d. y.
TERGUDRVAN = Paraveli
Melgars Nidrsi
(See 40)
KADRKUTAN = Mosur (8)
Nidrsi Kars
NIPKUDR = Matchidz (21)
Nidrsi Taradr
No ch.
PURSAS = Siners (8)
Nidrsi Kars
No ch.
MOKUDR = Natcham (3) = Sigar (27)
Nidrsi Kars Kanddrs
i. m. i. m.
NUDJEN = Idjamani
Kars Nidrsi
(See 8)
MALN
Nalur

43.

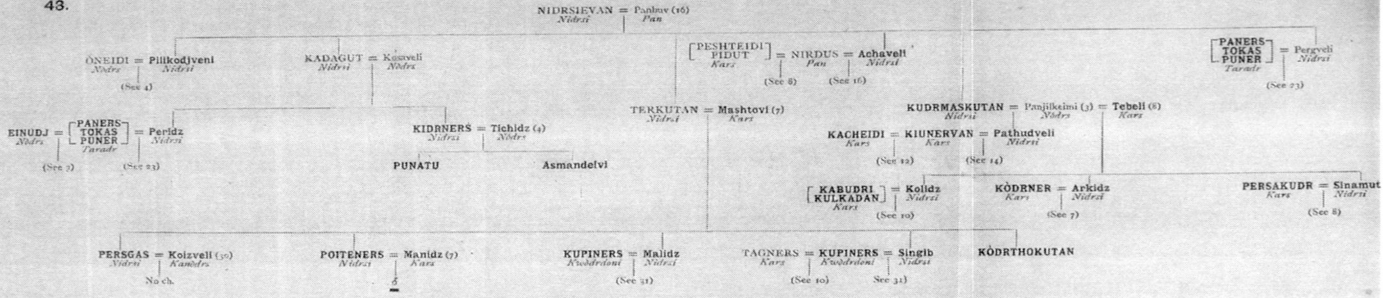
NIDRSIEVAN = Panluv (16)
Nidrsi Pan
ONEIDI = Pilikodjveni
Nodrs Nidrsi
(See 4)
KADAGUT = Kosaveli
Nidrsi Nodrs
PESHTEIDI PIDUT = NIRDUS = Achaveli
Kars Pan Nidrsi
(See 6) (See 16)
PANERS TOKAS PUNER = Pergveli
Taradr Nidrsi
(See 23)
EINUDJ = PANERS TOKAS PUNER = Peridz
Nodrs Taradr Nidrsi
(See 3) (See 23)
KIDRNERS = Tichidz (4)
Nidrsi Nodrs
PUNATU
Asmandelvi
TERKUTAN = Mashtovi (7)
Nidrsi Kars
KUDRMASKUTAN = Panjilkeimi (3) = Tebeli (8)
Nidrsi Nodrs Kars
KACHEIDI = KIUNERVAN = Pathudveli
Kars Kars Nidrsi
(See 12) (See 14)
KABUDRI KULKADAN = Kolidz
Kars Nidrsi
(See 10)
KODRNER = Arkidz
Kars Nidrsi
(See 7)
PERSAKUDR = Sinamut
Kars Nidrsi
(See 8)
PERSGAS = Koizveli (30)
Nidrsi Kanodrs
No ch.
POITENERS = Manidz (7)
Nidrsi Kars
KUPINERS = Malidz
Kwodrdoni Nidrsi
(See 31)
TAGNERS = KUPINERS = Singib
Kars Kwodrdoni Nidrsi
(See 10) See 31)
KODRTHOKUTAN

44.

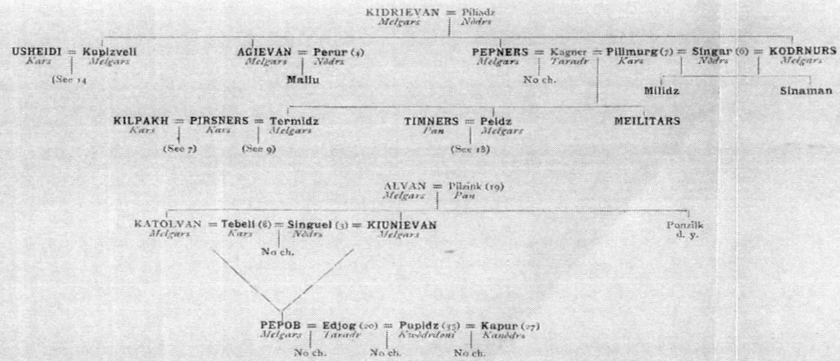
KIDRIEVAN = Piliadz
Melgars Nodrs
USHEIDI = Kupizveli
Kars Melgars
(See 14
AGIEVAN = Perur (4)
Melgars Nodrs
Mallu
PEPNERS = Kagner = Pilimurg (7) = Singar (6) = KODRNURS
Melgars Taradr Kars Nodrs Melgars
No ch.
Milidz
Sinaman
KILPAKH = PIRSNERS = Termidz
Kars Kars Melgars
(See 7) (See 9)
TIMNERS = Peidz
Pan Melgars
(See 18)
MEILITARS
ALVAN = Pilzink (19)
Melgars Pan
KATOLVAN = Tebeli (8) = Singuel (3) = KIUNIEVAN
Melgars Kars Nodrs Melgars
No ch.
Punzilk
d. y.
PEPOB = Edjog (20) = Pupidz (35) = Kapur (27)
Melgars Taradr Kwodrdoni Kanodrs
No ch. No ch. No ch.

45.

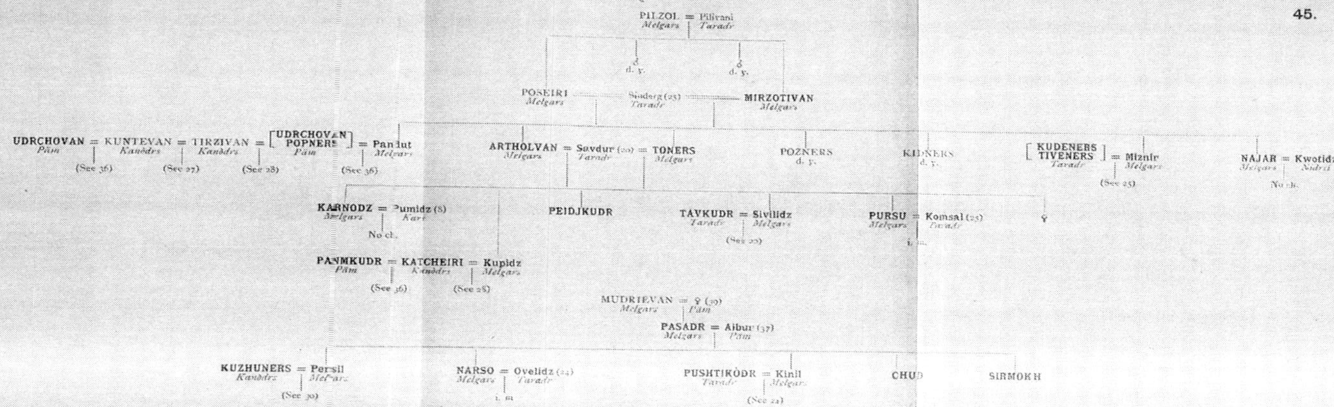
PILZOL = Pilirani
Melgars Taradr
♂ d. y.
♂ d. y.
POSEIRI Melgars
Sindarg (23) Taradr
MIRZOTIVAN Melgars
UDRCHOVAN = KUNTEVAN = TIRZIVAN = [UDRCHOVAN POPNERS] = Pandut
Pām Kanōdrs Kanōdrs Pām Melgars
(See 36) (See 27) (See 28) (See 36)
ARTHOLVAN = Sovdur (20) = TONERS
Melgars Taradr Melgars
POZNERS d. y.
KIDNERS d. y.
[KUDENERS TIVENERS] = Miznir
Taradr Melgars
(See 25)
NAJAR = Kwotidz
Melgars Nidrsl
No ch.
KARNODZ = Pumidz (8)
Melgars Kars
No ch.
PEIDJKUDR
TAVKUDR = Sivilidz
Taradr Melgars
(See 20)
PURSU = Komsal (25)
Melgars Taradr
i. m.
♀
PANMKUDR = KATCHEIRI = Kupidz
Pām Kanōdrs Melgars
(See 36) (See 28)
MUDRIEVAN = ♀ (39)
Melgars Pām
PASADR = Aibur (37)
Melgars Pām
KUZHUNERS = Persil
Kanōdrs Melgars
(See 30)
NARSO = Ovelidz (24)
Melgars Taradr
i. m.
PUSHTIKODR = Kinil
Taradr Melgars
(See 22)
CHUD
SIRMOKH

46.

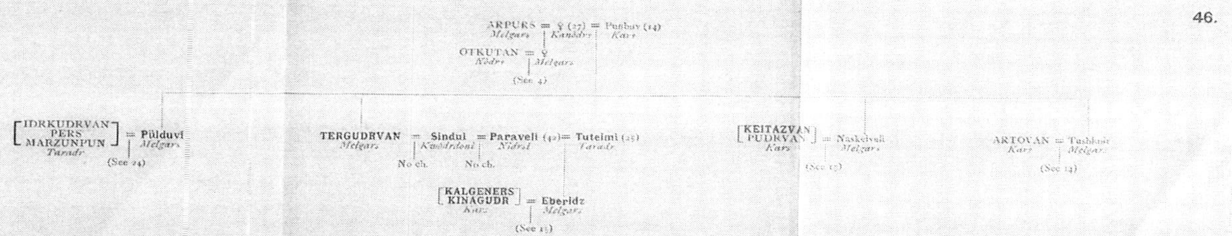
ARPURS = ♀ (27) = Pushuv (14)
Melgars Kanōdrs Kars
OTKUTAN = ♀
Kōdrs Melgars
(See 4)
[IDRKUDRVAN PERS MARZUNPUN] = Pülduvi
Taradr Melgars
(See 24)
TERGUDRVAN = Sindul = Paraveli (42) = Tuteimi (25)
Melgars Kanōdrdoni Nidrsl Taradr
No ch. No ch.
[KALGENERS KINAGUDR] = Eberidz
Kars Melgars
(See 15)
[KEITAZVAN PUDRVAN] = Naskeivali
Kars Melgars
(See 17)
ARTOVAN = Tushkair
Kars Melgars
(See 14)

47.

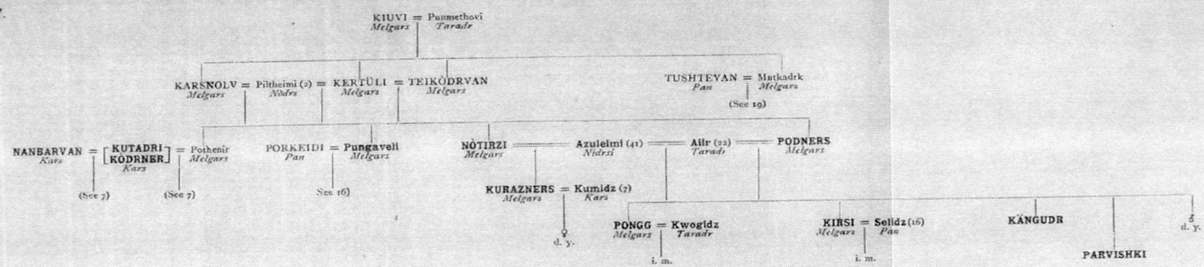
KIUVI = Punmethovi
Melgars Taradr
KARSNOLV = Piltheimi (2) = KERTÜLI = TEIKODRVAN
Melgars Nödrs Melgars Melgars
TUSHTEVAN = Mutkadrk
Pan Melgars
(See 19)
NANBARVAN = [KUTADRI KODRNER] = Pothenir
Kars Kars Melgars
(See 7)
(See 7)
PORKEIDI = Pungaveli
Pan Melgars
See 16)
NOTIRZI — Azuleimi (41) — Ailr (22) — PODNERS
Melgars Nidrsi Taradr Melgars
KURAZNERS = Kumidz (7)
Melgars Kars
♀
d. y.
PONGG = Kwogidz
Melgars Taradr
i. m.
KIRSI = Selidz (16)
Melgars Pan
i. m.
KÄNGUDR
PARVISHKI
♂
d. y.

48.

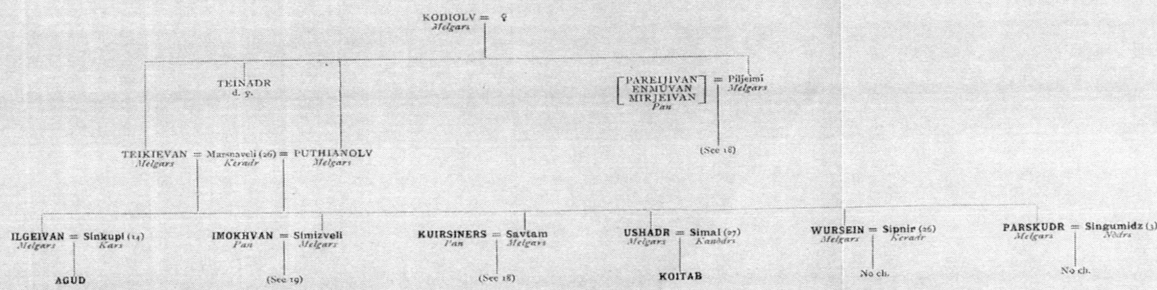
KODIOLV = ♀
Melgars
TEINADR
d. y.
[PAREIJIVAN ENMUVAN MIRJEIVAN] = Piljeimi
Pan Melgars
(See 18)
TEIKIEVAN = Marsnaveli (26) = PUTHIANOLV
Melgars Keradr Melgars
ILGEIVAN = Sinkupi (14)
Melgars Kars
AGUD
IMOKHVAN = Simizveli
Pan Melgars
(See 19)
KUIRSINERS = Savtam
Pan Melgars
(See 18)
USHADR = Simal (27)
Melgars Kanödrs
KOITAB
WURSEIN = Sipnir (26)
Melgars Keradr
No ch.
PARSKUDR = Singumidz (3)
Melgars Nödrs
No ch.

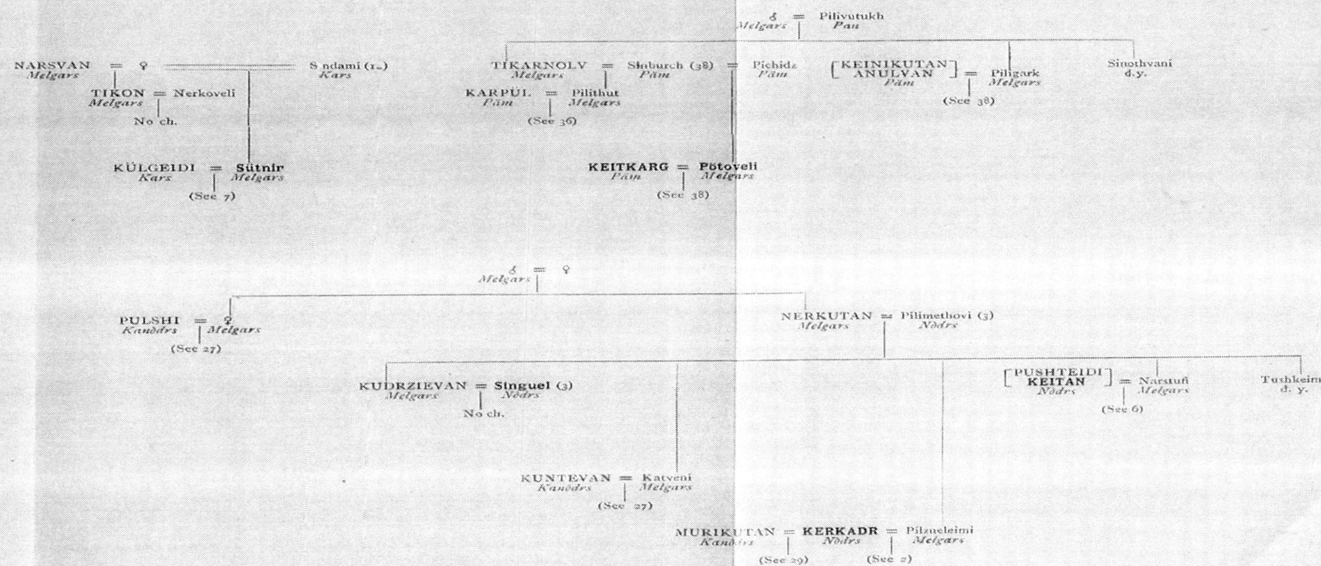

♂ Melgars = Pilivutukh Pau
NARSVAN Melgars = ♀ = S ndami (12) Kars
TIKON Melgars = Nerkoveli
No ch.
KÜLGEIDI Kars = Sütnir Melgars
(See 7)
TIKARNOLV Melgars = Shuburch (38) Päm = Pichidz Päm
KARPUL Päm = Pilithut Melgars
(See 36)
KEITKARG Päm = Pötoveli Melgars
(See 38)
KEINIKUTAN ANULVAN Päm = Piligark Melgars
(See 38)
Sinothvani d.y.
♂ Melgars = ♀
PULSHI Kanödrs = ♀ Melgars
(See 27)
NERKUTAN Melgars = Pilimethovi (3) Nödrs
KUDRZIEVAN Melgars = Singuel (3) Nödrs
No ch.
KUNTEVAN Kanödrs = Katveni Melgars
(See 27)
MURIKUTAN Kanödrs = KERKADR Nödrs = Pilzneleimi Melgars
(See 29)
(See 2)
PUSHTEIDI KEITAN Nödrs = Narstuñ Melgars
(See 6)
Tushkeimi d. y.

50.

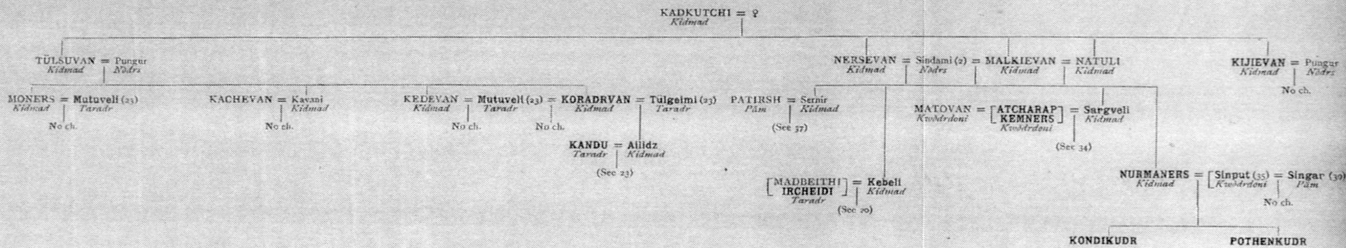
KADKUTCHI = ♀
Kidmad
TÜLSUVAN = Pungur
Kidmad Nödrs
NERSEVAN = Sindami (2) = MALKIEVAN = NATULI
Kidmad Nödrs Kidmad Kidmad
KIJIEVAN = Pungur
Kidmad Nödrs
No ch.
MONERS = Mutuveli (23)
Kidmad Taradr
No ch.
KACHEVAN = Kavani
Kidmad
No ch.
KEDEVAN = Mutuveli (23) = KORADRVAN = Tülgeimi (23)
Kidmad Taradr Kidmad Taradr
No ch.
No ch.
KANDU = Alildz
Taradr Kidmad
(See 23)
PATIRSH = Semir
Păm Kidmad
(See 37)
MADBEITHI
IRCHEIDI = Kebeli
Taradr Kidmad
(See 20)
MATOVAN = ATCHARAP
KEMNERS = Sargveli
Kwödrdoni Kwödrdoni Kidmad
(See 34)
NURMANERS = Sinput (35) = Singar (39)
Kidmad Kwödrdoni Păm
No ch.
KONDIKUDR
POTHENKUDR

51.

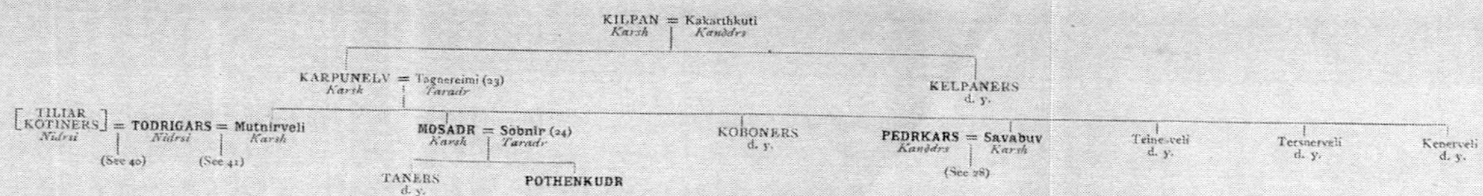
KILPAN = Kakarthkuti
Karsh Kanödrs
KARPUNELV = Tagnereimi (23)
Karsh Taradr
KELPANERS
d. y.
TILIAR
KOTINERS = TODRIGARS = Mutnirveli
Nidrsi Nidrsi Karsh
(See 40)
(See 41)
MOSADR = Sobnir (24)
Karsh Taradr
TANERS
d. y.
POTHENKUDR
KOBONERS
d. y.
PEDRKARS = Savabuv
Kanödrs Karsh
(See 28)
Teinesveli
d. y.
Tersnerveli
d. y.
Kenerveli
d. y.

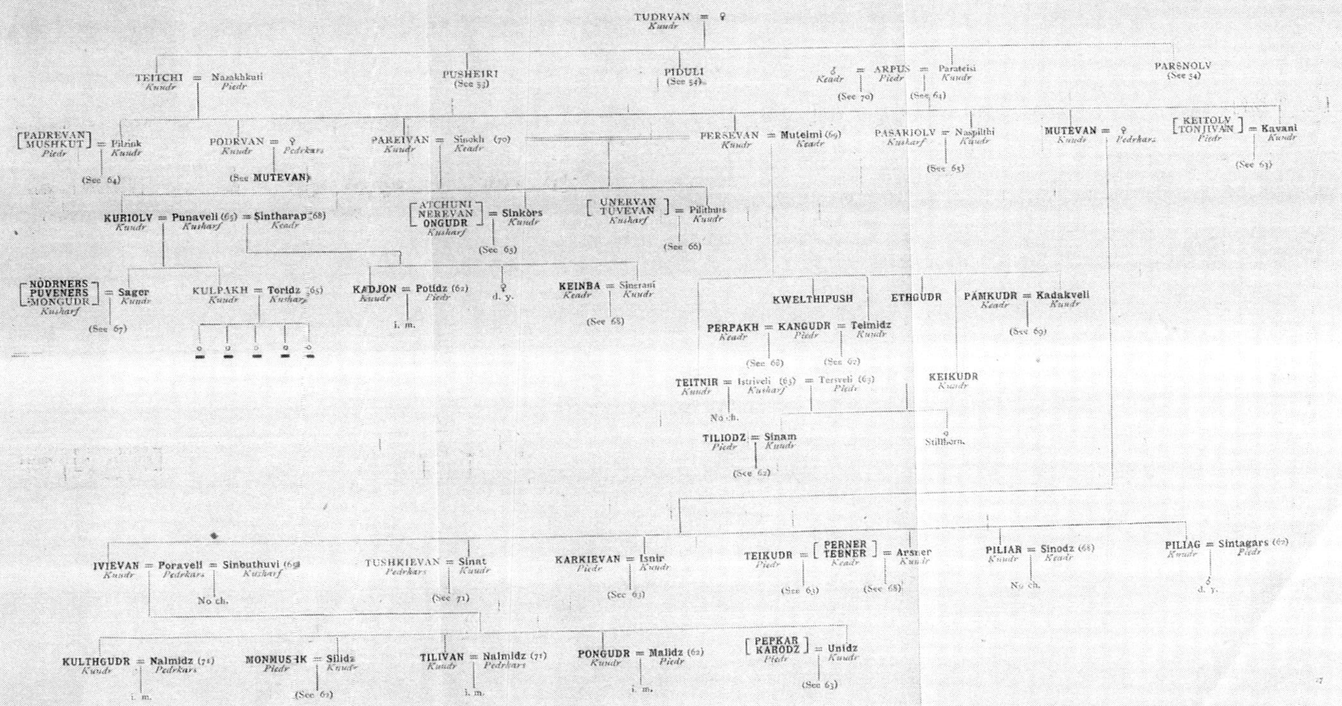
TUDRVAN = ♀
Kuudr
TEITCHI = Nazakhkuti
Kuudr Piedr
PUSHEIRI
(See 53)
PIDULI
(See 54)
♂ = ARPUS = Parateisi
Keadr Piedr Kuudr
(See 70)
(See 64)
PARSNOLV
(See 54)
[PADREVAN MUSHKUT] = Pilzink
Piedr Kuudr
(See 64)
PODRVAN = ♀
Kuudr Pedrkars
(See MUTEVAN)
PAREIVAN = Sinokh (70)
Kuudr Keadr
PERSEVAN = Muteimi (69)
Kuudr Keadr
PASARIOLV = Naspilthi
Kusharf Kuudr
(See 65)
MUTEVAN = ♀
Kuudr Pedrkars
[KEITOLV TONJIVAN] = Kavani
Piedr Kuudr
(See 63)
KURIOLV = Punaveli (65) = Sintharap (68)
Kuudr Kusharf Keadr
[ATCHUNI NEREVAN ONGUDR] = Sinkors
Kusharf Kuudr
(See 65)
[UNERVAN TUVEVAN] = Pilithuis
Kusharf Kuudr
(See 66)
[NODRNERS PUVENERS MONGUDR] = Sager
Kusharf Kuudr
(See 67)
KULPAKH = Toridz (65)
Kuudr Kusharf
KADJON = Potidz (62)
Kuudr Piedr
i. m.
♀
d. y.
KEINBA = Sinerani
Keadr Kuudr
(See 68)
KWELTHIPUSH
ETHGUDR
PAMKUDR = Kadakveli
Keadr Kuudr
(See 69)
PERPAKH = KANGUDR = Telmidz
Keadr Piedr Kuudr
(See 66)
(See 67)
TEITNIR = Istriveli (63) = Tersveli (63)
Kuudr Kusharf Piedr
No ch.
KEIKUDR
Kuudr
TILIODZ = Sinam
Piedr Kuudr
(See 62)
♀
Stillborn.
IVIEVAN = Poraveli = Sinbuthuvi (69)
Kuudr Pedrkars Kusharf
No ch.
TUSHKIEVAN = Sinat
Pedrkars Kuudr
(See 71)
KARKIEVAN = Isnir
Piedr Kuudr
(See 63)
TEIKUDR = [PERNER TEBNER] = Arsner
Piedr Keadr Kuudr
(See 63)
(See 68)
PILIAR = Sinodz (68)
Kuudr Keadr
No ch.
PILIAG = Sintagars (67)
Kuudr Piedr
♂
d. y.
KULTHGUDR = Nalmidz (71)
Kuudr Pedrkars
i. m.
MONMUS IK = Silidz
Piedr Kuudr
(See 62)
TILIVAN = Nalmidz (71)
Kuudr Pedrkars
i. m.
PONGUDR = Malidz (62)
Kuudr Piedr
i. m.
[PEPKAR KARODZ] = Unidz
Piedr Kuudr
(See 63)

53.

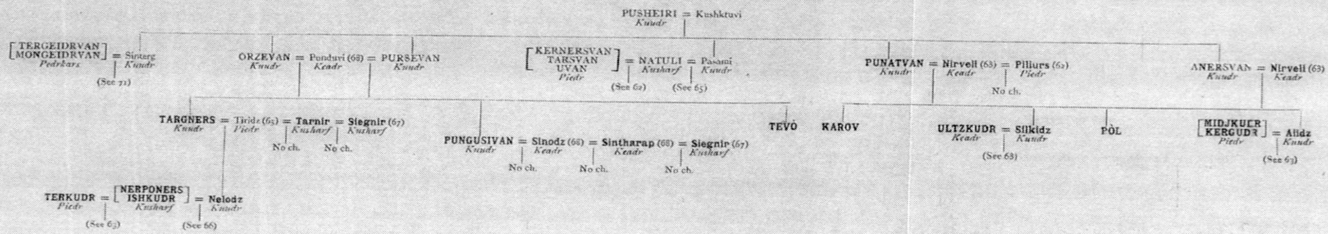
PUSHEIRI = Kushktuvi
Kuudr
TERGEIDRVAN MONGEIDRVAN = Sinterg
Pedrkars Kuudr
(See 71)
ORZEVAN = Punduvi (68) = PURSEVAN
Kuudr Keadr Kuudr
KERNERSVAN TARSVAN UVAN = NATULI = Pasami
Piedr Kusharf Kuudr
(See 62) (See 65)
PUNATVAN = Nirveli (63) = Pillurs (62)
Kuudr Keadr Piedr
No ch.
ANERSVAN = Nirveli (63)
Kuudr Keadr
TARGNERS = Tiridz (65) = Tarnir = Siegnir (67)
Kuudr Piedr Kusharf Kusharf
No ch. No ch.
PUNGUSIVAN = Sinodz (66) = Sintharap (68) = Siegnir (67)
Kuudr Keadr Keadr Kusharf
No ch. No ch. No ch.
TEVO
KAROV
ULTZKUDR = Silkidz
Keadr Kuudr
(See 63)
PÖL
MIDJKUDR KERGUDR = Alidz
Piedr Kuudr
(See 63)
TERKUDR = NERPONERS ISHKUDR = Nelodz
Piedr Kusharf Kuudr
(See 63) (See 66)

54.

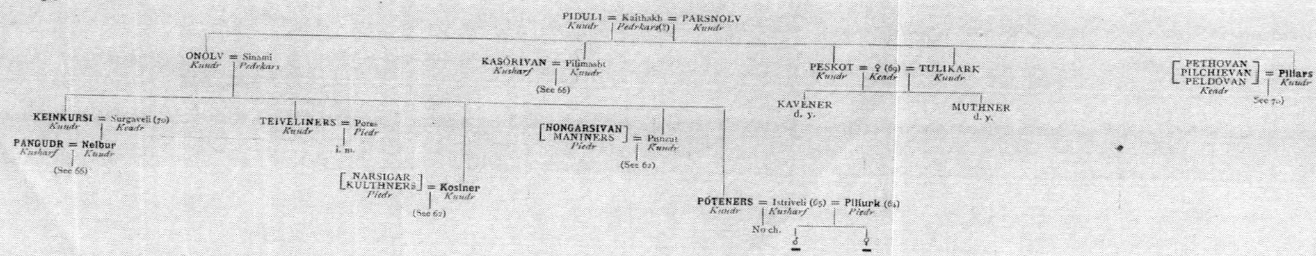
PIDULI = Kaithakh = PARSNOLV
Kuudr Pedrkars(?) Kuudr
ONOLV = Sinami
Kuudr Pedrkars
KASÖRIVAN = Pilimasht
Kusharf Kuudr
(See 66)
PESKOT = ♀ (69) = TULIKARK
Kuudr Keadr Kuudr
KAVENER
d. y.
MUTHNER
d. y.
PETHOVAN PILCHIEVAN PELDOVAN = Pillars
Keadr Kuudr
See 70)
KEINKURSI = Surgaveli (70)
Kuudr Keadr
PANGUDR = Nelbur
Kusharf Kuudr
(See 66)
TEIVELINERS = Pores
Kuudr Piedr
i. m.
NARSIGAR KULTHNERS = Kosiner
Piedr Kuudr
(See 62)
NONGARSIVAN MANINERS = Punzut
Piedr Kuudr
(See 62)
PÖTENERS = Istriveli (65) = Pillurk (64)
Kuudr Kusharf Piedr
No ch.
♂
♀

55.

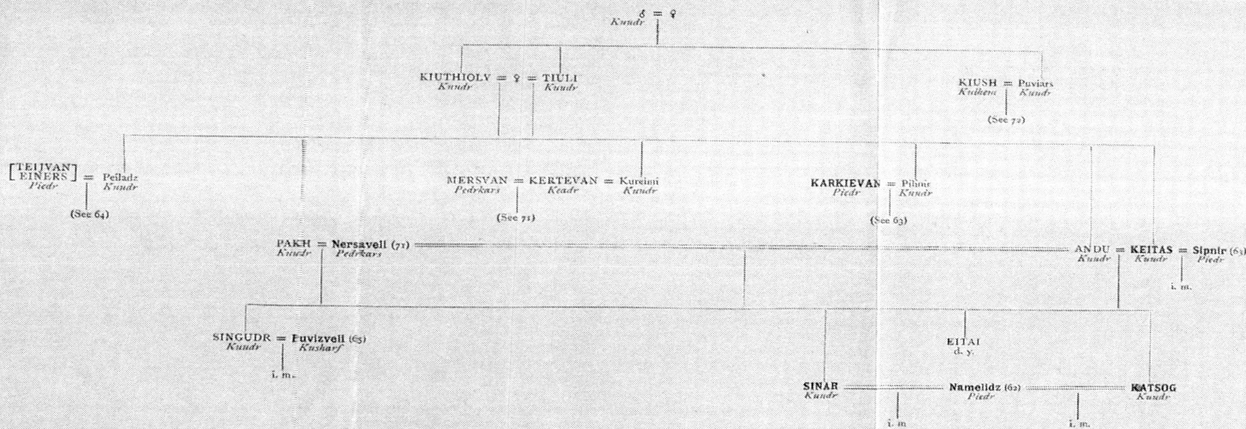

♂ = ♀
Kuudr
KIUTHIOLY = ♀ = TIULI
Kuudr
Kuudr
KIUSH = Puviars
Kulhem
Kuudr
(See 72)
TEIJVAN
EINERS
Piedr
= Peiladz
Kuudr
(See 64)
MERSVAN = KERTEVAN = Kureimi
Pedrkars
Keadr
Kuudr
(See 71)
KARKIEVAN = Pilinir
Piedr
Kuudr
(See 63)
PAKH = Nersaveil (71)
Kuudr
Pedrkars
ANDU = KEITAS = Sipnir (63)
Kuudr
Kuudr
Piedr
i. m.
SINGUDR = Fuvizveil (65)
Kuudr
Kusharf
i. m.
EITAI
d. y.
SINAR
Kuudr
Namelidz (62)
Piedr
KATSOG
Kuudr
i. m.
i. m.

56.

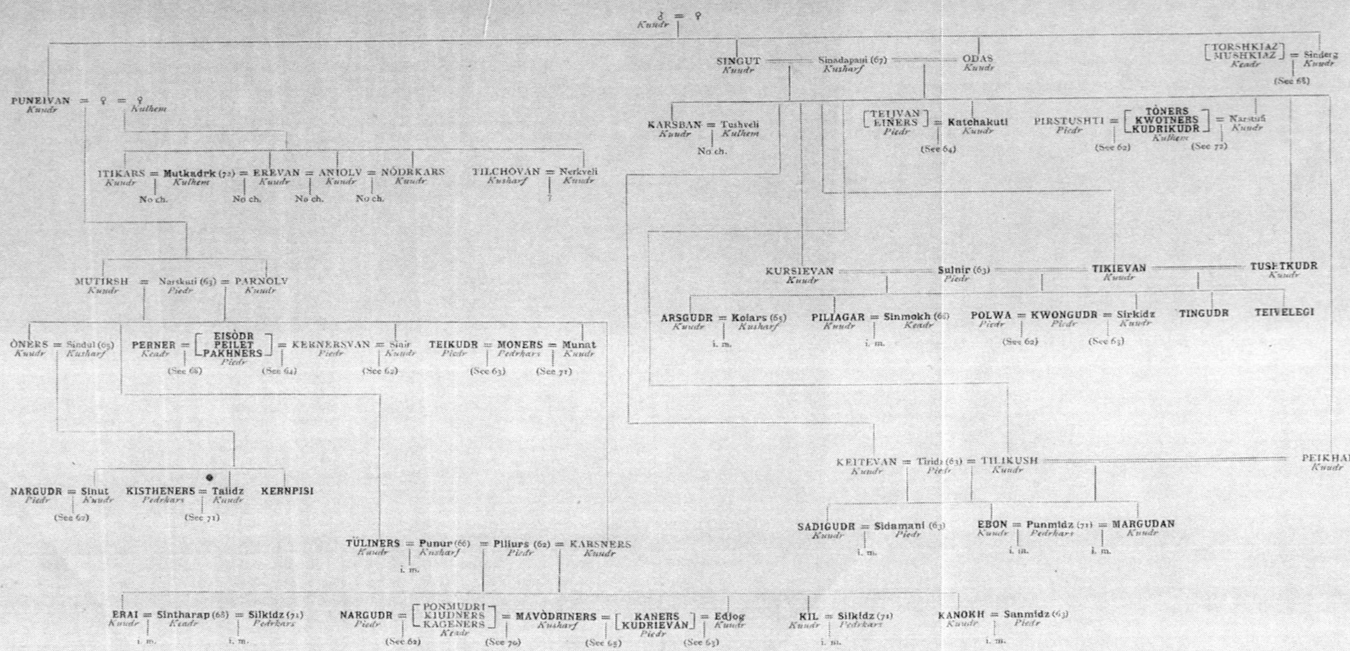

♂ = ♀ Kuudr
SINGUT Kuudr = Sinadapani (67) Kusharf = ODAS Kuudr
[TORSHKIAZ MUSHKIAZ] Keadr = Sinderg Kuudr (See 68)
PUNEIVAN Kuudr = ♀ = ♀ Kulhem
KARSBAN Kuudr = Tushveli Kulhem No ch.
[TEIJVAN EINERS] Piedr = Katchakuti Kuudr (See 64)
PIRSTUSHTI Piedr = [TÒNERS KWOTNERS KUDRIKUDR] Kulhem = Narstuti Kuudr (See 62) (See 72)
ITIKARS Kuudr = Mutkadrk (72) Kulhem = EREVAN Kuudr = ANIOLV Kuudr = NÒDRKARS Kuudr No ch. No ch. No ch. No ch.
TILCHOVAN Kusharf = Nerkveli Kuudr ?
KURSIEVAN Kuudr = Sulnir (63) Piedr = TIKIEVAN Kuudr = TUSETKUDR Kuudr
MUTIRSH Kuudr = Narskuti (63) Piedr = PARNOLV Kuudr
ARSGUDR Kuudr = Kolars (65) Kusharf i. m.
PILIAGAR Kuudr = Sinmokh (66) Keadr i. m.
POLWA Piedr = KWONGUDR Piedr = Sirkidz Kuudr (See 62) (See 63)
TINGUDR
TEIVELEGI
ÒNERS Kuudr = Sindul (65) Kusharf
PERNER Keadr = [EISÒDR PEILET PAKHNERS] Piedr = KERNERSVAN Piedr = Siair Kuudr (See 68) (See 64) (See 62)
TEIKUDR Piedr = MONERS Pedrkars = Munat Kuudr (See 63) (See 71)
KEITEVAN Kuudr = Tiridz (63) Piedr = TILIKUSH Kuudr = PEIKHAR Kuudr
NARGUDR Piedr = Sinut Kuudr (See 62)
KISTHENERS Pedrkars = Talidz Kuudr (See 71)
KERNPISI
SADIGUDR Kuudr = Sidamani (63) Piedr i. m.
EBON Kuudr = Punmidz (71) Pedrkars = MARGUDAN Kuudr i. m. i. m.
TÜLINERS Kuudr = Punur (66) Kusharf = Piliurs (62) Piedr = KARSNERS Kuudr i. m.
ERAI Kuudr = Sintharap (68) Keadr = Silkidz (71) Pedrkars i. m. i. m.
NARGUDR Piedr = [PONMUDRI KIUDNERS KAGENERS] Keadr = MAVÒDRINERS Kusharf = [KANERS KUDRIEVAN] Piedr = Edjog Kuudr (See 62) (See 70) (See 65) (See 63)
KIL Kuudr = Silkidz (71) Pedrkars i. m.
KANOKH Kuudr = Sanmidz (63) Piedr i. m.

30

57.

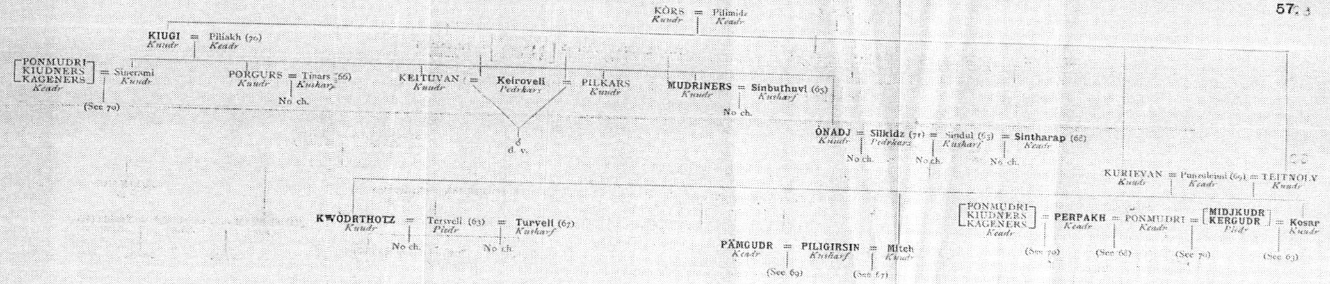
KÖRS = Pilimidz
Kuudr Keadr
KIUGI = Piliakh (70)
Kuudr Keadr
PONMUDRI KIUDNERS KAGENERS = Sinerami
Keadr Kuudr
(See 70)
PORGURS = Tinars (66)
Kuudr Kusharf
No ch.
KEITUVAN = Keiroveli = PILKARS
Kuudr Pedrkars Kuudr
d. y.
MUDRINERS = Sinbuthuvi (65)
Kuudr Kusharf
No ch.
ÖNADJ = Silkidz (71) = Sindul (65) = Sintharap (68)
Kuudr Pedrkars Kusharf Keadr
No ch. No ch. No ch.
KURIEVAN = Punzuleimi (69) = TEITNOLV
Kuudr Keadr Kuudr
KWÖDRTHOTZ = Tersveli (63) = Turveli (67)
Kuudr Piedr Kusharf
No ch. No ch.
PÄMGUDR = PILIGIRSIN = Mitch
Keadr Kusharf Kuudr
(See 69) (See 67)
PONMUDRI KIUDNERS KAGENERS = PERPAKH = PONMUDRI = MIDJKUDR KERGUDR = Kosar
Keadr Keadr Keadr Piedr Kuudr
(See 70) (See 68) (See 70) (See 63)

58.

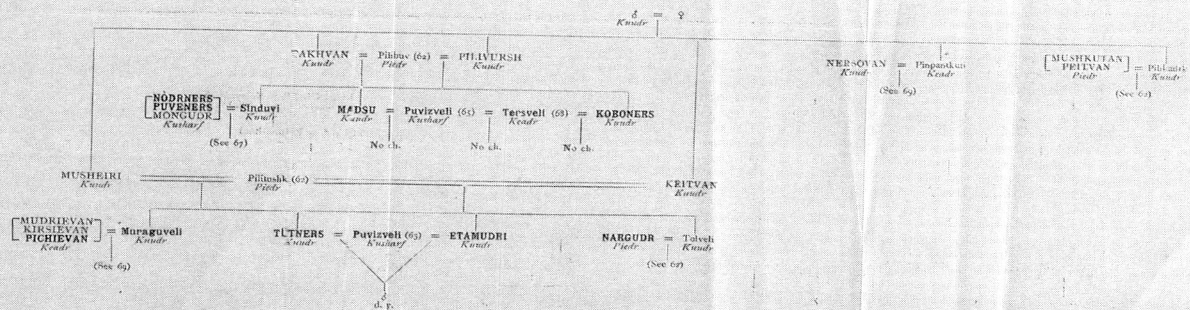
♂ = ♀
Kuudr
AKHVAN = Pilibuv (62) = PILIVURSH
Kuudr Piedr Kuudr
NÖDRNERS PUVENERS MONGUDR = Sinduvi
Kusharf Kuudr
(See 67)
MADSU = Puvizveli (65) = Tersveli (68) = KOBONERS
Kuudr Kusharf Keadr Kuudr
No ch. No ch. No ch.
MUSHEIRI = Pilitushk (62) = KEITVAN
Kuudr Piedr Kuudr
MUDRIEVAN KIRSIEVAN PICHIEVAN = Muraguveli
Keadr Kuudr
(See 69)
TÜTNERS = Puvizveli (65) = ETAMUDRI
Kuudr Kusharf Kuudr
d. y.
NARGUDR = Tolveli
Piedr Kuudr
(See 67)
NERSOVAN = Pinpantkun
Kuudr Keadr
(See 69)
MUSHKUTAN PEITVAN = Pilizadz
Piedr Kuudr
(See 62)

59.

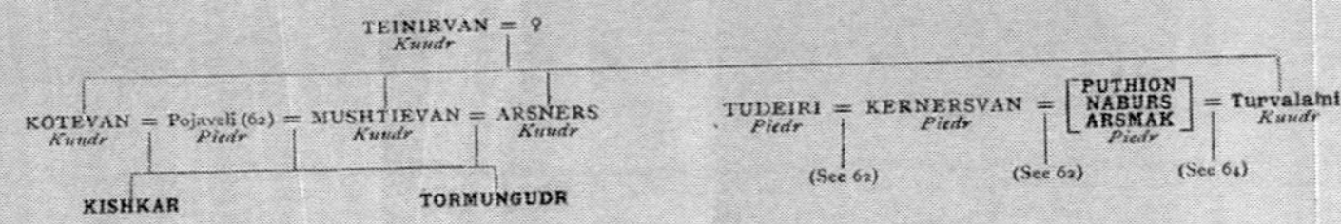
TEINIRVAN = ♀
Kuudr
KOTEVAN = Pojaveli (62) = MUSHTIEVAN = ARSNERS
Kuudr Piedr Kuudr Kuudr
KISHKAR
TORMUNGUDR
TUDEIRI = KERNERSVAN = PUTHION NABURS ARSMAK = Turvalami
Piedr Piedr Piedr Kuudr
(See 62)
(See 62)
(See 64)

60.

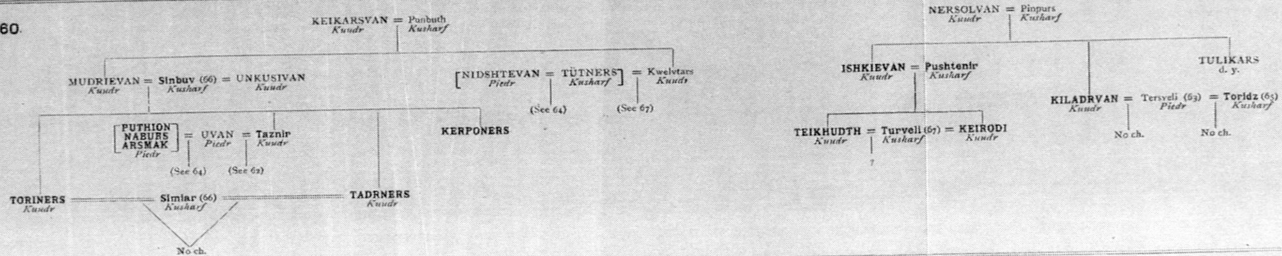
KEIKARSVAN = Punbuth
Kuudr Kusharf
MUDRIEVAN = Sinbuv (66) = UNKUSIVAN
Kuudr Kusharf Kuudr
NIDSHTEVAN = TÜTNERS = Kwelvtars
Piedr Kusharf Kuudr
(See 64)
(See 67)
PUTHION NABURS ARSMAK = UVAN = Taznir
Piedr Piedr Kuudr
(See 64)
(See 62)
KERPONERS
TORINERS
Kuudr
Simiar (66)
Kusharf
TADRNERS
Kuudr
No ch.
NERSOLVAN = Pinpurs
Kuudr Kusharf
ISHKIEVAN = Pushtenir
Kuudr Kusharf
TULIKARS
d. y.
KILADRVAN = Tersveli (63) = Toridz (65)
Kuudr Piedr Kusharf
No ch.
No ch.
TEIKHUDTH = Turveli (67) = KEIRODI
Kuudr Kusharf Kuudr
?

61.

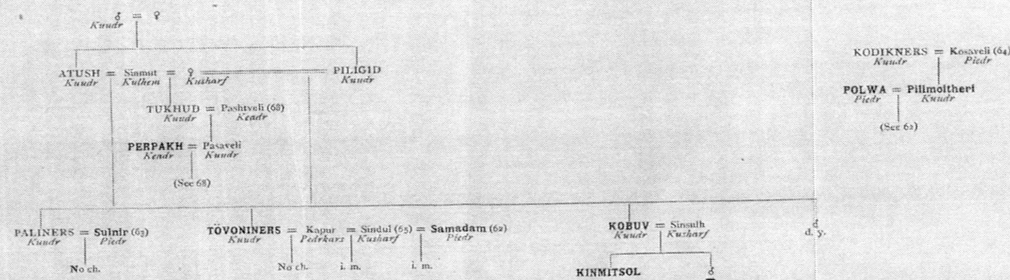
♂ = ♀
Kuudr
ATUSH = Sinmut = ♀
Kuudr Kulhem Kusharf
PILIGID
Kuudr
TUKHUD = Pashtveli (68)
Kuudr Keadr
PERPAKH = Pasaveli
Keadr Kuudr
(See 68)
PALINERS = Sulnir (63)
Kuudr Piedr
No ch.
TÖVONINERS = Kapur = Sindul (65) = Samadam (62)
Kuudr Pedrkars Kusharf Piedr
No ch.
i. m.
i. m.
KOBUV = Sinsulh
Kuudr Kusharf
KINMITSOL
♂
d
d. y.
KODIKNERS = Kosaveli (64)
Kuudr Piedr
POLWA = Pilimoltheri
Piedr Kuudr
(See 62)

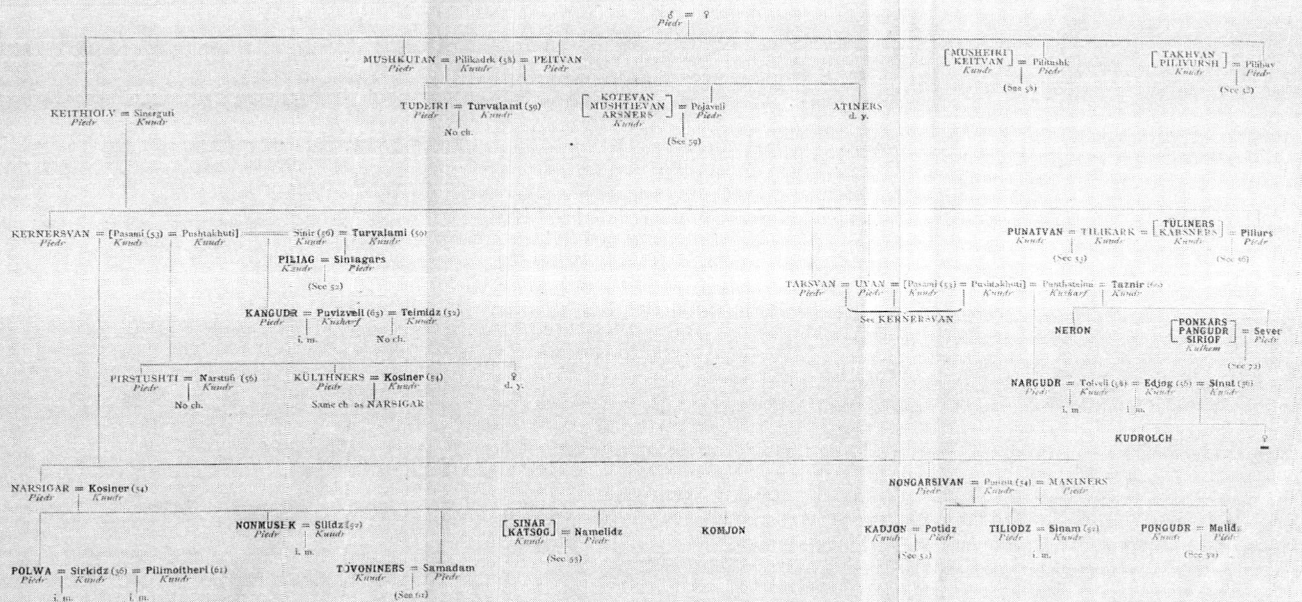

♂ = ♀
Piedr
MUSHKUTAN = Pilikadrk (58) = PEITVAN
Piedr Kuudr Piedr
MUSHEIRI KEITVAN = Pilitushk
Kuudr Piedr
(See 58)
TAKHVAN PILIVURSH = Pilibav
Kuudr Piedr
(See 48)
KEITHIOLV = Sinsrguti
Piedr Kuudr
TUDEIRI = Turvalami (59)
Piedr Kuudr
No ch.
KOTEVAN MUSHTIEVAN ARSNERS = Pojaveli
Kuudr Piedr
(See 59)
ATINERS
d. y.
KERNERSVAN = [Pasami (53) = Pushtakhuti] = Sinir (56) = Turvalami (59)
Piedr Kuudr Kuudr Kuudr Kuudr
PILIAG = Sintagars
Kuudr Piedr
(See 52)
KANGUDR = Puvizveli (65) = Telmidz (52)
Piedr Kusharf Kuudr
i. m.
No ch.
PIRSTUSHTI = Narstufi (56)
Piedr Kuudr
No ch.
KULTHNERS = Kosiner (54)
Piedr Kuudr
Same ch. as NARSIGAR
♀
d. y.
PUNATVAN = TILIKARK = TULINERS KARSNERS = Pilurs
Kuudr Kuudr Kuudr Piedr
(See 53)
(See 46)
TARSVAN = UYAN = [Pasami (53) = Pushtakhuti] = Panthatsiun = Taznir (62)
Piedr Piedr Kuudr Kuudr Kusharf Kuudr
See KERNERSVAN
NERON
PONKARS PANGUDR SIRIOF = Sever
Kulkem Piedr
(See 72)
NARGUDR = Toiveli (58) = Edjog (56) = Sinut (36)
Piedr Kuudr Kuudr Kuudr
i. m.
i. m.
KUDROLCH
♀
NARSIGAR = Kosiner (54)
Piedr Kuudr
NONMUSEK = Silidz (52)
Piedr Kuudr
i. m.
SINAR KATSOG = Namelidz
Kuudr Piedr
(See 55)
KOMJON
POLWA = Sirkidz (36) = Pilimoitheri (61)
Piedr Kuudr Kuudr
i. m.
i. m.
TOVONINERS = Samadam
Kuudr Piedr
(See 61)
NONGARSIVAN = Pusinu (54) = MANINERS
Piedr Kuudr Piedr
KADJON = Potidz
Kuudr Piedr
(See 52)
TILIODZ = Sinam (52)
Piedr Kuudr
i. m.
PONGUDR = Malidz
Kuudr Piedr
(See 52)

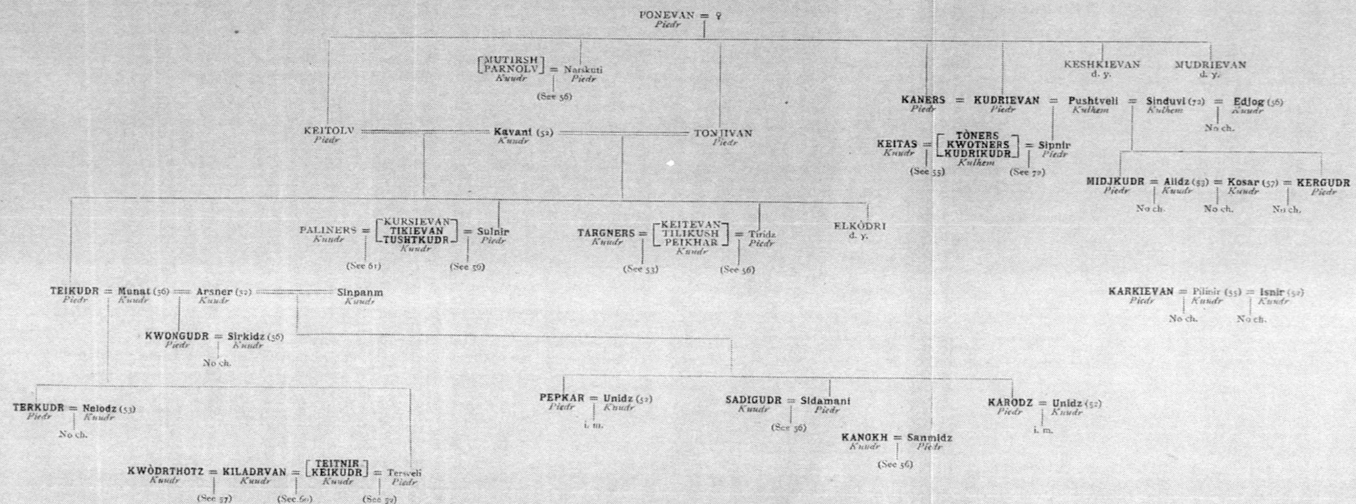
PONEVAN = ♀ Piedr
MUTIRSH PARNOLV Kuudr = Narskuti Piedr (See 56)
KESHKIEVAN d. y.
MUDRIEVAN d. y.
KANERS Piedr = KUDRIEVAN Piedr = Pushtveli Kulhem = Sinduvi (72) Kulhem = Edjog (56) Kuudr No ch.
KEITOLV Piedr = Kavani (52) Kuudr = TONJIVAN Piedr
KEITAS Kuudr = TONERS KWOTNERS KUDRIKUDR Kulhem = Sipnir Piedr (See 55) (See 72)
MIDJKUDR Piedr = Alidz (53) Kuudr = Kosar (57) Kuudr = KERGUDR Piedr No ch. No ch. No ch.
PALINERS Kuudr = KURSIEVAN TIKIEVAN TUSHTKUDR Kuudr = Sulnir Piedr (See 61) (See 59)
TARGNERS Kuudr = KEITEVAN TILIKUSH PEIKHAR Kuudr = Tiridz Piedr (See 53) (See 56)
ELKÒDRI d. y.
TEIKUDR Piedr = Munat (56) Kuudr = Arsner (52) Kuudr = Sinpanm Kuudr
KWONGUDR Piedr = Sirkidz (56) Kuudr No ch.
KARKIEVAN Piedr = Pilinir (55) Kuudr = Isnir (52) Kuudr No ch. No ch.
TERKUDR Piedr = Nelodz (53) Kuudr No ch.
PEPKAR Piedr = Unidz (52) Kuudr i. m.
SADIGUDR Kuudr = Sidamani Piedr (See 56)
KARODZ Piedr = Unidz (52) Kuudr i. m.
KANOKH Kuudr = Sanmidz Piedr (See 56)
KWÒDRTHOTZ Kuudr = KILADRVAN Kuudr = TEITNIR KEIKUDR Kuudr = Terweli Piedr (See 57) (See 60) (See 52)

64.

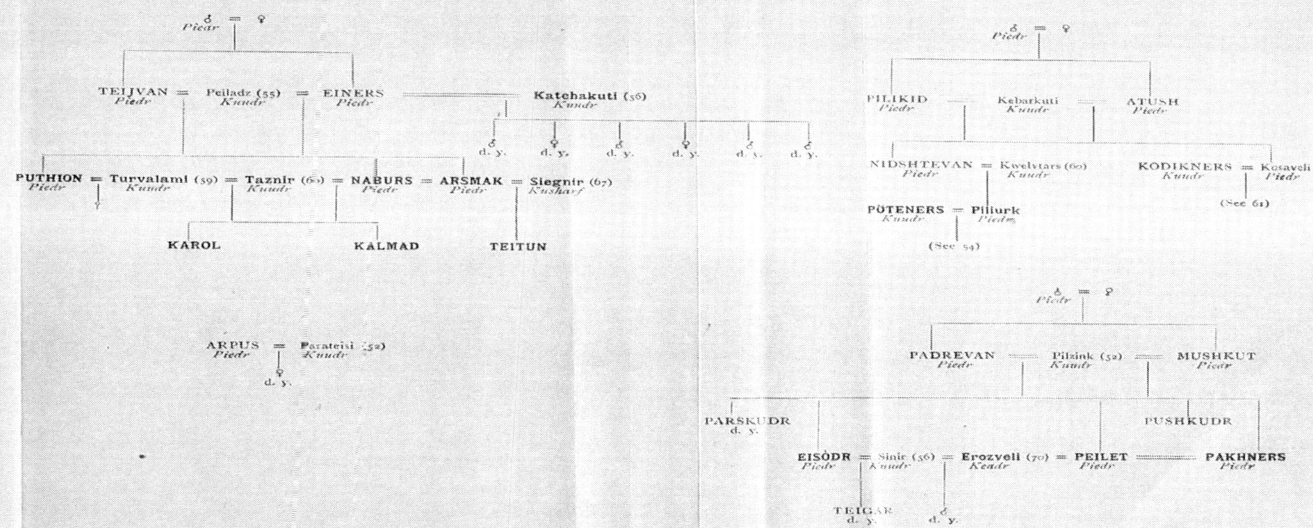

♂ = ♀
Piedr
TEIJVAN = Peiladz (55) = EINERS
Piedr Kuudr Piedr
Katehakuti (56)
Kuudr
♂ d. y.
♀ d. y.
♂ d. y.
♀ d. y.
♂ d. y.
♂ d. y.
PUTHION = Turvalami (59) = Taznir (63) = NABURS = ARSMAK = Siegnir (67)
Piedr Kuudr Kuudr Piedr Piedr Kusharf
♀
KAROL
KALMAD
TEITUN
ARPUS = Parateisi (52)
Piedr Kuudr
♀ d. y.
♂ = ♀
Piedr
PILIKID — Kebarkuti — ATUSH
Piedr Kuudr Piedr
NIDSHTEVAN = Kwelvtars (60)
Piedr Kuudr
KODIKNERS = Kosaveli
Kuudr Piedr
(See 61)
PÖTENERS = Piiurk
Kuudr Piedr
(See 54)
♂ = ♀
Piedr
PADREVAN — Pilzink (52) — MUSHKUT
Piedr Kuudr Piedr
PARSKUDR
d. y.
PUSHKUDR
EISÖDR = Sinir (56) = Erozveli (70) = PEILET — PAKHNERS
Piedr Kuudr Keadr Piedr Piedr
TEIGAR
d. y.
♂ d. y.

65.

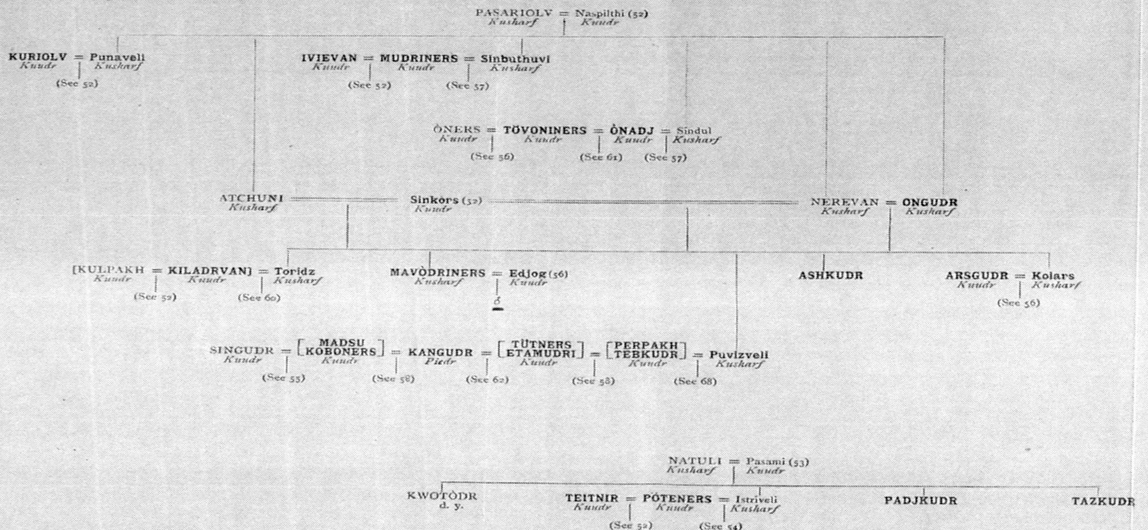
PASARIOLV = Naspilthi (52)
Kusharf
Kuudr
KURIOLV = Punaveli
Kuudr
Kusharf
(See 52)
IVIEVAN = MUDRINERS = Sinbuthuvi
Kuudr
Kuudr
Kusharf
(See 52)
(See 57)
ÖNERS = TÖVONINERS = ÒNADJ = Sindul
Kuudr
Kuudr
Kuudr
Kusharf
(See 56)
(See 61)
(See 57)
ATCHUNI
Kusharf
Sinkòrs (52)
Kuudr
NEREVAN = ONGUDR
Kusharf
Kusharf
[KULPAKH = KILADRVAN] = Toridz
Kuudr
Kuudr
Kusharf
(See 52)
(See 60)
MAVÒDRINERS = Edjog (56)
Kusharf
Kuudr
ASHKUDR
ARSGUDR = Kolars
Kuudr
Kusharf
(See 56)
SINGUDR = [MADSU KOBONERS] = KANGUDR = [TÜTNERS ETAMUDRI] = [PERPAKH TEBKUDR] = Puvizveli
Kuudr
Kuudr
Piedr
Kuudr
Kuudr
Kusharf
(See 55)
(See 58)
(See 62)
(See 58)
(See 68)
NATULI = Pasami (53)
Kusharf
Kuudr
KWOTÒDR
d. y.
TEITNIR = PÒTENERS = Istriveli
Kuudr
Kuudr
Kusharf
(See 52)
(See 54)
PADJKUDR
TAZKUDR

66

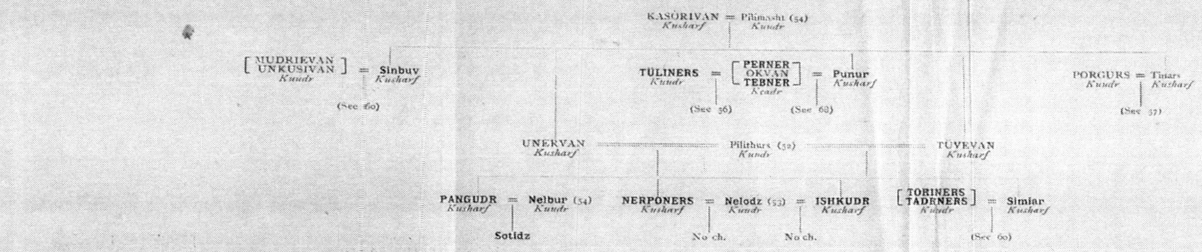
KASÖRIVAN = Pilimasht (54)
Kusharf Kuudr
[MUDRIEVAN UNKUSIVAN] = Sinbuy
Kuudr Kusharf
(See 60)
TÜLINERS = [PERNER OKVAN TEBNER] = Punur
Kuudr Kuudr Kusharf
(See 56) (See 68)
PORGURS = Tinars
Kuudr Kusharf
(See 57)
UNERVAN
Kusharf
Pilithurs (52)
Kuudr
TÜVEVAN
Kusharf
PANGUDR = Nelbur (54)
Kusharf Kuudr
Sotidz
NERPONERS = Nelodz (53) = ISHKUDR
Kusharf Kuudr Kusharf
No ch. No ch.
[TORINERS TADRNERS] = Simiar
Kuudr Kusharf
(See 60)

67.

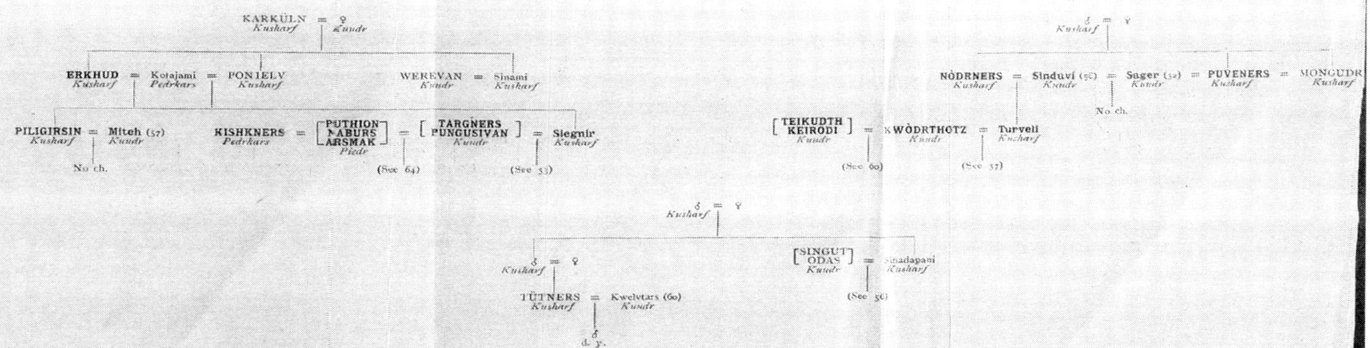
KARKÜLN = ♀
Kusharf Kuudr
ERKHUD = Kotajami = PONIELV
Kusharf Pedrkars Kusharf
WEREVAN = Sinami
Kuudr Kusharf
PILIGIRSIN = Miteh (57)
Kusharf Kuudr
No ch.
KISHKNERS = [PUTHION ABURS ARSMAK] = [TARGNERS PUNGUSIVAN] = Siegnir
Pedrkars Piedr Kuudr Kusharf
(See 64) (See 53)
♂ = ♀
Kusharf
NÒDRNERS = Sinduvi (56) = Sager (52) = PUVENERS = MONGUDR
Kusharf Kuudr Kuudr Kusharf Kusharf
No ch.
[TEIKUDTH KEIRODI] = KWÒDRTHOTZ = Turyeli
Kuudr Kuudr Kusharf
(See 60) (See 57)
♂ = ♀
Kusharf
♂ = ♀
Kusharf
TÜTNERS = Kwelvtars (60)
Kusharf Kuudr
♂
d. y.
[SINGUT ODAS] = Sinadapani
Kuudr Kusharf
(See 56)

8.

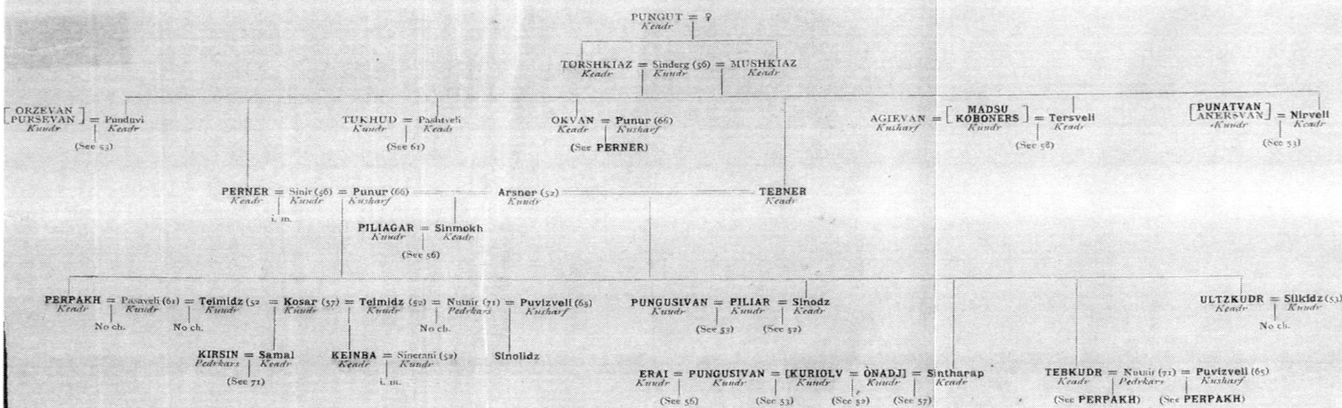
PUNGUT = ?
Keadr
TORSHKIAZ = Sinderg (56) = MUSHKIAZ
Keadr Kuudr Keadr
[ORZEVAN PURSEVAN] = Punduvi
Kuudr Keadr
(See 53)
TUKHUD = Pashtveli
Kuudr Keadr
(See 61)
OKVAN = Punur (66)
Keadr Kusharf
(See PERNER)
AGIEVAN = [MADSU KOBONERS] = Tersveli
Kusharf Kuudr Keadr
(See 58)
[PUNATVAN ANERSVAN] = Nirveli
Kuudr Keadr
(See 53)
PERNER = Sinir (56) = Punur (66)
Keadr Kuudr Kusharf
i. m.
Arsner (52)
Kuudr
TEBNER
Keadr
PILIAGAR = Sinmokh
Kuudr Keadr
(See 56)
PERPAKH = Pasaveli (61) = Telmidz (52) = Kosar (57) = Telmidz (52) = Nutnir (71) = Puvizveli (65)
Keadr Kuudr Kuudr Kuudr Kuudr Pedrkars Kusharf
No ch. No ch. No ch.
KIRSIN = Samal
Pedrkars Keadr
(See 71)
KEINBA = Sinerani (52)
Keadr Kuudr
i. m.
Sinolidz
PUNGUSIVAN = PILIAR = Sinodz
Kuudr Kuudr Keadr
(See 52) (See 52)
ERAI = PUNGUSIVAN = [KURIOLV = ÒNADJ] = Sintharap
Kuudr Kuudr Kuudr Kuudr Keadr
(See 56) (See 53) (See 52) (See 57)
ULTZKUDR = Silkidz (53)
Keadr Kuudr
No ch.
TEBKUDR = Nutnir (71) = Puvizveli (65)
Keadr Pedrkars Kusharf
(See PERPAKH) (See PERPAKH)

69.

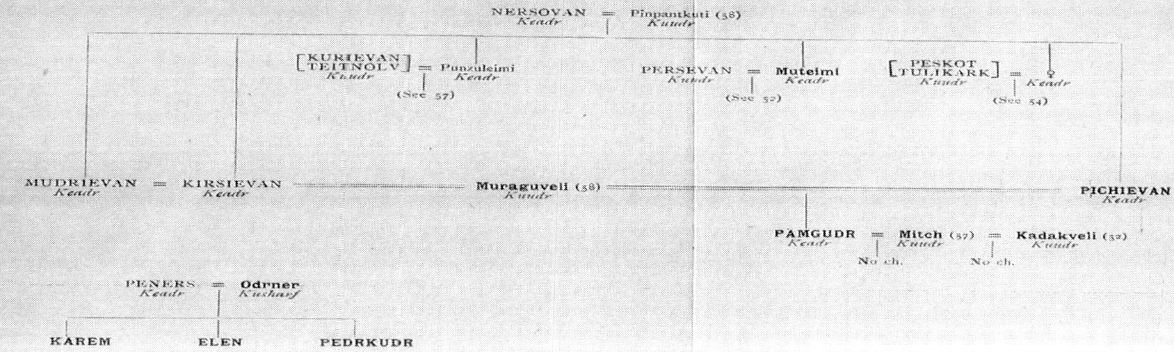
NERSOVAN = Pinpantkuti (58)
Keadr
Kuudr
KURIEVAN
TEITNOLV
Kuudr
= Punzuleimi
Keadr
(See 57)
PERSEVAN = Muteimi
Kuudr
Keadr
(See 52)
PESKOT
TULIKARK
Kuudr
= ♀
Keadr
(See 54)
MUDRIEVAN = KIRSIEVAN
Keadr
Keadr
Muraguveli (58)
Kuudr
PICHIEVAN
Keadr
PAMGUDR = Mitch (57) = Kadakveli (52)
Keadr
Kuudr
Kuudr
No ch.
No ch.
PENERS = Odrner
Keadr
Kusharf
KAREM
ELEN
PEDRKUDR

70.

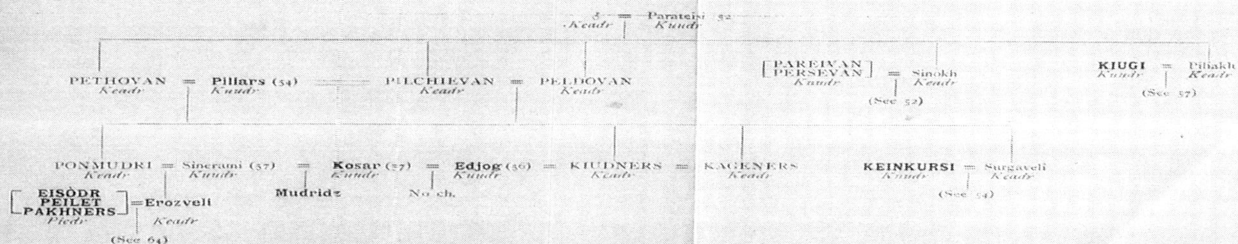
♂ = Parateisi 52
Keadr
Kuudr
PETHOVAN = Pillars (54)
Keadr
Kuudr
PILCHIEVAN = PELDOVAN
Keadr
Keadr
PAREIVAN
PERSEVAN
Kuudr
= Sinokh
Keadr
(See 52)
KIUGI = Pilakh
Kuudr
Keadr
(See 57)
PONMUDRI = Sinerami (57) = Kosar (57) = Edjog (56) = KIUDNERS = KAGKNERS
Keadr
Kuudr
Kuudr
Kuudr
Keadr
Keadr
KEINKURSI = Surgaveli
Kuudr
Keadr
(See 54)
Mudridz
No ch.
EISÒDR
PEILET
PAKHNERS
Piedr
=Erozveli
Keadr
(See 64)

71.

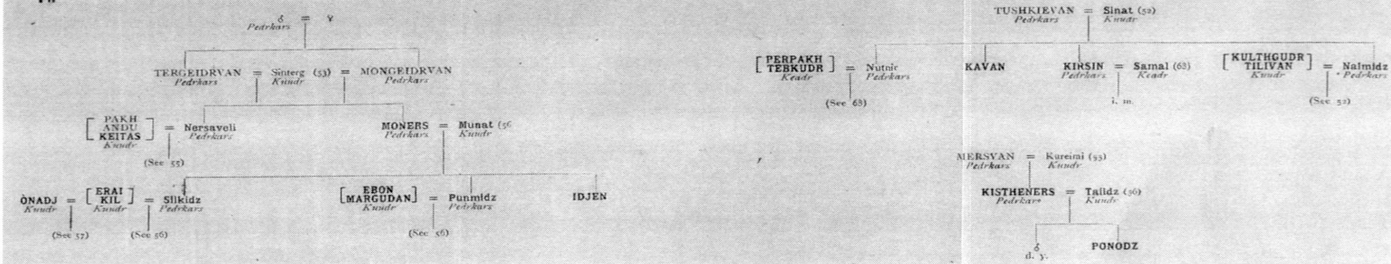

♂ Pedrkars = ♀
TERGEIDRVAN Pedrkars = Sinterg (53) Kuudr = MONGEIDRVAN Pedrkars
PAKH ANDU KEITAS Kuudr = Nersaveli Pedrkars
(See 55)
MONERS Pedrkars = Munat (56 Kuudr
ÒNADJ Kuudr = ERAI KIL Kuudr = Silkidz Pedrkars
(See 57)
(See 56)
EBON MARGUDAN Kuudr = Punmidz Pedrkars
(See 56)
IDJEN
TUSHKIEVAN Pedrkars = Sinat (52) Kuudr
PERPAKH TEBKUDR Keadr = Nutnir Pedrkars
(See 68)
KAVAN
KIRSIN Pedrkars = Samal (68) Keadr
i. m.
KULTHGUDR TILIVAN Kuudr = Nalmidz Pedrkars
(See 52)
MERSVAN Pedrkars = Kureimi (53) Kuudr
KISTHENERS Pedrkars = Talidz (56) Kuudr
♂ d. y.
PONODZ

72.

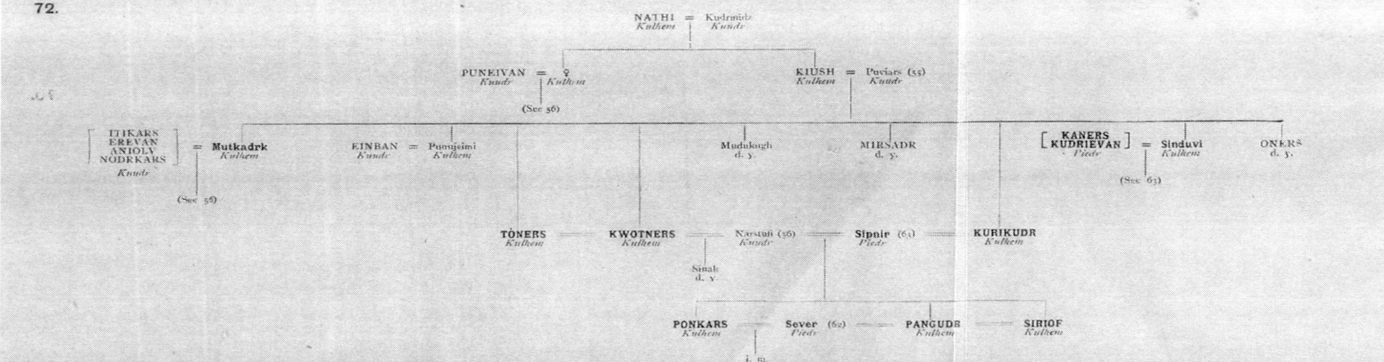

NATHI Kulhem = Kudrmidz Kuudr
PUNEIVAN Kuudr = ♀ Kulhem
(See 56)
KIUSH Kulhem = Puviars (55) Kuudr
ITIKARS EREVAN ANIOLV NODRKARS Kuudr = Mutkadrk Kulhem
(See 56)
EINBAN Kuudr = Punujeimi Kulhem
Mudukugh d. y.
MIRSADR d. y.
KANERS KUDRIEVAN Piedr = Sinduvi Kulhem
(See 63)
ONERS d. y.
TONERS Kulhem
KWOTNERS Kulhem
Narstuti (56) Kuudr
Sinak d. y.
Sipnir (63) Piedr
KURIKUDR Kulhem
PONKARS Kulhem
Sever (62) Piedr
i. m.
PANGUDR Kulhem
SIRIOF Kulhem